Information Systems

Foundation of E-Business

Fourth Edition

Information
Systems
Foundation of E-Business

Fourth Edition

Steven Alter

Prentice Hall

Upper Saddle River, NJ 07458

Publisher: Natalie Anderson
Executive Editor, MIS: Bob Horan
Associate Editor: Kyle Hannon
Editorial Assistant: Erika Rusnak
Media Project Manager: Joan Waxman
Marketing Manager: Sharon K. Turkovich
Marketing Assistant: Jason Smith
Managing Editor (Production): Gail Steier de Acevedo
Production Editor: Vanessa Nuttry
Permissions Coordinator: Suzanne Grappi
Associate Director, Manufacturing: Vincent Scelta
Manufacturing Buyer: Natacha St. Hill Moore
Design Manager: Pat Smythe
Art Director: Kevin Kall
Interior Design: Amanda Kavanagh
Cover Design: Lorraine Castellano
Manager, Print Production: Christy Mahon
Print Production Liaison: Ashley Scattergood
Project Management and Composition: Pre-Press Company, Inc.
Cover Printer: Lehigh Press
Printer/Binder: Quebecor World

Credits and acknowledgments borrowed from other sources and reproduced, with permission, in this textbook appear on page 564.

Microsoft Excel, Solver, and Windows are registered trademarks of Microsoft Corporation in the U.S.A. and other countries. Screen shots and icons reprinted with permission from the Microsoft Corporation. This book is not sponsored or endorsed by or affiliated with Microsoft Corporation.

Library of Congress Cataloging-in-Publication Data
Alter, Steven.
    Information systems : foundation of e-business/Steven Alter.—4th ed.
        p. cm.
    Includes bibliographical references and index.
    ISBN 0-13-061773-3
    1. Management information systems. 2. Electronic commerce. I. Title.

    T58.6.A44 2001
    658.4'038'011—dc21   2001033943

10 9 8 7 6 5 4 3 2 1
ISBN 0-13-061773-3

preface

Now, like it or not, "e" stands for everything: e-banking, e-books, e-travel, e-training, e-entertainment, and even e-engineering.[1]

The "e" in e-business will soon be irrelevant.[2]

E-business is rapidly becoming a way of life. It's our perspective that the name for e-business in the year 2000 will simply be: business.[3]

Information Systems, Foundation of E-Business, is the new name of this fourth edition of a book whose first three editions were called *Information Systems, A Management Perspective*. This edition retains its management flavor, but it also emphasizes and integrates the significant trends toward e-business and e-commerce that have become pervasive in the last few years.

E-BUSINESS: WHY THE MESSENGER ISN'T THE MESSAGE

In a few short years, e-business grew from an IBM advertising campaign into a tidal wave of hope and hype mixed with fear and uncertainty about becoming obsolete or being blindsided by unknown competitors. The seeds of e-business have evolved continually over almost five decades since the first computer applications in business. Back in the 1960s "e" was the first letter in electronic data processing (EDP). Later it was the first letter in electronic mail (e-mail) and electronic data interchange (EDI). The Web arrived in the early 1990s and it brought new forms of electronic commerce (e-commerce). And now we have e-business, which leapt to prominence when an IBM advertising campaign popularized e-business as an umbrella term for a long-term trend.

The day before IBM's e-business ad campaign appeared on Oct. 7, 1997, the *Wall Street Journal* said Louis Gerstner, IBM's CEO, wanted "to position IBM as a cutting-edge company and shake off for good its image as a stodgy, if reliable, supplier of computers to giant corporations."[4] Within several months an *Informationweek* article[5] noted that anyone who hadn't been in Fiji for the past few months had doubtless heard the latest computer industry buzz phrase: electronic business. Today "e" is everywhere. Open a newspaper, listen to a strategy consultant's sales pitch, learn about the latest NASDAQ IPO and the discussion almost can't avoid mentioning e-business, e-commerce, e-enterprise, e-economy, and e-just about anything else.

Although "e" is often associated with the Internet, the long history of EDP, e-mail, EDI, and e-commerce shows that the Internet is not the message even if it is the latest electronic messenger. The message is about work systems that make extensive use of computer and communication technologies in order to perform work more efficiently, satisfy new and existing customer desires, and allow people to live more interesting and fulfilling lives. The message is full of optimism and hope, but the reality has been mixed. Applications of technology have enabled processes and products that would have been impossible without today's cost-effective technology. Unfortunately some technology applications have also led to problems and disappointments.

Information systems are the foundation of e-business because e-business is really about making extensive use of computer and communication technologies in critical business processes. Some of these uses are directed within the firm, such as designing products, coordinating value added work, and integrating across an enterprise. Others are associated

with e-commerce, such as selling and providing service through electronic links. Yet others, such as supply chain management and customer relationship management, span the firm and its business partners. More and more of today's important work systems are inextricably linked to the information systems that support them. Most of today's important work systems in large organizations rely on information systems so completely that they cannot operate efficiently without the information systems. Increasingly, if the information system goes down, so does the work system. And from the other direction, it is increasingly obvious that the purpose and effectiveness of most information systems can be understood mainly in terms of their direct role in work systems.

In summary, I renamed this book *Information Systems: Foundation of E-Business* to emphasize the essential role of information systems in the systems through which today's businesses operate.

- Businesses operate through work systems.
- Work systems increasingly use e-business approaches.
- Information systems are the foundation of e-business.

The implications for a business professional are clear. Anyone who intends to play an important role in today's business needs to understand information systems in order to understand the work systems through which organizations operate. Anyone who lacks this understanding will be at a great disadvantage. Today's business professionals need more than the ability to do personal work on a computer and a general familiarity with business and technical terms. Contributing fully to current organizations requires an ability to participate in e-business systems, evaluate them, and contribute to system development efforts. This requires an organized approach for thinking about systems, an approach that can be used successfully today and will still be valid five or ten years from now when today's technical and business terms are no longer at the cutting edge.

WHAT'S THE HEADLINE?

Books related to information systems and e-business are often written from one of two viewpoints. Either business issues are the headline or technology is the headline. Major choices in writing this book reflect its emphasis on business even though the technology topics are covered thoroughly:

- The book is organized around a framework that business professionals can use for visualizing any computerized or non-computerized system in any organization. The basic unit of analysis is the work system, a system in which human participants and/or machines perform a business process using information, technology, and other resources to produce products and/or services for internal or external customers. This unit of analysis is appropriate for today's business professionals for a number of reasons:

    Information systems are actually work systems.
    E-business systems are actually work systems.
    Information systems exist to support other work systems.
    Information systems are increasingly integrated with the work systems they support.
    Information system projects are actually time-limited work systems.

    In other words, the concept of work system is like a common denominator covering most situations in which information systems are built or used. Having a central conceptual core makes it much easier to understand the importance of the many business and technical terms that constitute the vocabulary of information systems.

- The coverage of the work system framework, system-related principles, and the general topic of how to think about systems from a business viewpoint appear at the beginning of the book, not the end or in an isolated chapter about "problem solving." Accordingly, Chapters 1 and 2 introduce the framework and explain how business professionals can analyze systems for themselves. The chapters that follow discuss the elements of a work system, the business process (3), information and databases (4), customers and products (6), human and ethical issues (7), and technology (8, 9, and

10). The other chapters discuss types of information systems (5) and topics related to building and maintaining information systems (11, 12, 13).

- Wherever there is a choice, topics are presented with a business emphasis rather than a technology emphasis. For example, the discussion of databases appears in Chapter 4 as part of a discussion of information and databases, rather than in a later chapter grouped around technology headings such as computer hardware, software, and telecommunications. Similarly, intranets and extranets are introduced in Chapter 5, Types of Information Systems, as part of a discussion of information systems that support communication activities. Later, Chapter 10, Networks and Telecommunications, discusses telecommunications applications and common types of networks before delving into important technical topics that business professionals should be familiar with.

WHAT'S NEW?

The changes in this new edition include an improved representation of the work system framework, introduction of principle-based analysis of systems, integration of e-business and e-commerce topics, and updating to include many topics that were not as important when the previous edition was published.

Improved representation of the work system framework

As in the previous edition, this edition establishes a framework for describing a system and applies that framework to a chapter opening case to make sure the organizing principles and basic concepts are always apparent. This edition goes further by providing an improved version of the framework used in the previous edition. This framework has been renamed the work system framework (instead of the WCA framework) to emphasize that the analysis of computerized and non-computerized systems should start from a core of ideas related to work systems. Context and infrastructure have been added as elements of the framework. This reflects the reality that work system success depends on issues in the surrounding context and on the operation of infrastructure that is not owned or controlled within the work system. Adding these two elements to the framework makes it much easier to explain how to think about a system from a business viewpoint. The previous edition looked at a single framework from five different perspectives, and some readers found that too cumbersome. The new approach eliminates the idea of five separate perspectives and makes it easier to focus on what the system is, how well it operates, and how it might be improved.

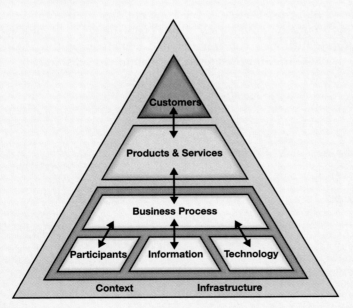

Introduction of principle-based analysis

Regardless of how clearly conceptual material and technical terminology are presented, students often have difficulty visualizing how it applies to real business situations or to their everyday lives. This edition introduces the principle-based systems analysis (PBSA) method, which anyone can use as a starting point for identifying and organizing issues and improvement goals related to any system. The PBSA method is based on a set of principles linked directly on the elements of the work system framework. (See Table P.1) The analysis of any system comprises defining a problem and the system, using the principles to look at each element of the system in an appropriate amount of depth, and then making a recommendation that addresses the problem and conforms to all of the principles to the extent possible.

The combination of the framework and the related principles provide motivation for pursuing the in-depth coverage within the chapters. For example, the chapter on business processes contains sections related to documenting process operation, understanding process characteristics, evaluating performance, and understanding concepts related to communication and decision making. Each of these topics provides a direction for digging deeper when trying to apply the principle "do the work efficiently."

Integration of e-business and e-commerce topics

The Internet, e-business, and e-commerce are important forces in today's business and are also the object of enormous hype and wishful thinking. It is increasingly clear that e-business should not be viewed as a different, newly invented type of business activity. It is true that the Internet has provided many opportunities for major improvements in serving customers and doing work efficiently, but it is not as though extensive use of computer and communication technology was invented in the last few years. To provide appropriate and balanced coverage of what is becoming the norm in today's business, the new edition contains a large number of new or updated examples and cases that involve e-business and illustrate that information systems are the foundation of e-business. For example, the chapter opening cases about companies such as Dell, Amazon, Schwab, eBay, DoubleClick, and Napster all contain e-business content even though the main point of each case is about the topic of the chapter, regardless of whether it is business processes, information, technology, or human and ethical issues.

Chapter by chapter changes

Table P.2 shows that the chapters in the book are organized around the work system framework and summarizes how each chapter contributes to an understanding of IT-enabled systems. Although the number and sequence of the chapters have not changed, many of the individual chapters were improved substantially.

TABLE P.1

Principles related to elements of the work system framework	
Element of the framework	**Principle**
Customer and Product	Please the customer.
Business Process	Do the work efficiently.
Participants	Serve the participants.
Information	Create value from information.
Technology	Minimize effort consumed by technology.
Infrastructure	Make infrastructure a genuine resource.
Context	Minimize unintended conflicts and risks.

How each chapter contributes to an understanding of systems

Primary emphasis	Chapter
	Chapter 1, "Moving toward E-Business as Usual," starts by explaining what e-business is and summarizing the basic concepts for understanding how businesses operate through systems. Next it discusses the process of building a system and the technical advances that made today's IT-enabled systems possible. It closes by citing challenges such as embracing technology without succumbing to hype and overselling, while also accepting the difficulty of anticipating how technology will be adapted in practice. Chapter 2, "Understanding Systems from a Business Viewpoint," explains the work system framework and shows how it leads directly to a set of principles that apply to almost any system in a business or other organization. After discussing relationships between information systems and work systems it explains a principle-based analysis method that anyone can use anyone as a starting point for identifying and organizing issues and improvement goals related to any system.
	Chapter 3,"Business Processes," shows how to examine a business process. It starts with process modeling and graphical methods for summarizing a process. After discussing process characteristics that determine how well processes perform, it looks at a set of process performance variables. The final section covers communication and decision making activities that play key roles in many processes.
	Chapter 4, "Information and Databases," introduces basic concepts related to computerized data files and discusses data modeling, a general technique for understanding information requirements. It then covers different types of databases and summarizes the capabilities of database management systems that store and control databases. It discusses performance concepts for evaluating information and closes by explaining the importance of formal models.
	Chapter 5, "Types of Information Systems," contains two major sections. The first introduces important information system categories such as CAD, EDI, SCM, MRP, CIM, CRM, and EFT that are linked to specific functional areas of business. The second section looks at idealized types of information systems such as TPS, MIS, and DSS that are equally applicable across all of the functional areas.
	Chapter 6, "Customer, Product, and E-Commerce," starts with ideas related to the customer and the product for any system and then uses these ideas as the basis for a discussion of e-commerce. The initial concepts include three dimensions for visualizing the products and services a work system produces, the phases in the customer experience related to a product, and the criteria a customer uses to evaluate the product of a work system. The coverage of e-commerce discusses challenges such as establishing and integrating systems, attracting customers, and providing an effective self-service environment.
	Chapter 7, "Human and Ethical Issues," focuses on positive and negative impacts of work systems and information systems on people at work. It points out that the success of any system in business depends on its participants. It closes by discussing ethical issues such as privacy, accuracy, property, and access.
	Chapter 8, "Computers in a Networked World," starts with measures of performance for technology, provides an overview of different types of computer systems, and presents some of the technical choices for capturing data, storing and retrieving data, and displaying data. Chapter 9, "Software, Programming, and Artificial Intelligence," starts by identifying different types of software and discussing the process of programming. It shows how the nature of programming has changed and uses related ideas to trace the evolution of programming languages. It provides an overview of operating systems and then closes with a discussion of the difficulty in trying to program intelligence into machines. Chapter 10, "Networks and Telecommunications," looks at different types of networks that link communication devices and computers. It surveys major networking technologies, emphasizes the importance of standards, and closes by discussing policy issues that affect the future of telecommunications.
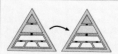	Chapter 11, "Information Systems Planning," looks at the strategic and practical issues involved when deciding how to incorporate IT into a firm's business strategy. It covers a series of strategic issues, methods for selecting among proposed information system investments, and issues related to project management. Chapter 12, "Building and Maintaining Information Systems," identifies the phases of any information system project, and shows how these phases are performed in four different approaches for building information systems.
	Chapter13, "E-Business Security and Control," discusses different types of risks related to accidents and computer crime. It explains some of the business conditions that increase vulnerability and then presents a value chain for system security, with special attention to security issues and techniques related to Web-based commerce and transactions.

Chapter 1, "Moving toward E-business as Usual," was renamed and rewritten to emphasize the essential role of information systems in e-business and e-commerce. The coverage of the value chain and supply chain previously in Chapters 2 and 6 was moved to Chapter 1 to help demonstrate why any substantial understanding of today's leading business practices (and e-business) requires an understanding of information systems.

Chapter 2, "Understanding Systems from a Business Viewpoint," was renamed and rewritten to clarify and simplify the approach for analyzing any IT-enabled system from a business viewpoint. The revised work system framework is explained along with the newly introduced principle-based systems analysis (PBSA) method. This eliminates the cumbersome aspects of looking at one framework from five perspectives and makes it easier to focus on what the system is, how well it operates, and how it might be improved.

Chapter 3, "Business Processes," now ends with topics related to communication and decision making because these are an important part of most business processes. Communication and decision making were moved from Chapter 5. "Rhythm" was added to the list of business process characteristics. The section on process performance has a new distinction between activity rate and output rate and has merged the coverage of "flexibility" into the discussion of process consistency.

Chapter 4, "Information and Databases," was reorganized to make its flow easier to grasp. Basic concepts about files are now introduced before the more abstract topic of entity-relationship diagrams. Data warehousing was moved here from Chapter 5 in order to link data warehousing more directly with database topics.

Chapter 5, "Different Types of Information Systems," was reorganized into two major sections. The first introduces important information system categories such as CAD, EDI, SCM, MRP, CIM, CRM, and EFT that are linked to specific functional areas of business. The second section looks at idealized types of information systems such as TPS, MIS, and DSS that are equally applicable across all of the functional areas. The sections on communication and decision making were moved to Chapter 3. The concept of "execution systems" was eliminated because these systems are covered along with the functional area systems. Enterprise systems were introduced as a new category. Expert systems and other decision-related systems derived from AI research are now included with other methods for supporting decision making. They were moved to this chapter from Chapter 9, Software, Programming, and Artificial Intelligence, because their real world applications are most easily understood by placing them with other methods for supporting decision making.

Chapter 6, "Product, Customer, and E-commerce," provides a more extensive coverage of e-commerce and provides a new section on e-commerce challenges such as establishing and integrating systems, attracting customers, and providing an effective self-service environment. It also replaces the product positioning concept with a more useful three-dimensional grid for describing the products and services a system produces. It replaces the term "customer involvement cycle" with the simpler term "customer experience."

Chapter 7, "Human and Ethical Issues," contains updated examples that emphasize e-commerce and Internet-related issues that were not as important when the previous edition was published.

Chapter 8, "Computer Hardware," contains updated examples and factual updates.

Chapter 9, "Software, Programming, and Artificial Intelligence," provides more coverage of operating systems and simplifies the coverage of types of software. Although topics such as expert systems and neural networks were moved to Chapter 5 to emphasize applications rather than intellectual origins, trends toward making computers more intelligent are still covered in three places in the chapter.

Chapter 10, "Networks and Telecommunications," has a new section on different types of networks, ranging from home networks to wide area networks and the Internet. The discussion of telecommunications standards was moved earlier in the chapter. Wireless networking and IP telephony receive more coverage. The section on telecommunications policy is updated.

Chapter 11, "Information Systems Planning," incorporates updated examples.

Chapter 12, "Building and Maintaining Systems," starts with a new example about building an e-commerce Web site to demonstrate that building and maintaining e-commerce sites involve the same issues as building and maintaining virtually any important information system.

Chapter 13, "E-Business Security and Control," provides many updated examples along with an expanded coverage of e-business security and control techniques such as public key encryption and digital signatures.

PEDAGOGICAL FEATURES

This book's pedagogical features start with the typical pedagogical features of a good current textbook. Each chapter contains study questions, a chapter summary, keywords, review questions, and discussion questions. Pedagogical features that help differentiate this book include the following:

Streamlining. This fourth edition maintains the streamlining that was accomplished in the third edition. Information systems texts tend to get longer and longer as new topics emerge. Careful integration of the topics around a powerful framework allows this fourth edition to stay at 13 chapters after being reduced from 20 and 15 chapters in previous editions.

Unifying framework. All good books in this field provide a thorough coverage of terminology. This book's most unique pedagogical feature is its use of a unifying framework that motivates the book's outline and is the core of a systems analysis approach that any business professional can use. Direct and indirect references to the framework keep the big picture visible and show how current terminology is related to a simple set of ideas that the students can use long after a new generation of business and technical practices emerges.

Real world cases. Another key pedagogical feature is its inclusion of real world cases. Some students learn best by focusing on examples and seeing how they are related to concepts and theories. Others learn best by focusing on a theory and seeing how examples validate it. This book is designed to serve both groups. Each chapter starts with an interesting, current, real world case and ends with two more. These cases genuinely support the material in the chapter and are not thrown in as an afterthought. Furthermore, the body of every chapter contains real world examples that are integrated into the explanation of the concepts rather than being put in isolated boxes. To provide a balanced representation of the real world and to avoid implying that technology is a magic bullet, the cases and examples include both successes and failures. Table P.3 explains how each opening case illustrates important topics within each chapter.

Debate topics, reality checks, and Web checks. The debate topic following each chapter-opening case is designed to encourage active interest and participation by students. The reality checks following major sections within the chapters serve a similar purpose. The Web checks ask the students to see how points in the text are reflected in the Web sites of companies mentioned in cases and examples.

Look Aheads and Reminders. Many topics are introduced in one chapter as part of an overview and are then explained later. Since students use hypertext links to navigate the Web, they have become more likely to use these forward and backward references to obtain more complete explanations that exist elsewhere in the text.

TABLE P.3

Chapter opening and chapter ending cases

Ch.	Chapter opening case	Chapter ending cases
1	Dell Computer - Its strategy relies on e-commerce and an efficient supply chain and value chain for purchasing and production. What is the relative significance of the efficient supply chain vs. sales over the Internet?	• Hershey – order fulfillment breakdowns during peak season because of information system glitches • Levi Strauss – the challenge of customization in the clothing industry
2	Amazon.com – It was originally a pure Internet business but eventually had to acquire its own warehouses in order to fulfill orders efficiently. What is a good system view of this company?	• Aramark Uniform Services – satisfying customers in a service industry • PanAmSat – impacts of a mishap with a single communication satellite that provides part of the infrastructure for many customers
3	Charles Schwab – Its original business model as a discount broker changed with self-service online trading, but it also needed to provide other types of information and service for its best customers. How are business process concepts relevant?	• E-stamp.com – costs and benefits of using a Web-based postage system in the process of producing and mailing packages • Cisco Systems – using the Internet for internal efficiency
4	eBay – It built a huge consumer-to-consumer auction business for used merchandise. How does it rely on an online database? How does it address issues related to trust?	• U.S. Air Force bombs an embassy – the impact of inadequate information in the bombing the Chinese embassy in Belgrade in 1999 • Patient Bill of Rights – the database that would be required to support the legislation
5	Boeing – It used CAD to build an airplane without using physical models. How does this project exemplify features of different types of information systems?	• Dow Corning – integrating information systems when a company acquires other companies to meet customer needs • Enron – the world's largest e-commerce site for commodity transactions
6	Otis Elevator – It sells complex machinery and supports it through a remote service center and other methods. Is this an e-business and does that question even matter?	• Ernst & Young – how a major consulting company set up a high profile site for Web-based consulting and how this evolved • WebVan – Can an Internet grocer make a profit?
7	DoubleClick – It provides clickstream data that is valuable for targeted marketing. What is the right balance between marketing needs and privacy?	• National Directory of New Hires – Is the privacy risk warranted? • Visionics – applying facial recognition software in driver registration
8	Napster – It used the Web to create a contro-versial peer-to-peer network. Is this a step toward the network becoming the computer?	• Transmeta Corp. – building a new chip for mobile computing • Gemstar International – Will its e-book provide enough benefits?
9	Microsoft – It programs software products using a method called synch and stabilize. Does this method allow too many bugs to remain in the software?	• Chrysler – Will extreme programming improve quality and reduce defects? • Cycorp – attempting to codify everyday real-world knowledge
10	FedEx – It uses a wide area network to track packages from sender to destination. Will manufacturers increasingly outsource delivery to firms with this type of capability?	• NTT DoCoMo – Wireless Internet access explodes in Japan. Will this technology have a similar impact in the United States? • Exodus Communications – What are the growth directions for a leader in complex Web hosting?
11	Kmart – Its new strategy calls for huge investments in information systems to improve its supply chain capabilities. How important is its new Web site as part of its strategy?	• Economist Intelligence Unit – launching a Web-based business intelligence unit • Cemex – What role does e-business play in a leading cement company's strategy?
12	Yahoo Store – It provides a template for building an online store without programming. How does this demonstrate the phases of building and maintaining a system?	• NIBCO – what it takes to succeed in a "big-bang" implementation of SAP • FAA – the long path toward overhauling the air traffic control system
13	VISA – It advised online merchants to take extra precautions due to the high level of fraud in online purchases. Do these guidelines cast undue suspicion on legitimate customers?	• Love Bug virus – how a hacker in the Philippines caused $10 billion in damage • London Ambulance Service – a new system causes a disaster

Web site. This book's Web site is designed to supplement the coverage in the book and will be updated periodically to make sure it provides links to the most current case material. Included with many of these examples are several questions for discussion. In addition, it provides a list of Web sites that delve more deeply into major issues discussed in the chapters.

TEACHING SUPPLEMENTS

Instructor's Resource CD-ROM (0130646164). A complete set of teaching supplements is available for instructors who adopt this book. These supplements are designed to enhance the accessibility, versatility, and teachability of the text material. The Instructor's Resource CD-ROM includes the Instructor's Manual, Test Item File, PowerPoint slides, Image Library, and Test Manager.

Instructor's Manual. This supplement explains approaches for teaching with this text. It is available on the Instructor's Resource CD-ROM and for download from the password protected instructor's section of **www.prenhall.com/alter**. It contains teaching suggestions for each chapter, suggested answers for Reality Checks, Debate Topics, and Web checks, and answers to end-of-chapter questions and cases.

PowerPoint slides. The slides illuminate and build upon key concepts in the text. Most figures and photos found in the text are provided and organized by chapter for your convenience in the Image Library on the Instructor's Resource CD-ROM. These images and lecture notes can be easily imported into Microsoft PowerPoint to create new presentations or to add to existing presentations.

If desired, the PowerPoint slides can be printed and used as transparency masters.

Testbank and Test Manager. The testbank contains approximately 80 multiple choice, true-false, and essay questions per chapter. The questions are rated by difficulty level and answers are referenced by section. For instructor convenience, the Prentice-Hall Test Manager is included in the Instructor's Resource CD-ROM

MyPHLIP/Companion Website. Available at **www.prenhall.com/alter** is a Web site that provides an Interactive Study Guide, access to the Instructor's Manual, PowerPoint slides, and Internet links. Features of this new site include the ability to customize your home page, real-time news headlines, In the News (IS related news articles summarized by a selected team of professors and supported by exercises and activities), and Internet Exercises that are continually added to the site.

Prentice Hall's Guide to E-Commerce and E-Business. This useful guide to e-business and e-commerce introduces students to many aspects of e-business and the Internet. It allows students to discover the role the Internet can play in continuing their education, distance learning, and looking for jobs. This guide is free when packaged with this text.

Online Courses

 www.prenhall.com/blackboard

Prentice Hall's on-line content, combined with Blackboard's popular tools and interface, result in robust Web-based courses that are easy to implement, manage, and use—taking your courses to new heights in student interaction and learning.

 www.prenhall.com/coursecompass

CourseCompass is a dynamic, interactive on-line course management tool powered exclusively for Pearson Education by Blackboard. This product allows you to teach market-leading Pearson Education content in an easy-to-use cutomizable format.

Tutorial Software

For instructors looking for Application Software support to use with this text, Prentice Hall is pleased to offer PH Train IT and PH Assess IT for Office 2000. These tutorial and assessment products are fully certified up to the expert level of the Microsoft Office User Specialist (MOUS) Certification Program. These items are not available as stand-alone items but can be packaged with this text at an additional charge. Please go to www.prenhall.com/phit for an online demonstration of these products or contact your local Prentice Hall representative for more details.

ACKNOWLEDGMENTS

Many individuals and organizations have contributed to this book, either directly or indirectly. I especially want to thank students in undergraduate, MBA, and executive MBA classes at the University of San Francisco who provided an excellent testing ground for both the ideas in this book and the approach for conveying those ideas.

This book benefited greatly from the efforts of many reviewers. Numerous review cycles identified strengths that could be amplified and shortcomings that could be eliminated or minimized. Although it is impossible to respond to every request and answer every criticism (in both books and information systems), and although I am responsible for any confusions or misunderstandings that remain, I did my best to incorporate the many insightful ideas and criticisms provided by the following reviewers:

Cynthia M. Beath, Southern Methodist University

Robert Behling, Bryant College

Linda J. Behrens, University of Central Oklahoma

Harry Benham, Montana State University, Bozeman

Susan A. Brown, Indiana University

Elia V. Chepaitis, Fairfield University

William Cummings, University of Illinois

Donald L. Davis, University of Southern Mississippi

Evan Duggan, University of Alabama at Tuscaloosa

Joel Dunn, University of North Carolina - Chapel Hill

David Fickbohm, Golden Gate University

Mary Beth Fritz, University of Florida

Jonathan L. Gifford, George Mason University

Ernest A. Kallman, Bentley College

Edward M. Kaplan, Bentley College

Gary Ledin, Jr., Sonoma State University

William Leigh, University of Central Florida

Michael D. Myers, University of Auckland, New Zealand

William Myers, Belmont Abbey College

Scott Orr, IUPIU

Leah R. Pietron, University of Nebraska at Omaha

Samuel A. Rebelsky, Grinnell College

Erik Rolland, University of California

Roger Smith, Yale University

Stephen J. Snyder, University of W. Florida

Louise L. Soe, California State Polytechnic University, Pomona

Craig A. VanLengen, Northern Arizona University

Murali Venkatesh, Syracuse University

C. Thomas Wu, Naval Post Graduate School

Brian A. Yahn, Northern Alberta Institute of Technology

Daniel Zappala, University of Oregon

Kay Zemoudeh, California State University at San Bernardino

The task of producing this fourth edition involves a lot of work beyond writing the chapters. Bob Horan's efforts as editor helped assure that this book would meet the needs of the market and would be produced in a timely manner. Before Bob came on board, David Alexander played the important editorial role of encouraging the continued development of a text whose unique approach had been developed originally at a sister company. Sharon Turkovich, marketing manager, provided both marketing ideas and direct marketing support needed to make the book a success. A dedicated and well coordinated effort in producing the book made that process effective and timely. Kyle Hannon, associate editor, coordinated editorial, marketing, and production efforts related to the book and its supplements. Vanessa Nuttry, the Prentice-Hall production editor, worked closely with Jan Turner, project manager at Pre-Press Company, which produced the book. Amanda Kavanagh produced an interesting interior design, Pre-Press Company rendered the diagrams, and Teri Stratford researched the photos, all of which made this book more effective for students and instructors. The combined efforts of all these individuals realized the intentions in the original manuscript and produced an attractive book on schedule.

This book is dedicated to Linda, without whose help it would have been written more quickly but with less inspiration.

about the author

of Information Systems: Foundation of E-Business

Steven Alter is Professor of Information Systems at the University of San Francisco. He holds a B.S. in Mathematics and Ph.D. in Management Science, both from MIT. While on the faculty of the University of Southern California, he revised his Ph.D. thesis and published it as *Decision Support Systems: Current Practice and Continuing Challenges*, one of the first books on this type of information system. Professor Alter's journal articles have appeared in *Harvard Business Review, Sloan Management Review, MIS Quarterly, Communications of the ACM, Communications of AIS, TIMS Studies in Management Sciences, Interfaces, Data Processing, Futures,* and *The Futurist.*

Prior to joining the University of San Francisco, he served for eight years as a founding vice president of Consilium, Inc. (acquired by Applied Materials in 1998). He participated in building and implementing early versions of manufacturing software used by major semiconductor and electronics manufacturers in the United States, Europe, and Asia. His many roles included starting departments for customer service, documentation and training, technical support, and product management.

Upon returning to academia he decided to work on a problem he observed in industry, the difficulty business people have in articulating what they expect from computerized systems and how these systems can or should be used to change the way work is done. His initial efforts in this area led to the 1992 publication of the first edition of this text. The subsequent editions have benefited from additional research on how business professionals understand information systems. His related articles in *Communications of AIS*, the online journal of the Association for Information Systems include:

"A General, Yet Useful Theory of Information Systems" (March, 1999)

"Same Words, Different Meanings: Are Basic IS/IT Concepts Our Self-Imposed Tower of Babel?" (April, 2000)

"Are the Fundamental Concepts of Information Systems Mostly about Work Systems?" (April, 2001)

His hobbies include music, hiking, skiing, yoga, and international travel. He is a member of the Larkspur Trio Dot Com, which occasionally presents reasonably proficient amateur performances of trios for violin, cello, and piano. One enthusiastic reviewer raved, "They certainly played up to their potential." The photo was taken while he was traveling to ICIS 2000, the International Conference on Information Systems in Brisbane, Australia, for which he organized a debate entitled "Does the Trend toward E-Business Call for Changes in the Fundamental Concepts of Information Systems?" Despite coaxing, the koala seemed to have no views on this topic.

brief contents

Preface   v

CHAPTER 1   Moving Toward E-Business as Usual   2

CHAPTER 2   Understanding Systems from a Business Viewpoint   40

CHAPTER 3   Business Processes   84

CHAPTER 4   Information and Databases   132

CHAPTER 5   Types of Information Systems   178

CHAPTER 6   Customer, Product, and E-Commerce   224

CHAPTER 7   Human and Ethical Issues   266

CHAPTER 8   Computers in a Networked World   304

CHAPTER 9   Software, Programming, and Artificial Intelligence   346

CHAPTER 10   Networks and Telecommunications   384

CHAPTER 11   Information Systems Planning   428

CHAPTER 12   Building and Maintaining Information Systems   470

CHAPTER 13   E-Business Security and Control   510

Notes   551
Credits   564
Company Index   565
Author Index   567
Glossary/Index   571

contents

Preface   v

CHAPTER 1   Moving Toward E-Business as Usual   2

OPENING CASE: Dell Computer: Building Customized Personal Computers   3

BUSINESSES OPERATE THROUGH SYSTEMS   7
Systems and Subsystems   8
Business Processes and the Value Chain   10
The Trend Toward E-Business   14

PHASES IN BUILDING AND MAINTAINING SYSTEMS   19
Project Success or Failure   20

INFORMATION TECHNOLOGY AS A DRIVING FORCE FOR INNOVATION   21
Greater Miniaturization, Speed, and Portability   22
*Greater Connectivity and Continuing Convergence of Computing
and Communications*   25
Greater Use of Digitized Information and Multimedia   26
Better Software Techniques and Interfaces with People   28

**OBSTACLES WHEN APPLYING INFORMATION TECHNOLOGY IN THE
REAL WORLD**   29
Unrealistic Expectations and Techno-hype   29
Difficulty Building and Modifying IT-Based Systems   30
Difficulty Integrating IT-Based Systems   31
Organizational Inertia and Problems of Change   32
Genuine Difficulty Anticipating What Will Happen   33

CHAPTER CONCLUSION   35

CASES   38
Levi Strauss: Selling Customized Casual Clothing
Hershey Foods: Why a Candy Maker Missed Chocolate Deliveries for Halloween

CHAPTER 2   Understanding Systems from a Business Viewpoint   40

OPENING CASE : Amazon.com: An Evolving Business Model   41

THE NEED FOR FRAMEWORKS AND MODELS   43

THE WORK SYSTEM FRAMEWORK   45
Balance between the Elements of a Work System   47
Viewing Information Systems and Projects as Work Systems   47

WORK SYSTEM PRINCIPLES   48

RELATIONSHIPS BETWEEN WORK SYSTEMS AND INFORMATION SYSTEMS   50
Trend toward Overlap   51

NEED FOR A BALANCED VIEW OF A SYSTEM   52

THE PRINCIPLE-BASED SYSTEMS ANALYSIS METHOD   53
The General Idea of Systems Analysis   53

Organizing the Analysis around Work System Principles   54
Applying PBSA to Work Systems, Information Systems, and Projects   58
Limitations and Pitfalls   58

MEASURING WORK SYSTEM PERFORMANCE   63

CLARIFICATIONS RELATED TO THE ELEMENTS OF A WORK SYSTEM   65
Customers   65
Products and Services   67
Business Process   68
Participants   68
Information   69
Technology   72
Infrastructure   72
Context   74

CONCEPTS AND VOCABULARY FOR LOOKING AT A WORK SYSTEM IN DEPTH   76

CHAPTER CONCLUSION   80

CASES   82
     Aramark Uniform Services: Satisfying Customers in a Service Industry
     PanAmSat: Recovering from a Satellite Failure

CHAPTER 3   Business Processes   84

OPENING CASE: Charles Schwab   85

PROCESS MODELING: DOCUMENTING A BUSINESS PROCESS   87
Data Flow Diagrams   88
Flowcharts and Structured English   91

PROCESS CHARACTERISTICS   94
Degree of Structure   96
Range of Involvement   99
Level of Integration   100
Rhythm   104
Complexity   105
Degree of Reliance on Machines   106
Prominence of Planning and Control   107
Attention to Errors and Exceptions   108

EVALUATING BUSINESS PROCESS PERFORMANCE   110
Activity Rate and Output Rate   112
Consistency   112
Productivity   114
Cycle Time   115
Downtime   116
Security   117

MORE ABOUT COMMUNICATION AND DECISION-MAKING   118

BASIC COMMUNICATION CONCEPTS   118

BASIC DECISION-MAKING CONCEPTS   121

CHAPTER CONCLUSION   126

CASES   129
     E-Stamp: Internet Postage for Letters and Packages
     Cisco Systems: Using the Web for Internal Efficiency

CHAPTER 4 Information and Databases 132

OPENING CASE: eBay: Providing Online Auctions for Personal Property   133

BASIC IDEAS FOR DESCRIBING DATA   135
Types of Data   135
What Is a Database?   137
Files   138
Logical versus Physical Views of Data   139
The Process of Accessing Data   140

DATA MODELING: DEFINING AND ORGANIZING DATA   141
Entity-Relationship Diagrams   141
Identifying the Data in a Database   142

TYPES OF DATABASES   145
Relational Databases   145
Multidimensional Databases   146
Data Warehouse   149
Geographic Information Systems   149
Text and Image Databases   149
Hypermedia Databases and the Web   152

DATABASE MANAGEMENT SYSTEMS   156
Defining the Database and Access to Data   156
Methods for Accessing Data in a Computer System   157
Processing Transactions   160
Controlling Distributed Databases   160
Backup and Recovery   160
Supporting Database Administration   161

EVALUATING DATA AS A RESOURCE   162
Information Quality   162
Information Accessibility   166
Information Presentation   167
Information Security   167

MODELS AS COMPONENTS OF INFORMATION SYSTEMS   168
Mental Models and Mathematical Models   169
What-If Questions   170
Virtual Reality: The Ultimate Interactive Model?   170

CHAPTER CONCLUSION   172

CASES   175
        U.S. House of Representatives: Patients' Bill of Rights Act of 1998
        U.S. Air Force: Could the Accidental Bombing of an Embassy Have Been Avoided?

CHAPTER 5 Types of Information Systems 178

OPENING CASE: Boeing: Using CAD to Design a New Airplane   179

INFORMATION SYSTEM CATEGORIES RELATED TO SPECIFIC FUNCTIONAL AREAS OF BUSINESS   181
Product Design Systems   182
Supply Chain Systems   182
Manufacturing Systems   185
Sales and Marketing Systems   186
Finance Systems   188

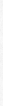

INFORMATION SYSTEM CATEGORIES THAT APPLY IN ANY FUNCTIONAL
AREA OF BUSINESS   189

OFFICE AUTOMATION SYSTEMS   190

COMMUNICATION SYSTEMS   192
Teleconferencing   193
E-mail, Voice Mail, and Fax   194
Instant Messaging and Chat Rooms   195
Groupware   195
Intranets and Extranets   196
Knowledge Management   196
Group Support Systems   197

TRANSACTION PROCESSING SYSTEMS   199
Batch versus Real-Time Processing   200

MANAGEMENT AND EXECUTIVE INFORMATION SYSTEMS   200
From MIS to EIS   202
Do MIS and EIS Really Solve Manager's Problems?   202

DECISION SUPPORT SYSTEMS   205
Simulation and Optimization   207
OLAP and Data Mining   207
Expert Systems   208
Neural Networks   210
Fuzzy Logic   212
Case-Based Reasoning   213
Intelligent Agents   214

ENTERPRISE SYSTEMS   215

LIMITATIONS AND USES OF INFORMATION SYSTEM CATEGORIES   216

CHAPTER CONCLUSION   219

CASES   222
Owens Corning: Integrating Across Business Units
Enron: The World's Largest E-Commerce Web Site for Commodity Transactions

CHAPTER 6   Customer, Product, and
E-Commerce   224

OPENING CASE: Otis Elevator: Providing Better Service for Customers   225

CUSTOMER'S VIEW OF PRODUCTS AND SERVICES   226
Three Dimensions of Products and Services   227
Characteristics of Information Products   231
Characteristics of Services   232
Customization and Adaptability   233

THE CUSTOMER EXPERIENCE   235
Determining Requirements   237
Acquiring the Product   238
Using the Product or Receiving the Service   241
Maintaining and Retiring the Product   243

CUSTOMER'S CRITERIA FOR EVALUATING PRODUCTS AND SERVICES   244
Cost   245
Quality   246
Responsiveness   246

Reliability   246
Conformance to Standards and Regulations   247

DIVERSE CONCERNS OF DIFFERENT CUSTOMERS   248

INFORMATION SYSTEMS AND COMPETITIVE ADVANTAGE   249
Mission-Critical Information Systems   249
Strategic Information Systems   250
Competitive Advantage Creates Competitive Necessity   250

CHALLENGES AS COMMERCE BECOMES E-COMMERCE   251
Establishing and Integrating Systems   252
Setting Prices   253
Attracting Customers   255
Providing an Effective Self-Service Environment   256
Providing Excellent Customer Service   258
Achieving Profitability and Sustainable Differentiation   259

CHAPTER CONCLUSION   261

CASES   263
Ernst & Young: Providing Consulting though the Web
Webvan: Can an Internet Grocer Make a Profit?

CHAPTER 7   Human and Ethical Issues   266

OPENING CASE: DoubleClick: Collecting Data About Web Usage   267

TECHNOLOGY AND PEOPLE   268
Human-Centered Design versus Machine-Centered Design   269
User Friendliness   270
Technology as a Metaphor and Influence   271

POSITIVE AND NEGATIVE IMPACTS ON PEOPLE AT WORK   272
Health and Safety   273
Autonomy and Power   275
Use of Valued Skills   277
Meaningfulness of Work   279
Social Relationships   280

DEPENDENCE ON PEOPLE FOR INFORMATION SYSTEM SUCCESS   281
Skills and Knowledge   282
Involvement and Commitment   282
Resistance to Change   284
Unanticipated Innovations   285

SYSTEMS AND ETHICS   286
Ethical versus Legal Issues   286
Ethical Theories   287
Privacy   287
Accuracy   291
Property   292
Access   295

BALANCING POSITIVE AND NEGATIVE IMPACTS   297

CHAPTER CONCLUSION   299

CASES   302
U.S. Congress: Creating a National Directory of New Hires
Visionics: Applying Facial Recognition Software in Driver Registration

CHAPTER 8 Computers in a Networked World **304**

OPENING CASE : Napster.com: Using the Web to Change the Rules of an Industry 305

PERFORMANCE VARIABLES FOR INFORMATION TECHNOLOGY 307
Functional Capabilities and Limitations 308
Ease of Use 309
Compatibility 309
Maintainability 309

UNITS OF MEASURE FOR TECHNOLOGY OPERATION 309
Measuring Amounts of Data 310
Measuring Time 310
Measuring the Rate of Data Transfer 310
Measuring Clock Speed and Transmission Frequency 310
Measuring the Speed of Executing Instructions 311
Technology Performance from a Business Viewpoint 311

OVERVIEW OF COMPUTER SYSTEMS 312
Basic Model of a Computer System 312
Types of Computers 312

FOUR APPROACHES TO COMPUTING IN ORGANIZATIONS 315
Centralized Computing 317
Personal Computing 317
Distributed Computing 318
Network Computing 318
Client/Server and Beyond 319

HOW COMPUTERS MANIPULATE DATA 322
Converting any Type of Information to Bits 323
Machine Language 326
Impact of Miniaturization and Integration on Performance 327
Other Approaches for Improving Performance 329

DATA INPUT: CAPTURING DATA 330
Keyboards and Pointing Devices 331
Optical Character Recognition 331
Capturing Pictures, Sounds, and Video 333

STORING AND RETRIEVING DATA 334
Paper and Micrographics 335
Magnetic Tapes and Disks 336
Optical Disks 336
Flash Memory 337
Smart Cards 337

DATA OUTPUT: DISPLAYING DATA 338
Screen Outputs 338
Paper Outputs 338
Audio Outputs 339

CHAPTER CONCLUSION 340

CASES 343
Transmeta Corporation: Building a New Chip for Mobile Computing
Gemstar International: Will Its E-Book Reader Provide Enough Benefits?

CHAPTER 9 — Software, Programming, and Artificial Intelligence   346

OPENING CASE : Microsoft: Programming Software for a New Release   347

THINKING ABOUT THE CURRENT LIMITS OF SOFTWARE   348

TYPES OF SOFTWARE   350
Application Software   350
System Software   351

PROGRAMMING VIEWED AS A BUSINESS PROCESS   352
Programming as a Translation Process   352
Organizing Ideas   352
Testing Programs   354
The Changing Nature of Programming   356
The Trend toward Object-Oriented Programming   358

FOUR GENERATIONS OF PROGRAMMING LANGUAGES   361
Machine Languages   361
Assembly Languages   361
Higher Level Languages   362
Fourth Generation Languages   366

OTHER MAJOR DEVELOPMENTS IN PROGRAMMING   367
Special-Purpose Languages   367
Spreadsheets   367
Computer-Aided Software Engineering Systems   368

OPERATING SYSTEMS   370
Operating Systems for Personal Computers   370
Operating Systems for Multiuser Computer Systems   373
Why Operating Systems Are Important   373

STEPS TOWARD MAKING COMPUTERS "INTELLIGENT"   374

CHAPTER CONCLUSION   378

CASES   381
Chrysler: Using "Extreme Programming" to Improve Quality and Minimize Defects
Cycorp: Building a Knowledge Base to Support Commonsense Reasoning

CHAPTER 10 — Networks and Telecommunications   384

OPENING CASE: FedEx Applies Telecommunications in Package Delivery   385

APPLYING TELECOMMUNICATIONS IN BUSINESS   387
Vital Role of Telecommunications in E-Business   387
Convergence of Computing and Communications   388
Making Sense of the Terminology and Details   390

TYPES OF NETWORKS   392
A Typical Home Network   392
A Local Area Network in a Business   392
A Telephone Network   394

The Internet (from a User's Viewpoint)   396
A Wide Area Network   396

FUNCTIONS AND COMPONENTS OF TELECOMMUNICATIONS NETWORKS   397
Generating and Receiving Data   400
Transmitting Analog versus Digital Data   401
Directing Data from Source to Destination   404
Transmitting Data through Wired and Wireless Media   406

TELECOMMUNICATIONS STANDARDS   412

MORE ABOUT NETWORK TECHNOLOGY   414
More about LANs   415
More about WANs   416
Wireless Networking   418
IP Telephony   418

TELECOMMUNICATIONS POLICY   419

CHAPTER CONCLUSION   423

CASES   426
NTT DoCoMo—Pioneering the Wireless Internet via Cell Phone
Exodus Communications: Growth Directions for a Large Internet Service Provider

CHAPTER 11   Information Systems Planning   428

OPENING CASE: Kmart Plans a New Information System Thrust   429

THE PROCESS OF INFORMATION SYSTEM PLANNING   431
What Is an Information System Plan?   431
Challenges in IS Planning   432
Principles for IS Planning   435
Planning Role of the IS and User Departments   436
Allocating Resources between New and Old Information Systems   437
Project Roles of IS Professionals   438

STRATEGIC ALIGNMENT OF BUSINESS AND IT   440
Consistency with Business Priorities   440
Reengineering and Downsizing   441
Enterprise-wide and Interorganizational Systems   443
Information System Architecture   444
Centralization versus Decentralization   445
Describing a Business-Driven IT Infrastructure   448
Outsourcing   450
International Issues   451

SELECTING SYSTEMS TO INVEST IN   453
Cost/Benefit Analysis   453
Risks   456
Financial Comparisons   456

PROJECT MANAGEMENT ISSUES   458
Division of Labor between the IS Department and Users   458
Keeping the Project on Schedule   459

SYSTEMS ANALYSIS REVISITED   462
Information Sources for Analyzing Systems   462
Performing Interviews   463

CHAPTER CONCLUSION   465

CASES   467
    Economist Intelligence Unit: Launching a Web-Based Business Intelligence Service
    Cemex: Incorporating IT into a Cement Company's Strategy

CHAPTER 12   Building and Maintaining Information Systems   470

OPENING CASE: Yahoo! Store: Building Your Own Online Store   471

PHASES OF ANY INFORMATION SYSTEM   **474**
    Initiation   *475*
    Development   *476*
    Implementation   *477*
    Operation and Maintenance   *478*

OVERVIEW OF ALTERNATIVE APPROACHES FOR BUILDING INFORMATION SYSTEMS   **479**

TRADITIONAL SYSTEM LIFE CYCLE   **480**
    Initiation   *481*
    Development   *481*
    Implementation   *484*
    Operation and Maintenance   *487*

PROTOTYPES   **489**
    Phases   *489*
    Advantages and Disadvantages   *491*

APPLICATION PACKAGES   **492**
    Phases   *494*
    Advantages and Disadvantages   *497*

END-USER DEVELOPMENT   **498**
    Phases   *498*
    Supporting the Users   *500*
    Advantages and Disadvantages   *501*

DECIDING WHICH COMBINATION OF METHODS TO USE   **502**
    Comparing Advantages and Disadvantages   *502*
    Combining System Development Approaches   *503*

CHAPTER CONCLUSION   504

CASES   507
    Nibco: A "Big Bang" Implementation of ERP
    FAA: Trying to Overhaul the Air Traffic Control System

CHAPTER 13   E-Business Security and Control   510

OPENING CASE: Visa Advises Extra Precautions for Online Merchants   511

THREAT OF ACCIDENTS AND MALFUNCTIONS   **512**
    Operator Error   *513*
    Hardware Malfunctions   *515*

Software Bugs   516
Data Errors   516
Accidental Disclosure of Information   517
Damage to Physical Facilities   517
Inadequate System Performance   518
Liability for System Failure   518

THREAT OF COMPUTER CRIME   519
Theft   520
Sabotage and Vandalism   524

FACTORS THAT INCREASE THE RISKS   526
The Nature of Complex Systems   526
Human Limitations   527
Pressures in the Business Environment   528

METHODS FOR MINIMIZING RISKS   528
Controlling System Development and Modifications   528
Providing Security Training   530
Maintaining Physical Security   531
Controlling Access to Data, Computers, and Networks   531
Controlling Traditional Transaction Processing   538
Maintaining Security in Web-Based Transactions   540
Motivating Efficient and Effective Operation   541
Auditing the Information System   543
Preparing for Disasters   543

CHAPTER CONCLUSION   544

CASES   547
The Love Bug: How a Student Hack Caused $10 Billion in Damage
London Ambulance Service: A New System Causes a Disaster

Notes   551
Credits   564
Company Index   565
Author Index   567
Glossary/Index   571

Information
Systems

Foundation of E-Business

Fourth Edition

Moving Toward E-Business as Usual

chapter1

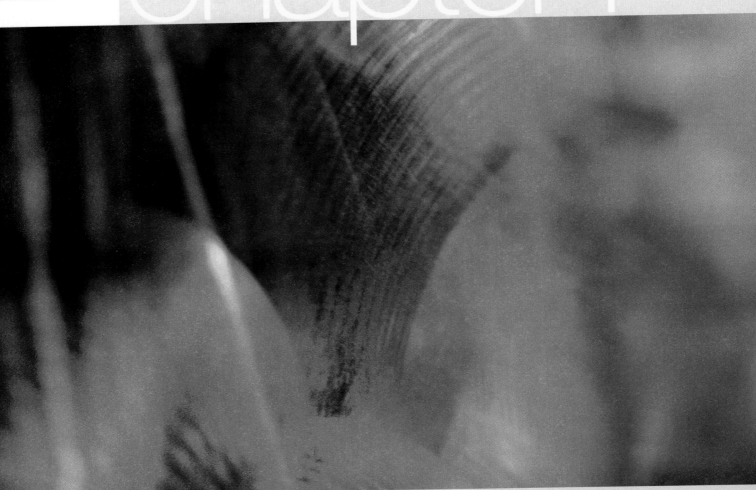

STUDY QUESTIONS

- What is e-business and how is it different from e-commerce?
- What are this book's four main themes?
- How are ideas about systems and the value chain relevant to e-business?
- What are the phases in building and maintaining systems?
- What technology trends have enabled IT-based innovation in business?
- What obstacles and real-world limitations have slowed the pace of implementation for IT-based innovations?

OUTLINE

Businesses Operate through Systems
    Systems and Subsystems
    Business Processes and the Value Chain
    The Trend Toward E-Business

Phases in Building and Maintaining Systems
    Project Success or Failure

**Information Technology as a Driving Force
for Innovation**
    Greater Miniaturization, Speed, and Portability
    Greater Connectivity and Continuing
      Convergence of Computing and
      Communications
    Greater Use of Digitized Information and
      Multimedia
    Better Software Techniques and Interfaces
      with People

Obstacles When Applying IT in the Real World
    Unrealistic Expectations and Techno-hype
    Difficulty Building and Modifying IT-Based
      Systems
    Difficulty Integrating IT-Based Systems
    Organizational Inertia and Problems of Change
    Genuine Difficulty Anticipating What Will
      Happen

Chapter Conclusion
    Summary
    Key Terms
    Review Questions
    Discussion Questions
    Cases

OPENING CASE

DELL COMPUTER: BUILDING CUSTOMIZED PERSONAL COMPUTERS

Dell Computer is one of the great success stories of the past decade. The computer business Michael Dell started while still a student at the University of Texas grew to a multibillion-dollar enterprise guided by the insight that it could bypass computer dealers and could sell directly to customers ranging from individuals to large companies buying thousands of computers. Many of Dell's large competitors traditionally built PCs starting from demand estimates and contracts with distributors that sold the computers to individuals or businesses. They decided how many computers to assemble based on this information, shipped them to distributors, and hoped the computers would be sold before becoming outdated. Dell used a different approach. It could eliminate markups charged by dealers and vastly reduce the risks of carrying large inventories by taking orders directly from the customers and building computers only when it had customer orders specifying the options individual customers wanted. Dell implemented this strategy through a combination of outsourcing and mass customization. As this system developed, Dell became more and more efficient in providing a wide range of options, yet manufacturing the computers efficiently and delivering them through a delivery service within two weeks. Dell reached the point at which it typically received payment for the computers before having to pay suppliers for the components. This means that Dell's inventory holding cost is negative.[1]

Dell's approach to mass customization is to create an efficient order fulfillment process that provides rapid delivery and low prices while also providing important options related to computer power, storage, the type of monitor, and other features. Because many customers wanted specific software installed on the computers before delivery Dell created a network within its factory that made it possible to select one of many possible configurations and load it efficiently. The internal processes that make this mass customization approach possible start with estimates of demand and long-term contracts with only 200 suppliers, 30 of whom account for 78% of total purchases.[2] Dell maintains electronic links to its suppliers that tell them exactly when the parts are needed. These electronic links help make sure that Dell uses only the most current parts and does not have to store large inventories. Dell tracks inventory velocity and related measures closely and has reduced its inventory to 11 days, meaning that its risk of holding obsolete inventory is minimal. When its inventory balance is not quite right, it can use its direct sales model to steer customers toward products that can be built with the available inventory.[3]

As an aggressive outsourcer, Dell has been a leader in permitting partners and suppliers to do work that might otherwise be done by company employees. At each stage in its value chain, Dell asks whether there is any reason to do the work internally. Dell does not manufacture the semiconductor chips used in its computers and does not attach the chips to the computer motherboards. Instead, it buys computer motherboards from suppliers with which it has long-term contracts. Similarly, it does not make monitors, but purchases them from suppliers such as Sony. Since there is no advantage in receiving a shipment of Sony monitors, repackaging them, and shipping them to the customers, Dell asks Airborne Express or UPS to pick up computers at the Dell plant in Austin, match the computers with monitors from the Sony plant in Texas, and ship both to the customer at the same time. In a similar fashion, most of the 10,000 technicians who service Dell computers in the field are actually employees of other firms operating under contract with Dell. Furthermore, since there is no special value in insisting that only Dell employees have access to Dell's help desk tools and information, people from major customers such as MCI can access this information directly through www.dell.com.

Dell was also an early leader in using the Web for sales and achieved $3 million of sales per day by 1998. Actually, there were and still are a number of ways to buy from Dell. Consumers can order through the Web without talking to anyone, order through a sales representative without using the Web, or set up a tentative order on the Web and then talk to a sales representative. Only half of Dell's customers "use Dell's web pages to configure their orders. And only 15% of customers place the order electronically. The remaining 35% design the order online and then submit it in some way that requires Dell to take a second step to feed it into the system, such as e-mailing or faxing."[4]

Sales to large companies occur through more traditional industrial sales relationships. This combination of different methods provides a comfortable shopping experience for different types of customers with different preferences and experience levels.

WEB CHECK [✓]

Look at Dell's Web site, www.dell.com, and see how it presents its product options and how it explains its manufacturing process.

DEBATE TOPIC

Which is more important to Dell, the fact that it sells computers over the Web or the fact that its manufacturing process permits it to build and deliver customized computers efficiently?

This text has a very practical purpose, namely, to help you understand and analyze information systems from the viewpoint of a **business professional**, a person in a business or government organization who manages other people or works as a professional in fields such as sales, manufacturing, consulting, and accounting. Understanding information systems from this viewpoint is important because business professionals inevitably encounter information systems in today's business world. Most readers of this book will not only use information systems extensively, but will also be called upon to analyze systems by identifying their strengths and weaknesses, recommending changes, and helping to implement these changes.

The opening case about Dell Computer exemplifies the way today's leading-edge businesses operate through systems that rely extensively on information technology (IT). Turn off the Internet and the telephone system and Dell's order entry system would be dead in the water. Turn off the computer and communication technology used for its manufacturing and delivery systems and Dell would not be able to fulfill orders regardless of how cleverly Dell attracted customers to its Web site.

WORK SYSTEM SNAPSHOT
Dell Computer: Manufacturing a Computer to Order

CUSTOMERS
- Computer buyers

PRODUCTS & SERVICES
- Customized personal computers, built to order and delivered.

BUSINESS PROCESS
- Receive order and payment information from buyer (either through the Web or through a sales representative).
- Place the computer on the manufacturing schedule.
- Perform manufacturing steps including assembling the computer, installing software, and testing whether the computer operates correctly.
- Pack the computer for shipment.
- Ship the computer directly to the consumer.

PARTICIPANTS	INFORMATION	TECHNOLOGY
• Computer buyer • Dell sales representative • Manufacturing staff • Packaging staff • Delivery service	• Specification of the computer to be built • Identification and address of customer • Payment information • Manufacturing information	• Customer's PC (if the customer orders or obtains information online) • Sales rep's computer • Any computers and networks used to track and manage manufacturing • The Internet (infrastructure)

Definition of E-Business   The Dell case demonstrates the trend toward **e-business**, the practice of performing and coordinating critical business processes such as designing products, obtaining supplies, manufacturing, selling, fulfilling orders, and providing services through the extensive use of computer and communication technologies and computerized data. Table 1.1 compares this definition of e-business with several others. This book's definition emphasizes the way a business operates rather than the fact that it uses the Internet as part of its infrastructure. This definition is designed to include leading-edge business methods that existed in 1990, before the Internet was used for e-commerce, while also including business methods that will exist in 2010, when other technologies may have supplanted the Internet for important applications. It resonates with a comment from Charles Schwab, the founder of the leading brokerage firm with the same name:

> "E-business has been built on technology, but it's not about technology. . . . I am often asked about how the Internet has changed our business at Charles Schwab. The perhaps surprising answer is: 'It really hasn't.' Rather than fundamentally *changing* our business, the Internet has *enhanced* the way we have been operating since I founded the company in 1971."[5]

Dell Computer is often seen as a prime example of an e-business, but an either/or classification as an e-business is not what really matters. When Michael Dell started the company in his dorm room it could not have been considered an e-business. Its use of information technology expanded over the years as the company grew in size and sophistication and as it learned to integrate the Internet and other technologies into its critical business functions.

Dell developed its e-business capabilities from scratch, but many retailers, financial institutions, airlines, and manufacturers had well-established physical stores, sales forces, or distribution channels long before the Internet was used for commerce. Today most of these companies use online selling in addition to their traditional methods. For these companies and for Dell, the Internet provided a way to reduce costs,

TABLE 1.1

Alternative Definitions and Views of E-Business

The first definition of e-business is the one used in this book. The others are listed in general order of similarity. The least similar definitions give more weight to the use of the Internet and to business transformation.

"E-business is the practice of performing and coordinating critical business processes such as designing products, obtaining supplies, manufacturing, selling, fulfilling orders, and providing services through the extensive use of computer and communication technologies and computerized data."

"Electronic business" . . . "includes everything having to do with the application of information and communication technologies (ICT) to the conduct of business between organizations or from company to consumer."[6]

"E-business includes e-commerce but also covers internal processes such as production, inventory management, product development, risk management, finance, knowledge management, and human resources."[7]

"The use of the Internet and other digital technology for organizational communication and coordination and the management of the firm."[8]

"E-business is the complex fusion of business processes, enterprise applications, and organizational structure necessary to create a high performance business model."[9]

"It is important to note that e-business is much more than electronic commerce. E-business involves changing the way a traditional enterprise operates, the way its physical and electronic business processes are handled, and the way people work."[10]

IBM defines e-business as "a secure, flexible and integrated approach to delivering differentiated business value by combining the systems and processes that run core business operations with the simplicity and reach made possible by Internet technology."[11]

"E-business is about using Internet technologies to transform the way business processes are performed. Its most visible form is online purchasing, both wholesale and retail."[12]

"In its simplest sense, e-business is the use of Internet technologies to improve and transform key business processes. Most companies understand this and have begun the evolution from traditional business practices to e-business."[13]

"E-business: any Internet initiative—tactical or strategic—that transforms business relationships, whether those relationships be business-to-consumer, business-to-business, intrabusiness, or even consumer-to-consumer. . . . E-business is really a way to drive efficiencies, speed, innovation, and new value creation in an organization."[14]

"By connecting your traditional IT systems to the Web you become an e-business."[15]

speed operations, and provide value for customers. What matters to these firms is not whether a particular date marked their transformation from traditional businesses to e-businesses, but rather whether their use of the Internet and other technologies contributed to their competitive success. Internet technology fostered e-business by providing far less expensive ways to handle data required for critical business processes, but e-business is not about the Internet. Regardless of the attention and hype that "dot-com" businesses attracted in the last few years, the Internet is actually only one of many technologies that play essential roles in today's leading businesses. The Internet is a wonderful and powerful tool, but other tools may steal the spotlight tomorrow.

Work Systems, Information Systems, and E-Business   The tabular "system snapshot" accompanying the Dell case illustrates this book's approach for making sense of IT applications today and in the future. Although Dell happens to use the Internet in several ways its customers can submit orders, the case emphasizes the larger system of order fulfillment that plays an essential role in Dell's success. This system is not the Internet or the World Wide Web, but rather a **work system**, a system in which human participants and/or machines perform a business process using information, technology, and other resources to produce products and/or services for internal or external customers.

This book emphasizes a particular class of work systems called information systems. An **information system** is a work system whose business process is devoted to capturing, transmitting, storing, retrieving, manipulating, and displaying information, thereby supporting other work systems.

This introductory chapter is called "Moving Toward E-Business as Usual" because most companies are becoming e-businesses and because information systems are the foundation of e-business. Successful companies in today's business world increasingly operate using an e-business style that emphasizes customer focus, responsiveness,

[**L O O K   A H E A D**]
Chapter 2 will explain work systems in depth and will extend the comparison between work systems and information systems.

accuracy, and efficiency. Continued success in a world of "e-business as usual" is largely based on a company's ability to build, implement, and maintain information systems that help people do their work, support effective collaboration, codify individual business processes, integrate those processes with other processes including those of suppliers, and maximize value received by customers.

E-business is becoming business as usual because organizations that cannot adapt to this environment are increasingly noncompetitive unless they are fortunate enough to have unique products, skills, or a location that others cannot match. We still encounter many companies whose products and services seem lackluster, but other than lucky exceptions, companies that cannot meet today's high expectations will gradually be taken over or will go out of existence.

Four Themes   This introductory chapter presents the book's four main themes, which follow. All of the material in this book contributes depth to your understanding of these themes and what they mean to you as a business professional who will almost certainly participate in the development and use of systems in organizations.

1. Businesses operate through systems in which people perform business processes using technology and information. The basic ideas for thinking about these systems are the same regardless of whether the Internet is involved.
2. Business professionals participate in all the major phases of building and maintaining these systems, and therefore need knowledge and skills necessary for effective participation.
3. Advances in IT have been and continue to be a driving force in business innovation in general and e-business in particular.
4. The success of IT-enabled systems is in no way guaranteed even when the latest technology is used.

The section on the first theme introduces the work system framework and describes a company's supply chain, value chain, and customer experience in terms of work systems. The next section summarizes the process of building and maintaining systems, and notes that business professionals play important roles throughout. The discussion of the third theme looks at the amazing technological progress that has made the current e-business approaches possible. The chapter concludes by discussing some of the real-world limitations and uncertainties that often make it difficult to use IT effectively in organizations. As you read this book, your challenge is to appreciate the enormous potential in this area while also cultivating a practical way to think about any system that uses IT in business.

BUSINESSES OPERATE THROUGH SYSTEMS

Consider these three situations: buying a pizza, hiring a new employee, and manufacturing an automobile. On the surface these seem unrelated, but all of them can be described using the same basic terms that the Work System Snapshot used to summarize the order fulfillment system in the Dell Computer case. If you look in detail at how any of these activities are performed you would find the following: Human participants are performing a business process using information and other technology in order to produce some combination of products and services for a customer.

The **work system framework** shown in Figure 1.1 can be used to summarize the three situations as well as Dell's inventory control and order fulfillment systems. This framework will be used throughout the book as a way of clarifying what system is being discussed, how well it is operating, and how it might be improved. It will be explained in detail in Chapter 2 along with a related method for understanding and analyzing systems in organizations.

The work system framework is quite general and it can be used to think about a work system regardless of whether information technology is used. It is possible to buy a pizza by walking to a pizza store, placing an order, and paying in cash. It also may be

FIGURE 1.1

Work system framework

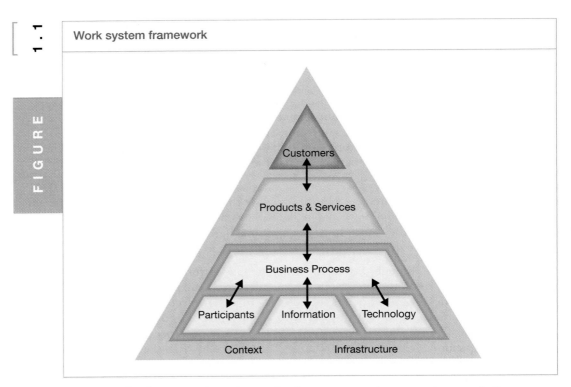

The concept of work system can be used to visualize almost any system that operates in an organization.

possible to order the pizza over the Web, have it delivered by a delivery service that is hooked into a wireless network, and pay for it using a debit card that links directly with a computerized banking system. The framework can describe both possibilities. Similarly, it can describe a totally noncomputerized way of hiring someone just as it can describe a hiring system that includes finding résumés on the Web, using e-mail to contact applicants, using the company's Web site to publicize opportunities at the company, and using other Web-based information sources to verify information provided by applicants. It can also summarize many different methods of manufacturing cars, ranging from highly customized cars built from scratch for the ultra-rich through high-volume models ordered through the Web and manufactured with components obtained through Web-based transactions and coordination.

These examples illustrate several important points: First, there are many different ways to do any particular type of work. A crucial management responsibility is to identify ways to do work more efficiently and to produce better products and services. Second, notice how the work in each case might be done with or without extensive use of the Internet and other information technologies. In all of these cases, using the Internet for part of the work may yield important advantages, but the main goals are about providing value for customers and doing work efficiently.

Systems and Subsystems

Concepts about systems provide the basic terminology for understanding how firms provide value for customers and how they perform work efficiently.

A **system** is a set of interacting components that operate together to accomplish a purpose. Systems that play a role in our everyday lives include our bodies' circulatory and digestive systems as well as society's transportation and communications systems. In this book we are concerned with systems that use IT while performing work in business and government organizations.

A **subsystem** is a component of a system, even though it can also be considered a system in its own right. The systems with which we are concerned are always sub-

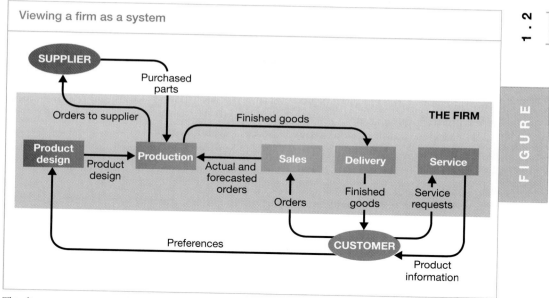

FIGURE 1.2

Viewing a firm as a system

This diagram represents a firm as a system consisting of five subsystems: product design, production, sales, delivery, and service.

systems of larger systems and typically contain subsystems that perform different parts of the work. Understanding the significance of any particular system usually requires at least some understanding of the larger system it serves. To demonstrate this, Figure 1.2 represents a manufacturing firm as a system consisting of five subsystems: product design, production, sales, delivery, and service. Each of these subsystems can be subdivided further into smaller subsystems that are not shown in the figure. Some of those smaller subsystems are information systems that help people perform the work and that help coordinate tasks done in different parts of the larger system.

Other terms frequently used when discussing systems include the system's purpose, boundary, environment, input, and output:

- A system's **purpose** is the reason for its existence and the reference point for measuring its success. For example, the purpose of Dell's order fulfillment system is to efficiently produce and deliver what the customer ordered.
- A system's **boundary** defines what is inside the system and what is outside. For example, someone primarily concerned with the way orders are entered over the Web might view the delivery step as outside the scope of the system.
- A system's **environment** is everything pertinent to the system that is outside of its boundaries. The environment in the Dell case includes Dell's competitive challenges, Dell's corporate culture, and the laws that apply to interstate shipping.
- A system's **inputs** are the physical objects and information that cross the boundary to enter it from its environment. In the Dell case these range from customer requirements to physical components that are assembled into computers.
- A system's **outputs** are the physical objects and information that go from the system into its environment. The order fulfillment system's primary output is the delivery of the computer.

Figure 1.2 illustrates these terms. The box around the five subsystems is the *boundary* between the system (the firm) and its *environment*. The environment is everything outside the boundary, such as the suppliers and customers. The suppliers and customers are shown explicitly because they provide *inputs* and receive *outputs*. The inputs into the firm include parts purchased from suppliers and information such as preferences, orders, and service requests from customers. The outputs to the customers include finished goods and information such as warranties and advice about how to use the product.

Unlike the systems one encounters in a chemistry experiment, work systems in businesses need to change frequently to accommodate to changing conditions in their environments and changing customer needs. These changes may occur anywhere in the system. The computer hardware and software may be changed if they are inadequate. Whether or not the hardware and software change, aspects of the business process may change. The participants may also change in a number of ways, such as by acquiring new skills, becoming more adept at the work, being reassigned to other work, or leaving the organization.

For now we will focus on business processes and temporarily will move the participants, information, and technology to the background.

Business Processes and the Value Chain

When viewing an entire business or a part of a business, the way work is performed can be summarized in terms of a set of business processes. A **business process** is a related group of steps or activities in which people use information and other resources to create value for internal or external customers. These steps are related in time and place, have a beginning and end, and have inputs and outputs.[16, 17] Figure 1.2 shows that the design process creates the product design that goes to internal customers who do the work of producing the product. In turn, the production process creates finished goods that go to other internal customers who perform the delivery process. The delivery process provides finished goods to an external customer.

The scope of a business process is the specific set of subprocesses and activities it includes. **Subprocesses** are parts of a process that are processes in their own right because they consist of well-defined steps related in time and place, have a beginning and end, and have inputs and outputs. For example, the process of producing a textbook includes subprocesses such as writing the manuscript, revising the manuscript, designing the book's layout, producing the artwork, and printing the book. In contrast to the term subprocess, however, we will use the term *activity* to denote more general, often less well-defined things that people do in businesses, such as communicating with others, motivating employees, and analyzing data. In some cases, an important role of IT is to convert a poorly defined activity into a better-defined subprocess that is done in a predictable way and produces consistent outputs. For example, this happens when voice mail is installed to improve message taking.

A process's **value added** is the amount of value it creates for its internal or external customer. At Dell Computer, for example, the process "assemble a computer" starts with the computer's component parts and ends with a completely assembled computer. The value added is the difference between the value of the components and the value of the assembled computer.

The most obvious question to ask about any business process or step within a business process is whether it adds any value at all. Consider what happened when the employees at a General Electric plant met to identify ways to improve internal processes. The editor of an award-winning plant newsletter complained that seven approvals were needed before each monthly edition could be released. The plant manager's public response: "This is crazy. I didn't know that was the case. From now on, no more signatures." Producing the newspaper added value for internal customers, but getting signatures added nothing but delay and wasted effort.[18]

Business Processes and Functional Areas of Business Businesses have traditionally organized around the **functional areas of business**, the departments of a firm related to specific business disciplines, such as Production, Sales and Marketing, and Finance. Most businesses are organized around the functional areas because this provides a focus for work and because it promotes professionalism and expertise. Unfortunately, organizing in terms of business functions sometimes reinforces an inward-looking orientation, sometimes called operating through **functional silos**. This inward focus devotes too much attention to what happens within the functional area (the "silo") while showing little concern for coordinating across the functional areas

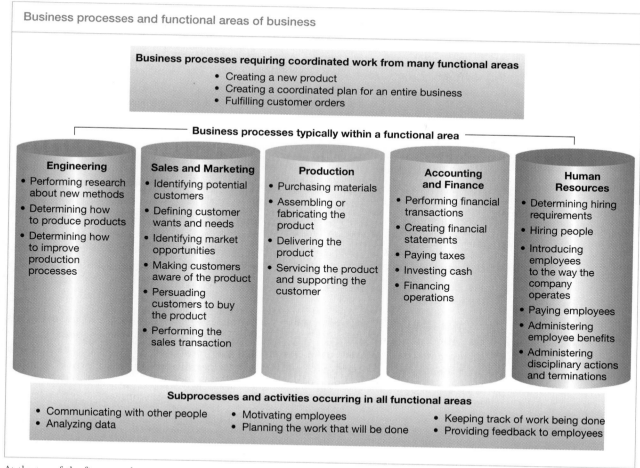

Business processes and functional areas of business

FIGURE 1.3

Business processes requiring coordinated work from many functional areas
- Creating a new product
- Creating a coordinated plan for an entire business
- Fulfilling customer orders

— Business processes typically within a functional area —

Engineering
- Performing research about new methods
- Determining how to produce products
- Determining how to improve production processes

Sales and Marketing
- Identifying potential customers
- Defining customer wants and needs
- Identifying market opportunities
- Making customers aware of the product
- Persuading customers to buy the product
- Performing the sales transaction

Production
- Purchasing materials
- Assembling or fabricating the product
- Delivering the product
- Servicing the product and supporting the customer

Accounting and Finance
- Performing financial transactions
- Creating financial statements
- Paying taxes
- Investing cash
- Financing operations

Human Resources
- Determining hiring requirements
- Hiring people
- Introducing employees to the way the company operates
- Paying employees
- Administering employee benefits
- Administering disciplinary actions and terminations

Subprocesses and activities occurring in all functional areas
- Communicating with other people
- Analyzing data
- Motivating employees
- Planning the work that will be done
- Keeping track of work being done
- Providing feedback to employees

At the top of the figure are business processes that require coordinated effort involving several functional areas. The center shows business processes that typically occur within a particular functional area. The bottom of the figure shows business processes and activities that occur in all functional areas.

and maximizing customer value. After recognizing the disadvantages of functional silos, many firms have moved a bit closer to organizing around customer-oriented processes.

Business processes are often associated with functional areas of business, but the business process is a more fundamental idea for understanding how businesses perform their work and provide value for customers. The existence of three different types of processes identified in Figure 1.3 illustrates the problem of overemphasizing functional areas when thinking about IT applications:

- *Processes that cross functional areas:* Essential processes such as creating a new product, creating a coordinated plan for an entire business, and fulfilling customer orders usually span multiple functional areas. Seeing these processes from the viewpoint of just one functional area is often misleading and contrary to the way today's business leaders want their organizations to operate.
- *Processes related to a specific functional area:* Other essential processes such as manufacturing products, identifying potential customers, and paying taxes are typically viewed as belonging to a particular functional area. The best way to learn about these processes and the information systems that support them is by learning about the functional area rather than by learning about information systems per se.
- *Activities and subprocesses occurring in every functional area:* These common activities and subprocesses include communicating with other people, analyzing data, planning the work that will be done, and providing feedback to employees. These activities often use information systems in one way or another, and are not at all unique to a particular functional area.

All three groups of processes and activities rely heavily on IT, yet only one of the three groups tends to exist primarily within the functional silos. To present as realistic a picture as possible, this book contains many examples from different functional areas but doesn't make functional areas a key emphasis. Instead, it focuses on analyzing information systems from a business professional's viewpoint regardless of the functional area.

R E A L I T Y C H E C K [✓]

Describing a Business as a System

The text states that ideas pertaining to systems, in general, can be used for thinking about how a business operates.

1. Summarize your understanding of the inputs, outputs, and major subsystems of any business with which you are familiar.

2. Explain your view of the advantages and disadvantages of dividing any business or government organization into specialized functional areas.

The Value Chain   The set of processes a firm uses to create value for its customers is often called its **value chain**.[19] The value chain includes **primary processes** that directly create the value the firm's customer perceives and **support processes** that add value indirectly by making it easier for others to perform the primary processes. The idea of the value chain is important because the way work is organized within a firm should be related to the way the firm provides value for its customers.

Figure 1.4 identifies some of the processes in a hypothetical restaurant's value chain. These primary processes include purchasing, taking orders, and serving food. Essential support processes not mentioned in the figure include cleaning the kitchen, hiring employees, paying taxes, and managing the restaurant. Managing can be viewed as a support process because it is not directly involved with doing the work that provides value for customers. This particular value chain probably does not belong to a fast-food restaurant. In most fast-food restaurants, the customers seat themselves instead of waiting to be seated. In addition, many fast-food restaurants cook the food before receiving the orders and receive payment before serving the food.

Attaining agreement about a useful view of any firm's value chain is an important step in improving its effectiveness. Although a value chain may seem obvious after a useful view of it is produced, that view is often far from obvious in advance. For example, the value chain in Figure 1.4 leaves out deciding what menu to offer and developing recipes. For some purposes, these might have been the heart of the issue. Deciding what to include and what to exclude requires judgment and careful attention to the purpose of the analysis.

FIGURE 1.4

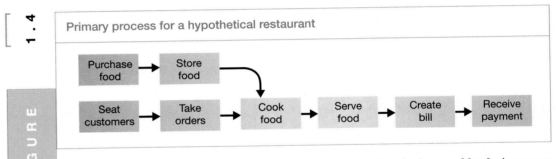

Primary process for a hypothetical restaurant

Based on the primary processes shown, this probably is not the value chain for the type of fast-food restaurant that cooks the food before taking orders.

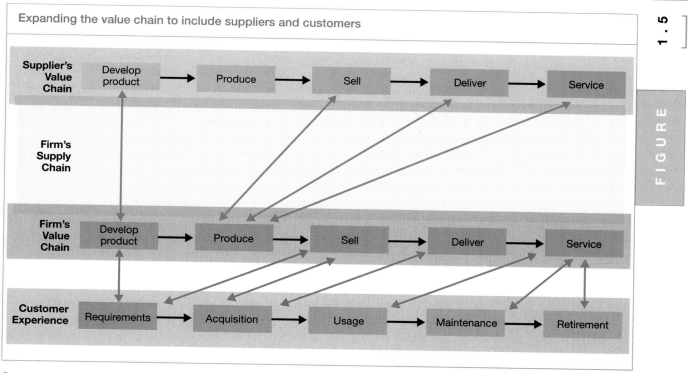

Expanding the value chain to include suppliers and customers

FIGURE   1.5

Opportunities to increase value for the customer may exist not only within the internal value chain, but also within the suppliers' processes, methods of coordinating with the suppliers, and customers' entire experience related to acquiring and using the product.

The Supply Chain and the Customer Experience   Figure 1.5 extends the idea of the value chain by showing four separate layers involved in performing work efficiently and maximizing value to the customer:

- The supplier's value chain
- The supply chain between the supplier and the firm
- The firm's value chain
- The customer's experience in acquiring and using the product

Processes inside the firm's suppliers and inside the firm itself include developing, producing, selling, delivering, and servicing the product's components or the product itself. The **supply chain** is the transactions, coordination, and movement of goods between the firm's suppliers and the firm. The customer experience includes every aspect of the customer's involvement with the firm's product. This includes determining requirements, acquiring the product, using it, maintaining it, and retiring it.

Each process in Figure 1.5 is an opportunity to improve internal efficiency or increase value to the customer, regardless of whether the improvements occur within the firm's internal operation or for a supplier's or customer's direct benefit. For example, supply chain management systems can help a firm manufacture its product with less waste and less inventory. The basic approach is to create standardized electronic links and long-term agreements with suppliers. This helps the firm price its products competitively. Within the firm, information systems can improve sales processes by providing better information for salespeople and customers. These systems can also improve service processes by maintaining customer records and hastening response. When the customer becomes involved, information systems can help fit the product to the customer's requirements and can make the product easier to use and maintain.

The Role of Information Technology   The role of IT in organizational business processes such as manufacturing and selling has expanded greatly. The first generations of computer technology were primarily used for record keeping and monitoring performance by telling managers today what happened yesterday and last week. Advances leading to online processing made it possible to capture and use information virtually from the moment it was generated. Much previously manual record keeping has been automated by capturing information as a by-product of doing work rather than as a separate clerical step.

Computerized systems can now help monitor the work as it is being done, thereby warning workers about obvious or likely errors before those errors cascade to create additional problems elsewhere. Many previously manual processes have been automated completely. In some cases this eliminated jobs; in other cases it allowed people who previously performed manual steps to work more like programmers specifying what machines should do.

In addition to affecting the nature of work and the workplace, use of technology has also led to changes in the way firms compete. IT has helped firms improve their internal operations, thereby reducing internal costs and accelerating product development. Lower internal costs make profits possible even at lower selling prices. The sooner a product is on the market, the sooner it can generate profits. Quicker time to market is especially important for technology products in which prices drop rapidly as soon as many similar products become available. IT also supports sales and marketing processes in many ways. It provides salespeople better information about prospective customers; it helps salespeople identify and demonstrate the right product choices; it helps companies calculate individualized prices based on the needs and resources of specific customers. IT applications also make the actual purchase transactions simpler and faster.

The role of IT does not end once the customer has purchased the product. IT can support customer service activities by keeping track of both general information about each customer and information related to specific customer interactions, such as repairs or warranty claims. IT can also be built into products and services as an important component of what the customer is buying. For example, we may think of automobiles as physical objects, but they are increasingly served and controlled using IT-based devices such as antilock brakes.

The Trend toward E-Business

E-business was defined earlier as the practice of performing and coordinating critical business processes through the extensive use of computer and communication technologies and computerized data. Concepts including the value chain, supply chain, and customer experience help demonstrate that the trend toward e-business involves much more than having a cool Web site. Leading e-business companies like Dell Computer use information technology extensively across their entire supply chain, internal value chain, and customer experience. Dell was one of the first manufacturers to use the Internet for high-volume sales to consumers. It was also a leader in using information systems to integrate its supply chain with its manufacturing processes. This is how it achieved a negative cost of capital while many of its competitors were still struggling to reduce excess inventory levels.

Many other firms that are not typically associated with high technology have also made significant strides in the direction of e-business. For example, the *Wall Street Journal* quoted the vice president of e-business at Clorox as saying "Even bleach is an e-business." Although Clorox has exchanged electronic purchase orders and invoices with its largest customers for several decades, over half of its shipping notices, payments, and order acknowledgements are entered into corporate databases from telephone calls, faxes, or e-mail messages. Clorox is planning to set up a Web-based exchange to handle orders with all suppliers and retailers. It estimates its internal costs for ordering from suppliers might be reduced to $15 per order from $100. The plan's success will depend in part on whether its suppliers become more wired themselves over the next several years.[20]

Figure 1.6 illustrates that having a cool, or at least useable, Web site is only the tip of the iceberg in e-business. The part of e-business that a customer experiences directly is often called **electronic commerce** (**e-commerce**). This refers to using the Internet and other communication technology for marketing, selling, and servicing products. E-commerce often includes tasks such as:

- Informing a customer of a product's existence
- Providing in-depth information about the product

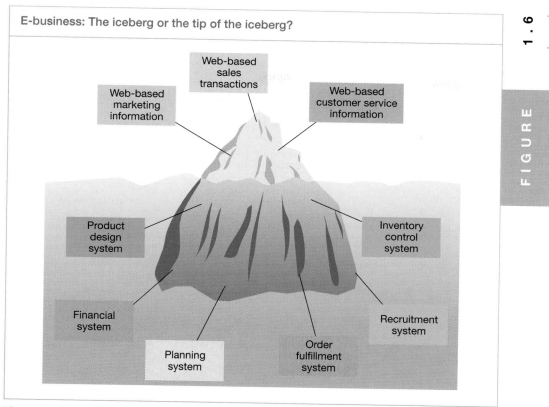

FIGURE 1.6

E-business: The iceberg or the tip of the iceberg?

The customer may directly experience Web-based marketing, sales transactions, and customer service, but e-business involves a great deal more that customers never see.

- Establishing the customer's requirements
- Performing the purchase transaction
- Delivering the product electronically if the product happens to be software or information
- Providing customer service electronically

The distinction between B2B and B2C is cited frequently in discussing e-commerce opportunities. **B2B** (business-to-business) refers to using the Internet as a primary channel for selling products to other businesses. **B2C** (business-to-consumer) refers to using the Internet as a primary channel for selling products to consumers. In some cases B2B operations are different from B2C operations because some consumers might be more influenced by fads, flashy presentation, and impulses to buy. In contrast, the premise of B2B focuses more on repetitive purchasing processes involving specific requirements and cost comparison. On the other hand, the fact that Dell Computer's Web site has separate sections for B2B, B2C, and even B2G (business-to-government) shows that many firms operate in all of these areas and that some types of B2B and B2C may be quite similar.

As in traditional market situations, e-commerce provides many alternatives for linking the buyer and the seller. In cases such as Dell Computer, a manufacturer sets up a Web site and sells directly to customers. In other cases, a retailer or distributor like Amazon.com uses a Web site to sell products produced by many different firms. In yet other situations, a Web site may be designed as an auction or clearinghouse to permit different buyers to bid for merchandise that is offered for sale. In all these examples, the use of a Web site is only one of several possible ways to handle the interactions. For example, electronic commerce activities directed at a limited set of pre-qualified customers might control access to a Web site using passwords or might bypass the Web altogether by using a private network that may or may not have a Web-like interface. Table 1.2 presents a number of examples that illustrate the range of business models directly based on e-commerce.

E-Commerce Business Models

Notice that some of the examples fall into several of these broad e-commerce categories.

Business model	How it works	Examples
E-retailer	Use the Internet to sell directly to consumers or businesses	amazon.com egghead.com buy.com travelocity.com expedia.com
Clicks and bricks	Use both the Internet and traditional stores to sell to customers	The Gap Office Depot Eddie Bauer Barnes & Noble
Financial services	Provide financial services such as stock brokerage using the Web	Charles Schwab E*Trade Merrill Lynch Morgan Stanley Dean Witter
E-auction	Run auctions through the Web	eBay Freemarkets, Inc.
E-marketplace	Provide information and commercial transactions related to a specific group of companies in a specific industry	Ariba CommerceOne VerticalNet
Content aggregator	Provide many types of information for consumers and the general public, thereby encouraging Web users to visit the site each time they use the Web	America Online (AOL) Yahoo! CNET.com Lycos
Content provider	Provide content over the Internet	New York Times Wall Street Journal Disney Google Northern Lights AskJeeves
Web hosting, Internet service providers, and other infrastructure services	Provide services related to running Web sites and providing access to the Web	Exodus Communications EarthLink At Home Corp. Akamai Technologies America Online (AOL) Microsoft Network

Regardless of how a firm interacts with its customers, operating in an e-business style requires responsiveness, accuracy, and efficiency that can be accomplished only through highly developed supply chains and value chains supported by information systems that customers may never experience directly. The difficulties many Internet retailers experienced in fulfilling orders during the 1999 holiday season also demonstrate this phenomenon. Whether or not these companies had great Web sites, their inability to perform essential processes such as obtaining inventory, processing orders, and providing quick delivery led to customer disillusionment and contributed to the disastrous stock market results in the spring of 2000. Similarly, some of the traditional retailers who established online stores in addition to their existing stores experienced disappointing results because their internal systems were not responsive enough to both traditional and online channels. For example, product returns from their online sales could not be brought to their traditional stores because the information systems supporting the online sales were not integrated with systems supporting the traditional stores.

If one looks beyond specific stories and the unique opportunities in specific situations, the trend toward e-business is largely about different assumptions about how work systems should and must operate in order for companies to be competitive. Table 1.3

TABLE
1.3

Using the Work System Framework to Understand the Trend toward E-Business

Basic assumptions about work systems change as firms move toward e-business.

Assumptions about Products and Services, Customers, and Business Environment

Past Assumptions	Assumptions with E-Business
Rate of change is rapid as IT becomes integrated into organizations.	Rate of change is accelerating. New business models and new forms of competition abound.
Organizations must remain reasonably stable for the sake of efficiency.	New ways to deploy IT enable faster organizational change and new ways to organize around virtual teams, outsourcing, and dynamic work roles.
Planning is important, particularly long-range, strategic plans.	Planning remains important, but the ability to respond quickly to variability and surprises is more important. Contingency planning is more important than producing an initial optimum plan.
Build or purchase application software that supports the organization.	Build or purchase technology infrastructure that supports the organization today and permits it to adapt to continuing changes in its competitive environment.
Customer purchases products by selecting from the supplier's product list.	Customer and supplier negotiate requirements and the supplier customizes the product to suit the customer.
Prices are somewhat negotiable, depending on the type of product and market.	Prices are highly dynamic.

Assumptions about Business Processes

Past Assumptions	Assumptions with E-Business
Business processes are designed to compensate for the unavailability of important information.	Business processes are designed based on the availability of important information.
Delays between planning, execution, and control activities are lengthy.	Cycles of planning, execution, and control are rapid and occur conveniently at different levels of detail.
Information systems record information about the process but do not play a direct role in doing the work.	Information systems are integrated into the business process and perform or control major process steps.
Information systems are separate from value added steps in the business process.	Value added steps in the business process collect information automatically and store that information as a by-product that can be used for planning and control.

Assumptions about Work System Participants

Past Assumptions	Assumptions with E-Business
Information technology is unfamiliar and somewhat frightening.	Information technology is familiar and not frightening.
People have reasonably stable jobs and careers.	Rapid change in work life forces people to adapt frequently to new situations.
Participants play their independent assigned roles in the work system.	Participants are under greater pressure to perform well individually and as a team.
Managers have little patience with mathematical rationales and technical methods.	Managers are even less interested in complex rationales and optimization methods because of the rapid change in their environments.

Continued

TABLE

Using the Work System Framework to Understand the Trend toward E-Business, *continued*

Assumptions about Information Used in Work Systems

Past Assumptions	Assumptions with E-Business
Track customers, inventories, and business activities at an aggregate level because data capture is expensive. Worry about details never captured or lost in the aggregation.	Track customers, inventories, and business activities at a unit level through the use of bar codes and other automatic data capture methods. It is feasible to aggregate and segment at any level of detail.
Can obtain information only after substantial delays for collection, compilation, and summarization.	Obtain detailed information in near real time.
Available information is incomplete. Analytical models are needed to fill in some of the blanks.	Complete information is available. Though still useful for many purposes, analytical models are not as necessary because more of the details are available and because simulations are easy to perform and inexpensive.
Since communication bandwidth is limited and expensive, communication through text and numerical data is cost effective. Simple phone calls are not too expensive, but video-conferencing and other extensive exchanges of multimedia information are expensive.	Since communication bandwidth is inexpensive, it is possible to access computerized information through networks and contact individuals through whatever media are most effective.

Assumptions about the Technology Used in Work Systems

Past Assumptions	Assumptions with E-Business
Awkward and confusing interfaces make IT difficult to use unless users receive extensive training and use IT frequently.	The interface will be simpler and more intuitive. Hands-on use of information technology is second nature and not remarkable.
Limited ability to store and retrieve information constrains analysis and decision-making.	Virtually unlimited ability to store and retrieve information means that any information that can be captured is available for analysis and decision-making.
Image and audio information plays little role in decision-making because the information cannot be processed effectively.	Greater ability to process images and audio information, leading to better, and more qualitative, decision-making tools.
Limited ability to summarize and display information graphically.	Many powerful ways to summarize and display information graphically supplement and in some cases supplant more quantitative methods.
Connectivity to other parts of the organization and to customers and suppliers is limited.	Connectivity to other parts of the organization and to customers and suppliers is extensive and growing rapidly.

compares past assumptions versus assumptions under e-business for most of the elements in the work system framework. One reason for the success of Dell and other e-business leaders is that these companies have made most of the new assumptions into realities sooner than their competitors.

Thus far we have discussed the book's first major theme, that business operates through systems and that these systems can be described as work systems in which human participants perform a business process using information and other technology in order to produce some combination of products and services for a customer. E-business is a style of operating an organization by making extensive use of information technology within critical work systems. The next major theme involves the phases of building and maintaining any work system (including information systems).

PHASES IN BUILDING AND MAINTAINING SYSTEMS

Figure 1.1, the framework for visualizing any work system, is one of two "common denominators" that apply throughout this book when thinking about systems in organizations. That framework is used for describing how a system currently operates or how it might operate differently in the future. As shown in Figure 1.7, the other common denominator is a way to see how systems in organizations are built and maintained. This is described in terms of four phases: initiation, development, implementation, and maintenance. These phases apply to information systems just as they apply to work systems in general since information systems are a special type of work system. Chapter 12, "Building and Maintaining Systems," will show how these phases summarize different types of system life cycles that operate differently depending on whether the software is developed internally or acquired from a vendor. It will also explain why highly technical work such as programming usually takes up less than 20% of this effort.

Initiation is the process of defining the need to change an existing work system, identifying the people who should be involved in deciding what to do, and describing in general terms how the work system should operate differently and how any information system that supports it should operate differently. This phase may occur in response to recognized problems, such as data that cannot be found and used effectively, or high error rates in data. In other cases, it is part of a planning process in which the organization is searching for ways to improve and innovate, even if current systems pose no overt problems. This phase concludes with a verbal or written agreement about the directions in which the work system and information system should change, plus a shared understanding that the proposed changes are technically and organizationally feasible.

Development is the process of acquiring and configuring hardware, software, and other resources needed to perform both the required IT-related functions and the required functions not related to IT. This phase starts by deciding exactly how the computerized and manual parts of the work system will operate. It then goes on to acquire the needed resources. If the hardware isn't already in place, development includes purchasing and installing the hardware. If the software isn't in place, it includes purchasing the software, producing it from scratch, or modifying existing software. Regardless of how the hardware and software are acquired, this phase includes creating documentation explaining how both the work system and the information system are supposed to operate. The development phase concludes with thorough testing of the entire information system to identify and correct misunderstandings and programming errors. Completion of development does not mean "the system works." Rather, it means only

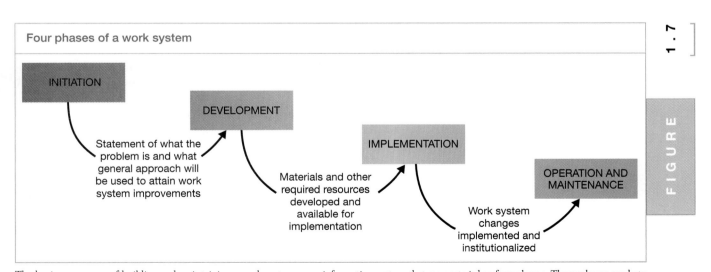

Four phases of a work system

FIGURE 1.7

The business process of building and maintaining a work system or an information system that supports it has four phases. These phases apply to all systems in business even though the details of the individual phases may be quite different for different systems.

that the computerized parts of the work system operate on a computer. Whether or not the "system works" will be determined by how it is actually used in the organization.

Implementation is the process of making a new work system operational in the organization. This phase starts from the point when the software runs on the computer and has been tested. Activities in implementation include planning, user training, conversion to the new information system and work system, and follow up to make sure the entire system is operating effectively. The implementation phase may involve major changes in the way organizations or individuals operate. Conversion from the old to the new must be planned and executed carefully to prevent errors or even chaos. For information systems that keep track of transactions such as invoices and customer orders, the conversion process requires some users to do double work during a pilot test, operating simultaneously with the old and new systems. Running two information systems in parallel helps identify unanticipated problems that might require information system or work system modifications before implementation is complete.

Operation and maintenance is the ongoing operation of the work system and the information system, plus efforts directed at enhancing either system and correcting bugs. At minimum, this requires that someone be in charge of ensuring that the work system is operating well, that the information system is providing the anticipated benefits, and that the work system and information system are changed further if the business situation calls for it.

The main point about the four phases is that the work of building and maintaining systems in organizations is not just technical work. Regardless of how the four phases are performed, business professionals play an important role in all four of the phases. For example, regardless of whether the software is developed from scratch or purchased from a software vendor, business professionals have to be involved throughout the four phases. In the initiation phase they decide whether the system is worth building from a business viewpoint. In the development phase they help define exactly how the work system should operate, thereby providing guidelines for the technical staff that is programming the software in the information system. Because the implementation phase is the process of changing from the old way of doing work to the new way, it is clearly the responsibility of the business professionals and their managers. Similarly, the wholehearted support and commitment of business professionals is usually necessary for successful operation and maintenance.

[**L O O K   A H E A D**]

Table 12.4 lists the steps and deliverables in a traditional system life cycle. Notice the high degree of user participation in most steps not involving programming.

Project Success or Failure

Table 1.4 lists common reasons for failures during each of the four major phases of building and maintaining a system. Failure during the initiation phase means that the project is terminated before the technical work starts. No one wants a project to fail, but failure at this phase is much less expensive and disruptive than failure at other phases because much less time and effort is lost. In development failures, the work is done on the detailed design and programming but the information system never runs successfully on the computer. In implementation failures, the programs run on the computer but the organization does not fully embrace the new ways of doing work. As a result, the intended benefits do not occur. Failure during operation and maintenance occurs when the information system users revert back to previous work practices or when the information system is not kept up to date with changing business requirements.

Notice that project success or failure is not just a technical issue. For example, a project directed at building a new Web site for e-commerce might fail because technology such as programming languages and databases is not used appropriately. It might also fail for many other reasons:

- The e-commerce approach might have too little support among company employees and managers who traditionally did their work in a different way.
- The Web effort might be too expensive for the company to finance.
- The requirements for the Web site might not be obvious.
- The company's IT staff might not have enough familiarity with Web site design.

TABLE 1.4

Common Reasons for Project Failure at Different Project Phases

Information system projects can be terminated at any of the four phases. Terminating a failing project sooner is better than letting it waste resources unnecessarily.

Phase	Common Reasons for Project Failure
Initiation	• The reasons for building the system have too little support. • The system seems too expensive.
Development	• It is too difficult to define the requirements. • The system is not technically feasible. • The project is too difficult for the technical staff assigned.
Implementation	• The system requires too great a change from existing work practices. • Potential users dislike the system or resist using it. • Too little effort is put into the implementation.
Operation and Maintenance	• System controls are insufficient. • Too little effort goes into supporting effective use. • The system is not updated as business needs change.

- The implementation of modified internal work systems might involve too much change to absorb easily.
- The Web site might have security flaws or other inadequate controls.
- The Web site might not be updated as competitors bring in their own Web-based innovations.

REALITY CHECK [✓]

Phases in Building and Maintaining Systems

This section describes four phases in building and maintaining systems.

1. Use the phases to describe a project of any type that you have done.
2. Identify the important challenges in each phase of your project and explain whether the challenges you encountered are related to the general discussion of the phases.

INFORMATION TECHNOLOGY AS A DRIVING FORCE FOR INNOVATION

The dramatic progress that has occurred in information technology has been a driving force in business innovation by making it possible to perform work in ways that were not previously possible. Here are a few examples of impacts of progress in information technology:

- The ability to miniaturize electronic circuits and make electronic devices portable has made it possible for people to carry cell phones, laptop computers, and computerized personal organizers such as Palm Pilots, thereby making it possible to do work more effectively outside of a traditional workplace. Without the technical progress, new ways of doing and managing work would not have been feasible.
- The comparatively low cell phone charges in Europe have encouraged widespread adoption of cell phones. In turn, this has led to initial examples of **m-commerce** (mobile commerce), such as using a cell phone to pay for parking spaces or soft drinks in vending machines. In this type of m-commerce, the cell phone call initiates electronic transfer of money from an account linked to the cell phone. Eventually, m-commerce may replace cash in many of the small transactions of everyday life.
- The use of bar codes in industry and government has enabled many innovations in tracking inventories and shipments. Consider the U.S. Army's experience during

the 1991 Persian Gulf War, during which it sent 40,000 tractor-trailer-sized containers to Saudi Arabia with no identifying information. It was necessary to open each container to find out whether it contained tires, generators, or something else. There were also many over-shipments because, according to *Fortune*, supply sergeants traditionally ordered everything three times in the expectation that two requisitions would go astray in unmarked containers. A review of logistics operations following the war led to a vastly improved approach in which bar codes on the containers are used to access a database listing their contents and global positioning satellites are used to signal their location.[21]

- Increased storage capacity of hard disks in personal computers plus improved data compression methods have made it possible to store large audio and video files on personal computers. This ability plus the ability to extract electronically coded songs from music CDs and the ability to transmit data between computers have created a major threat to the music industry: How will record labels and artists receive compensation for their efforts if music lovers can obtain audio files over the Internet for free?

Examples such as these touch aspects of business ranging from day-to-day operations through industry strategies and structure. A first step in understanding the role and impact of technological progress is simply to look at the functions IT can perform. Surprisingly, these can be boiled down to six basic data processing operations: capturing, transmitting, storing, retrieving, manipulating, and displaying data. Consider a grocery store's customer checkout system:

1. It *captures* data using the bar code.
2. It *transmits* data to a computer that looks up the item's price and description.
3. It *stores* information about the item for calculating the bill.
4. It *retrieves* price and description information from the computer.
5. It *manipulates* the information when it adds up the bill.
6. It *displays* information when it shows each price it calculates and prints the receipt.

Table 1.5 defines the six functions and shows some of the technologies that focus on each of them. Some of these technologies have been used and improved for decades, whereas others have appeared only recently. Given the rapid innovation of the last few decades there is no question that other technologies will emerge.

The entire history of computing in this century has been about performing the six functions of IT faster and more efficiently through an amazing sequence of technological breakthroughs. Since the 1960s, key characteristics of computer hardware technologies such as price, reliability, and density have been improving at a rate of 30% to 50% per year. Even at a rate of 20%, the equivalent of hardware capabilities costing $100 in 1960 would have cost $10.74 in 1970, $1.15 in 1980, $0.12 in 1990, and little more than a penny in 2000. To put this in perspective, if automotive technology had improved at that rate since 1960, a new car would cost less than a movie ticket, and we could drive across the United States on several ounces of gasoline.

Most experts believe the current rate of improvement will continue for at least another decade, extending trends that have operated for years. Major directions for these improvements include:

- Greater miniaturization, speed, and portability
- Greater connectivity and continuing convergence of computing and communications
- Greater use of digitized information and multimedia
- Better software techniques and interfaces with people

Each of these trends continues to have important implications for business operations.

Greater Miniaturization, Speed, and Portability

The increasing speed and power of electronic components is the force underlying the immense progress to date in computers and telecommunications. These enhancements result directly from **miniaturization**, the process of creating smaller electronic compo-

Six Functions of Information Technology

TABLE 1.5

Function	Definition	Example of devices or technologies used to perform this function
Capture	Obtain a representation of information in a form permitting it to be transmitted or stored	Keyboard, bar code scanner, document scanner, optical character recognition, sound recorder, video camera, voice recognition software
Transmit	Move information from one place to another	Broadcast radio, broadcast television via regional transmitters, cable TV, satellite broadcasts, telephone networks, data transmission networks for moving business data, fiber optic cable, fax machine, electronic mail, voice mail, Internet
Store	Move information to a specific place for later retrieval	Paper, computer tape, floppy disk, hard disk, optical disk, CD-ROM, flash memory
Retrieve	Find the specific information that is currently needed	Paper, computer tape, floppy disk, hard disk, optical disk, CD-ROM, flash memory
Manipulate	Create new information from existing information through summarizing, sorting, rearranging, reformatting, or other types of calculations	Computer (plus software)
Display	Show information to a person	Laser printer, computer screen

nents with greater capabilities. Miniaturization of computers started when the solid-state transistor (an off-on device that can represent a 0 or 1) superseded the vacuum tube (an older off-on device). It started to increase exponentially with the 1959 invention of the **integrated circuit**, a device incorporating multiple transistors on a single silicon chip the size of a fingernail. Integrated circuits were smaller, used less electricity, and were more reliable because they replaced many separate parts that previously had to be wired together (see Figure 1.8).

The degree of progress that has occurred through miniaturization of electronic components is difficult to imagine because it defies our typical experience. Back-to-back improvements of 10 or 15% starting from a respectable base are viewed as significant achievements. In contrast, Table 1.6 shows that the capacity of computer memory chips has increased at a rate predicted in the early 1970s by Gordon Moore, a cofounder of Intel. Consistent with this prediction, which is often called **Moore's Law**, chip capacities have doubled approximately every 18 months for over 20 years, and will probably continue to do so for years to come. Memory chips containing the equivalent of over 256 million transistors are now being sold. This is just one of many aspects of the technical progress that has occurred.

The increase in speed and reliability due to miniaturization has paved the way toward the development of computers, VCRs, fax machines, bar code scanners, cellular phones, telephone switches, fiber optic phone cables, and many other types of information technology. Raw computing power in the year 2000 was probably 100 times cheaper than it was in 1990.

The miniaturization of electronic components plus advances in communication technology has also led to much greater **portability** of computer and communications devices; devices are considered portable when their users can carry them around conveniently. Previous generations of computers and telephones were far from portable. Early computers required specially air-conditioned rooms, and telephones were anchored in place by wire connections. Just being able to store hundreds of pages of data on a pocket-sized

FIGURE 1.8

Comparison of a vacuum tube computer and an integrated circuit

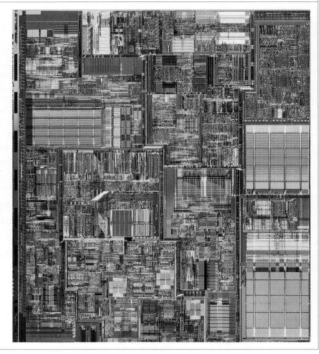

The first general purpose computers contained thousands of vacuum tubes, each of which represented a single off-on switch. The Pentium IV microprocessor is a single integrated circuit about the size of a fingernail. It contains complex logical circuitry along with the equivalent of millions of off-on switches.

TABLE 1.6

Progress in Memory Chip Capacity Since 1973

This table shows that the storage capacity of computer memory chips has been doubling approximately every 18 months. For each type of chip the date given is one or two years after its first commercial introduction, but before its sales peaked and started to decline as the next generation came into use. The date was estimated by combining data on product introductions and product sales patterns.[22,23] (The term *kilobit* refers to approximately one thousand bits since a kilobit chip actually contains 1,024 off-on units. Similarly, a megabit chip actually contains 1,024 times 1,024 bits.)

Approximate date of widespread commercial availability	Type of chip	Capacity in number of bits
1973	1 kilobit	1,024
1976	4 kilobit	4,096
1979	16 kilobit	16,384
1982	64 kilobit	65,536
1985	256 kilobit	262,144
1988	1 megabit	1,048,576
1991	4 megabit	4,194,304
1994	16 megabit	16,777,216
1997	64 megabit	67,108,864
2000	256 megabit	268,435,456

diskette was an important step toward portability, even if the computer remained anchored in place. Today, the equivalent of over 450 diskettes can be stored on a single CD-ROM that costs less than a dollar and can be generated from a personal computer whose CD drive has both read and write capability, an option that costs less than $100.

Although large computers and major telephone installations are still in fixed locations, today's individual users have many choices of portable devices. The popularity of cell phones has clearly demonstrated that telephones no longer must be anchored by wires. The first common portable computers were laptops, which business professionals could carry conveniently for use on airplanes and other locations away from the office. Personal digital assistants (PDAs) equipped with wireless communication capabilities support new work patterns for mobile workers ranging from salespeople to police officers (see Figure 1.9).

Although portable computers are more convenient for users, the downside is that portability makes it much more difficult to control the flow of information. A single diskette in a person's pocket can contain a company's entire customer list; the hard disk in a laptop computer can store over 1,000 times that amount of information. The risks created by carrying around this much confidential information are evident from what happened when someone stole a laptop computer from a car parked for five minutes in downtown London in late 1990. The car belonged to a wing commander in Great Britain's Royal Air Force. The laptop contained some of General Schwartzkopf's plans for attacking Iraq. (The commander was court-martialed, demoted, and fined. The computer was returned anonymously a week later.)[24] A decade later, a laptop owned by the CEO of the telecommunications company Qualcomm was stolen from his hotel room while he was attending a conference.

Greater Connectivity and Continuing Convergence of Computing and Communications

Connectivity is the ability to transmit data between electronic devices at different locations. Increasingly, computerized data can be transmitted almost instantaneously nearly anywhere in the world. The scope of connectivity includes interactive communication between people, electronic mail, transmittal of faxes, and transmission of business data

---

FIGURE 1.9

Using a PDA in mobile work

The combination of a cellular phone and a PDA helps this salesperson work more effectively.

between computers. Connectivity is important to businesses because it reduces some of the disadvantages of being separated geographically. It also makes it easier to obtain important business information, much of which comes from outside sources, such as customers and suppliers.

Connectivity means more than just transmitting a signal from one place to another, however. Because many organizations own hardware and software purchased from a variety of vendors, true connectivity often depends on the ability of these heterogeneous components to work together conveniently and inexpensively. This is often called **interoperability**. Software products that perform the same or complementary functions are often rated in terms of interoperability. For example, the interoperability of two word processing programs is determined by the extent to which a document produced using one word processor looks the same and is handled the same way when it is displayed by another word processor, perhaps on a different type of computer. In this case, interoperability requires compatible internal coding of data, compatible program logic, compatible user interfaces, and compatible communication with storage devices and printers.

The need for connectivity and interoperability has generated customer demand for **open systems**, which are technical systems that use clearly described, nonproprietary industry standards available to anyone. Hardware and software buyers insisted on the movement toward open systems in order to make it easier to switch hardware or software brands without a complete technical overhaul. Deploying open systems supports a range of opportunities to compete more effectively. Within the firm, these trends make it easier and cheaper to build information systems and transmit data. Reducing these costs makes it more practical to use information systems to help people work together and to link more effectively with customers. On the other hand, open systems are not always a boon to hardware and software suppliers. Many of them have tried to resist an open systems approach because they see open systems as a direct threat to a strategy of providing unique, incompatible capabilities that lock in customers by making brand switching difficult.

Greater connectivity supports the continuing **convergence of computing and communications** whereby communication capabilities have become essential to many computer systems, and computing capabilities have become essential to communication systems (see Figure 1.10). Consider the way salespeople at many firms access wide area networks using laptop computers or touch-tone telephones to obtain pricing information and enter orders. Similarly, companies deploying computers in branch offices often require communication networks to perform company-wide computing tasks such as consolidating results and sharing data. This convergence even affects individuals in their everyday lives (see Figure 1.11).

Greater Use of Digitized Information and Multimedia

Information exists in five different forms—predefined data items, text, pictures, sounds, and video (sequences of pictures and sound), each of which can be digitized. **Digitization** involves coding the data as an equivalent or approximately equivalent set of numbers. For example, the letters in the word "cab" might be coded 33-31-32 if the coding rule were to add 30 to the position of each letter in the alphabet. Likewise, a picture can be digitized by dividing it into tiny dots on a grid and assigning a number to represent the color and intensity of the dot. Because any type of data can be digitized, any type of data can be stored, manipulated, and transmitted by computerized systems.

The method used to digitize pictures and sounds originally limited the feasibility of processing these types of data on computers. The problem was that digitized pictures and sounds require much more storage and transmission capability than pure text. For example, all the paragraphs of straight text in this book can be stored on several pocket-sized diskettes, but a single high-resolution photograph could require a similar amount of storage as all of that text.

Fortunately, advances in miniaturization and speed of electronic components made large-scale use of digitized data affordable. These advances started solving the problem

[**L O O K   A H E A D**]

Figure 8.9 illustrates the process of digitizing an image.

Convergence of computing and communications

FIGURE 1.10

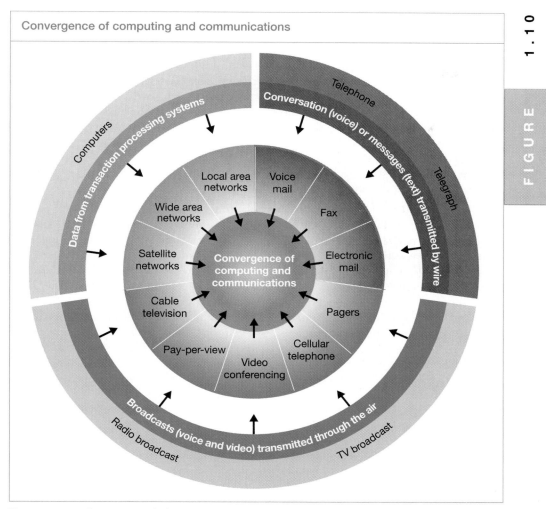

The convergence of computing and telecommunications sprang from separate innovations related to telegraphs (1794), telephones (1876), radio broadcasting (1906), television broadcasting (1925), and computers (around 1945). Existing combinations of computers and telecommunications will continue to evolve into new applications in the future.

Example of the convergence of computing and communications

FIGURE 1.11

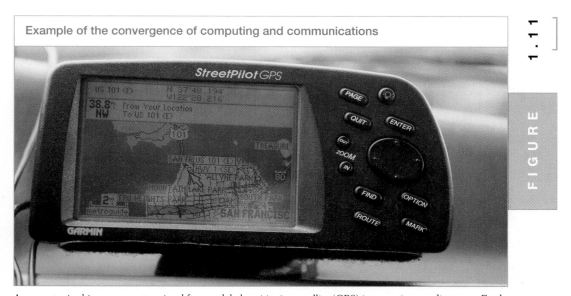

A computer in this car converts a signal from a global positioning satellite (GPS) into precise coordinates on Earth, and displays the location on a map while giving synthesized spoken instructions for finding the destination.

by providing processing speeds and storage capacities needed to store, manipulate, and transmit pictures and sounds. This made widespread use of fax machines and video-conferencing economically feasible. These advances also made the extensive use of multimedia feasible. **Multimedia** is the use of multiple types of data, such as text, pictures, and sounds, within the same application. The first steps toward multimedia involved things such as combining drawing software with word processors. Current software for creating presentations now includes capabilities to handle photographs, sound clips, and video clips. Anyone who uses the World Wide Web sees that multimedia has emerged from its infancy and can be used extensively in education, entertainment, and business applications.

Better Software Techniques and Interfaces with People

The first computerized systems were difficult to develop and use. People who created these systems used development methods and programming languages that are primitive in comparison to today's methods. They had to share computers that were often overloaded and frequently produced results after substantial delays. They had to use computer terminals that were small, blurry, and unable to handle different font sizes or graphics (see Figure 1.12). They lacked database management systems and other tools that separated technical aspects of data handling from the logic of the application. Advances in many directions have made it easier to define how the computer system is supposed to operate and how to program and debug it. These advances generally involve permitting programmers (or users) to specify what they want the computer to accomplish rather than specifying every detail of how the computer should store, retrieve, and manipulate the data. The software advances themselves were made possible by advances in miniaturization and speed that made computers much more powerful.

The same types of advances that made programming easier also made the use of computers easier. Today, millions of workers use desktop computers interactively, even though they may know little about computer technology. Computer monitors designed to display text, graphics, and even photographic images have replaced early computer terminals with limited ability to handle graphics. Interactive techniques for requesting, filtering, and displaying information have replaced earlier methods of delivering management data using inflexible computer-generated listings that only programmers could specify. Users of current computer systems can often specify what they need by pointing and filling in blanks instead of mastering complicated computer languages and

Comparison of a current computer monitor with a terminal from the 1980s

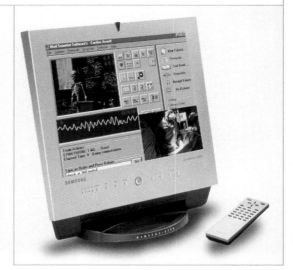

Comparison of the older computer monitor with the powerful flat panel monitor illustrates how far display technology has come since the 1980s.

remembering awkward command codes. Computer users have ready access to word processors, spreadsheets, and presentation tools that personal computers could not handle a decade ago. Even though we don't know exactly how computers will be used in the future, ongoing advances in both hardware and software make it safe to predict that they will be even easier to use than they are today.

R E A L I T Y C H E C K   ✓

Progress in Processing Data

This section identified four important trends in processing data.

1. Explain how these trends have affected you directly.
2. Identify areas where you wish the trends had affected you but you have not felt any impact yet.

OBSTACLES WHEN APPLYING INFORMATION TECHNOLOGY IN THE REAL WORLD

One of this book's central goals is to help you see information technology and information systems for what they really are—powerful, valuable tools, but not magic. When applied thoughtfully, these tools can bring important benefits for individuals, organizations, and customers. When misapplied, they can waste tremendous amounts of time, effort, and money. We will close this introductory chapter by identifying some of the obstacles to applying IT successfully in the real world of business. These obstacles include unrealistic expectations, difficulty building and modifying information systems, difficulty integrating systems that are built for different purposes, organizational inertia and problems of dealing with change, and genuine difficulty anticipating what will happen.

Unrealistic Expectations and Techno-hype

Computer technology has always received more than its share of speculation and hype. In 1952, an early Univac computer used simple statistical methods to "predict" the winner of the Presidential election. The day following the election, a newspaper headline read: "Big Electronic Gadget Proves Machines Smarter Than Men."[25] What might have seemed like a giant brain at the time had considerably less computing power than a personal computer you can put in a shopping cart at an office supply store today.

In today's business world, computer mystique has expanded to encompass business and social environments that use computers extensively. Many books and articles have described what businesses must do to succeed in the information age—the age of smart machines, intelligent corporations, total quality, globalization, and continual change and reengineering. Separating hype from reality in these discussions is sometimes difficult, especially when the message is conveyed in a loosely disguised infomercial for technology vendors or consulting firms.

Hardware and software vendors often add to the confusion by claiming that they "sell solutions." The work system framework in Figure 1.1 shows why this is misleading. Unless the totality of a problem is poor technology that can be replaced without changing anything else, technology is almost never a solution by itself. Addressing a real business problem usually requires the organization to do something differently, and this usually requires changes in at least several parts of the work system. Even if the required changes involve better use of IT, other factors may be much more important. For example, a company may invest in a top-of-the-line computer system with the most current software on the market, but if the right people aren't in place to operate the software, or if the people working on the computer aren't properly trained, the investment may be wasted.

[L O O K   A H E A D]

Figure 9.10 shows the range of images that are associated with artificial intelligence.

Even when they have no reason to express a bias, people often exaggerate or misstate the role of technology. "Auto screws up" might seem a strange headline for an article about a traffic accident, but the business magazine *Forbes* used "When machines screw up" as the title of an article about an ill-fated decision to use computers to grant mortgage loans in as little as 15 minutes. According to the article, the problem had much less to do with computers than with an overly aggressive business decision to sidestep basic loan qualification procedures.[26] In another example, a *Business Week* article about the German company SAP and its highly integrated enterprise software package said that its interwoven programs "can speed decision making, slash costs, and give managers control over global empires at the click of a mouse."[27] Although this software certainly can help in speeding decision-making and slashing costs, it cannot perform the magic trick of giving managers control over global empires with a click of a mouse. Exaggerations or poetic license of this type might seem a trivial matter, except that we often hear that computers made errors, were slow and inaccurate, or were responsible for problems. A careful look usually reveals that the real problems were human business decisions related to the design or execution of business processes. Confusions about what computers can and cannot do make it more difficult to use IT to the fullest.

There has also been a lot of hype about the Internet. Consider the following sentence, taken out of context, but similar to many other claims and predictions about the Internet: "The Internet promises to change your whole manufacturing process, allowing you to communicate instantly with suppliers, partners, and customers on a worldwide basis."[28] It is true the Internet makes it possible to transmit information to almost any point in the developed world within seconds. However, by itself the Internet can't promise anything; it is just a computer network and does not have the ability to make promises. The Internet may be used to improve certain steps in manufacturing processes, but it probably won't change "your whole manufacturing process" since many steps will probably remain the same. And the fact that you can send a message around the world in a second does not mean you can communicate instantly with suppliers, partners, and customers around the world. What if your message arrives in the middle of the night? What if the recipient isn't ready to look at your message because it not part of an established process? What if the recipient isn't willing or able to change a production run that is already underway? These objections might seem like nit-picking, but in an environment of excessive hype it is worthwhile to be skeptical about claims that technical tools have the power to change the way people and organizations work.

Difficulty Building and Modifying IT-Based Systems

Today it is much easier to build IT-based systems than it ever has been, but the task is still difficult. The fact that IT still has a long way to go is illustrated by the enormous effort that went into the **Year 2000 (Y2K) problem**, which was related to the way many information systems use just two digits to identify the year portion of a date. Coding dates as mm/dd/yy was fine if the year was 1988 and a computer was calculating how many more years of payments will occur for a loan due to be paid off in 1992. The calculation is "92 – 88 = 4." However, if the same program performed the same calculation ten years later for a loan due to be paid off in 2002, the result would be nonsense because the calculation is "02 – 98 = –96"; in other words, the mortgage was paid off 96 years ago. Any subsequent calculations that use this result would generate more nonsense. Because almost all business data processing systems use date calculations, and because errors in these calculations could have created a cascade of erroneous results, finding and correcting computer programs that contained two-digit year codes or used calculations based on those codes cost industry and government a huge amount of money, by one estimate $300 to $600 billion.[29]

Even with technological problems such as difficulty undoing the two-digit year codes, much of the difficulty in building and maintaining business systems is elsewhere. We can see this by referring back to the four phases of a system's life cycle (see

Figure 1.7). It would be convenient if there were some "correct" guaranteed method for performing these phases either for work systems or information systems that support them. Unfortunately it is generally agreed that no best method exists. To the contrary, different situations call for different processes that will be explained later in the book. Regardless of which method is used, the likelihood of success is highest when the system is small, self-contained, and easily understood. As the situation becomes more complicated, people analyzing both the work system and the information system have to contend with more details, more complexity, and a higher likelihood that the stakeholders will not agree wholeheartedly about what should happen.

These generalizations are consistent with the findings of surveys concerning the success rate for information systems. A study by the Standish Group in the mid-1990s obtained data about 8,380 systems from 365 respondents across a spectrum of large and small organizations. The summary result was that only 16.2% of the information systems were completed on schedule and within budget; 52.7% were late, went over budget, or produced fewer functions than planned, and 31.1% were canceled before completion. The factors most strongly associated with success were user involvement, executive support, clear statement of requirements, proper planning, and realistic expectations. None of these are technical matters. The factors most strongly associated with cancellation were incomplete requirements, lack of user involvement, lack of resources, and unrealistic expectations.[30] A subsequent Standish Survey found somewhat better results several years later, mostly based on doing smaller projects that had fewer uncertainties. A Meta Group survey in 1997 produced similar findings, with over 30% of new software projects canceled before completion and more than 50% of projects at least 80% over budget. A Gartner Group survey of 1,375 IT professionals in September 2000 found that roughly 40% of IT projects fail to meet business requirements, that the average canceled IT project is scheduled to last 27 weeks and is canceled on week 14, and that project team members are keenly aware of a project's doom six weeks before it is finally canceled.[31]

Difficulty Integrating IT-Based Systems

One of the most difficult issues related to building and maintaining IT-based systems is the requirement that these systems be integrated with the organization's other systems. This issue arises frequently when hardware and software best suited for one purpose must be used in conjunction with hardware and software acquired for a different purpose. For example, two separate factories within the same firm may have purchased different factory management software because their products and processes are different. If the firm subsequently decides to develop a new enterprise-wide management reporting system, one of the factories or possibly both may have to scrap a system designed around local problems in order to address an issue for the entire organization. Even regardless of the software, the two factories may have inconsistent product codes, process codes, and other data that make it extraordinarily difficult to combine their results in company-wide management reports. In both cases, each factory may have deployed its resources in what seemed the best way, only to find that that best way was not optimal for the entire firm.

An attempt to create an effective information system for handling Medicare insurance claims demonstrates how difficult integration problems can be. In 1994, the Clinton administration initiated a project that was to provide for timely payment of Medicare claims and to reduce fraudulent claims. The U.S. Secretary of Health and Human Services declared, "We're going to move from the era of the quill pen to the era of the superelectronic highway." The ultimate goal was to create a single national system for paying doctors, hospitals, nursing homes, HMOs, and others who provide care for Medicare patients. The system would pay one billion bills a year and would help reduce fraud by detecting suspicious billing patterns, including unnecessary services and submission of multiple claims for the same services. GTE was hired as the main contractor; however, as the project team got deeper into the analysis of the project, they discovered that a unified Medicare information system would have to integrate 72 separate systems built and operated by different insurance companies. Integrating these systems would require team members to develop an understanding of how each of the 72 systems worked and then to define commonalities that would unify all of them. In 1997, the administration canceled the project, which was behind schedule and over budget, and told GTE to stop work. A GTE spokesman said that the project had been far more complex than anyone anticipated. Approximately $100 million had been spent.[32]

One of the reasons why the Y2K problem absorbed so much time and effort involved integrated supply chains. These systems are designed to enforce consistent transactions and communication links between suppliers and customers, thereby minimizing costs and delays in ordering materials. If Y2K problems had caused a supplier's information system to generate incorrect information, the mistakes would have been passed on to their supply chain partners. Even partners who had completely cleaned up their own programs would have ended up suffering Y2K problems. Seeing the possibility of enormous lawsuits because the threat of Y2K had been recognized for many years, some law firms actually geared up for a lot of business in this area, only to be disappointed when the Y2K problem did not cause major disruptions.

Organizational Inertia and Problems of Change

A distressing reality for those who are enthusiastic about any particular technology-based innovation is that it is simply difficult to change the way an organization operates. Here is one observer's way of summarizing this issue:

- All technical progress exacts a price; while it adds something on the one hand, it subtracts something on the other.
- All technical progress raises more problems than it solves, tempts us to see the consequent problems as technical in nature, and prods us to seek technical solutions to them.
- The negative effects of technological innovation are inseparable from the positive. It is naive to say that technology is neutral, that it may be used for good or bad ends; the good and bad effects are, in fact, simultaneous and inseparable.
- All technological innovations have unforeseeable effects.[33]

Restated in terms of systems within organizations, this says that any particular change that has positive consequences in some areas may have negative consequences in other areas. For example, new efficiencies may mean that fewer employees are needed or that hard-earned skills are no longer important (see Figure 1.13). Differences of opinion and uncertainties about the positive and negative impacts of proposed changes often contribute to **organizational inertia**, the tendency to continue doing things in the same way, and therefore to resist change. Inertia related to information systems starts with the fact that formal systems are only a component of organizational operations and decision processes. Just changing an information system may not have much impact unless other things are changed, such as the way work is organized and the incentives that are established for the participants.

Unless a business problem is both evident and painful to all concerned, overcoming inertia often consumes a lot of effort across all four phases of the system life cycle summarized in Figure 1.7. During the initiation phase, this effort is related to identifying stakeholders, understanding their views of the situation, and considering those views in deciding on the focus and scope of the project. Extensive involvement of work system participants in the development phase helps ensure that the work system details are specified appropriately and that work system participants feel ownership of the way the system eventually operates. During the implementation phase, people who were initially uninvolved or only marginally involved must be educated about why the problem is important, how the system changes address the problem, and how the system will affect them. During the operation and maintenance phase, someone must monitor the way the work system is operating to make sure it doesn't slide back into

Example of the positive and negative impacts of technical change

FIGURE 1.13

In telephone systems of the 1930s, switchboard operators at telephone company offices and customer offices plugged in wires to connect telephone calls. Automating this task had a positive impact by making it much more convenient to use telephones, but it also had the negative impact of eliminating jobs that some switchboard operators relied on.

the old way of doing things. In some cases, the time and effort spent overcoming inertia may exceed the time and effort spent in building the computer-related parts of system development.

Genuine Difficulty Anticipating What Will Happen

A final aspect of real-world limitations to IT-based innovation is that no one really knows how any particular innovation will develop or will be adapted over time. For example, the electronic transfer of money seemed like a good idea and has had numerous advantages for legitimate businesses; however, it also allows criminals to move drug money surreptitiously.

Even inventors, business leaders, and major researchers often have great difficulty foreseeing the development and potential application of their inventions. Table 1.7 presents many examples of this phenomenon. What might now seem like an inevitable unfolding of technical advances in each of these areas was not at all obvious at the time. Many technologies have succeeded when other technologies with the same initial potential failed for various business and technical reasons. Many currently commonplace technologies, such as fax machines and the use of a mouse in computing, languished for years before becoming commercially important. Today's researchers and business managers know some of the technical capabilities that will come out of the lab three to five years from now, but even in that short time frame, there will probably be surprises, especially in the ways the new technical capabilities are combined in new, unanticipated applications. The brief and incredible history of the World Wide Web is a case in point. The WWW was invented in 1992; within five years it became a phenomenon that has had an impact on most large businesses and universities. If you look back at what was written in 1991 and 1992, however, you would see that these developments were quite unexpected.

TABLE

1.7

Technology Predictions or Business Assessments That Missed the Mark

These predictions or assessments show how difficult it is even for experts to predict the development and application of technology.

Expert and topic	Expert's prediction or comment
Alexander Graham Bell, inventor of the telephone, around 1876	He thought the telephone network would be primarily an entertainment instrument, transmitting concerts and operas to homes.[34]
Chairman of Western Union when offered exclusive patent rights to the telephone in 1876	"What use would this company have for an electrical toy?"[35]
Mercedes Benz, 1900, on the future demand for cars	"In 1900 Mercedes Benz did a study that estimated that the worldwide demand for cars would not exceed one million, primarily because of the limitation of available chauffeurs."[36]
General Electric, RCA, IBM, Remington Rand, refusing a chance to develop the basic patent for copy machines	Chester Carlson invented xerography in 1938 but spent years trying to find a corporate sponsor for his invention. Only after a long series of refusals did he persuade Battelle Memorial Institute in Ohio to continue the research.[37]
Thomas Watson, Sr., CEO of IBM, in the early 1950s	The worldwide demand for data-processing computers is less than 50 machines.[38]
Xerox Corporation, on funding early development work on the laser printer	Garry Starkweather of Xerox invented the laser printer in 1971 by modifying existing copier technology. Before he built a prototype he was instructed to stop working on the project. He might have had to leave the company to pursue the project if he had not learned of the new Xerox research lab in California where other researchers were interested in being able to print computer screen images.[39]
Herbert Simon and Allen Newell, early researchers in artificial intelligence, in 1958	Within ten years, a digital computer will be the world's chess champion unless the rules bar it from competition.[40]
Ken Olson, CEO of Digital Equipment Corporation, 1977	"There is no reason for any individual to have a computer in their home" (attributed to Ken Olson, at a convention of the World Future Society in Boston, 1977).[41]
IBM's view of the MS-DOS operating system in the early 1980s	The DOS operating system was first purchased by Microsoft for $50,000. IBM did not realize the significance of the operating system and did not insist on owning it. Eventually, ownership and future development of the operating system became more important and profitable than the hardware it ran on.
Microsoft's view of Lotus Notes in 1988	Lotus Development Corporation started developing this system in 1984. In 1988, it tried to sell it to Microsoft for $12 million, but Microsoft would go no higher than $4 million. In 1993, Lotus Notes generated $100 million in revenue and was central to Lotus Development Corporation's strategy. In 1995, IBM purchased Lotus Development Corporation for $3.5 billion, largely because of the possibilities presented by Notes.[42]
IT executives' view of personal computers and Microsoft Windows	At the Gartner Group's Symposium/Expo 95, a survey of 600 IT executives revealed that less than 20% had anticipated in 1985 that personal computers would become dominant desktop devices. Similarly, less than 20% had anticipated in 1990 that Microsoft Windows would become the dominant operating system.[43]

R E A L I T Y C H E C K [✓]

Obstacles to Applying IT in the Real World

This section identified five obstacles to applying IT.

1. Identify examples of techno-hype that you have encountered and explain whether you think these were accidentally or intentionally misleading in any important way.

2. Describe several situations in which you have encountered any of the other four obstacles to applying IT in the real world.

CHAPTER CONCLUSION

What is e-business and how is it different from e-commerce?

E-business is the practice of performing and coordinating critical business processes such as designing products, obtaining supplies, manufacturing, selling, fulfilling orders, and providing services through the extensive use of computer and communication technologies and computerized data. This broad definition is designed to include leading-edge business methods that existed in 1990, before the Internet was used for e-commerce, and also to include business methods that will exist in 2010, when other technologies may have supplanted the Internet for important applications. E-commerce is a subset of e-business related to using the Internet and other communication technology for marketing, selling, and servicing products.

What are this book's four main themes?

First, businesses operate through systems in which people perform business processes using technology and information. The basic ideas for thinking about these systems are the same regardless of whether the Internet is involved. Second, business professionals participate in all the major phases of building and maintaining these systems, and therefore need knowledge and skills necessary for effective participation. Third, advances in IT have been and continue to be a driving force in business innovation in general and e-business in particular. Fourth, the success of IT-enabled systems is in no way guaranteed even when the latest technology is used.

How are ideas about systems and the value chain relevant to e-business?

Systems concepts are basic vocabulary for talking about e-business because e-business operates through systems, specifically work systems that make extensive use of computer and communication technology and computerized data. A firm's value chain is the set of processes it uses to create value for its customers. Looking at each process as a work system is a good way to start the analysis of how to improve a value chain.

What are the phases in building and maintaining systems?

Both work systems and information systems that support them go through four phases: initiation, development, implementation, and operation and maintenance. Initiation is the process of defining the need to change an existing work system, identifying the people who should be involved in deciding what to do, and describing in general terms how the work system should operate differently and how any information system that supports it should operate differently. Development is the process of acquiring and configuring hardware, software, and other resources needed to perform both the required IT-related functions and the required functions not related to IT. Implementation is the process of making a new work system operational in the organization. Operation and maintenance is the ongoing operation of the work system and the information system, plus efforts directed at enhancing either system and correcting bugs.

What technology trends have enabled IT-based innovation in business?

Major directions for these improvements include greater miniaturization, speed, and portability; greater connectivity and continuing convergence of computing and communications; greater use of digitized information and multimedia; and better software techniques and interfaces with people.

What obstacles and real-world limitations have slowed the pace of implementation for IT-based innovations?

Implementation of IT-based innovations has been delayed by a combination of unrealistic expectations, difficulty building and modifying information systems, difficulty integrating systems that are built for different purposes, organizational inertia and problems of dealing with change, and genuine difficulty anticipating what will happen.

business professional
e-business
work system
information system
work system framework
system
subsystem
purpose
boundary
environment

inputs
outputs
business process
subprocess
value added
functional areas of business
functional silos
value chain
primary processes
support processes

supply chain
electronic commerce
    (e-commerce)
B2B
B2C
initiation
development
implementation
operation and maintenance
mobile commerce (m-commerce)

miniaturization
integrated circuit
Moore's Law
portability
connectivity

interoperability
open systems
convergence of computing and
    communications
digitization

multimedia
Year 2000 (Y2K) problem
organizational inertia

REVIEW QUESTIONS

1. In what ways is Dell Computer an e-business?

2. In what way is an information system a special type of work system?

3. What is the difference between a system and a subsystem?

4. What is a business process?

5. Distinguish between business processes that cross functional areas of business and those that are specific to functional areas.

6. What is a functional silo and why is that important?

7. Why does it make sense to extend the value chain to include aspects of the supply chain and customer experience?

8. What is the difference between e-business and e-commerce?

9. What are the phases of building and maintaining a system?

10. Why is it important for business professionals to be involved throughout the four phases of building and maintaining a system?

11. What are the six basic data processing operations?

12. Why does Moore's Law describe a phenomenon unlike other things in the history of business?

13. How does portability of computers make it difficult to control the flow of information?

14. Explain why open systems can be viewed both as an opportunity and as a threat.

15. How do continuing trends toward connectivity and interoperability provide opportunities to compete more effectively?

16. In what ways have computers and the Internet been the object of unrealistic expectations and hype?

17. What was the Year 2000 problem?

18. How is organizational inertia related to information systems?

19. How does the history of past business and technology predictions explain why the growth of the World Wide Web was a major surprise?

DISCUSSION QUESTIONS

1. Review the alternative definitions of e-business in Table 1.1. Assume that you wanted to decide whether a particular business, such as The Gap or McDonald's or IBM is an e-business. Which definitions would be comparatively easy to use and which would be comparatively difficult to use? Why?

2. Table 1.3 listed a number of past assumptions about work systems and identified how those assumptions change with e-business. Identify several of the new assumptions that describe e-business practices that you have experienced. Identify several new assumptions that seem exaggerated or unrealistic. Explain some of the differences between the first group of assumptions you identified and the second group.

3. A quote in the section on the difficulty of handling organizational change says that technological change always creates new problems and has both positive and negative consequences. Explain how this might affect you personally in your career.

4. Some people say that there is nothing special about techno-hype because it is discounted just like other forms of advertising and exaggeration that we hear every day. Explain why you agree or disagree.

5. Review Table 1.7, which listed a large number of predications or business assessments that missed the mark. Explain why you do or do not find these examples surprising. Explain any implications for a business trying to analyze possibilities for using new e-business approaches in the next several years.

6. Competition between individuals, organizations, cities, and countries has existed for centuries. Do you believe that computerized information systems are changing the nature of global competition? Why or why not?

C A S E   **Levi Strauss: Selling Customized Casual Clothing**

In 1995 Levi Strauss brought customization to the women's casual clothing industry by introducing its Personal Pair product. To purchase these customized jeans the customer willing to pay an extra $10 to $15 had to go to a properly equipped Levi's retailer where a salesperson took four measurements: inseam, waist, hips, and rise. The salesperson entered these numbers into a computer, which identified one of over 400 pairs of nonadjustable "fitting jeans" that were only for try-on use. The customer tried on the trial pair and told the salesperson about any adjustments that would improve the fit. The salesperson used these suggestions to produce the precise measurements for the customized jeans. In effect, these were a manufacturing specification for a factory in Tennessee. A computer network transmitted the specification to the factory, where the customized jeans were assembled and mailed directly to the customer or to the store within three weeks. Sewed into the waistband was a bar code with an individual customer reference number. The customer could order another pair easily because the personal measurement information is saved in a database.[44] The Personal Pair program achieved a repeat-purchase rate of 38%, more than triple the repeat purchase rate on other Levi's products.[45] By 1997, the program accounted for 25% of women's jeans sales at Original Levi's Stores.[46]

The fall of 1998 brought the next iteration, Original Spin, which was sold to women and men. "Customers choose a base jean model—classic, low-cut, or relaxed—then choose from color, fly, and leg opening options. Legs can be tapered, straight, boot cut, flare, or wide; flies, zip or button. Then there are four color choices. A trained sales associate measures a customer's waist and seat. Inseam length is determined based on what shoes will be worn with the jeans and whether the customer likes cuffs. A computer uses these measurements to suggest a pair of fitting jeans. Customers try them on and decide whether they want their jeans the same or tighter, looser, shorter, or longer. Levi's jeans produced from the Original Spin process cost $55, and every pair has a guarantee of a full refund, a new pair, or credit."[47]

Moving further in the direction of customization, by early 2000 retailers could send measurements and order information to Original Spin's Web server. There, measurements were converted to a pattern using Levi's proprietary, computerized pattern-making algorithms that create unique patterns based on each buyer's size and desired features. In contrast, earlier attempts at mass customization used a massive pattern database and matched each customer's measurements as closely as possible to a stored pattern. To help assure quick order turnaround, the company reconfigured a Texas plant to handle the special orders with workcells of seven or eight people producing one pair of pants at a time using the customer's pattern and an automated cutting table.[48]

In another aspect of its business, Levi Strauss started to sell jeans to consumers through Levi's and Dockers Web sites in late 1998 with the proviso that its retail partners would not be able to sell its merchandise over the Web. This created channel conflict, competition between a manufacturer and its retailers. Disgruntled retailers decided to put more retail effort into other brands. Online sales were disappointing and in October 1999 Levi Strauss reversed its strategy. It kept several different Web sites but used them for consumer information and advertising rather than direct sales.

The late 1990s did not treat Levi Strauss well. It suffered sagging sales, heavy layoffs, and plant closings. After peaking at $7.1 billion in 1996, company-wide sales dropped to $6.9 billion in 1997, and further to $6 billion in 1998. What's more, exorbitant advertising campaigns have done little to lure teens from the store racks of rival designers.[49]

QUESTIONS

1. Compare the way Levi Strauss produces customized jeans with the way Dell Computer produces customized computers. Other than the fact that one product is clothing and the other is a computer, what are the main similarities and differences?

2. Review the definition of e-business. In what ways does Levi Strauss seem to be an e-business?

3. Even people who are not interested in fashion typically have at least some experience in buying clothes. Based on your personal knowledge as a customer of this industry, explain your view about the importance of e-business for success in this industry.

Hershey Foods: Why a Candy Maker Missed Chocolate Deliveries for Halloween

The Halloween and holiday season of 1999 was a major disappointment for Hershey Foods, the largest U.S. candy maker. In July 1999 it had gone live with a new $112 million information system that combines SAP's R/3 enterprise software with software from Manugistics Group and Siebel Systems. IBM was the system integrator. Glitches in the system left many distributors and retailers with empty candy shelves in the season leading up to Halloween. Despite the complexity of the system, Hershey decided to go live with a huge piece of it all at once, an approach that is both rare and dangerous.[50] With a number of vendors involved it was difficult to assign responsibility for the problems.

Hershey had embarked on this project in 1996 partly to satisfy retailers who wanted to keep their own costs down by receiving deliveries when they are really needed. The new information system is used by Hershey's 1,200-person sales force and other departments "for handling every step in the process, from original placement of an order to final delivery. It also runs the company's fundamental accounting and touches nearly every operation; tracking raw ingredients; scheduling production; measuring the effectiveness of promotional campaigns; setting prices; and even deciding how products ought to be stacked inside trucks." The project was supposed to go live during the slow period in April, but development and testing were not yet complete. The July startup occurred as Halloween orders were arriving. In July, Hershey informed customers that computer problems might cause delays and some customers soon started receiving incomplete shipments. In September, it announced that its turnaround time for orders would double to 12 days.[51]

In September, Hershey announced it would miss third-quarter earnings forecasts due to the problems rolling out new systems designed to take customer orders and make store deliveries. That particularly hurt Hershey during the Halloween season, when it sacrificed some market share to competitors such as Mars and Nestlé. Hershey blamed lower-than-expected sales in December on a slowdown in customer order demand partly due to earlier customer-service and order-fulfillment issues. Hershey predicted its sales would be off by as much as $150 million for the year.[52]

The problems with the information system were reported in Hershey's 1999 annual report: "We have experienced the well-publicized problems associated with the implementation of the final phase of our enterprise-wide information system. While this has been a painful process for us and for our customers, we should remember that the system is designed to make Hershey more competitive through lower costs, better customer service, and increased sales. It has not been the easiest journey, but we still expect to arrive at our intended destination."[53]

QUESTIONS

1. Summarize what happened in each of the phases of building and maintaining systems and the extent to which Hershey encountered the problems mentioned in Table 1.4.

2. Review the section on obstacles to applying IT in the real world. Explain the extent to which Hershey seems to have encountered these obstacles.

3. Based on the definition of e-business and the limited information in the case, explain the extent to which Hershey wanted to become and actually became more of an e-business.

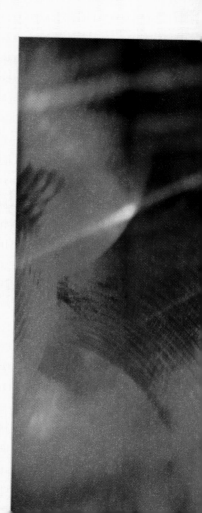

Understanding Systems
from a Business Viewpoint

chapter2

- Why is it important to have a framework for analyzing information systems?
- What eight elements can be used for summarizing any work system?
- What principles can be used to explore how well a work system is operating?
- What is the relationship between information systems and work systems?
- Why is it important to define the problem and the work system together when analyzing a system?
- What are the steps in systems analysis and how can work system principles be used in performing these steps?
- What is the difference between a participant and a user when thinking about a work system?

The Need for Frameworks and Models

The Work System Framework

Work System Principles

Relationships between Work Systems and Information Systems

Need for a Balanced View of a System

The Principle-Based Systems Analysis Method
 The General Idea of Systems Analysis
 Organizing the Analysis around Work System Principles
 Applying PBSA to Work Systems, Information Systems, and Projects
 Limitations and Pitfalls

Measuring Work System Performance

Clarifications Related to the Elements of a Work System
 Customers

 Products and Services
 Business Process
 Participants
 Information
 Technology
 Infrastructure
 Context

Concepts and Vocabulary for Looking at a Work System in Depth

Chapter Conclusion
 Summary
 Key Terms
 Review Questions
 Discussion Questions
 Cases

Understanding Systems from a Business Viewpoint

O P E N I N G   C A S E

AZON.COM: AN EVOLVING BUSINESS MODEL

Amazon.com was launched in 1995 as the first major bookseller on the World Wide Web and touted itself as the earth's biggest bookstore. The way Amazon.com provided value for its customers was quite different from the approach of traditional stores. It was a virtual bookstore that could sell any of 2.5 million books, 10 times the number in the largest chain store, even though it has no apparent physical location and actually stocked very little inventory. It gave discounts on some items, just as most chain stores did, but it charged a shipping fee and always had a delay for shipping. If a shopper knew what book to consider, information about it could be found immediately. If a shopper did not know what to consider, it was possible to search on author, title, or subject. In some cases, it was possible to see excerpts from published book reviews, comments by other readers, or even a sample chapter to see some of the book's content and style. Amazon.com could also use a profile of the books the buyer had ordered to identify other books that might be of interest.

Although first out of the box, Amazon soon faced growing competition as other booksellers responded by creating their own online bookstores. In May 1997, Barnes & Noble opened its own online bookstore and sued Amazon over its assertion about being the earth's biggest bookstore. Barnes & Noble argued that Amazon's assertion amounted to false advertising because it keeps only a few hundred titles in stock at any given time. "[Amazon] isn't a bookstore at all," Barnes & Noble claimed. "It is a book broker making use of the Internet exclusively to generate sales to the public." Barnes & Noble's new Web site trumpeted itself as "The World's Largest Bookseller Online."[1]

Amazon's business model faced severe challenges in the next few years, and by the end of 2000, its business had evolved in several directions. Amazon initially kept its costs low by carrying little inventory, and filling orders by obtaining the books from several wholesalers, packing them, and shipping them to customers from a central facility. By 1999 it was building five large warehouses so that it could fill orders in a timely, efficient manner.[2] Suddenly it had to deal with inventories, even if it didn't have the expense of physical store locations. Amazon also started selling other types of products, such as CDs, toys, housewares, and consumer electronics. At various times it had offered discounts of as much as 50% on bestsellers,[3] but in an effort to attain profitability it reduced these discounts substantially.

The investment community was split about Amazon's long-term prospects. On the one hand, it was one of the best known and mostly widely publicized e-retailers. Due to Amazon's strong brand recognition, customers associated Amazon with online shopping and tended to go to its Web site rather than other, less known competitors. It had developed a highly effective customer experience for people who did not want to go to a physical store. It had even patented a one-click checkout method that made purchases on its Web site especially convenient. Its delivery record was viewed as comparatively reliable. On the other hand, Amazon had never been profitable and continued its string of quarterly losses through 2000. For the first three quarters of 2000, revenues increased 86% to $1.79 billion, but the net loss totaled $866.1 million. Some investment analysts believed Amazon would not become profitable in the near future and some even questioned whether Amazon had enough money to stay in operation through all of 2001. After hitting a high of $113 in December 1999, Amazon's stock price dropped to as low as $19 in late 2000.

WEB CHECK [✓]

Look at the amazon.com and barnesandnoble.com Web sites. Assuming you wanted to buy a book online, decide which site you would favor and explain why.

DEBATE TOPIC]

Is there any reason to believe that purely online retailers such as Amazon.com have major long-term advantages over retailers such as Barnes & Noble that have both physical stores and e-commerce sites?

a mazon's business model evolved over the first five years of its existence as it found that it needed to have its own warehouses and as it started selling more types of products. Even a strong, highly recognized Web presence had not generated profits because Amazon's supply chain and value chain were not efficient enough to support Amazon's pricing. Putting aside the impact of the Internet stock market bubble on Amazon's management, the evolution of Amazon's internal systems reflected what managers in any company would do in order to satisfy their customers while trying to achieve profitability. Amazon's managers were continually looking for ways to improve its work systems so that it could reduce costs without reducing service or increasing prices too much.

This chapter presents ideas that any business professional can use for visualizing and analyzing any of the work systems used by Amazon at any point in its history. These ideas start with the work system framework that was introduced in Figure 1.1. This chapter defines the elements of that framework more thoroughly and identifies general principles related to these elements. The principles are the basis of the principle-based analysis method, which takes its name from the fact that the analysis stems directly from the principles.

The starting point for this type of analysis is a work system snapshot such as the table accompanying the case. This table summarizes the work system in terms of human participants performing a business process using information and technology to produce products and services for internal or external customers. Viewing a system this way is especially useful when business professionals deal with software and hardware companies that talk about "selling systems." Hardware and software are important, but these are clearly just a part of what business professionals really care about—systems for doing work in their organization.

As the chapter unfolds, you will see how any business professional can understand a lot about even a technically complex information system by starting with the work system

W O R K   S Y S T E M   S N A P S H O T

Amazon.com provides a different way to shop for books

CUSTOMERS

- People who purchase books
- Wholesalers that supply the books
- Amazon.com's shipping department

PRODUCTS & SERVICES

- Information about books that might be purchased
- Information describing each book order
- Books that are eventually delivered

BUSINESS PROCESS

- Purchaser logs on to www.amazon.com.
- Purchaser identifies desired books or gives search criteria.
- Purchaser looks at book-related information and decides what to order.
- Purchaser enters order.
- Amazon.com finds the books in its inventory and packs them for shipping. If the books are not in its inventory, Amazon orders them from a wholesaler and ships them to the customer after they arrive at the Amazon warehouse.
- Shipping department packages order and sends it to the purchaser.

PARTICIPANTS	INFORMATION	TECHNOLOGY
• People interested in purchasing books • Order fulfillment department of wholesaler • Shipping department of Amazon.com	• Orders for books • Price and other information about each book • Purchase history and related information for each customer	• Personal computers used by purchaser • Computers and networks used by Amazon.com for order processing • The Internet (infrastructure)

and then looking at the role of the information system in supporting the work system. By the end of the chapter, you will have a general approach for starting the analysis of any system in a business. You will be able to use this method to think about how a video store keeps track of its videos, how a stock market operates, or how a marketing manager decides where to advertise. Like any general method for studying or designing systems, the ideas presented here and developed throughout the rest of the book are not a cookbook. You cannot just follow a recipe or fill in the blanks. Studying these ideas will not make you an expert in information systems, but it will improve your ability to describe information systems, understand their role in businesses, and participate in their development and use.

THE NEED FOR FRAMEWORKS AND MODELS

This chapter explains how to use a framework to create a model that helps in thinking about a system in an organization. To clarify the basic approach, we will start by defining the terms *framework* and *model*.

A **framework** is a brief set of ideas and assumptions for organizing a thought process about a particular type of thing or situation. It identifies topics that should be considered and shows how the topics are related. Here are some frameworks you have probably encountered:

- In economics, the concept of supply and demand as an explanation for how markets operate and how people make buying and selling decisions
- In biology, the classification into species, which helps biologists understand relationships between different types of animals
- In sports such as football, the rules that determine how to play the game and what types of actions are permitted.

Examples of models

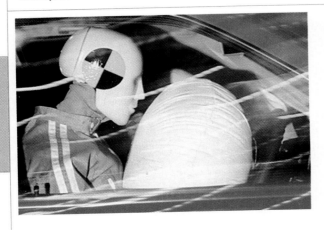

The mechanical dummy is a model used for testing the safety of automobile designs in crash situations. The spreadsheet is a model managers use to plan for the coming year.

A framework is typically used to create a **model,** a useful representation of a specific situation or thing. Models are useful because they describe or mimic reality without dealing with every detail of it. They typically help people analyze a situation by combining a framework's ideas with information about the specific situation being studied. Figure 2.1 shows examples of how a model can be used. A dummy is a model that represents a person in order to permit testing that would otherwise be impractical or unsafe. Other types of models frequently used in conjunction with automobiles include computerized drawings, wind-tunnel models, and simulators for training drivers. A less dramatic example in Figure 2.1 is a spreadsheet model used to decide whether a planned sales effort will probably meet profit goals by month. This model supports the decision by providing an organized way to combine past results and assumptions about the future.

Models always emphasize some features of reality and downplay or ignore others. For example, a plastic scale model of a car's exterior could illustrate what it would look like, but would be useless for understanding how the car's shape affects its handling during rainstorms. Likewise, the spreadsheet model might emphasize the company president's assumptions about next year's sales, but might totally ignore the sales manager's unannounced plan to leave the firm and jump to a competitor next month.

The entire history of science can be viewed as the development and testing of frameworks and models for understanding the world. When people believed that the sun rotated around the earth, they interpreted their observations of the sun, moon, planets, and stars in terms of models based on this framework. Shifting the framework so that the earth rotated around the sun made it easier to understand their observations and led people to examine things they might have never considered otherwise.

Frameworks and models are important in business and society as well as science because they help us make sense of the world's complexity. For example, the work system snapshot accompanying the introductory case was a simple descriptive model of the way Amazon.com operates. It summarized, in a single table, a complex situation for which a detailed description could have been 100 pages long. This chapter will explain why this type of summary is a useful starting point for analyzing a system.

Why Are Frameworks Important?

A framework is a set of ideas that helps to organize thoughts about a particular type of situation. Although everyone generalizes from personal experience, the idea of using a framework to think about particular types of situations may not be as obvious.

1. Identify some of the frameworks you have studied or used in areas such as government, languages, history, literature, music, sports, or everyday life.

2. Identify situations in which you have disagreed with someone about either the framework that should be used for resolving an issue or the way to use a particular framework.

THE WORK SYSTEM FRAMEWORK

As introduced in Figure 1.1, the concept of *work system* provides a useful lens for examining almost any computerized or noncomputerized system in an organization. It can be applied across the entire gamut of systems ranging from a firm's entire value chain to its smallest systems in which several individuals occasionally do a particular type of specialized work. A **work system** is a system in which human participants and/or machines perform a business process using information, technology, and other resources to produce products and/or services for internal or external customers. Typical business organizations have work systems for obtaining materials from suppliers, producing and delivering end products, finding customers, creating financial reports, hiring employees, coordinating work across departments, and many other functions.

Figure 2.2 shows the **work system framework** and defines the eight elements that should be included in even an initial understanding of a work system. The trapezoid surrounding the business process, participants, information, and technology indicates that those four elements constitute the system performing the work. The work system's outputs are the products and services received and used by its customers. Including the product and customer in the picture even though they are not part of the system reflects the notion that any system exists to produce outputs for its customers. Regardless of whether a work system is operating consistent with its initial design or its formal documentation, it is not fully successful unless it generates products and services customers want. Including the related infrastructure and context that is outside the system is a reminder that any system's operation and success depends to some extent on external factors beyond the direct control of the system's participants and managers.

Note that a work system is different from business process, business function, organization, and other terms commonly used to describe business operations. A work system (as defined in Figure 2.2) is smaller than an entire organization or business function because organizations typically contain multiple work systems and operate through them.

On the other hand, a work system is larger than a business process because it explicitly includes the participants, information, and technology. Looking at the entire work system does not diminish the importance of the business process, which is pictured as the core of the work system and which usually is viewed as the fundamental element of a value chain. Considering the entire work system is useful, however, because the same business process can be performed with drastically different levels of efficiency and effectiveness depending on who does the work and what information and technology they use. For example, the best programmers are many times more productive than mediocre programmers.[4] The same can be said for the best salespeople, fashion designers, and sports stars. Looking at the entire work system also may help in seeing whether the business process actually operates as it was designed. In some cases the difference between the idealized business process (how it was designed) and the

FIGURE 2.2

Definition of elements of the work system framework

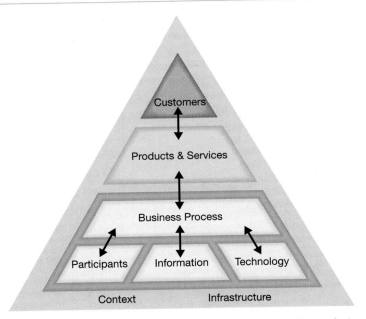

- The **customers** are the people who use and receive direct benefits from the products and services produced by the work system. They may be external customers who receive the organization's products and/or services or they may be internal customers inside the organization.

- The **products & services** are the combination of physical things, information, and services that the work system produces for its customers. The work system exists to produce these products and services.

- The **business process** is the set of work steps or activities that are performed within the work system. These steps may be defined precisely in some situations or may be relatively unstructured in others. In some situations, different participants might perform the same steps differently based on differences in their skills, training, and interests.

- The **participants** are people who perform the work steps in the business process. Some participants may use computers and information technology extensively, whereas others may use little or no technology.

- The **information** is the information used by the participants to perform their work. Some of the information may be computerized, but other important information may never be captured on a computer.

- The **technology** is the hardware, software, and other tools and equipment used by the participants while doing their work. The technology considered to be within a work system is dedicated to that system, whereas technical infrastructure is technology shared with other systems.

- **Context** is the organizational, competitive, technical, and regulatory realm within which the work system operates. These environmental factors affect the system's performance even though the system does not rely on them directly in order to operate.

- **Infrastructure** is shared human and technical resources that the work system relies on even though these resources exist and are managed outside of it. This typically includes human infrastructure such as support and training staff, information infrastructure such as shared databases, and technical infrastructure such as networks and programming technology.

These eight elements can be used to summarize almost any work system.

work that actually occurs (the real business process) stems from a mismatch between the idealized business process and the participants. For example, a Web site user who is both the customer and a participant in a self-service process may be unable or unwilling to follow the designer's intentions. Aside from serving people with different knowledge levels, the site might also have to support different business processes related to different goals for using the site.

Balance between the Elements of a Work System

The links between elements in the work system framework are represented as two-headed arrows for two reasons. First, the two-headed arrows imply that the elements should be in balance. This means that the products & services are appropriate for the customers, the business process is appropriate for producing the products & services, and the participants, information, and technology are appropriate for the business process. Going in the other direction, it means that the business process is appropriate for the participants and the available information and technology. The tendency toward balance between the elements also implies that a change in one element usually requires a corresponding change in other elements. For example, better information or technology may have no effect on work system performance if the limiting factors are characteristics of the business process or participants. Well-intended changes sometimes have negative impacts as well. For example, changing to more highly educated participants may generate better results for processes that need their skills, but it may degrade performance if the new participants become bored because the business process lacks challenge.

Viewing Information Systems and Projects as Work Systems

The work system concept is widely applicable because the terms, generalizations, and success factors that apply to every work system apply to special types of work systems such as information systems and projects.[5] An **information system** is a work system whose business process is devoted to capturing, transmitting, storing, retrieving, manipulating, and displaying information. Software products such as spreadsheets and word processing software are not information systems because they are not work systems in their own right. A **project** is work system that is designed to produce a particular product and then go out of existence.

Even an e-commerce Web site can be viewed as a work system. In this work system, the customer performs steps outlined by the logic of the Web site in order to buy things or to obtain information. The aesthetics and technical features of the Web site are obviously important, but from a business perspective the main issue is about how the customer becomes a work system participant who uses the Web site to accomplish specific objectives. Thinking about the Web site in work system terms immediately raises issues about different goals that a user might have and different processes the customer might use. An e-commerce site that might be ultra-convenient for ordering a frequently used personal item might be stunningly ineffective for figuring out what to order as a gift for someone else. The issue is not about technology, but rather, about two different work systems that happen to use the same Web site.

R E A L I T Y C H E C K ☑

Elements of the Work System Framework

The work system framework identifies eight elements needed to understand a work system.

1. Identify each of these elements in a work system with which you are familiar, such as registering for classes, renting a video, or ordering a meal at a restaurant.

2. From a customer's viewpoint, identify the product of the work system and explain how you would evaluate that product.

FIGURE

2.3

General principles related to the work system framework

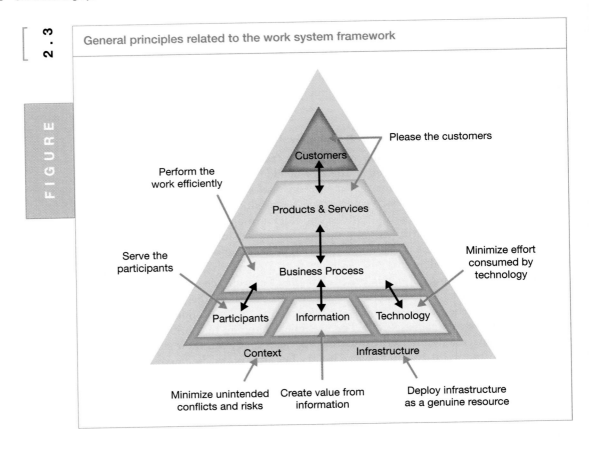

WORK SYSTEM PRINCIPLES

Figure 2.3 identifies seven **work system principles** that apply to any work system regardless of whether e-business is involved. Each of these principles is associated with specific elements of the framework.

- customers,   →   Please the customer
  products & services
- business process   →   Perform the work efficiently
- participants   →   Serve the participants
- information   →   Create value from information
- technology   →   Minimize effort consumed by technology
- infrastructure   →   Deploy infrastructure as a genuine resource
- context   →   Minimize unintended conflicts and risks

    Taken at face value each of the principles is straightforward enough to use for starting the evaluation or design of any work system. For example, the principle "please the customers" leads directly to the question "to what extent do the current products and services actually please the customers?" Likewise, the principle "create value from information" leads to examining whether the existing information is being used fully and whether better information would really help.

    These principles may seem obvious, but they are often not followed, as the examples in Table 2.1 show. Although the principles are mutually reinforcing in some situations, in other situations they pull in opposite directions and are at least somewhat contradictory. For example, pleasing customers is important, but it is also important to do the work efficiently. In some situations, genuinely pleasing the customers may be completely consistent with efficient internal operation; in others it may require expending excess resources and therefore doing the work inefficiently. Striving for suc-

Common Examples of Failing to Follow the Work System Principles in E-Commerce Web Sites	
Work system principle	**Common example of its opposite in e-commerce Web sites**
Please the customers	An e-commerce Web site does not provide the products and services customers want.
	An e-commerce Web site accepts the order but fulfillment is delayed or does not occur at all.
	An e-commerce Web site provides inadequate help in matching customer needs to product offerings.
Perform the work efficiently	The customer's process of entering orders and figuring out what to buy is convoluted and takes too long.
	The customer using an e-commerce Web site has to enter the same information several times.
	The firm's internal ordering and fulfillment processes operate inefficiently because they are not integrated with other organizational processes.
Serve the participants	An e-commerce Web site is collecting information that might be used in unauthorized ways.
	Internal personnel are frustrated by their inability to do their work efficiently and effectively.
Create value from information	The information captured through the customer's clicks is not recorded or analyzed.
	Existing information about the customer is not made available to help the customer place repeat orders.
	Sales and customer information is not used effectively to market or refine the product offering.
Minimize effort consumed by technology	Web site users have to expend too much effort and attention figuring out how to use and maintain their computers.
	Downloading the new data files for the antivirus software requires too much effort.
Deploy infrastructure as a genuine resource	The firm's infrastructure is overbuilt and many of its capabilities are not used.
	The firm's Web site is programmed in a way that reveals some of the Internet and World Wide Web's weaknesses.
Minimize unintended impacts and conflicts	Creation of an e-commerce Web site generates internal rivalry and hostility within the firm.
	Inadequate security of an e-business Web site results in theft of customers' credit card numbers.
	An e-business work system has unplanned downtime, resulting in customer inconvenience and lost sales.

TABLE 2.1

cess in any work system involves applying the success principles and finding compromises that address the contradictions as well as possible.

One reason for citing these general principles is that some work systems (especially information systems) are no longer adequate even if they operate exactly as they were originally designed to operate. The original design goals gradually may have become less important as the business situation changed. For example, a hiring system might have been developed to hire a large number of salespeople during a period of growth. Five years later the same goals might no longer apply even if the same hiring system still existed.

RELATIONSHIPS BETWEEN WORK SYSTEMS AND INFORMATION SYSTEMS

Relationships between work systems and information systems are important because improving an information system may be futile without separate changes in the work system. Table 2.2 provides examples illustrating the difference between an information system and a work system it supports. In each case, the information system plays an important role in a work system, but does not directly affect other aspects of it.

Figure 2.4 extends this point further by showing some of the possible relationships between information systems and work systems. In the first case, an information system is a small, dedicated component of a work system. An example might be an information system that helps a farmer by collecting and displaying information about soil conditions in different parts of the farm. The main work that is going on involves planting and tending to crops. The information system helps with decisions that are important but the bulk of the work system involves physical activities rather than information processing. In other situations the work system and the information system overlap significantly and may be almost indistinguishable from each other. An example is the work of granting and monitoring loans in a bank's student loan program. This work is information-intensive because it is mostly about processing information such as identification, qualifications, references, payments, and balance due. Whether or not computers are involved, the work system is mostly an information system.

The other two situations in Figure 2.4 involve information systems that affect two or more work systems that may operate independently. An example of the first type is an information system that helps mobile salespeople find sales prospects and keep track of their interactions with them. Some of this information might be used by the company's financial planning system because there may be a predictable relationship between the extent of sales contacts and the number and type of sales that eventually occur. In cases such as this one, the original information system for the sales force might have to be modified to make the information more useful for the financial planners. These modifications might not help the sales force and might even cause them more work with little benefit.

The final case in Figure 2.4 is a large information system that supports many different work systems. An example is an airline reservation system for a major airline. This type of information system is used by travel agents and airline sales agents to make reservations; it is used for direct purchases on the airline's Web site; it is used to gener-

	Distinction between Information Systems and Work Systems They Support	
	The table shows that each of the information systems listed supports some, but not all, of the important aspects of a work system.	
Information system	**Work system supported by the information system**	**Aspects of the work system not included in the information system**
Bar code scanners and computers identify the items sold and calculate the bill	Performing customer checkout	Establishing personal contact with customers, putting the groceries in bags
University registration system permits students to sign up for specific class sections	Registering for classes	Deciding which classes to take and which sections to sign up for in order to have a good weekly schedule
Word processing system used for typing and revising chapters	Writing a book	Deciding what to say in the book and how to say it
Interactive system top managers use to monitor their organization's performance	Keeping track of organizational performance	Talking to people to understand their views about what is happening
System that identifies people by scanning and analyzing voice prints	Preventing unauthorized access to restricted areas	Human guards, cameras, and other security measures

TABLE 2.2

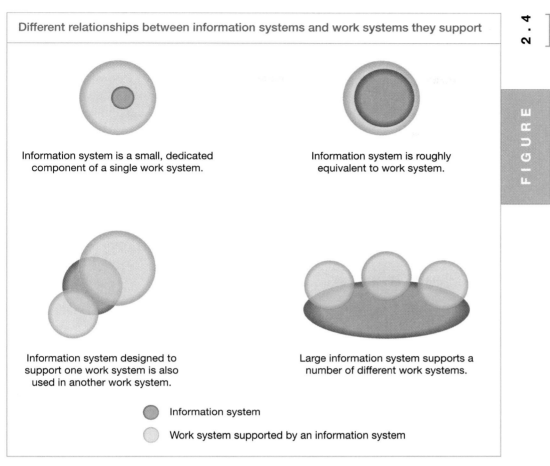

Different relationships between information systems and work systems they support

FIGURE 2.4

Information system is a small, dedicated component of a single work system.

Information system is roughly equivalent to work system.

Information system designed to support one work system is also used in another work system.

Large information system supports a number of different work systems.

⬤ Information system

◯ Work system supported by an information system

The many different types of relationships between information systems and work systems illustrate the wide range of roles that information systems may play.

ate tickets; it is used for yield management, the process of revising prices frequently and occasionally offering specials to maximize profits; it may be used to maintain personal profiles and frequent flyer information for individual flyers. All of these activities might be viewed as separate work systems, yet they use what the airline views as a single information system. In an example like this, the information system is more like the shared infrastructure used by a number of work systems and may be larger and more complex than any of them.

Trend toward Overlap

The first computerized information systems operated more like the simpler cases in Figure 2.4, the comparatively small, dedicated information system or the information system that is roughly equivalent to a work system devoted to processing information. The more complex situations are becoming more common, however. A significant overlap between the work system and the information system appears in most of this book's chapter-opening cases. The evolution of manufacturing information systems illustrates how this trend developed over time. The earliest of these systems used paper log sheets to record events in the work system (such as items completed at each step or items scrapped) and later compiled and reported that information to accountants and management for subsequent use. These information systems collected information about the work being done but did not directly help production workers perform manufacturing operations. Subsequent developments in interactive computing made it possible for the information system to help manufacturing workers by immediately checking data input for detectable errors and by making up-to-the-second information available whenever workers or managers needed it for current decisions. Highly automated manufacturing takes this a step further by automatically collecting data whenever a work step is completed, automatically making decisions about what item to work on next, and automatically downloading the correct machine recipe. In these situations, the information system and the work system overlap so much that the manufacturing is largely controlled by the information system. Turn off the information system and this type of manufacturing grinds to a halt.

The wide range of possible relationships between information systems and other work systems demonstrates why an organized method for thinking about systems is especially valuable. Just communicating about a system can be difficult because different people in the same conversation related to an information system often attach different meanings to common terms such as system, user, and implementation.[6] Another glance at Table 2.2 reveals part of the problem. Even in the same conversation some people may refer to the information system as "the system"; others sitting at the same table may refer to the work system as "the system." The remainder of this chapter presents a systems analysis method that not only helps in exploring a system by yourself, but also helps in clarifying what others mean when they speak or write about systems.

R E A L I T Y C H E C K [✓]

Take another look at Table 2.2 and Figure 2.4. Identify several situations in which you have encountered information systems that support other work systems. Describe the areas of overlap and nonoverlap between the information system and the work system.

NEED FOR A BALANCED VIEW OF A SYSTEM

Figure 2.5 uses the work system framework to illustrate three different viewpoints that are used frequently when thinking about work systems that use IT extensively.

- *Focusing on business results.* Emphasize the customer's satisfaction with whatever is being produced along with concern for the efficiency of the business process.
- *Focusing on people and organization.* Emphasize the work environment, job satisfaction, and whether the organization is operating smoothly.
- *Focusing on technology and information.* Emphasize processing of information in databases, transmission of information, and whether the technology is operating efficiently and effectively.

Each of these viewpoints is essential, yet an excessive emphasis on any of them fosters blind spots. Excessive emphasis on business results sometimes leads to superficial analysis of organizational and technical capabilities and wishful thinking about the power of technology. Excessive emphasis on people and organization sometimes generates too much concern about how people in the organization are getting along and too little concern about whether they are generating business results and whether the available technology and information are adequate. Excessive emphasis on technology and information sometimes generates technical solutions to comparatively minor problems that have little impact on business results or the internal operation of the organization.

Building and maintaining successful systems in organizations requires ongoing collaboration between business professionals who understand the business and organizational needs and IT professionals who understand how to create and maintain information systems. Since the IT professionals naturally tend to focus on technology and information, it is especially important that business professionals make sure the other two viewpoints are represented adequately. They cannot stop there, however. They need to make sure that all three viewpoints are part of the collaboration and that no major topics are simply swept under the table.

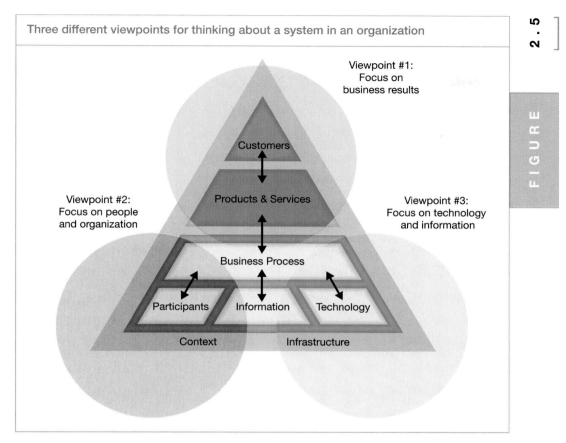

Three different viewpoints for thinking about a system in an organization

Each of these viewpoints is essential, yet overemphasis on any of them tends to ignore important issues raised by the other viewpoints.

THE PRINCIPLE-BASED SYSTEMS ANALYSIS METHOD

This section presents one of many possible ways to analyze any work system (including an information system or a project) from a business viewpoint. An organized analysis method can help business professionals understand a business situation more completely. This helps in explaining business needs to IT professionals who make the technical changes that make desired work system changes possible. A business professional's ability to analyze systems using an organized approach such as this one will become even more important as organizations continue to downsize.

The General Idea of Systems Analysis

Systems analysis is a very general process of defining a problem, gathering pertinent information, developing alternative solutions, and choosing among those solutions. When stated in its most general form, systems analysis can be applied to almost any problem involving people, resources, and action. This section expresses the general concept of systems analysis in a way that helps in analyzing work systems and information systems. Many of the same ideas also apply when thinking about physical systems, social systems, and business organizations as a whole, but those areas are not the focus of this book. Although different authors express it differently, systems analysis is basically a four-step decision-making process (shown in Figure 2.6):

- Defining the problem
- Describing the situation in enough depth
- Designing potential improvements
- Deciding what to do

FIGURE 2.6

Steps in systems analysis

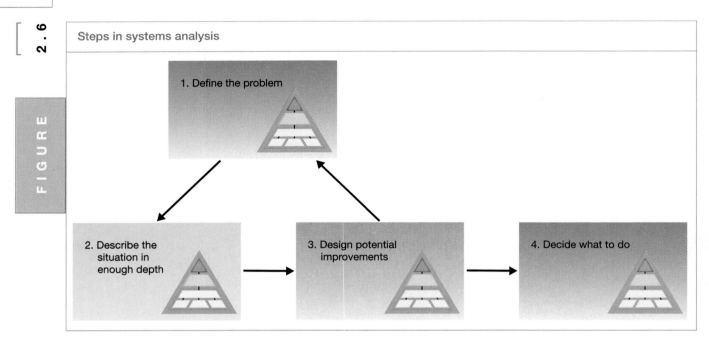

Systems analysis iterates between defining the problem, describing the current situation, and designing potential improvements. The final step is deciding what to do. The work system icon at each stage emphasizes that the framework can be used throughout the analysis process.

The steps in the figure are presented as though they apply to a single system. If the situation being analyzed contains several major subsystems, the steps can be used to examine each subsystem separately, and then to examine the overall system. Figure 2.6 shows that the process is iterative; that is, the cycle of steps can be repeated if necessary. This is consistent with the way people typically identify a problem they want to think about and then redefine the problem after gathering information that helps them understand it. An icon representing the work system framework appears in Figure 2.6 to reinforce the idea that the problem statement, the description of the current situation, the potential improvements, and the recommendations should all consider a specific work system and should pay an appropriate amount of attention to each of its elements.

A shortcoming of the very general four-step systems analysis process in Figure 2.6 is that it provides very little guidance about what to think about in each phase or how to do the analysis. To make this type of analysis easier and more practical to apply, we will integrate the seven work system principles (see Figure 2.3) into the analysis process.

Organizing the Analysis around Work System Principles

To provide some of the guidance missing from the very general process in Figure 2.6, this section introduces the principle-based systems analysis™ method, a practical approach business professionals can use for analyzing systems at whatever level of depth is appropriate in the situation. This method can be used in a number of ways:

- To help organize the analysis when business professionals must build their own small information systems using end-user tools.
- As a way to create an initial understanding of a situation and even a tentative recommendation before starting a collaboration with IT professionals.
- As a way to make sure that an ongoing collaboration between business and IT professionals balances business issues and computer system details. Maintaining this balance is especially important during discussions with software vendors, who often view the system as the software they sell rather than as the work system their customer is attempting to improve.
- As a way IT professionals can make sure they have an adequate understanding of the business situation.

The Principle-Based Systems Analysis Method

TABLE 2.3

The principle-based analysis (PBSA) method starts with defining the problem and the work system within which the problem exists. It then uses the seven work system principles to explore the situation and to find potential improvements. The last step is making a recommendation about what to do and why.

Systems analysis step	Steps in principle-based systems analysis
1. Define the problem	Define the problem and the work system together
2. Describe the current system in enough depth and 3. Design potential improvements	Use each work system principle in turn as a lens for summarizing the current situation and search for possible improvements Principle #1: Please the customers Principle #2: Perform the work efficiently Principle #3: Serve the participants Principle #4: Create value from information Principle #5: Minimize effort absorbed by technology Principle #6: Deploy infrastructure as a genuine resource Principle #7: Minimize unintended conflicts and risks
4. Decide what to do	Make a recommendation that addresses the problem while supporting the organization's priorities

Table 2.3 shows how the **principle-based systems analysis** (PBSA) method combines the general concept of systems analysis with the work system framework to provide an approach anyone can use when thinking about how to improve a work system. PBSA converts the four steps of systems analysis into three steps that can be pursued at whatever level of detail makes sense in the situation. Table 2.3 shows that these steps involve defining the problem, using the principles to explore the situation and identify possible improvements, and deciding upon a recommendation for action.

Defining the Problem and the Work System   The first step in analyzing a system is to define the problem by identifying the purpose of the analysis and the scope of the work system that is being analyzed. The purpose is typically to accomplish a goal such as increasing the efficiency of a business process, producing a better product, or solving an employee turnover problem.

The scope of the work system is not fixed before the analysis starts. Instead, it is a conscious choice based on the purpose of the analysis and a practical trade-off between making the topic too broad and complex versus making it too narrow and insignificant. An overly broad problem definition may make the work system scope so large that even completing the analysis could prove impractical, thereby making it exceedingly unlikely that any resulting project would succeed. An overly restrictive definition may mean that the major problems are not addressed. For example, assume that the purpose of the analysis is to increase sales at an e-commerce Web site. The work system might be defined narrowly in terms of how a user uses the Web site to decide what to order. This definition of the work system might be too restrictive. Defining the work system to include everything from attracting the user to the site through delivering the purchase might reveal that any problems related to the Web site itself are minor compared to problems about attracting customers to the site and demonstrating that the prices on the site are genuinely lower than prices at competitive Web sites and in physical stores.

Use of a tabular **work system snapshot** such as the table accompanying the opening case in each chapter helps in bounding the scope of the work system because it identifies the work system participants, the beginning and end of the business process, and the products and services being produced. A work system snapshot is a summary, a simplification of reality that leaves out many topics essential for understanding the situation. It is still useful, however, because it provides a balanced view of the system and clarifies what is and is not included. Notice that the work system snapshot does not include separate cells for infrastructure and context. This is to keep the snapshot as simple as possible and also to recognize that in some cases infrastructure and context may not raise important issues and may barely be mentioned.

Another important part of the problem definition is identifying constraints and priorities that affect the way the analysis will be done. **Constraints** refer to limitations that make particular changes infeasible even though they might otherwise seem beneficial. Typical constraints that apply in some situations include budgetary limits, restrictions in shifting personnel, the organization's technology standards, and policies related to privacy. **Priorities** are statements about the relative importance of different goals. Because many different types of improvements are typically at least conceivable in most situations, the analysis process tends to be more successful if a small number of high-priority issues remain the primary focus.

The initial systems analysis step of defining the problem is surprisingly difficult because different people looking at the same situation may have a very different idea of what the problem is. Sometimes the disagreements are conscious, but in many other cases, different people simply make different assumptions about what the system includes. For example, someone in a human resources department might assume that the company's recent hiring problems are related to difficulties processing résumés as part of that department's responsibilities, whereas others in the company might believe the problem is related to poor impressions that qualified applicants receive during on-site interviews.

When trying to deal with problems related to a work system it is especially important to avoid defining the work system in terms of a software package provided by a vendor or IT group. From a business viewpoint, the appropriate system is a system in which people are performing a business process. Software vendors often try to sway their clients into defining the problem in terms of capabilities that software supports. Influencing clients in this direction may be effective for software sales but it downplays or totally ignores issues unrelated to the software. The need to consider an entire work system rather than just the software capabilities might seem obvious, but confusion about whether "the system" is defined by particular application software is very common. For example, a business professional might believe that the system being analyzed is a work system for manufacturing air conditioners, whereas a software vendor or programmer might believe the system is a software product used to keep track of manufacturing work. These topics overlap, but they certainly aren't identical and comments about one "system" may not apply to the other.

Using Work System Principles to Explore the Situation and Search for Possible Improvements   The next phase of the analysis after defining the problem involves looking at different facets of the work system and trying to imagine potential improvements. Each of the seven work system principles is used in turn as a lens for focusing on a particular part of the work system, thinking about how well it is operating, and identifying possible directions for improvement. Since each principle summarizes an aspect of the way things should be, deviations from a principle indicate that potential changes should be identified and evaluated. For example, the principle "please the customer" implies that the direct causes of important customer dissatisfaction should be identified and considered carefully. Similarly, the principle "perform the work efficiently" implies that important inefficiencies should be identified and considered as part of the analysis.

While applying each principle, first describe the situation at a level of depth and completeness consistent with the purpose of the analysis. For example if the initial problem statement says that the business process takes too long, use of the principle "do the work efficiently" starts with getting more clarity about how the business process operates and finding out how long each step takes. Different analysts with different personal goals might approach this in different ways. For example, a manager preparing for a preliminary discussion that will happen tomorrow would look at this in less detail than an analyst trying to make sure that possible information system changes proposed during that preliminary discussion will have the right impact. Similarly, an IT professional would tend to look at technology-related issues in more depth than a business professional.

Applying each principle in turn frequently uncovers problems that were not included in the original problem definition. For example, the principle "serve the participants" might lead to the discovery that work system participants are up in arms about unpredictable personal work schedules that have caused family problems. The original problem statement may have focused on customer dissatisfaction, technical problems, or anything else, but the recommendation might have to address personal concerns of work system participants in order to have a desired effect on customer satisfaction.

While looping through the seven principles it is likely that some potential changes that initially seem to help in one part of the work system might have negative effects elsewhere. The work system framework explains why this very common type of conflict occurs. The two-headed arrows linking various elements in Figure 2.2 highlight the direct relationships between the elements and show why a change in any element may affect other elements. A change that is beneficial for one element of the framework may be beneficial in some other parts of the framework or may cause problems in other parts. Therefore, no change should be recommended until a variety of potential improvements have been considered. For example, although switching to more current technology might improve the results for a particular work system, this might cause problems due to inconsistencies with other work systems. A better overall approach might involve adding a step to a business process or providing better training.

Making a Recommendation That Addresses the Problem While Supporting the Organization's Priorities   Analyzing a system is a fruitless exercise unless the understanding developed in the analysis is used to set a course of action. Accordingly, deciding what to do is the last step in the PBSA method. The briefest possible recommendation simply identifies a direction for change and explains something about why this type of change is a good idea. A more complete recommendation includes:

- Recommended changes in each element of the work system
- Clarification of which changes involve just the work system, just the information system, or both the information system and the work system
- Explanation of how the proposed improvements will address the most important parts of the problem identified in step #1
- Justification of the overall recommendation in terms of organizational priorities and feasibility
- Identification of meaningful alternatives that were not chosen and why these were deemed less beneficial than the alternatives that are recommended
- Discussion of the how the project would be done and what resources it would require
- Tentative project plan including timing and deliverables

The recommendation typically excludes some of the potential improvements identified earlier by applying each work system principle in turn. Some of those improvements probably won't make much difference in terms of the problem identified in the first step. For example, obtaining more complete information might be somewhat beneficial, but not nearly as important as changing the business process so that it produces what the customers actually want. Other changes that might seem like improvements in one area might cause problems elsewhere and might actually degrade overall performance.

Ideally, the recommendation should be based on clearly stated decision criteria that help resolve trade-offs and uncertainties related to constraints, priorities, and implementation capabilities. Typical trade-offs involve conflicting needs of different work systems, conflicts between technical purity and business requirements, and choices between performance and price. The uncertainties encompass issues such as the direction of future technology and uncertainty about what is best for the business. Although it might be possible to force the ultimate decision into a formula, it makes more sense to use clear decision criteria as a way to compare options and provide sanity checks for proposals.

> **R E A L I T Y C H E C K** [✓]
>
> Using Systems Analysis in Everyday Life
>
> The systems analysis process described here is very general. Much of it can be applied to everyday life, even though we don't often think of everyday issues in terms of systems.
>
> 1. Identify any nontrivial problem you have had to deal with in your everyday life (not a problem assigned in a course) that required you to think about a situation and develop a plan of action. Use the work system framework and work system principles to think about the original situation and whether whatever actions were taken actually improved the situation.
>
> 2. Explain the areas where the work system principles seemed pertinent to your situation and the areas where they seemed peripheral or irrelevant.

Applying PBSA to Work Systems, Information Systems, and Projects

Since the PBSA method can be applied to any work system, it can be used in a project devoted to building or maintaining a system. During the initiation phase of the project, the PBSA method can help in defining the problem that is being addressed and in producing an initial recommendation for the desired changes and improvements. When deciding how to do the project, the PBSA method can help in deciding what methods to use. If the project encounters difficulties, the PBSA method can be used to analyze the situation and figure out how to get back on track.

The fact that information systems and projects are work systems also helps in understanding **success factors**, the situational characteristics that are usually associated with system or project success or whose absence is associated with system or project failure. Figure 2.7 illustrates how generalizations and success factors related to work systems in general are "inherited" by information systems and projects since these are special types of work systems. Furthermore, generalizations about information systems (or projects) in general also apply to specific types of information systems (or projects).

Table 2.4 expands on Figure 2.7 by listing typical success factors for work systems in general, for information systems, and for projects.[7] Its layout emphasizes the idea that success factors for work systems also apply to information systems and projects, but that additional, more specialized success factors may apply to each of them. For example, "management support" is a success factor related to the context within which a work system operates, regardless of whether that work system happens to be an information system or project. On the other hand, "extensive experience with information systems" and "positive beliefs about information systems" are success factors for information systems, but not for work systems in general. The same type of relationship applies for other work system success factors, such as participant motivation, information quality, and maintainability of technology.

Limitations and Pitfalls

The PBSA method is designed as organized guidelines that focus attention on issues business professionals understand and care about. It helps in thinking about different facets of an information system or related work system so that discussions with other business professionals and with IT professionals will be more effective. Unlike systems analysis methods for IT professionals, PBSA makes no attempt to create a rigorous technical specification of a desired information system.

The PBSA method is also designed to be adapted to the needs of a range of people who use it in different ways. Just glancing at the work system framework and the work system principles (Figure 2.3) while thinking about a system-related problem or proposed improvement is often sufficient for identifying important questions that need to be answered. An overview of this type meets the needs of people who want to visualize the situation but don't need to study it in depth. For the business and IT professionals who actually have to build or modify the system, each work system principle leads to deeper questions that should be examined carefully.

F I G U R E   2 . 7

Inheritance of generalizations and success factors related to work systems

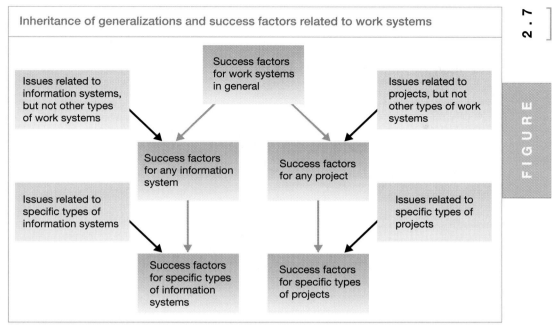

The diagram shows that success factors for work systems in general also apply to information systems and projects, both of which are specific types of work systems. Similarly, success factors for any information system (or project) apply to specific types of information systems (or projects). Table 2.4 uses the elements of the work system framework to list typical success factors for work systems along with additional success factors related to information systems and projects.

T A B L E   2 . 4

Success Factors for Work Systems, Information Systems, and Projects

Figure 2.7 illustrated the inheritance of generalizations and success factors from work systems to information systems and projects. This table uses the elements of the work system framework to present success factors for work systems in general plus additional success factors that apply only to information systems and projects. Although many success factors are listed, some important ones are probably missing.

CONTEXT
Work systems in general
• Management support • Consistency with culture • Cooperative decisions about work methods • Low level of turmoil and distraction

Information systems	**Projects**
• Extensive experience with information systems • Positive beliefs about information systems	• Management commitment • Management willingness to allocate necessary resources • Consensus on need for the project • Consensus on project governance • Informed agreement on requirements • Culture of cooperation on projects • Legal or competitive necessity

Continued

TABLE 2.4 Success Factors for Work Systems, Information Systems, and Projects, *continued*

INFRASTRUCTURE

Work systems in general

- Adequate technical infrastructure for the work system
- Adequate human infrastructure for the work system

Information systems	Projects
• Adequate support by the IT staff • Adequate training on content • Adequate training on technology	• Adequate training on methods and technologies used in the project

CUSTOMERS, PRODUCTS & SERVICES

Work systems in general

- Product design consistent with customer needs
- Adequate product performance

Information systems	Projects
• Customer involvement in designing and accepting the information system	• Limited scope of change (the greater the intended change, the lower the probability of success) • Realistic expectations • Customer involvement in designing and accepting the project's product

BUSINESS PROCESS

Work systems in general

- Fit of business process with other elements of the work system
- Adequate resources for business process
- Effective operational management

Information systems	Projects
• Comfortable fit with the work system being served	• Business process tailored to the project • Experience with the type of business process used for the project • Appropriate project management process • Attention to organizational implementation

PARTICIPANTS

Work systems in general

- Appropriate skills and understanding
- Interest in doing this type of work
- Motivation to do this work in this setting
- Ability to work together to resolve conflicts

Information systems	Projects
• Familiarity with using computers • Confidence computers will not be used for de-skilling, job elimination, etc.	• Involvement of project participants in all four phases of the project • Commitment to project success • Experience doing this type of project • Confidence by project participants that the project can be done with the available human and technical resources • Incentives favoring timely completion • Availability of subject matter experts (SMEs) who provide necessary knowledge

Continued

Success Factors for Work Systems, Information Systems, and Projects, *continued*

INFORMATION

Work systems in general

- Adequate information quality
- Adequate information accessibility
- Adequate information presentation
- Adequate information security

Information systems	**Projects**
• Information appropriately tailored to the situation	• Shared understanding of the project's goals, rationale, schedule, and resources • Schedules and deliverables designed to further the work (not delay it) and to help in identifying problems and slippages • Expert knowledge about the context and content of the work system being improved or created

TECHNOLOGY

Work systems in general

- Ease of use
- Adequate technology performance (having enough "horsepower")
- Maintainability
- Compatibility with technology in related systems

Information systems	**Projects**
• Adequate internal design • Adequate compatibility with technology in related systems • Adequate documentation	• Experience with whatever type of technology is being used for the project

Realistically, most business professionals cannot answer all questions related to every aspect of a work system, and they usually need help with questions related to technical topics. Nonetheless, doing their own analysis using PBSA clarifies their views and leaves them more able to communicate and negotiate effectively both with other business professionals and with the IT professionals responsible for filling in the technical details and operating the resulting computer system.

Although the PBSA method has many uses, it still has limitations. Like any general problem-solving approach, it is not a formula or cookbook. Regardless of whether you are analyzing a work system or an information system that supports it, you have to apply judgment to use it effectively. PBSA applies most directly when the business process in the work system or information system consists of identifiable steps occurring over time and producing a recognizable output. It is not as effective when applied to activities such as "management" or "communication" unless the steps in a specific management or communication process are being explored.

The PBSA method is a compromise between complexity and completeness. The eight elements in the work system framework were selected to be as understandable and broadly useful as possible. Other elements that could have received more emphasis include facilities, management, and organization. Facilities, such as computer rooms and wiring closets, were not treated as a separate topic because related questions are tangential to a business professional's understanding of systems. Instead of treating management as a separate element, PBSA handles it either as the planning and control part of a work system or as a separate work system. Likewise, organization is not in the framework but is related to how the work is performed and the context surrounding the work system. In similar fashion, the compromise between simplicity and usefulness in the seven work system principles was the result of a lengthy trial-and-error process aimed at providing insights at many different levels of detail.

Specific pitfalls related to the eight elements are shown in Table 2.5. Entries in the table provide hints about how to use the PBSA method carefully. The three most general pitfalls in using PBSA are inadequate problem definition, confusion about the difference between the information system and the work system, and careless or nonexistent performance measurement. A typical symptom of inadequate problem definition is that the work system snapshot is either too broad or too narrow in relation to the problem. The second pitfall is often revealed when a statement like "the system is easy to use" occurs in the middle of a discussion of a work system. This sometimes shows confusion about the difference between the work system and the information system since the term "easy to use" applies to technology, but not to work systems. Carelessness about performance measurement is very common and will be discussed in the next section.

TABLE 2.5

Common Systems Analysis Pitfalls Related to Elements of the Work System Framework		
Customers	**Products & Services**	
Ignoring the customer and the fact that the customer should evaluate the product	Forgetting that the purpose of a system is to produce a product for a customer	
Treating managers as customers even though they don't use the system's product directly	Forgetting that the product of a work system is often not the product of the organization	
Business Process		
Defining the business process so narrowly that an improvement has little consequence		
Defining the business process so broadly that it involves a wide range of products and customers and is difficult to analyze coherently; in particular, defining the business process as the firm's entire value chain (which usually contains a number of separate business processes)		
Confusing business process measures (such as consistency and productivity) with product measures (such as cost to the customer and quality perceived by the customer)		
Thinking about the business process as a theoretical set of steps and ignoring whether it is adequately supported by participants, information, and technology		
Participants	**Information**	**Technology**
Ignoring the incentives felt by participants and ignoring other pressures on them	Assuming that better information will generate better results	Believing that the technology is the system
Focusing on "users" rather than participants, thereby over-emphasizing IT and under-emphasizing how the work system operates and what it produces	Downplaying the importance of soft information not captured by formal systems	Assuming that better technology will generate better results
		Focusing on technology without thinking about whether it makes a difference in the work system
Context	**Infrastructure**	
Ignoring context issues such as organizational culture and politics, organizational policies, the competitive environment, and government and industry standards and regulations	Ignoring possible failures in technical infrastructure	
	Ignoring the need for human infrastructure to keep the work system in operation	

MEASURING WORK SYSTEM PERFORMANCE

Both business and IT professionals are sometimes willing to describe a system in detail and then recommend how it should be changed without ever clarifying how well it is performing now and how well it should perform in the future. To help you understand this common pitfall, this section clarifies the difference between architecture (how a system operates) and performance (how well a system operates), and then discusses measures of performance.

A work system's **architecture** includes the work system's main components, how the components are linked, and how they operate together. A work system snapshot such as the one at the beginning of this chapter summarizes a work system's architecture to clarify the system's scope and boundaries. A complete look at the system's architecture requires a much more detailed look at how the components are linked and how they operate together. Although the term "architecture" may sound technical, it applies equally to processes, information, technology, and organizations. For example, *information architecture* refers to how information is organized within a system, whereas *organizational architecture* refers to how the people and departments are organized.

Any attempt to evaluate or improve a work system involves more than understanding how it operates mechanically. Improving a system requires a careful look at system **performance**, which describes how well the system, its components, and its products operate. Table 2.6 identifies typical performance variables that can be measured and evaluated for each element of the work system framework other than the context and infrastructure. For example, quality, accessibility, presentation, and security are important for information, whereas skills, involvement, commitment, and job satisfaction are important for participants. Later chapters use many examples to explain these terms further.

Separately evaluating the performance of different elements is important because changes or improvements in one area may or may not generate better work system

TABLE 2.6

Typical Performance Variables Related to Different Elements of a Work System

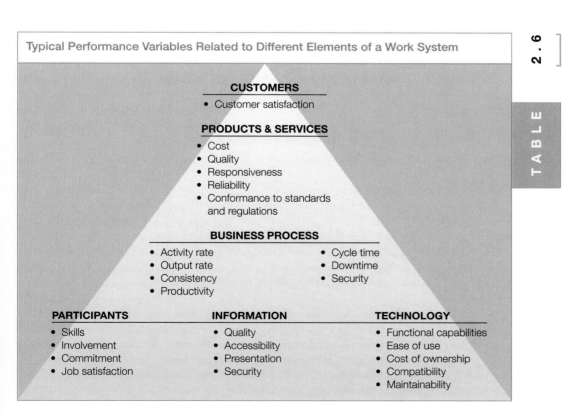

CUSTOMERS
- Customer satisfaction

PRODUCTS & SERVICES
- Cost
- Quality
- Responsiveness
- Reliability
- Conformance to standards and regulations

BUSINESS PROCESS
- Activity rate
- Output rate
- Consistency
- Productivity
- Cycle time
- Downtime
- Security

PARTICIPANTS
- Skills
- Involvement
- Commitment
- Job satisfaction

INFORMATION
- Quality
- Accessibility
- Presentation
- Security

TECHNOLOGY
- Functional capabilities
- Ease of use
- Cost of ownership
- Compatibility
- Maintainability

results. For example, substantial amounts of time, money, and effort are sometimes wasted improving the quality, accessibility, or presentation of information in ways that have little impact on work system results. This is what happens when someone uses a word processor to edit a document extensively, often with the net effect of improving the document's appearance much more than its substance. Similarly, people sometimes use spreadsheets on personal computers to run a model under numerous scenarios without ever thinking about whether those scenarios lead to genuine insight. In the same way, managers sometimes fund information systems that provide enormous amounts of information with little or no impact on decisions. These examples show why it is important to focus on overall work system performance before upgrading any particular component.

Considering many different performance variables is often important because there may be natural conflicts between some of them. For example, increasing the reliability of a product might be desirable, but this might require an undesirable increase in cycle time to provide more time for testing. Hence, the increase in cycle time might decrease the responsiveness that a customer perceives.

"More is better" almost always applies for some performance variables such as customer satisfaction and information quality. For others, however, more may not be better. The right levels of performance variables such as output rate, consistency, and security are a compromise between problems of excess and problems of deficiency. For example, too much consistency may mean participants cannot use their creativity to respond to changes, whereas too little makes the business process inefficient and the results chaotic. Even in today's harried business world, shorter cycle times may not always be beneficial. A good example of this is Xerox Corporation's conclusion that its business process for delivering products was sometimes too fast. It observed that customers cared much less about rapid delivery of a copier than about delivery on a committed delivery date when the installation site for the new equipment would be ready.[8]

You might wonder why cost is listed with the product, whereas productivity (which is related to internal costs) is listed with the business process. Similarly, reliability is listed with the product, whereas security is listed with the process. Things are broken out this way because the customer often does not care about the productivity of the business process that produced the product but is concerned with the total cost of ownership—the total amount of resources the customer must expend in acquiring, using, and maintaining the product. Likewise, the customer is concerned with the reliability of the product but may not feel a direct stake in the security of the business process.

Customers may not even perceive this distinction between external and internal aspects of performance, which is often summarized as the difference between efficiency and effectiveness. Efficiency involves doing things in the right way, whereas effectiveness involves doing the right things. **Efficiency** is an internal view focusing on how well resources are used within a work system to produce a particular output. Typical internal performance measures related to efficiency include business process measures such as consistency, productivity, and cycle time. **Effectiveness** is an external view related to whether the products and services produced are what the customer really wants. It is measured in terms of things the customer perceives directly, such as the cost, quality, and responsiveness. Although they are measured separately and should be considered separately, efficiency usually has an impact on effectiveness because work done well is more likely to produce good results than work done poorly.

Finally, notice how each of the performance variables can be described or measured at different levels of clarity. Quality experts are adamant that careful performance measurement is essential for process improvement. Table 2.7 illustrates the nature of such measurements by comparing them with vague descriptions and interpretations for a few characteristics. Notice how the measurements are stated more precisely and quantitatively than the vague descriptions.

TABLE 2.7

Comparing Vague Descriptions, Measurements, and Interpretations

Performance variables can be expressed at different levels of detail and precision, ranging from vague descriptions to careful measurements and interpretations. Here are examples showing vague descriptions, measurements, and interpretations for several performance variables related to work systems.

Performance variable	Vague description related to this variable	Measurement related to this variable	Interpretation related to this variable
Accuracy of information	The information doesn't seem very accurate.	97.5% of the readings are correct within 5%.	This is (or is not) accurate enough, given the way the information will be used.
Skills of participants	The salespeople are very experienced.	Every salesperson has 5 or more years of experience; 60% have more than 10 years.	This system is (or is not) appropriate for such experienced people.
Cycle time of a business process	This business process seems to take a long time.	The three major steps take an average of 1.3 days each, but the waiting time between the steps is around 5 days.	This is (or is not) better than the average for this industry, but we can (or cannot) improve by eliminating some of the waiting time.
Quality of the work system output	We produce top-quality frozen food, but our customers aren't enthusiastic.	65% of our customers rate it average or good even though our factory defect rate is only .003%.	Our manufacturing process does (or doesn't) seem OK, but we do (or don't) need to improve customer satisfaction.

CLARIFICATIONS RELATED TO THE ELEMENTS OF A WORK SYSTEM

This section presents a series of comments and clarifications about each element of the work system framework, especially infrastructure and context. The other elements are the subjects of entire chapters, which explain these topics in much more depth. Regardless of whether the PBSA method is used, effective analysis of business systems requires clarifications such as the ones presented here.

Customers

Figure 2.2 defined customers as the people who receive, use, and obtain direct benefits from the products and services produced by a work system. By this definition, someone buying a book from Amazon.com is the customer, but Amazon's managers and stockholders are not customers even though they care greatly about how many books are sold.

Internal and External Customers   A work system's customers may include both external and internal customers. **External customers**, such as people shopping on an e-commerce Web site, receive a work system's products and services as private individuals or as representatives of other firms or government organizations. In other words, external customers include both the people who receive the firm's products and services and governmental agencies or other external groups that receive taxes or information required by law or by membership in industry groups. **Internal customers**, such as employees who receive paychecks from a company's payroll system, work in the same firm and participate in other work systems within that firm. For example, a manufacturing department might consider a packaging department as its internal customer because the packaging department receives the manufactured items and performs the next steps in the value chain before the external customers receive the product. The idea of internal customers is sometimes pooh-poohed because firms exist to satisfy their external customers, but it is useful as a reminder that even internally directed systems are not fully successful unless they satisfy their customers as well.[9]

FIGURE 2.8

Who is a toy factory's customer?

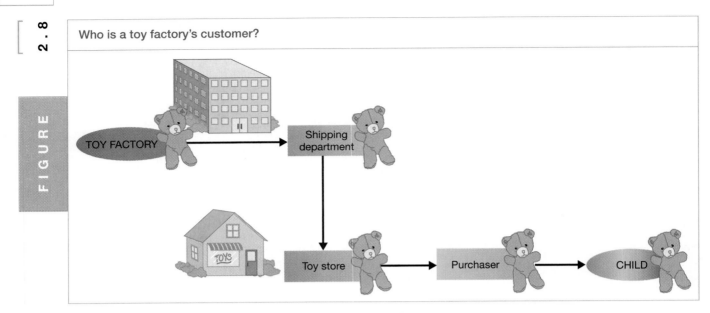

The product produced by a toy factory goes to a series of internal and external customers.

Multiple Customers with Different Concerns   It is easy to say that a work system has customers, but trying to identify these customers sometimes leads to surprises. For example, one might think that the customers of a toy company's manufacturing system are the children who use the toys; however, Figure 2.8 shows there is actually a chain of customer relationships between the manufacturing line and the children. For purposes of scheduling and balancing work inside the factory, the immediate customer of the manufacturing process is an internal customer, the shipping department, which is trying to meet its shipping schedule while using its staff efficiently. The direct customer of the shipping department is an external customer, the distributor. Its direct customer is the person who makes the purchase rather than the child who will eventually use the toy directly. This example shows that a work system may have many different customers and that the customers to consider when analyzing a system depend on the purpose of the analysis.

Having multiple customers with different concerns is often a complicating factor in building information systems. The most obvious customers are direct users and the managers of the business processes the information system supports. Direct users and managers performing different roles in a work system might have quite different information needs. The IT staff that will have to maintain and improve the resulting information system over time can also be considered an indirect customer. Reconciling different needs of all these customers can be difficult, especially if an information system that would satisfy all the end users' wishes would also be a nightmare to maintain.

Self-Service: Transforming Customers into Participants   External customers typically did not participate in the work system itself until the advent of **self-service work systems** that use ATMs, Web sites, telephone voice response systems, information kiosks, and other approaches to allow external customers to participate directly in value added work (see Figure 2.9). In an ideal situation, a self-service approach is beneficial for both the firm and the customer. For example, an ATM customer receives greater convenience and efficiency in depositing and withdrawing money, and the bank incurs lower expenses for buildings and tellers. One of the ideas behind Web-based e-commerce is to make the external customer a more direct participant in what were once primarily internal systems such as entering orders. Benefits from making the customers direct participants in these systems include not only eliminating data entry

FIGURE 2.9

Self-service makes the customer a participant

clerks, but also providing quicker response about product availability and delivery dates. Self-service certainly isn't guaranteed to please the customer, however. This is totally clear to anyone who has become lost in a maze of phone menus that ostensibly lead to customer service information but appear to be no more than a way to eliminate the customer support staff.

Products and Services

The output of a system is often called its product. The work system framework calls work system outputs "products & services" because we are concerned with systems that often produce a combination of products and services, each of which may involve a combination of information and physical things. For example, a custom tailor shop produces the clothing (a physical thing), measures the client and customizes patterns for the client's needs (a service), and may provide information about related products. In contrast, an online bank performs banking services and provides information but may not produce physical things for the customer unless it mails out its monthly statements on paper.

Customers Evaluate the Product   Quality experts frequently assert that the work system's customers should evaluate the system's products and services because the customers are in the best position to determine what meets their needs. In general, customer satisfaction revolves around two issues: whether the products and services produced by the system are what the customer actually wants and whether the customer's overall experience of acquiring and using the product is positive. The customer's evaluation of a product or service usually combines at least several areas of product performance including the cost to the customer, quality perceived by the customer, responsiveness, reliability, and conformance to standards or regulations. Although one or two of these performance variables may be more important than the others in specific situations, separate consideration of each often helps in thinking about ways to improve the product from the customer's viewpoint.

Business Process

A business process is a related group of steps or activities in which people use information and other resources to create value for internal or external customers. Business processes consist of steps related in time and place, have a beginning and end, and have inputs and outputs. Business processes are at least somewhat formalized, but they need not be totally structured. For example, some auto dealerships require that salespeople sell cars at a prespecified price, whereas others permit salespeople to negotiate on price within certain limits. An automobile is being sold in both cases, but one process is somewhat more structured because the price is fixed in advance. Improving business processes is frequently a direct way to improve the performance of most work systems. This can be done by adding, combining, or eliminating steps, or by changing the rationale or methods used by the steps.

Link between Process Characteristics and Process Performance   The efficiency of a business process and its ability to produce what the customers want are strongly influenced by process characteristics including the degree of structure, the range of involvement, the level of integration, rhythm, and complexity. The degree of structure is one of the most important characteristics for understanding e-business situations because people focusing on a Web site's technology or aesthetics sometimes ignore it. Business processes for registering a user or making a payment are highly structured. Other processes such as using a search engine are semistructured or unstructured because users can go in many different directions and sometimes enjoy finding unanticipated results. Increasing or decreasing the amount of structure in a business process may improve or degrade performance, depending on the situation and the performance variables that are being considered. The same is true of other process characteristics.

Participants

A work system is not a machine. Even when computers play a major role in a work system, its success depends partly on whether its participants have the skills and tools needed to do their work and the interest and commitment needed to make it succeed.

Participants in a work system are the people who perform the business process. Even highly automated systems typically include human participants, such as the human attendants who can sometimes be reached when none of the options in an automated voice mail system suffices. Although information systems are often viewed as computer systems, human participants in these systems typically play essential roles such as entering, processing, or using the information in the system. The importance of human participants in information system success and failure is often underplayed. There is a tendency to attribute success to the wonders of the computer. Simultaneously, human errors such as entering incorrect data or failing to follow required procedures are often reported as a "computer glitch."

Difference between Participants and Users   The difference between work system participants and technology users is important in understanding the significance of technology features and capabilities. In a widely cited case study,[10] a company's salespeople performed a number of important tasks, one of which involved extensive use of an information system that was hard to use. The company spent millions of dollars making the information system easier to use. The salespeople agreed it was easier to use after the improvements, but still barely used it because their other tasks were more directly linked to their ability to earn commissions. In this case and in many others, being a work system participant (a salesperson) was much more important to the participants themselves than being an information system user. When analyzing an information system it is often important to recognize that work system participants may give higher priority to aspects of the work system not related to the information system.

Even when looking at a Web site, referring to *participants* in a work system instead of *users* of a Web site emphasizes the way work system participants perform a business process, rather than the less significant topic of how they interact with a computer while performing certain business process steps. A confusing Web site that made it difficult to complete transactions would obviously hurt sales, but in many other cases the difference between an average interface and an above-average interface would have relatively little impact on the issues that determine work system success, such as providing the right information and selling the right products at the right prices. On the other hand, Box 2.1 shows how a human interface issue was the center of a controversy about the U.S. Presidential election of 2000.

Impacts on Participants   Designing a work system to serve its participants is a direct way to encourage the participants to perform their roles to the fullest. Assuring they have the right skills and providing the right tools makes it easier for them to achieve satisfaction from doing a job well. This also shows that the organization actually cares about what they are doing. Providing appropriate work conditions, such as a reasonable workload, stress level, degree of autonomy, and possibilities for personal growth, encourages interest and commitment by demonstrating that the organization genuinely cares about serving the participants.

Work systems have impacts on their participants even though many of these systems are designed as though their impacts on participants were irrelevant or unimportant. The nature of these impacts depends on a participant's individual characteristics because people bring vastly different capabilities and backgrounds to their work. Highly structured, repetitive systems may be fine for some participants, but unsatisfying for others with different skills or personality traits. Applying technology to change a work system may foster personal learning and growth by instilling jobs with a more appropriate degree of engagement and challenge. To the contrary, however, it may devalue job skills and make jobs tedious or even obsolete.

Information

The information in a work system potentially can take a variety of forms including numbers, text, sounds, pictures, and even video. Some of the information in a work system may be created or modified within the system; other information may be received from other work systems.

The value of information does not come from the information itself, but rather, from its use. This implies that better information may not affect work system results. Better information certainly won't help if it languishes in a database that is never used, which happens frequently enough that jokes referring to rarely used databases as "write-only memories" sometimes strike a responsive chord. The information in many corporate databases and document repositories is surprisingly difficult to access and use. Except where specific information is directly linked to repetitive business processes, much of the information and knowledge in many organizations is rarely used outside of particular departments, even if there is a technical capability to access it. Information has the highest likelihood of making a difference if it is integrated into structured business processes and used by people with the knowledge and training needed to interpret it and apply it correctly.

Data, Information, Knowledge   The distinction between data, information, and knowledge is important for deciding whether providing better information would have any effect on the results a work system produces. Figure 2.10 shows that data form the basis of information and that knowledge is needed to use information. **Data** are facts, images, or sounds that may or may not be pertinent or useful for a particular task. In our everyday lives, we absorb data from newspapers and television, from

BOX 2.1   HOW A HUMAN INTERFACE AFFECTED AN ELECTION CONTROVERSY

The results of the U.S. Presidential election of 2000 hinged on disputed results in Florida, where the initial difference between the candidates was only 300 votes out of over 5,800,000. Some voters complained that the confusing appearance of the ballot caused them to make mistakes in voting. "Of the 462,657 ballots cast in Palm Beach County, 19,120 were thrown out because the voter had punched two or more candidates for a single office. When Palm Beach County officials did a hand recount of a sample of about 4,600 ballots they found 144 that had two or more candidates selected."[11] The photo of the butterfly ballot used in Palm Beach County shows that Bush, Buchanan, Gore, and McReynolds appear alphabetically as the first four choices but that they appear on alternating sides of the ballot. Some voters found this confusing and said they made voting mistakes. The following table shows the distribution of accidental double punches by voters. If this pattern applied to the entire vote in Palm Beach County, it is possible that a confusing human interface affected the result of the election.

BY THE NUMBERS

Punching Two or More In Palm Beach County

Of the 462,657 ballots cast in Palm Beach County, Fla., 19,120 were thrown out because the voter had punched two or more candidates for a single office. When Palm Beach County officials did a hand recount of a sample of about 4,600 ballots, they found 144 that had two or more candidates selected. Of those 144, the most frequent combinations were as follows.

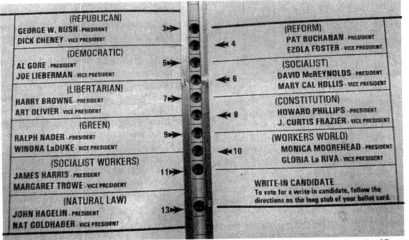

Detail of the butterfly ballot used in Palm Beach County, Fla.

Associated Press

CANDIDATES PUNCHED FOR PRESIDENT	POSITION ON BALLOT	BALLOTS WITH TWO OR MORE CANDIDATES SELECTED	
		NUMBER	PERCENTAGE
Patrick J. Buchanan and Al Gore *Reform and Democratic*		80	**56%**
Al Gore and David McReynolds *Democratic and Socialist*		21	**15**
George W. Bush and Patrick J. Buchanan *Republican and Reform*		11	**8**
Al Gore and Harry Browne *Democratic and Libertarian*		5	**3**
George W. Bush and Al Gore *Republican and Democratic*		3	**2**

Source: Palm Beach County canvassing board

The New York Times

billboards, and from other people. We receive so much data every minute that our conscious minds can't possibly pay attention to all of it. **Information** is data whose form and content are appropriate for a particular use. Converting data into information by formatting, filtering, and summarizing is a key role of information systems. People need knowledge to use information effectively. **Knowledge** is a combination of instincts, ideas, rules, and procedures that guide actions and decisions.

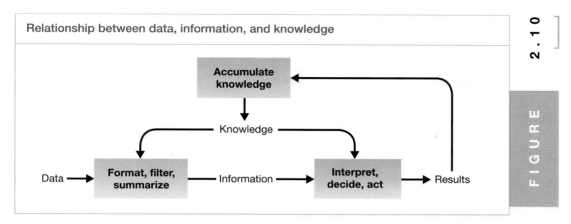

Relationship between data, information, and knowledge

FIGURE 2.10

People use knowledge about how to format, filter, and summarize data as part of the process of converting data into information useful in a situation. They interpret that information, make decisions, and take actions. The results of these decisions help in accumulating knowledge for use in later decisions.

The distinction between data and information is easy to remember and is cited frequently in explaining why vast operational databases often fail to satisfy managerial information needs. Data in these databases constitute information for people performing day-to-day operational tasks such as processing orders, but are not useful for managers, who need the data converted into information for management decision-making. There are many ways to do this, such as:

- Selecting the data pertinent to the situation and removing the irrelevant data
- Combining the data to bring it to a useful level of summarization
- Highlighting exceptions that may bias the results, or explaining more clearly what the data really say
- Displaying the data in an understandable way
- Developing models that convert data and assumptions into explanations of past results or projections of future results

In addition to showing the conversion of data into information, Figure 2.10 shows the process of accumulating knowledge and using that knowledge. It says that people act based on their information about the current situation plus their accumulated knowledge about using information. The results of action feed into the process of accumulating more knowledge, which in turn makes people more able to process data into information and more able to use that information in the future. For example, this is the process by which medical students become expert doctors. As medical students examine patients, treat them, and observe the results, their medical knowledge deepens.

Hard and Soft Data   Systems with human participants contain both hard and soft data. **Hard data**, clearly defined data generated by formal systems, must often be balanced with **soft data**, intuitive or subjective data obtained by informal means such as talking to people or interpreting stories and opinions. Although hard data is factual and explicit, soft data is often essential for understanding what really happened in a situation, or whether proposed actions might encounter resistance within an organization. Typical methods for identifying and defining the information in formal, computerized systems usually ignore important soft data, implying that some data in most work systems will never be formalized. Furthermore, even in formalized business processes, unanticipated situations sometimes make it necessary to create work-arounds, situation-dependent steps that bypass the formal process because they don't fit the situation. In these instances, the problem may not be the methods for building information systems, but rather with the human inability to anticipate everything that can possibly happen, even in relatively small systems. Information system designers primed to define information requirements for computerized systems sometimes find this realization disappointing.

Technology

This book focuses on work systems that use **information technology**, computer and communication hardware and software. **Hardware** refers to the devices and other physical objects involved in processing information, such as computers, workstations, physical networks, and data storage and transmission devices. **Software** refers to the computer programs that interpret user inputs and tell the hardware what to do. Software includes operating systems, end-user software such as word processors, and application software related to specialized business tasks such as recording credit card transactions or designing automobiles. (Although "pencil and paper" and chalkboards are also forms of information technology, our definition is stated in terms of hardware and software because we are concerned primarily with computerized systems.)

The key point about technology in a work system is that it has no impact whatsoever unless it is used within a business process. A business professional's analysis of a work system must include technology but should emphasize the way the technology will be used in the work system rather than the internal details of the technology. A business professional's view of technology is concerned primarily with its capability to support the desired work system and with its long- and short-term costs, risks, and other business implications.

Since work systems exist to produce products and services for customers, their participants' efforts should be directed at doing the necessary work rather than figuring out how to use or work around the available technology. Despite amazing advances in the power of information technology, installation, configuration, training, and ongoing usage still absorb large amounts of effort and attention that might otherwise be directed toward doing the work of producing what the customers want.

Minimizing effort consumed by technology is one of the most evident advantages of applications based on Internet technology. Permitting a user to click on underlined hypertext links is an incredibly simple method for capturing information about what the user wants to see or do next. Transmitting information to and from the user and a Web site anywhere in the world is also incredibly simple from a user's viewpoint. Simply enter the Web site's address to get started and the Internet's invisible infrastructure takes care of all subsequent information transmission automatically. Depending on the nature of the application, storage of information can occur on a Web server or on the user's computer through reasonably simple commands about how to name the information and where to store it. Information retrieval can be as simple as clicking on a command in a highly structured application or as complicated as using a search engine to find information in a novel situation. In addition, Web-based applications make it possible to display images, audio, and video information that could not be included in traditional computer applications.

Infrastructure

Infrastructure is the shared human, informational, and technical resources on which the work system relies in order to operate, even though these resources exist and are managed outside of the work system. It is useful to compare the IT-infrastructure that supports a work system with the public infrastructure that supports a city's residential, commercial, and civic activities. Part of a city's infrastructure is physical things, such as streets, public buildings, electric lines, and water lines. Also essential is the human side of infrastructure, shared services such as police, fire fighting, education, and public health. In a similar way, a firm's IT-infrastructure includes both technical and human components. Equally applicable to cities and to work systems, infrastructure itself is at least partially beyond the control of people who rely on it. This is demonstrated by infrastructure failures, such as telephone or electricity outages, and by work stoppages by public employees, such as police officers or bus drivers. This lack of control sometimes tempts business professionals to think of infrastructure as someone else's problem, but its essential nature demands that it not be ignored. The Internet is a good example of infrastructure because the millions of Web sites that rely on it don't own it and can't control it.

Every part of a firm's infrastructure should be deployed as a genuine resource regardless of whether it is a shared corporate database or a computer network or a support and training organization. In any of these cases, failure to manage infrastructure as a genuine resource means that the benefits from using it will not be fully realized. The shared database may be accurate and complete, but may still have little impact on decision-making; the computer network may operate flawlessly without improving operations; the training staff may have 200 training programs that have no impact on the underutilization of enterprise software whose acquisition and implementation cost millions of dollars. Overall, deploying infrastructure as a genuine resource requires ongoing responses to frequent feedback about how the infrastructure is being used and how it does or does not support important work systems. In other words, the infrastructure on which many work systems rely should be operated and managed like any other work system, with careful attention to how well it is performing and how it might improve.

Distinguishing between Technology and Infrastructure   Even though it is useful when trying to understand many work systems, the distinction between technology inside a work system and the external infrastructure on which it relies is often imprecise. For example, a computer that houses a firm's Web site might be considered technology within the work system of maintaining the site whereas a shared corporate database used and managed for many other purposes might be considered part of the external infrastructure. Similarly, the laptop computers insurance salespeople use during personal sales presentations might be viewed as the technology used within a sales work system, or alternatively as a part of the firm's technical infrastructure for receiving e-mail, linking to the Internet, and performing other general communication and data processing activities.

We will use the following guidelines to distinguish between a work system's technology and the infrastructure that supports it. Technology is part of the infrastructure if it is viewed as outside a work system, if it is shared among many work systems, if it is owned and managed by a centralized authority in charge of infrastructure, and if its details generally are hidden from users and seem inconsequential to them. Technology is not included in infrastructure if it is dedicated to a particular work system, if it is owned and controlled within the work system, if it is managed by whomever manages the work system, and if its hands-on users need to understand its technical details.

This book discusses both the infrastructure needed by an organization's value chain and the infrastructure used by IT professionals for information system development and operation. Typical elements of information system infrastructure include telecommunications networks for transmitting voice and computerized data, messaging services for handling e-mail and voice mail, centralized computers for large-scale data processing, database management systems (DBMSs) that permit sharing of data across application areas, and computer-aided software engineering (CASE) systems used for building information systems. Deficiencies in any element of the hardware, software, or human and service infrastructure can cripple an information system. Conversely, a well-managed infrastructure with sufficient processing power makes it much easier to maximize business benefits from these systems. Evaluating infrastructure is often difficult because the same infrastructure may support some applications excessively and others insufficiently. For example, a telephone network that is fine for voice conversations may be inadequate for video conferencing or data transfer. Likewise, a DBMS that is adequate for small information systems developed by end users may be totally inadequate for larger systems with stringent performance requirements.

Human Infrastructure   Human infrastructure is often less noticed than the hardware and software components of infrastructure, but it is equally essential for successful information system development and maintenance. Responsibilities of human and service infrastructure include managing IT facilities, managing the technical operation of hardware and software, helping business professionals use technology effectively, performing IT-related training, managing relationships with IT suppliers, recommending and enforcing IT standards, identifying and testing new technologies, establishing IT security, and planning for disaster recovery.[12]

This human infrastructure is often underfunded and underappreciated. For example, business professionals are often surprised by the effort and expense devoted to the human infrastructure that keeps information systems operating technically and trains and counsels users. The tendency toward organizational decentralization and outsourcing of many system-related functions makes it even more important to include human infrastructure in the analysis of new systems.

Information Infrastructure   Information infrastructure is codified information that is shared across a company. Ideally a company's information infrastructure should be stored in databases designed for use in different work systems in different parts of the company. Although "enterprise systems" have provided a path in this direction, a high level of information sharing across the company is still rare. One of the great frustrations of working in many firms is the inability to share information that was generated elsewhere in the firm but is important for a different purpose. Sometimes it is difficult to share the information because of the lack of technical links. In other situations the information is hoarded or otherwise controlled in an unhelpful way.

Context

Changes in work systems often generate unanticipated consequences. Some of these consequences occur within the work system, such as when work system participants use information in unauthorized ways or when overly qualified participants make too many errors because they are bored. Other unintended impacts and consequences occur when the operation and rationale of the work system conflict with the context within which the work system operates.

Context is the organizational, competitive, technical, and regulatory realm within which the work system operates, including external stakeholders, organizational policies and practices, organizational culture, resource availability, business pressures, and laws and regulations that affect the system. The context may create incentives and even urgency for change but may also create obstacles that make those changes infeasible. For example, state legislators and university administrators might favor distance education as a way to reduce costs, but a state university's faculty and students might create obstacles based on their view that face-to-face education is more effective. The relevant context may also include explicit rules and requirements such as government regulations, industry standards, and organizational policies. Table 2.8 identifies important aspects of the context surrounding a work system and links each topic to the element of the work system framework with which it is most directly associated.

Web-based e-commerce has spawned a large number of unintended impacts and conflicts. The Internet Tax Freedom Act of 1998 established a three-year moratorium on new state and local taxes on the use of the Internet and interactive computing services. Under this law a buyer pays sales tax for a Web-based purchase only if the merchant has a store or other corporate presence in the state where the buyer resides. State and local governments may not have anticipated the threat from tax-free sales on the Web; many e-commerce sites probably did not welcome the invention of shopping agents that compare prices offered by competitive sites; Web pioneers who touted it as a tool for freedom probably did not focus on its commercial use for pornography, gambling, and gun sales; global commerce enthusiasts may not have anticipated the difficulties of translating Web sites for different cultures and the complexity of handling national taxes and tariffs. Although it is impossible to anticipate all of the unintended impacts and conflicts that might occur from the trend toward e-business, it is possible to anticipate some of them. Whoever can accomplish that will be in a better position to benefit from the positive impacts while minimizing the negative impacts.

[**L O O K   A H E A D**]
Chapter 5 explains enterprise systems as one of six categories of information systems.

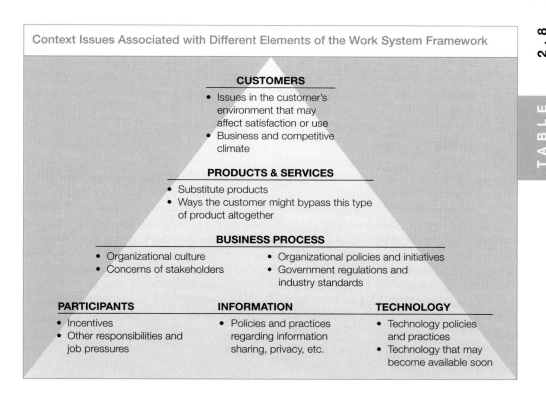

Context Issues Associated with Different Elements of the Work System Framework

CUSTOMERS
- Issues in the customer's environment that may affect satisfaction or use
- Business and competitive climate

PRODUCTS & SERVICES
- Substitute products
- Ways the customer might bypass this type of product altogether

BUSINESS PROCESS
- Organizational culture
- Concerns of stakeholders
- Organizational policies and initiatives
- Government regulations and industry standards

PARTICIPANTS
- Incentives
- Other responsibilities and job pressures

INFORMATION
- Policies and practices regarding information sharing, privacy, etc.

TECHNOLOGY
- Technology policies and practices
- Technology that may become available soon

The personal, organizational, and economic aspects of the context have direct impact on the work system success. Work systems that address external competitive threats and opportunities receive much greater attention than other systems along with a disproportionate share of human and monetary resources. Simultaneously, unavailability or diversion of the resources needed to build a system or operate it reduces its likelihood of success. Even if the firm has the necessary monetary resources, context factors ranging from historical precedents and budget cycles to internal politics and culture can be stumbling blocks. We will say a bit more about three aspects of the context: incentives, organizational culture, and nonparticipant stakeholders.

Incentives   Personal incentives of system participants are often a key determinant of whether a system will succeed. Regardless of how well designed a system appears to be, system participants tend to put little energy into a system that is unrelated to or inconsistent with their personal incentives. Medical care systems are notorious in terms of conflicting incentives. Their idealized goal is to keep people healthy, but the traditional monetary incentives for health care providers were based on the number of procedures and patient visits, rather than on health-related outcomes. With monetary incentives structured this way, the doctors make less if the system succeeds in keeping people healthy and they make more the worse it performs. The recent move toward HMOs and other arrangements based on a fixed fee for each person enrolled have shifted the nature of conflicting incentives. Paying medical care providers a fixed amount per person and forcing them to absorb the incremental cost of each unit of medical care gives providers a monetary incentive to limit medical care as much as possible without making patients too angry. The incentives in the old system drove the providers to perform additional visits, tests, and procedures, regardless of whether they were genuinely needed. The new system motivates them to provide fewer visits and procedures, even if they might be needed. Both approaches suffer from internal incentive conflicts and neither brings about an ideal alignment of participant goals with customer goals.

As though conflicting or misdirected incentives weren't bad enough, some systems contain counter-productive incentives and may even encourage participants to cheat. Consider the way arbitrary date cutoffs in budget systems create counter-productive incentives. Ideally these systems should assure proper resource allocation and use, but departments trying to avoid future budget cuts often feel pressure to consume whatever is left in the budget before the next cycle begins. A clear example was the admission by a former Air Force pilot that he had been directed to fly out over the ocean and drop a load of jet fuel because the budget year was almost over and his group had not yet used up its fuel allotment. The incentives in that control system motivated the opposite of the desired careful stewardship of resources.

Organizational Culture　Discussions of systems often focus on formal procedures for performing tasks, but the organization's culture is often just as important as the system's official rationale in determining system success. **Organizational culture** is the shared understandings about relationships and work practices that determine how things are done in a workplace. Culture is subtle because it is a combination of written and unwritten rules and practices that govern the way people behave. It covers issues such as the importance of status symbols, the degree to which decisions are made based on organizational hierarchy, the extent to which people show respect to each other, the degree to which dissent is considered acceptable, and the extent to which the organization treats employees as family members or as contractors for hire.

One of the difficulties in dealing with organizational culture is that discussing important cultural issues is virtually taboo in many organizations. Defining procedures and measuring activities or results is much easier than showing how the organization's managers don't "walk the walk" even if they "talk the talk." Yes, the organization espouses its desire to balance home and work life, but it requires that everyone arrive just before schools open. Yes, the organization espouses the value of everyone's contribution, but the only way to get an idea accepted is to convince the boss that she invented it. Yes, the organization espouses customer focus, but its engineers are more motivated by doing sophisticated engineering than by solving simple customer problems. Cultural contradictions such as these may readily be apparent to people who work in the setting, but people rarely want to be the messenger who makes the announcement.

Stakeholders　Also part of the work system context are **stakeholders**, people with a personal stake in the system and its outputs even if they are neither its participants nor its customers. Managers who have high visibility roles as system sponsors or champions are key stakeholders in many strategically important systems because they work toward the system's success and ultimately receive some of the credit or blame. Other stakeholders may be affected less directly if a system shifts the balance of power in an organization or works contrary to their personal goals. Information systems that create new communication patterns are likely to have a wide range of stakeholders. For example, new voice mail or e-mail systems sometimes enhance the visibility and status of individuals with expert knowledge about specific activities; easy access to these experts often reduces the power of some support staff positions, middle managers, and others who formerly served as information conduits.

IT staff members are important stakeholders of most information systems because they are responsible for system operation and enhancement. As professionals in the field, they have a deeper understanding than most business professionals about what it takes to build and maintain solid information systems. They also have a clearer view of technical relationships between different systems and a better understanding of policies and practices related to systems.

CONCEPTS AND VOCABULARY FOR LOOKING AT A WORK SYSTEM IN DEPTH

The introduction to the PBSA method noted that the four phases of systems analysis provide very little guidance regarding what to think about in each phase or how to do the analysis. The PBSA method introduced the seven work system principles as a lens for focusing on different parts of a work system, discovering issues, and identifying potential improvements. This provides much more guidance than just the four general steps of systems analysis, but it raises the same question at a different level: What ideas and concepts help in applying each of the seven principles? For example, in-depth use of the principle "perform the work efficiently" requires basic ideas for describing how a business process operates and how well it is performing. Similarly, applying the principle "create value from information" requires basic ideas for identifying the information in a work system and evaluating how good that information is.

This entire book is designed to fill in these ideas and concepts. Table 2.9 shows how the material in the book can help in applying the PBSA method in more depth. The table lists each of the steps in the PBSA method and identifies the parts of the book that provide the most direct guidance when performing that step. Table 2.9 shows that this book tries to combine two important goals:

- To provide a thorough coverage of information system concepts needed as part of general business literacy
- To provide a method for using those ideas in an organized way when thinking about any system

The many entries in Table 2.9 show that understanding systems in organizations involves much more than being able to identify technology or document the way a business process is supposed to operate. The work system framework, the work system principles, and the PBSA method provide an organized way to approach any system without getting overwhelmed in the details. A more thorough analysis requires much more effort, but the basic ideas about work systems remain in the foreground as a way to organize the analysis at whatever level of depth makes sense.

TABLE 2.9

Finding Ideas and Vocabulary That Support Each Step in the PBSA Method

Ideas and vocabulary needed to pursue PBSA in depth appear throughout this text. The order of the chapters is determined by the ease of absorbing the ideas rather than the specific order of the PBSA principles.

Step in the PBSA method	Location of related ideas and vocabulary in the text
1. Define the problem and the work system together.	Chapter 2, *Understanding Systems from a Business Viewpoint* • Definition of elements in the work system framework • Work system snapshot • Constraints and priorities • Explanation of the principle-based systems analysis (PBSA) method
2. Use work system principles for summarizing the current situation and searching for possible improvements.	Locations of ideas and vocabulary for each principle follow.
Principle #1: Please the customers	Chapter 2, *Understanding Systems from a Business Viewpoint* • Internal customers vs. external customers • Self-service work systems Chapter 6, *Customer, Product, and E-Commerce* • The phases in the customer experience related to products and services • Framework for visualizing alternatives for a system's products and services • Criteria a customer uses to evaluate a product • Competitive uses of information systems. *Throughout the book*: Numerous cases and examples in which customers have views about the products and services they receive.

Continued

TABLE 2.9

Finding Ideas and Vocabulary That Support Each Step in the PBSA Method, *continued*

Principle #2: Perform the work efficiently	*Chapter 1, Moving Toward E-Business as Usual* • Basic information-processing tasks performed by information technology *Chapter 3, Business Processes* • Graphical methods for documenting a business process • Process characteristics that affect how well processes are performed; impact of excess or deficiency for each characteristic • Variables used for evaluating business process performance • Trade-offs between these performance variables • Common activities within business processes: communication, decision-making, and management *Chapter 5, Different Types of Information Systems* • Comparison of seven different types of information systems, each representing a cluster of ideas related to performing different types of work efficiently *Chapter 8, Computers in a Networked World* • Performance variables for technology • Technology choices for capturing data, storing and retrieving data, and displaying data *Chapter 9, Software, Programming, and Artificial Intelligence* • The process of programming and the evolution of programming languages *Chapter 10, Networks and Telecommunications* • Applications of telecommunications • Different types of networks
Principle #3: Serve the participants	*Chapter 2, Understanding Systems from a Business Viewpoint* • Difference between users and participants *Chapter 7, Human and Ethical Issues* • Positive and negative impacts of work systems and information systems on people at work • Dependence of systems on participants • Ethical issues such as privacy, accuracy, property, and access
Principle #4: Create value from information	*Chapter 4, Information and Databases* • Basic concepts related to computerized data files and different types of databases • Data modeling, a general technique for understanding information requirements • Capabilities of database management systems that store and control databases • Performance variables related to information quality, accessibility, presentation, and security • Use of models to create value from information
Principle #5: Minimize effort absorbed by technology	*Chapter 8, Computers in a Networked World* • Performance variables for technology • Cost of ownership • Alternative computer architectures *Chapter 9, Software, Programming, and Artificial Intelligence* • The process of programming and the evolution of programming languages *Chapter 10, Networks, Telecommunications, and the Internet* • Relative advantages of different telecommunications options • Importance of standards
Principle #6: Deploy infrastructure as a genuine resource	*Chapter 2, Understanding Systems from a Business Viewpoint* • Difference between technology and infrastructure • Importance of technical, human, and information infrastructure *Chapter 9, Software, Programming, and Artificial Intelligence* • Programming methods as infrastructure • Importance of operating systems *Chapter 10, Networks and Telecommunications* • Telecommunications networks as infrastructure

Continued

Finding Ideas and Vocabulary That Support Each Step in the PBSA Method, *continued*

Principle #7: Minimize unintended conflicts and risks	*Chapter 1, Moving Toward E-Business as Usual* • Discussion of obstacles when applying IT in the real world *Chapter 2, Understanding Systems from a Business Viewpoint* • Discussion of context as the organizational, competitive, technical, and regulatory realm within which the work system operates *Chapter 10, Networks and Telecommunications* • Telecommunications policy as part of the context *Chapter 11, Information Systems Planning* • International issues that may be part of the context *Chapter 13, E-Business Security and Control* • Vulnerability to various types of accidents and computer crime *Throughout the book* • Cases and examples involving unintended conflicts and risks
3. Make a recommendation that addresses the problem while supporting the organization's priorities	*Chapter 2, Understanding Systems from a Business Viewpoint* • Problem definition including system boundaries, constraints, and priorities • Recognition that information systems and work systems they support might have overlapping and nonoverlapping changes *Chapter 11, Information Systems Planning* • Strategic and practical issues when deciding how to incorporate IT into a firm's business strategy • Methods for selecting among proposed information system investments • Issues related to project management. *Chapter 12, Building and Maintaining Information Systems* • Phases of any information system project • Comparison of four different approaches for building information systems (based on how these phases are performed) • Project failure *Chapter 13, E-Business Security and Control* • Value chain for system security

CHAPTER CONCLUSION

Why is it important to have a framework for analyzing information systems?

A framework is a brief set of ideas for organizing a thought process about a particular type of thing or situation. A framework helps people by identifying topics that should be considered and by showing how the topics are related. When studying information systems or other topics, a good framework helps people make sense of the world's complexity.

What eight elements can be used for summarizing any work system?

A work system is a system in which human participants and/or machines perform a business process using information, technology, and other resources to produce products and/or services for internal or external customers. Work systems operate within a surrounding context and rely on infrastructure that operates and is managed outside of the work system. The eight elements are the customers, products and services, business process, participants, information, technology, context, and infrastructure.

What principles can be used to explore how well a work system is operating?

The following principles apply to any work system: 1) please the customer; 2) perform the work efficiently; 3) serve the participants; 4) create value from information; 5) minimize effort consumed by technology; 6) deploy infrastructure as a genuine resource; 7) minimize unintended conflicts and risks. Although the principles are mutually reinforcing in some situations, in other situations they are at least somewhat contradictory. For example, pleasing customers is important, but it is also important to perform the work efficiently. It may not be possible to follow both principles simultaneously.

What is the relationship between information systems and work systems?

An information system is a particular type of work system that uses information technology to capture, transmit, store, retrieve, manipulate, or display infor-

mation used by one or more work systems. Information systems often play crucial roles in the work systems they support, but some aspects of those work systems are usually unrelated to information systems. The more information-intensive the work system is, the larger the role the information system plays.

Why is it important to define the problem and the work system together when analyzing a system?

The scope of the work system is not fixed before the analysis starts. Instead, it is a conscious choice based on the purpose of the analysis and a practical trade-off between making the topic too broad and complex versus making it too narrow and insignificant. It is especially important to avoid defining the work system in terms of a software package provided by a vendor or IT group.

What are the steps in systems analysis and how can work system principles be used in performing these steps?

Systems analysis is a general process of defining a problem, gathering pertinent information, developing alternative solutions, and choosing among those solutions. The principle-based systems analysis (PBSA) method combines this idea with the work system framework and work system principles. First, define the problem and the work system. Second, use each work system principle in turn to explore the situation and search for improvements. Third, make a recommendation that addresses the problem while supporting the organization's priorities.

What is the difference between a participant and a user when thinking about a work system?

Participants in a work system are the people who perform the business process. These work system participants may be users of technology during some of the steps in the process. When analyzing an information system it is often important to recognize that work system participants may give higher priority to aspects of the work system not related to information system usage.

framework
model
work system
work system framework
information system
project
work system principles
systems analysis
principle-based systems analysis
    (PBSA)
work system snapshot

constraints
priorities
success factors
architecture
performance
effectiveness
efficiency
internal customers
external customers
self-service work systems
data

information
knowledge
hard data
soft data
information technology
hardware
software
infrastructure
context
organizational culture
stakeholders

REVIEW QUESTIONS

1. What is the difference between a framework and model?

2. What is a work system?

3. Why is it important to maintain balance between the elements of a work system?

4. Why are information systems and projects both special types of work systems?

5. Explain why work system principles may be mutually contradictory.

6. What are the steps in a general systems analysis process?

7. In what way is a work system snapshot a simplification of reality?

8. Why are constraints and priorities important in systems analysis?

9. What are success factors and why do general success factors for work systems apply to information systems and projects?

10. Provide several examples of information systems that support aspects of a work system but not necessarily all of it.

11. What is the difference between efficiency and effectiveness, and how is this related to the work system framework?

12. What are some of the performance variables associated with each element of the framework?

13. What is the difference between internal customers and external customers?

14. In what situations would it be advantageous to transform customers of a business process into participants?

15. Who should evaluate the outputs produced by a work system?

DISCUSSION QUESTIONS

1. When anthropologists working in Xerox's Palo Alto Research Center asked clerks how they did their jobs, the descriptions corresponded to the formal procedures in the job manual. But when they observed clerks at work they discovered that the clerks weren't really following the procedures at all. Instead they relied on a rich variety of informal practices that weren't in any manual but were crucial to getting work done.[13] How is this finding related to the topics in this chapter?

2. In 1973 an official of the United Auto Workers (UAW) asked that the following notice be posted on the union's in-plant bulletin boards in General Motors plants: "Quality products are our concern too." A General Motors executive called him to complain that quality is solely management's responsibility and demanded that the bulletins be taken down.[14] Explain why this story is related to ideas in this chapter.

3. Explain why you believe it is or is not important for managers and system participants to be able to analyze information systems.

4. Explain why you do or do not believe that the study of information systems is basically a study of how information technology operates.

5. Explain how the following passage from Machiavelli's *The Prince*, written in 1513, is related to the PBSA method and the success factors for work systems, information systems, and projects: "It must be remembered that there is nothing more difficult to plan, more doubtful of success, nor more dangerous to manage than the creation of a new system. For the initiator has the enmity of the old institution and merely lukewarm defenders in those who would gain by the new ones."[15]

CASE   Aramark Uniform Services: Satisfying Customers in a Service Industry

Aramark is a $7 billion world leader in providing managed services—food services and facilities management, uniform and career apparel, and child care and early education programs. Headquartered in Philadelphia, Aramark has more than 160,000 employees serving 15 million people at 500,000 locations in 15 countries every day. In corporate communications to customers and employees Aramark makes a big point of working together to provide the best services possible in the most convenient way.

Aramark Uniform Services rents, leases, or sells uniforms for service employees working in industries including food processing, airlines, manufacturing, hotels, department stores, and many more. It claims to have the broadest range of uniform and career apparel products and services in the industry. The rental service includes clean uniforms delivered every week, automatic repairs and replacements, and free upgrades. The lease option allows the customers to clean the garments without having to purchase them but still repairs and replaces worn-out garments at no cost and allows size changes. The purchase option does not offer cleaning but allows a wider range of products and fabrics, and extensive embroidering and screen-printing for personalization. Its trademarked ApparelOne Process is designed to determine which option is best for a customer. The process starts with a needs assessment. The second phase is customization to meet the needs of each employee group and to define the right services. The third phase is to provide proactive improvement suggestions, immediate problem resolution, and one-stop, hassle-free service.[16]

Consistent with this service orientation, Aramark announced an improved customer invoice as follows: "Spend more time managing your business . . . And less time learning about our Invoice! . . . We listened when you told us our invoice could be improved by making the format more readable and less confusing. Accordingly, we have taken the first step in the process of continuous improvement." The changes included redesigning and simplifying invoice layout, removing unnecessary information, and simplifying item descriptions. The goals were to increase readability, reduce clutter, and reduce customer time spent reviewing invoices.[17]

Invisible to Aramark's customers is an enormous amount of data processing required to keep track of uniforms, services, and customer accounts. Until Aramark changed its internal data processing systems, it took three days to retrieve an invoice to resolve a customer complaint. The old paperwork system involved storage rooms full of file cabinets and approximately 100 employees who did nothing but file and retrieve invoices at branch offices. A new outsourcing arrangement with Xerox changed that.

"Aramark bills are now sent to a single Xerox-run processing center in Toledo, Ohio. Xerox scans and archives 2 million invoices a month into an electronic repository and mails out the monthly statements. The database is accessible to any one of Aramark's local offices through a secured Internet hookup." According to the director of marketing services, "If a customer calls with a dispute, we can instantly pull that image up on the screen and we can fax it directly to the customer, saying: Look, here's the guy who signed for it."[18]

Ironically the *Forbes* article that described this outsourcing arrangement presented it as a counterpoint to major internal problems at Xerox due to two bungled reorganizations. In one of them 53 administration centers in Europe and 36 in the United States were consolidated into 1 and 3 locations, respectively. "The result was chaos. The invoices and shipping orders piled up; Xerox sales reps had to spend up to 40% of their time getting the orders right and answering billing questions. Instead of cutting expenses, the transition ended up costing Xerox money and customer goodwill."

QUESTIONS

1. Assume that an Aramark customer wishes to rent uniforms. Based on the limited information provided here, produce a work system snapshot of the situation. Assume this is part of an analysis of customer satisfaction.

2. Review Tables 2.6 and 2.7. Identify specific measures of performance for the products & services, business process, and information you identified in the first questions.

3. Identify ideas in the chapter that might help explain how it is possible that Xerox could help clean up an invoicing mess at Aramark but had great difficulty with invoicing as a result of its own reorganization.

PanAmSat: Recovering from a Satellite Failure

A Galaxy 4 satellite operated by PanAmSat, a subsidiary of Hughes Electronics, tilted away from the earth at 6:13 P.M. on May 19, 1998 and began to spin because of a computer failure and the subsequent failure of a backup computer. This unexpected problem disabled 80% to 90% of the pager services in the U.S. along with a number of credit card authorization networks, television transmissions, and other networked services. PanAmSat's efforts to realign the satellite failed, but it was able to restore service within a day by rerouting the traffic the satellite normally handled. Of the 17 satellites PanAmSat had in orbit at the time, one was a spare. The recovery plan included rerouting signals for paging, retail-store services, and other services through its Galaxy 3R satellite and rerouting television signals through its Galaxy 6 satellite, which it was moving into roughly the same geosynchronous orbit over Kansas that the Galaxy 4 had occupied since its launch in 1993. Computer failure had transformed the Galaxy 4 from a $200 million link in the U.S. business infrastructure into a 3,700-pound piece of space junk with a 100-foot span of solar panels. The satellite was insured for $116 million, and the company did not expect to suffer a major financial loss as a result.

The immediate consequences of the satellite failure demonstrated the widespread dependence on communications infrastructure. Emergency communication to police departments and physicians was disrupted for hours. Customers at 5,400 Chevron stations could no longer pay by credit card at the pump because automated credit-card authorization requests were transmitted from antennas atop gas stations through the Galaxy 4 satellite. Customers in Wal-Mart stores had similar problems. At home, the nonresponse of family members and friends when paged repeatedly led to confusion and annoyance. The cost of satellite time suddenly jumped. It had ranged from $100 to $500 for a 15-minute block depending on the satellite's location; after the failure the prices jumped to $250 to $600. Annual prices of $900,000 to $2,500,000 seemed to be increasing by up to 50%.[19,20] Ten months later, a failure on GE Americom's satellite GE-3 disrupted a number of key networks including PBS broadcasting, CNN, and Turner Classic Movies.[21]

Although satellites typically have been extremely reliable, with a failure rate of less than 1%, the widespread impact of this event was a reminder of vulnerability to infrastructure-related weak links that affect business and society. It is possible to imagine ways to reduce risks through investment in redundant capacity, but the costs are prohibitive in many situations. For example, CBS television shifted to a backup satellite when the Galaxy 4 could not carry its planned broadcasts. CBS could afford the backup, but many paging businesses do not have the resources to keep a satellite idling in reserve.

QUESTIONS

1. Explain how this case is related to the discussion of infrastructure in this chapter.

2. PanAmSat's system of providing satellite communication infrastructure for other companies can be viewed as a work system. Assume that tomorrow you will join a team analyzing this work system in detail. To help organize your own thoughts use the work system framework to identify your assumptions about the business process, participants, information, and so on.

3. It is easy to say that business and government should assess risks and take appropriate action. Thinking about IT-based systems ranging from pagers to ATMs to air traffic control, suggest general guidelines a business or government might use for deciding what failure rate to tolerate and what level of resources to devote to disaster recovery.

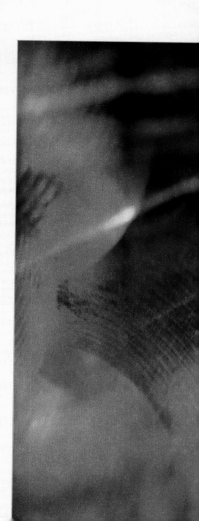

Business Processes

chapter3

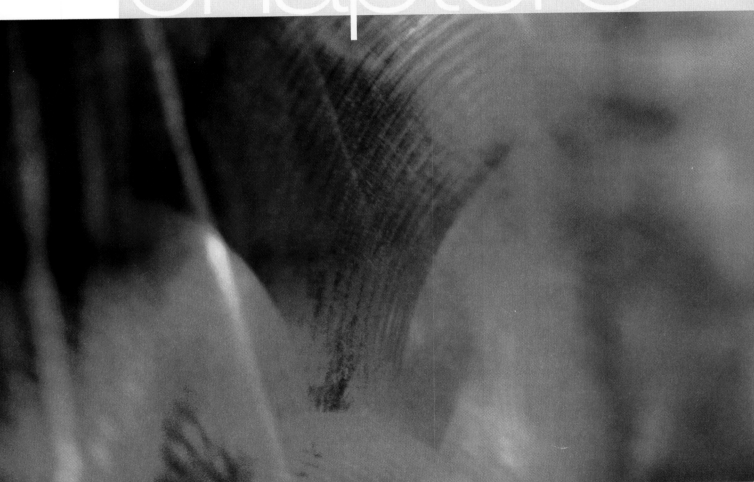

STUDY QUESTIONS

- What is the role of data flow diagrams in process modeling?
- What business process characteristics reflect system design choices that will affect business process performance?
- What is the difference between structured, semistructured, and unstructured tasks?
- What are the five possible levels of integration of business processes?
- Why are planning and control important elements of many business processes?
- Why is it sometimes necessary to reconcile inconsistent performance goals for a business process?
- How are social context and nonverbal communication important when communication technologies are used?
- What are the phases of decision-making and what are some of its common limitations?

OUTLINE

Process Modeling: Documenting a
Business Process
Data Flow Diagrams
Flowcharts and Structured English

Process Characteristics
Degree of Structure
Range of Involvement
Level of Integration
Rhythm
Complexity
Degree of Reliance on Machines
Prominence of Planning and Control
Attention to Errors and Exceptions

Evaluating Business Process Performance
Activity Rate and Output Rate
Consistency

Productivity
Cycle Time
Downtime
Security

More about Communication and
Decision-Making
Basic Communication Concepts
Basic Decision-Making Concepts

Chapter Conclusion
Summary
Key Terms
Review Questions
Discussion Questions
Cases

Business Processes

CHARLES SCHWAB

Charles Schwab & Co. was one of the leaders in changing the basic business processes through which stocks are bought and sold by individuals. According to one recent article, Schwab "is widely acknowledged as the only traditional retail operation—financial services or otherwise—to have successfully adapted its business to the Web."[1] Schwab was incorporated in 1971, and became a discount broker after the Securities and Exchange Commission (SEC) outlawed fixed brokerage commissions in 1975. Its strategy of undercutting the competition was a wild success: in just seven years, revenues grew from less than $5 million to more than $126 million. As of October 17, 2000, Schwab had $961 billion of assets under management, 7.4 million active accounts and 4.2 million online accounts. It had 368 branch offices and over 25,000 employees.[2]

Schwab was built based on the idea of eliminating the investment advisory role of stockbrokers and providing only transaction processing services. As part of this strategy, Schwab first offered online trading in 1984 through its proprietary Equalizer software. In 1989 it introduced Tele-Broker, a 24-hour telephone trading service that offered a 10% discount to customers willing to place stock orders and obtain quotes from a touch-tone phone. In 1993 it introduced a $169 Windows-based software package called Street Smart, which allowed investors to use their personal computers to obtain research reports from independent firms such as Standard & Poor's, obtain current prices, and enter buy and sell orders. Schwab also offered a 10% discount for customers who placed trades by computer and offered the software for free to anyone who transferred $15,000 into a Schwab account.[3]

The advent of the Web permitted even small investors to obtain investment information and enter buy or sell orders directly from their homes without ever talking to stockbrokers or paying their higher commission rates. Schwab began offering Web-based trading in 1996 through a separate unit called E-Schwab but soon reabsorbed that unit because its customers did not want to deal with two

Schwabs. Even after cutting its commission for trades of 1,000 shares or less by more than half to $29.95 in 1997, Schwab was still being undercut by some by some online brokerages that charged less than $10 per trade. The average commission for ten leading online brokerage firms dropped from $53 to $16 between 1996 and early 1998. These low commission rates led some observers to wonder whether individual investors would discard the standard long-term "buy and hold" strategy in favor of a riskier, active trading approach because transaction costs were less of a factor.[4]

During the next few years, Schwab expanded the investment information available to its customers and provided new guidance and decision-making tools for all investors. In a strategy aimed at upscale investors in 1999 it introduced its Signature Services for active and affluent traders with at least $100,000 in assets. These additional services included priority phone access, complimentary professional-quality research and investment management information, additional discounts for active traders, and access to information and online tools not available to all accounts.[5] In January 2000 it purchased New York-based U.S. Trust, a money-management firm providing services such as trust and estate services, private banking, financial planning, tax services, and equity research to clients with $500,000 to $10 million in assets.[6] Approximately 30% of Schwab's client assets and 10% of its client accounts were managed by 5,600 independent, fee-based investment advisors.[7] Schwab was a leader in online services, but had come a long way from its roots as a discount broker.

WEB CHECK [✓]

Compare the Charles Schwab Web site to the site of one of its discount broker competitors such E*Trade, Datek, or Ameritrade. Are there any significant differences in the services offered to an investor who is not wealthy?

DEBATE TOPIC

To what extent does self-service trading cause undue risk to Schwab's customers that they would not encounter if they were being served by a financial professional?

Charles Schwab established its reputation as a longtime pioneer in e-business by providing new types of services related to buying and selling stocks and other securities. Schwab's innovations center on removing the stockbroker from the process and allowing the customer to enter buy and sell orders via self-service methods that progressed from touch-tone phones, to custom computer applications, to Web-based trading. At each stage in this progression, the details of the business process changed, the process characteristics changed, and the measures of process performance changed accordingly.

This chapter explains ideas for describing and analyzing business processes within a work system. The previous chapters defined a business process—a related group of steps or activities in which people use information and other resources to create value for internal or external customers. These steps are related in time and place, have a beginning and end, and have inputs and outputs.[8,9] The chapter's organization reflects the relationship between process architecture and process performance. First it explains process modeling, a method of documenting process architecture by identifying major processes and dividing them into linked subprocesses. Next it looks at major process characteristics, such as degree of structure, range of involvement, and level of integration. These process characteristics are important determinants of process performance. It discusses process performance variables such as rate of output, consistency, productivity, cycle time, and downtime. These inward-looking variables focus on the process rather than the product, and therefore differ from the product performance variables that a customer perceives. The final section presents additional ideas related to communication and decision-making, activities that occur in most business processes.

Many of the process characteristics and performance variables discussed in this chapter are familiar from everyday life, so you might wonder why they are discussed in a book on information systems. The reason is that these terms provide a practical vocabulary about business processes and how these processes can be improved.

WORK SYSTEM SNAPSHOT
Charles Schwab provides self-service stock trading

CUSTOMERS
- Charles Schwab account holders who buys and sells stocks

PRODUCTS & SERVICES
- Execution of buy and sell transactions
- Online stock data and stock analysis
- Monthly account reports

BUSINESS PROCESS
- Evaluate current status of account
- Decide what to buy or sell
- Enter the buy or sell order online
- Receive confirmation of completed trade
- Receive monthly reports and other brokerage information

PARTICIPANTS	INFORMATION	TECHNOLOGY
• Account holder • Financial professional (if desired) • Schwab back-office staff	• Market price and purchase price of stocks • Analysts' reports • Buy or sell orders • Account holder's current portfolio of stocks, bonds, and other assets	• Personal computer • Schwab's hardware and software for tracking portfolios and trades • The Internet (infrastructure)

PROCESS MODELING: DOCUMENTING A BUSINESS PROCESS

Process modeling is itself a business process that involves naming business processes and subdividing them into their basic elements so that they can be understood and improved. Process modeling is an essential part of information system development because it helps clarify the problem the information system attempts to solve and the way it goes about solving that problem.

If this were a systems analysis text for IT professionals, we would cover a number of different process-modeling techniques in some depth. Because this is an information systems text for business professionals, we will look carefully at one process-modeling technique, the data flow diagram, and will also mention flowcharts and structured English in less detail. Data flow diagrams are valuable for building information systems because they show how the structure of the business process depends on the storage and flow of data. Flowcharts are a technique for representing the flow of calculations, especially when the sequence of calculations varies depending on the results of intermediate calculations. Other process-modeling techniques based on mathematical models can be used for other purposes, such as determining the time and resources a process will use under different circumstances.

We will illustrate process modeling using a well-known example, the redesign of Ford's purchasing and payables system. This story (see Box 3.1) is often cited as an example of **business process reengineering (BPR)**, the complete redesign of a business process using information technology. "Work system reengineering" might be more accurate than the established term BPR because reengineering affects the entire work system, not just the business process.

BOX 3.1

**FORD REENGINEERS ITS
PAYABLES PROCESS**

In the early 1980s Ford Motor Company decided to reduce its Accounts Payable staff from 500 to 400. Before paying a supplier, Accounts Payable verified that invoices from suppliers were consistent with what the Purchasing Department ordered and what the Receiving Department actually received. Ford representatives visited its Japanese affiliate, Mazda, to look for fresh ideas and were amazed that only five people performed Mazda's Accounts Payable function. Mazda had to be doing something totally different to account for the staffing difference.

The main difference involved the business process. When a shipment arrived at Mazda, the Receiving Department staff looked up the purchase order. If the material matched the purchase order completely, the Receiving Department entered a receipt confirmation into the database. Accounts Payable now had a very simple job of paying the supplier because Mazda had ordered the material and the supplier had delivered it. If the material did not match the purchase order completely, the shipment was simply returned. Refusing to accept an incorrect shipment meant that Accounts Payable never had to figure out how to reconcile inconsistencies between the purchase order, material delivered, and the invoice sent by the supplier.

Ford had used a very different method. The Receiving Department accepted some orders that did not match the purchase order exactly. The subsequent arrival of an invoice triggered Accounts Payable to try to verify how much material had been ordered and had arrived. Cases where the material received didn't match the purchase order required looking in several places and possibly making phone calls to figure out what to do.

After comparing their version and Mazda's version of the same business process, Ford decided to change its process by creating a shared database, changing its Receiving Department rules. In 1986, Ford employed 500 people paying bills in the old way. By 1990, only 125 were needed.[10,11,12] Notice how the new information system was only part of the solution and succeeded only because of the reorganized workflow. Before changing its information systems Ford fixed its business process by eliminating steps that did not add value.

Data Flow Diagrams

Data flow diagrams (DFDs) represent the flows of data between different processes within a system. They provide a simple, intuitive method for describing business processes without focusing on the details of computer systems. Virtually anyone who works in a business can understand a carefully designed DFD and can point out errors or omissions. DFDs are an attractive technique because they describe what users do rather than what computers do and involve only four symbols: the process, data flow, data store, and external entity (see Figure 3.1).

The four DFD symbols focus the analysis on flows of data between subprocesses, rather than on the information technology used. This approach makes sense to business professionals, whose main concern is to make sure the information system supports or enforces a specific set of activities performed using specific methods.

An important limitation of DFDs is that they focus only on flows of information. There is no symbol for flows of material, such as the physical things actually ordered by Ford using its Purchasing system. In addition, DFDs do not include the symbols used in flowcharts for expressing decision points, sequences of operations, and other things that must be clarified before writing a computer program. The advantages of DFDs mirror their limitations. The fact that so few symbols are included makes it easy for users to understand DFDs and helps them focus on the business process. Other techniques such as flowcharts are used later to document decision criteria, timing of subprocesses, and other details not handled by DFDs.

Describing Business Process Organization and Hierarchy   Figure 3.2 shows that the starting point when using DFDs is to create a **context diagram**, which verifies the

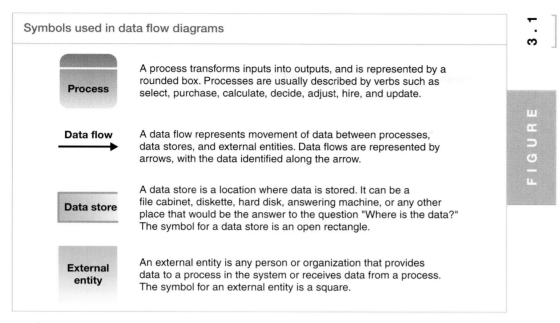

Symbols used in data flow diagrams

Process
A process transforms inputs into outputs, and is represented by a rounded box. Processes are usually described by verbs such as select, purchase, calculate, decide, adjust, hire, and update.

Data flow
A data flow represents movement of data between processes, data stores, and external entities. Data flows are represented by arrows, with the data identified along the arrow.

Data store
A data store is a location where data is stored. It can be a file cabinet, diskette, hard disk, answering machine, or any other place that would be the answer to the question "Where is the data?" The symbol for a data store is an open rectangle.

External entity
An external entity is any person or organization that provides data to a process in the system or receives data from a process. The symbol for an external entity is a square.

FIGURE 3.1

Data flow diagrams use only four symbols but can be applied to aid in understanding how the structure of a business process depends on the storage and flow of data.

scope of the system by showing the sources and destinations of data used and generated by the system being modeled. At the center of the context diagram, the Purchasing system is represented as a single process. Surrounding that process are boxes representing the external entities that provide data for the Purchasing system or receive data from it. The external entities in this case are the Material Planning Department and the supplier. They are considered external to the business process because we are focusing on the flows of information related to ordering material, receiving it, and paying the supplier. System boundaries would be different for a different analysis.

In addition to bounding the system and summarizing flows of data, the context diagram might convey significant organizational issues and even surprises for some of the participants. First of all, it says that the system is called "Purchasing" even though it generates payments and therefore must include a payables process. Just this concept of

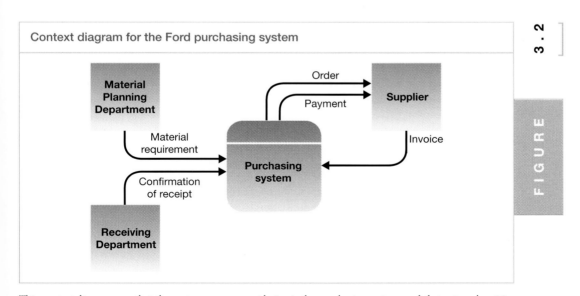

Context diagram for the Ford purchasing system

FIGURE 3.2

This context diagram says that the system we are considering is the purchasing system, and that external entities include the supplier and two internal departments.

FIGURE **3.3**

Data flow diagram showing the main processes in Ford's original purchasing system

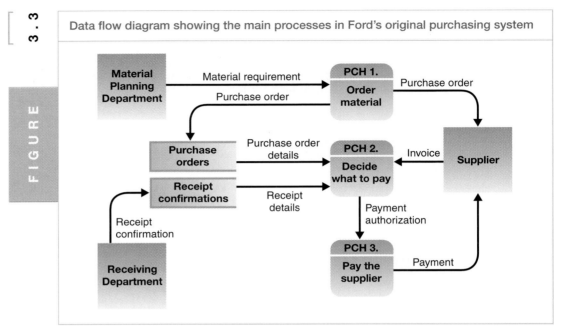

This top-level data flow diagram breaks the business process into three separate processes: PCH 1, order the material; PCH 2, decide what to pay; PCH 3, pay the vendor. (PCH is an abbreviation for "purchasing.")

a more integrated system might be very controversial. It also says that the material requirement comes from only one source, the Material Planning Department. People reviewing it might object that other groups should be able to submit orders. This example shows how using data flow diagrams helps in identifying and resolving issues about responsibility and authority before the technical system design begins.

After using the context diagram to establish the scope of the system, the next step is to identify processes and break them down into subprocesses to describe exactly how work is done. DFDs make it possible to look at business processes at any level of detail by breaking them down into successively finer subprocesses. This type of analysis is needed to understand what an information system should do in this situation.

Figure 3.3 shows what might have been the first step toward breaking down the original Purchasing system into its constituent processes. The original Purchasing system might be divided into three major processes: PCH 1, order the material; PCH 2, decide what to pay; PCH 3, pay the vendor. Notice how the second process involves reconciling data generated from three different places at three different times. This might be a hint that a more effective process could be used. As is described in Box 3.1, the new business process gave the Receiving Department access to the purchase order file. If the material received matched the purchase order precisely, they accepted it and added a receipt confirmation to the purchase order file. Otherwise they simply returned it and the complex reconciliation process disappeared.

Compared to the context diagram, Figure 3.3 provides more information about how the business process operates but still doesn't give enough information to understand it fully. Doing that would require breaking each of the three processes into subprocesses. For example, depending on how Ford truly ordered material, the process PCH 1 might be broken into the four subprocesses in Figure 3.4. Each of these subprocesses could be broken down into smaller subprocesses until drawing additional diagrams added no further understanding. The completed analysis would cover many pages but would permit a person to look at the business process in whatever level of detail was important for thinking about a particular issue.

You might wonder whether all this detail is necessary, especially for a manager or end user. In fact, it is absolutely necessary because managers and users are the ones who understand how processes operate in the organization. For example, Ford's man-

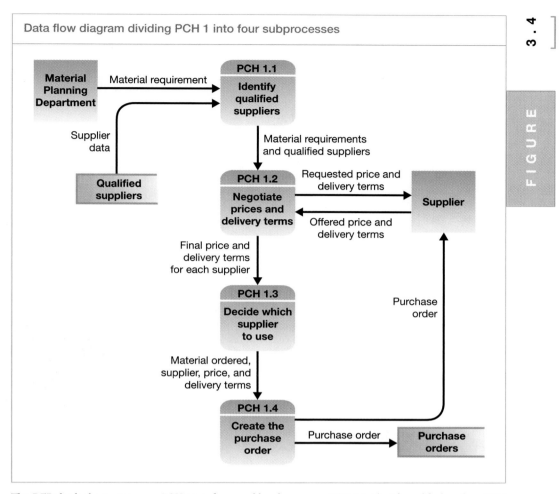

Data flow diagram dividing PCH 1 into four subprocesses

FIGURE 3.4

This DFD divides business process PCH 1 into four possible subprocesses: PCH 1.1, identify qualified vendors; PCH 1.2, negotiate prices and delivery terms; PCH 1.3, decide what vendor to use; PCH 1.4, create the purchase order.

agers would certainly find fault with Figure 3.4 because much of Ford's purchasing is done through long-term agreements. However, this is the point. Much of the value in developing DFDs results from resolving disagreements about how work is done currently or how it should be done in the future. If users and managers cannot or will not describe things at this level of detail, any attempt to build a new information system will probably fail due to disagreements about what it should do.

The data flow diagram is only one of many process-modeling techniques. This technique is easily understood by both system users and system developers, and it is used widely during the initial phases of information system development to clarify the boundaries and internal operation of the business process being studied. It is also incorporated directly into most computer-aided software engineering (CASE) systems (discussed in Chapter 9).

Flowcharts and Structured English

Even when DFDs are used extensively, other techniques often are used to fill in the details not adequately expressed by DFDs. For example, although they express data flows between processes, DFDs express neither the sequence and timing of processes nor the detailed logic of processes, such as the precise rules for selecting among alternative actions such as accept or reject. Furthermore, they do not represent the physical devices used by the data processing system. Flowcharts and structured English are two techniques used to document these essential details.

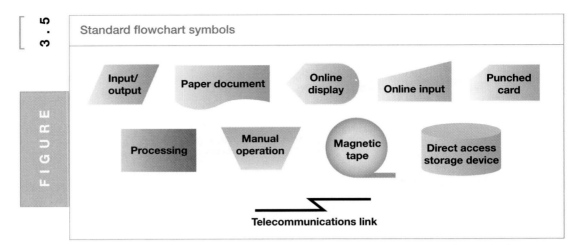

FIGURE 3.5

Standard flowchart symbols

Input/output · Paper document · Online display · Online input · Punched card

Processing · Manual operation · Magnetic tape · Direct access storage device

Telecommunications link

These are some of the standard flowchart symbols. The punched card symbol is one of many that have become obsolete due to changes in storage technology.

Flowcharts are diagrams expressing the sequence and logic of procedures using standardized symbols to represent different types of input/output, processing, and data storage. Figure 3.5 shows some of the many standard flowcharting symbols used to represent both the logical flow of a process and the physical devices that capture, store, and display the data. Flowcharts were once the primary diagramming tool used for documenting systems. They are still used in many ways but have often been replaced by DFDs as tools for discussing information system logic with users and for documenting the flow of data between business processes.

Figure 3.6 shows an example of the type of flowchart you might use directly to document business rules and calculations within a subprocess after the data flows between processes have been clarified using DFDs. The diamond-shaped decision box in Figure 3.6 exemplifies the type of procedural detail that DFDs do not capture, but that flowcharts represent effectively. As with DFDs, flowcharts can be represented on many hierarchical levels and spread across many pages.

For specifying exactly how a procedure operates, pictures may not be as terse and precise as a carefully constructed set of declarative sentences. **Structured English** is a way to represent the precise logic of a procedure by writing out that logic using a few limited forms such as sequence, iteration, and selection using if-then or if-then-else formats. As an example, look at the following specification of how to decide whether the material received is equivalent to the material in an order.

> Retrieve the purchase order
>
> For each item on the purchase order
>> if quantity received = quantity ordered
>>
>> then item code is "match"
>
> If item code = "match" for all items in the purchase order
>> then purchase order receipt code is "match"
>
> If purchase order receipt is "match"
>> then approve payment for order
>>
>> else return material received

Structured English is sometimes called pseudocode because it resembles the code in a computer program, except that it ignores the grammar or peculiarities of any particular programming language. This level of description is so detailed that it requires careful scrutiny. For example, many people might read the nine lines of structured English without realizing that they ignore the possibility of receiving merchandise that was not

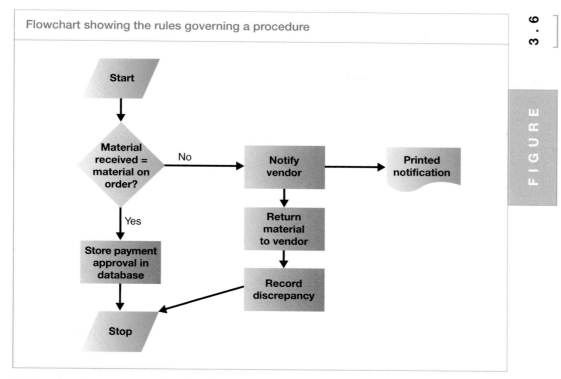

Flowchart showing the rules governing a procedure

FIGURE 3.6

This flowchart demonstrates something data flow diagrams cannot do. It shows different paths depending on conditions such as whether the material received is equal to the material on order.

on the purchase order at all. If those nine lines were converted directly to a computer program, the program would contain a bug that would eventually cause problems.

This section has illustrated three techniques that are used to document business processes. DFDs are a primary tool for process modeling, which includes naming business processes and subdividing them into their basic elements so that they can be studied and improved. Flowcharts and structured English are used to fill out the details that cannot be expressed well using DFDs.

You might be surprised that defining the architecture of an existing or proposed system is largely about giving names to subprocesses and data. The naming process is surprisingly difficult and often raises controversy. For example, an item on an invoice might be called an item, line item, stock item, or something else. Likewise, commitment date might refer to when a product will be completed, when it will be shipped, or when the customer will receive it. Such distinctions might seem like nit-picking, but are absolutely essential for building systems regardless of whether computers are involved. Clarifying data definitions is especially important for avoiding confusion if people working in different departments could use the same term in different ways.

It is also important to realize that formal documentation of a process typically represents the **idealized business process**, the way the business process is supposed to be performed assuming that work system participants follow the rules. In many real situations, work system participants diverge from the idealized process. Sometimes this happens because participants are inattentive or poorly trained. In other cases, the work system participants want to do their jobs well but the idealized process cannot deal with situations that arise in practice. For example, the rule might say that a grade of at least B in course X is a prerequisite for taking course Y; Chris never took course X but was a successful teaching assistant for that course last semester based on prior knowledge; Chris seems totally qualified to take course Y and is allowed to do so, contrary to the rule. This type of divergence from the idealized process is called a **workaround**. Workarounds are necessary when the rules built into a business process or information system become an obstacle to getting work done or making reasonable decisions. Workarounds are surprisingly common because even well-designed formal processes often fail to anticipate unique situations that were not included in the original analysis. High rates of workarounds indicate that the process was designed poorly or that an external change has made part of the process inadequate. Workarounds involving information systems occur frequently and cause many problems because information in the database no longer reflects reality.

R E A L I T Y C H E C K [✓]

Using Data Flow Diagrams to Document Process Architecture

This section has emphasized DFDs as a method for summarizing process architecture.

1. Write a one-level DFD (similar to Figure 3.3) for a process that you are familiar with, such as registering for classes, renting a video, or using an ATM to withdraw money from a bank account. Include at least two subprocesses.

2. Write a DFD for one of the subprocesses (as is done in Figure 3.4) and explain how you could keep track of everything if you needed to produce DFDs for subprocesses of the subprocesses.

PROCESS CHARACTERISTICS

The previous section explained process modeling as a way to document processes, subprocesses, and information flows. Although looking at process steps in detail is essential, it is also important to look at the big picture in terms of process characteristics that often affect business process performance (see Figure 2.3). Summarizing a process in terms of these characteristics helps in talking about process design without becoming swamped in details.

Consider the example of stock trading through an online broker such as Charles Schwab. Here is how important process characteristics help in describing online trading:

Degree of structure: The trading process is highly structured since the buy or sell orders must be entered in a particular manner and many rules apply, such as limits on purchasing on margin. The shift to self-service does not change the degree of structure by creating different steps that bypass the stockbroker.

Range of involvement: The move toward online trading reduces the range of involvement because it bypasses the stockbroker.

Level of integration: Permitting the customer to place the buy and sell transactions over the Web means that the external customer provides direct, non-intermediated entries into the firm's internal order-processing system. The customer does not have to coordinate with a stockbroker.

Rhythm: Customers enter orders at their convenience. The trades take place during trading hours whenever a bid and ask price match. The rhythm for individual trades is therefore event-driven. When viewed in the aggregate, the ebb and flow of trading may define a series of distinguishable rhythms for trading volume and market volatility.

Complexity: The general simplicity of the ordering process is one of the reasons why online trading is practical. On the other hand, the vast amount of information that has become available makes trading decisions more complex to those who want to use that information.

Reliance on machines: Online trading relies totally on the company's ability to provide an operational Web site. This is why Web site downtime at the online brokerages has attracted so much attention.

Prominence of planning and control: Online trading is mostly about execution. Once entered, the order is executed when certain conditions are met. The order entry process has a few built-in controls, such as not allowing excessive purchases on margin. Depending on the brokerage, various planning capabilities may be available, but typically these are directed at analyzing individual stocks rather than planning for the overall portfolio.

Attention to errors and exceptions: Entering trade orders and executing trades are both highly structured processes, but errors and exceptions sometimes do occur, ranging from customer errors to computer problems. Since these are financial transactions, the online brokerages need highly structured methods for identifying and recovering from errors.

Impacts of Excess or Deficiency   Someone thinking about improving an online trading process might look at these characteristics as a lever for improvements since it might be possible to increase or decrease the level of each characteristic. The issues of excess and deficiency in Table 3.1 illustrate why a move toward e-business involves much more than installing new technology and processing information more efficiently. Better performance through e-business involves redesigning business

Impacts of Excess or Deficiency in Important Process Characteristics

Process characteristic	Problem if the level is too high	Problem if the level is too low
Degree of structure	• System participants are prevented from using their judgment. • System participants feel like cogs in a machine because they have too little autonomy.	• Easily foreseeable errors occur because well-understood rules are not applied consistently. • Outputs are inconsistent.
Range of involvement	• Work is slowed down because too many people get involved before steps are completed.	• Work is performed based on narrow or personal considerations, resulting in decisions that may not be the best for the overall organization.
Level of integration	• Steps in the process are too intertwined. Participants in different business processes interfere with each other. To change one step it is necessary to analyze too many other steps or processes.	• Steps in the processes are too independent. The process needs greater integration to produce better results.
Rhythm	• If the rhythm is too pronounced and inflexible, the process is less able to respond quickly to changes in customer needs.	• If the rhythm is undefined or easily overridden, performing the process efficiently may become more difficult.
Complexity	• Participants, managers, and programmers have difficulty understanding how the system operates or what will happen if parts of it are changed.	• The system cannot distinguish different cases that should be handled differently.
Degree of reliance on machines	• People become disengaged from their work. • People's skills may decrease. • Mistakes occur because people overestimate what the computers are programmed to handle.	• Productivity and consistency decrease as bored people perform repetitive work that computers could do more efficiently.
Prominence of planning and control	• Too much effort goes into planning and controlling within the process, and not enough goes into execution.	• Insufficient effort in planning and control leaves the business process inconsistent and unresponsive to customer requirements.
Attention to errors and exceptions	• The process focuses on exceptions and becomes inefficient and inconsistent.	• The process fails altogether or handles exceptions incorrectly, resulting in low productivity or poor quality and responsiveness perceived by customers.

TABLE 3.1

processes, and this means recognizing and resolving the trade-offs for each of these process characteristics. Discussions of e-business rarely cover this territory, but it is at the heart of whether an e-business approach will succeed.

Degree of Structure

The term *information system* implies that the purpose of these systems is to provide information. This is often true, although the purpose of many information systems could be described more accurately as "to systematize and structure business processes through information."

The **degree of structure** of a task or a business process is the extent to which it can be scripted in advance, including the order of the steps, the information that is required, the ways to validate that information, and the relationships between inputs and outputs. For example, an ATM system is highly structured because it is completely governed by rules stating how it will respond to each possible input. In contrast, the process of creating a perfume advertisement is quite unstructured. Because most tasks and decisions are neither totally structured nor totally unstructured, it is useful to compare structured, semistructured, and unstructured tasks.

Structured, Semistructured, and Unstructured Tasks   A totally **structured task** is so well understood that it is possible to say exactly how to perform it and how to evaluate whether it has been performed well. For example, totaling the previous month's invoices is a typical structured task. Specific characteristics of a highly structured task include the following:

- Information requirements are known precisely.
- Methods for processing the information are known precisely.
- Desired format of the information is known precisely.
- Decisions or steps within the task are clearly defined and repetitive.
- Criteria for making decisions are understood precisely.
- Success in executing the task can be measured precisely.

In a **semistructured task,** the information requirements and procedures are generally known, although some aspects of the task still rely on the judgment of the person doing it. The way a doctor diagnoses an illness is often a semistructured task. It contains some structure because the physician understands common medical facts and diagnosis methods; on the other hand, it is not totally structured because many medical situations are ambiguous and require judgment and intuition.

An **unstructured task** is so poorly understood that the information to be used, the method of using the information, and the criteria for deciding whether the task is being done well cannot be specified. Unstructured decisions tend to be performed based on experience, intuition, trial and error, rules of thumb, and vague qualitative information. Examples include the selection of a company president or the choice of a picture for the cover of a fashion magazine. The decision about the president involves intangible factors such as how well the candidate gets along with people in the organization and the likelihood that the candidate would find the job challenging but not overwhelming. The magazine decision is based on aesthetic issues such as taste and intuition about what magazine readers would enjoy.

The desired degree of structure is the crux of major controversies related to processes such as making medical decisions, granting mortgages, and admitting students to college. Consider the process of granting mortgages, which raises a number of economic, ethical, and legal issues for banks and loan officers. Banks are often accused of redlining certain districts, thereby unfairly preventing people in minority groups from receiving loans. Although there are many viewpoints about the appropriate goals of a mortgage approval process, from a system design viewpoint the question can be framed as an issue about how structured the decision should be. If it is unstructured, loan officers will make whatever decision they want based on intuition and any methods they want to use. If it is highly structured, formulas, models, and external con-

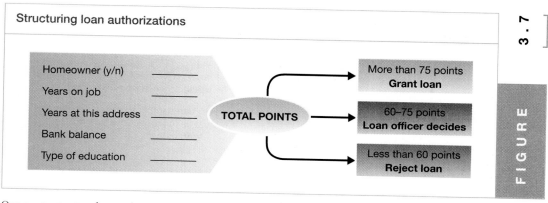

One way to structure loan authorizations is to assign a certain number of points for each response on a loan application. If the application scores more than a high cutoff amount, the loan is automatically granted. Applications with less than a low cutoff are automatically rejected. Applications between the high and low cutoffs are in a gray area and the loan officer makes the decision based on judgment.

straints will determine much of what they decide (see Figure 3.7). The degree of structure is important even in less politically or emotionally charged processes such as purchasing inventory and debugging software. Over-structuring reduces flexibility and generates consistency at the cost of both customer satisfaction and internal performance. Under-structuring leads to inconsistency and delays, which often reduce the quality and reliability the customer perceives.

Although the degree of structure is one of the most important characteristics for understanding e-business situations, people focusing on a Web site's technology or aesthetics sometimes ignore it. E-business processes run the gamut from highly structured to semistructured and even to unstructured. E-business purchasing transactions such as placing an item in a shopping cart, finalizing an order, and submitting the credit card information must be highly structured to assure consistency and completeness. In contrast, e-business applications that support professional activities such as designing, teaching, selling, and repairing often require a semistructured approach that provides enough freedom to exercise judgment and inspiration along with enough structure to provide useful information and support nontrivial methods. Similarly, e-business search processes such as deciding which product to buy or finding information using a search engine might be semistructured through the use of options or suggestions, or might be quite unstructured.

Using Information Systems to Impose Structure   Successful information systems impose the amount of structure that is appropriate for the activity being supported. Imposing too much structure stifles creativity and makes the participants in the process feel as though they have no responsibility for the outcome. Imposing too little structure results in inefficiencies and errors.

Table 3.2 shows that information systems can impose different degrees of structure on business processes. The extent to which a system structures a task can be divided into three broad categories with a number of gradations. Information systems that provide information and tools impose the least structure. This is consistent with the typical approach to personal computing, allowing people to do whatever computing they want to do, however they want to do it. Systems that enforce rules and guidelines impose more structure. This idea is consistent with parts of the total quality movement, which maintains that quality depends on using consistent methods and achieving consistent results. Systems that substitute technology for people automate tasks totally and impose the most structure. Substituting technology for people is a basic reason for using most machines.

Table 3.2 says nothing about whether imposing more structure is better or worse in general. Imposing a minimal amount of structure on well-understood tasks may permit

TABLE 3.2   Different Levels of Imposing Structure on Work

Degree to which structure is imposed	Approach for imposing structure	Example
Highest: Substitution of technology for people	Replace the person with technology.	An automatic teller machine performs work that a teller would otherwise perform.
	Automate much of the work.	A construction company uses a program to generate bids for construction contracts. The computerized bids are usually changed only slightly.
High: Enforcement of rules or procedures	Control each step in the work.	A bank's loan approval system is based on a formula using data from a fill-in-the-blanks form.
	Provide real-time guidance for work steps performed by people.	An interactive shop-floor control system tells workers what machine settings to use and warns them when exceptions occur.
Low: Access to information or tools	Use a model to evaluate or optimize a potential decision.	A pharmaceutical company uses a model to help allocate funds among research proposals. People make the decision.
	Provide specialized tools that help people do their work.	An architecture firm uses a computer-aided design system to help design buildings.
	Provide information that is filtered, formatted, and summarized to make it useful.	A management information system provides performance information for managers.
	Provide a general purpose tool to help people do work.	Provide a telephone, spreadsheet, or word processor.

excessive variability in results. Imposing too much structure on poorly understood tasks may prevent people from using their intelligence to produce good results and may generate problems when unanticipated circumstances occur.

The different degrees of structure apply in different situations. Automating tasks by substituting technology for people is pertinent for parts of business processes that handle information in a totally structured way. Enforcement of rules and procedures applies to process steps that are largely repetitious but involve some degree of judgment. Providing tools and information applies to process steps that are truly novel or unstructured. Providing tools and information in unstructured situations may be ineffective, however, because most potential users may have no idea how to apply tools and information successfully in inherently unstructured situations. Despite the best efforts of software vendors, an information and tools strategy often fails unless it is reasonably apparent how work system participants will use the tools and information to perform their work.

The concept of structure can also be used to identify mismatches between an information system's goal and the way it tries to accomplish its goal. If its goal is to enforce consistency, providing access to information may not be powerful enough. If its purpose is to help people do their work, a system that enforces procedures may be overly restrictive or counterproductive. Looking at information systems this way also highlights a common problem in implementing systems. In some cases, the developer sees the system as a way to provide access to information, whereas the potential users see it as a personal threat because it may automate their work.

Finally, notice that it is often misleading to try to generalize about the degree of structure in a type of business process, such as granting automobile loans. Different businesses performing the same type of process may do it differently based on their business strategy or skills. One bank might use precise formulas and procedures to make automobile loan decisions and leave little discretion to the loan officer. Other banks might use formulas and procedures only as guidelines, leaving the task semi-structured; yet other banks might leave the decision to the loan officer's discretion.

Range of Involvement

It sounds simple to say too many cooks spoil the broth, but the right range of involvement in business processes is often elusive. **Range of involvement** is the organizational span of people involved in a business process. When the range of involvement is too narrow, decisions are made from an excessively local viewpoint, often missing opportunities for the overall enterprise. When the range of involvement is too great, business processes seem to move at a glacial pace. Many state and local governments feel this issue acutely in business complaints about the large number of different permits and approvals that are needed to open a new business or modify a building.

Too Many Participants or Too Few   The case manager approach often touted in discussions of reengineering illustrates the importance of reducing unnecessarily wide spans of involvement. Before a reengineering project at IBM Credit, which provides customers with financing for IBM products, the process for analyzing equipment loan requests and responding to the customer averaged six days and sometimes took up to two weeks. Salespeople hated the delays because this gave the customers six extra days to change their minds. When two managers walked a financing request through the steps while asking people to do the work immediately, they were amazed to find the actual work took only 90 minutes. During most of the six days the requests simply sat on people's desks waiting for action. The existing process operated like an assembly line whose steps included logging the salesperson's loan request on a slip of paper, entering the request into a computerized system, checking for creditworthiness, modifying the standard loan document based on customer requests, determining the interest rate for the loan, and producing a quotation letter sent to the sales representative by overnight courier. IBM Credit moved to a **case manager approach**, in which a single individual is in charge of the entire processing of a case, has direct access to all the standard information required, and uses discretion to call upon specialists in other departments for more complex cases. The new system cut the turnaround to four hours with no staffing increase. It also increased the number of deals handled by the staff, reduced the error rate, and increased flexibility through adoption of three variations on the process to handle cases of different complexity.[13]

Too few cooks in the kitchen can also be a problem, however, when it is necessary to enforce organizational standards and quality expectations. This is why some large programming groups try to maintain quality and prevent unwarranted software modifications through a process called software change control. One person checks out a program and changes it, another person checks the program and its documentation, and yet another person replaces the program in the program library and records the fact that a change took place. A smaller range of involvement might seem more efficient, but it would not enforce quality or security standards as effectively. The individual work might proceed more quickly and might be more fun, but the software produced might contain more errors and might not be as maintainable over the long term.

[L O O K   A H E A D]

Figure 13.5 illustrates the process of software change control.

Doers versus Checkers   A way to be more specific about the range of involvement in a business process is to categorize participants as doers, the people who perform the value added tasks; and checkers, the people who check to make sure the tasks were done or will be done properly by others. The total quality management (TQM) movement generally pushes for reducing the range of involvement in processes by insisting that work system participants have the knowledge to do their work and the responsibility for checking it. Successful TQM efforts have improved quality and reduced cycle times by providing more of a feeling of ownership and by eliminating unnecessary quality control inspections. In contrast, financial auditors insist on the segregation of duties to reduce the likelihood of financial fraud. Having one person create a purchase order, another approve it, and a third approve the payment makes it less likely that people will collude, but also means that three people are involved in the work that one or two might do.

Despite the positive aspects of using e-business to increase or decrease the range of involvement, changes in either direction may not be beneficial. Yes, it is desirable to obtain tax forms by using the Web instead of speaking to IRS clerks, but what about requiring a manager to pre-approve a large expenditure or requiring doctors to issue prescriptions instead of allowing their patients to buy any antibiotic that might be available on the Web? Should the manager and the doctor be eliminated as unnecessary intermediaries or should e-business strengthen their roles in reducing fraud or decreasing the likelihood that improper medication will be used? Deciding how much involvement by which participants is necessary involves trade-offs. Having too many cooks in the kitchen degrades cycle time and productivity, but having too few cooks degrades consistency and conformance through myopic decision-making and insufficient supervision.

Level of Integration

It is often unclear what people mean when they use the terms "integration" and "integrated system" because these terms are used in many different ways—sometimes in relation to technology and databases and sometimes in relation to business processes. As with degree of structure and range of involvement, the right level of integration in a business process is often not obvious. Insufficiently integrated systems are disorganized and unproductive, but overly integrated systems are complex and hard to control. We will start with a single general definition but will then look at five separate levels of integration, each of which may provide a clue about the right level of integration in a system being analyzed.

Integration is mutual responsiveness and collaboration between distinct activities or processes. The extent of integration between two processes or activities is related to the speed with which one responds to events in the other. This speed depends on both the immediacy of communication and the degree to which the processes respond to the information communicated. Information systems can play roles in both aspects of integration, first by supporting the communication, and second by making it easier for each business process to use the information to respond effectively.

As an example, consider the way integration between the sales effort and the production effort has become a major competitive issue in many industries. The more integrated these processes are, the faster the production process responds to new orders from sales. For example, Honeywell's consumer products group is establishing online links to both customers and suppliers. When Jiffy Lube orders 1,000 oil filters, Honeywell's new system will immediately notify suppliers to begin making the metal casings, filter elements, and tops, and to ship them to Honeywell for final assembly.[14] Similarly, Costco and other large retailers have outsourced inventory replenishment decisions to certain major suppliers. With this form of integration, Kimberly-Clark analysts in Wisconsin track Costco's inventory of Huggies diapers at stores around the country, make timely shipping decisions, and feed these decisions directly to internal scheduling for diaper production.[15] Information systems play a crucial role in integration because they convey the information and process it (see Figure 3.8).

Five Levels of Integration A basic question in business process redesign involves the desired level of integration between different business processes. Figure 3.9 summarizes five different levels of integration. The first two levels are conditions that make it easier to work together, although they are not inherently related to responsiveness and typically exist for reasons totally outside of any particular business process. Long-time employees of dissimilar organizations that have merged are painfully aware that cultural differences make it more difficult to communicate and work together. Similarly, the lack of common standards such as using the same word processing soft-

FIGURE 3.8

The starting point for integrating between customers and suppliers

Inventory data collected using a portable bar code scanner and computer feeds into an inventory replenishment system that sends computerized orders directly to suppliers.

ware, same database definitions, or even the same business vocabulary creates obstacles that make it more difficult to maintain processes and technologies, whether or not they are directly related. A glaring example in e-commerce is the operational inefficiency and service lapses resulting from inconsistent product-numbering conventions across the traditional and online operations of many retailers.

Sharing information, the third level of coordination, is the least obtrusive way to attain responsiveness between processes. Information sharing occurs when all the lawyers working on a large legal case can easily access any document about the case, or when the sales force can access a manufacturing database to determine available capacity for additional orders. Information sharing is comparatively unobtrusive because the people who produced the information do not have to take additional action to make the information useful to others. This approach to integration sounds easier than it really is because personal and political incentives in the organization often motivate people not to share.

FIGURE 3.9

Five levels of integration between business processes

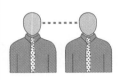

Common culture: *shared understandings and beliefs*

People involved in two independent processes share the same general beliefs and expectations about how people communicate and work together. These shared beliefs make it easier to work together and resolve conflicts whenever necessary.

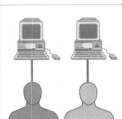

Common standards: *using consistent terminology and procedures to make business processes easier to maintain and interface*

Two different business processes use the same standards but otherwise operate independently. For example, two different departments may use the same type of personal computer or the same word processing software. Operating with agreed upon standards of this type may create economies of scale for the technical staff, who may be able to learn and service a smaller number of technical options. It also may enhance the possibility of other forms of integration in the future.

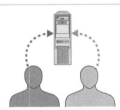

Information sharing: *access to each other's data by business processes that operate independently.*

Two different business processes share some of the same information even though the information sharing does not directly involve mutual responsiveness. For example, a sales department and a manufacturing department might share the manufacturing database so that sales would know what capacity was still available for additional orders.

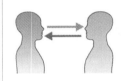

Coordination: *negotiation and exchange of messages permitting separate but interdependent processes to respond to each other's needs and limitations*

Different business processes maintain their own unique function and identity, but pass information back and forth to coordinate their efforts toward a common objective. For example, sales tells manufacturing what they can sell; manufacturing responds with a tentative output schedule; they negotiate to come up with a mutually feasible plan and then go about their individual work.

Collaboration: *such strong interdependence that the unique identity of separate processes begins to disappear*

Two different business processes merge part or all of their identity to accomplish larger objectives of the firm. For example, based on the need to get more easily manufacturable products to market sooner, many firms have moved toward product development processes that involve close collaboration between marketing, engineering, and manufacturing.

Groups of business processes in a firm can be totally unrelated to each other or can be integrated at any of these five levels.

Coordination, the fourth level of integration, can be defined as managing dependencies among activities. These dependencies might involve the synchronization of inputs and outputs among activities, such as not starting manufacturing steps until the materials have arrived. They might involve the sharing of resources, such as machines or people who can't do two things at once. They also might involve the fit between outputs, such as when several engineers are designing different parts of the same product.[16] Coordination is more obtrusive than information sharing because it calls for negotiations or two-way information flows that provide mutual responsiveness even though the processes operate separately. In a production planning cycle, for example, Sales tells Manufacturing what it can sell, Manufacturing responds with a tentative output schedule, and then they negotiate to come up with a mutually feasible plan before going about their individual work.

Coordination has become a significant issue for "clicks and mortar" merchants who sell through the Web and through retail stores. During the 1999 holiday shopping season Home Depot realized "that its consumer customers and its small-business customers were expecting a seamless integration with the Home Depot retail outlets. They didn't want to just order from a Web site and receive goods a few days later via UPS; they wanted to order online and pick up items (or return and exchange items) at the stores. They also wanted an integrated account for online and offline transactions." Home Depot's team stopped work on its online catalog and delayed launching its e-business effort to redesign it to be coordinated with its retail stores.[17]

By attaining collaboration, the fifth level of integration, interdependence between processes is so strong that their unique identity begins to disappear. To develop products more quickly and to make them easier to manufacture, for example, many firms have moved toward product development processes that involve close collaboration between marketing, engineering, and manufacturing. These highly collaborative processes try to minimize the problems of less integrated approaches in which Marketing handed requirements to Engineering, which then produced a product design that could not be manufactured economically. Full collaboration between different parts of a business is effective for some product design processes, but in most other situations it contradicts the efficiencies of applying the division of labor and assigning different types of tasks to different people.

The difference between information sharing, coordination, and collaboration is especially important for thinking about potential benefits of moving toward e-business. Although often touted as a major benefit of e-business approaches, genuine coordination or collaboration requires much more than just sharing the same information. Network technology can provide information access, but coordination and collaboration require active commitment by the participants. The level of integration designed into a business process should therefore be consistent with the level of integration the participants are ready to accept and commit to.

Integration Trade-offs   E-business supports the possibility of greater integration between business processes and across an entire supply chain and value chain, but also makes it possible to integrate in a relatively loose manner that facilitates recovery if computer glitches or other problems render part of the process temporarily inoperable. The general trade-off here is between overly integrated systems that are complex and hard to control versus insufficiently integrated systems that are disorganized and unproductive. Lack of integration causes extra work and delays within a business process when pertinent information from another business process is not accessible. For example, as part of fraud-avoidance, most current ATM systems have a delay between the time an ATM deposit is made and the time it is recognized as money available for use. This is especially apparent on weekends, when a Friday night deposit may not be recognized until Monday, the next working day. This time lag shows that the process of making deposits is not tightly integrated with the process of accounting for checking account balances.

Although the tight integration of processes might seem desirable, forcing processes to respond to each other too frequently may make it difficult for each process to get its work done. This is one of the reasons why many factories that produce noncustomized products "freeze" their schedules a week or two at a time. Their managers believe that changing production schedules continually in response to daily events in the sales department causes too much chaos and inefficiency in production. The difficulty in responding rapidly while also maintaining high production quality and efficiency is one of the reasons why responsiveness to customers is a genuine competitive issue.

Information system designers sometimes avoid highly integrated information systems for their own reasons. They often prefer to build two separate information systems plus an interface that operates on a schedule, such as daily or weekly. This approach is often far simpler than real-time integration, which would assure that any event recorded by either system is immediately reflected in the other. Thinking of the connection between two systems as an interface divides a large problem into two smaller problems that can be solved individually. Often this means that a usable information system will be available sooner. Building an interface is especially appropriate where the desired capabilities of a new system are open to debate or when the business situation is changing rapidly. The lower level of integration that results may have negative consequences, however. For example, there might be a long delay in the interface between a customer returns system and the inventory system used for customer orders. This delay could result in situations when material returned by one customer could be shipped for another order except that the inventory system does not yet recognize the return has occurred.

Tightly integrated (also called tightly coupled) systems are also more prone to catastrophic failure than less integrated systems. Tightly coupled systems have little slack, require that things happen in a particular order, and depend on all components to operate within particular ranges. When one component fails, the others may also fail immediately. The most tightly coupled systems in our society include aircraft, nuclear power plants, power grids, and automated warfare systems.[18] In contrast, loosely coupled systems are decentralized, have slack resources and redundancies, permit delays and substitutions, and allow things to be done in different orders. Failures tend to be localized and therefore can be isolated, diagnosed, and fixed quickly. Thus, high levels of integration have both advantages and disadvantages that should be analyzed carefully.

Rhythm

The rhythm of a process is the frequency and predictability with which it occurs. The rhythm of a process may be periodic (occurring on a fixed cycle), event-driven (initiated by particular events), or haphazard (starting up for no typical reason). From a producer viewpoint, operating on a predictable, linear schedule is usually the most efficient way to operate. The customer typically isn't as interested in the producer's internal operations and is more concerned about obtaining the right product at the right time and right place.

A variety of external relationships with customers, complementers, suppliers, and competitors should strongly influence many rhythms within the organization. Even the rhythms of general management often deserve rethinking. For example, why should general management use an annual planning cycle instead of tailoring the planning to the nature of the market? In one diversified company, management went to a six-month cycle for electronic components with short product life cycles, maintained annual reviews for products with a one- to three-year life cycle, and set strategic reviews every 18 months for heavy industrial equipment.[19]

One of the great strengths of e-business approaches is the ability to support more responsive business rhythms often expressed in terms such as just-in-time (JIT), "lot size of one," and "anytime, anyplace" operation. The idea is that the work system is always open for business and can respond to customer requests immediately. No more fixed rhythm of 8:00 to 5:00; no more fixed rhythm of waiting until we do the next batch on Thursday because that is a relatively light day for the back office. Processes based on e-business make it possible to place orders or obtain information anytime, anywhere; if the fulfillment process is operating on a 24×7 basis it may start immediately upon receipt of the order.

The technical capability to deliver anytime, anyplace communication and information access does not imply that rhythm is becoming unimportant. The fact that we receive e-mail all day long does not imply that we need to respond all day long because that would disrupt the rhythm of other work. On the other hand, networked communication is making it easier to maintain certain types of rhythm in otherwise disjointed situations. For example, a research study on global virtual teams found that "while the individual coordination meetings helped in decision making and relationship building, the rhythm of meetings over time provided continuity and long term stability. They reduced ambiguity in the task by structuring expectations and making response times predictable. It was this sense of rhythm that enabled members to work efficiently and confidently alone or in ever-changing subgroups between coordination meetings."[20]

Complexity

The U. S. federal income tax system demonstrates the issue of complexity. A simple system might just collect a fixed or sliding percentage of personal income and leave it at that. Such a system, however, would not explicitly address additional social, political, and economic goals, such as making it easier to own a house, making it easier to send children to day care, recognizing the depletion on oil wells, or granting special favors to major political contributors. Each additional tax code feature recognizes another goal, for better or for worse, but also adds to the number of differentiated components and creates a wider range of interactions between components. The resulting complexity has become virtually unmanageable, as was demonstrated by the 39% error rate in the advice the IRS tax hotline gave to taxpayers on 1986 changes in tax laws.[21] Subsequently the IRS issued statements saying that the taxpayer, not the IRS, is responsible for any taxpayer errors resulting from incorrect information the IRS provides. A decade later, things had become even worse. The *Wall Street Journal* introduced the July 29, 1997 budget deal by saying the "mind-numbing complexity of the budget pact is good news for tax advisers. Even veteran tax lawyers are astonished by how tricky many of the new provisions are."[22,23]

Remove all the references to the tax system in this story and we are left with the fundamental trade-off about complexity. Systems that are too simple don't handle the complexity of the problem (much like a word processor that can't number pages automatically). Systems that are too complex are hard to understand and hard to fix. Each additional function or feature shifts the balance away from simplicity and toward complexity.

Managing Complexity   A system's **complexity** is a combination of how many types of elements it contains and the number and nature of their interactions. As complexity increases, systems are more difficult to develop and manage because more factors and interactions must be considered, evaluated, and tested. Complexity also makes it more difficult to understand what is going on and even more difficult to anticipate the consequences of changes throughout the system.

The most direct strategy for reducing complexity is to eliminate **low value variations**, different versions of processes and information that exist based on historical accident rather than conscious design. For example, Du Pont once printed paychecks over 3,300 times a year. Some plants and divisions paid on the first and fifteenth of the month, others at the middle and end of the month, and yet others every other Monday. Seeing little advantage in this way of doing things, Du Pont converted most of its payroll to the same bimonthly cycle, and consolidated to 36 payrolls. This eliminated over 100 jobs and saved $12 million annually.[24] Eliminating low value variations was a key factor in the adoption of electronic data interchange by most large companies. Part of the $55 large companies like General Motors had to spend to process a paper invoice was related to deciphering data and formatting inconsistencies between invoices and other forms sent by suppliers. These inconsistencies added to costs and typically provided no value. Many industry groups have responded to these problems by banding together to create industry-wide EDI formats and then telling their suppliers that the use of EDI is a requirement for doing business. More recently, EDI concepts have moved to the Internet and provide the promise of wider cost savings.

Another approach for managing complexity is to recognize variations explicitly and treat them differently instead of trying to treat different problems using a fundamentally similar process. A business process might have a single name, such as "approve building permit," but that doesn't mean it has to be performed the same way in every instance. Consider, for example, why minor home improvement projects sometimes have to wait six months for a public hearing because they have to go through the same process as an application for a multimillion-dollar office complex.[25] The sensible thing to do in such cases is to recognize that one size does not fit all and that complex requests with major ramifications call for a more complex process than small requests.

Degree of Reliance on Machines

The general approach for the division of labor between people and machines is to assign tasks in a way that emphasizes the strengths and deemphasizes the weaknesses of each. In general, tasks assigned to computers are totally structured, can be described completely, and may require a combination of great speed, accuracy, and endurance. Tasks with relatively little processing (such as keeping track of orders and invoices) can also be assigned to computers to assure organized and predictable execution. In contrast, tasks people must perform are those requiring common sense, intelligence, judgment, or creativity. People handle these tasks better than computers because they are flexible and can identify and resolve situations never encountered before.

The trend toward e-business is based on integrating computer and communications technology into business processes. As with other process characteristics, increasing the reliance on machines brings both advantages and disadvantages. Today's technology has incredible capabilities for performing totally structured tasks that require speed, accuracy, and endurance. As is apparent when shopping at a store with a noncomputerized inventory system, doing things manually that could be done by computers is slow and inefficient and often makes it difficult to provide excellent service for customers. Even when the amount of processing is small, computerizing basic business transactions helps assure organized and predictable execution. On the other hand, over-reliance on machines makes systems inflexible and may also lead to disengagement by human participants. An obvious downside of highly computerized processes is that the process stops when the computer goes down. Highly successful e-businesses have suffered embarrassing computer outages that shut down their Web sites for hours at a time. If they experience difficulty keeping their sites in operation, how reliable are the sites of smaller organizations with less IT horsepower? Furthermore, the proven ability of both hackers and auditors to break into Web sites and other computer installations shows an additional type of risk that must be contained.

Not a Magic Bullet   Although computers and other machines enable business processes that might have seemed unbelievable in the past, people have often relied too heavily on automation to solve problems machines alone cannot solve. A widely discussed example from the 1980s is the way General Motors spent over $40 billion on highly automated factories, but reaped few rewards. Many of the robots never worked properly due to a variety of technical, social, and political circumstances. The fallacy of viewing automation as a magic bullet was demonstrated by the NUMMI joint venture involving GM and Toyota. The plant used comparatively little automation and had many of the same workers as a previous GM plant at the same location, but attained much higher productivity mostly by changing the expectations for both labor and management.

In addition to not being a solution in many cases, excessive reliance on machines can be inefficient, ineffective, or even dangerous due to a shortcoming in the technology or in the way the technology affects system participants. An example of this type of problem occurred when the autopilot in a Boeing 747 began to malfunction as the plane was flying over Thunder Bay, Canada, on a dark night. The autopilot gradually began banking the plane to the right, but the motion was so gentle that the pilots did not notice the problem until too late. The plane banked 90 degrees, a position in which the wings provided no lift, and it began to dive toward earth. It fell two miles before the pilots could pull out of the dive. After more than a year of investigation, engineers could not agree on the cause. Airplane manufacturers and many pilots believe autopilot systems are safer and less error prone than human pilots under most circumstances; however, the question certainly remains about how much pilots should rely on machines that were designed to assist and supplement the pilot's capabilities, but not replace them.[26]

This type of incident demonstrates why relying on machines to automate decision-making is risky unless every aspect of the decision is so well understood that any mistake will be minor. The fundamental issue is that no system design team, regardless of how brilliant, can anticipate every condition a system will face. What if the incoming data are wrong? One of the many problems faced in the attempt to automate baggage delivery at the new Denver International Airport was simply dirt on sensors, which occasionally made it impossible to locate baggage. What if the computations contain a bug? Will there be a backup method if the automated process fails for some reason? And what if the backup method fails? If the future of e-commerce is to include widespread use of the "intelligent agents" and "shop-bots" for important functions, issues such as these will have to be addressed convincingly.

Even if the software and human procedures in a work system operate perfectly relative to its design specifications, over-reliance on machines may cause problems or even disasters because there is no guarantee that the system will operate correctly under unanticipated circumstances. A potentially apocalyptic example illustrates why major decisions should not be automated completely. On October 5, 1960, a missile warning system indicated that the United States was under a massive attack by Soviet missiles with probability exceeding 99.9%. Fortunately, human decision makers concluded that something must be wrong with the information they were receiving. In fact, the early warning radar at Thule, Greenland, had spotted the rising moon,[27] but nobody had thought about the moon when specifying how the information system should operate.

Prominence of Planning and Control

Participants in a business process need to know what to do, when to do it, and how to make sure work is being done properly. We can think of this as a cycle of planning, execution, and control. **Planning** is the process of deciding what work to do, what outputs to produce, and when. **Executing** is the process of doing the work. **Controlling** is the process of using information about past work performance to assure that goals are attained and plans carried out.

Planning, execution, and control occur wherever people do work. For example, a carpenter making a bookcase plans the work, performs the work, and uses carpentry techniques to ensure that the work is being done correctly. A manager implementing an organizational change goes through the same three steps. The manager's plan outlines the process of explaining the change, training the people, and converting from the old method to the new method. The execution is the explanation, training, and conversion. The control is the collection and use of information to make sure that the change is occurring.

Figure 3.10 shows flows of information between planning, execution, and control. Planning determines work standards, what work will be done, and when. As work is executed, it generates information that is used in control processes. A control system

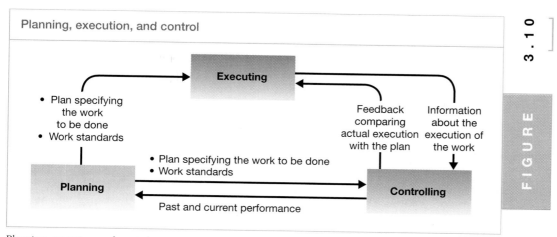

Planning, execution, and control

Planning, execution, and control are separate activities. Execution receives the output of planning and provides information inputs into the control process.

FIGURE 3.10

feeds information back to execution to keep the execution on track and also to the planning process to ensure that future plans use realistic assumptions. To keep execution on track, recent performance is compared with work standards or work schedules and actions are taken to compensate for any deviations. Planning and control are information-intensive activities because a plan is information and because control involves the use of information to check how well the plan is being met and to take any necessary corrective action.

The relationships in Figure 3.10 might seem obvious, but a careful look at many work systems would find ineffective links between planning the work, doing the work, and receiving feedback. The link between the plan and the execution is often so tenuous that the plan offers little guidance, especially since it is often out of date by the time some of the work steps are being performed. Providing usable feedback is also problematic since it is often compiled too late to be used effectively, such as reporting significant decreases in productivity one month after a large project is completed. In other cases feedback and direct forms of control are so excessive that the work situation may seem stifling to the participants and may limit their ability to respond to novel situations.

There are many ways to improve the cycle of planning, execution, and control. Planning for individual work can be supported by creating a standard planning format and then supplying information such as customer specifications or machine availability in a computerized form so that planning calculations can be automated. Organizational planning can be improved by creating standard formats and processing procedures for the structured parts of planning, such as transmitting and distributing plans, calculating planned results, and merging numbers from different organizations.

Execution can be improved by focusing information systems on execution per se, rather than mostly on planning or control activities. The emergence of powerful interactive computing makes this much more feasible today than it was even ten years ago, although its practicality depends on the nature of the work. Information-intensive processes such as designing a product or creating customer bills focus on information and require some type of information system. In contrast, information systems are less central for processes such as making a violin or training people to work effectively with peers.

Control processes can be improved in a number of ways using information systems, such as by making the collection of control data an automatic by-product of doing the work. Beyond combining data collection with work tasks, it is also possible to integrate control activities into the work itself. For example, instead of having a historically oriented control system that tells what went wrong last week or last month, it is sometimes possible to use information systems to provide immediate feedback to the people doing the work.

Table 3.3 shows how information requirements for planning, execution, and control are different. Planning is about the future, whereas execution is about the present and control is about learning from the past. The differences in information requirements for these activities explain why some information systems are not helpful for particular decisions. The information system supporting a business process may be useful for control decisions but ineffective for execution or planning decisions. For example, an information system for managers may summarize last month's sales performance effectively but still not address crucial questions about how to proceed into new markets.

Attention to Errors and Exceptions

Discussions of business processes often focus on how they are supposed to work in typical situations rather than how they should respond when an error, exception, or malfunction occurs. Since these things happen in all real business processes, part of the process architecture is the way the process should respond to these conditions. Focusing on what to do about likely errors, exceptions, and malfunctions is especially important when computers are involved because computerized business processes are

Comparison of Planning, Execution, and Control		
Step in the cycle	**Time focus**	**Important issues related to information**
Planning	Future	• Having reliable methods of projecting into the future by combining models, assumptions, and data about the past and present
Execution	Present	• Providing information that tells people what to do now to meet the plan and adjust for any problems that have occurred recently • Using current information to identify problems or errors in current work • Collecting information without getting in the way of doing the work
Control	Past	• Having reliable methods of using data about the past to develop or adjust plans, and to motivate employees • Provide information current enough that it can be used to guide current actions

TABLE 3.3

often more structured and less flexible than manual processes and therefore have more difficulty handling exceptions.

As an example consider an order-processing system built under the assumption that incomplete orders cannot be processed and that a complete order includes the customer's shipping address. What if the customer wants to order a product that takes a long time to build but has not decided where it should be shipped? Should the order be accepted without the shipping address? Regardless of the system developer's original intention, many real-world order takers would treat this as an exception and would try to trick the information system by entering a "temporary" shipping address so that the computer system would accept the order. The fact that the shipping address was actually a workaround would probably be long forgotten by the time the material was ready to ship, perhaps to a fictitious location.

The approach for handling exceptions, errors, and malfunctions in any situation is a trade-off between wasting time and resources by being unsystematic versus diverting energy from the work system's major goals through excessive formalization of exception processing. Consider the question of how an accounts receivable process should handle adjustments to customer bills for reasons such as incorrect shipments, incorrect bills, and unsatisfactory merchandise. A highly informal process might give inconsistent responses to similar situations and would not accumulate useful information about the reasons for adjustments. An overly formalized process might have so many categories and cross-checks that it would become a bottleneck in the process.

Inadequacies of Safety Systems   Unfortunately, subsystems for detecting and correcting errors are just as prone to errors as any other part of a work system. An example well known to software developers is a bug in the software that reset Therac-25 X-ray machines when the operator tried to correct an incorrectly entered setting. Several patients received fatal doses of radiation because of this bug.[28] More recently, the safety systems in a Lufthansa Airbus 320 caused a crash landing in Warsaw. The airplane had received faulty wind-speed information and came in too fast, creating a lift that lightened the load on the landing gear. The flight control software concluded the plane was not on the ground and prevented the jets from braking the aircraft by reversing thrust. The resulting crash killed two people and injured 45.[29]

Although automation-related malfunctions such as these are often dramatic, inattention and carelessness by human participants is probably a far more significant factor in the failure of safety systems. On an everyday level, look at the number of people who don't wear automobile seat belts or bicycle helmets. The National Transportation Safety Board says that 68% of people in cars use seat belts. Increasing that to 85% would save 4,200 deaths per year and $7 billion in medical and other costs, yet in 1997, 36 states that require seat belt use explicitly forbade the police to stop drivers because they or their front seat passengers were not wearing them.[30] Safety guidelines for investments or employee safety are also ignored in many situations. For example, the Chernobyl nuclear meltdown accident occurred when operators broke many essential safety rules, including the one about not shutting down the safety system. The fact that most safety systems seem to work most of the time is reassuring, but examples such as these show that procedures for handling exceptions, errors, and malfunctions are an important part of any work system that involves substantial resources or risks.

R E A L I T Y C H E C K ✓

Business Process Characteristics

The text discussed eight process characteristics and explained how these are related to choices about information systems.

1. Think about a business process with which you are familiar, such as registering for classes, borrowing books from a library, or voting in an election. Based on your personal experience, describe that business process in terms of the eight characteristics.

2. Explain differences in the process if each characteristic were increased or decreased.

EVALUATING BUSINESS PROCESS PERFORMANCE

We have now seen how to document a business process and how to summarize its characteristics. Concepts for evaluating process performance are the next part of the picture. We will focus on seven of many possible performance variables that can be used.

Table 3.4 illustrates the need to look at each of these seven variables separately because each variable involves genuine choices, with too much often as bad as too lit-

TABLE 3.4

Finding the Right Level for Each Process Performance Variable

Process performance variable	Problem if the level is too high	Problem if the level is too low
Activity rate	• Wasted effort and build-up of unneeded inventory	• Inefficient resource usage and imbalanced work-in-process
Output rate	• Lower productivity and consistency by increasing rates of errors and rework	• Lower productivity due to the cost of unused capacity
Consistency	• Inflexibility, making it difficult to produce what the customer wants	• Too much variability in the output, reducing quality perceived by the customer
Productivity	• Too much emphasis on cost per unit and too little emphasis on quality of the output	• Output is unnecessarily expensive to produce
Cycle time	• Lack of responsiveness to customer • Excess costs and waste due to delays	• Product damaged or compromised while waiting until the customer needs it • Delivery before the customer is ready
Downtime	• Lower productivity, longer cycle times, less consistency	• Exhausted participants if little or no downtime is allowed in some processes
Security	• Excess attention to security gets in the way of doing work	• Insufficient attention to security permits security breaches

tle along any of the dimensions. In many cases these variables are mutually reinforcing. For example, reducing cycle time or increasing consistency often increases productivity by reducing waste. In other cases, over-emphasis on any one of them may have negative consequences for others. For example, excessive attention to consistency may slow down the work and reduce productivity; attempts to reduce cycle time may reduce productivity by consuming excessive amounts of effort; extreme vigilance related to security may reduce the effort available for producing output.

Business process participants and managers should be involved in designing and evaluating information systems because they have the most direct insight about the advantages and disadvantages of different levels of process performance. Table 3.5 lists common performance measures for each process performance variable and identifies some of the ways information systems can be used to improve performance in regard to that variable. Looking at each variable in turn helps in understanding most information system applications.

TABLE 3.5

Process Performance Variables and Related Roles of Information Systems

Process performance variable	Typical measures	Common information system role
Activity rate	• Number of work steps completed per day	• Track the rate at which work steps are occurring • Help in deciding which steps to do when, thereby keeping the inventory balanced and the work flow steady
Output rate	• Average units completed per hour or week • Peak load units per hour or week	• Increase rate of output by performing some of the work automatically • Increase rate of output by systematizing the work
Consistency	• Defect rate • Percentage variation • Rework rate	• Systematize work to reduce variability of the product • Provide immediate feedback to identify and correct errors • Help process participants analyze the causes of defects
Productivity	• Output per labor hour or machine hour • Ratio of outputs to inputs (in dollars) • Scrap rate • Cost of rework	• Help people produce more output with the same effort • Automate data processing functions people perform inefficiently • Systematize work to reduce waste • Schedule work to improve resource utilization
Cycle time	• Elapsed time from start to finish • Total work-in-process inventory divided by weekly output (a useful approximation in some situations)	• Perform data processing work more quickly • Make it possible to combine steps, thereby eliminating delays • Make it possible to perform steps in parallel, thereby eliminating delays • Systematize work to reduce waste and rework
Downtime	• Total time out of operation compared to length of the time period • Total time out of operation compared to scheduled uptime	• Track the process and equipment to identify things that are going out of spec • Perform backups and provide recovery methods to minimize computer-related downtime
Security	• Number of process breaches in a time interval • Seriousness of process breaches in a time interval	• Systematize record keeping about the business process • Systematize record keeping about computer access and usage • Track all nonstandard transactions such as changes to completed transactions

Activity Rate and Output Rate

Activity rate and output rate are separate performance variables that focus on the amount of work being done per unit of time. Like other performance variables, activity rate and output rate are determined by a combination of the way the business process is designed, the preparation and enthusiasm of the participants, the quality of the available information, and the operation of the technology.

Output rate is the amount of output (completions) that a process produces per unit of time, whereas **activity rate** is the number of interim work steps that are performed per unit time. This distinction is important mainly for processes that take a long time to complete or are complicated. For example, a construction company trying to stay on schedule while building a bridge would find it far more useful to track its activity rate in work steps per week rather than its output rate in bridges completed per week. Similarly, semiconductor manufacturers who are very concerned about meeting weekly output schedules also track activity rates because the processes involve over one hundred separate steps. These companies recognize that the work system's goal is to produce output, not activity, but that the activity rate is an important predictor of increases or decreases in output. If the rate of activity drops, the rate of output will probably drop in turn.

Variability in activity and output rates is an important issue in designing business processes and in controlling how they operate. Most processes operate at maximum efficiency when they produce the same type of output at a consistent rate. In contrast, the demand for output varies in many situations. Information systems can reduce the related inefficiencies in a number of ways. They can be used to help smooth demand by increasing the cost borne by the customer as demand increases. This is how some electric utilities charge more for electricity during the day in order to shift demand toward low-usage times at night. They can also be used to minimize the impact of demand variations by smoothing flows between intermediate steps in production.

Both of these variables differ from **capacity,** which is the theoretical limit of the output a system can produce in a given time period. Establishing the right capacity and ideal activity rate for a business process is a challenge because every unit of excess capacity typically has some monetary cost. In addition, excess capacity often permits sloppiness in the system, as was demonstrated repeatedly when downsized companies increased output and responsiveness to customers despite cutting layers of management and other staff. Similar effects apply when the excess capacity involves equipment or inventory. For example, a major advantage of minimizing the amount of the idle inventory sitting in warehouses or on factory floors is that nonexistent inventory cannot be broken, lost, stolen, or made obsolete. Minimizing inventory buffers also helps in identifying production problems, which become apparent quickly because they cannot hide behind excess inventory.

An important related characteristic of both business processes and the information systems that support them is **scalability**, the ability to significantly increase or decrease capacity without major disruption or excessive costs. The least scalable processes involve huge capital outlays for individual units of production, such as power plants or airports. Increased scalability is one of the important benefits of Web-based computing.

Consistency

Consistency in a business process means applying the same techniques in the same way to obtain the same desired results. Because one of the TQM movement's main tenets is that unwarranted variation destroys quality, TQM calls for careful specification of exactly how a process should be performed and careful monitoring to ensure that it is being performed consistent with those specifications.

One of the main benefits of some information systems is that they force the organization to do things consistently. For example, companies in the airfreight business such as Federal Express and United Parcel Service do very detailed tracking as each package passes each step. Part of the value of this tracking is that it enforces consis-

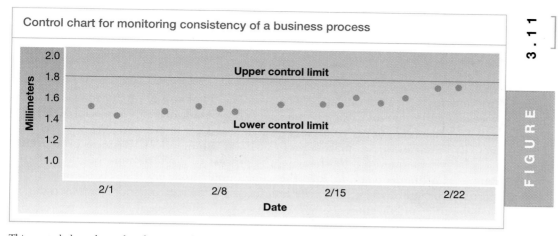

FIGURE

3.11

This control chart shows data for a manufacturing process that is going out of control even though it has not yet exceeded a control limit. Machine operators looking at this control chart should stop the process and fix it before the output of their production step must be scrapped or reworked.

tency in the way work is done. System participants know that if they deviate from the rules in their handling of a package, the information system will be able to show it was handled in a proper way until it got to them.

Some information systems are designed to provide information that helps people perform business processes in a consistent manner. Figure 3.11 shows a control chart, a device used widely to monitor business process consistency. The control chart graphs a process measurement such as the average width of a sample of machined parts or the average length of time customers had to wait on hold. The process is considered "in control" if it stays within limits, has expected variability, and has no trend toward going out of limits. This type of tool helps in identifying problems before they have significant impacts on quality or productivity.

Unfortunately, excessive consistency in some processes creates a straitjacket that prevents system participants from handling exceptions well or even doing their work effectively. Consider the description by a reform-minded undersecretary of defense about what happened when the Department of Defense (DOD) wanted to buy mobile radios during the Persian Gulf War. The best available radio was a commercial product from Motorola, but DOD rules required the contractor to have a DOD-approved system in place for justifying the selling price. Motorola did not have such a system and DOD would not change its rules, even in time of war. The situation was resolved when Japan bought the radios and donated them to the United States.[31]

This example illustrates that emphasizing consistency often makes it more difficult to be flexible. The **flexibility** of a business process is the ease with which it can be adjusted to meet immediate customer needs and adapted over the long term as business conditions change. The competitive advantages of flexibility are apparent: Customers prefer the product features they really want, rather than the product features suppliers think they want. It is also possible to make business processes too flexible, however. Excessive flexibility in a business process leads to chaos because process participants need reference points for keeping themselves organized and productive.

There are a number of approaches for achieving flexibility within a framework of consistency. One general principle is to avoid restricting things about the process that can be left to the judgment of the process participants. For example, don't force the participants to fill out computerized forms in a particular order unless the sequence really matters. Another principle is to delay as long as possible those choices that convert information into a physical result that is hard to change. According to this principle, installation of physical customer options should be delayed as long as possible if those options would make a customized product hard to sell to another customer. A third principle is to perform the business process using technical tools and methods that are flexible themselves. For example, use programming methods that generate programs that are comparatively easy to change. Figure 3.12 shows that automation does not necessarily imply flexibility.

Productivity

Productivity is the relationship between the amount of output produced by a business process and the amount of money, time, and effort it consumes. It is measured in terms such as units of output per labor hour or dollar sales per month. As a firm's overall productivity improves, it can make a profit at lower selling prices. Business process productivity can be improved by changing the process to produce more output from the same level of inputs or to produce the same output from lower levels of inputs. One approach for improving productivity is to increase the rate of work, thereby reducing the labor time and inventory costs related to a particular level of output.

Eliminating waste and rework is another approach to improving productivity, and it is surprisingly important. Quality experts often estimate that 20% to 30% of costs are actually just **waste**, which can be defined as any activity that uses resources without adding value. Taaichi Ohno, a Toyota executive who was a pioneer in lean production methods, identified seven causes of waste:

1. Defects in products
2. Overproduction of goods not needed
3. Inventories of goods awaiting further processing or consumption
4. Unnecessary processing
5. Unnecessary movement of people
6. Unnecessary transport of goods
7. Time spent waiting for process equipment to finish its work, or for an upstream activity[32]

FIGURE 3.12

Automation versus flexibility

A high degree of automation does not necessarily imply a high degree of flexibility. This highly automated frame-welding process is not designed to be as flexible as many other manual or computerized processes.

Looking at a list like this sometimes helps people realize that waste is built into the way many processes operate. This was certainly the case for the Ford example at the beginning of the chapter. Built-in waste is also present when the steps that customize a product to the requirements of different customers are performed too early in the process. At minimum, the customized units will remain in inventory longer. At worst, demand will change and unnecessarily customized units will have to be scrapped or reworked.

Most early computerized information systems supported productivity improvement by collecting detailed information and summarizing what happened yesterday, last week, or last month. More recently, information systems have attempted to increase productivity by supporting automation and by providing interactive tools used directly by professionals in their work.

Perhaps surprisingly, there is substantial question about whether information technology investments actually increase productivity. Looking at just computers, statistical studies relating computer investments to company performance have found little discernible impact on aggregate productivity, although recent research has started to find more positive results.[33,34] Part of the question here is that computer investments involve many costs beyond the purchase price. In businesses, hidden or unobserved costs related to support, training, facilities, maintenance, administration, and time spent by end users doing programming can push total spending over $10,000 per PC according to many studies.

Computers can also reduce productivity by tempting people to waste time making endless refinements in documents and spreadsheets. For example, a study of Internal Revenue Service examiners who were given laptop computers found that they performed examinations faster but didn't increase the number of examinations they performed. Instead they spent more time writing aesthetically pleasing reports and sometimes playing games. A survey by accounting software maker SBT Corp. asked customers to estimate how much time they spent "futzing with your PC." They came up with 5.1 hours a week doing things such as waiting for computer runs, printouts, or help; checking and formatting documents; loading and learning new programs; helping co-workers; organizing and erasing old files; and other activities such as playing games.[35] Citing this estimate, a consultant with McKinsey, a leading consulting firm, quipped that if the estimate is correct, personal computers may have become the biggest destroyer of white-collar productivity since the management meeting was invented.[36]

Cycle Time

It is easy to say time is a scarce resource, but many business processes operate as though time barely matters. For example, in conventional batch manufacturing the time during which value is actually being added often constitutes less than 5% of total manufacturing cycle time. Over 95% of the time, the product is either sitting in batches awaiting processing or being moved to another work center.[37] Delays of this type can be just as important in information-based processes, such the processing of insurance or loan applications.

The use of time in a business process can be summarized as **cycle time**, the length of time between the start of the process and its completion. Cycle time is determined by a combination of the processing time for performing each step in the process, the waiting time between completing one step and starting another, and the dependencies between steps. Waiting time when no value is being added is often a major problem in factories that produce physical goods and in "paperwork" processes such as the IBM Credit example mentioned earlier.

Bottlenecks are another important source of delays and excessive cycle times. A **bottleneck** is an essential work step where a temporary or long-term capacity shortage delays work on most of the items being produced or processed. In these situations, maximizing utilization of the bottleneck may be the key to reducing total cycle time. Information systems can help in these situations by helping people decide on the right order of work to improve flow through the bottleneck.

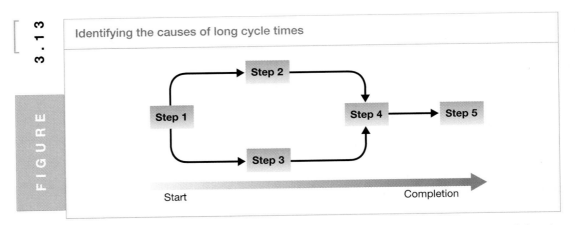

FIGURE   3.13

Identifying the causes of long cycle times

Five steps must occur before this process is complete. The total cycle time depends on factors including the elapsed time for each step, the amount of waiting time before each step begins, and the dependencies preventing one step from starting until several other steps are finished.

Self-imposed and legally imposed deadlines are another important aspect of time in business processes. Concerns about the freshness of packaged foods and pharmaceuticals leads manufacturers to stamp expiration dates on packages and remove stale product. Time is also a regulatory issue, such as the way the Securities and Exchange Commission required that settlement time, the time between stock or bond purchases and payment, be reduced from five days to three days in 1995. A current push to reduce this further is based on the belief that it would reduce the chances for fraud.

Just drawing a picture like Figure 3.13 can often help in identifying bottlenecks and unnecessary steps that expand total cycle times. In this example steps 2 and 3 can overlap in time but cannot begin until step 1 completes. In turn, step 4 cannot start until both 2 and 3 complete. Part of the analysis for reducing delays in business processes involves drawing this type of diagram and examining the processing time, waiting time, and dependencies for each step. Sometimes the delays jump out at you. For example, if step 3 is a meeting involving people from different groups, there may be a two-week delay before any work on step 4 can begin. An attempt to reduce the process's cycle time would probably include an analysis of whether it is possible to eliminate the meeting, handle it by phone, or identify work that does not need to wait for the meeting to happen.

Downtime

The bane of computerized systems, **downtime** is the amount or percentage of time during which the process is out of operation. Downtime of a process may occur because a computer system is out of operation unexpectedly or for planned maintenance. It may also occur for any number of other reasons involving the system participants and the context. Even planned maintenance sometimes becomes an unacceptably long period of downtime. Wal-Mart surprised many observers by completely closing its Web site on October 3, 2000 for a complete makeover just before the holiday season. It remained down for 28 days before reopening with greatly improved appearance and usability.[38]

Computer downtime is especially important in e-business because the process depends on the computer and communication technology so completely. Web sites of e-commerce leaders including Schwab, E*Trade, and eBay have suffered embarrassing spates of unplanned downtime due to internal computer problems. In a totally different type of situation, coordinated denial of service attacks by hackers brought down the Web sites of Yahoo!, Amazon, Buy.com, CNN, and E*Trade. These attacks were perpetrated by bombarding the Web sites with information sent repeatedly from a large number of computers that had been infiltrated and infected with a malicious program.[39]

Security

The **security** of a business process is the likelihood that it is not vulnerable to unauthorized uses, sabotage, or criminal activity. Although companies avoid discussing security issues publicly, a number of security problems are well known. One of these involves telephone fraud, in which someone steals another person's telephone credit card number and then uses it illegally. In another form of telephone fraud, the criminal penetrates a company's internal telephone system and then uses it to make outgoing calls. Telephone fraud costs at least several billion dollars per year.

The security of a business process depends on procedures that ensure accuracy and prevent unauthorized access (see Figure 3.14). Although preventing unauthorized access to computerized systems is obviously essential, even systems with adequate control over computer access may have insufficient controls over clerical procedures that surround the system. Although accuracy is also obviously important, many systems contain insufficient methods for checking the accuracy of input data, identifying errors in the data in the system, and correcting those errors.

Information systems can improve security or can weaken it. They improve security when they contain effective safeguards against unauthorized access and use. They weaken security when they remove control from people and lead the people in the system to become complacent about security concerns and to "trust the computer." Chapter 13 will discuss both the problems and the safeguards in some detail.

Vigilance of the participants is perhaps the most general characteristic leading to system security. Many system- and organization-related disasters prove the point. In 1987 a Pacific Southwest Airlines jet crashed because a recently fired employee brought a gun onto the airplane and shot the pilot and co-pilot. Unaware that he had been fired, airport security personnel had waved him past the security checkpoints even though regulations required that he show an ID card. Even security agencies can show insufficient vigilance. In 1994 the director of the U.S. Central Intelligence Agency (CIA) issued a scalding assessment of the failure to catch Aldrich Ames, a spy

Using an iris scanner for controlling access

FIGURE 3.14

This iris scanner identifies people using the features of the iris of the eye.

whose actions in exchange for more than $2 million from 1985 to 1994 had destroyed the CIA's network of spies inside the Soviet Union and caused the deaths of 10 double agents. Though the CIA knew Ames was an alcoholic who repeatedly flouted its rules, it promoted him to run the counterintelligence branch within the Soviet division. The CIA director said the inattention of senior officials was almost universal and went on for years. "One could almost conclude not only that no one was watching, but that no one cared."[40]

R E A L I T Y **C H E C K** ✓

Evaluating Process Performance

This section has discussed a number of variables used to evaluate process performance.

1. Consider the business process you selected earlier. Identify the process performance variables that seem most important and least important in this situation. Explain how you might measure those variables.

2. Assume someone actually measured each variable. Make an estimate of what the person would find currently and what the person might find if the business process were revamped to operate as well as possible.

MORE ABOUT COMMUNICATION AND DECISION-MAKING

Business processes consist of different types of activities including:

Processing data: performing any combination of capturing, transmitting, storing, retrieving, manipulating, or displaying data. These are the tasks information systems can perform.

Communicating: conveying ideas and information to another person so that person can understand it. Communication requires understanding by the recipient, in contrast to transmitting data, which is basically about moving data from one place to another.

Making decisions: using information to define, evaluate, and select among possible options. This can be done by people based on varying degrees of concentration and thought or can be done automatically by machines.

Thinking/creating: absorbing and combining ideas in a nonprogrammed way to create new information and ideas. The fluid, unstructured nature of thinking and creating differentiates this from merely manipulating data.

Taking physical action: any purposeful combination of movements including assembling or fabricating something and moving it from place to place.

Chapter 1 introduced the six data processing operations and most of this book talks about the role of data processing within business processes. IT applications sometimes support thinking/creating and sometimes control physical actions, and these will be mentioned briefly in Chapter 5. This chapter closes by saying a bit more about communication and decision-making, each of which brings a number of concepts that are useful in understanding business processes. Table 3.6 shows that information systems can affect communication and decision-making performance in many different ways.

Basic Communication Concepts

The ways information systems can help improve communication include:

- Permitting communication that could not take place otherwise
- Making communication situations more effective

TABLE 3.6

Ways Information Systems Can Improve Communication and Decision-Making within Business Processes

This table is organized in terms of the process performance variables of business processes in Table 3.5.

Process performance variable	How information systems can improve communication	How information systems can improve decision-making
Activity rate and Output rate	• Make sure communication does not cause delays in performing work steps • Communicate more information or more types of information to more people	• Make sure information for decision-making is readily available • Make more decisions using better, more complete information
Consistency	• Make sure different people receive the same communication	• Make sure repetitive decisions are made in a consistent manner
Productivity	• Achieve more communication with less effort • Permit efficient communication in many different forms	• Make better decisions with less effort • Maintain decision quality across a wider range of situations
Cycle time	• Eliminate undesirable delays in communication	• Eliminate unnecessary delays in decision-making
Downtime	• Provide backup channels to continue communication even if the regular channel is not available	• Automate certain decisions to minimize the impacts of process downtime
Security	• Make sure communications go only to the intended recipients	• Make sure decisions are controlled only by those authorized to make the decisions

- Eliminating unnecessary person-to-person communication by making information available through the Web or other computerized means
- Making communication systematic to minimize wasted effort and confusion

Basic communication concepts are useful in describing and evaluating these uses of communication technology within business processes.

Social Context   **Social context**, the situation and relationships within which communication takes place, starts with **social presence**, the extent to which the recipient of communication perceives it as personal interaction with another person. We feel social presence strongly because we all learn how to communicate in face-to-face situations where social presence is powerful. Social context also includes organizational position, relationships, cultural norms, age, gender, and the topic being discussed.

Much of what is communicated in face-to-face situations is communicated through **nonverbal communication,** such as facial expressions, eye contact, gestures, and body language. This is why two different people saying exactly the same words may communicate different thoughts and feelings. This is also why different degrees of social presence are desirable in different communication situations. In some situations, getting the message across requires a strong feeling of social presence. In others, such as communication of orders and bills between companies, social presence is unimportant.

Different communication technologies filter out nonverbal information and decrease social context cues to varying extents. A face-to-face meeting provides richer communication than a telephone call because the telephone filters out body language, eye contact, and facial expressions. Similarly, a telephone call provides richer communication than a computerized text message because text filters out voice inflection and intensity.

Personal, Impersonal, and Anonymous Communication   The form and content of communication vary depending on whether communication is personal, impersonal, or anonymous. In **personal communication** the personal relationship between the sender and receiver affects both form and content even in business situations. Even though an employee's performance review conveys factual information in a business setting, it is based in a personal relationship and therefore is an example of personal communication. In **impersonal communication** the specific identity and personality of the sender and recipient affect the communication less, if at all, because the sender and receiver act as agents implementing the policies and tactics of business organizations. Impersonal communication occurs when you pay a credit card bill because what matters most is receipt of the payment before the deadline. The sender's identity is purposely hidden in **anonymous communication**, which is used in situations ranging from the suggestion box to crime tips for the police.

IT can make communication more personal or more impersonal. For example, using an automated voice messaging system makes parts of communication more impersonal because the caller leaves a message without speaking to a person. In contrast, IT has been used in customer service to create the appearance of personal service by making customer information readily available to customer service agents as soon as they answer a call.

Time, Place, and Direction of Communication   Communication can be described in terms of whether the sender and recipient are present at the same time, whether they are present at the same place, and whether the communication is inherently one-way or two-way. *Same-time* (also called synchronous) communication occurs when both sender and recipient are available simultaneously. *Different-time* (also called asynchronous) communication occurs when the participants are not available simultaneously, and therefore requires recording of a message. As electronic communication technologies advanced, the first step was often same-time transmission, such as telephone, live radio, and live television. Different-time communication became possible as cost-effective recording technologies appeared, ranging from taping TV programs to recording phone messages.

Table 3.7 shows how common communication technologies can be categorized by the time and place of communication. Technologies that link people across a distance are commonly thought of as communication technology, but IT can support communication in other ways as well. Various technologies can support communication during face-to-face meetings. Even online databases from data processing systems such as inventory and reservations systems serve a role in communication by substituting computer queries for unnecessary person-to-person communication when all that is needed is data.

TABLE 3.7

Communication Technologies Classified by Time and Place of Communication

This table classifies communication technologies based on the time/place relationship between the sender and recipient. Notice that electronic mail and voice mail can be used when the sender and recipient are in the same place (such as in the same office) or in different places.

	Same time	Different time
Same place	• Presentation systems • Group support systems (GSS)	• Transaction databases • World Wide Web • Electronic mail • Voice mail
Different place	• Typical telephones • Computer conferencing • Video telephones and conferencing • Nonrecorded radio or TV broadcast	• Transaction databases • World Wide Web • Electronic data interchange (EDI) • Electronic mail • Voice mail • Fax • Prerecorded radio or TV broadcast

Effects of Communication Situations

The text differentiates between different degrees of social presence in communication (personal, impersonal, and anonymous) and between different combinations of time, place, and direction of communication (same-time versus different-time, same-place versus different-place, and one-way versus two-way).

1. Thinking about things you have done at work or in school, give examples of communication illustrating each variation on these two aspects of the communication situation.

2. For each example identify ways it might have been possible to improve the communication by changing these aspects of the communication situation in some way.

Basic Decision-Making Concepts

An understanding of decision-making is essential because information systems are designed to support decision-making in one way or another. The phases of decision-making are covered first, followed by rationality and common flaws in decision-making.

Steps in a Decision Process   Figure 3.15 combines several models researchers have proposed for describing decision processes. Decision-making is represented as a problem-solving process preceded by a separate problem-finding process. **Problem-finding** is the process of identifying and formulating problems that should be solved.[41] Although often overlooked, problem-finding is the key to effective decision-making because a seemingly good solution to the wrong problem may miss the point. For

Steps in decision-making

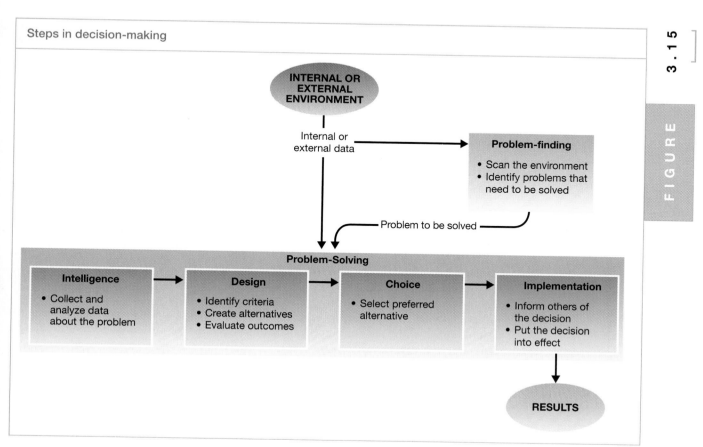

FIGURE 3.15

The diagram shows decision-making as a four-phase problem-solving process preceded by a problem-finding process.

example, we might come up with many solutions to the problem of how to expand our airports, but it might be better to formulate the problem as "How can we avoid expanding our airports by using transportation substitutes such as video conferencing?"

Problem-solving is the process of using information, knowledge, and intuition to solve a problem that has been defined previously. The problem-solving portion of Figure 3.15 says that most decision processes can be divided into four phases: intelligence, design, choice, and implementation.

- **Intelligence** includes the collection and analysis of data related to the problem identified in the problem-finding stage. Key challenges in the intelligence phase include obtaining complete and accurate data and figuring out what the data imply for the decision at hand.
- **Design** includes systematic study of the problem, creation of alternatives, and evaluation of outcomes. Key challenges in this phase include bounding the problem to make it manageable, creating real alternatives, and developing criteria and models for evaluating the alternatives.
- **Choice** is the selection of the preferred alternative. Key challenges here include reconciling conflicting objectives and interests, incorporating uncertainty, and managing group decision processes.
- **Implementation** is the process of putting the decision into effect. This includes explaining the decision to the appropriate people, building consensus that the decision makes sense, and creating the commitment to follow through. Key challenges involve ensuring that the decision and its implications are understood and that others in the organization will follow through, whether or not their preferred alternative is chosen.

The first three phases of the problem-solving process are Simon's classic model of decision-making.[42] The intelligence phase converts data into information for designing alternatives. The design phase creates the alternatives, one of which is selected during the choice phase. Implementation is the fourth phase because the problem is not solved until the decision is put into operation. Perhaps surprisingly, many information systems designed to support decision-making have their greatest impact not in making decisions, but in implementation activities such as explaining and justifying decisions.

The model is an idealization that separates decision-making into separate phases, but real decision processes are iterative and return to previous phases. This can happen if the intelligence phase determines that the problem was not defined properly, or if the design phase determines that more information is needed. In similar fashion, the choice or implementation phases might identify needs for additional information or issues requiring the development of additional alternatives.

Rationality and Satisficing   Describing the phases in decision-making is a starting point for explaining how people make decisions, but it raises questions as well, such as whether people are rational decision makers and what that means.

Rationality is a common model for explaining how people should make decisions. Classical economic theory says that rational decision makers maximize their welfare by performing the first three phases of problem-solving thoroughly. First, they gather all pertinent information and interpret it. Second, they identify all feasible alternatives and evaluate them based on criteria that maximize the good of the individual or organization. Third, they choose among the alternatives based on consistent and explicit trade-offs between the criteria.

For centuries economists have argued about whether people show rationality by making economic decisions that maximize their own welfare. The way most people use e-commerce Web sites reveals something important about rationality. Even though a great deal of price comparison information is available, less than half of all Web shoppers actually use it when they make purchases. Instead of searching for the best possible price, they typically identify one or several options and select the one that seems best without doing an exhaustive search.

Choosing a satisfactory alternative rather than searching for an optimal alternative is called **satisficing.** The concept of satisficing came from Simon's attempt to describe the way people actually behave rather than the way they should behave if they genuinely tried to optimize all or even most decisions. Satisficing is consistent with a theory of **bounded rationality,** whereby people make decisions in a limited amount of time, based on limited information, and with limited ability to process that information. Think about any decision you made recently: where to live or what to do next weekend. As you examine the way you made the decision, you will probably conclude that you could not obtain all of the relevant information. In fact, you probably couldn't even define all possible alternatives, much less consider them seriously. You may also have had difficulty defining the criteria to use in choosing the desired alternative.

Information systems have value in decision-making because they reduce some of the bounds on rationality by providing more information, helping generate and evaluate alternatives, and helping select among them. Except in extremely structured decisions, however, you might still feel that you don't have all the information you would like to have and that you aren't totally sure how to create and evaluate the alternatives.

Common Flaws in Decision-Making   Both business professionals and psychologists have observed common flaws in the way people make decisions. To supplement the examples that follow, Table 3.8 defines each problem and mentions some of the ways information systems might be used to avoid the related errors. Although few information systems are designed specifically to counter these problems, recognizing them helps in understanding what information systems can and cannot do for us.

- *Poor framing*: Decision makers often allow a decision to be "framed" by the language or context in which it is presented. In one experiment, two groups of students were given identical information about a business strategy. One group was told that the strategy had an 80% probability of success; the other was told that it had a 20% probability of failure. The majority of the "80% success" group gave the go-ahead, whereas the majority of the "20% failure" group did not. The only difference was the way the issue was framed.[43]

TABLE 3.8

How Information Systems Might Help Counteract Common Flaws in Decision-Making

Common flaw	Description	How an information system might help
Poor framing	Allowing a decision to be influenced excessively by the language used for describing the decision	Provide information encouraging different ways to think about the definition of the issue
Recency effects	Giving undue weight to the most recent information	Provide information showing how the most recent information might not be representative
Primacy effects	Giving undue weight to the first information received	Show how some information is inconsistent with the first information received
Poor probability estimation	Overestimating the probability of familiar or dramatic events; underestimating the probability of negative events	Make it easier to estimate probabilities based on pertinent data
Overconfidence	Believing too strongly in one's own knowledge	Provide counterexamples or models showing that other conclusions might also make sense
Escalation phenomena	Unwillingness to abandon courses of action decided upon previously	Provide information or models showing how the current approach might give poor results
Association bias	Reusing strategies that were successful in the past, regardless of whether they fit the current situation	Provide information showing how the current situation differs from past situations
Groupthink	Bowing to group consensus and cohesiveness instead of bringing out unpopular ideas	Provide information inconsistent with the current consensus and prove its relevance

- *Recency effects:* People frequently make decisions based on information received most recently. This is why an indecisive executive's advisors sometimes jockey to be the last person to give advice. This effect is sometimes called availability bias, meaning that the most easily visualized or most readily available information has the greatest weight in the decision.

- *Primacy effects:* It is often difficult for people to change an opinion or position about an issue once they have defined it. Because they are stuck on that spot, this effect is sometimes called anchoring. Negotiators sometimes exploit this idea by establishing a bargaining position and gradually giving in just a little.

- *Poor probability estimation:* People tend to overestimate the probability of familiar, dramatic, or beneficial events and greatly underestimate the probability of negative events. This is why people overestimate the frequency of deaths from causes such as accidents, homicides, and cancer, and underestimate the frequency of deaths from unspectacular causes and diseases that are common in nonfatal form such as diabetes, stroke, tuberculosis, and asthma.[44]

- *Overconfidence:* Both experts and the general public tend to be overconfident about the accuracy of what they know. As they think about an issue and reach initial conclusions, they tend to remember supporting facts and ignore contrary ones. This may be one reason why one year before the space shuttle Challenger disaster, NASA estimated the probability of such an accident as one in 100,000, even though the historical proportion of booster rockets blowing up is 1 in 57.[45]

- *Escalation phenomena:* Decision makers often find it difficult to abandon courses of action that have already been adopted and therefore ignore feedback indicating the course of action is failing. Decision makers who are not caught in escalation phenomena cut their losses by changing strategies and do not throw good money after bad.

- *Association bias:* Decision makers trying to repeat their past successes may choose strategies more related to a past situation than the current one.

- *Groupthink:* This is what happens when the need to maintain group consensus and cohesiveness overpowers the group's desire to make the best decision. A famous example is the acceptance of faulty assumptions by President Kennedy and his advisors during the disastrous decision to support the Bay of Pigs invasion of Cuba. They assumed a force outnumbered 140 to 1 could prevail because the Cuban people would immediately join invaders trying to overthrow the government.[46]

Automating Decisions Table 3.2 summarized the idea of imposing various degrees of structure on a business process and mentioned approaches including providing access to tools and information, enforcing rules and procedures, and substituting technology for people. In reference to decision-making, the last option is tantamount to automating the decision.

Automating decisions can have important advantages if a great deal of information must be processed or if small time delays affect the outcome. For example, automatic collision avoidance systems in airplanes perform high-speed evasive actions more reliably than human pilots. In the very different realm of finance, brokerage firms use computerized program trading systems to find short-term discrepancies between prices of large groups of stocks and options to buy or sell these groups of stocks in the future. On finding such discrepancies, the system can lock in a guaranteed profit by buying stocks in one market and selling options in the other. Another reason to automate decisions is to improve consistency or efficiency and make errors less likely. Systems for automating inventory reordering are of this type.

Automating a decision can be seen as a two-step process. First, decide exactly how the decision should be made. Second, create an automatic system for making the decision that way. A computer may play an important role in this second step or may simply automate exactly what a person might do. Consider a college admissions office deciding whom to admit. The dean has decided to divide applicants into two groups, those whose College Board scores exceed a cutoff and those whose scores are lower. Anyone below the cutoff will receive a rejection letter. Regardless of whether this process is carried out by a computer or by a clerk, the dean has eliminated any discretion the admissions office had. Although a person receiving a computer-generated rejection letter might feel that a computer made the decision, the real decision was whether to use a fixed rule as part of the admissions process and exactly what rule to use. In other words, the key issues in automating decisions are often not about computers, but about advantages and disadvantages of delegating a decision to an automatic process instead of human judgment.

Automatic decision-making is acceptable only when every aspect of the decision is so well understood that any mistakes will be minor. For example, an automatic inspection machine on a canning line in a food-processing factory may incorrectly designate some good fruit as bad. As long as the percentage of error is tolerably small, this automated system may be cheaper and just as reliable as a system using human inspectors. Automatic decision-making is inadvisable and potentially disastrous when the consequences of errors are large and when important errors are likely due to the possibility of erroneous data or of unanticipated factors that need to be considered. Except where occasional mistakes are unimportant, human judgment and intuition should be part of any decision process.

R E A L I T Y C H E C K ✓

Decision-Making Concepts

The text names the phases of decision-making, discusses the idea of rationality, and identifies common flaws in decision-making.

1. Identify several decisions you have made recently and explain how well or poorly these ideas fit with what happened.

2. Identify aspects of these decisions that seemed easier or more difficult, and explain how the ideas in this section are related to what was easy and what was difficult.

CHAPTER CONCLUSION

What is the role of data flow diagrams in process modeling?

Process modeling is a method of defining business process architecture by identifying major processes and dividing them into linked subprocesses. Data flow diagrams (DFDs) represent the flows of data between different processes in a business. They provide a simple, intuitive method for describing business processes without focusing on the details of computer systems. DFDs make it possible to look at business processes at any level of detail by breaking them down into successively finer subprocesses. The four symbols used in DFDs are the process, data flow, data store, and external entity.

What business process characteristics reflect system design choices that affect business process performance?

Eight characteristics determined by system design include degree of structure, range of involvement, level of integration, rhythm, complexity, degree of reliance on machines, prominence of planning and control, and attention to errors and exceptions.

What is the difference between structured, semistructured, and unstructured tasks?

The degree of structure of a task or a business process is the degree of predetermined correspondence between its inputs and its outputs. A totally structured task is so well understood that it is possible to say exactly how to perform it and how to evaluate whether it has been performed well. In a semistructured task, the information requirements and procedures are generally known, although some aspects of the task still rely on the judgment of the person doing the task. An unstructured task is so poorly understood that the information to be used, the method of using the information, and the criteria for deciding whether the task is being done well cannot be specified.

What are the five possible levels of integration of business processes?

Integration is mutual responsiveness and collaboration between distinct activities or processes. The five levels of integration include common culture, common standards, information sharing, coordination, and collaboration.

Why are planning and control important elements of many business processes?

Participants in a business process need to know what to do, when to do it, and how to make sure the work was done properly. Planning is the process of deciding what work to do and what outputs to produce when. Executing is the process of doing the work. Controlling is the process of using information about past work performance to assure that goals are attained and plans carried out. Planning and control activities provide the direction and coordination needed to attain the objectives of an entire organization or any of its business processes.

Why is it sometimes necessary to reconcile inconsistent performance goals for a business process?

Performance variables for a business process may be mutually reinforcing, but may also conflict with each other. For example, reducing cycle time or increasing consistency often increases productivity by reducing waste. In other cases, over-emphasis on any one of them may have negative consequences for others.

How are social context and nonverbal communication important when communication technologies are used?

Social context is the situation and relationships within which communication takes place. Much of what is communicated in face-to-face situations is communicated through nonverbal communication, such as facial expressions, eye contact, gestures, and body language. Technologies that filter out nonverbal information decrease social context cues and therefore limit communication. Technology may hinder communication if it is mismatched with the needs of the situation.

What are the phases of decision-making and what are some of the common limitations of decision-making?

Decision-making is a problem-solving process preceded by a problem-finding process. The phases of decision-making are intelligence, design, choice, and implementation. In the real world, rationality is always bounded by the amount of time available to make the decision and the limited ability of people to process information. Additionally, many common flaws in decision-making have been observed, such as poor framing, recency and primacy effects, poor probability estimation, overconfidence, and groupthink.

KEY TERMS

process modeling
business process reengineering
   (BPR)
data flow diagram (DFD)
context diagram
flowchart
structured English
idealized business process
workaround
degree of structure
structured task
semistructured task
unstructured task
range of involvement
case manager approach
integration
common culture
common standards

information sharing
coordination
collaboration
complexity
low value variations
planning
executing
controlling
output rate
activity rate
capacity
scalability
consistency
flexibility
productivity
waste
cycle time
bottleneck

downtime
security
social context
social presence
nonverbal communication
personal communication
impersonal communication
anonymous communication
presentation technologies
problem-finding
problem-solving
intelligence
design
choice
implementation
rationality
satisficing
bounded rationality

REVIEW QUESTIONS

1. What is process modeling?

2. What four symbols comprise a DFD, and what does each symbol represent?

3. What is a context diagram?

4. Why is it important to describe business processes at different levels of detail?

5. Why would a user of DFDs ever want to see information expressed in flowcharts or structured English?

6. Describe differences between structured, semistructured, and unstructured tasks.

7. How is the case manager approach related to range of involvement?

8. Define each of the five levels of integration.

9. What kinds of problems sometimes result from tight integration?

10. Will information sharing always result in coordination or collaboration between business processes?

11. In what ways can planning, execution, and control be improved?

12. Why is it important to discuss treatment of exceptions, errors, and malfunctions as part of the analysis of a business process?

13. Define each of the process performance variables. Describe how an information system can improve performance relative to each of them.

14. Identify some of the common forms of waste in business processes.

15. Why is it important to differentiate between personal, impersonal, and anonymous communication?

16. Why is it sometimes important to make communication systematic?

17. How is problem-finding related to problem-solving?

18. What is the relationship between rationality and satisficing?

1. General Electric once had 34 different payroll systems but reduced that number to one by 1994. It went from five financial processing centers to one. These moves allowed it to cut finance operation payroll by 40% and from 1,000 to 600 people over a decade.[47] Explain whether these productivity-related changes could raise any ethical issues for General Electric.

2. Federal Express charges incurred by the New York office of a financial services firm soared during a three-month period. People in the firm had discovered that sending a memo or file from the thirteenth floor to the fifth was slower using the company's inter-office mail system than using Federal Express. With the faster option, Federal Express picked up the package, transported it to Memphis, Tennessee, sorted it, and sent it back to the same building for delivery.[48] How is this example related to ideas in this chapter?

3. Great Western Bank in Chatsworth, California, started using a computerized 20-minute job interview in which the interviewee performs tasks ranging from making change to responding via microphone to video clips involving tense customer service situations. Bank managers say the system helps weed out the four out of ten candidates who would be a waste of time to interview in person. Some weary job hunters find that being interviewed by a computer is even more depersonalizing than a normal job interview.[49] Explain your view of the trade-off, if any, between productivity issues and ethical issues in this situation.

4. Assume you are a manager in a company where a computerized calendar system has been installed. The system requires that you specify the times you are available for meetings, thereby making it possible for people you work with to set up a meeting without a lot of phone calls and delays. Explain why this increase in integration may affect you personally in some positive ways and some negative ways.

5. Consider the following claim: "Most information systems seem to be designed specifically to structure work and to eliminate judgment on the part of workers." Cite examples and explain whether you believe this claim about the purpose of most information systems is true. Explain the circumstances under which you believe it is best to structure work even if that reduces workers' ability to exercise judgment.

6. You are a manager looking for an office assistant. You place an ad in a newspaper and receive 500 résumés. Someone has screened the résumés and has identified 400 applicants who meet all objective criteria you can think of, such as typing speed, business experience, and education. Describe the process you would use to decide whom to hire and explain how that process is or is not consistent with the ideas about decision-making presented in this chapter.

CASE   E-Stamp: Internet Postage for Letters and Packages

Every business that uses the U.S. Postal Service (USPS) to send packages and letters to customers and other businesses needs to use postage stamps to pay for postal service. Aside from producing mailings that look neat and are easy for the U.S. Postal Service to handle, businesses need to keep track of postage expenditures and make sure that stamps are not lost or destroyed. Various generations of postage meters have served these purposes for approximately 80 years. The postage meter is a machine that prints the equivalent of a stamp directly on an envelope or on a label that can be pasted on an envelope or package. For obvious reasons the Postal Service controls the leasing of the meters.

The market for postage meters and related services has many segments. An example of a product for large mailing needs is the Pitney Bowes DocuMatch Integrated Mail System, which "prints personalized documents and matching envelopes, adds preprinted sheets, accumulates and folds this material, adds a business reply card, inserts the complete mailpiece and seals the envelope. The final output is matched mail produced in-house at an average rate of 900 pieces per hour."[50] In contrast, the small-office and home-office (SOHO) market has much simpler requirements but is quite large. Monthly lease fees for postage meters for this market are around $20 to $40 and ink and reset fees can add another $20 to $30, depending on use patterns. Customers buy postage electronically, recharging their meters via modem.[51]

E-Stamp Corporation was founded in the mid-1990s to develop Web-based postage meters for the SOHO market. On August 9, 1999, after five years of discussion and negotiation with E-Stamp, the USPS formally approved the use of Internet postage. E-Stamp Internet Postage uses a digital stamp called Information Based Indicia (IBI). The indicia features a bar code the USPS uses to process mail quickly and efficiently. Account information and postage are stored locally on the user's printer in a small, tamper-proof electronic "vault" that allows the user to print postage directly at any time without connecting to the Internet. E-Stamp's hardware and software cost around $50 and can be purchased over the Web or from an office supply store.

E-Stamp's Internet postage system operates as follows: The user logs onto the Web and purchases postage in an amount up to $500 using a major credit card. Once the postage payment is recorded in the vault, the user can generate digital stamps at any time without reconnecting to the Internet. The account balance in the vault is reduced by the value of each digital stamp generated. The user enters the class of postage and either enters the package's weight manually or uses E-Stamp's integrated scale. The postage amount is calculated automatically. Data from an address-matching CD is used to ensure that the address has the proper nine-digit zip code.[52]

Disappointingly, consumers did not embrace online postage. Since the USPS refused to grant reduced rates, $100 of postage costs $110 and most small businesses will not pay 10% extra for the convenience of using the Web. The vaults are an additional startup expense. Furthermore, the USPS requires that both the digital stamp and the address be printed at the same time. If the address and the indicia information do not match, the Postal Service will return the envelope. This makes it difficult to use envelopes with preprinted addresses. To get around that, it is possible to print the indicia and address on separate labels. The user presses the indicia label on the preprinted envelope and throws away the address label.[53]

A July 2000 press release containing corporate results for Q2 of 2000 announced that it shipped 18,000 new E-Stamp® Internet postage starter kits during the second quarter, bringing total units shipped to 97,000. However, it listed revenues of $1.6 million and an operating loss of $28.1 million. E-Stamp announced "a shift in its business strategy including placing a greater emphasis on shipping and logistics as well as a refocusing of efforts within its Internet postage business. . . . E-Stamp will redirect its marketing, sales and development activities away from the stand-alone Internet postage piece of its business toward building its growing e-shipping, e-logistics and supplies businesses. The company will refocus its mailing activities specifically on attracting higher value SME [small to medium enterprise] customers."[54] E-Stamp's stock price had reached as much

as $44 in November 1999, but had plummeted to less than $0.50 by mid-November 2000. Later that month E-Stamp announced it would stop selling Internet postage.[55]

QUESTIONS

1. Summarize the steps in the business process of using Internet postage. Compare this with the steps of using a regular postage meter or going to a post office.

2. Explain whether there is any significant difference in terms of the process characteristics discussed in the chapter.

3. Explain whether there is any significant difference in terms of the process performance variables discussed in the chapter.

4. What seem to be the main competitive advantages and disadvantages of Internet postage?

C A S E   **Cisco Systems: Using the Web for Internal Efficiency**

With over $21 billion in sales and over 38,000 employees, Cisco Systems is one of the most highly valued companies in the world. It had the good fortune of providing routers and other components of the Internet's infrastructure just as the Internet was taking off. Other firms were in the same line of business, but Cisco found distinctive methods for servicing its customers, performing its internal operations, coordinating with its suppliers, and successfully acquiring and assimilating other firms whose products complemented those that Cisco already had. Cisco places so much emphasis on customers that customer satisfaction is an explicit part of the personal goals for a majority of its employees. Cisco actually outsources much of its production, and in many cases passes orders on to suppliers who send the product directly to customers without additional handling by Cisco.

One part of Cisco's success is related to the way it uses information systems, both its internal Oracle enterprise software and Internet-based systems that provided data and communication links for customers and employees. One advantage Cisco had in this regard was that it was founded in 1984 and therefore was not encumbered by the remnants of incompatible and poorly programmed data processing systems from the 1970s.

"Despite its central role as a maker of Internet equipment, Cisco discovered the power of the Internet almost by accident. In the early 1990s, Cisco created a simple text 'bulletin board' for customer questions and comments. In late 1993, Cisco engineers looking for a better way to interact with customers turned to Mosaic, the first Web browser. Cisco began using Mosaic, but there still was no commercial Web—customers had to dial into Cisco's computers directly." Cisco began using the Internet for selling in 1995. By 2000, customers, suppliers, distributors, and other business partners had access to portions of Cisco's internal Web site. In February 2000, 97% of its orders arrived via the Internet.[56]

Cisco's employees have come to expect that everyday data processing tasks that annoy and frustrate employees of most companies will be done quickly and efficiently through Web-based applications. For example, engineers, salespeople, and others who need to travel to customer sites can enter their expense reports using the Internet instead of turning in handwritten reports that will certainly involve delays and will have a higher chance of misinterpretation and errors.

Cisco uses a system of top-down transparency in which managers at every level in the company have extensive, up-to-date information on sales and other important business transactions. Cisco's sales database is updated three times a day, allowing Cisco management to keep close tabs on whether sales goals are being met. At any time, Cisco's chief financial officer can obtain the company's revenues, margins, orders, discounts given on those orders, and top ten customers—all for the previous day. Financial data that once took weeks to gather and verify are now collected automatically as part of doing business. This helps the company react more quickly to market shifts and competitive threats. It also allows Cisco executives to maintain tight control without suffocating employees' entrepreneurial spirit. Cisco has even shortened the time it needs to close its books at the end of each quarter from the ten days four years ago to one day today while cutting spending on finance from 2% of sales to 1%.[57]

QUESTIONS

1. This brief description of Cisco mentioned a number of different business processes. Identify at least three of these. For each process, identify several possible performance variables and related measures of performance.

2. Review the chapter's discussion of integration. Identify the different types of integration that seem to apply at Cisco and identify any ways in which Cisco might be more integrated than it already is. Also identify any possible personal or organizational downsides to its current degree of integration.

3. Compare Cisco to another organization with which you are familiar. What would that organization have to do to operate its important processes in a style more similar to the way Cisco operates?

CHAPTER FOUR

Information and Databases

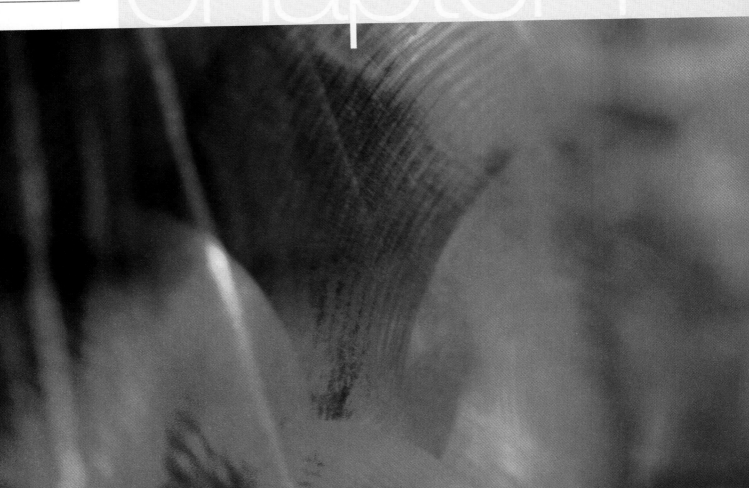

chapter4

STUDY QUESTIONS

- What are the different types of data, and when is each type particularly useful?
- What is the difference between a database and a database management system?
- Why is a single file often insufficient for storing the data in an information system?
- What is the role of entity-relationship diagrams in data modeling?
- What is the difference between relational, multidimensional, and text databases?
- What is a data warehouse and what is the process of creating and maintaining a data warehouse?
- What are the purposes of a DBMS, and what functions does a DBMS perform?
- How is the World Wide Web different from a typical prestructured database?
- What factors determine the usefulness of information?
- What is the purpose of building and using mathematical models?

Basic Ideas for Describing Data
Types of Data
What Is a Database?
Files
Logical versus Physical Views of Data
The Process of Accessing Data

Data Modeling: Defining and Organizing Data
Entity-Relationship Diagrams
Identifying the Data in a Database

Types of Databases
Relational Databases
Multidimensional Databases
Data Warehouse
Geographic Information Systems
Text and Image Databases
Hypermedia Databases and the Web

Database Management Systems
Defining the Database and Access to Data
Methods for Accessing Data in a Computer
  System

Processing Transactions
Controlling Distributed Databases
Backup and Recovery
Supporting Database Administration

Evaluating Data as a Resource
Information Quality
Information Accessibility
Information Presentation
Information Security

Models as Components of Information Systems
Mental Models and Mathematical Models
What-If Questions
Virtual Reality: The Ultimate Interactive Model?

Chapter Conclusion
Summary
Key Terms
Review Questions
Discussion Questions
Cases

Information and Databases

OPENING CASE

EBAY: PROVIDING ONLINE AUCTIONS FOR PERSONAL PROPERTY

eBay is one of the great successes of e-business. It started in 1995 when Pierre Omidyar's fiancée mentioned that she would like to be able to use the Internet to trade Pez dispensers with other collectors. Omidyar, an engineer at General Magic, decided to start an online auction in which individuals could sell collectibles and used items to other individuals. By mid-2000 eBay had 15.8 million registered users, and was hosting nearly 4 million auctions, with over 450,000 new items in 4,320 categories joining the "for sale" list every 24 hours. Its revenues for Q2 of 2000 were $97.4 million.[1] Unlike traditional auction houses for high-priced items and antiques, such as Sotheby's and Christie's, eBay holds no inventories, even for the duration of the auction. eBay developed in many directions that might not have been imagined initially. For example, items offered in many of its auctions come not from individuals, but from businesses that use eBay as a distribution channel. The top twenty sellers were responsible for 72,000 listings.[2]

The auctions operate as follows: Both prospective sellers and prospective buyers register with eBay if they have not already done so. Each person registers under a UserID—either an e-mail address or a nickname. A prospective seller describes the item in words, provides a picture if appropriate, specifies a minimum selling price, and explains how the item will be delivered. eBay creates an auction with a start and end date and lists that auction along with other ongoing auctions in the same category. Potential buyers register with eBay and look up the category they are interested in. eBay displays a list of all ongoing auctions. The potential buyer participates in the auction by looking at the highest bid entered thus far and entering a higher bid. The winning bidder is whoever has offered the highest bid before the auction closes. The winning bid is a legal contract to pay for the item.

Trust is a crucial issue in these auctions because the buyers and sellers do not know each other personally and may not be able to verify the exact identity of the other party. Among the questions are whether the seller is representing the item properly, whether the seller will deliver the item as promised, and whether the bidders are both willing and able to buy whatever they bid on. Recognizing these trust issues, eBay has developed a number of trust mechanisms. Its Feedback Forum allows an eBay user to check any accumulated feedback about buyers and sellers who have used eBay in the past. It automatically provides up to $200 in insurance (minus a $25 deductible) for buyers. It provides a link to a fee-based escrow service that allows the buyer to leave the payment in the custody of a third party until the buyer confirms delivery. Buyers and sellers can voluntarily request an ID verification by Equifax Secure, which posts an "ID Verify" icon on the buyer or seller's feedback profile after checking their eBay registration information for consistency with consumer and business databases.[3] To reduce the impact of occasional problems with Web site outages, eBay adopted a policy of extending all eligible auctions for 24 additional hours whenever an outage lasting more than two hours occurs.

Despite these trust mechanisms, cases of both buyer and seller fraud have occurred. Some buyers have attempted to purchase items with stolen credit cards.[4] Some sellers have sold items that were not described correctly. In some instances, rings of "shill bidders" have acted as partners by entering phony bids to boost the prices received in particular auctions.[5]

WEB CHECK [✓]

Look at eBay's Web site to find explanations of its trust mechanisms. Which would you use if you decided to buy an expensive audio system in an eBay auction?

DEBATE TOPIC

It is fundamentally unreasonable to buy things at auction and pay the seller when the buyer does not know the seller's identity and does not have a referee to make sure the seller is telling the truth and will follow through.

The eBay case illustrates the importance of information and databases. eBay is a pure information business. It handles no inventories and makes no deliveries. It creates value for its customers and earns its revenues by processing the information required to operate online auctions. To create this type of business eBay had to define exactly what information is needed to run online auctions and had to create and maintain the computer programs that capture the information, store it, assure its integrity, and provide convenient access to both bidders and sellers.

Given the essential role of information and databases in e-business, business professionals must know how to identify the information they want, decide whether it is adequate, and explain their suggestions for improvements to programmers and system designers. If you are unable to do these things, it is unlikely that you will be able to participate effectively in designing, using, and improving information systems for your organization.

This chapter presents ideas needed to describe and analyze the information and databases used in information systems. The first three sections provide the underpinnings related to defining data and databases and the last three sections focus on data as a resource. The first section defines what a database is and summarizes basic terminology such as types of data, terms describing files, and physical versus logical views of data. The second section (data modeling) explains how to summarize the content and organization of the data in a database. The third section compares different types of databases including relational databases, multidimensional databases, data warehouses, text databases, and hypermedia databases. It also discusses the World Wide Web.

Building on these explanations of how to describe data and how it is organized, the sections focusing on data as a resource begin with a discussion of how database management systems (DBMS) use data definitions and relationships to provide capabilities that make data more of a resource. Next comes a discussion of the value of information and the importance of information quality, availability, presentation, and security. The

W O R K   S Y S T E M   S N A P S H O T
Buying an item in an eBay online auction

CUSTOMERS

- Buyers of items sold through an online auction

PRODUCTS & SERVICES

- Purchase and receipt of items
- Information about the items

BUSINESS PROCESS

- Recognize interest in purchasing an item of a particular type
- Use eBay Web site to identify auctions selling these items
- Sign up as a potential buyer (if not done previously)
- Bid for the item and track other bids
- Pay for items purchased, making escrow or insurance arrangements if desired
- Take delivery

PARTICIPANTS	INFORMATION	TECHNOLOGY
• Bidders	• Terms of the auction	• DBMS storing data about items, sellers, and bidders
• Sellers	• Description of the item	
• Escrow and insurance firms	• User ID of the seller and buyer	• Bidder's PC
	• Bids	• eBay Web site
	• Past eBay feedback about the buyer and seller	• the Internet (infrastructure)

final section looks at the role of models in converting data into information needed for decision-making.

BASIC IDEAS FOR DESCRIBING DATA

We experience information in everyday life and usually don't have to be rigorous in the way we talk about it. Rigorous terms are needed for identifying and describing data in computerized systems, however, because building, using, and maintaining these systems requires precise answers to three questions:

- Exactly what data does the system include?
- How is the data organized?
- How can users obtain whatever information they need?

In the eBay case, the data was about items for auction, sellers, bidders, and bids. The case did not talk about data organization because it stressed other points, but eBay managers or employees involved with the auction system would need to know how to obtain whatever information they need. The starting point for attaining this type of understanding is a set of basic concepts about data and databases.

[**R E M I N D E R**]

Remember the distinction between data, information, and knowledge presented in Figure 2.10.

Types of Data

The five primary types of data in today's information systems include predefined data items, text, images, audio, and video. Traditional business information systems contained only predefined data items and text. More recent advances in technology have made it practical to process pictures and sounds using techniques such as digitization, voice messaging, and video conferencing.

Predefined data items include numerical or alphabetical items whose meaning and format are specified explicitly and then used to control calculations and transactions that use the data. For example, credit card number, transaction date, purchase amount, and merchant ID are predefined data items in information systems that authorize and record credit card transactions. Most of the data in transaction-oriented business systems is of this type, and the operation of these systems is programmed based on the meaning and precise format of these data items. An extremely costly example of the importance of format is the Y2K problem mentioned in Chapter 1. This problem would never have occurred if the data item *year* had been defined as a four-digit number in all information systems.

Text is a series of letters, numbers, and other characters whose combined meaning does not depend on a prespecified format or definition of individual items. For example, word processors operate on text without relying on prespecified meanings or definitions of items in the text; rather, the meaning of text is determined by reading it and interpreting it. We will discuss text databases later in this chapter.

Images are data in the form of pictures, which may be photographs, hand-drawn pictures or graphs generated from numerical data. Images can be stored, modified, and transmitted in many of the same ways as text. Editing of images provides many other possibilities, however, such as changing the size of an object, changing its transparency or shading, changing its orientation on the page, and even moving it from one part of a picture to another. Figure 4.1 shows images that were produced by different types of information systems. The computer-generated chart shows an image whose meaning is defined by the specific data items it summarizes. The meaning of the other images is much more open to interpretation based on the viewer's experience and knowledge.

Audio is data in the form of sounds. Voice messages are the kind of audio data encountered most frequently in business. Other examples include the sounds a doctor hears through a stethoscope and the sounds an expert mechanic hears when working on a machine. The meaning of audio data is determined by listening to the sounds and interpreting them.

Video combines pictures and sounds displayed over time. The term *video* is used here because it is becoming the catch-phrase for multiple types of data display that involve both sound and pictures, such as a video conference. The meaning of video data is determined by viewing and listening over a length of time.

Although this book discusses these five types of data extensively, other types of data can be important in certain situations as well. For example, taste and smell are important in the restaurant and wine businesses, and the development of a fine sense of touch for robots is a key technical challenge in that area. Significant research is underway related to providing computerized capabilities involving smell, taste, and touch.

The five primary types of data serve different purposes and have different advantages and disadvantages. Predefined data items provide a terse, coded description of an event or object, but lack the richness of text, images, audio, or video. When Nissan truck designers commissioned a photographer to take pictures of small trucks in use as commuter and family cars, they were startled to discover how little their trucks were actually being used for the purposes being advertised and reported in market surveys. One surprise was how many people were eating in trucks, "not just drinks, but whole spaghetti dinners!"[6] Information of this type probably would not have emerged from survey questionnaires or sales statistics.

Richer information is not necessarily better, however—it can be worse. For example, a car dealer's accountants just want to know how much the car was sold for; they have no desire to read a story, listen to a sales pitch, or watch a video. Predefined data items help them by reducing the sale of a car to a few facts they need to do their jobs. These facts might also be fine for a manager who needs to know whether weekly sales targets have been met. If the manager wants to understand why salespeople are having trouble meeting their goals, it might be more useful to observe their work.

[**L O O K   A H E A D**]

Figure 8.9 shows why images can be stored, modified, and transmitted in many of the same ways as text.

Images produced by information systems

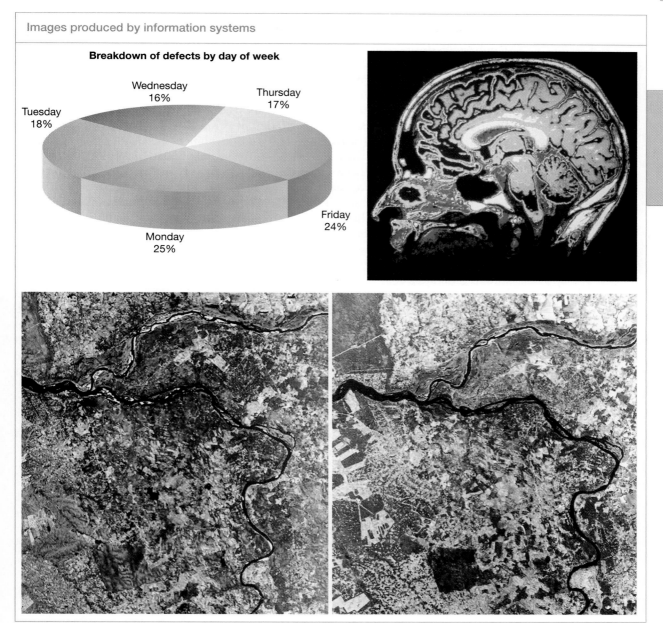

4.1

FIGURE

Different types of information systems produced these images. The pie chart summarizes network utilization data in an easily understood format. The MRI image of a patient's brain provides diagnostic information for a radiologist. The MRI combines multiple images into a form providing the clearest, most usable information. The LANDSAT satellite photos of part of the Amazon rain forest were used in an analysis of the rate of deforestation in that region. The rate was estimated by comparing a sequence of images taken at different times.

What Is a Database?

The data in a computerized system is often called a database, although the term is used in many ways. For example, people sometimes refer to the World Wide Web as a giant database even though there are no controls on the content or organization of the data. This chapter will discuss many types of databases, including text databases and hypermedia databases.

When used by itself, the term **database** refers to a structured collection of electronically stored data that is controlled and accessed through computers based on predefined relationships between predefined types of data items related to a specific business, situation, or problem. A database may include any of the five types of data.

By this definition, paper memos in a file cabinet are not a database because they are not accessed through a computer. Similarly, the entire World Wide Web is not a database of this type because it lacks predefined relationships between predefined types of data items (even though, as we discuss later, a particular Web page might contain links to other pages and might provide access to a database).

Databases come in different forms and are used in many different ways. Most of the work systems discussed thus far in this book use databases for storing and retrieving information needed for day-to-day operation of firms. The databases in these systems contain data about things such as inventory, orders, shipments, customers, and employees. Some of the everyday use focuses on retrieving and updating specific information, such as adjusting the units-on-hand of a product after each sale, or recording an order from a customer. Other everyday uses of databases produce summaries of current status or recent performance. Examples include a listing showing the total units on hand for each product group, or a listing showing total sales last week broken out by state.

In some situations the same database is used for both updating specific information and generating status and performance reports. In other situations, it is more practical to use one database (often called the production database) for real-time updating and to generate a copy of that database periodically for status and performance reports for management. If this is done, the copy will be up to one shift or one day out of date, depending on how frequently the downloads occur, but that is usually current enough for purposes related to reporting.

Notice the difference between the term database and **database management system (DBMS)**. A DBMS is an integrated set of programs used to define, update, and control databases. We will look at data concepts and databases first, and will discuss DBMS capabilities later as part of the discussion of treating data as a resource.

Files

The file is the simplest form of data organization used in business data processing. A **file** is a set of related records that contain the same fields in the same order and format. A **record** is a set of fields, each of which is related to the same thing, person, or event. A **field** is a group of characters that have a predefined meaning. A **key** is a field that uniquely identifies which person, thing, or event the record describes. Figure 4.2 illustrates the meaning of these terms. It is an excerpt from a hypothetical employee file that contains one record for each employee. Each record contains a set of fields, such as social security number, last name, and birth date. The social security number is the key because even two employees with the same name will have different social security numbers.

The order of records in a file also matters. The four records in the table are sorted by last name. Their order would have been different if they had been sorted by social security number. Sorting the data by social security number might be more appropriate for other applications, such as submitting payroll taxes.

The general description of a file uses just a few terms (file, record, field, and key) that are widely applicable and easily understood. With data in the form of a file, users or programmers easily can specify the subset of the data they need. They can select the records based on the values in individual fields. For example, they can say they want all the students who live in Oakdale or all students born before 1981. They can also identify the specific fields they want. For example, for a mailing list they can select the names and addresses, but not social security numbers.

Organizing data as a file works well when the information needed for the situation is limited to the attributes of a single type of thing, such as students, customers, or items listed in an auction. For example, if the business problem involved finding information about individual students, an expanded version of the student file in Figure 4.2 might be a good solution. Each record is about a particular student (identified by social security number), and the attributes include name, address, and date of birth.

Unfortunately, organizing all the data in a situation as a single file is often impractical. In the eBay case, for example, there is separate data about bidders, sellers, and

FIGURE 4.2

Excerpt from an employee file

the key

Example of a field

Example of a record

Social security number	Last name	First name	Street address	City	State	ZIP code	Date of birth
044-34-5542	Bates	Alvin	243 Third St.	Middleton	MA	02137	05/07/78
434-98-8832	Chang	Brenda	87 Palm Ave.	Oakdale	MA	02143	09/30/80
888-23-9038	Schmidt	Dieter	663 Cress Way	Cresston	MA	02184	12/17/79
334-59-3087	Toliver	Gail	743 First St.	Middleton	MA	02137	07/02/78

This excerpt from a hypothetical employee file illustrates that "last name" is an example of a field, that the data for Brenda Chang is an example of a record, and that "social security number" serves as the key because it identifies the person each record refers to.

auctions. Most business situations involve data about different types of things and therefore require use of multiple files. If you were using a paper and pencil system to keep track of this data, you would probably organize it into separate file folders related to each of these types of entities. eBay obviously can't use paper and pencil because it has millions of bidders, but the more general problem is that the data in different files is linked. The auctions involve items from sellers and bids from bidders. If all the data about the sellers and bidders went into the file about the auctions the data would soon be jumbled, especially since duplicate data about individual sellers and bidders would be repeated with each auction in which they were involved. As we will see, relational databases provide methods that allow eBay to maintain data specifically about particular auctions, sellers, and bidders, while keeping track of relationships such as who bid what amounts in which auctions.

Logical versus Physical Views of Data

Another basic idea about data in computerized information systems is that the person using the data does *not* need to know exactly where or how the data are stored in the computer. For example, a real estate agent wanting a list of all three-bedroom apartments rented in the last two weeks should ideally be able to say, "List all three-bedroom apartments rented in the last two weeks." Even if the information system accepts only coded questions in special formats, the user should not have to know the computer-related details of data storage.

In fact, even most programmers do not need to know exactly where each item resides in the database. Instead, users and programmers need a model of how the database is stored. The technical workings of the computer system then translate between the model of the database and the way the database is actually processed technically. Hiding unnecessary details in this way is totally consistent with the way many things happen in everyday life. For example, people can drive a car without knowing exactly how its electrical system operates.

The terms *logical view of data* and *physical view of data* are often used to describe the difference between the way a user thinks about the data and the way computers actually handle the data. A **logical view of data** expresses the way the user or programmer thinks about the data. It is posed in terms of a **data model,** a sufficiently

FIGURE 4.3

Different logical views of a database for different users

This shows three possible views of data about a company's employees. (This example illustrates the concept of different views of data in a file or database.) It shows a small subset of the data fields about a particular employee that might exist in an employee file. For that small subset it shows three of the many possible views:
1. Data used for sending letters to employees' homes
2. Data used for medical insurance
3. Data used for generating paychecks and paying withholding taxes

detailed description of the structure of the data that helps the user or programmer think about the data. This data model may reveal little about exactly how or where each item of data is stored.

Figure 4.3 shows how different users with different purposes might have different logical views of the same data file or database. Establishing and enforcing separate views of data for different users is one of the important methods of maintaining information security inside a company.

Logical views of data are important, but methods must also exist for actually finding and processing data via the computer. The technical aspects of the information system (the programming language, database management system, and operating system) work together to convert a logical view into a **physical view of data**; that is, exactly what the machine has to do to find and retrieve the data. The physical view is stated in terms of specific locations in storage devices plus internal techniques used to find the data. Because this book is directed at business professionals rather than programmers, it emphasizes logical views of data.

The Process of Accessing Data

Given a logical view of what the data is and how it is organized, the next part of a user's view involves data access. Concepts related to data access include push versus pull and preprogrammed versus ad hoc.

Push versus Pull   A basic choice in designing many information systems involves the difference between push and pull systems. In a **push system**, the information is provided to the user automatically. In a **pull system**, the user must request the information explicitly each time it is to be used. Each of these approaches has been used extensively.

Early information systems were typically set up as push systems, in which managers sometimes received enormous daily or weekly printouts (often called *reports*). Such systems were frequently the butt of jokes because the printouts often went into the trash without ever being used. The advent of interactive computing in the 1970s and 1980s made it more possible to use pull systems because the users now had a means to ask for specific listings or queries directly.

Push versus pull is an important question for many users of the Internet. Regardless of whether they often use the Internet in pull mode to obtain information they need for a novel purpose, some users also like using it in a push mode to obtain specific information that they want to see on a daily basis, such as news reports and stock prices.

Preprogrammed versus Ad Hoc   To provide preprogrammed access to data, programmers speak with users and identify a small set of queries that can be programmed once and then used repetitively. To permit ad hoc access, the users must have data access tools that allow them to specify individual queries that will generate the information they want at any particular time. Accordingly, push systems are preprogrammed because the user identifies the specific information to be provided on a schedule or whenever a triggering event occurs, such as a large swing in a company's stock price. Information requests in pull systems are ad hoc because they are specified for an information need that may never recur. Providing easy ways to specify ad hoc queries was one of the major breakthroughs in information systems. Before ad hoc query capability was available, users often had to ask programmers to produce special programs whenever they needed information not included in existing preprogrammed reports.

DATA MODELING: DEFINING AND ORGANIZING DATA

The previous section introduced the idea that a database might include data files devoted to different kinds of things, and that the data in these files might be related. This section provides the basic concepts needed to describe data and relationships within a database. Consistent with current system development ideas, the general discussion of these questions is introduced through **data modeling**, the process of defining what data is used or produced in an information system and how that data is organized. Data modeling goes hand in hand with the process modeling introduced in Chapter 3. The basic tool for data modeling is called an entity-relationship diagram.

Entity-Relationship Diagrams

Assume you were designing a registration system for a university. What data should the database contain? This question can be broken down into three parts:

> *What are the kinds of things this information system collects data about?* The specific things it collects data about are **entities**. The kinds of things it collects data about are called **entity types**. In a registration system, the entity types usually include courses, professors, students, course sections, classrooms, and perhaps many others. Entity instances of each type might include Economics 101, Professor Jones, Dana Watts, the Monday night section of Economics 101, and classroom E324.

> *What is the relationship between the entity types?* Relationships between entity types govern the entities of each type. The **relationship** between two entity types is the way specific entities of one type might be related to specific entities of the other type. For example, "student" and "section" are entity types. A student can be enrolled in no sections, one section, or several sections.

> *What specific data does the database contain for each entity type?* A database contains the same data items for each entity within a particular entity type. The specific data items stored for each entity type are called its **attributes**. For example, attributes of "student" may include address, telephone number, and whether or not fees have been paid. The attributes of "course" may include a description and a list of prerequisites.

These questions are the basis of **entity-relationship diagrams (ERDs)**, a technique for identifying the entity types in a situation and diagramming the relationships between those entity types. ERDs help in identifying the data in a system and making sure it is represented properly. They help create a shared understanding of the basic ideas underlying the specific data in the system. This technique forces people involved in the analysis to focus on the business situation instead of just listing every relevant item they can think of.

Figure 4.4 contains an entity-relationship diagram for part of a registration system. It uses one of several common notations for ERDs. This diagram identifies six entity

FIGURE 4.4

Entity-relationship diagram for part of a university registration system

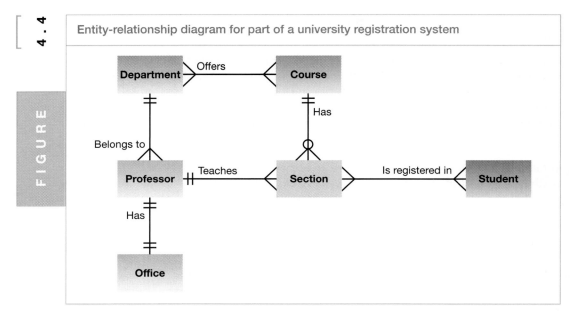

This entity-relationship diagram (ERD) identifies six entity types and shows relationships among them. The different types of relationships in ERDs are explained in Figure 4.5.

types and the relationships between those entity types. For example, it says that a course may have no sections or may have one or more, and that each section has a single professor and one or more students.

The relationships in Figure 4.4 apply at some universities, but they aren't true in others. Looking at the ERD raises questions such as:

- Does each professor really belong to exactly one department? Is it possible for a professor to belong to several departments or none?
- Is it possible to have several professors assigned to the same section? This would be the case for a team-taught course.
- Does each section really have a professor, or is the more appropriate term "instructor" since people teaching some courses may not be professors?
- Is it permissible for a course to have no sections? This would be permissible if a course in the catalogue is not offered during a particular semester, but the rules of the school would determine whether that is allowed.
- Is it permissible for a section to have no students? This would certainly be true until the first student signed up for it, but a section that had no students would make no sense after the semester started.

Asking questions such as these is essential in building information systems. They help determine what data will be included and excluded, how the database will be structured, and some of the ways the system will eventually detect errors. In addition, they provide an excellent communication medium for system participants who often have trouble explaining the current and desired situation to the technical staff building the system. The term *entity-relationship diagram* sounds very technical, but these diagrams are actually used for the nontechnical purpose of identifying the types of things within the system's scope and the relationships among these types of things (see Figure 4.4).

Identifying the Data in a Database

After identifying the entity types and their relationships, it is much easier to identify the data that should be in the system. For each entity type and relationship, this data consists of the attributes that are significant in the situation. Table 4.1 lists some of the possible attributes that might be included in the registration system for each entity type in Figure 4.4. As the analysis of the system continues, these attributes might be renamed or modified, and many other attributes would surely be added.

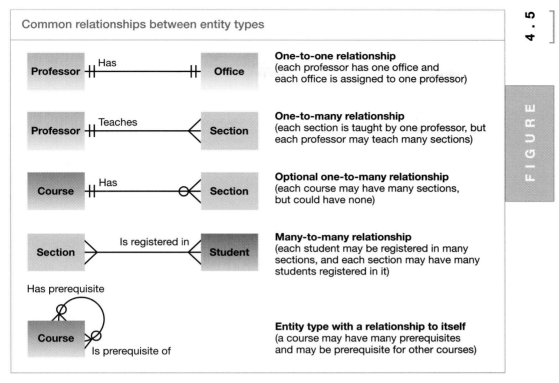

Common relationships between entity types

FIGURE

4.5

Professor ╫──Has──╫ Office

One-to-one relationship
(each professor has one office and
each office is assigned to one professor)

Professor ╫──Teaches──< Section

One-to-many relationship
(each section is taught by one professor, but
each professor may teach many sections)

Course ╫──Has──O< Section

Optional one-to-many relationship
(each course may have many sections,
but could have none)

Section >──Is registered in──< Student

Many-to-many relationship
(each student may be registered in many
sections, and each section may have many
students registered in it)

Has prerequisite

Course

Is prerequisite of

Entity type with a relationship to itself
(a course may have many prerequisites
and may be prerequisite for other courses)

The ERD in Figure 4.4 includes four common relationships: one-to-one, one-to-many, optional one-to-many, and many-to-many. Shown here are examples from Figure 4.4 plus one additional relationship not included in that figure. Other relationships not shown include either-or relationships and relationships between entity types and subentity types.

Believe it or not, the innocuous looking list in Table 4.1 could create a lot of debate among the users and designers analyzing the system. Here are some possible issues:

- Is any data missing about each entity type? For example, should the system include course prerequisites or the average grades given by this professor in this course in previous years? Including the prerequisites would be necessary if the system is supposed to check automatically that the student has taken all prerequisites. Including the average grades given by the professor might help students decide which section to attend but would also raise many contentious issues.

- Are some attributes unnecessary or inappropriate? For example, do we want to use the professor's or student's social security number, birth date, gender, or ethnicity? Attributes such as these might be needed, might be extraneous, or might be improper or illegal to use or divulge.

- Is there any ambiguity in what the various attributes mean? For example, does the professor's address refer to home or office? To avoid mistakes, separate attributes might be named "office address" and "home address." Even seemingly obvious terms often have different meanings to different people. For example, the *Wall Street Journal* reported that EuroDollar, the European arm of Chrysler's Dollar Rent-A-Car, gave one-week specials but considered a week to be five days. A traveler who kept a car for seven days was surprised to receive a bill for one week plus two days.[7]

- Do the same attributes appear in two places? Notice how office telephone is an attribute of professor and telephone extension is an attribute of office. This kind of thing causes confusion for two reasons. First, there are two different terms for the same thing, and second, the information system needs to have each item in one place to make sure it is updated correctly. Telephone extension should be either an attribute of the professor or an attribute of the office, but not both.

It would be easy to generate many more questions about the details of how things are named and what attributes of which entity types should be included in the system.

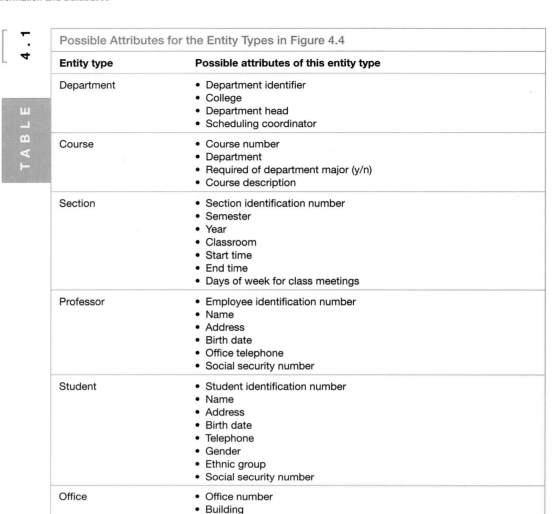

TABLE 4.1

Possible Attributes for the Entity Types in Figure 4.4	
Entity type	**Possible attributes of this entity type**
Department	• Department identifier • College • Department head • Scheduling coordinator
Course	• Course number • Department • Required of department major (y/n) • Course description
Section	• Section identification number • Semester • Year • Classroom • Start time • End time • Days of week for class meetings
Professor	• Employee identification number • Name • Address • Birth date • Office telephone • Social security number
Student	• Student identification number • Name • Address • Birth date • Telephone • Gender • Ethnic group • Social security number
Office	• Office number • Building • Telephone extension

This analysis can be tedious and requires great attention to detail. Notice, however, that the main questions are about the situation and the logic of the registration process, not about the details of computer technology. Answering these questions incorrectly could result in work wasted developing an information system ill-suited to the situation.

Data modeling is a comparatively new idea in building information systems. The first paper on the entity-relationship diagram was published in 1976,[8] but the need for this step is now widely accepted and has been incorporated into system development methods because it summarizes the business view of the data stored in the database.

R E A L I T Y C H E C K ✓

Data Modeling

We have introduced the idea of data modeling and have explained how entity relationship diagrams work.

1. Study Figure 4.4 and modify it to make it more consistent with your understanding of how your university's registration system operates. Add or remove entity types and relationships as necessary.

2. Study Table 4.1 and modify it to include other attributes you think might be important in the registration process. Include attributes of any entity types you added in question #1.

TYPES OF DATABASES

We have talked about data modeling to provide the general outline of how the data should be organized from a user's viewpoint. The purpose of this section is to introduce different types of databases, starting with the relational database, the type of database that links directly to the data modeling that was just described.

Relational Databases

The relational data model is the predominant logical view of data used in current information systems because it provides an easily understood way to combine and manipulate data in multiple files in a database. Posed in terms of this model, a **relational database** is a set of two-dimensional tables in which one or more key-fields in each table are associated with corresponding fields in other tables. (The term "relational" comes from the fact that relational database theory starts with the term *relation* instead of the term *file*. A **relation** is a keyed table consisting of records.)

Relational databases have the advantage of meshing with data modeling techniques. Entity-relationship diagrams provide a simple starting point for thinking about the tables in a relational database. The starting point includes a table for each entity type and for each relationship in the diagram. Figure 4.6 shows how Microsoft Access represents the entity-relationship diagram for a sample database supporting a retail chain's order entry system. Notice how each order is linked to a customer, a store, and an employee, and how an order can contain multiple line items, each of which must be a legitimate item in the item table. The representation of each table was adjusted to show only a few of the many attributes for each entity type.

Designing a database for efficiency requires a technique called **normalization**, which organizes the database and pares it down to its simplest form. Among other

Entity-relationship diagram from a relational database

FIGURE 4.6

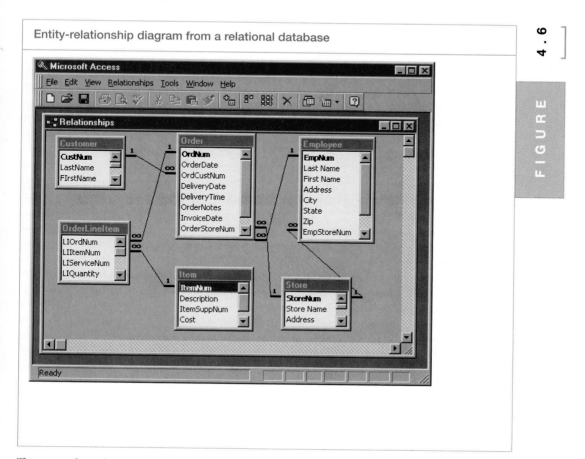

This entity-relationship diagram was generated from a sample database in Microsoft Access.

FIGURE 4.7

Posing a query in Microsoft Access

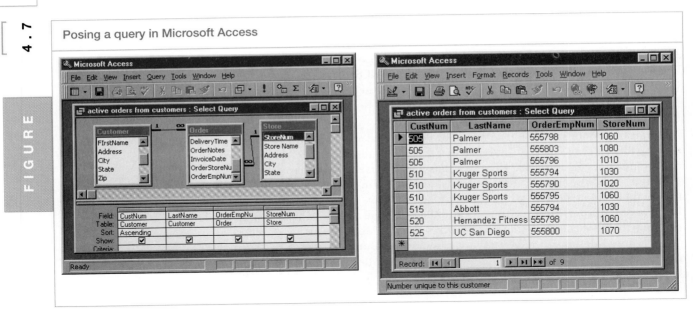

This shows a query that lists the employee number and store number for each order from each customer.

goals, normalization eliminates redundancies (such as recording Sam's home address in three different places) and inconsistent dependencies (such as recording Sam's home address in an order file rather than a customer file).[9] Going beyond just normalization, database designers must also organize the database to achieve internal efficiency by reflecting the way the users will access the data. This may be a simple question for a small database but quite challenging for a large database with stringent response-time requirements.

Although the internal structure of a relational database may be quite complicated, its straightforward appearance to users makes it comparatively easy to work with by combining and manipulating tables to create new tables. The industry-standard programming language for expressing data access and manipulation in relational databases is called **SQL (Structured Query Language)**, but it is often possible to pose straightforward database queries without using SQL. Figure 4.7 shows how links between several tables are the starting point for specifying the query without requiring the use of arcane computer languages. Figure 4.8 shows an alternative approach in which a natural language query system uses a situation-specific dictionary to translate a natural language query into SQL.

Relational databases have become popular because they are easier to understand and work with than other forms of database organization. Early implementations of relational databases were slow and inefficient, but faster computers and better software have reduced these shortcomings. For example, some relational DBMSs contain optimization methods that determine the most efficient order for performing the steps in a particular query. Most new information systems for processing transactions in business are developed using relational databases even though many existing systems still use older data models called the hierarchical data model and the network data model. Because users are shielded from the details of these older data models, we will treat them as specialized concerns of the technical system staff and will not discuss them here.

Multidimensional Databases

Relational databases bring many advantages, but they have shortcomings when the situation requires frequent analysis of massive databases. In many situations transac-

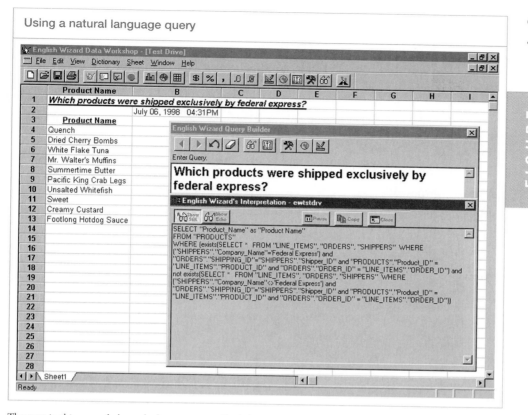

Using a natural language query

FIGURE 4.8

The user in this example has asked a question in English. Using a dictionary of terms developed for this particular database, a query program called English Wizard translates the question into an SQL query and produces the answer.

tion data collected in a relational database or other type of database is downloaded daily or weekly into a separate historical database designed for data analysis. The database used for data analysis is often a **multidimensional database** consisting of a single file, each of whose columns can be viewed as a separate dimension. The benefit of storing data in this form is that its structure makes calculations and summarization more efficient.

Figure 4.9 shows a multidimensional database of the type that might be used when a national market research organization collects weekly data about sales of thousands of products in thousands of stores across the United States. This database is a single table, each of whose records is a particular week's sales of a particular product in a particular store. The data can be analyzed from many different viewpoints to find trends and correlations involving individual products, groups of products, individual stores, and groups of stores. Note that the questions in the figure focus on calculations that look across multiple products, stores, and weeks. This type of analysis is sometimes called **slicing and dicing** the data because it involves identifying a subset of the database and performing particular calculations on that subset in order to answer a particular question. A typical marketing manager might want to look for trends by asking less specific questions, such as:

- Which products have the highest rate of sales growth in the last three months?
- Which product groups had the highest month-to-month sales growth last month in stores with above average month-to-month sales growth in total sales?
- Which groups of customers are increasing their purchases of these products?

These questions would have to be restated in an unambiguous form in order to specify a database query that a computer could process.

FIGURE   4 . 9

Slicing and dicing the data in a multidimensional database

The database is sales of four different products in three different stores and three different weeks.

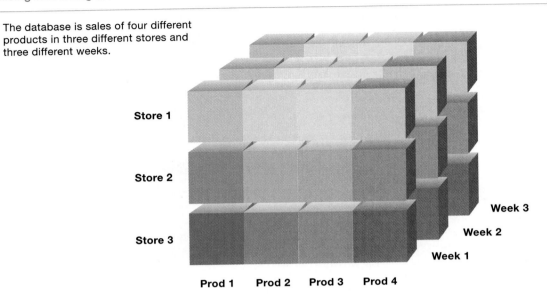

Store 1

Store 2

Store 3

Week 3

Week 2

Week 1

Prod 1   Prod 2   Prod 3   Prod 4

What are the total sales of products 1 and 2 in week three? (Select the sales for the two products in all three stores in week three and then total.

What are the total sales of product 4 across all three stores and all three weeks? (Select the sales for product 4 in all three stores and all three weeks and then total.)

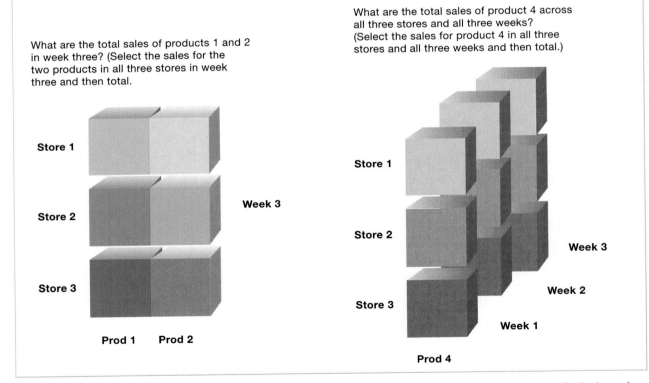

Store 1

Store 2

Store 3

Week 3

Prod 1   Prod 2

Store 1

Store 2

Store 3

Week 3

Week 2

Week 1

Prod 4

Each cell represents results for a particular product in a particular region in a particular week. The process of slicing and dicing the database selects the information needed to answer specific questions.

Data Warehouse

Multidimensional databases are the technical basis of most data warehouses. A **data warehouse** is a combination of a database and software designed to support business analysis and management decision-making rather than minute-to-minute processing of business transactions. The data stored in a data warehouse is downloaded periodically from transaction databases, creating a separate database that often resides on a different computer and uses specialized data warehouse software. This separation minimizes mutual interference that might otherwise occur if data analysis calculations had to access large amounts of active transaction data as the transactions continued. Since the data warehouse for an entire company contains data about specific concerns of different departments or areas of knowledge, a small data warehouse or a subset of a larger data warehouse devoted to a particular business function or department is sometimes called a **data mart**.

The process of creating and maintaining a data warehouse involves much more than just making a second copy of data. The full process includes the following steps: extraction, consolidation, filtering, cleansing, transformation, aggregation, and updating (see Figure 4.10). Extraction involves periodically downloading new transaction data from a transaction database. Consolidation is combining data from different databases into the appropriate organization for analysis. For example, customer-related data might come from a sales database, a technical support database, and a warranty database. Filtering is the elimination of data that is not needed for analysis purposes. Cleansing involves finding identifiable coding errors and duplications and correcting them to the extent possible. For example, software designed for cleansing data might be able to find multiple records that refer to the same customer but use slightly different names. Transformation is modification of data so that it is consistent with the data definitions, data formats, and coding schemes used in the data warehouse. For example, the codes for product types might be converted into a different coding scheme that is used in the data warehouse. Aggregation is the summarization of data into appropriate units for analysis. For example, daily source data might be aggregated into weekly data, or data for various versions of the same product might be aggregated into summary data for the product. The final step is updating the data warehouse by adding the new data.

[L O O K   A H E A D]

Data warehouses are used extensively for data mining, a topic included in the discussion of decision support systems in Chapter 5.

Geographic Information Systems

Organizing data so that it can be accessed by pointing at a region on a map has become useful in a wide variety of applications. Information systems that support this type of application are often called **geographic information systems (GIS)** because they permit a user to access data based on spatial or geographic coordinates. A GIS therefore includes both a database in the traditional sense and a way to retrieve or manipulate subsets of the data by selecting locations on a map. Many marketing and planning applications use GIS to visualize the density of current and potential customers or users in particular areas (see Figure 4.11). GIS can be used by police departments to visualize the relationship between crime frequency and police coverage in different precincts. They can also be used to control mobile resources such as trucks or emergency vehicles. The important difference between GIS and other types of information systems is not in the database per se, but in the way users access the data through maps.

Text and Image Databases

Databases of the types discussed thus far all consist of predefined data items. In other words, each record in these databases consists of fields that are defined in advance. Although these databases are the basis of most business information systems, text and image databases are becoming increasingly important as search techniques have become fast enough to find information within text documents and as computers have become powerful enough to process images efficiently. A **text database** is a set of text

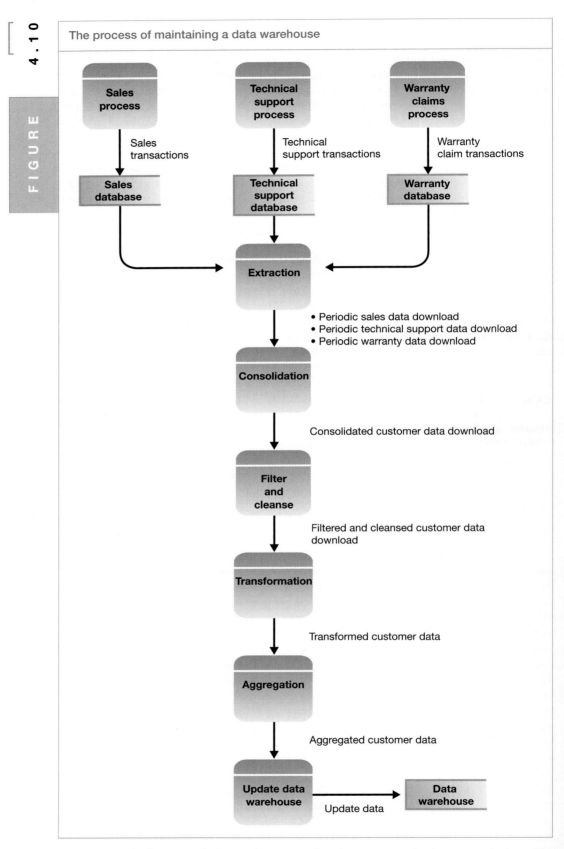

FIGURE **4.10**

The process of maintaining a data warehouse

In this example, the data in a single data warehouse comes from three customer-related transaction databases. The process of maintaining the data warehouse includes data extraction, consolidation, filtering, cleansing, transformation, aggregation, and updating.

FIGURE 4.11

Using a geographic information system

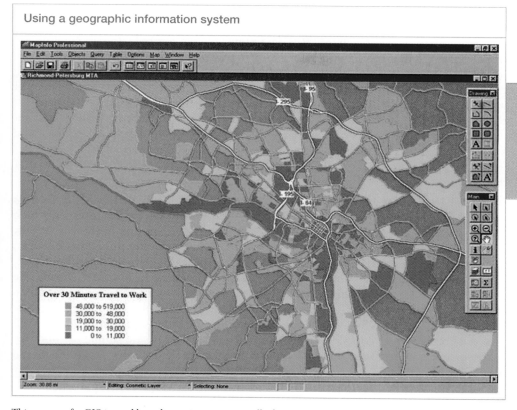

This output of a GIS is used by radio stations trying to sell advertising time and by businesses trying to use radio to sell to customers from particular areas.

documents stored on a computer so that individual documents and information within the documents can be retrieved. It is typically possible to search for particular words or groups of words within the documents, and to retrieve documents based on keywords that categorize the document. An example of a text database is the LEXIS-NEXIS database of legal information and news, which was initially available through proprietary software but was revamped for Web-based access in 1998. Its 30,700 news, business, and legal information sources provide nexis.com with 2.8 billion searchable documents, several times the size of the Web.[10] Corporate and government databases of important documents are another example of text databases. For example, the U.S. Congress uses a text database of bills under consideration and past legislation. Similarly, large pharmaceutical companies rely on text databases of their past and current research and clinical trials.

It is possible for a text database to consist of completely independent documents that are indexed into categories, but the ability to link any point in a document to another related document is valuable in many situations. **Hypertext** documents are online documents containing underlined phrases or icons that a user can click in order to move immediately to related parts of the current document or to other documents with related information. In effect, this means that selectable menu items are embedded in documents. Ted Nelson invented the idea of hypertext in the 1960s. It was barely used for several decades but is now the basic method of navigating within and between Web pages. The author of the hypertext document creates the link by identifying and storing an address for the related information. As is familiar to anyone who uses the Web, clicking on the hypertext instructs the computer to follow the link, retrieve a separate document if necessary, and display the part of that document referenced by the link. When using the Web, the link may go to another part of the same Web page or may go to a completely different page.

Image databases are databases that store images and their descriptions rather than just predefined data items or text. Image databases are increasingly important as the use of computerized images becomes more commonplace. For example, the efficient operation of catalog companies requires that they or their commercial suppliers of images maintain image databases so that the catalogs can be updated conveniently. A catalog company wanting to put its catalog on a Web site cannot just post an electronic copy of its catalog. In addition to creating a Web site that is convenient to use, it often must reformat the images and convert them to the lower resolution (72 dots per inch) of computer screens. Storing and revising a large number of images in different versions could become a nightmare without an image database to store and organize all the images.

Hypermedia Databases and the Web

In 1991, Tim Berners-Lee and several colleagues at the CERN physics lab in Geneva invented the World Wide Web as a way to extend the capabilities of the Internet, which had been created by U.S. Department of Defense research starting in the late 1960s. The original research goals were about creating reliable interconnections between groups of computer networks that might or might not use incompatible technologies. The result would be an "internetwork," soon abbreviated as an internet. During the 1980s the Internet grew from a research project to a network used widely in academic and research circles as a way to communicate by e-mail and share research documents, but the Internet of that time was difficult to use. The breakthrough in creating the Web involved providing an intuitive graphical interface, interactivity, and simple methods for retrieving documents posted on any computer attached to the Internet, regardless of the type of computer.

The Web is not a database because its contents are not defined and controlled. However, it illustrates the capabilities of a **hypermedia database**, a database that uses hypertext links to organize documents that may include any combination of text, images, data files, audio, video, and executable computer programs. For a hypermedia database to operate, it is necessary to have a way to identify individual documents, retrieve them when they are needed, and display them appropriately. Although the Web is not a database, its design provides methods for doing these things. Individual documents are identified as Web pages. A **Web page** is a hypertext document directly accessible via the Internet. The information on a Web page is conveyed to the user's computer in a format called **hypertext markup language (HTML)**. The fact that this is an agreed upon standard makes it possible to achieve interoperability between many different types of computers.

A Web page is identified through its **uniform resource locator (URL)**, which serves the same type of role as a telephone number. Just as a telephone number identifies the telephone that is to receive the call, the URL identifies the Web page that is to be retrieved. Users of the Web retrieve the information they want by typing the URL or by clicking on hypertext links that lead to other Web pages stored on servers that can be reached through the Web infrastructure. For example, a Web user wanting to access the Web site for Prentice-Hall, this book's publisher, would type www.prenhall.com.

The Web page is transmitted from the server to a browser program running on the user's computer. The **browser** provides the user's interface to the Web by converting the HTML into the screen display the user sees. Common browsers include Netscape and Internet Explorer. To illustrate what a browser does, Figure 4.12 shows the HTML and the corresponding screen display for a Web page that requests feedback about this book's previous edition.

The HTML tags shown in Figure 4.12 are the codes through which HTML defines the formats the browser will use when displaying the Web page. For example, any text that appeared between <B> and </B> would appear in a bold font. An important shortcoming of HTML is that its tags provide information about format but not about the meaning of the information. A number of industry groups are working on an extension of HTML called **XML (extensible markup language)**, which contains tags that define data in the same way that data field definitions define data in databases. For example, if

FIGURE 4.12

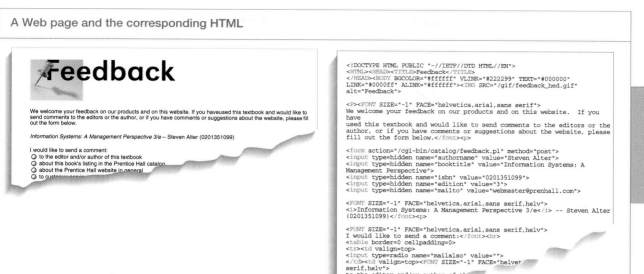

A Web page and the corresponding HTML

```
<!DOCTYPE HTML PUBLIC "-//IETF//DTD HTML//EN">
<HTML><HEAD><TITLE>Feedback</TITLE>
</HEAD><BODY BGCOLOR="#ffffff" VLINK="#222299" TEXT="#000000"
LINK="#0000ff" ALINK="#ffffff"><IMG SRC="/gif/feedback_hed.gif"
alt="Feedback">

<P><FONT SIZE="-1" FACE="helvetica,arial,sans serif">
We welcome your feedback on our products and on this website.  If you
have
used this textbook and would like to send comments to the editors or the
author, or if you have comments or suggestions about the website, please
fill out the form below.</font><p>

<form action="/cgi-bin/catalog/feedback.pl" method="post">
<input type=hidden name="authorname" value="Steven Alter">
<input type=hidden name="booktitle" value="Information Systems: A
Management Perspective">
<input type=hidden name="isbn" value="0201351099">
<input type=hidden name="edition" value="3">
<input type=hidden name="mailto" value="webmaster@prenhall.com">

<FONT SIZE="-1" FACE="helvetica,arial,sans serif,helv">
<i>Information Systems: A Management Perspective 3/e</i> -- Steven Alter
(0201351099)</font><p>

<FONT SIZE="-1" FACE="helvetica,arial,sans serif,helv">
I would like to send a comment:</font><br>
<table border=0 cellpadding=0>
<tr><td valign=top>
<input type=radio name="mailalso" value="">
</td><td valign=top><FONT SIZE="-1" FACE="helver
serif,helv">
to the editor and/or author of th
</td></tr><tr><td vali
<input
</
```

Notice how the HTML contains tags within angle brackets. These tags, such as <table border=0 cellpadding=0> determine the format that appears on the screen.

the hypothetical tags <order number> and <order date> were included in an XML Web page, the user's computer could display the page while recording the data in a database.

Browsers provide several methods for retrieving a Web page. The first method is to type a URL into a designated field on the screen and press Enter. The second method is to click on a hypertext link within a Web page. That link may be presented to the user in the form of a URL or it may just be an underlined word or phrase that the author of the Web page associated with a particular URL when the Web page was created. Other possibilities involve selecting a URL previously recorded in a file on the user's computer when the corresponding Web page was viewed in the past. URLs for these Web pages may have been recorded automatically in a history file or the user may have designated these sites as "favorites" in order to revisit them without searching for them.

Regardless of how the URL is selected, the following sequence occurs (see Figure 4.13):

1. The browser sends the textual URL such as www.prenhall.com to a domain name server to determine the numerical port address (such as 121.45.98.053) for the host computer that will supply the Web page.
2. The browser builds a request for the page that includes the port address of the server, a description of what is requested, and a return address.
3. The computer that is running the browser transmits this message onto the Internet, whose infrastructure routes it to the server that will supply the information.
4. The server processes the request, sometimes returning an existing page and sometimes building a new page in response to information the user provided by filling out an interactive form. In either case, the Web page is coded in HTML.
5. The server sends the coded Web page back to the user's computer via the Internet.
6. The browser receives the HTML and automatically uses this data to display the page on the screen in an appropriate format.

Included with the HTML may be **applets**, small programs that operate on part of the data transmitted to the user's computer as part of the Web page. For example, an applet might cause a logo to rotate as part of the appearance of the Web page, or it might perform calculations based on data the user enters.

[**L O O K   A H E A D**]

Other chapters will look at other aspects of the Internet. Chapter 6 will discuss "cookies" within its coverage of e-commerce. Chapter 10 will look at data transmission protocols on the Internet. Chapter 13 will cover encryption and other techniques used for information and transaction security.

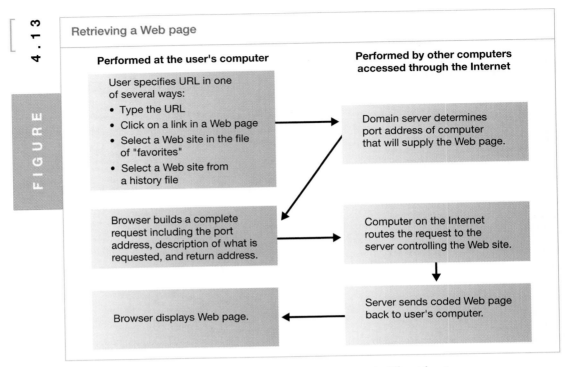

Retrieval of a Web page requires passing messages between computers in different locations.

Indexes and Search Engines   The previous discussion assumed that the user knows the URL of the desired page or that the author of a Web page has provided hypertext links to the specific Web pages that a user might want. What if this has not happened in advance and the user needs to find the desired information by asking for it without a link or URL? The query tools in a relational DBMS allow the user to express the query in terms of predefined data items and relationships, and therefore make it possible to specify exactly what information is needed for a particular query (see Figure 4.7). In contrast, query tools for searching the Web must operate in a different way because the Web lacks predefined data definitions. Methods for finding desired information on the Web and in text databases include indexes, search engines, and keywords.

An **index** is a list structure organized to identify and locate documents or portions of documents related to specific topics. The index at the end of this book identifies and locates references to all the key terms in the book, and to many other terms. A multi-layer index such as the one used in Yahoo! tries to divide all topics on the Web into a hierarchy of successively finer topics and subtopics. At any level of subtopics Yahoo! can identify finer subtopics or Web pages related to the current subtopic. Building and maintaining this type of index of the Web is enormously more ambitious than creating the index of a book because the Web's vast content changes continually.

A **search engine** is a program that finds documents or Web pages that seem to be related to groups of words or phrases supplied by the user. A user who wants to find out about vacations in Alaska can simply type "Alaska vacation" in a search engine's query box and click Enter. The search engine looks at a special alphabetical index that includes words used in each Web site that it covers. It identifies every site that contains Alaska and vacation and lists those sites. Entering this term into the Lycos, Google, and Excite search engines resulted in 87,000, 132,000, and 572,000 hits, respectively. The responses included things ranging from kayaking trips to apartments for rent. Identifying exactly what is needed is clearly a problem in a search of this type. Different search engines provide different means for specifying the search, such as saying that certain words must be included and that others may be included. Some search engines provide the capability to look for other sites that use words similar to those used by any particular site found by an initial search.

Search engines usually are designed to give extra weight to keywords associated with a particular site. As used in subject indexes in libraries, **keywords** are terms that describe a general area of information in which a document or Web site may be classified. Keywords are often useful, but they may be somewhat unreliable because the keyword may not be stated in exactly the same terms the user might express. For example, a book on information systems might be listed only under the traditional heading of management information systems. Another problem with keywords is that the mere presence of a particular word does not prove that a document is pertinent to the user's inquiry. Consider the topics *apple, jaguar,* and *shark,* each of which refers to a number of different things. For example, a search engine's response to the word *shark* might include documents about sea creatures, hockey teams (the San Jose Sharks), seafood prices (price of shark in fish markets), and even criminal activities (loan sharking). This is why search engines permit users to enter combinations of words and phrases to help eliminate the documents that use key terms in an irrelevant sense.

Compared with a traditional prestructured database, the World Wide Web's techniques of hypertext, browsing, and search engines have created a very different metaphor for dealing with collections of information. Table 4.2 shows some of the differences between a hypertext/search metaphor and a traditional database metaphor.

WEB CHECK [✓]

Identify a topic you are interested in. Compare the results from an index such as Yahoo! with the results from a search engine such as Lycos, Google, and Excite.

TABLE 4.2

Differences between Using a Traditional Database and Using the World Wide Web

	Traditional database	World Wide Web
Basic structural elements	Tables, records, fields, keys	Web pages and hyperlinks
Basic organizing principle	Predefined tables and relationships that have a specific meaning in a specific business context	Author-defined links from any location in a Web page to any other location on the same Web page or to another Web page
Finding specific information	Identify specific records or fields in those records and the DBMS will find them	Identify a specific Web address (URL) and the browser will request and display the page if it is available
Finding information related to the information most recently accessed	No typical method	Click on a hypertext link
Method for identifying data required in a query	State selection criteria in terms of specific values of specific data items in specific tables	Identify words or terms that should appear in the Web pages selected by the search engine
How the computer finds the data by searching	DBMS finds the pertinent tables in the database and selects the appropriate data from the records that meet the criteria	Search engine finds Web pages containing each word or phrase in the query and then prioritizes these based on the priorities in the query
Treatment of impossible or ridiculous queries	DBMS rejects queries not phrased in terms of tables, fields, and relationships in the database	The search engine performs whatever search is requested
Likelihood that a query will produce usable results	DBMS returns exactly what is requested; if the user asks the wrong question, the result may not be useful	Many of the Web pages found by a search engine may be unrelated to what the user wanted
Methods for controlling data quality	During data entry the DBMS checks for obvious errors such as missing values, out-of-range values, etc.	The Web has no organized method of controlling quality of information in Web pages

Finding Data in Databases and through the World Wide Web

The comparison between databases and the World Wide Web emphasized the way the structure of a database makes it easier to retrieve and control information.

1. Identify a database you are familiar with or have at least encountered in some way. Assuming it is a relational database, identify the tables you think it contains and the types of questions it can answer for users.

2. Think about how you have used the World Wide Web to search for information. Explain how that process differed from the process in the previous question and how the process affected the quality of the results you obtained.

DATABASE MANAGEMENT SYSTEMS

Thus far the chapter has focused on identifying different types of databases and introducing concepts for defining the data in a database. Since data should be treated as an organizational resource, the remainder of the chapter will focus on various aspects of this topic. This section will look at how database management systems are used to control databases and maintain data integrity. The next section will look at topics used in evaluating data as a resource. The last section will summarize the role of computerized models in obtaining benefits from an information system.

A database management system (DBMS) is an integrated set of programs used to define databases, perform transactions that update databases, retrieve data from databases, and establish database efficiency. Some DBMSs for personal computers can be used directly by end users to set up small information systems, whereas other DBMSs are much more complex and require professional programming. DBMSs include a query language that allows end users to retrieve data. DBMSs make data more of a resource and facilitate programming work, thereby making access to data more reliable and robust.

Controlling and Organizing Data to Enhance Its Value   DBMSs provide many capabilities that help in treating data as a resource. DBMSs improve data access by providing effective ways to organize data. They improve data accuracy by checking for identifiable errors during data collection and by discouraging data redundancy. They encourage efficiency by providing different ways to organize the computerized database. They encourage flexibility by providing ways to change the scope and organization of the database as business conditions change. They support data security by helping control access to data and by supporting recovery procedures when problems arise. They support data manageability by providing information needed to monitor the database.

Making Programming More Efficient   DBMSs also contain numerous capabilities that make programming more efficient. They provide consistent, centralized methods for defining the database. Also, they provide standard subroutines that programmers use within application programs for storing and retrieving data in the database. DBMSs free the programmer or end user from having to reinvent these complex capabilities.

DBMSs for different purposes provide vastly different features. A DBMS for a personal computer contains far fewer capabilities than a DBMS for a mainframe. The following discussion focuses on the range of DBMS functions rather than on the capabilities in any one DBMS. Business professionals unaware of these issues do not appreciate what it takes to use a DBMS successfully.

Defining the Database and Access to Data

DBMS applications start with a **data definition**—the identification of all the fields in the database, how they are formatted, how they are combined into different types of records, and how the record types are interrelated. A central tool for defining data in a

DBMS is a repository called a **data dictionary**. For each data item, the data dictionary typically includes:

- The name of the data item
- The definition of the data item
- The name of the file in which the data item is stored
- An abbreviation that can be used as a column heading for reports
- A typical format for output (for example, $X,XXX.XX or MM-DD-YY)
- A range of reasonable values (for example, the codes used for months)
- The identification of data flow diagrams where it appears in system documentation
- The identification of user input screens and output reports where it appears

Data dictionaries can be used throughout the system development process. In the early stages they serve as a repository of terms. This is especially useful for coordination when many people are working on the project at the same time. In the example in Table 4.2, the data dictionary might have helped identify the confusion between office telephone as an attribute of the professor and telephone extension as an attribute of the office. During programming, data dictionaries make it unnecessary to write the same data multiple times and help check for errors and inconsistencies. Instead of cluttering programs with subroutines that check input data, equivalent data checks can be inserted automatically from the data dictionary when the program is compiled. This is an example of setting something up once and reusing it so that the programmer doesn't have to recreate it repeatedly.

A data dictionary defines the data in the system, and therefore consists of **metadata**, data that defines data in the database. Aside from defining the data, metadata helps in linking computer systems from different vendors. This can be done by using interfaces that include the data (such as the data about courses and sections) along with metadata defining the meaning and format of the data.

The data definition for a database is often called a **schema**. Because some users may not be allowed access to part of the data in the database, many DBMSs support the use of subschemas. A **subschema** is a subset of a schema and therefore defines a particular portion of a database. Figure 4.3 did not use the terms schema and subschema, but the way it divided the file into data available for different purposes demonstrated the basic idea.

Although schemas and subschemas are logical views of how the database is organized, in order to store or retrieve data, DBMSs need a physical definition of exactly where the files reside in the computer system. This physical definition can be quite complicated if the database contains many different files or is spread across multiple storage devices in multiple locations. A DBMS must also reserve the areas in physical storage where the data will reside, and must organize the data for efficient retrieval. Because the number of records in any file in a database can grow or shrink over time, a DBMS must provide ways to change the amount of space reserved for each file in the database. After the database is defined, a DBMS plays a role in processing transactions that create or modify data in the database.

Methods for Accessing Data in a Computer System

A computer system finds stored data either by knowing its exact location or by searching for the data. Different DBMSs contain different internal methods for storing and retrieving data. This section looks at three methods that could be used: sequential access, direct access, and indexed access. Programmers set up DBMSs to use whatever method is appropriate for the situation, and shield users from technical details of data access.

Sequential Access　The earliest computerized data processing used **sequential access**, in which individual records within a single file are processed in sequence until all records have been processed or until the processing is terminated for some other reason. Sequential access is the only method for data stored on tape, but it can also be used for data on a direct access device such as a disk. Sequential processing makes it unnecessary to know the exact location of each data item because data are processed according to the order in which they are sorted.

Although sequential processing is useful for many types of scheduled periodic processing, it has the same drawback as a tape cassette containing a number of songs. If you want to hear the song at the end of the tape, you have to pass through everything that comes before it. Imagine a telephone directory that is stored alphabetically on a tape. To find the phone number of a person named Adams, you would mount the tape and search until the name Adams was encountered or passed. If the name were Zwicky, you would need to search past almost every name in the directory before you could find the phone number you needed. On the average, you would have to read past half of the names in the directory. As if this weren't bad enough, you would also need to rewind the tape. These characteristics of sequential access make it impractical to use when immediate processing of the data is required.

Direct Access   Processing events as they occur requires **direct access**, the ability to find an individual item in a file immediately. Magnetic disk storage was developed to provide this capability. To understand how direct access works, imagine that the phone directory described earlier is stored on a hard disk. As illustrated in Figure 4.14, a user needing Sam Patterson's telephone number enters that name into the computer system. A program uses a mathematical procedure to calculate the approximate location on the hard disk where Sam Patterson's phone number is stored. Another program instructs the read head to move to that location to find the data. Using the same logic to change George Butler's phone number, one program calculates a location for the phone number, and another program directs the read head to store the new data in that location.

Finding data on disk is not as simple as this example implies because procedures for calculating where a specific data item should reside on a disk sometimes calculate the same location for two different data items. This result is called a **collision.** For example, assume that the procedure calculates that the phone numbers for both Liz Parelli and Joe Ramirez should be stored in location 45521 on a disk. If neither phone number is on the disk and the user wishes to store Joe's number, it will be stored in location 45521. If the user stores Liz's number later, the computer will attempt to store it in location 45521, but will find that this location is already occupied. It will then store Liz's phone number in location 45522 if that location is not occupied. If it is

FIGURE 4.14

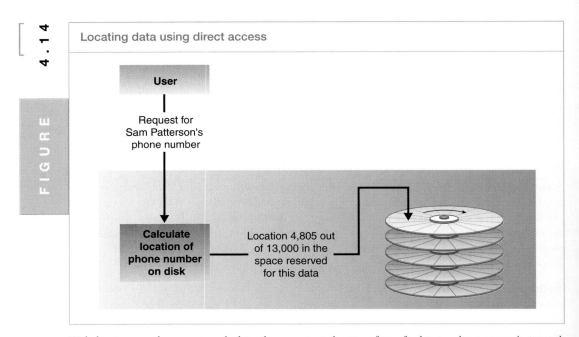

Locating data using direct access

User

Request for Sam Patterson's phone number

Calculate location of phone number on disk

Location 4,805 out of 13,000 in the space reserved for this data

With direct access, the computer calculates the approximate location of specific data in a direct access device such as a hard disk.

occupied, the computer will look at successive locations until it finds an empty one. When Liz's number is retrieved at some later time, the computer will look for it first in location 45521. Observing that the number in this location is not Liz's, it will then search through successive locations until it finds her number.

Because users just want to get a telephone number and don't care about how and where it is stored on a hard disk, the DBMS shields them from these details. Someone in the organization has to know about these details, however, because ignoring them can cause serious problems. When direct access databases are more than 60% to 70% full, the collisions start to compound, and response time degrades rapidly. To keep storage and retrieval times acceptable, the amount of disk space available for the database must be increased. Someone must unload the database onto another disk or a tape and then reload it so that it is more evenly distributed across the allocated disk space. Maintaining the performance of large databases with multiple users and frequent updating requires fine-tuning by experts.

Indexed Access   A third method for finding data is to use **indexed access**. An *index* is a table used to find the location of data. The example in Figure 4.15 shows how indexed access to data operates. The index indicates where alphabetical groups of names are stored. For instance, Palla to Pearson are on track 43. The user enters the name Sam Patterson. The program uses the index to decide where to start searching for the phone number.

Using indexes makes it possible to perform both sequential processing and direct access efficiently. Therefore, access to data using such indexes is often called the **indexed sequential access method (ISAM)**. To perform a sequential processing task, such as listing the phone directory in alphabetical order, a program reads each index entry in turn and then reads all of the data pointed to by that index entry. If the index entries and the data pointed to by the index entries are in alphabetical order, the listing will also be in alphabetical order.

Although they solve many problems, using indexes also causes complications. Assume that all the space on a track of a disk is used up and that another telephone number needs to be stored that belongs on that track. This situation is called an overflow. ISAM will put the data in a special overflow area but then may have to look in two places when it needs to retrieve a telephone number. Database performance degrades

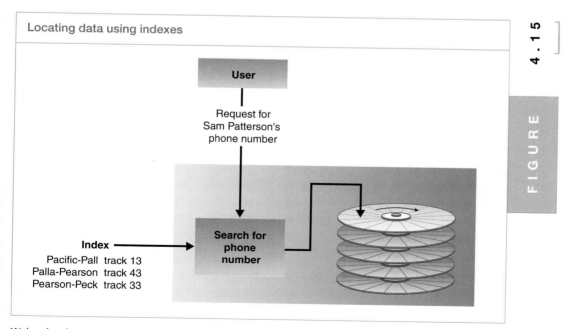

Locating data using indexes

FIGURE **4.15**

Index
Pacific-Pall   track 13
Palla-Pearson   track 43
Pearson-Peck   track 33

User

Request for
Sam Patterson's
phone number

Search for
phone
number

With indexed access, the computer uses an index that stores the location of ranges of data such as an alphabetical subset of a telephone directory.

as more data goes into the overflow area. As a result, it is occasionally necessary to unload the data, store it again, and revise the indexes. Once again, these are the details the DBMS and technical staff take care of because most users have neither the desire nor the need to think about them.

Processing Transactions

When a DBMS stores or retrieves a particular item of data, it performs part of the translation from a query or program instruction into machine language instructions. A programmer using a DBMS uses its data manipulation language to write commands such as "Find the next inventory record." In this command, the term *next inventory record* is a logical reference to the data. A **logical reference** identifies the data the programmer wants but doesn't say exactly how to find the data. The DBMS converts the logical reference into a physical reference, such as "retrieve the record at location 8452 on hard disk #5."

The DBMS also plays an important role in controlling access to data items when many transactions are occurring simultaneously, as happens in many business systems. Suppose that two concurrent transactions need to use or update the same data item. What prevents one transaction from reading the data, performing some other operations, and coming back to complete the transaction unaware that another transaction has changed the data? To avoid this type of problem DBMSs support **locking,** the ability to lock a specific page or record temporarily, thereby preventing access by any other process until it is unlocked. In transaction processing, a program locks a record when the transaction first accesses it and unlocks the record when the transaction is finished.

Controlling Distributed Databases

Ideally, a database should exist in one location and should always be updated there to maximize data integrity. Unfortunately this is not always feasible because many organizations are dispersed nationally or internationally. If the database is completely centralized in one location, each data update or retrieval from remote locations incurs data transmission costs. These costs led to the development of **distributed databases**, parts of which exist in different locations. Distributed databases have their own challenges, however, because decentralizing parts of the database to remote locations makes it more difficult to obtain a complete view of the entire database. General trade-offs between centralized and distributed database architectures include issues such as the cost of data transmission, the cost of synchronizing distributed parts of the database, and the degree to which the entire database must be current at all times.

A common alternative to distributed databases is database **replication**, in which the DBMS permits programmers to define complete or partial copies (called *replicas*) of the same master database at remote locations. Transactions performed using any of the remote copies are later transmitted to the other databases so that the entire database stays consistent enough to avoid confusion.

Backup and Recovery

Downtime in crucial transaction processing systems can virtually shut down a company. Therefore, the capability of a DBMS to recover rapidly and continue database operations after a computer or database goes down is essential. DBMSs contain backup and recovery capabilities for this purpose. **Backup** is storing additional copies of data in case something goes wrong. For example, if mechanical failure of a disk destroys the data it contains, backup data stored elsewhere prevents data loss.

Recovery capabilities restore a database to the state it was in when a problem stopped further database processing. As shown in Figure 4.16, the recovery process starts with the last complete backup plus a journal listing all the transactions since the last backup. The recovery process reruns all the transactions up to the one when the system crashed. That last transaction may be lost if it is not in the journal. Once the recovery is complete, processing of new transactions can continue. As with many other DBMS capa-

Backup and recovery

FIGURE 4.16

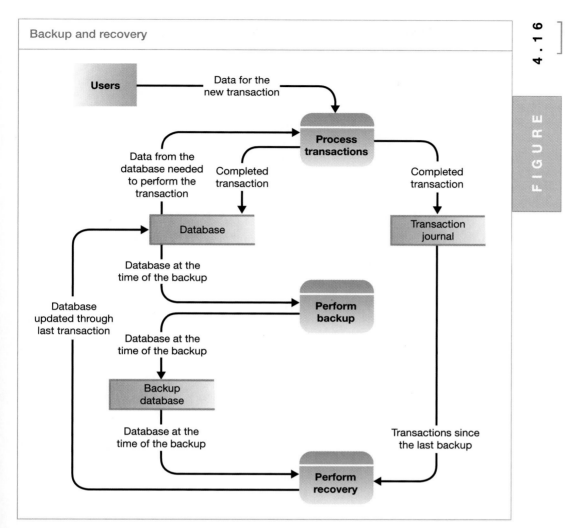

The normal processing of transactions uses the database and updates it. The backup process creates a separate backup copy of the database as of a specific time. When the transaction processing system goes down, the recovery process reruns transactions to bring the database back to its status at the time when processing stopped.

bilities, backup and recovery are functions that a programmer would have to reinvent with each information system if a DBMS didn't provide them. DBMS capabilities for backup and recovery are successful only when people who administer the database use them properly.

Supporting Database Administration

Like an automobile, a database is a valuable resource that must be monitored and maintained. The process of managing a database is often called **database administration.** The database administrator is responsible for things such as planning for future database usage, enforcing database standards, controlling access to data, and maintaining efficient database operation. Planning for future usage starts with monitoring trends in database size and activity. Along with user comments, this data helps in deciding what resources will be necessary to support future database use. Enforcement of database standards includes procedures for ensuring data accuracy and proper backups. Control of database access is accomplished by defining subschemas and monitoring data access. Maintaining efficient database operation involves monitoring the database and making sure that response times and other key indicators are acceptable. The internal record-keeping by the DBMS supplies much of the data needed for these functions.

R E A L I T Y C H E C K   [✓]

Database Management Systems

Roles of DBMSs include database definition, data access, transaction processing, control of distributed databases, backup and recovery, and database administration.

1. Think of a situation in which you have used a database or probably will use a database in the future. In what ways are these DBMS roles important in that situation?

2. The six roles are basically about formalizing rules and methods for handling data. Explain when this type of formalization is or is not advantageous.

EVALUATING DATA AS A RESOURCE

The use of DBMS is a method for making data more of a resource. We now turn to the question of how to evaluate data as a resource. The usefulness of information is determined partially by factors related to the information itself, and partially by the knowledge of the user and the way business processes are organized. The three main factors related to information usefulness are:

- **Information quality**: how good the information is, based on its accuracy, precision, completeness, timeliness, and source.
- **Information accessibility**: how easy it is to obtain and manipulate the information, regardless of how good it is.
- **Information presentation**: the level of summarization and format for presentation to the user, regardless of how good the information is and how accessible it is.

Since preventing inappropriate or unauthorized use of information is also crucial, a fourth area for evaluating information is **information security**, the extent to which information is controlled and protected from inappropriate, unauthorized, or illegal access and use.

Table 4.3 shows that each factor can be subdivided into more detailed characteristics and that information systems can support improvements in each area. Some characteristics such as accuracy can be measured without regard to the way the information is used. Others such as timeliness and completeness depend on how the information is used and sometimes on the user's personal work style. For example, some managers feel comfortable making decisions with much less information than other managers might say they need. All of these characteristics involve trade-offs between cost and usefulness. For example, keeping data more current often increases data costs.

Because the characteristics related to the four factors involve very different issues, it should not be surprising that information usefulness itself is difficult to measure. For example, although it is easy to say that a particular fact, graph, or newspaper article seems useful, it is difficult to evaluate its use without discussing other available information. Decision theorists have developed what is probably the best formulation of this issue, but their approach is more elegant than practical. Their concept of the **value of information** assumes that the purpose of acquiring information is to reduce uncertainty about a particular decision. If the decision would be the same with or without the information, it has no value for that decision because it does not reduce the uncertainty about what to do. It follows that the monetary value of information can be estimated by comparing the expected monetary value of the decision with the information and without it. Although it is difficult to assess the value of information in these terms, the underlying idea is still helpful for thinking about information systems. Whether or not it can be measured easily, the usefulness of the information in a system is related to the extent to which it influences decisions.

Information Quality

Information quality is related to a combination of accuracy, precision, completeness, age, timeliness, and the source of the information.

TABLE 4.3

Determinants of Information Usefulness and Related Roles of Information Systems

Characteristic	Definition	Related information system role
Information quality		
• Accuracy	Extent to which data represents what it is supposed to represent	Control data to ensure accuracy; identify likely errors
• Precision	Fineness of detail in the portrayal	Provide information with adequate precision
• Completeness	Extent to which the available information is adequate for the task	Provide information that is complete enough for the user and situation; avoid swamping the user with excessive information
• Age	Amount of time that has passed since the information was produced	Update information more frequently and transmit it to user more quickly
• Timeliness	Extent to which the age of information is appropriate for the task and user	Provide information quickly enough that it is useful
• Source	The person or organization that produced the information	Verify source of information; provide information from preferred sources; analyze information for bias
Information accessibility		
• Availability	Extent to which the necessary information exists and can be accessed effectively by people who need it	Make information available with minimum effort
• Admissibility	Whether or not use of the information is legal or culturally appropriate in this situation	No automatic approach even though it is possible to provide legal guidelines in an organized form
Information presentation		
• Level of summarization	Comparison between number of items in the original data and number of items displayed	Manipulate the data to the desired level of summarization
• Format	Form in which information is displayed to the user	Manipulate the data to the desired format
Information security		
• Access restriction	Procedures and techniques controlling who can access what data under what circumstances	Use passwords or other schemes to prevent unauthorized users from accessing data or systems that process data
• Encryption	Converting data to a coded form that unauthorized users cannot decode	Encrypt and decrypt the data

Accuracy and precision   The extent to which the information represents what it is supposed to represent is its **accuracy**. Increasing accuracy is an important purpose of information systems. For example, the scanner systems used in supermarkets and department stores provide more accurate information about what has been received, what has been sold, and therefore what inventory is currently on hand. Accurate information of this type makes it possible to provide the same level of customer satisfaction with lower costs for inventory.

The related term *precision* is sometimes confused with accuracy. Whereas accuracy is the extent to which the information represents what it is supposed to represent, **precision** is the fineness of detail in the portrayal. Assume that you had $5,121.68 in the bank. A statement that you had around $5,000 would be accurate but not as precise as the figure on your bank statement. On the other hand, a statement that you had $512,168.47 might appear to be very precise, but would actually be inaccurate, to say the least.

It is possible to measure both accuracy and precision, although the measures depend on the type of data and the situation. The typical measure of accuracy is error rate, the

FIGURE 4.17

Illustration of the precision of images

The precision of images can be measured in dots per inch. The image on the left contains 72 dots per inch. The same image is presented on the right at 2470 dots per inch, the standard precision for reproducing photos in books. Laser printers typically produce images at 300 to 600 dots per inch.

number of errors compared to the number of items. The measure of precision for numerical data is the number of significant digits. Figure 4.17 shows how the precision of an image can be measured as the number of dots per inch. The more dots per inch, the more precise the picture. This measurement is commonly used to describe the precision of printers, computer screens, scanners, and other image and print-related devices.

The two components of inaccuracy are bias and random error. **Bias** is systematic inaccuracy due to methods used for collecting, processing, or presenting data. An example of bias with far-reaching consequences is the way the U.S. consumer price index (CPI) is calculated. A study by the economic analysis firm DRI/McGraw-Hill in the mid-1990s concluded that the CPI overstated inflation by 1.2 points and therefore caused excessive cost-of-living-adjustments (COLAs) in social security and other federal programs calibrated to the CPI. Many economists agreed that the CPI was biased and believed retirees had reaped a windfall as a result, but that changing the calculation would have major political ramifications.[11]

Figure 4.18 looks at bias in a different way. It uses different degrees of "intended truthfulness" to show the range of bias that may occur in business information. Bias is rarely an issue in the raw data from transaction processing systems (such as point-of-sale and purchasing), which are built and documented carefully and scrutinized in many ways. However, as is often noted, data from these systems can be presented using biased graphs and models that exaggerate or minimize specific issues. Bias also pervades informal systems in many organizations, especially in the way verbal information and recommendations are repeatedly filtered and sanitized until their meaning changes. Bias may sometimes exist even when formalized modeling and forecasting methods are used. For example, a study called "The Politics of Forecasting: Managing the Truth" surveyed firms that used these methods and found that 45% of the respondents said that senior management frequently tried to intervene in the forecasting process to adjust revenue, cost, or profit projections to a more favorable level; only 16% reported that this happened rarely or never.[12]

A key point revealed by Figure 4.18 is that bias is expected, and in many cases even desired, in much important business information. For example, executives trying to

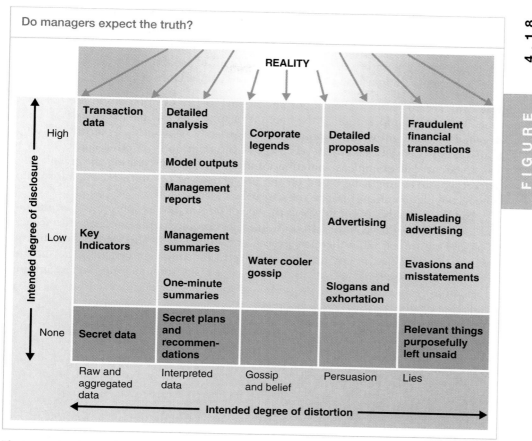

FIGURE 4.18

Do managers expect the truth?

The transaction data produced by formal information systems is only part of the important information people encounter in business. Raw data can be aggregated into key indicators. Data can be interpreted. Project proposals are produced based on personal goals and beliefs. Each of these cases involves a different form of expected bias in important information.

decide which manager's proposal to adopt are not always looking for impartiality. Rather, they often are looking for a combination of integrity, persuasion, and the passion to follow through and implement the proposal. The implied challenge is to be clear about whether interpretations and suggestions are meant to be unbiased, or whether they are meant to persuade and therefore stress some points and minimize others that might also be important.

The other component of inaccuracy, **random error** (also called noise), is inaccuracy due to inherent variability in whatever is being measured or the way it is being measured. The concept of random error is important for interpreting fluctuations in measures of performance reported by information systems. Consider a repair shop monitoring its work quality based on the percentage of customers who return with complaints. The average complaint percentage last year was 3%, but last week just 1% of the customers complained. This change may indicate that quality is going up or may just be part of the inherent variability in the percentage. Part of the random error in the data in an information system often results from inadequate data entry controls and procedures for correcting mistakes. Difficulty enforcing controls on data collected from numerous sources is a major reason for the widely publicized errors in commercial credit databases that landlords and merchants sometimes use to check on a tenant's or customer's creditworthiness.

Completeness   **Completeness** is the extent to which the available information seems adequate for the task. Except for totally structured tasks, it is often impossible to have totally complete information because some other factor might always be considered. In a practical sense, information is seen as complete if the user feels it is unnecessary to obtain more information before finishing the task or making a decision.

Like it or not, people must often work with incomplete information. For example, doctors at a drop-in clinic often need to diagnose and treat seriously ill patients without having access to their patients' full medical history. Similarly, business managers are often confronted with crises that need some kind of resolution immediately, even if more information might lead to a better or more comfortable decision.

Age and Timeliness   Other important characteristics of information are related to time. The **age** of information is the amount of time that has passed since it was produced. The age of information produced daily, weekly, or monthly by a firm's information systems is easy to determine. The age of information from other sources may be less apparent. For example, population information used in creating the sample for a marketing survey might be based on the last census or on more recent information such as population changes since the census.

Timeliness is the extent to which the age of information is appropriate for the task and user. Different tasks have different timeliness requirements. For example, second-to-second control of many chemical processes requires up-to-the-second data. In contrast, marketing departments tracking an advertising campaign generally are satisfied with day-old or week-old information. For other tasks such as long-range planning, information from months or even years ago may be satisfactory for the long-range trends that change slowly and predictably.

The recall of 1,800 Saturn automobiles illustrates the importance of timely information. These cars were shipped containing defective cooling liquid. Information from Saturn's dealer information network revealed a sudden increase in water pump changes within three days of the initial occurrence. All affected cars were recalled within two weeks, avoiding a calamity in the field. Without the information system, the defect would not have been detected until warranty claims began to arrive.[13]

Source   The **source** of information is the person or organization that produced it. The source is often a tip-off about bias—such as when one economic forecaster tends to be more optimistic than another. For example, during a vice-presidential debate on October 5, 2000, Joseph Lieberman, the Democratic candidate said, "the Senate Budget Committee estimates that Dick Cheney (the Republican candidate) has just referred to are the estimates of the partisan Republican staff of the Senate Budget Committee. We're using the numbers presented by the nonpartisan Congressional Budget Office."[14]

Information sources may be internal or external to the firm. Most computerized information systems focus on internal data, although external data is really needed for many purposes. This is why market research firms gather and sell data related to supermarket sales and advertising by the major competitors in a local market. Combining and reconciling data from internal and external sources is crucial in analyzing the business environment.

Sources of data can also be formal or informal. Formal sources include information systems, progress reports, published documents, and official statements from company officers. Informal sources include personal communications such as meetings and conversations during and outside of work, conversations with customers and competitors, and personal observations of work habits, work environments, and work relationships. Interpreting data from informal sources often involves much more intuition and experience than interpreting data from well-defined formal sources. Even inaccurate data from formal sources is usually organized and reasonably clear. In contrast, data from informal sources is often disorganized. When a manager hears a tense confrontation between two employees, the data may be fragmented, incomplete, and hard to understand. Yet that data may be important if those two individuals need to work together to accomplish the organization's goals. In such situations, managers must use intuition and experience to fill in gaps and decide what to do.

Information Accessibility

Information accessibility involves two issues: whether the information is available and, in some cases, whether it is legally admissible. **Availability** of information is the extent to which the necessary information exists in an information system and can be accessed effectively by people who need it. For example, data on a corporate mainframe computer may not be available in a timely fashion if a potential user cannot download it to a personal computer. Similarly, even information that can be derived from paper documents in a file cabinet in the user's own office may be unavailable if the analysis process will take too long because the information is on paper.

Information availability is an important determinant of how business processes operate. Consider the way Web-based e-commerce has made price information for goods ranging from office supplies to automobiles much more readily available. The availability of this information has effects on both buyers and sellers. Buyers have much greater ability to make comparisons conveniently and to receive merchants' sales efforts armed with facts about what their competitors are offering. On the other side, sellers have had to change some of their selling techniques because they know that their customers are better informed.

Admissibility of information depends on whether laws, regulations, or culture require or prohibit its use. This is an important factor when the use of age, gender, marital status, ethnicity, or medical condition might be viewed as relevant by some people and totally inappropriate by others. Such situations occur frequently in the course of business decisions such as hiring and promotion, assigning work tasks, determining insurance rates, and making loans. Issues related to admissibility of information are sometimes confusing because the use or reporting of such information is required in some cases and prohibited in others. Consider the idea of not discriminating against people based on age. How does this fit with the refusal of some rental car companies to rent to licensed drivers less than 25 years old?

Information Presentation

Information may be difficult to absorb and understand if it is presented in the wrong format or if it contains too many details. This is why graphs are sometimes used instead of tables of numbers, and why items of data are summarized into a smaller number of items. There are always alternative ways to present information to users, and the alternatives often have some advantages and some disadvantages. Graphs often make it easier to see general patterns, but they may hide particular items that are important exceptions. A similar thing can be said about summarized data presented in tables. For example, a 5% sales increase at a 600-product company might be interpreted differently if you knew that sales of 10 new products had actually gone down. This is why it is important to look for exceptions and other unusual conditions.

Terms used to describe data presentation include level of summarization and format. **Level of summarization** is a comparison between the number of individual items on which data are based and the number of items in the data presented. For example, a report combining 600 products into 4 product groups is more summarized (and less detailed) than a report combining the 600 products into 23 product groups. From a user's viewpoint, **format** is the way information is organized and expressed. Format involves things ranging from the number of decimal places displayed to the different ways to present the same material graphically.

Differences between individuals are also important to consider when thinking about summarization and format of information. For example, given the same information, some people will understand it more completely if it is presented graphically, whereas others will understand it better in tabular form. Fortunately, current information technology makes it comparatively easy for users to look at information in whatever form is most valuable for them personally.

Information Security

Because information used by the wrong people or in the wrong way can cause harm, it is necessary to round out the picture by mentioning information security, the extent to which information is controlled and protected from inappropriate, unauthorized, or illegal access and use.

[L O O K   A H E A D]

Passwords, encryption, and related topics are explained in Chapter 13.

Access restriction is the procedures and techniques used for controlling who can access what information under what circumstances. Although information systems typically are considered a means of providing information, many of their important capabilities involve access restrictions. The most obvious access restriction method is using passwords and other schemes for preventing unauthorized access to computers or specific data. **Encryption** means converting data into a coded form that unauthorized users cannot decode.

Access restrictions in most businesses are related to management choices about how to run a business with maximum effectiveness and minimum friction. For example, many organizations consider employee salaries privileged information even though top management salaries are reported for publicly traded companies. Yet other access restrictions are attempts to conceal information because it is embarrassing or counterproductive. Consider the 1998 release of internal memos showing that strategies and advertising campaigns of the R. J. Reynolds Tobacco Company had specifically targeted smokers as young as 13. A 1985 internal report on pretests of the Joe Camel ad campaign said these ads were well received by youngsters "due to the fun/humor aspects of the cartoons." A 1987 memo stamped "RJR secret" spoke of a new brand aimed at "primarily 13–24 year old male Marlboro smokers." The congressman who released these documents and also forwarded them to the Justice Department had presided over a 1994 congressional hearing in which the chairman of R. J. Reynolds denied that the company had ever conducted market research aimed at children.[15]

One of the ironies of the information age is that information technology cuts both ways in the area of access restriction. Passwords and other techniques can be used to restrict access, but the mere fact that so much information is recorded makes it much more difficult to keep embarrassing information hidden. U.S. presidents certainly have not been immune. Richard Nixon's Oval Office tapes played a major role in the investigation of the Watergate cover-up. Internal White House e-mail during the Reagan administration was important evidence during the investigation of illegal arms sales to Iran. The e-mail had been erased, but not before it had been stored on backup tapes. More recently, videotapes of 1996 fundraisers showed President Clinton seeming to acknowledge that some in the audience were foreigners, and then saying "I thank you for your financial contributions."[16] Because it is illegal for foreigners to contribute to federal election campaigns, the videotapes fueled an ongoing controversy about White House fundraising.

R E A L I T Y C H E C K [✓]

Evaluating Information

Information usefulness is discussed in terms of information quality, accessibility, and presentation.

1. Identify a systematic use of information that you have encountered, such as the use of standardized test grades to determine class placement, the use of medical records, or the use of teacher evaluations. Based on your experience, evaluate that information in terms of the various determinants of usefulness.

2. Considering the same information, explain how you might measure each of the characteristics discussed in this section.

MODELS AS COMPONENTS OF INFORMATION SYSTEMS

When managers and other business professionals need to make decisions, even accurate, timely, and complete data obtained through information systems and other sources may not provide the kind of coherent picture needed to make the decision comfortably. The person may need a model for converting the data into estimates or tentative conclusions directly related to the decision.

Recall from Chapter 2 that a model is a useful representation of something. Figure 2.1 showed examples of models. The dummy in the figure represents a person in a crash test. This example is an ideal use of a model because it permits testing that otherwise would be impractical or unsafe. The spreadsheet in the figure is a model that represents a situation mathematically rather than physically. Models stress some features of reality and downplay or ignore others. They are useful because they mimic reality without dealing with every detail of it.

Many information systems are actually models. Consider an information system that collects and reports sales results for a large company. Monitoring the company's sales by observing every sale would create an overwhelming amount of information. Instead, sales can be monitored by looking at a simple model such as the number of new customers and dollar volume for each salesperson. This model misses some of the richness of reality but contains enough information to support parts of an effective management process.

Mental Models and Mathematical Models

Two types of models are especially important in information systems: mental models and mathematical models. **Mental models** are the unwritten assumptions and beliefs that people use when they think about a topic. A sales manager's mental model might say that no salesperson with less than two years of experience can be trusted fully, or that repeat customers are more important than new customers. Figure 4.19 uses a diagram to show some of the interrelated variables in a manager's mental model of a marketing decision involving a new line of imported motorcycles. Because the motorcycle is produced elsewhere, the analysis focuses on advertising and hiring salespeople.

Mental models determine what information we use and how we interpret it. If our mental models don't include a particular type of information, we tend to ignore that information. The relationship between mental models and information usage affects information systems. For example, the sales manager who is very concerned about new prospects will find an information system inadequate unless it includes information about new prospects.

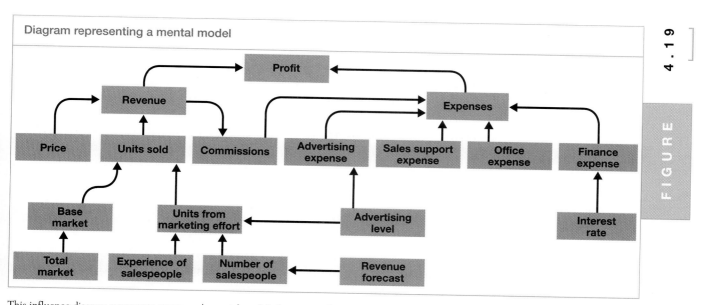

Diagram representing a mental model

FIGURE 4.19

This influence diagram represents a manager's mental model of a new-product marketing decision. Some aspects of this mental model might seem surprising, such as the belief that the number of units sold depends on the base market and additional units from marketing effort, but doesn't depend on price. To produce monetary estimates of revenues and profits, it would be necessary to describe each relationship precisely as part of a mathematical model.

Although mental models are essential for organizing and interpreting information, they are often inconsistent. For example, a senator's mental models might include a series of ideas about the burden of excess debt plus a set of other ideas about the necessity of using debt to finance business growth. Such inconsistencies between vague mental models often make it difficult to think through the consequences of decisions. This is one of the advantages of mathematical models.

A **mathematical model** is a series of equations or graphs that describe precise relationships between variables. The explicit nature of a mathematical model forces people to say exactly what they mean, which clarifies and organizes various mental models that may be pertinent to a decision.

Both mental and mathematical models provide ways to distill the meaning of information for a particular situation. Mental models identify the factors that are important and the general way the factors interact. Mathematical models express these ideas precisely and produce more precise conclusions.

More important, mathematical models compensate for our inability to pay attention to hundreds of things at the same time. Putting a large number of tiny models into a single mathematical model helps organize an analysis and ensures that many factors have been considered, even if a person cannot think about all of these factors at the same time. Keeping track of which factors have been considered, and in what way, is especially important when a group discusses a decision. Because each individual has different mental models, a mathematical model helps everyone focus on the same issues and visualize what has or has not been included.

What-If Questions

Mathematical models convert data into information by performing calculations that combine many elements, by evaluating tentative decisions, and by responding to what-if questions. Tentative decisions are possible decisions that users try out as part of the decision-making process. Users try these out by setting values of decision variables in the model. In a planning model for a bank, these decisions might include the number of people hired and the prices to be charged for services such as checking accounts. The model might start with tentative decisions and then calculate the value of other variables, such as expenses, profit, and estimated market share. These calculated variables could be used to think about whether the tentative decisions are wise.

Mathematical models also make it easy to ask **what-if questions**, which explore the effect of alternative assumptions about key variables. For example, a bank's planning model may contain the assumption that it will be able to make loans next year at 7% interest. Bank managers might want to see whether the bank will still be profitable if the interest rate drops to 5% or if it takes six extra months to roll out a new service.

Using an organized sequence of what-if questions to study the model's outputs under different circumstances is called **sensitivity analysis**. A sensitivity analysis determines how much the results of the model change when a decision or important assumption changes by a small amount or a progression of amounts. If a large change in a variable generates a small change in the results, that variable probably doesn't affect the decision very much. If a small change in a variable generates a disproportionate change in the results, this indicates that something is wrong either with the model or with the user's understanding of the model.

Virtual Reality: The Ultimate Interactive Model?

Virtual reality is a special type of model that is becoming important in entertainment and may become important in business. **Virtual reality** is a simulation of reality that engages the participant's senses and intellect by permitting the participant to interact with the simulated environment. The person wearing the helmet in Figure 4.20 is being trained to interact with an environment using a virtual reality simulation using a data glove. Flight training for pilots is one of the most extensive uses of virtual reality. It can also be used to support telepresence, the ability to view and manipulate things in a distant, dangerous, or unreachable environment such as the surface of the

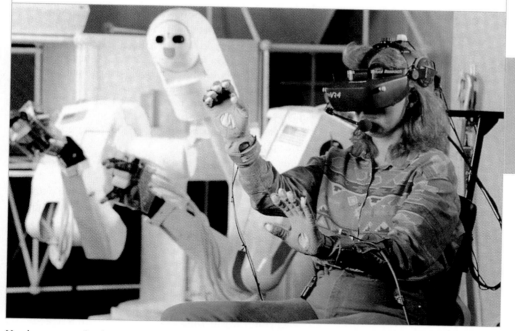

A virtual reality application

FIGURE 4.20

Hand movements by the engineer in the foreground are controlling the movements of the white robot in the background. NASA developed this VR robot for use in dangerous environments such as planetary exploration or work in the presence of radioactivity.

moon, the part of a chemical plant where a dangerous spill has just occurred, or the interior of a blood vessel. In one of the first uses of virtual reality in entertainment, VR movie theaters that appeared in Los Angeles and Las Vegas in 1993 used sight, sound, and motion to simulate a flight through an adventure environment. Instead of feeling like people sitting in a theater seat munching popcorn, audience members feel like participants because of the intense, coordinated sensations of movement, light, and sound.

The idea of virtual reality clarifies the breadth and scope of information systems. Most systems covered in this book provide useful information because they model reality as a small number of specific types of data, such as orders, customers, and schedules. They purposely filter out huge amounts of extraneous information that might have been captured. Virtual reality goes in the opposite direction by bombarding the user with sensory information, sometimes to the point of overload. A challenge for future information systems is to enhance the scope and richness of information while remaining coherent and understandable.

REALITY CHECK ✓

Models as Components of Information Systems

This section explained why models are often needed to convert data into information.

1. Think about the information needs of the president of a university or coach of a football team. In what ways might models be important to draw conclusions from information that is probably available from transaction databases, from external text databases, and from informal sources?

2. Assume you were helping a university president analyze the possible impact of a sequence of tuition increases over the next several years. What factors would you include in the model, and what potentially relevant factors do you think you would leave out?

CHAPTER CONCLUSION

What are the different types of data, and when is each type particularly useful?

The types of data include predefined data items, text, images, audio, and video. Predefined data items are used to reduce reality to a manageable number of salient facts that can be recorded and retrieved for performing specific tasks. Text can convey more information about unique circumstances of a situation. Images, audio, and video add more richness.

What is the difference between a database and a database management system?

The data in a computerized system is often called a database, although the term is used in many ways. For our purposes, a database is a structured collection of data stored, controlled, and accessed through a computer based on predefined, situation-specific relationships between the data items. A database management system (DBMS) is an integrated set of programs used to define, update, and control databases.

Why is a single file often insufficient for storing the data in an information system?

A file is a set of related records. In data modeling terms, a file contains data about the entities of the same entity type. It is often impractical to identify all the data in a situation using a single file because many situations involve relationships between entities of different types.

What is the role of entity-relationship diagrams in data modeling?

Data modeling is the process of creating a graphical model identifying the types of entities in a situation, relationships between those entities, and the relevant attributes of those entities. It helps create a shared understanding of the data in the system and forces users to focus on the business situation instead of just listing relevant data items. The entity-relationship diagram is a technique for identifying the entity types in a situation and diagramming the relationships between those entity types.

What is the difference between relational, multidimensional, and text databases?

A relational database is a set of two-dimensional tables in which one or more key-fields in each table are associated with corresponding key- or non-key-fields in other tables. Relational databases have become popular because they are easier to understand and work with than other forms of database organization. A multidimensional database consists of a single file, each of whose columns can be viewed as a separate dimension. These databases are typically used for analyzing data and typically are updated through downloads from transaction databases. A text database is a set of documents stored on a computer so that individual documents and information within the documents can be retrieved.

What is a data warehouse and what is the process of creating and maintaining a data warehouse?

A data warehouse is a combination of a database and software designed to support business analysis and management decision-making rather than minute-to-minute processing of business transactions. The process of creating and maintaining a data warehouse includes the following steps: extraction, consolidation, filtering, cleansing, transformation, aggregation, and updating.

What are the purposes of a DBMS, and what functions does a DBMS perform?

The two major purposes of a DBMS are making data more of a resource for an organization and making programming work more effective and efficient. A DBMS is used by programmers and end users to perform a variety of functions, including defining the database, providing data access, performing the transactions that update the database, controlling distributed databases, performing backup and recovery, and supporting database administration.

How is the World Wide Web different from a typical prestructured database?

Instead of predefined tables, relationships, fields, and keys, the structural elements of the WWW are hypertext Web pages and hyperlinks. Its organizing principle is author-defined links to other locations on the WWW. Specific information is located through a URL rather than through identifying data items in a structured database. Instead of selecting data from prestructured database records that meet the user's criteria, WWW search engines search for Web pages containing the desired words or phrases.

What factors determine the usefulness of information?

Information quality is based on accuracy, precision, completeness, age, timeliness, and source. Information accessibility is related to how easy it is to obtain and manipulate the information, regardless of its quality. Information presentation is related to the level of summarization and format for presentation to the user, regardless of information quality and accessibility. A fourth factor is information security, the extent to which information is controlled and protected from inappropriate, unauthorized, or illegal access and use.

What is the purpose of building and using mathematical models?

Models are useful because they mimic reality without dealing with every detail of it. Mathematical models are sets of equations or graphs that describe precise relationships between variables. They compensate for our inability to pay attention to hundreds of things at the same time and help organize an analysis. They also create information by evaluating tentative decisions and responding to what-ifs.

predefined data items
text
image
audio
video
database
database management system
   (DBMS)
file
record
field
key
logical view of data
data model
physical view of data
push system
pull system
data modeling
entity
entity type
relationship
attributes
entity-relationship diagram (ERD)
relational database
relation
normalization
SQL (Structured Query Language)
multidimensional database
slicing and dicing
data warehouse

data mart
geographic information system
   (GIS)
text database
hypertext
image database
hypermedia database
Web page
hypertext markup language
   (HTML)
uniform resource locator (URL)
extensible markup language (XML)
browser
applet
index
search engine
keyword
data definition
data dictionary
metadata
schema
subschema
sequential access
direct access
collision
indexed access
indexed sequential access
   method (ISAM)
logical reference
locking

distributed database
replication
backup
recovery
database administration
information quality
information accessibility
information presentation
information security
value of information
accuracy
precision
bias
random error
completeness
age
timeliness
source
availability
admissibility
level of summarization
format
access restriction
encryption
mental model
mathematical model
what-if question
sensitivity analysis
virtual reality

1.   What five types of data are found in information systems?

2.   What is a file?

3.   What is the difference between a database and a database management system?

4.   What is the difference between a logical and physical view of data?

5.   What is data modeling?

6.   What is the difference between an entity and an entity type?

7.   Describe some typical attributes of the entity type *patient*.

8.   What is an entity-relationship diagram, and why is this technique important?

9.   Why does defining the data in a database sometimes generate debate?

10.   Explain why it is often impractical to organize all data in a given situation as an individual file.

11.   What is a relational database?

12.   What is a data warehouse?

13.   What is the difference between a conventional paper document and a hypertext document?

14.   What is the difference between HTML and XML?

15.   How is an index different from a search engine?

16. What is metadata?

17. Explain the difference between a schema and a subschema, and why this is important.

18. Define backup and recovery, and explain why these capabilities are needed in a DBMS.

19. Identify characteristics that constitute information quality, accessibility, and presentation of information.

20. Explain how bias is a component of inaccuracy and whether total objectivity is always desired.

21. Describe the difference between mental and mathematical models.

22. What are the advantages of asking what-if questions?

DISCUSSION QUESTIONS

1. The chapter's discussion of accuracy raised the issue that people may intentionally shade or distort the truth. A survey published in the British medical journal *Lancet* asked doctors in Europe how they would break bad news about a cancer diagnosis. The survey found that doctors in Scandinavia, Great Britain, and the Netherlands would be the frankest with their patients, but doctors in southern and eastern Europe generally said they would be evasive even if asked directly by their patients.[17] Explain why this is or is not related to truthfulness of management explanations and recommendations.

2. Virginia Senator John Warner, ranking Republican on the Intelligence subcommittee, said, "I was astonished at the magnitude of the site." The Clinton Administration had just declassified information about a $310 million project to create a 70-acre office complex for the National Reconnaissance Office, which procures the nation's space-satellite systems. Senator Warner said that the full scope of the project, which had been approved and started during the Bush Administration, hadn't been authorized or appropriated by Congress, as is required by law.[18] How are ideas in this chapter related to this situation? What does this situation imply about information systems in general?

3. Identify some of the important databases the following individuals might encounter in their work. Identify some of the files in these databases, and the important fields in each file: a) factory manager, b) owner of a construction company, c) loan officer in a bank, d) mechanic working in a large automobile repair shop.

4. A distributor of building supplies for construction contractors has a database involving three types of entities: suppliers, products, and customers. Identify some of the important attributes of each type of entity. Based on your own background and intuition, try to sketch out an entity-relationship diagram and a set of relations that might be applicable in this case.

5. A family uses a database to identify all of its belongings. Assuming the database consists of a single file, identify 10 fields that might appear in the database. Explain advantages and disadvantages of having different files for different types of belongings. Show the structure of a database that has different types of records for different types of belongings. Think about how you would include things such as the person in the family who owned the item, what room in the house it was in, and when it was purchased.

6. Explain how models might be used in making the following decisions: a) deciding how much to pay for an apartment building, b) deciding which products to carry in a grocery store, c) deciding how to allocate a stock portfolio, d) deciding whom to marry.

CASE   U.S. House of Representatives: Patients' Bill of Rights Act of 1998

The rapid growth of health maintenance organizations (HMOs) and managed care was a hot button issue because it involved contradictory goals. On one side, people wanted to be able to choose their own doctors and to receive convenient, high-quality medical care. On the other side, reducing medical costs was a key issue for anyone paying medical insurance premiums, primarily businesses and government organizations, but also self-employed individuals who pay for themselves. Doctors, hospitals, and HMOs were caught in the middle because greater patient choice and higher quality care are more expensive to deliver. The resulting tug of war left many stakeholders unhappy. Patients complained that the insurance companies or HMOs chosen by their employers forced them to switch doctors, use inconvenient hospitals, or accept inadequate treatment. They also complained they could not get outcome data to help in choosing a physician. The doctors complained they wasted inordinate amounts of time trying to convince insurers that particular treatments were necessary. The insurers and HMOs complained they couldn't make a profit.

H.R. 3605, the Patients' Bill of Rights Act of 1998, was introduced in the House of Representatives on March 31, 1998 to address some aspects of these issues. It contained provisions related to access to medical care, quality assurance, patient information, and grievance and appeals procedures. Section 112 (one of 19 sections of the bill) concerned the collection of standardized data about medical care. It started by saying, "A group health plan and a health insurance issuer that offers health insurance coverage shall collect uniform quality data that include a minimum uniform data set. . . . The Secretary [of Health and Human Services] shall specify (and may from time to time update) the data required to be included in the minimum uniform data set . . . and the standard format for such data. Such data shall include at least: (1) aggregate utilization data; (2) data on the demographic characteristics of participants, beneficiaries, and enrollees; (3) data on disease-specific and age-specific mortality rates and (to the extent feasible) morbidity rates of such individuals; (4) data on satisfaction of such individuals, including data on voluntary disenrollment and grievances; and (5) data on quality indicators and health outcomes, including, to the extent feasible and appropriate, data on pediatric cases and on a gender-specific basis.[19]

The data collection provisions of H.R. 3605 were intended to support the patient's choice of physicians, but some observers believed they might actually have the opposite impact. The plans with the least choice for patients are HMOs and other organizations that permit only member physicians to provide services except under extreme circumstances. The plans with maximum flexibility for the patient are preferred provider plans, which allow patients to obtain medical services from any physician, but charge the patients more for physicians who are not a member of the plan. The costs of the data collection called for in Section 112 of H.R. 3605 would be substantially lower for HMOs than for preferred provider plans. This is because the HMOs have greater central control over patient medical records and over the process of routing patients to specialists. In contrast, large preferred provider plans may have thousands of doctors with no central repository of medical records and little consistency in record keeping. The process of sifting through different doctors' records to track the type and quality of treatment each patient received would be much more complicated for the preferred provider plans. If the law passed, they would therefore be required to spend more on their internal record keeping and therefore would have to raise their rates. This would tilt the economic advantage further in the direction of the HMOs that provide less choice.[20]

QUESTIONS

1. Assume you were asked to define the database needed for collecting information about every examination or treatment that every patient receives in a clinic or hospital. Identify some of the most important entity types and some of the important attributes of those entity types. (You might want to draw the ERD by hand to support your own thinking.)

2. Assume typical questions for evaluating medical care include things like how frequently diabetics are checked for high blood sugar and what types of drug treatments are used for different types of cardiac patients. Propose a process that might be used for gathering and analyzing the data in an HMO. Explain how this might be done in a preferred provider plan.

Continued

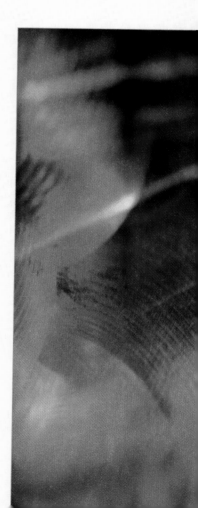

3. Assume you wanted to report information related to the five items listed in the proposed Patient's Bill of Rights. Explain how the database summarized in your answer to the first question might be used to provide this information. Identify any information called for in the proposed Patients' Bill of Rights that could not be derived from the database.

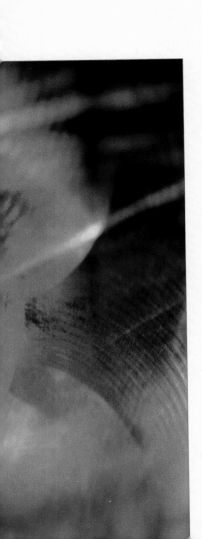

C A S E   **U.S. Air Force: Could the Accidental Bombing of an Embassy Have Been Avoided?**

Bombs dropped by a U.S. Air Force fighter jet during the 1999 NATO offensive against Serbia struck the Chinese embassy in Belgrade, killing three people and injuring 20 others. China had opposed the NATO intervention in Serbia and the bombing caused further strains in the relationship between the U.S. and China. Some observers believed the bombing was not an accident and a backlash of anti-American sentiment occurred in China. The bombs had actually hit the targeted building, but that building was the Chinese embassy instead of Serbia's Federal Directorate of Supply and Procurement, which was actually over 1,000 feet away and did not resemble the embassy physically. The embassy had moved to this site four years earlier. An 11-month inquiry into the incident led to the firing of one middle manager at the CIA and punishment of six others for their roles in providing incorrect information about the target. Chinese officials were not satisfied with this result. One spokesman said, "To pretend that the United States did not know the position of the Chinese Embassy in Yugoslavia is not credible . . . It was impossible for the U.S. side to mix up these two buildings. . . . The Chinese Embassy in Belgrade had 'unmistakable markings' that should have prevented its bombing."[21]

In events leading to the bombing, NATO had given the Serbian leadership an ultimatum about ending abusive treatment of ethnic Albanians in the Serbian province of Kosovo. Serbia did not conform and NATO decided to begin air strikes under the assumption that several days of bombing would force Serbian President Milosevic to agree to NATO's demands. Milosevic did not capitulate until the bombing had gone on for 78 days. When the bombing began NATO had 219 military targets for the bombing, but over half of those were hit within the first several days. Realizing that a much more extensive bombing campaign might be required, NATO's commander asked for a list of 2,000 potential targets including electric grids and commercial facilities. Around 650 targets were bombed during the campaign.

Bombing targets were initially suggested by NATO's Joint Analysis Center in Britain and at the Air Force's European headquarters in Germany. Determining these targets is a complicated process that uses intelligence reports and satellite photographs. As the known targets were being hit, the call for more targets brought other agencies into the process. The CIA's Counter-Proliferation Division proposed the Directorate of Supply and Procurement as a target because of long-held suspicions that it was involved with smuggling missile parts to other countries. These concerns were actually unrelated to the NATO action. The person who tried to locate the Directorate used three maps: two Yugoslav commercial maps from 1989 and 1996, and a U.S. government map produced in 1997. None showed the location of the Chinese embassy, which was built in 1996. The method for locating the building was based on triangulating between other addresses on the assumption that street addresses are numbered uniformly.[22] Only after the disaster did the CIA turn up in its files two maps that accurately placed the embassy: one was a map handed out by a Belgrade bank that showed a branch office near the embassy; the other listed the embassy and its grid coordinates in its index but did not mark the building on the map itself.[23]

"According to administration, defense and intelligence officials, the bombing was caused by a fundamentally flawed process for trying to locate the directorate's headquarters in the New Belgrade section of the Yugoslav capital. Armed with only an address, 2 Bulevar Umetnosti, the officer who was dismissed used an unclassified military map to try to pinpoint the building's location, based on a limited knowledge of addresses on a parallel street. . . . On the map, which the National Imagery and Mapping Agency produced in 1997, the building that turned out to be the embassy was not identified. Instead, the map showed the embassy in its former location in central Belgrade."[24] The potential target was given an official number, 0251WA0017. Looking at satellite images after the bombing, an intelligence official said that the building looked more like a hotel than an office building.

While announcing the punishments for those involved in the fiasco, the CIA director also singled out another officer who heard about the proposed target informally and despite having no direct authority in the matter called NATO to raise doubts and contacted several others at the National Imagery and Mapping Agency and the NATO task force responsible for the bombing runs. For a variety of reasons his concerns were not conveyed to senior officers who could have called off the attack.[25]

QUESTIONS

1. Use the work system framework to describe the system of determining targets and to identify some of the problems with that system. Identify any important points that might be missing from the brief description.

2. Assume that the relevant data existed in a database. Use the ideas in this chapter to identify the data in that database, giving special attention to how the database might be organized. Explain why you believe it would or would not be possible to compile this type of database.

3. In what way did the context, the factors outside of the work system, affect what happened?

Types of Information Systems

chapter5

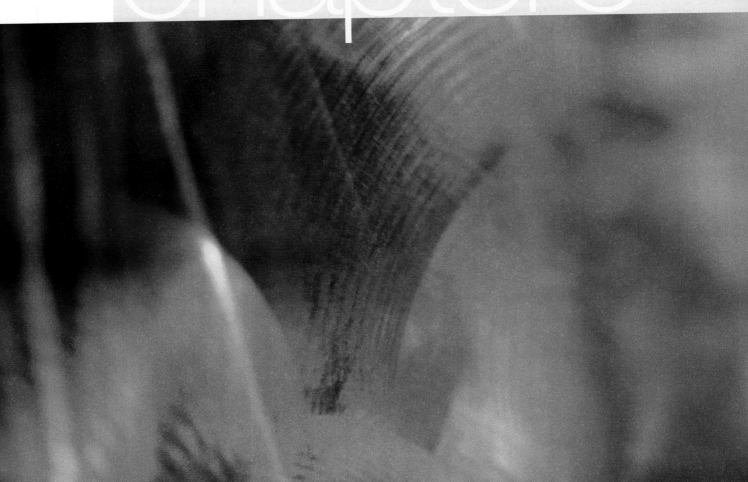

STUDY QUESTIONS

- Summarize the purpose of functional area information systems including CAD, MRP, EDI, SCM, CIM, POS, SFA, CRM, and EFT.
- What are the general differences between the idealized types of information systems that can be used in any functional area?
- What different approaches are used in communication systems?
- In what ways do information systems support various management roles?
- Identify some of the data- and model-related techniques used in different types of DSS.
- What are some of the goals and difficulties associated with enterprise systems?
- How are features of one type of information system transferable to systems of other types?

OUTLINE

Information System Categories Related to Specific Functional Areas of Business
Product Design Systems
Supply Chain Systems
Manufacturing Systems
Sales and Marketing Systems
Finance Systems

Information System Categories That Apply in any Functional Area of Business

Office Automation Systems

Communication Systems
Teleconferencing
E-mail, Voice Mail, and Fax
Instant Messaging and Chat Rooms
Groupware
Intranets and Extranets
Knowledge Management
Group Support Systems

Transaction Processing Systems
Batch versus Real-Time Processing

Management and Executive Information Systems
From MIS to EIS
Do MIS and EIS Really Solve Managers' Problems?

Decision Support Systems
Simulation and Optimization
OLAP and Data Mining
Expert Systems
Neural Networks
Fuzzy Logic
Case-Based Reasoning
Intelligent Agents

Enterprise Systems

Limitations and Uses of Information System Categories

Chapter Conclusion
Summary
Key Terms
Review Questions
Discussion Questions
Cases

Types of Information Systems

OPENING CASE

NG: USING CAD TO DESIGN A NEW AIRPLANE

Boeing began designing its new 777 airliner by spending a year working with eight airlines to obtain consensus about design issues such as the width of the fuselage, the shape of the overhead compartments, and the use of folding wingtips so that a larger plane would fit into existing airport gates. To complete this work, Boeing had to design 130,000 unique parts. By including rivets and fasteners Boeing engineers could say that the airplane they were producing would be "3 million parts flying in very close formation." The traditional approach to designing an airplane was to produce drawings for each part and assembly, manually check the drawings for compatibility and placement, build a scale model, and discover and fix the mismatches. Boeing decided to move to a paperless design process using CATIA, a mainframe-based computer-aided design (CAD) tool originally developed by the French aircraft manufacturer Dassault.

The basis of the new paperless design process was a CAD specification of the precise shape and location of every component. CATIA could use data to generate realistic pictures of individual components or combinations of adjacent components. Creating these specifications and making sure they were compatible was the principal work product of 238 engineering teams of up to 40 engineers. The data storage capacity for the system was 3.5 terabytes (trillion bytes), and the data was made available to 7,000 workstations spread around the world. Online access to the database of CAD specifications permitted an engineer working on any part to access the specifications, and hence electronic drawings, of any related part. Traditional delays in finding, copying, and moving paper drawings were eliminated.

Having all of the design data in an electronic database made it possible to test automatically for mutual interference between components. An electronic preassembly program called CLASH displayed flashing red zones whenever two separate components were designated to be in the same location, such as when one engineering team planned to run an electric cable through a location reserved for ductwork by another team. To test whether maintenance technicians could actually reach every location that required maintenance the CAD team created simulated human forms that could be put into any location in the position needed to do the work. Physical mock-ups were constructed for some aircraft subsystems, but the CLASH program was so effective at detecting interference between parts that further mock-ups were not used. The completed CAD specifications were fed into computer-controlled fabrication equipment, whose error rate in a fuselage 20.33 feet in diameter was less than one part in 10,000.[1, 2]

WEB CHECK [✓]

IBM's Web site cites CATIA as an IBM e-business solution for "product life cycle management and engineering."[3] Use a search engine to find an introduction to the latest version of CATIA and identify its main features and benefits.

DEBATE TOPIC [ ]

There is a trend toward using CAD and linking it to computer-controlled fabrication equipment. Is this a major threat to the job security of both product designers and factory workers?

The Boeing CAD case starts this chapter because it illustrates facets of the different types of information systems that this chapter will discuss:

Office automation systems: CAD is basically a tool for recording and manipulating information. In some ways it is like a word processor and spreadsheet for design engineers.

Communication systems: Effective communication and collaboration between thousands of engineers at locations around the world was essential for the success of the project.

Transaction processing systems: Each time an engineer changed the design, the new information had to be validated, stored in a database, and made available for subsequent retrieval. This reflects the spirit of transaction processing systems used in retail and wholesale businesses to enter orders and record shipments.

Management information systems and executive information systems: Although not mentioned in the case, Boeing management needed information to plan and manage the project. This involves information systems directed at managers and executives.

Decision support systems: During the course of the design work the software provided various types of guidance, including identifying mutual interference between components.

Enterprise systems: The term "enterprise system" typically focuses on creating an enterprise-wide infrastructure of transaction data, but the spirit of Boeing's coordinated design effort requires a somewhat similar use of databases and communication capabilities that keep a large, geographically dispersed enterprise operating together.

The previous chapters introduced the value chain, explained how to think about work systems and information systems in a particular situation, and introduced many ideas related to business processes, information, and databases. This chapter shows the range of possibilities for using information systems to improve communication, decision-making, and entire business processes within organizations.

The first part of the chapter looks at some of the information systems often associated with specific functional areas. Such systems include CAD, MRP, SCM, CIM, CRM, and others. The second part of the chapter describes the different idealized types of information systems that might be used in any functional area of business. These systems include OAS, communication systems, TPS, MIS, DSS, and enterprise systems.

WORK SYSTEM SNAPSHOT
Using CAD to design the Boeing 777

CUSTOMERS

- Boeing's manufacturing department
- Airline maintenance departments

PRODUCTS & SERVICES

- Specification of the precise function, shape, and location of each component and assembly
- Verification that the components are physically compatible

BUSINESS PROCESS

- Decide on major features of airplane
- Design individual components
- Test for compatibility with other components and other subsystems
- Transmit the specifications to manufacturing

PARTICIPANTS	INFORMATION	TECHNOLOGY
• Representatives of airlines • Boeing engineers at many locations	• General design goals • CAD specification of the shape, location, materials, and function of each component	• CAD database and computer for storing the data • Engineering workstations • Data network

Although it is important to recognize commonly used vocabulary of the IS field, you will see that the names of different types of information systems have changed over the years as innovators invented new methods and combined old ones into new forms. One result is that system classifications are always in flux. People name and describe a new type of system, such as a decision support system or executive information system. Ten years later, the name still exists but some of the original characteristics are no longer as important or have become commonplace. Eventually many information systems contain characteristics from several system categories. Furthermore, any particular information system that might fit a particular category today might not fit tomorrow when additional features are added.

Many real-world systems like the Boeing design system incorporate aspects of different types of information systems. This means that information system categories are less useful as rigid classifications and more useful as aids in identifying possible directions for improvement in any particular situation. Understanding the categories helps in visualizing the potential applicability of different approaches for applying IT and in recognizing strengths and weaknesses of those approaches.

INFORMATION SYSTEM CATEGORIES RELATED TO SPECIFIC FUNCTIONAL AREAS OF BUSINESS

Chapter 1 identified typical business processes in different functional areas of business (refer back to Figure 1.3). It also explained the supply chain, internal value chain, and customer experience (refer back to Figure 1.5). E-business applications have improved, and in some cases revolutionized the way these functional areas operate in many companies. This section looks at some of the important innovations in information systems and commercial software that are directly related to product design, supply chain, manufacturing, sales and marketing, and finance. Although most of these e-business innovations were underway before commercial Internet applications began in the early

1990s, the Internet has provided many new ways to extend and improve methods that were already in use. The second part of the chapter will look at the different types of information systems that might be used anywhere in the value chain.

Product Design Systems

The first step in creating value for the customer is designing the product based on a combination of the customer's desires, the designer's imagination, and the firm's goals and capabilities. As was illustrated by the Boeing case, **computer-aided design (CAD)** software has helped change the nature of design processes once the basic concept of the new product has been envisioned. CAD software accepts coded descriptions of components or processes and can display the resulting product specification graphically. CAD starts with the ability to draw the shape of an object but extends much further. It includes the ability to create photo-realistic representations that allow a designer to see exactly what an object will look like without ever producing a physical model. Many types of CAD also include the ability to evaluate the object being designed. For example, an electrical engineer might test a circuit, or an architect might verify that a building is strong enough before it is built. CAD software can also perform calculations such as the area of the rooms and the amount of paint required. By automating both drawings and calculations, it is easy to evaluate the cost and acceptability of design alternatives. Taking this a step further, CAD software such as the CLASH program used by Boeing can apply the laws of geometry and physics to check for design flaws such as two objects occupying the same space, moving parts that will interfere with each other, or excessive physical stresses that may cause structural failure. Systems for designing electrical circuits and semiconductor chips can run exhaustive simulations to determine whether correct outputs will be produced under all foreseeable conditions.

A surprising aspect of CAD is its wide range of applications. When CAD was originally conceived, it was a tool comparable to a word processor for engineering drawings. CAD has moved out of the engineer's domain and has become an integral tool in organizational processes for creating and testing products and product modifications. The visualization capabilities in advanced CAD systems permit the customer to have a simulated walk-through of a building that has never been built or to view how a washing machine works even though it has not yet been manufactured. This is the type of capability that Boeing used to design the Boeing 777 airliner without ever creating a physical scale model. Although most CAD applications are used for electronic, mechanical, and architectural design, CAD has also moved into a broad range of activities that use two- or three-dimensional representations. Orthopedic surgeons and plastic surgeons use CAD to design operations; clothes designers use CAD to design clothes; even hairdressers can use a form of CAD to try out alternative hairstyles before they cut hair (see Figure 5.1).

Supply Chain Systems

Chapter 1 introduced the concept of the supply chain, the transactions, coordination, and movement of goods between suppliers and the firm. Regardless of whether the firm is a manufacturer or a retailer, its supply chain for raw materials and components should assure reliable, low-cost acquisition of whatever it needs. For a manufacturer, all necessary materials should arrive just before the manufacturing schedule calls for its use. If it arrives too late, manufacturing will be disrupted. If it arrives too early, money and warehouse space will be tied up in unused inventory for too long, and the material may even become obsolete if the product changes. The challenge is similar for retailers. If the merchandise arrives too early it will tie up money while it sits on shelves or racks. If it arrives too late the customer will have already gone somewhere else and it may be necessary to sell the merchandise at deep discounts before the next product season.

Supply chain systems start with information about what inventory is available, when previously ordered material will arrive, and when material will probably be needed based on manufacturing schedules or sales forecasts. This information is used to:

CAD in unexpected places

FIGURE 5.1

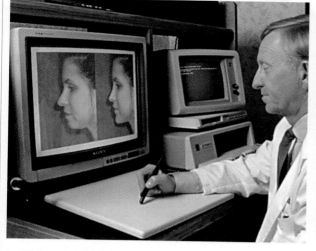

CAD has been used for a wide range of applications, some of which might seem surprising.

- Determine material requirements for future weeks or months
- Generate new orders
- Send the orders to suppliers
- Obtain commitment dates for likely receipt
- Verify that the ordered material actually arrived

Delays between these steps reduce procurement efficiency. The slower the system operates, the more likely it is that demand will change before the material arrives. If demand increases, the material will be insufficient and customers will be inconvenienced or will go elsewhere. If demand decreases, the excess material will tie up money and may become obsolete before it is ever used.

The first commercial software packages that addressed major parts of the supply chain were called **material requirement planning (MRP)** systems. These systems attempted to integrate purchasing and production activities. MRP systems start with a firm's output requirement by week or other period and work backward to calculate a schedule of how many units of the finished product and intermediate products must be started, when the units must be started, and when the necessary materials must be ordered. They also permit user adjustments in case lead times are inadequate or in case capacity is insufficient.

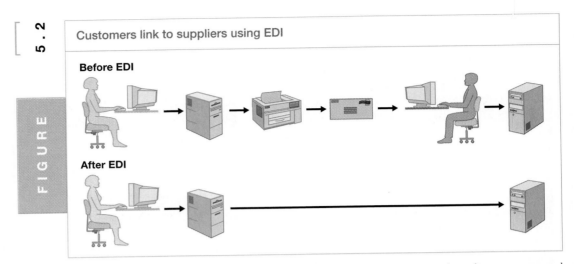

FIGURE 5.2

Customers link to suppliers using EDI

Before EDI, purchase orders and many other communications between customers and suppliers were generated by computer, mailed, and then manually reentered into another computer. EDI eliminates delays and increases accuracy by providing electronic transmission of data between the customer's computer and the supplier's computer. Web-based versions of EDI reduce costs even further by using widely available, non-proprietary infrastructure.

Initially, data processing related to purchasing was viewed as a largely internal process of ordering the right material at the right time. This view became outdated for many large distributors and manufacturers when networks made it possible to transmit data between companies. Links between large companies and their suppliers became more effective with the use of **electronic data interchange** (**EDI**), the electronic transmission of business data such as purchase orders and invoices from one firm's computerized information system to that of another firm. The initial EDI systems used proprietary software and networks, but some of the same EDI functions are now available at lower cost through the Web. Since electronic data transmission is virtually instantaneous, the supplier's information system can check for availability and respond quickly with a confirmation. Figure 5.2 illustrates some of the advantages of EDI. Before EDI, the data from one computerized system was printed on paper, mailed, and reentered into another computer. In terms of dollars, a company typically spent $55 to process a paper purchase order, whereas EDI could reduce that amount to $2.50,[4] and Web-based versions of EDI can cut the cost even further.

The more current idea of **supply chain management** (**SCM**) goes beyond automating data transfers. It is the overall system of coordinating closely with suppliers so that both the firm and its suppliers reap the benefits of smaller inventories, smoother production, and less waste. Standardizing and automating both internal data processing and data transfer between suppliers and their customers is fundamental for SCM because this makes procurement systems faster and more effective.

SCM system and EDI (whether Web-based or not) are essential ingredients in a trend toward integration between suppliers and their customers. The more integrated they are, the quicker suppliers respond to customer requests and the quicker customers respond to schedule changes at the supplier. This trend toward integration applies if the supplier and customer are separate firms or if they are departments within a single firm. This tighter integration across several consecutive stages of a product's value chain was possible a decade ago, as illustrated by the links between Dillard's Department Stores, the apparel manufacturer Haggar, and the textile manufacturer Burlington Industries. When Dillard's inventory of a pants style went below a specified level, it automatically sent an electronic message to Haggar. In turn, Haggar electronically notified Burlington Industries if it didn't have enough cloth to manufacture the pants Dillard's requested.[5]

Manufacturing Systems

A manufacturing system is a firm's system of producing physical (or informational) products that it sells. The impact of IT on manufacturing systems came in several waves. The first uses were in keeping track of inventory and work-in-process and in performing record keeping about who did what work, when they did it, and how well they did it. Separate manual record keeping has gradually been replaced by the use of bar codes and automatic sensors. In addition, computerized controls have been built into the manufacturing equipment itself. The most highly automated factories operate under conditions that once seemed like science fiction. For example, as early as 1983 a Fanuc factory in Japan producing 10,000 electric motors a month operated with people doing maintenance during the day and only robots working at night. The factory contained 60 machining cells and 101 robots and produced 900 types and sizes of motor parts in lots ranging from 20 to 1,000.[6] Automated machinery actually is only one type of component of an automated factory. In totally automated factories, all production is scheduled and performed automatically. This requires extensive information systems that integrate automatic material movement, automatic scheduling of all work steps, automatic execution of work steps, and automatic sensing of quality.

Despite progress in automating manufacturing systems, most current factories are only partially automated because it is possible to get better results by automating some functions and leaving others to the flexibility, common sense, and ingenuity of human workers. The success of the only partly automated NUMMI joint venture between General Motors and Toyota is a case in point (mentioned in Chapter 3).

Even when the major work steps are only partially automated, IT has often had a major impact in manufacturing through various degrees of **computer-integrated manufacturing (CIM)**, which includes computerized data collection and integrated data flows between design, manufacturing, planning, accounting, and other business functions. When people in one department complete their tasks, the data produced are immediately available for use by people in other departments. Technical advances in the last decade that have made CIM more of a reality include increased computer power at much lower cost, better data management capabilities, and distributed computing and telecommunications. Reasons for adopting CIM include reduced cost, better quality, better customer service, greater flexibility in responding to customer requirements, and quicker time-to-market with new products.

The use of CAD, CIM, and other computer-based techniques is gradually changing the logic of manufacturing. It is increasingly divided between two computerized phases. First is a design phase, which creates a computerized description of the product including the options that customers can select. Next is a manufacturing phase, which uses the computerized description directly. As manufacturing moves in this direction, there is an increase in the **information content of products**, the degree to which the value of products resides in product specification information rather than in just physical objects.

Heightened customer expectations have made more extensive customization a key competitive issue for many products. The ability to link CAD systems to order entry systems and to transmit order details directly into the factory is making it more practical to tailor anything from clothes to machines based on the customer's requirements or wishes. Today many firms are moving toward **mass customization**, the use of mass production techniques to produce customized products or services. Mass customization is an attempt to retain the advantages of mass production while providing value related to customization. From the manufacturer's viewpoint, the product or service is mass-produced. From the consumer's viewpoint, the product or service is customized. Figure 5.3 shows an example of mass customization. Matsushita's National Bicycle increased its share of the Japanese sports bicycle market from 5% to 29% by moving from inexpensive, noncustomized bicycles to customized bicycles that start from measurements determining the exact size of frame the rider needs.[7]

FIGURE 5.3

Building a customized bicycle

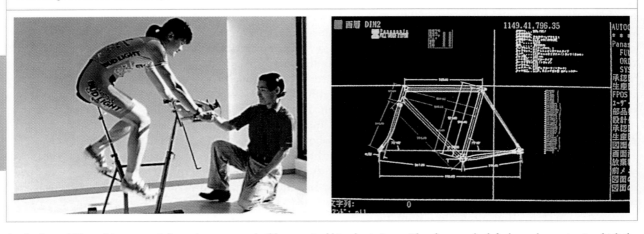

A subsidiary of Matsushita uses an information system to build customized bicycles in Japan. The photo on the left shows the session in which the customized dimensions of the bicycle are determined. These measurements are entered into a special computer-aided design (CAD) system that creates a diagram (shown on right) that is transmitted directly to the factory.

Sales and Marketing Systems

The previous sections on product design and manufacturing show how IT makes it easier to provide the product the customer wants, when and where the customer wants it. IT also enables companies to use radically different sales and marketing approaches than were possible when IT applications were less developed. E-commerce is but one of the newer approaches, and a number of e-commerce business models were mentioned in Table 1.2.

Even without electronic links to customers, IT has had a major impact on traditional sales activities such as keeping track of customers or taking orders. One of the most important innovations in keeping track of customers occurred as a by-product of **point-of-sale (POS)** systems that use bar codes to generate customer bills at checkout counters. Many supermarkets now give their repeat customers an ID card for check cashing and for rewarding customer loyalty with discounts on selected items. Using the ID cards in conjunction with POS systems provides the extra benefit to the store, namely, a cumulative history of every item the repeat customer purchased on each trip to the store.

Combining POS data with other data related to magazine subscriptions, personal affiliations, and Web usage can lead to valuable and sometimes controversial indications of preferences and buying patterns linked to individuals. These are the basis of **direct marketing**, the process of selling through communications addressed to specific individuals who are likely to be interested in the product. Direct marketing is based on **addressability**, the ability to direct specific messages to specific individuals via paper mail, telephone, or e-mail. Direct marketing tries to improve upon newspaper advertising, broadcast advertising, and mass mailings that often have a low yield rate because most of the people who see the message are not interested.

Combining customization techniques with addressability creates possibilities of directing different messages to different customers. This has been used for years in the world of print journalism. For example, *American Baby* adapts the mix of editorial and advertising pages to the age of the baby in each subscriber's household. It does this through a process called selective binding, in which different pages are included in a magazine depending on subscriber characteristics stored in a subscriber database. Even 10 years ago, *Farm Journal* recognized 5,000 different subclassifications of farm type and geographic region and produced a different edition for each.[8] Small companies can also use direct marketing techniques based on addressability. Some small clothes retailers maintain a customer list and record the color and size of each item sold to each customer. This enables them to send out pre-Christmas mailings to their customers' spouses mentioning Christmas gifts that might go well with "the tan slacks Pat purchased last month." Since Web servers can keep track of every access from a particular computer and since Web pages are transmitted in an electronically coded form, it is possible to create a similar degree of personalization by customizing Web pages for a particular user based on that user's past visits to the site.

Direct marketing using a telephone is called **telemarketing**. Although it requires nothing more than a telephone and a list of telephone numbers, important aspects of telemarketing can be automated. Having the telephone numbers on a computer makes it possible to dial phone numbers automatically, and even redial automatically if the line is busy. Once the telephone connection is established, the computer can display a script outlining the main points to be covered in the call. The script can even move into different branches depending on responses entered into the computer by the telemarketing agent. If any follow-up action is required, the system can record that data in the database for later use. If a product or service is sold, the sales transaction can be processed immediately. Any data gathered during the phone call can remain in the database to improve the targeting of future telemarketing efforts toward this account. For example a stockbroker might learn that a potential client will have funds to invest at a future time and is interested in long-term bonds.

Sales work has also been facilitated through sales force automation systems and customer relationship management systems. As with many information system categories, SFA and CRM overlap substantially because the popular name gradually changed from SFA to CRM. **Sales force automation (SFA)** traditionally focused on data handling and data retrieval tasks related to personal scheduling, opportunity tracking, contact management, note and information sharing, tracking the progress of sales cycles, and providing revenue forecasts to headquarters as an input to financial planning. Contrary to the name, most commercial SFA packages do not actually automate sales work. A common problem with SFA packages is that they require salespeople to do a lot of data entry work. Many salespeople resent this because a major part of their efforts devoted to SFA mostly support headquarters rather than their own attempts to earn commissions.

Customer relationship management (CRM) addresses the somewhat broader topic of planning, controlling, and scheduling pre-sales and post-sales activities. These include everything in SFA, but also recognize that from a firm's viewpoint, the relationship with a customer starts with the sales cycle and continues through customer service activities, product maintenance, and repeat sales. An important part of CRM is the collection of data from customer interactions such as service calls, call center responses, sales transactions, and Web-site activity. Analyzing these types of customer relationship data potentially helps in identifying patterns that are useful in crafting marketing campaigns and building targeted sales pitches. It also potentially helps in figuring out how to serve different groups of customers more effectively and profitably.

Another important sales application sometimes linked with SFA and CRM is the ability to generate a correctly priced sales proposal on the spot without delays for getting back to headquarters. This is a traditional problem of salespeople who travel to customer sites to sell products ranging from perishable farm produce to life insurance to heavy equipment. In each case, the sales process is undermined by any inability to respond immediately to questions about product availability or final prices after discounts are applied. Cellular phones, e-mail, voice mail, and even networked database access all make it easier to get messages from an office without interrupting anyone else. Data and models on laptop computers or accessible through the Web make it easier to demonstrate options and to provide accurate pricing information because the same rules that might be used at the office can be programmed into the laptop.

Finance Systems

The field of finance includes the business of finance as well as the finance departments within all firms, regardless of what those firms produce. Firms in the business of finance include banks, credit card companies, stock brokerages, home mortgage companies, currency traders, and suppliers of financial information. The "products" in the business of finance include bank accounts, money market funds, credit cards, loans, and buying and selling of stocks, bonds, foreign currencies, real estate, and even entire businesses. The finance function within a typical business is a support activity that handles transactions involving money, produces financial statements, and pays taxes. These are all essentially information system functions, and they have been computerized for decades. The difference in the 1990s, however, is that this information has been integrated more effectively and made more readily available for decision-making in matters ranging from how to treat slow-paying customers to how to invest the firm's working capital so that it generates revenue even when it is not being used immediately.

To better understand the impact of IT on finance systems, consider the changing form and use of money, which was first invented because people found that bartering for everything was inconvenient. Using money made it possible to exchange value without possessing the specific commodity the trading partner wanted. Money had its own problems, however. What if you wanted to buy something but didn't have your cash at hand? Or what if you wanted to pay a bill without traveling to the merchant's place of business and handing over cash? Or what if you simply didn't want to carry large amounts of cash? Information systems are the basis of a number of alternatives that were developed or are still being developed:

- *Checking accounts* are basically information systems that keep track of account balances and permit people to write checks if they have enough money in their bank accounts. But checking accounts operate using paper checks that take days to clear though a complex settlement process.
- *Credit cards* permit users to make payments through short-term loans. Credit cards require large-scale information systems for approving transactions quickly, consolidating monthly customer statements, and paying merchants.
- *Debit cards* are based on a similar idea, but operate differently. Instead of providing credit to be paid off later, debit cards move money immediately from the cardholder's account to the merchant's account.
- *Smart cards*, such as prepaid phone cards, copy cards, and electronic meal tickets, provide another card-based option in which a person transfers an amount such as $10 or $20 onto a card containing a memory chip. The **smart card** is used via simple vending machines that deduct the amount of a purchase from the stored amount on the card and add that amount to an account that is receiving the payment.
- *Electronic cash* is currently being promoted in several forms as a way to make small payments for access to information on the World Wide Web or for other small transactions for which credit card systems are prohibitively expensive. The basic idea is similar to that of a smart card except that the record keeping takes place on a PC instead of a smart card. A person acquires the **electronic cash** by transferring funds to a company that issues electronic cash by updating information on the purchaser's personal computer. When the electronic cash user makes a purchase, the electronic balance on the computer is reduced by the purchase price and the merchant's account on a different computer is increased by the same amount.

Electronic cash is actually a newer, limited version of **electronic funds transfer (EFT)** that has been used for several decades. EFT uses electronic messages to settle accounts between banks and other businesses. Use of EFT is more efficient than transferring physical money because it only requires transmission of suitably encrypted electronic messages.

Information systems are also essential for the operation of stock and commodity markets. These markets simply could not operate at their current scale without computerized systems for entering buy and sell orders, transmitting them to the traders, recording the transactions, and making payment within three days. This reliance on computerized systems became highly visible during the stock market crash on October 19, 1987, when over 500,000,000 shares were traded on the New York Stock Exchange. This was more than twice the previous high volume. Because of this unprecedented data processing load, the online information about stock prices lagged as much as two hours behind the trading on the floor of the stock market, contributing to the panic during the crash. Subsequent IT investments increased capacity to well over a billion shares per day.

Real-time (immediate) access to the latest stock, bond, and commodity price information has also permitted large firms to automate certain buy and sell decisions using a technique called **program trading**. An approach to program trading that exploits the availability of real-time information is using the speed of computers to search for temporary discrepancies between current prices of large groups of stocks and options to buy or sell these stocks in the future. Upon finding such discrepancies, the system can lock in a guaranteed profit by buying stocks in one market and selling options in the other. A fundamentally different approach to program trading uses statistical analysis and models to identify price conditions under which specific buy or sell orders have a high probability of making money. Some observers believe this form of program trading tends to reinforce instability when market values are changing rapidly. In response, the New York Stock Exchange has created rules called "circuit breakers," which disallow program trading if aggregate price indicators, such as the Dow Jones Industrial Average, have changed more than a particular amount in any day.

Even individual investors with small portfolios are benefiting from current finance systems. As was explained in the Charles Schwab case in Chapter 3, the first online brokerage services for consumers became available in the mid-1980s and the first Web-based brokerage services appeared in 1996. By the year 2000, millions of individuals had online brokerage accounts and could place trades with far lower brokerage commissions than had been the norm just five years earlier.

The preceding examples of functional area systems across the value chain barely scratch the surface, but they illustrate that e-business approaches have been with us for several decades and show that IT is playing an increasingly important role in the way business is conducted.

R E A L I T Y C H E C K ✓

E-Business Applications in Every Business Function

This section mentioned several e-business applications in a number of business functions.

1. Give examples of how some of these IT-based innovations have affected you directly.

2. Identify other IT-based innovations that have affected one or more business functions in important ways.

INFORMATION SYSTEM CATEGORIES THAT APPLY IN ANY FUNCTIONAL AREA OF BUSINESS

The previous sections focused on types of information systems associated with specific functional areas of business. The remainder of this chapter looks at six types of information systems that apply in any functional area.

Any discussion of types of information systems faces a difficult problem because the categories simply won't hold still. The first computerized systems were used to collect and summarize data about financial transactions or work that had been done in the past. The advent of real-time computing made it possible to integrate computers into the process of doing the work itself. The advent of personal computers made it possible to provide personal tools individuals could use to keep track of their own information, independent of what the rest of the organization was doing. Moreover, the vast expansion of communication capabilities and computer networks made new types of team-oriented systems possible.

Perhaps more problematic from a purist's viewpoint, the categories are not mutually exclusive. Information system categories differ in this regard from categories used in the natural sciences, where there is often detailed agreement about small differences between biological species or chemical compounds. In contrast, information system categories often overlap and change as new applications combine new capabilities with old ones.

Despite this classification problem, general categories must be discussed because the terms are used frequently in business and because each category supports communication and decision-making from a different and important viewpoint. Table 5.1 summarizes the basic idea of each type of information system along with the ways each type supports communication and decision-making. Table 5.2 gives a brief example of each in the functional areas of sales, manufacturing, and finance. After introducing each system type, the chapter concludes with general issues related to all the system types.

OFFICE AUTOMATION SYSTEMS

An **office automation system (OAS)** facilitates everyday information processing tasks in offices and business organizations. These systems use a wide range of tools such as spreadsheets, word processors, and presentation packages. Although telephones, e-mail, v-mail, and fax can be included in this category, we will treat communication systems as a separate category.

OASs help people perform personal record keeping, writing, and calculation chores efficiently. Of all the system types, OASs and communication systems are the most familiar to students. Tools generally grouped within the OASs category include:

Spreadsheet programs, which provide efficient methods for performing calculations that can be visualized in terms of the cells of a spreadsheet. The first spreadsheet program was VisiCalc, which helped create the demand for the first personal computers in the late 1970s.

Text and image processing systems, which store, revise, and print documents containing text or image data. These systems started with simple word processors but have evolved to include desktop publishing systems for creating complex documents ranging from brochures to books.

Presentation packages, which help managers develop presentations independently, instead of working with typists and technical artists. These products automatically convert outlines into presentation pages containing appropriately spaced titles and subtitles.

Personal database systems and *note-taking systems*, which help people keep track of their own personal data (rather than the organization's shared data). Typical applications include an appointment book and calendar, a to-do list, and a notepad.

When using these tools for personal productivity purposes, users can take any approach they want because the work is unstructured. Some individuals use these tools extensively and enjoy major efficiency benefits, whereas others do not use them at all. The same tools can also be used for broader purposes, however, in which they are incorporated into larger systems that structure and routinize tasks in organizations. For example, a corporate planning system may require each department manager to fill in and forward a preformatted spreadsheet whose uniformity will facilitate the corporation's planning process.

TABLE 5.1

Typical Ways Each Type of Information System Supports Communication and Decision-Making

Although people often think of information systems as tools for decision-making, each type of information system supports both communication and decision-making in a number of ways.

System type	Typical user	Impact on communication	Impact on decision-making
Office automation system: provides individuals effective ways to process personal and organizational business data, to perform calculations, and to create documents	• Anyone who stores personal data, creates documents, or performs calculations	• Provides tools for creating documents and presentations, such as word processors and presentation systems	• Provides spreadsheets and other tools for analyzing information • Communication tools also help in implementing decisions
Communication system: helps people work together by interacting and sharing information in many different forms	• Anyone who communicates with others, including office workers, managers, and other professionals	• Telephones and video conferencing for communication • E-mail, v-mail, fax, for communication using messages and documents • Access to memos and other shared information • Scheduling meetings • Organizing and expediting interactions during meetings • Controlling flow of work	• Telephones and teleconferencing for decision-making • E-mail, v-mail, fax, other tools for obtaining information • Support sharing information related to making joint decisions
Transaction processing system (TPS): collects and stores information about transactions; controls some aspects of transactions	• People whose work involves performing transactions	• Creates a database that can be accessed directly, thereby making some person-to-person communication unnecessary	• Gives immediate feedback on decisions made while processing transactions • Provides information for planning and management decisions
Management information system (MIS) and executive information system (EIS): converts TPS data into information for monitoring performance and managing an organization; provides executives information in a readily accessible interactive format	• Managers, executives, and people who receive feedback about their work	• Provides a basis of facts rather than opinions for explaining problems and their solutions • May combine e-mail and other communication methods with presentation of computerized data	• Provides summary information and measures of performance for monitoring results • May provide easy ways to analyze the types of information provided in less flexible form by older MIS
Decision support system (DSS): helps people make decisions by providing information, models, or analysis tools	• Analysts, managers, and other professionals	• Analysis using DSS helps provide a clear rationale for explaining a decision	• Provides tools for analyzing data and building models • Analysis using a DSS helps define and evaluate alternatives
Enterprise system: creates and maintains consistent data processing methods and an integrated database across multiple business functions	• People who enter transaction information • Managers and executives • Anyone who needs transaction information from other business functions	• Maintains a database that can be accessed directly, thereby making some person-to-person communication unnecessary • Establishes and maintains uniformity that makes communication easier	• Maintains a database that provides uniform, consistent information for decision-making • Establishes and maintains uniformity that makes it easier to use information while making decisions

TABLE   5.2

Examples of Each Type of Information System in Three Functional Areas of Business

One of the reasons the various categories are mentioned frequently is that each is used in every functional area of business.

System type	Sales examples	Manufacturing examples	Finance examples
Office automation system	• Spreadsheet to analyze different possible prices • Word processor to create sales contract	• Spreadsheet to analyze a production schedule • Word processor to write a memo about how to fix a machine	• Spreadsheet to compare several loan arrangements • Word processor to write a memo about new financial procedures
Communication system	• E-mail and fax used to contact customer • Video conference to present new sales materials to sales force • Workflow system to make sure all sales steps are completed • System to coordinate all work on a complex sales contract	• E-mail and v-mail used to discuss a problem with a new machine • Video conference to coordinate manufacturing and sales efforts • Workflow system to make sure engineering changes are approved	• V-mail and fax to communicate with bank about loan arrangements • Video conference to explain effect of financing on factory investments • Workflow system to make sure invoice approval precedes payment • System for exchanging the latest information related to a lawsuit
Transaction processing system (TPS)	• Point of sale system for sales transactions • Keeping track of customer contacts during a sales cycle	• Tracking movement of work-in-process in a factory • Tracking receipts of materials from suppliers	• Processing credit card payments • Payment of stock dividends and bond interest
Management information system (MIS) and executive information system (EIS)	• Weekly sales report by product and region • Consolidation of sales projections by product and region • Flexible access to sales data by product and region	• Weekly production report by product and operation • Determination of planned purchases based on a production schedule • Flexible access to production data by product and operation	• Receivables report showing invoices and payments • Monthly financial plan consolidation • Flexible access to corporate financial plan by line item
Decision support system (DSS)	• Model helping insurance salespeople test alternatives • Marketing data and models to analyze sales	• Model determining current priorities for machine operator • Production data and models to analyze production results	• Analysis of characteristics of customers who pay bills promptly • Stock database and models to help in selecting stocks to buy or sell
Enterprise system	• Help a sales rep enter an order and establish that enough capacity exists to meet the schedule	• Help the manufacturing manager to schedule maintenance based on minimizing disruption to sales	• Help the finance department track the cost of production back to purchase orders

COMMUNICATION SYSTEMS

Electronic **communication systems** help people work together by exchanging or sharing information in many different forms. New communication capabilities have changed the way many businesses operate by making it possible to do many things at a distance that previously required being present in a specific location. This section covers a wide range of these tools. Teleconferencing systems make it possible to hold same-time, different-place meetings. A variety of technologies including e-mail, voice mail, fax, instant messaging, and chat rooms make it possible to transmit specific messages to specific individuals or groups of individuals. Groupware systems start with messaging but go further by facilitating access to documents and controlling team-related workflow. Intranets and extranets extend the scope of groupware by using Web technology to provide dispersed groups of employees, suppliers, and customers ready access to information ranging from employee manuals and product catalogs through news bulletins and schedules. Knowledge management systems often use intranets to facilitate the sharing of knowledge, not just information. Group support systems help facilitate meetings.

Teleconferencing

The use of electronic transmission to permit same-time, different-place meetings is called **teleconferencing**. We can think of a traditional telephone call as a minimal teleconference, but the term normally is applied to other options including audio conferencing, audiographic conferencing, and video conferencing. (We will include computer conferencing in the discussion of groupware.)

The distinction between these approaches is related to the type of information that is shared. **Audio conferencing** is a single telephone call involving three or more people participating from at least two locations. If several people on the call are in the same office, they can all participate using a speakerphone, which includes a high-sensitivity microphone and a loudspeaker that can be heard by anyone in a room. **Audiographic conferencing** is an extension of audio conferencing, permitting dispersed participants to see pictures or graphical material at the same time. This is especially useful when the purpose of the meeting is to share information that is difficult to describe, organize, or visualize, such as a spreadsheet or model used to perform calculations under different assumptions (see Figure 5.4). **Video conferencing** is an interactive meeting involving two or more groups of people who can see each other using display screens. The least expensive forms of video conferencing are tiny cameras and four-inch screens added to telephones or separate video conferencing windows displayed on computer screens. In typical business video conferencing, remote participants appear on a television screen.

Video conferencing simulates a face-to-face meeting without requiring unnecessary travel, which absorbs time and energy, not to speak of the cost of airplane and hotel bills. However, the effectiveness of video conferences decreases if the participants lack a prior social bond. For example, doing sales calls via video conference might seem tempting but might not foster the personal relationship needed to succeed in many sales situations.

Options for teleconferencing

5.4

FIGURE

These photos show examples of two extensions of the original idea of the telephone. The first shows an audiographic conference in which financial analysts in different cities are working together on the same spreadsheet model. The second shows how a video conference provides more social presence than a regular phone call and costs much less than getting on an airplane.

On the other hand, Citibank and other banks have begun to experiment with stripped-down branch offices that have no tellers but permit customers to open accounts by video conferencing with multilingual staffers in another state.[9]

E-mail, Voice Mail, and Fax

Different-time, different-place communication has been used for centuries in the form of books and letters. Messaging systems make it possible to transmit specific messages to specific individuals or groups of individuals. They use technologies such as electronic mail, voice mail, and fax to make different-time, different-place communication more effective. E-mail, voice mail, pagers, and fax were news to many people ten years ago, but are now so commonplace that they are part of popular culture. Each has a number of advantages but also raises a number of issues, such as:

Social context: E-mail, v-mail, and fax all filter out some of the social context. Ideas communicated using these tools may seem less forceful or caring compared to the same ideas communicated personally. These tools should be used only when social presence is unimportant for understanding the message.

Danger of misinterpretation: The meaning of speech is conveyed partly in the inflection of a voice. Consider the sentences, "That really helped" and "I think you made a mistake." Depending on the context and inflection of the speaker's voice, the first comment could be complimentary or sarcastic. The second could be anything from a mild observation to a reason for firing someone. E-mail and fax provide no clue about inflection, and v-mail filters out body language. People using these tools need to be especially careful not to say things that could be misconstrued, such as jokes.

Power relationships: Use of e-mail and v-mail may create new communication patterns, sometimes involving people who have never communicated previously. With these tools, high-level managers find it easy to obtain information directly from people lower in the organization without going through intermediate managers and chains of command. People in the middle may find themselves out of the loop, as happens with assistants who formerly served as conduits to their bosses.

Privacy and confidentiality: Confidentiality problems may arise because fax outputs can be read by whoever is near the machine, which is often in a clerical work area. The issue of privacy took a bizarre turn in the Iran-gate investigation of illegal arms sales to Iran. Government officials who sold the arms had communicated with each other using e-mail but carefully covered their tracks by erasing the messages. Investigators found backup tapes that had been produced before many of the messages were erased. In this way, the use of e-mail left a trail that eventually aided the investigation.

Electronic junk mail: All three technologies can distribute messages that waste the recipient's time. Users may find that half their e-mail messages are something like "Has anyone seen a green sweater left in room 10-250?" This might seem trivial except that many people receive 50 or more mail messages daily. Junk fax may tie up fax machines when important faxes should be arriving or may use up all the paper in the machine. Some states have considered legislation against it. Companies sending these faxes argue that prohibiting this practice would violate their right to free speech.

Information overload: Messaging capabilities such as v-mail, e-mail, cellular telephones, and pagers have made communication so much more immediate that people in fast-moving firms sometimes feel overwhelmed with the amount of communication they receive. Sometimes there is an expectation that people will respond quickly and thoroughly, even from home. For managers and professionals already overloaded with information and work, this is not always a welcome development. Some complain that e-mail, v-mail, and fax have generated higher workloads, more stress, and an inability to get away from work.

One problem of having three alternative forms of electronic messages is the inconvenience of having to look in too many places to retrieve messages. The idea of **unified messaging** addresses this problem by combining e-mail, voice mail, and sometimes fax into a single mail box that can be accessed from any location. Unified messaging was first available in the mid-1990s and could become more popular as telephone companies, Internet service providers, and Web portals start offering these services to mobile professionals.[10]

Instant Messaging and Chat Rooms

The Internet brought several additional forms of online messaging that have seen wide use. One of these is **instant messaging**, the ability to direct a message to someone on your "buddy list" who happens to be online when you are. All you do is click on a list that highlights your "buddies" who happen to be online, type a message, and it appears immediately on your buddy's screen. The other form of messaging is an online **chat room**, an ongoing, informal computer conference that someone can join, participate in, and then leave. Chat rooms became popular as forums for discussing almost any imaginable topic—teenagers use both chat rooms and instant messaging as a form of socializing. The popularity of these capabilities was a key part of AOL's explosive growth to over 20 million subscribers. Unlike a traditional phone system, instant messaging systems from different carriers do not necessarily link to each other. In fact, Microsoft's Messenger Service was designed to allow its users to talk to AOL users, but AOL blocked access for a variety of competitive and privacy-related reasons.

Instant messaging and chat rooms both have developed into business tools. For example, Yellow Freight System's customer service agents field customer inquiries about rates and delivery times via the same buddy list method that the teenagers use. Similarly, the online brokerage of Bank One urges its customers to add its online nickname to their buddy lists. Among other things, this could be used to inform customers when transactions are completed.[11]

In a reversal that rivals the writeable CD-ROM (a ROM is a read-only memory), some chat rooms have begun to support **voice chat**, which means using chat room capabilities but talking into a microphone and listening to others using headphones. Hundreds of thousands of people have downloaded voice chat software. For example, the Saddlebrook, New Jersey, Police Department started using voice chat for communication with residents who want to discuss issues with the police while remaining anonymous.[12]

Groupware

Coined in the late 1980s,[13] the term **groupware** refers to software and related procedures that help teams work together by sharing information and by controlling internal workflows. This relatively new and still somewhat unshaped type of communication system has attained wide recognition due to the increasing need for dispersed teams to work together effectively at a distance as a result of downsizing and rapid organizational change. Groupware starts with messaging but goes further by facilitating access to documents and controlling team-related workflows. Many groupware products are related to specific group-related tasks such as project management, scheduling meetings ("calendaring"), and retrieving data from shared databases. Lotus Notes, a prominent product in this category, is designed for sharing text and images and contains a data structure that is a cross between a table-oriented database and an outline. For example, a law firm in Seattle uses Lotus Notes to permit everyone working on a particular case to have access to the most current memos and other information about that case, even if they are traveling. Other companies use Lotus Notes to store and revise product information for salespeople selling industrial products, thereby replacing the massive three-ring binders they formerly lugged around.

Yet other groupware functions are performed via **computer conferencing**, the exchange of text messages typed into computers from various locations to discuss a particular issue. When done through the Internet this is sometimes called a **newsgroup**. A computer conference permits people in dispersed locations to combine their ideas in useful ways even though they cannot speak to each other face-to-face. Any conference participant may be able to add new ideas, attach comments to existing messages, or direct comments to specific individuals or groups. Proponents of computer conferencing recognize some disadvantages of working through computers but emphasize major advantages, such as preventing a single forceful individual from dominating a meeting. Also, because everything is done through a computer, a record of how ideas developed is automatically generated.

A different type of groupware product focuses primarily on the flow of work in office settings. These products provide tools for structuring the process by which information for a particular multistep task is managed, transferred, and routed. A typical example is the approval of planned travel expenses. In this case, one person must propose the expenditure and someone else must approve it. The workflow application is set up to make the approval process simple and complete. In effect, groupware is being used as a small transaction processing system for multistep transactions. (See the section on transaction processing.)

Intranets and Extranets

The widespread use of the World Wide Web has led many firms to apply the information-sharing concepts of groupware on a much larger scale by creating a fourth type of communication system, intranets and extranets. **Intranets** are private communication networks that use the type of interface popularized by the Web but are accessible only by authorized employees, contractors, and customers. They are typically used to communicate nonsensitive but broadly useful information such as recent corporate news, general product information, employee manuals, corporate policies, telephone directories, details of health insurance and other employee benefits, and calendars. In some cases employees can use intranets to access and change their personal choices regarding health insurance and other benefits. Once security issues are addressed adequately, intranets for accessing general-purpose corporate data may lead to widespread use of intranets as a front end to transaction processing systems and management information systems described in the following sections.

The simplest intranets basically serve as electronic bulletin boards and employee manuals that make internal company information such as benefits rules, company calendar, sales promotions, and recent press releases readily available to company employees and contractors. Complex intranets can provide access to information in databases around the world. For example, in 2000, Electronic Data Systems (EDS) won a $7 billion contract to create a worldwide intranet for the U.S. Navy and Marines. This intranet would be linked to important military databases and would allow maintenance workers around the world "to pinpoint the availability of an airplane part anywhere in the Navy or Marine Corps system, or to contact the part manufacturer online."[14]

WEB CHECK [✓]

Look at your college's Web page. How might it be different if it were only an intranet directed to enrolled students, instructors, and other employees?

Extranets are private networks that operate similarly to intranets but are directed at customers rather than at employees. Extranets provide many types of information customers need, such as detailed product descriptions, frequently asked questions about different products, maintenance information, warranties, and how to contact customer service and sales offices. Much of this information was formerly difficult for customers to access because paper versions of it at the customer site became scattered and outdated. By using extranets, companies are making this type of information increasingly available at a single interactive site that is easy to navigate.

Knowledge Management

Today's leading businesses are increasingly aware that the knowledge of their employees is one of their primary assets. In consulting companies and other organizations that rely heavily on unique competencies and methods, knowledge has more competitive significance than physical assets because the physical assets can be replaced or replenished more easily.

Knowledge management systems are communication systems designed to facilitate the sharing of knowledge rather than just information. As with groupware, the idea of knowledge management is still emerging and is applied in many different ways in different firms. Tacit knowledge and explicit knowledge require different types of knowledge management efforts. **Tacit knowledge** is understood and applied unconsciously. Examples include an experienced manager's understanding of "human nature" and a member of a culture knowing how to act based on the culture's unwritten norms. It is acquired and shared through experience and social interaction. **Explicit knowledge** is precisely and formally articulated and is often codified in databases of corporate procedures and best practices. The computer applications underlying the management of explicit knowledge are often built on technologies such as intranets, electronic mail, groupware, databases, and search engines. Functions supported by these technologies include codifying knowledge (such as best practices), organizing it in repositories for later access, finding knowledge (using search engines and other schemes), and providing organized ways to find people who possess the required knowledge.[15, 16]

The human element is paramount in both sides of knowledge management. The companies with the best results to date stitch technologies together into a system that operates effectively and that is genuinely supported by the culture. For example, employee reviews in many consulting companies give significant weight to demonstrated contributions to knowledge sharing. This type of recognition is especially important if the firm's culture otherwise encourages internal competition and hoarding of knowledge for personal advancement. In many cases, the most effective use of knowledge requires involvement of the person who is the expert. When a British Petroleum drilling ship in the North Sea encountered an equipment failure, it put the equipment in front of a video camera and used a satellite link to contact a drilling expert in Scotland. His rapid diagnosis of the problem prevented delays and a possible shutdown.[17]

Due to the two sides of knowledge, the tacit and the explicit, different people who refer to knowledge management may mean completely different things. A knowledge management system sold by a software vendor is about codifying and accessing explicit knowledge. The human resources expert Jeffrey Pfeffer has argued that building intranets might give the appearance of knowledge management but in his view it is really just building an infrastructure that can be used "to transfer only explicit, codified information. Talk to people who work at consulting firms. They all have such 'knowledge management systems.' They are almost never used. No one has the time. There are a few simple principles to keep in mind: 1) The most important knowledge is tacit knowledge; 2) tacit knowledge and, for that matter, most explicit knowledge is exchanged best through personal interaction; 3) all work is knowledge work in today's economy; 4) firms lose knowledge when they lose their people."[18]

Group Support Systems

A form of groupware called a **group support system (GSS)** supports communication by helping facilitate meetings. The original idea was an offshoot of DSS research and was originally called group decision support systems (GDSS), although many of the people associated with these systems have shifted the term to GSS because many meetings are directed at brainstorming, discussions, and other purposes that may not be linked directly to decisions.

In its original concept, a GDSS was a specially outfitted conference room containing hardware and software that facilitates meetings (see Figure 5.5). This technology may include advanced presentation devices, computer access to databases, and capabilities permitting the participants in a meeting to communicate electronically. These rooms improve same-time, same-place communication by a group of people working together in a meeting. The meeting's purpose could be anything from brainstorming

A GDSS

This computerized conference room has been used for research and pilot studies of group decision-making. It combines carefully designed physical space with extensive software capabilities for recording and processing ideas, votes, and other data generated by meeting participants.

about possible new product features to reviewing business operations or responding to an emergency. Today's typical GSS capabilities include:[19]

- *Display*. A workstation screen or previously prepared presentation material is displayed to the entire group.
- *Electronic brainstorming*. Participants enter and share comments anonymously through their computer screens.
- *Topic commenting*. Participants add comments to ideas previously generated by themselves or others.
- *Issue analysis*. Participants identify and consolidate key items generated during electronic brainstorming.
- *Voting*. Participants use the computer to vote on topics, with a choice of prioritization methods.
- *Alternative evaluation*. The computer ranks alternative decisions based on preferences entered by users.

GSS has been more of a research topic than common practice in business, although experience to date suggests GSS has significant potential for improving both the efficiency and effectiveness of certain types of decision-making. Typical meetings in a pilot study for internal problem solving at IBM generated a large number of high-quality ideas. The meetings took about half as long as participants' estimates of the length of regular meetings on the same topics.[20] An important GSS phenomenon is the impact of entering and transmitting ideas anonymously. Unlike typical meetings, very little cross-talk occurs during anonymous brainstorming sessions, and participants tend to comment on the topic at hand. Anonymity encourages participation by all members of the group, independent of their status. It tends to reduce groupthink, pressures for conformity, and dominance of forceful individuals. It also tends to heighten conflict because people's comments in this context may be more assertive and less polite than spoken comments. It remains to be seen whether or not this type of guided group interaction will become commonplace, although some GSS capabilities have already been introduced into computer conferencing.

TRANSACTION PROCESSING SYSTEMS

A **transaction processing system (TPS)** collects and stores data about transactions and sometimes controls decisions made as part of a transaction. A transaction is a business event that generates or modifies data stored in an information system. TPSs were the first computerized information systems that were used widely. We encounter computerized TPSs frequently, including every time we write a check, use a credit card, or pay a bill sent by a company. A TPS used to record a sale and generate a receipt is primarily concerned with collecting and storing data. If the TPS validates a credit card or helps a clerk determine whether to accept a personal check, it also controls decisions made within the transaction. Figure 5.6 contains a TPS data entry screen.

TPSs are designed based on detailed specifications for how the transaction should be performed and how to control the collection of specific data in specific data formats and in accordance with rules, policies, and goals of the organization. Most contain enough structure to enforce rules and procedures for work done by clerks or customer service agents. Some TPSs bypass clerks and totally automate transactions, such as the way ATMs automate deposits and cash withdrawals. A well-designed TPS checks each transaction for easily detectable errors such as missing data, data values that are obviously too high or too low, data values that are inconsistent with other data in the database, and data in the wrong format. It may check for required authorizations for the transaction. Certain TPSs such as airline reservation systems may automate decision-making functions such

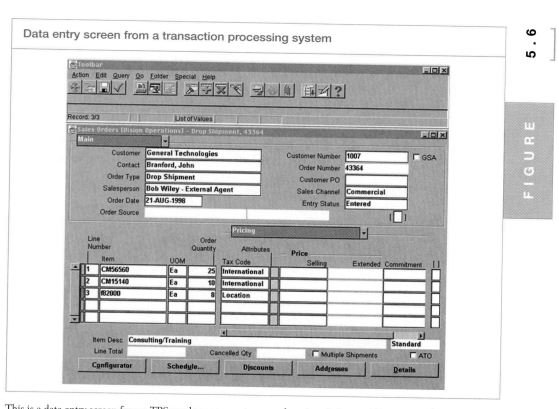

FIGURE 5.6

Data entry screen from a transaction processing system

This is a data entry screen from a TPS used to enter customer orders. A well-designed TPS can minimize data entry errors by automatically filling in data such as customer address or unit price once the user has entered the customer or product number.

as finding the flight that best meets the customer's needs. Finally, when all the information for the transaction has been collected and validated, the TPS stores it in a standard format for later access by others.

As anyone knows who has tried to make a reservation when a computerized reservation system is down, organizations rely heavily on their TPSs. Breakdowns disrupt operations and may even bring business to a complete halt. As a result, a well-designed TPS has backup and recovery procedures that minimize disruptions resulting from computer outages.

Batch versus Real-Time Processing

The two main types of transaction processing are batch processing and real-time processing. With **batch processing**, information for individual transactions is gathered and stored but isn't processed immediately. Later, either on a schedule or when a sufficient number of transactions have accumulated, the transactions are processed to update the database. With **real-time processing**, each transaction is processed immediately. The person providing the information is typically available to help with error correction and receives confirmation of transaction completion. Batch processing was the only feasible form of transaction processing when data were stored only on punched cards or tapes. Real-time transaction processing requires immediate access to an online database.

Batch processing is currently used in some situations where the transaction data comes in on paper, such as in processing checks and airline ticket stubs. A batch approach is also used for generating paychecks and other forms of paper output that will be distributed after a delay. Unfortunately time delays inherent in batch processing may cause significant disadvantages. The central database may never be completely current because of transactions received while the batch was being processed. Worse yet, batching the transactions creates built-in delays, with transactions not completed until the next day in some cases. Even systems with interactive user interfaces may include lengthy delays before transactions are completed. For example, weekend deposits into many ATMs are not posted to the depositor's account until Monday. Even though the ATM's user interface is interactive, the larger system doesn't perform real-time processing.

Batch process may seem very old-fashioned, but securities firms still settle their trades using a batch process. In other words, the trades are recorded in real time, but the payment system uses an overnight batch process that may take up to three days. The Securities and Exchange Commission urged the brokerage industry to settle all trades within 24 hours, but the industry said the conversion would take four years and would cost $8 billion. Part of the problem is that every company in the industry would have to switch to nearly real-time transactions between brokerages and banks.[21]

Compared to batch processing, real-time processing has more stringent requirements for computer response and computer uptime. As is obvious when a travel agent says, "Sorry, the computer is down," the jobs and work methods of the people using a real-time TPS are designed under the assumption that the system will be up and available.

MANAGEMENT AND EXECUTIVE INFORMATION SYSTEMS

A **management information system (MIS)** provides information for managing an organization. The idea of MIS predates the computer age. For example, as long ago as the middle 1500s, the Fugger family in Augsberg, Germany, had business interests throughout Europe and even into China and Peru. To keep in touch, they set up a worldwide news-reporting service through which their agents wrote letters about critical political and economic events in their areas of responsibility. These letters were collected, interpreted, analyzed, and summarized in Augsberg and answered through instructions sent to the family's agents. This paper-based system encompassing plan-

FIGURE 5.7

Division/ Branch	Sales	Plan	Perf vs. Plan	Sales Per Rep.	% Repeat Sales
Southeast					
Atlanta	1217	1189	1.02	112	51
Miami	1643	1734	0.95	137	34
New Orleans	1373	1399	0.98	108	44
Tampa	2300	2106	1.09	145	53
Total	6533	6428	1.02	129	46
Midwest					
Chicago	6323	6523	0.97	144	66
Detroit	6845	6448	1.06	137	53
Minneapolis	5783	6300	0.92	150	71
St. Louis	5345	5318	1.01	129	55
Total	24296	24589	0.99	140	61
Far West					
Phoenix	2337	2445	0.96	104	44
Portland	3426	3276	1.05	120	52

A management report from a hypothetical MIS

This figure represents a management report showing last month's sales results for an office supplies company that is expanding out of its major Midwest markets into the Southeast and Far West.

ning, execution, and control helped the family move more rapidly in the mercantile world than their rivals.[22] Instructions went out to the agents; the agents executed their work; and the agents reported their results.

Computerized MISs generate information for monitoring performance, maintaining coordination, and providing background information about the organization's operation. Users include both managers and the employees who receive feedback about performance indicators such as productivity. Figure 5.7 shows a sample report from a hypothetical MIS. Notice how it provides summary information rather than the details of individual sales transactions.

The concept of MIS emerged partly as a response to the shortcomings of the first computerized TPSs, which often improved transaction processing but provided little information for management. Computerized MISs typically extract and summarize data from TPSs to allow managers to monitor and direct the organization and to provide employees accurate feedback about easily measured aspects of their work. For example, a listing of every sale during a day or week would be extremely difficult to use in monitoring a hardware store's performance. However, the same data could be summarized in measures of performance, such as total sales for each type of item, for each salesperson, and for each hour of the day. The transaction data remains indispensable, and the MIS focuses it for management.

As part of an organization's formal control mechanisms, an MIS provides some structure for the comparatively unstructured task of management by identifying important measures of performance. The fact that everyone knows how performance is measured helps in making decisions and helps managers motivate workers. For example, in a sales group expecting $1,000 per day of evenly distributed sales, the MIS might report that a salesperson met weekly and monthly sales targets but usually did poorly on one group of products. In this typical situation, the MIS reports information but leaves it to the people to decide how to improve performance.

From MIS to EIS

An **executive information system (EIS)** is a highly interactive system providing managers and executives flexible access to information for monitoring operating results and general business conditions. These systems are sometimes called *executive support systems (ESS)*. EIS attempts to take over where the traditional MIS approach falls short. Although sometimes acceptable for monitoring the same indicators over time, the traditional MIS approach of providing prespecified reports on a scheduled basis is too inflexible for many questions executives really care about, such as understanding problems and new situations.

EISs provide executives with internal and competitive information through user-friendly interfaces that can be used by someone with almost no computer-related knowledge. EISs are designed to help executives find the information they need whenever they need it and in whatever form is most useful. Typically, users can choose among numerous tabular or graphical formats. They can also control the level of detail, the triggers for exception conditions, and other aspects of the information displayed. Most EISs focus on providing executives with the background information they need, as well as help in understanding the causes of exceptions and surprises. This leaves executives better prepared to discuss issues with their subordinates.

A typical sequence of EIS use is shown in Figure 5.8. The EIS user starts with a menu listing available types of information, such as sales results, manufacturing results, competitive performance, and e-mail messages. The categories are customized for individual executives. The user selects a category from the menu and receives an additional menu identifying available subcategories plus the specific online reports that can be obtained. The executive can often customize these reports by choosing options, such as selecting a subset of the data, sorting, or providing more detail. For example, while looking at last month's sales results, a user might select the branches with less than 2% improvement, sort these sales branches from highest to lowest percentage improvement, and obtain more detail for these branches by looking at results for individual departments within these branches. In addition, users can generate graphical displays such as trend charts and pie charts to make it easier to visualize what is happening.

For an EIS to operate, technical staff members must ensure that the right data are available and are downloaded to the EIS from other systems in a timely manner. The data in EISs are usually replenished periodically from internal company databases and external databases. Although technical advances in data display and networking capabilities have made EISs much easier to maintain, EISs continually modified to keep up with current business issues still require major efforts and substantial technical maintenance.

Although EIS users are executives and managers, ideally anyone in a business should be able to get the right information in the right format. Even when commercial EIS software is used, the time and effort to customize and maintain an EIS limits use to high-level managers. Ideally, the flexibility and ease of access built into EIS should also be built into other information systems. Ten years ago, it was much more expensive to provide EIS capabilities to executives. Ten years from now, the interfaces in information systems at all organizational levels may mimic or exceed those in today's EIS.

Do MIS and EIS Really Solve Managers' Problems?

The foregoing discussion describing typical MIS and EIS capabilities said little about whether these information systems actually provide the information managers need. In fact, different managers have very different types of responsibilities. An MIS for a first-line manager deeply involved in the details of how work is done would be very different from an MIS for a high-level manager, who is more concerned with making an entire organization operate effectively. Top managers are also concerned with developing and instilling a long-range vision of where the organization is going. Most introductory management texts start discussing what managers do by identifying the classical

Use of an executive information system

FIGURE 5.8

(a)

	A	B	C	D	E	F	G	H
1				Profit before tax report for September, 1999				
2								
3		Actual	% of total	Budget	% of total	Variance	% Variance	
4								
5	Microwave	2248	48.63	2197	0.46	51	2.3	
6	Mixers	1337	28.92	1390	0.29	-53	-3.8	
7	Coffee ma	590	12.76	630	0.13	-40	-6.3	
8	Toasters	448	9.69	550	0.12	-102	-18.5	
9		----------	----------	----------	----------	----------	----------	
10		4623	100.00	4767	100.00	-144	-3.0	
11								
12								
13								
14								
15								
16								
17								
18								

Sheet1 **Sheet2** Sheet3

(b)

	A	B	C	D	E	F	G	H
1				Profit summary for Microwave Ovens, September 1999				
2								
3		Actual	% of total	Budget	% of total	Variance	% Variance	
4								
5	Net sales	14014	100.00	13167	100.00	847	6.4	
6	Cost of sal	-7987	-1.33	-7367	-1.27	-620	8.4	
7		----------		----------		----------	----------	
8	Gross mar	6027	100.00	5800	100.00	227	3.9	
9								
10	Product D	1635	0.46	1223	0.37	412	33.7	
11	Selling	1449	0.40	1675	0.51	-226	-13.5	
12	Gen. & Ad	494	0.14	406	0.12	88	21.7	
13		----------		----------		----------	----------	
14	Expenses	3578	100.00	3304	100.00	274	8.3	
15								
16	Net profit	2449	0.17	2496	0.19	-47	-0.1	
17								
18								

Sheet1 Sheet2 **Sheet3**

(c)

	A	B	C	D	E	F	G	H
1				1998 Product Development expenses for Toasters				
2								
3								
4		Actual	Budget	Variance				
5	Jan.	1359	1440	-81				
6	Feb.	1420	1474	-54				
7	Mar.	1466	1450	16				
8	Apr.	1468	1450	18				
9	May	1507	1600	-93				
10	Jun.	1591	1550	41				
11	Jul.	1613	1470	143				
12	Aug.	1630	1350	280				
13	Sept.	1635	1223	412				
14								
15	Year to date	13689	13007	682				
16								
17								

This sequence, using a spreadsheet, demonstrates how an executive can use an EIS to study a firm's financial results by "drilling down" to understand specific items in more detail. (a) The executive scans the firm's standard financial report summarizing actual versus budgeted revenues and expenses for the month of September. The executive wants to look at the Microwave division in more detail and with an EIS would use a mouse or touch screen to identify the area where more detailed data is needed. (b) The more detailed data for the Microwave division shows that product development expenses are 33.7% over budget for the month. This variance calls for a deeper look. (c) The executive looks at monthly actual versus budget for this category and sees that expenses have not fallen as they were supposed to. This background information will help the executive ask probing questions when discussing the situation with the managers in charge of product development.

management functions, such as planning, organizing, leading, and controlling. After identifying these functions, many texts point out that these functions do not adequately describe what managers actually do.

Figure 5.9 identifies the types of information systems that support a list of managerial roles based on a well-known characterization of managerial work by Mintzberg. The roles are grouped into three categories: interpersonal, informational, and decisional. Even though the mix of roles would differ greatly between the CEO of General Motors and a branch accounting manager, most managers perform most of these roles to some extent. For example, as part of organizing a department, a manager could play interpersonal roles such as figurehead for the organizational effort, leader for meetings, and liaison to other departments. Informational roles in the process could include monitoring activities, disseminating the principles behind the new organization, and serving as organizational spokesperson. Decisional roles could include the entrepreneur defining the new goals, the negotiator resolving conflicts, and the disturbance handler.

Figure 5.9 shows that different types of information systems support the different management roles. The relevance of communication systems to all of the management roles illustrates that management is a highly interactive job. Typical managers spend

FIGURE 5.9

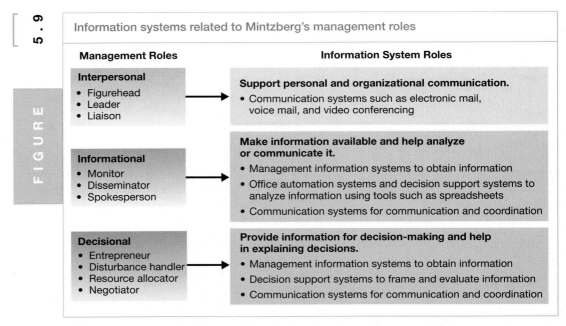

Information systems related to Mintzberg's management roles

Management Roles	Information System Roles
Interpersonal • Figurehead • Leader • Liaison	**Support personal and organizational communication.** • Communication systems such as electronic mail, voice mail, and video conferencing
Informational • Monitor • Disseminator • Spokesperson	**Make information available and help analyze or communicate it.** • Management information systems to obtain information • Office automation systems and decision support systems to analyze information using tools such as spreadsheets • Communication systems for communication and coordination
Decisional • Entrepreneur • Disturbance handler • Resource allocator • Negotiator	**Provide information for decision-making and help in explaining decisions.** • Management information systems to obtain information • Decision support systems to frame and evaluate information • Communication systems for communication and coordination

Different types of information systems support different types of management roles.

little time doing detailed analytical work. To the contrary, brevity, variety, and fragmentation characterize managerial work. Many managers prefer verbal media rather than written media and work through their network of personal contacts.[23]

Since the information that managers use should be consistent with their work style, much of that information does *not* come from formalized information systems. Rather, it comes from networks of contacts inside and outside the organization and from gathering information about particular issues of current importance. Managers also absorb information from being present in an organization and from "management by walking around."[24] Table 5.3 extends this theme by categorizing common sources of management information as formal or informal and internal or external. Formal information may come from computer-based systems, written documents, or scheduled meetings. Informal information comes from a range of sources such as lunchtime gossip, trade shows, and what managers learn while walking around.

Recognizing this range of information sources helps clarify why formal systems provide managers with only part of the information they need even though they do provide a lot of essential information. The high degree of variety and action in managerial work implies that information systems used by managers should be flexible and easy to use. Because managers often deal with exceptions and nonroutine situations, the particular information they need tomorrow may not be the same as the informa-

TABLE 5.3

Common Sources of Management Information

Character of the information	Internal sources	External sources
Formal, computer-based	Key indicators generated by internal tracking systems	Public databases
Formal, document-based	Planning reports, internal audits	Industry reports, books, magazines
Formal, verbal	Scheduled meetings	Industry forums
Informal	Lunch conversations, gossip, management-by-walking-around	Trade shows, personal contacts

tion they need today. If a formal information system does not readily support tomorrow's needs, an action-oriented manager will simply bypass it and find some other source of information.

DECISION SUPPORT SYSTEMS

A **decision support system (DSS)** is an interactive information system that provides information, models, and data manipulation tools to help make decisions in semistructured and unstructured situations where no one knows exactly how the decision should be made. The traditional DSS approach includes interactive problem solving, direct use of models, and user-controllable methods for displaying and analyzing data and formulating and evaluating alternative decisions. This approach emerged in the 1970s in response to dissatisfaction with the traditional limitations of TPS and MIS. TPS focused on record keeping and control of repetitive clerical processes. MIS provided reports for management that were often inflexible, and was unable to produce the information in a form that managers could use effectively. In contrast, DSSs were intended to support managers and professionals doing largely analytical work in less structured situations with unclear criteria for success. DSSs are typically designed to solve the structured parts of the problem and help isolate places where judgment and experience are required.

Many of the originally innovative DSS concepts have now become commonplace in the convenient interactive use of spreadsheets, databases, and other interactive tools. Other decision-making applications often included under the DSS heading include highly customized simulation or optimization models focusing on a specific business situation. DSSs now apply a wide range of repetitive or nonrepetitive decision-making. They support repetitive decision-making by defining procedures and formats, but still permit the users to decide how and when to use the system's capabilities. They support nonrepetitive decision-making by providing data, models, and interface methods that can be used however the user wants (see Figure 5.10).

Despite the widespread penetration of DSS concepts into computer usage, many DSS efforts have languished and have had little impact. The concept of a work system

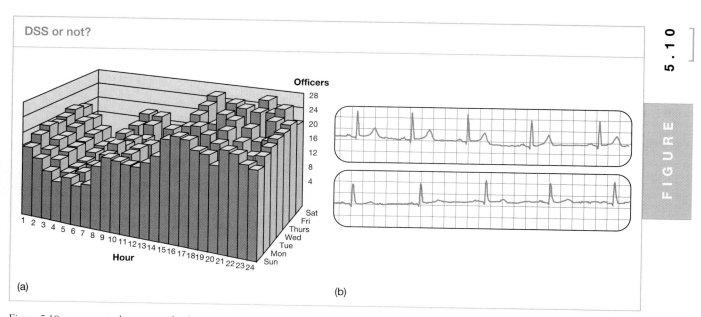

DSS or not?

Officers

Hour

(a)

(b)

FIGURE 5.10

Figure 5.10a represents the output of a decision support system used by the San Francisco Police Department to schedule police officers. This three-dimensional graph shows the average requirements for police officers for each hour in each day of the week. Figure 5.10b shows an electrocardiogram generated by a doctor's nurse so that the doctor can look for irregularities in the heartbeat pattern of a patient. Although both examples support decision-making, the second is not usually included in discussions of DSS because the physician uses a printout instead of using a computer directly.

is a good starting point for understanding what makes real-world applications of DSS succeed. Figure 2.7 and Table 2.4 showed that success factors for work systems in general also apply to information systems. Most DSS disappointments probably come from the absence of important work system success factors in the situation.

The rest of this section will identify some of the data- and model-related techniques applied in different types of DSS. Table 5.4 summarizes the approach and the source of a number of prominent techniques used in DSS. It starts with the most model-intensive approaches (simulation and optimization), continues with the most data-intensive approaches (OLAP and data mining), and then mentions a number of approaches that evolved from methods developed in artificial intelligence (AI) research. Most readers probably have at least some experience with statistics, simulation, and possibly optimization. The topics related to AI are not used as frequently, are

[L O O K   A H E A D]

Artificial intelligence, the field of research related to the demonstration of intelligence by machines, is discussed at the beginning and end of Chapter 9, "Software, Programming, and Artificial Intelligence."

TABLE 5.4

Important Techniques Sometimes Used in Supporting Decision-Making		
Techniques	**Related discipline**	**Approach**
Simulation	Research on different simulation techniques	Create a mathematical model of the situation. Define the main decision variables and operate the model under different assumptions or with different starting conditions to help explore alternative paths for the real situation.
Optimization	Mathematical optimization techniques	Create a mathematical model of the situation. Design the model so that optimization techniques can be used to search for optimal values of decision variables.
OLAP and data mining	Statistics (mathematical techniques) and computer science (database techniques)	Use statistical techniques to analyze business results and find hidden relationships.
Expert systems	AI research on language and knowledge representation	Summarize an expert's view of an area of knowledge in terms of facts and rules. Apply the facts and rules to a particular situation to help someone else decide what to do.
Neural networks	Statistics (mathematical techniques) and AI research related to perception	Start with a large set of coded examples that represent the range and frequency of possibilities in the situation being studied. Apply automated statistical "learning" techniques to find the statistical parameters that best represent correlations between groups of characteristics within the training set.
Fuzzy logic	Research on alternative formal logic systems	Control decision processes using logic systems that replace "either–or" logic with logic based on relative degrees of inclusion in sets.
Case-based reasoning	AI research on representing knowledge	Create a database of examples that may help in making decisions. Add another example to the database when the database does not cover a new situation.
Intelligent agents	AI research on controlling systems that operate on many levels	Specify decision parameters for a computerized "agent" that searches one or more databases to find a specific answer, such as the lowest price for a particular camera.

unfamiliar to most readers, and are often not grouped with DSS even though they support decision-making in a number of important applications.

Simulation and Optimization

The diagram in Figure 4.19 represented a manager's mental model of the way certain variables influence the profit in a particular situation. When used as part of a DSS, a mental model is formalized as a mathematical model using a spreadsheet or other programming method. Some of the relationships in the model are accounting identities, such as the fact that profit equals revenue minus expenses. Others are assumptions or empirical generalizations derived from data.

This type of model is typically used as a **simulation model** because it calculates the simulated outcome of tentative decisions and assumptions entered by the user. Most current simulation models for financial decisions are built using spreadsheet software that nonprogrammers can use and that is well suited for most planning and budgeting decisions. Other programming tools are more effective for creating simulations in other types of situations. An **optimization model** uses a fundamentally different approach for generating information used in decision-making. Instead of starting with tentative decisions, optimization models start with optimization criteria supplied by the user and then use mathematical search techniques to determine the optimal decisions based on the criteria and any constraints that apply. Both simulation models and optimization models are typically used in an iterative fashion by asking **what-if questions** to try out different assumptions and to test the effect of uncertainties related to certain relationships or assumptions.

The results calculated by simulation and optimization models are usually viewed as inputs to decision processes, but are not the only determinant of the decision since models typically ignore other factors that need to be considered. In general, the mathematical model supports the decision process by distilling disparate facts, accounting relationships, empirical relationships, and assumptions into information that is focused directly on the decision.

OLAP and Data Mining

Simulation and optimization models represent a model-oriented approach to DSS. A data-oriented approach focuses on analyzing data and extracting nuggets of insight that may help in making better decisions. The use of online data analysis tools to explore large databases of transaction data is called **online analytical processing (OLAP)**. The idea of OLAP grew out of difficulties analyzing the data in databases that were being updated continually by online transaction processing systems. When the analytical processes accessed large slices of the transaction database, they slowed down transaction processing. The solution was periodic downloads of data from the active TPS database into a separate database for analysis work. The discussion of data warehouses in Chapter 4 explained how the data is extracted, consolidated, filtered, transformed, and aggregated (see Figure 4.10). Use of a data warehouse makes it possible to perform both transaction processing and OLAP efficiently without mutual interference.

Data mining is the use of data analysis tools to try to find the patterns in large transaction databases such as the customer receipts generated in a large sample of grocery stores across the United States. Careful analysis of this data might reveal patterns that could be used for marketing promotions, such as a correlation between diaper sales and beer sales during the evening hours. For example, MCI used data mining to identify customers who were likely to switch to other carriers. It analyzed data on 140 million households and looked at as many as 10,000 characteristics, such as income, lifestyle, and details of past calling patterns. Eventually it found 22 statistical profiles of customers who are likely to switch. MCI's chief information officer said that these highly confidential profiles could not have been developed without data mining.[25] In another example, Chase Manhattan Bank discovered that a lot of customers with multiple accounts were actually unprofitable. This finding contradicted long-held beliefs and helped the bank refocus its marketing approach.[26] In yet another example, Florida Hospital in Orlando analyzed the probability that patients would pay whatever part of their bill was not covered by insurance. The analysis helped them decide whether to forward delinquent accounts to a collection agency or try to collect from these accounts for another 30 to 60 days, thereby avoiding collection agency fees.[27]

The problem with data mining is that many patterns occur strictly by chance and have no value in making business decisions. For example, a data mining program might discover that sales of ice cream in Iowa are correlated with sales of concrete in India. Unlike what usually would happen with a meaningful pattern, a spurious pattern such as this would probably disappear if the same data were gathered next year. According to Mark Hulbert, who writes a newsletter that ranks investment newsletters, a number of investment newsletters use data mining approaches to search for "strategies" that would have been successful in the past. An example might be "buy the five lowest priced stocks among the 10 highest yielding Dow companies." Test 100 random strategies similar to this and one probably will look best. But there is no reason to believe this is anything but a statistical accident.[28] This explains why some "proven strategies" will run out of luck.

Expert Systems

Operating from a very different starting point, **expert systems** support professionals engaged in design, diagnosis, or evaluation of complex situations requiring expert knowledge in a well-defined area. The first expert systems were developed in the 1970s as part of AI research about developing ways for computers to "understand" situations in order to translate between languages and respond to queries from people. Expert systems have been used to make credit decisions, diagnose diseases, configure computers, analyze chemicals, analyze machine vibrations, and support many other problem-solving processes. They are used either as interactive advisors or as automated tools for converting data into recommendations or other conclusions. Common reasons for developing expert systems include preserving an expert's knowledge, improving the performance of less experienced people doing similar tasks, and enforcing some consistency in the way people do particular types of work.

Expert systems try to mimic the reasoning an expert would use and are often called **knowledge-based systems** because they represent knowledge in an explicit form so that it can be applied automatically. Many expert systems represent knowledge as **if-then rules** stated in the form: *If* certain conditions are true, *then* certain conclusions should be drawn. A hypothetical if-then rule that might be used to decide whether to grant a business loan is:

> *If: The applicant is current on all debts, and the applicant has been profitable for two years, and the applicant has strong market position,*
> *Then: The applicant is an excellent credit risk.*

The five major components of an idealized expert system are illustrated in Figure 5.11. The **knowledge base** is a set of general facts and if-then rules supplied by an expert. The *database* of facts related to the specific situation being analyzed may start as a blank slate each time the system is used or may begin with data gathered previously. The **inference engine** uses rules in the knowledge base plus whatever facts are currently in the database to decide what question to ask next, either to the user or to other databases. The *interface* is the way the expert system interacts with the user. The **explanation module** is available to the user as a way to find out how a particular fact was inferred or why a particular question is being asked.

As illustrated in Figure 5.12, expert system logic combines forward chaining and backward chaining. **Forward chaining** starts with data and tries to draw conclusions from the data, especially if trying to determine all of the conclusions implied by the data when there is no clear goal. **Backward chaining** starts with a tentative conclusion and then looks for facts in the database supporting that conclusion. As part of backward chaining, the expert system may identify facts that would confirm or deny the conclusion and then look up these facts in a database or ask the user questions related to these facts.

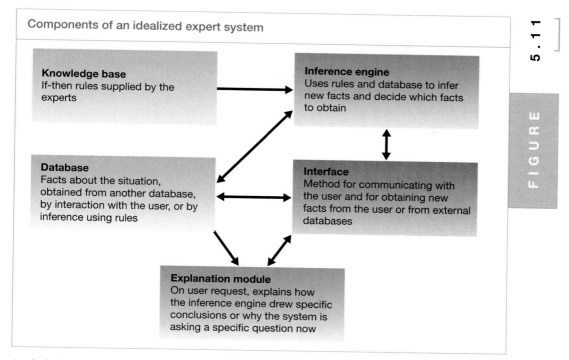

An idealized expert system can be described in terms of five components.

The term "expert system" is actually a misnomer. Although they contain some of the knowledge of a human expert, these systems are not true experts because they lack common sense and have no real understanding of the data and logic they are using. This is why it is risky to trust expert systems to make decisions independently. In contrast, human experts learn by experience, restructure their knowledge, break the rules when necessary, determine the relevance of new facts, and recognize the limits of their knowledge when they encounter unfamiliar situations.[29] They can often see that data is probably erroneous or that a particular rule or procedure was designed for one situation and doesn't really apply in another. Except in problems that are totally understood,

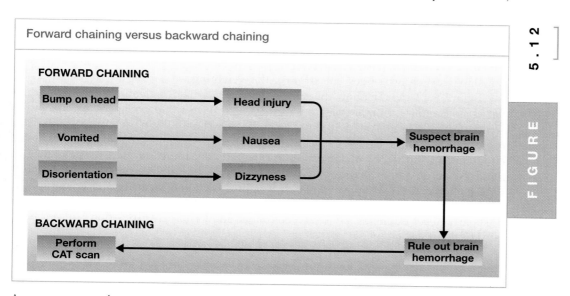

An emergency room physician examines a 3-year-old injured in an automobile accident. The child has a bump on his head, has vomited, and seems disoriented. Although the physician would immediately decide to perform tests to rule out a brain hemorrhage, an expert system confronted with this information might go through intermediate forward chaining steps.

appropriate uses of expert systems divide responsibilities between the expert system and a person. The person is responsible for making the decision and exercising common sense. The expert system structures part of the analysis, makes sure that important factors haven't been ignored, and provides information that helps the person make a good decision.

R E A L I T Y C H E C K ✓

What Can We Trust Expert Systems to Do?

1. You are a passenger on an airplane and have just learned that it will be landed automatically by an expert system. How would you feel about that? Why?

2. You are a pilot and have just learned that the airline plans to buy airplanes containing an expert system that controls takeoffs and landings. How would you feel about that? Why?

Neural Networks

Although the concept of an artificial neural network is an early offshoot of AI research, it is actually a statistical method for finding and representing patterns in data. The term *neural network* comes from attempts to model the way the human brain operates. A **neural network** is an information system that recognizes objects or patterns based on examples that have been used to train it. Each training example is described in terms of a set of characteristics and a result, such as whether or not a loan was repaid. In its "learning phase" the neural network uses statistical methods to optimize a set of internal weights that relate each input to each of the possible results. Neural networks often do well with identification and discrimination tasks even when some information is missing because they operate by applying numerical weights to many different characteristics. This is a numerical attempt to mimic the typical human ability to work with partial information, such as trying to recognize someone who is wearing sunglasses or a hat.

Figure 5.13 represents a simplified neural network for deciding whether to approve or deny mortgage loans based on years at the current address, years at the current job, the ratio of salary to the loan amount, health, and credit rating. For each characteristic the input layer contains a separate neuron that is linked to each of seven neurons in the hidden layer. Each of those neurons is linked to the two neurons in the output layer. In all, this neural network contains 15 nodes and 56 links. The numerical weighting of each link is represented in the picture by the thickness of the line. The stronger the relationship between two nodes, the stronger the weighting.

Figure 5.13 explains how the neural network learns by adjusting these weightings based on examples. In real cases, a network might have 1,000 examples, and the entire sequence might be repeated 50 times to make sure the weightings converge to the best representation of the data. In some ways this process resembles the process by which a child learns to speak, by making sounds and gradually adjusting them into clearly pronounced words. After the training, the neural network would be ready to assist in mortgage loan decisions. Because it uses a weighting scheme involving many inputs, the neural network might give reasonably good results even when some data is missing or in slightly novel examples, such as a combination of characteristics that had not been used in the training.

Neural networks operate based on a totally different approach from expert systems, which rely on an expert's ability to express knowledge through an explicit knowledge representation such as rules. In contrast, neural networks are used for tasks that have no predefined formulas or procedures. If a task can be performed well using known procedures, there is no reason to build a neural network. Neural networks have been applied to a wide range of problems, such as predicting business failures, rating bonds,

FIGURE   5.13

Using neural networks

Create a starting point for training: The starting point for the learning process is a neural network with random weights assigned to all the associations between the hidden layer and the input and output layers. Some of these initial weights may not make much sense because these initial values are an arbitrary starting point and are eventually washed out by exposure to numerous repetitions of examples that contain the patterns the neural network is learning.

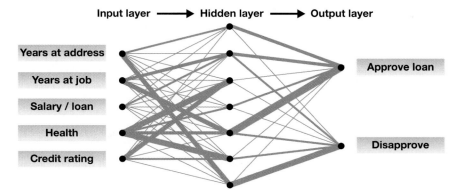

Adjust the weights based on each example: This step is repeated for every example in the training set. The mathematical techniques for modifying the weights (and hence, learning) involve changing the weights in a way that minimizes the overall error that would occur when all the examples thus far are considered. You can see that a number of the weights have changed. For example, the link emanating from *years at job* and *ratio of salary* to loan has increased in weight because these two variables must be strong indicators of good loans in the training set.

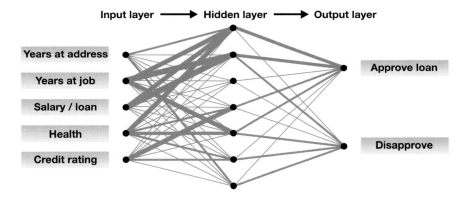

Use the neural network: Once the neural network is trained, it can be used for making decisions. If a loan application arrived from someone with long job tenure and a high ratio of salary to loan amount, this neural network would probably approve the loan.

The process of using neural networks starts by defining the network's structure. This is done by identifying the nodes in the input and output layer, creating the links to and from hidden layers, and deciding on the mathematical technique that will be used for learning. The next steps are creating a starting point for its training, training it, and then using it.

trading commodities, detecting fraud, generating forecasts, controlling refrigerators, and identifying explosives based on gamma ray patterns. They are especially applicable in situations where a large database of examples is available and where even experts cannot give rules for converting situational characteristics into recognizable patterns.

At first blush a computerized system that learns automatically might seem like magic: turn it on and watch it learn. Of course it isn't that simple. People who create neural networks must decide what factors to use as input nodes and output nodes, how to arrange the hidden layers, and what mathematical learning technique to use. If the database is too small or if it is not representative, the neural network may learn incorrect weightings. For example, a prototype of a loan approval system often approved loans for applicants with low income and rejected loans for applicants with high income because the training data had contained many low-income individuals who were good credit risks. The neural network learned to treat low income as a favorable characteristic.[30] In another case, a neural network was trained to distinguish between tanks and other battlefield objects. However, all the pictures of the tanks had been taken with one camera and were slightly darker than the pictures of the other objects, which had been taken by another camera. The neural network had actually learned to distinguish between the cameras, not between tanks and other objects.[31]

R E A L I T Y C H E C K [✓]

Vulnerability to Training Errors in Neural Networks

Neural networks are vulnerable to training errors, but people also make mistakes because they establish stereotypes based on just a few examples.

1. Identify some of the stereotypes you have heard people talk about that are probably based on just a few examples that may be unrepresentative.

2. Explain whether you think it is healthy or unhealthy to form stereotypes this way. For example, is it unhealthy to conclude that ice is dangerous after slipping once, or that people from Chicago are helpful after being helped once in Chicago?

Fuzzy Logic

Fuzzy logic is often used in conjunction with neural networks because it addresses some of the same issues. **Fuzzy logic** is a form of reasoning that makes it possible to combine imprecise conditions stated in a form similar to the types of descriptive categories people use. The term was coined in 1964 by Lofti Zadeh, a professor at Berkeley. Fuzzy logic was invented to minimize a problem that occurs in expert systems and in many types of formal reasoning. The expert system rule cited earlier recognized only whether it is true or false that the applicant has been profitable for two years. The trivial difference between a $1 profit and a $1 loss would affect the decision just as much as the difference between a $100 million profit and a $1 loss. Fuzzy logic recognizes that better decisions might result from combining a number of different rules based on a set of conditions such as very profitable, somewhat profitable, slightly profitable, slightly unprofitable, and so on. Furthermore, instead of forcing a precise cutoff between "somewhat profitable" and "slightly profitable," the reasoning system could treat these categories as somewhat overlapping, thereby reasoning in a manner similar to the way a person would reason.

Figure 5.14 shows how fuzzy logic might be used to control an air conditioner. Instead of forcing cool and cold to be mutually exclusive, the fuzzy controller would allow these conditions to overlap because a particular temperature might have some "degree of membership" in coldness and some degree of membership in coolness. A rule about coolness could apply at the same time other rules about coldness or another characteristic applies. The fuzzy controller could come to a decision by combining all of the rules based on the relative degree of coldness, coolness, and other characteristics. This type of logic avoids artificial cutoffs that may lead to poor decisions when using either–or rules.

Fuzzy logic has been used in household appliances such as refrigerators and Matsushita's fuzzy washing machines, which use sensors and fuzzy rules to automatically adjust the wash cycle to the kind and amount of dirt (muddy or oily) in the wash water and the size of the load.[32] Fuzzy logic attained such prominence in Japan that appliances are labeled as fuzzy or not, and people have argued about whether a particular appliance truly deserves the label. Applications in video cameras include auto-

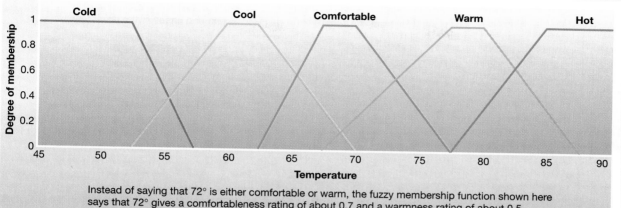

Example of fuzzy variables, fuzzy rules, and how they are combined

FIGURE 5.14

Instead of saying that 72° is either comfortable or warm, the fuzzy membership function shown here says that 72° gives a comfortableness rating of about 0.7 and a warmness rating of about 0.5. If an air conditioner were based on crisp rules, it would have to decide whether the current temperature was comfortable or warm. Only one case could apply. But a fuzzy controller could use the following two rules simultaneously:
(1) If it is comfortable, then continue the current cooling level.
(2) If it is warm, then increase the cooling a little.
At a temperature of 72° both rules would fire, but their effect would be weighted by the degree of comfortableness (in the first rule) and the degree of warmness (from the second rule). Many other rules might fire at the same time. The fuzzy controller could weight all of these results to decide whether to increase, decrease, or leave the cooling constant.

matic focusing, automatic exposure, automatic white balancing, and image stabilization. The autofocus technique reduces the amount of time needed to hunt for the right focus by using 13 rules, such as "If the sharpness is high and its differential is low, then the focus motor speed is low." The image stabilization detects unwanted movements caused by bumping and bouncing of platforms and jitters caused by shaking hands, and then corrects the shaken image as much as possible.[33] Even with its commercial success in Japan, some observers believe that the use of fuzzy logic is much less important than simply building in sensors that monitor whatever process is being performed.

Case-Based Reasoning

Assume you are working at a manufacturer's customer service help desk, answering calls about many different models of many different products. Although there are shelves of manuals, finding the right information in those manuals takes a long time. Worse yet, the manuals explain how the product is supposed to work but often say little about the things that go wrong and how the customer could solve these problems. When Compaq Computer installed a case-based reasoning system to support the people at its help desk, the system paid for itself within a year.[34]

Case-based reasoning (CBR) is a decision support method based on the idea of finding past cases most similar to the current situation in which a decision must be made. CBR systems therefore maintain a history of past cases related to the topics under consideration. When a new situation arises, or a new call comes to the help desk, the decision maker identifies the characteristics of the situation and receives a list of related situations that have been analyzed in the past. Often the past solutions provide important clues or directly answer the current question. When the issue is resolved, the decision maker can add the case just solved as an additional instance in the database. In this way, a case-based reasoning system starting empty or with just a few cases can gradually be expanded to make it a valuable resource (see Figure 5.15).

FIGURE **5.15**

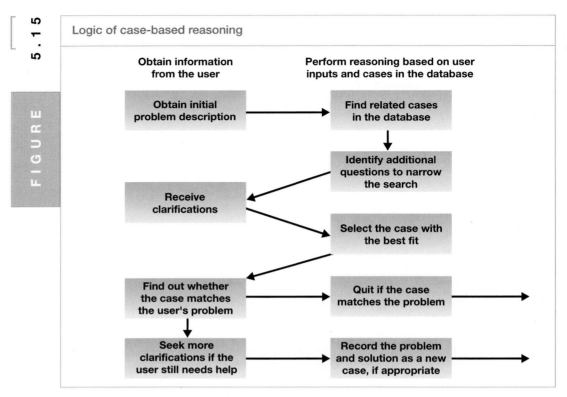

Logic of case-based reasoning

Case-based reasoning operates by finding a case in a database that is most closely related to the user's problem. When a new problem is solved, the information about that case is added to the database.

Like a neural network, CBR operates based on data rather than rules. The data consists of past cases and their characteristics and CBR merely attempts to display the case most similar to the situation the user is analyzing. Someone setting up a CBR application must identify the initial categories of cases and the way the cases will be compared and retrieved. Although it can be used with a small database, attaining the potential of CBR requires a database of several hundred examples. It also requires the administrative role of collecting reports of new cases, verifying that these cases differ from cases currently in the database, and coding and indexing the new cases for inclusion and retrieval. Without this type of administrative effort the CBR database fills up with redundant and confusing entries.

Intelligent Agents

Our nervous systems have the amazing ability to control multiple simultaneous processes at different levels of conscious awareness. Truly intelligent machines would require a capability to operate many simultaneous foreground and background processes and bring background processes into the foreground immediately when necessary. This type of machine does not yet exist, but initial research on this problem led to the concept of an **intelligent agent**, an autonomous, goal-directed computerized process that can be launched into a computer system or network to perform background work while other foreground processes are continuing. Although past AI research explored many ideas related to intelligent agents,[35] the initial applications of intelligent agents look more like mainstream programming than AI.

The idea of intelligent agents has been used to some extent in e-commerce in the form of **shopbots** that search the Web to find the lowest price for a particular item. The effectiveness of shopbots has been limited to date by the refusal of some Web merchants to allow shopbots to access the information on their sites. Other possible intelligent agents include an e-mail agent, a data mining agent, and a news agent. Each of these would operate in the background, performing information-related tasks that save time or increase the usefulness of information. The e-mail agent would scan incoming e-mail to identify the comparatively few incoming messages that call for the recipient to be interrupted instead of just going on a list to be read at the recipient's convenience. The data-mining agent would sort and filter data in a database to identify trends, surprises, and other new information a user might want. The news agent would scan articles on a computerized news service to cobble together a personalized daily news bulletin containing only articles of interest to a particular individual. Ideally this type of agent would be able to learn about the individual's changing interests instead of being told what to do by programming or check-off lists.

ENTERPRISE SYSTEMS

The introduction to the chapter introduced reasons why the CAD system used by Boeing's engineers is different from every other type of system we have discussed thus far. Its capabilities for entering, storing, and modifying data are superficially similar to office automation capabilities, but the scope, power, and degree of specialized knowledge built into a large CAD system make it far larger and more complex than a typical OAS. The CAD system supported communication between thousands of engineers, but calling it a communication system seems off the mark because it does so much more and contains so much specialized knowledge about mechanical design. Every entry into the database was a transaction, but this was much more than a typical TPS. Managers probably had a way of using the CAD data to track progress, but this wasn't an MIS. The CAD system certainly supported important decisions about designing the airplane, but it wasn't just about decisions either. The CAD system served as the coordinating infrastructure for thousands of people doing related work.

Imagine that an integrated information system could serve a similar function by encompassing the entire firm's major transaction processing systems within an integrated database. This would provide a consistent, readily accessible repository of information used in business processes such as purchasing, inventory control, manufacturing, sales, delivery, billing, accounts receivable, and personnel. Achieving this degree of integration is the idealized goal of **enterprise systems**, firm-wide information systems that serve as a common, integrated information infrastructure for basic business processes. If all of these functions were seamlessly integrated through a common database, the wasted effort in translating between inconsistent information systems within the same company would disappear. With this level of integration, a salesperson anywhere in the world would be able to find out whether the capacity and inventory are available for a new order, would be able to determine a feasible delivery date, and would feel confident that information about this order would not be lost. Furthermore, the salesperson would know that the expenses related to the sales call would be allocated to the right sales group and that the reimbursement would be handled expeditiously.

This type of enterprise system seemed beyond reach until the mid-1990s when several software vendors started selling **enterprise resource planning** (ERP) systems. As with many IT terms, the term *ERP* evolved out of a previous generation of systems. In this case the previous systems were MRP systems, which attempted to integrate purchasing and production scheduling activities. ERP took part of its name from MRP but changed "materials" to "enterprise" to indicate a much broader scope. As a result, resource planning (the RP in ERP) actually describes only a small part of the capabilities of a complete ERP system, which include, among others:

- Operations and logistics: inventory management, MRP, production planning, quality management, shipping
- Financials: accounts receivable and payable, cash management, general ledger, profitability analysis
- Sales and marketing: order management, sales management, pricing, sales planning
- Human resources: employee time accounting, payroll, travel expenses[36]

Enterprise systems are quite controversial because the effort to define requirements, configure or modify software, and implement in the organization is enormous.

These systems involve much more than changing the format of databases. Often it is necessary to change business processes to suit the limitations of the available software instead of changing software to fit the desired business processes. Nonetheless, some organizations have found that the integration resulting from this large investment seems to be worthwhile.

ERP software is currently sold by software vendors such as SAP, Oracle, Peoplesoft, and J.D. Edwards. These vendors analyzed basic business processes such as purchasing and accounting in many firms and then created database structures that incorporate many of the process variations they found. This design strategy makes their products enormously complicated. Just figuring out which of the many options to use often takes several hundred person-months of time. In many situations, departments must give up existing customized systems that address their unique problems in order to use the more general software and its integrated database. When Owens Corning acquired a number of other companies and needed to integrate its sales and manufacturing efforts, a large ERP project addressed a pressing need and was successful. (See the Owens Corning case at the end of this chapter.) In other situations where the need for integration within the firm is not as pressing and where the ERP system may force departments to change their processes in order to fit the software, ERP projects sometimes become enormous drains of effort with little reward. Some companies such as Dell Computer looked at ERP and decided their business was changing too rapidly to implement information systems that were so large and monolithic.[37] In other cases only one or two modules are implemented, resulting in systems that may be called ERP because the software was sold by an ERP vendor, but that are far more complicated than they need to be and don't accomplish the integration they may have set out to accomplish.

LIMITATIONS AND USES OF INFORMATION SYSTEM CATEGORIES

The chapter introduction noted that information system categories are imprecise and are in continual flux. As a result it is sometimes difficult to understand what someone else means by using the categories or related terms. For example:

- Someone speaking of a Web-based communication system might mean any combination of e-mail, voice mail, instant messaging, chat rooms, intranets, and extranets.
- Someone speaking of a DSS might mean potentially useful, general-purpose software or might mean a specific information system that is currently playing an important role in a work system.
- Someone speaking of a sales force automation system might mean an information system that helps the salespeople, or might mean an information system into which salespeople are obligated to enter data needed by the headquarters finance group.
- Someone speaking of an ERP system might mean an enterprise-wide information system or might mean a single module purchased from an ERP vendor.
- Someone speaking of a knowledge-based system might mean an expert system and might mean some other kind of system that codifies or uses knowledge.

Table 5.5 summarizes this type of issue by comparing a typical goal of each system category with some of the ways that goal is often garbled or subverted in practice.

Even though the categories overlap to some degree and are sometimes used inconsistently, each of the general categories that apply in any functional area emphasizes certain features that may be relevant in many situations. Table 5.6 identifies some of these features and notes some of the transferable features of each system type. These features can be turned into a design question when looking at any particular system. For example, the absence of DSS-like features in a TPS might indicate a direction for future improvement. Conversely, the controls typically built into a TPS might be the model for building similar controls into a DSS or even an MIS. As new information systems are built, it will be more difficult to classify real information systems using current categories, a small price to pay for more powerful and usable systems.

How Typical Goals of Information System Categories Are Sometimes Garbled or Subverted

Every category of information system has some typical goals. In practice these goals are sometimes garbled or subverted. This applies across information system categories that refer to functional area systems and categories that refer to idealized systems used in any functional area.

Category	Typical goal	How the goal is sometimes garbled or subverted
CAD	Design products through computerized specifications that can be stored, changed, and shared conveniently.	Use CAD as a tool for individual work but don't achieve consistency needed to gain additional benefits from internal and external coordination.
MRP	Order materials so that they arrive when needed to meet the production schedule.	The lead times built into MRP are averages or estimates. Incorrect lead times result in the same problems that MRP tries to solve.
EDI	Transfer data between suppliers and their customers electronically to improve efficiency.	Large companies shift costs to suppliers who may be forced to revamp their own systems.
SCM	Create an integrated supply chain that minimizes delays and waste.	If the supply chain is too tightly integrated, a mishap in one area will ripple quickly to other areas.
CIM	Create an integrated manufacturing environment that permits sharing of data across all manufacturing operations.	Computerize data used in manufacturing but don't integrate various manufacturing processes enough to gain important benefits.
POS	Record every sale of every item to maintain complete control of inventory.	If the POS system goes down, the sales process stops or it is necessary to do workarounds that often result in errors.
Direct marketing and Telemarketing	Send marketing communications to potential customers who would be interested.	Send catalogs and other mailings that seem like junk mail. Annoy potential customers by interrupting them.
SFA	Provide benefits to sales force by automating their data handling.	Provide new information to headquarters to support sales and financial planning, but require the sales force to do a lot of extra data entry.
CRM	Understand the customers more completely and provide a clearer view of the complete relationship with customers.	Cause the sales force to handle a lot of data that they don't use very much.
OAS	Use general-purpose office applications to make office work efficient.	Use office software as a tool for individuals but don't achieve the consistency needed to make the office more efficient.
Communication systems	Link employees, customers, and suppliers electronically to facilitate communication and coordination.	Overwhelm employees with too much communication and too many communication options.
TPS	Process transactions efficiently and record them accurately.	Ignore judgment that should be exercised when aspects of the transaction do not conform with the idealized assumptions about the situation.
MIS and EIS	Provide managers and executives the information they really need.	Provide convenient ways to obtain ad hoc summaries of recent operational results, but do very little to link these results to strategies or plans.
DSS	Provide data, models, and analysis tools that support decision-making.	Provide data, models, and tools, but fail to integrate these into processes. As a result the DSS is not used effectively.
Enterprise systems	Coordinate major systems across a firm and permit seamless access to any information needed for decision-making.	To operate within the limits of commercially available software, impose limits on business processes, sometimes making them less efficient.

TABLE 5.6

Transferable Features of Particular Types of Information Systems

Certain features and characteristics are usually associated with each of the types of information systems. This table identifies some of these features that can be transferred to systems of other types.

Type of system	Transferable features
Office automation systems	• Multiple forms of information, sometimes used in combination • Immediacy and interactivity of communication • Avoidance of unproductive work
Communication systems	• Emphasis on communication in addition to data processing • Consideration of social presence and other communication characteristics when building systems • Recognition of the need to handle different combinations of the same or different time or place • Sharing information between different people working on different parts of a task • Controlling workflows and approval loops within a group • Incorporating efficient methods of scheduling meetings
Transaction processing systems	• Control • Procedures and rules • Repetition
Management and executive information systems	• Emphasis on measures of performance • Use of standard formats and performance measures by people in different departments • User-friendly interface • User-friendly methods for analyzing data
Decision support systems	• User-controlled interaction with computers • Use of models and data • Information systems applied to semistructured tasks • Direct treatment of explicit knowledge
Enterprise systems	• Make consistently defined information available across different business functions • Emphasis on uniform coding schemes and standardized processes

R E A L I T Y C H E C K [✓]

Types of Information Systems

The text identifies six types of information systems that apply in every functional area.

1. For each type of system, either identify an example that you have encountered or explain when you think you will first encounter an example.

2. In each of the situations explain how the system affects communication and decision-making.

CHAPTER CONCLUSION

Summarize the purpose of functional area information systems including CAD, MRP, EDI, SCM, CIM, POS, SFA, CRM, and EFT.

The purposes of these systems are as follows:

- Computer-aided design (CAD) systems accept coded descriptions of components or processes, display the resulting product specification graphically, and often perform other functions such as testing for theoretical feasibility.
- Material requirement planning (MRP) systems attempt to integrate purchasing and production activities by working backward from a finished goods schedule.
- Electronic data interchange (EDI) systems transmit electronically coded business data such as purchase orders and invoices between firms.
- Supply chain management (SCM) systems coordinate schedules between suppliers and their customers so that both benefit from smaller inventories, smoother production, and less waste.
- Computer-integrated manufacturing (CIM) systems include computerized data collection and integrated data flows between design, manufacturing, planning, accounting, and other business functions.
- Point-of-sale (POS) systems use bar codes to collect transaction data related to purchases and inventory movement.
- Sales force automation (SFA) systems automate data handling related to personal scheduling, contact management, note and information sharing, tracking the progress of sales cycles, and providing revenue forecasts to headquarters.
- Customer relationship management (CRM) systems address the somewhat broader topic of planning, controlling, and scheduling pre-sales and post-sales activities, and include analysis of data captured through customer interactions such as service calls, call center responses, sales transactions, and Web-site activity.
- Electronic funds transfer (EFT) systems use electronic messages to settle accounts between banks and other businesses.

What are the general differences between the idealized types of information systems that can be used in any functional area?

The general differences are as follows:

- Office automation systems (OASs) provide tools that support general office work such as performing calculations, creating documents, scheduling meetings, and controlling the flow of office work.
- Communication systems help people work together by exchanging or sharing information.

- Transaction processing systems (TPSs) collect and store data about transactions and control aspects of transaction processing and related decision-making.
- Management and executive information systems (MISs and EISs) summarize data from transaction processing systems and other data sources to convert it into information useful for managing an organization, monitoring performance, and planning.
- Decision support systems (DSSs) help people make decisions by providing information, models, or tools for analyzing information.
- Enterprise systems serve as a common, integrated, information infrastructure for basic business processes.

What different approaches are used in communication systems?

Different approaches used in communication systems include teleconferencing, messaging, groupware, intranets and extranets, knowledge management, and group support systems.

In what ways do information systems support various management roles?

Management roles can be grouped into three categories: interpersonal, informational, and decisional. For interpersonal roles, information systems support personal and interpersonal communication. For informational roles, information systems make information available and help in analyzing it or communicating it. For decisional roles, information systems provide information for decision-making and help in explaining decisions.

Identify some of the data- and model-related techniques used in different types of DSS.

These techniques include simulation, optimization, online analytical processing (OLAP), data mining, expert systems, neural networks, fuzzy logic, case-based reasoning, and intelligent agents. The last five come from artificial intelligence research and are worth mentioning even though they are not as common as the first four.

What are some of the goals and difficulties associated with enterprise systems?

Ideally, any authorized employee, supplier, or customer should be able to access any required operational information. Enterprise systems (often called ERP systems) use an integrated database to try to achieve a high degree of integration within and across different business functions. Enterprise systems are quite controversial because the effort to create them is enormous. Often it is necessary to change business processes to suit the needs of the information system instead of vice versa.

How are features of one type of information system transferable to systems of other types?

Each system category emphasizes certain features that may be relevant in many situations. For example,

the absence of DSS-like features in a TPS might indicate a direction for future improvement.

KEY TERMS

computer-aided design (CAD)
material requirement planning (MRP)
electronic data interchange (EDI)
supply chain management (SCM)
computer-integrated manufacturing (CIM)
information content of products
mass customization
point-of-sale (POS) system
direct marketing
addressability
telemarketing
sales force automation (SFA)
customer relationship management (CRM)
smart card
electronic funds transfer (EFT)
electronic cash
program trading
office automation system (OAS)
communication systems
teleconferencing

audio conferencing
audiographic conferencing
video conferencing
unified messaging
instant messaging
chat room
voice chat
groupware
computer conferencing
newsgroup
intranet
extranet
knowledge management system
explicit knowledge
tacit knowledge
group support system (GSS)
transaction processing system (TPS)
batch processing
real-time processing
management information system (MIS)
executive information system (EIS)

decision support system (DSS)
simulation model
optimization model
what-if questions
online analytical processing (OLAP)
data mining
enterprise system
enterprise resource planning (ERP)
expert system
knowledge-based system
if-then rules
knowledge base
inference engine
explanation module
forward chaining
backward chaining
neural network
fuzzy logic
case-based reasoning (CBR)
intelligent agent
shopbots

REVIEW QUESTIONS

1. What are some of the applications of CAD systems?
2. What is the difference between EDI systems and supply chain management (SCM) systems?
3. How is CAD related to mass customization?
4. Why do sales force automation (SFA) and customer relationship management (CRM) systems overlap?
5. Compare electronic cash with electronic funds transfer (EFT).
6. What are examples of tools typically grouped with office automation systems?
7. What is the difference between intranets and extranets?
8. Why is the difference between tacit and explicit knowledge important for understanding knowledge management?
9. What kinds of functions do group support systems (GSS) contain?
10. What is the difference between MIS, DSS, and EIS?
11. Why is it difficult to keep EISs current?
12. How is data mining related to DSS?
13. Define expert systems and explain how they improve the use of knowledge.
14. When are expert systems useful, and why can't they exercise common sense?

15. Identify the components of an idealized expert system.

16. Explain how a neural network operates.

17. What are the advantages of reasoning using fuzzy logic?

18. Define case-based reasoning, and explain how a CBR system typically operates.

19. What is an ERP system?

20. What typical features of particular types of information systems are often transferable?

1. Although executives typically are described as people who work on long-term, strategic issues, the discussion of EIS emphasizes the use of these systems to monitor recent organizational performance. Assuming you were an executive concerned with long-term issues, explain why you would or would not find this type of EIS useful. Explain some of the things an EIS would have to do if it were to focus specifically on long-term strategic issues.

2. Some people believe that e-mail, v-mail, and fax have reduced the quality of work life for many professionals by making it difficult to escape work for an evening or weekend. These observers believe any-time, any-place may be a fine goal for serving customers, but may not be appropriate as an expectation of company employees. Discuss the pros and cons of this issue.

3. Why is there a distinction between management information systems and decision support systems? After all, one of the basic purposes of management information systems is to provide information that is used for decision-making.

4. Assume that all current telephones were replaced with picture phones that could transmit both audio and video and could operate as video extensions of v-mail. Explain whether this would have any important impact on you personally.

5. Describe the process of attaining knowledge in anything you have ever studied outside of school, such as how to play baseball, play an instrument, or dance. Explain why it would or would not be possible for an expert system or neural network to learn how to do these things.

6. The manager of a $100 million company pension fund at Deere & Co. used a neural network to outperform common stock market indicators. At one point the neural network suggested the fund should invest 40% of its assets in bank stocks. The manager's boss overruled the neural network, but bank stocks increased in value more than the stocks that were selected for the portfolio.[38] Explain why this experience should or should not convince the people not to overrule the neural network.

Owens Corning manufactures building supplies such as fiberglass insulation and roofing materials, and sells them to building contractors and to building supply distributors such as Home Depot. In 1991 the company faced challenges on all fronts. It was deeply in debt due to a financial restructuring five years earlier, and its revenues were shrinking slowly. Internally it had 200 incompatible systems dedicated to specific tasks such as invoicing for specific product lines. Externally, the company was out of step with the direction the market was moving. The company was organized around different product lines, meaning that retailers dealt with four service centers and four sets of bills. Builders and remodelers also saw few benefits in this product line orientation because they were less concerned with selecting the right brand of a particular material such as insulation and far more concerned with timely, convenient acquisition and delivery of all the materials for a project. Furthermore, although the company wanted to provide a complete "envelope" for a house, including shingles, waterproofing, siding, and other materials, there were significant gaps in the product line.

Owens Corning embarked on a long-term effort to reorient the entire company. It acquired 14 smaller manufacturers to fill in the products it lacked. It reorganized sales so that salespeople sold the entire company's whole line instead of just one product line. One of its most daunting tasks was a complete overhaul of its hodgepodge of outdated and incompatible information systems. A new head of IS was hired in 1994. After reviewing the state of the existing information systems in the light of the company's strategy, he and his staff decided that an integrated information system was needed so that salespeople could enter orders, reserve inventory, and produce consistent bills.

In what was virtually a "bet the company" strategy, Owens Corning embarked on a two-year rush project to replace its old order fulfillment, manufacturing, inventory, distribution, and financial accounting software with SAP's R/3 program, an integrated, but notoriously complex, enterprise software package. The head of IS insisted that half the staffing for this project would have to come from the business units, not the IS group, and that its success would be defined in business terms, such as a 50% reduction in inventory.

By mid-1995 the project team of 250 people was housed at Toledo headquarters to maximize internal coordination and minimize delays in answering questions. It was divided into five groups, each focused on a different set of processes. Each group included representatives from local business units and IS and business professionals from across the company. Councils with members from all five groups made sure that each process meshed with other processes. In some areas, such as production planning, SAP's capabilities were not as good as those in homegrown systems. However, because the company's strategy required greater integration, the project team and local business operations sometimes had to be satisfied with "good-enough reengineering" rather than insisting on the best way to perform each process. Project cost through 1997 was $110 million for a combination of analyzing how to use SAP, setting it up on the computers, and training people to use it. Estimated benefits were $15 million in 1997, $50 million in 1998, and $80 million in 2000.[39, 40]

QUESTIONS

1. Owens Corning took a huge gamble in devoting so much money to an unproven reengineering project. Explain why you do or do not believe a more incremental approach would have been more prudent.

2. What explanation should be given to the individuals and groups in the company whose information systems will become less effective as a result of the switch to SAP?

3. In 2000, several years after the events covered in this case, Owens Corning declared bankruptcy in response to asbestos liability claims dating from asbestos exposure suffered decades ago by many workers. Explain why the bankruptcy does or does not change your views of the case.

CASE   Enron: The World's Largest E-Commerce Web Site for Commodity Transactions

Enron is a leading energy and communications company based in Houston. It has over 32,000 miles of pipeline and has built or acquired production or distribution facilities as it has moved into other industries. Its traditional business was buying and selling gas and electricity by purchasing from public utilities with surplus supplies and selling to utilities that need more. Starting from its base as the dominant player in the U.S. gas and electric power trading it branched out, became the leading gas and power trader in Europe, and also built other trading operations in paper, coal, and plastics. In January 2000 it announced it would begin trading "telecommunications bandwidth," excess capacity on fiber optics networks.[41] It now controls over 10,000 miles of fiber.

In late 1999 it opened EnronOnline, an e-commerce site for Enron's trading operations in energy and other areas. Within one year, it had the highest amount of dollar transactions of any e-commerce site in the world. As of October 11, 2000, Enron had used the site for executing over 350,000 online transactions involving commodities with a gross value of $183 billion. Within a year of its launch, over 60% of the world's wholesale gas trades were on EnronOnline.[42] At an average of over one-half million dollars per trade, it was a far cry from buying several books at a B2C site.

Unlike a typical B2B exchange that provides services for buyers and sellers but does not own anything that is being traded, Enron is actually a principal in all of the transactions on its site. It guarantees delivery or payment on all sales executed through EnronOnline. If a public utility uses the site to sell a fixed amount of gas to be delivered over 30 days in June, Enron will actually use its pipeline facilities to receive and resell that gas at whatever price it can get at that time. Conversely, if Enron contracts to deliver a guaranteed supply of gas to a utility if its local temperatures go over 95 degrees, it will actually make sure the delivery occurs unless it sells the contract to someone else.

The fact that Enron participates in a large number of trades and controls a large number of buy and sell contracts at any time gives it a great deal of flexibility to recombine those contracts in new ways to meet needs of utility buyers. In some ways this is like doing a jigsaw puzzle whose pieces are existing and potential contracts for future delivery. EnronOnline lets buyers and sellers act on prices that can change by the minute. Buyers and sellers see real-time price spreads of both the sell price and the buy price. By the time monthly prices had been quoted on the telephone those prices might have changed. Reuters and Dow Jones have offered subscription-based real-time commodity pricing for some time, but Enron's service provides real-time pricing for 800 products at no charge. The switch to EnronOnline removed the company's 500 traders from the order process, allowing them to handle 10 times the previous order volume by focusing solely on bidding based on Enron's own needs and costs. Transactions that once took three minutes over the phone now take a few seconds, including credit checks.[43]

QUESTIONS

1. How is EnronOnline different from the B2B exchanges introduced in Chapter 1?

2. Explain why the case either says or implies that Enron's traders use each of the six types of information systems. If there is any reason to believe Enron does not use a particular type of information system, explain why.

3. Ten years ago very few people in the power industry would have anticipated the development of EnronOnline. Explain why you do or do not believe the entire trading process could be automated. Start by explaining what information and knowledge would have to be used.

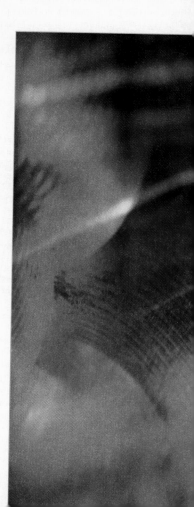

Customer, Product, and E-Commerce

chapter6

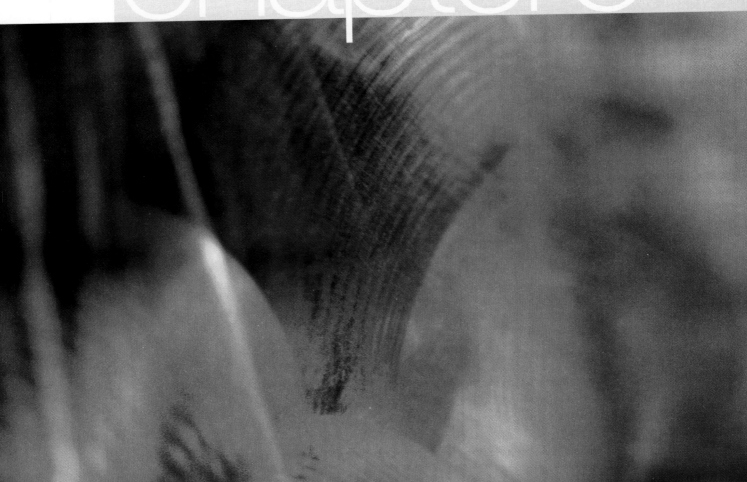

STUDY QUESTIONS

- What three dimensions can be used to describe and look for improvements in the products and services produced by a work system?
- What are the unique characteristics of information products and service products?
- What are the stages in an idealized customer experience related to a product or service?
- How are information systems related to competitive advantage?
- Why is it difficult to achieve sustainable competitive advantage through information systems?
- What are some of the challenges of electronic commerce?

OUTLINE

Customer's View of Products and Services
Three Dimensions of Products and Services
Characteristics of Information Products
Characteristics of Services
Customization and Adaptability

The Customer Experience
Determining Requirements
Acquiring the Product
Using the Product or Receiving the
    Service
Maintaining and Retiring the Product

**Customer's Criteria for Evaluating Products
and Services**
Cost
Quality
Responsiveness
Reliability
Conformance to Standards and
    Regulations

Diverse Concerns of Different Customers

Information Systems and Competitive Advantage
Mission-Critical Information Systems
Strategic Information Systems
Competitive Advantage Creates Competitive
    Necessity

**Challenges as Commerce Becomes
E-Commerce**
Establishing and Integrating Systems
Setting Prices
Attracting Customers
Providing an Effective Self-Service Environment
Providing Excellent Customer Service
Achieving Profitability and Sustainable
    Differentiation

Chapter Conclusion
Summary
Key Terms
Review Questions
Discussion Questions
Cases

Customer, Product, and E-Commerce

O P E N I N G C A S E

OTIS ELEVATOR: PROVIDING BETTER SERVICE FOR CUSTOMERS

Otis Elevator uses Otisline to achieve the responsiveness and quality essential to compete in the elevator service business. Otisline is a centralized system for dispatching mechanics to elevators requiring service. It uses a centralized database containing complete service records for each elevator installed. Prior to Otisline, the local Otis field office dispatched mechanics during normal working hours, and answering services dispatched them after hours and on weekends and holidays using a duty roster. These answering services often handled multiple elevator service companies and rarely displayed great interest or ingenuity in ensuring that elevator service calls were answered promptly. Record keeping related to service calls was haphazard.

Otisline improved service by handling all calls for service at a centralized service center that receives 9,000 calls per day. Highly trained, often multilingual operators use complete information about each elevator to make sure that the right mechanic gets to the scene promptly. The system maintains detailed records and reports exception situations such as elevators with high levels of maintenance.[1]

The use of information technology extends to the service technicians and to the elevators. Using handheld computers linked to a nationwide wireless network, Otis field service technicians across the country can communicate instantly with a central office in Connecticut for technical assistance and job dispatching. Communication can be initiated from a location as remote as the inside of an elevator shaft. Before this wireless network was available, field workers needing to contact the office were forced to secure the elevator, leave the work site, search for a phone, call, and sometimes wait on hold while the elevator was out of order. Beyond supporting the dispatching function, Otisline serves as a central conduit for exchanging crucial information among field service mechanics, salespeople, design and manufacturing engineers, and managers. For example, salespeople use Otisline to access an integrated database used for providing immediate quotes to customers.

Additional product enhancements related to IT include remote elevator monitoring, direct communication with trapped passengers, and monthly reports on each elevator for subsequent analysis of performance patterns. Customers purchase the remote monitoring function for an additional monthly charge. It uses a microprocessor to report elevator malfunctions to the dispatching office via modem.[2] In some cases this information can be used to fix problems before they cause elevator failure. By 2000 Otis was advertising several "e" features. E*Service provided Web-based access to maintenance records for an elevator. E*Display was the option of equipping elevators with flat panel displays that could show news, sports, advertising, or other broadcast or video information. E*Direct was a method for "choosing an ideal system in a few simple steps." This included calculating the requirements for vertical transportation, selecting among options, pricing the project, and tracking the order's progress.[3]

WEB CHECK [✓]

Look at Otis Elevator's Web site and the ways Otis emphasizes information technology and "e" features compared to other features of its product offerings.

DEBATE TOPIC [ ]

Otis's "e" capabilities probably are an expected part of a product offering in today's world, but they are mostly window-dressing compared to the basics of building and servicing elevators.

This case illustrates ideas that can help any business professional think about the customer and product of virtually any work system. Otis Elevator is in the elevator business, not the information system business, yet its information systems are an important part of what it offers customers. Otisline is cited often as an example of the competitive use of information systems because it benefits Otis Elevator's customers as well as internal operations. Otisline helps in centralizing dispatching and attaining better control of the maintenance process, thereby supporting better customer service than would otherwise be available. Internal benefits include better coordination, better feedback about how to improve the product, and better information to salespeople.

The coverage of customers, products, and e-commerce is combined in this chapter because many of the same concepts that apply to customer satisfaction for a firm's products and services also apply to customer satisfaction for inward-directed work systems. This chapter starts with the most general ideas by discussing a customer's view of the products and services produced by a work system. Next is an overview of the stages of an internal or external customer's experience with products and services. This is followed by criteria internal and external customers often use for evaluating products and services. Following an overview of the competitive use of information systems, the basic ideas are applied in a discussion of e-commerce challenges that include establishing and integrating systems, setting prices, attracting customers, providing an effective self-service environment, providing excellent customer service, and achieving profitability and sustainable differentiation.

Throughout this chapter the term "product" is used in several different ways just as it is used in everyday life. In some places, products are distinguished from services, as in "a shirt is a product" and "medical care is a service." In other places, the term product is used in a colloquial sense, as in "the Mayo Clinic has a good product" (which happens to be medical services). As in everyday life, readers should use the context to interpret the meaning whenever these terms are used.

CUSTOMER'S VIEW OF PRODUCTS AND SERVICES

Even a brief look at the products and services produced by a work system should include something about the nature of the products and services, the characteristics of the entire customer experience, and the criteria the customers use for evaluating what they receive.

W O R K   S Y S T E M   S N A P S H O T

Otis Elevator: Repairing elevators and providing service

CUSTOMERS

- Building owners and people who use elevators

PRODUCTS & SERVICES

- Elevator maintained in good operating condition
- Timely elevator repair
- History of service for each elevator

BUSINESS PROCESS

- Receive call about a problem
- Dispatch mechanics
- Perform repair steps
- Track progress until the elevator is fixed
- Update records
- Monitor the elevators and perform preventive maintenance

PARTICIPANTS

- Trained operators who answer calls for service
- Local mechanics

INFORMATION

- Notification of problem
- Current status of all calls for service
- Maintenance history of each elevator
- Qualification and availability of mechanics

TECHNOLOGY

- Computer at headquarters
- Handheld terminals
- Commercial wireless network

Three Dimensions of Products and Services

A simplistic way to look at a company's product or the product of a work system is to try to characterize it as an information product, physical product, or service product. An **information product**, in its purest form, consists of information and nothing else, such as a list of names downloaded using the Internet. Similarly, a pure **physical product**, such as a pound of sugar, has no significant information or service components. A pure **service product** is a set of actions that provide value to a customer who receives neither information nor physical things.

As summarized in Table 6.1, the difference between products and services is that the product's value comes from usage by the customer after it is produced, whereas the value of service comes from the execution of service tasks. For example, the value of an office copier comes from using the copier, whereas the value of a copying service is that someone else makes the copies. The examples in Table 6.1 show that customers can sometimes receive the same benefits through a product or a service, and that the choice between a product or service approach often depends on trade-offs related to price, convenience, and other variables.

Most products produced for external customers involve a combination of information, physical, and service components, even if one or two of the three dominate the product's value. Consider a new automobile, for example. Clearly it is a physical product purchased as several thousand pounds of steel and plastic with numerous aesthetic and practical features, but it certainly has a service component, either explicitly in the form of warranties or implicitly in the form of the reputation of the dealer and manufacturer. In the last decade its information content has also risen dramatically. The information content of older cars was limited to paper manuals and dashboard gauges. Newer cars have information-based features ranging from antilock brakes and collision

TABLE 6.1

Contrast between Products and Services

In many situations, similar benefits can be generated through products and/or services. The trade-offs in any particular situation depend on price, convenience, and other variables. The examples below identify products and services that might satisfy the same needs.

	Product	Service
Definition	• A work system output consisting of physical things and/or information that the customer obtains and uses later	• A work system output consisting of a set of actions performed for a customer without producing a product that the customer uses later
Direct source of benefits for the customer	• Possession and usage of the product	• Actions that are performed for the customer
Examples: products and services that might substitute for each other	• Automobile	• Transportation service
	• Office copy machine	• Copying service
	• Book about self-treatment for an ailment	• Examination and treatment by a health professional
	• Cosmetics	• Beauty treatment by a cosmetician
	• Guide book and maps	• Guide service

avoidance devices to location finders that use digital maps and signals from global positioning satellites (see Figure 6.1). Services ranging from warranty repairs through emergency road service are also part of the mix for some brands.

As an example of an information product whose physical traits have almost vanished, consider what has happened to encyclopedias in the last decade. They once were three or four shelf-feet of hardbound reference books, but over half of those sold today are in the form of CD-ROMs weighing ounces. By 1998, all 50 million words in a 32-volume Encyclopedia Britannica that previously cost $1,500 were available in a $100 product consisting of two CD-ROMs. Aside from requiring less physical space, the electronic encyclopedias provide some of the advantages of an interactive information product, such as the ability to show video segments, perform simulations, and link directly to material on other topics.[4]

FIGURE 6.1

Information systems built into automobiles

Information systems play an increasingly important role in automobiles as many basic driving functions are controlled or supported using computers.

The Internet and other networking options have magnified the possibilities for extending the value of products by adding more information and service. Link electronic street maps to current traffic information and the driver can avoid traffic jams instead of driving into them. Hide a location transmitter in a car and the mystery about finding a stolen car disappears. For Encyclopedia Britannica, shrinking the shelf of books to a comparatively inexpensive CD-ROM was only a part-way measure. By May 2000, Britannica was offering a print version of the encyclopedia for $1,250, a single-disk electronic version called Britannica DVD 2000 for $50 after the rebate, and an annual subscription for Web-based access for $50. The DVD version included the complete text from the Britannica 32-volume print set, plus additional articles not available in print. It had 83,000 articles, 15,000 images, and 5 hours of video; access to over 125,000 Internet links via Britannica.com; and a dictionary. Next came an attempt to offer the entire encyclopedia for free through the Web and to earn revenues on advertising linked to the topics the users are looking at. The multishelf behemoth still existed for those who wanted it, but it had also spawned a pure information product and a subscription service (see Figure 6.2).

The examples of cars and encyclopedias illustrate why simplistic dichotomies such as product versus service or physical product versus information product are less and less useful in today's networked environment. Almost every product offering involves some combination of information, service, and physical things. Customers don't want just a product; they want a product that includes appropriate service. When they receive service they don't want random actions. They want the service defined well enough that it could be considered a product. This is how Stan Davis and Christopher Meyer said it in the title of Chapter 2 of their book *Blur*: "The Offer: No product without service; No service without product."[5]

Figure 6.3 shows a basic model for thinking about the products and services that a work system currently produces and might produce in the future. In addition to product

---

Different forms of an information product

In the last several years the information within the leather-bound volumes became available on CD-ROM, on DVD, and then on the Web.

FIGURE   6 . 3

Three dimensions for describing the products
and services produced by any work system

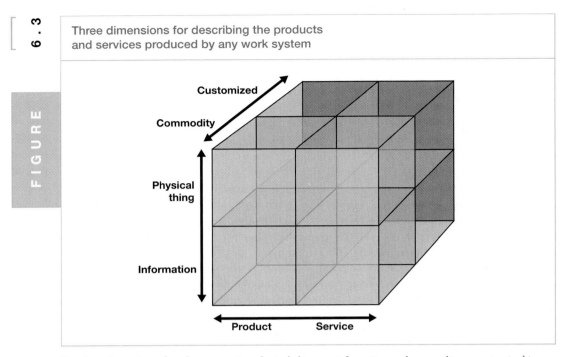

The three dimensions of product vs. service, physical object vs. information, and commodity vs. customized immediately reveal 8 possible areas for increasing customer satisfaction.

versus service and information versus physical thing it includes a third dimension for commodity versus customized. A product or service is a commodity if each customer receives basically the same type of value and little is done to adjust the products or services to the particular likings or whims of the customer. When a product or service is customized, the requirements stage of the customer experience includes consideration of and active response to the customer's unique desires.

Figure 6.3 shows that the simple dichotomies such as product versus service lead to eight separate approaches, each of which might be applied as part of the products and services produced by any work system. Figure 6.4 uses the example of an automobile to illustrate how the three dimensions can help in thinking about ways to increase the customer's satisfaction. The figure shows that the essence of an automobile is the basic car—a physical product that is essentially a commodity because anyone with enough money can buy it and it can be produced with no special consideration of taste or desires of that buyer. The "commodity-service" component also involves physical things and is the standard service that a dealership provides. The "commodity-information" component is the standard information in the warranty, owner's manual, and dashboard displays. The customized components include customer options in the car itself (the physical product) and any customized service that might be offered. Possible directions to extend the product and increase its value to the customer include opportunities to provide information as a customized product, commodity service, or customized service. For example, perhaps there is a way to include customized information, such as a meaningful ongoing history of this particular car's usage and repair records.

There is no guarantee that the ideas starting with "perhaps" are good ideas, but the eight approaches that might be built into the products and services produced by a work system do provide eight different directions for potential improvement. In some cases, this might be an improvement within an approach that is already being used. In others, it might involve using new approaches.

The relative balance of information, service, and customization is especially important for many IT-intensive products. Consider, for example, a commercial marketing information service that provides weekly item-level sales data from a sample of supermarkets across the country. Its output might be positioned as an information product

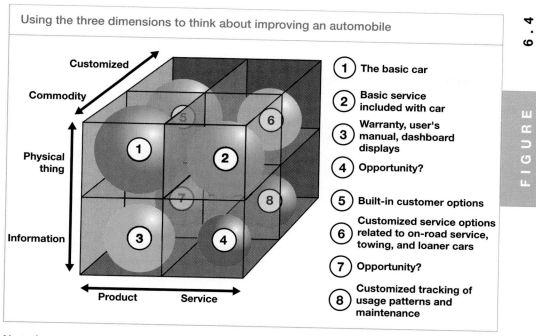

FIGURE 6.4

Using the three dimensions to think about improving an automobile

1. The basic car
2. Basic service included with car
3. Warranty, user's manual, dashboard displays
4. Opportunity?
5. Built-in customer options
6. Customized service options related to on-road service, towing, and loaner cars
7. Opportunity?
8. Customized tracking of usage patterns and maintenance

Notice how a typical automobile is basically a commodity product with physical, information, and service components, and that some of these can be customized under some circumstances.

containing an enormous database, a fixed set of preprogrammed reports, and a set of tools for ad hoc queries. Alternatively, it could be positioned as a combination of information and service by including an analysis service in addition to the database. This service would involve data analysis and marketing experts who would help corporate clients find the surprises and the trends in the data they receive. Whether the analyst role exists at all, and whether it is placed in the producer organization or the customer organization is a key determinant of both customer satisfaction and cost to the customer. Advances in hardware and software have made the range of choices much wider because it is now more feasible for the customers to manipulate the data themselves.

Notice that incorporating additional approaches may not mean that the customer will be happier. In fact, even within an approach, less may be better than more. Consider, for example, someone using a library or the Internet to research a particular question. More may not be better if the goal is to get to the answer quickly without being overwhelmed with information. Likewise, users of physical products often want less instead of more when they prefer products that are smaller, lighter, and less obtrusive. Similarly, owners of copy machines and elevators do not want more service; rather, they want the original product designed so that it will require a minimum of maintenance-related service.

Characteristics of Information Products

A number of characteristics of information have become increasingly important as computer and communication technologies have become more powerful. For example, information is intangible, copyable, transportable, nonconsumable, and manipulable:[6]

- *Intangible:* Information has no weight—you can't touch it or feel it.
- *Copyable:* Information can be copied numerous times at almost no cost.
- *Nonconsumable:* When you copy or use information, it does not change even though its value may change.
- *Transportable:* Information can be moved at almost no cost.
- *Manipulable:* Manipulating information is much easier than manipulating physical things. This is why Boeing found advantages in using CAD to design an airplane without building physical models. (Refer to the opening case in Chapter 5.)

These characteristics have major ramifications in many areas, such as publishing, which has taken on a new meaning in the world of electronic documents. Traditional publishing involved designing and producing a fixed document, such as a magazine or book, and distributing paper copies of it. Electronic publishing still involves producing the document and distributing it, but the shift to electronic documents brings a wide range of new possibilities. During the production process the document itself can be customized to the needs or tastes of specific readers. A multimedia document can augment text and graphics with audio, video, and models the user can execute. User controls that can be designed into the document include scroll bars, outlining, active internal links, links to other electronic documents, and even links to pages on the Web. The document can then be distributed in paper form or by using a variety of electronic media including diskettes, CD-ROMs, and access through the Web. The document can be sold as a fixed, resellable object like a CD, or it can be sold more like software, based on a license that may be time-limited and may provide upgrades.

The control and ownership of electronic documents is a key issue because most authors will not write unless they are paid. If electronic documents can be copied for free, only the first copy will be purchased and both publishers and authors will stop producing. Operating under the heading of **digital rights management (DRM)**, software firms and publishing companies have a number of initiatives that address these issues. For example, Adobe's DRM scheme permits the author or publisher to make the document freely available or to allow only a particular number of users, with each use requiring an explicit permission transferred through a Web site.[7]

A final aspect of information products is the intriguing possibility of profiting from giving away a version of the product for free. An example is the way Adobe has given away over 100 million free downloads of its Acrobat document reader but charges publishers for the software that converts documents into Acrobat format so that they can be distributed. The logic of the **free version of a product** is relatively simple: Potential users who might be interested simply receive the product and try it out. Transmitting the free version of an information product costs almost nothing, especially if it is downloaded or accessed using the Internet, and may be an opportunity to "capture" the customer by getting the customer to use the product and incorporate it into everyday work. On recognizing the product's value, the customer should then be willing to pay for some combination of powerful optional features, new releases, service contracts, education, consulting, and complementary products that augment the free product.[8]

Characteristics of Services

Services also have special characteristics since they are typically produced and consumed simultaneously, with the customer receiving value from actions rather than from possessing and using information or physical things. Table 6.2 shows that services can often be divided across two dimensions. The first is the type of service, namely, whether it is a physical service, information service, or knowledge service. A physical service involves action directed at physical things, such as giving a massage or moving a piano, whereas information or knowledge services are about actions related to conveying or using information or knowledge. The second dimension involves the way the service is delivered. The possibilities here include personal service delivered by an individual whose identity matters to the customer, impersonal service delivered by someone whose identity doesn't matter to the customer, and automated service delivered by a computer or other machine.

The difference between personal and impersonal but nonautomated service is important because it shows that there is more to service than whether a competent person does the work. The difference between impersonal and truly personal service is related to whether the service is a series of isolated encounters or part of an ongoing relationship.[9] Service through **supplier-customer encounters** occurs through interactions between customers and providers who are strangers. Service through a **supplier-customer relationship** occurs when a customer has repetitive contact with a particular provider and when the customer and provider get to know each other personally.

TABLE   6 . 2

Different Ways of Performing Services Providing Related Benefits

Services providing a particular type of benefit to the customer can be performed in a number of different ways. One way to categorize the service approach is along the dimension from personal to impersonal to automated. The service can also focus on physical things, information, or knowledge.

Type of service	Delivery approach		
	Personal	*Impersonal*	*Automated*
A physical service	Physical therapy	A ten-week group exercise program in a gym	Use of an exercise machine that controls exercise rate
An information service	Keeping track of an individual's medical records and making them available when needed	Providing books and pamphlets about fitness and medicine	Automatically sensing heart rate and other vital signs while an individual is exercising in a gym
A knowledge service	Medical treatment by a family physician who knows the patient	Medical treatment by a previously unknown physician in a clinic	Computerized diagnosis of a particular condition

Obtaining cash from a bank can be framed as an encounter with an ATM machine or faceless teller, or as part of an ongoing relationship with the staff of a local bank. Similarly, delivery of medical care can be framed as a series of encounters between the patient and whichever health care provider happens to be available, or as part of an extended relationship with particular providers. E-business approaches can improve either type of service delivery. For example, one way to improve an encounter style of medical service is by supplying complete and up-to-date patient information to any provider. Providing the information is not a replacement for a relationship with a medical care provider, but it decreases the chances that a total stranger will overlook something important that is already known and has been recorded. Similarly, e-business approaches can contribute to a relationship style of medical care delivery by making record keeping and billing more efficient, and thereby permitting more attention to the relationship.

The distinction between different types of services and different forms of delivery is not merely academic because it highlights alternatives for providing service. For example, impersonal services might be automated more readily than personal services because the customer would not care as much that something previously done by an anonymous individual is now being done by a computer. Similarly, knowledge services and physical services might be replaced by self-service information services.

LOOK AHEAD

The Ernst & Young case at the end of the chapter discusses innovative Web-based consulting services that tried to replace expensive personal service with less expensive impersonal services.

Customization and Adaptability

Regardless of how a work system's product combines information, physical, and service components, the customer may want to control the product's function or appearance at any point in time, or may want to adapt its features and functions over time as needs change. This is important for analyzing work systems because control and adaptability the customer wants can sometimes be accomplished in different ways including customization during the production process, the "smart" product, the interactive product, and the programmable product.

Customization   The key issue in customization is to provide the product features and functions the customer really wants rather than just those that have already been defined or those that are easy to produce. Building efficient customization into the process that produces the product requires that production be based on specifications unique to a particular customer order. These specifications must be obtained from the customer and converted into a form that controls the production of the specific product or service the customer receives. The range of customization options included in a production process has major ramifications for how the business process operates, how efficient it can be, and how well the product matches customer desires. The previous chapter explained that *mass customization* describes the ideal situation, namely, producing the product as though it were a commodity but using IT-based tools to customize it so that it fits customer needs exactly.

Smart Products, Interactive Products, Programmable Products   Adaptability and control can be accomplished in several ways after the customer acquires the product. A **smart product** is preprogrammed to obtain information from its environment and act appropriately, such as the way automatic floodlights turn on for three minutes after detecting motion, and the way computerized vending machines in Japan keep track of their own inventory levels and replenishment needs. Smart products with more complex functions range from heat-seeking missiles to databases programmed to identify new and emerging trends. An **interactive product** provides immediate responses to interactive commands. The widespread use of the World Wide Web shows that simple forms of the interactive approach are quite acceptable to a broad range of people. For example, many people are willing to enter data into mortgage calculators and to pose queries to search engines. In contrast, the use of complex models and complex interactive queries by nontechnical users is very rare. A **programmable product** accepts instructions from the user and executes them later. Thermostats and timers for VCRs and coffee makers are examples of the programmable approach in which the user enters instructions that are later executed automatically when particular conditions related to temperature or time are met. The fact that so few consumers actually use the programmable features of a VCR demonstrates that building programmability into products for nontechnical users may be ineffective until the programming tools are simpler and more intuitive.

Controllability and adaptability are crucial characteristics to consider when thinking about information as the product of an information system. The extreme inflexibility of early MISs was largely due to the programming methods and hardware technology available at the time. The ability to incorporate current tools, such as database management systems, into the technical underpinnings has made today's MISs much more flexible. In addition to accelerating design and programming processes, data retrieval and formatting functions in the newer tools have become part of the product itself. Current MISs may still generate the same set of computerized printouts every week, but they also bring many possibilities for direct control by permitting users to specify what information should be reported and in what format. This is an increasingly important part of the information system's product because business issues are in continual flux and because once customers learn how to use an information system, they often visualize new adaptations that may generate unanticipated benefits.

Figure 6.5 shows how the three dimensions in Figure 6.3 can be used to visualize possible improvements to a hypothetical MIS that provides a standard set of weekly paper-based printouts for management. Along the commodity versus customization dimension, the standard reports can be augmented by customized reports. Along the information versus physical product dimension, the paper-based reports can be augmented or replaced by electronic reports. Along the product versus service dimension, the idea of the reports as a product can be augmented through the service of personal help in generating and customizing reports.

R E A L I T Y C H E C K ✓

The Customer's View of the Product

This section described products as a mix of information, service, and physical characteristics.

1. Identify several products in which all three dimensions are important.

2. Explain how these products might be changed by providing more or less along each dimension.

Using the three dimensions to visualize options improving an MIS

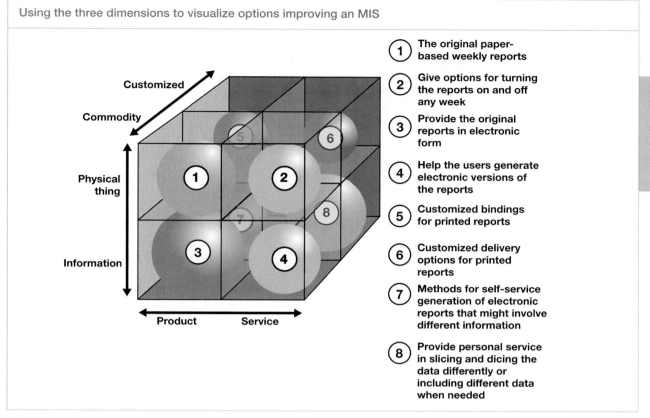

(1) The original paper-based weekly reports

(2) Give options for turning the reports on and off any week

(3) Provide the original reports in electronic form

(4) Help the users generate electronic versions of the reports

(5) Customized bindings for printed reports

(6) Customized delivery options for printed reports

(7) Methods for self-service generation of electronic reports that might involve different information

(8) Provide personal service in slicing and dicing the data differently or including different data when needed

Assume that an old-fashioned information system was designed to generate and distribute a series of paper-based management reports once a week. Designers planning improvements to the system might consider options across all three dimensions in Figure 6.3.

THE CUSTOMER EXPERIENCE

Anyone who has ever waited in line to pay for gasoline or to check in at an airport knows that customer satisfaction involves much more than just the characteristics of products and services that customers receive. Over 50 years ago, well before the computer revolution, Konosuke Matsushita, founder of the Matsushita Electric, stated "We are responsible for delivering satisfaction to the customer not only by designing good products, but also by providing those products through carefully laid out distribution systems in which we should follow through to eliminate any inconvenience to our customers, such as difficulty in repair work."[10]

Matsushita's broad view of the overall product offering is consistent with the first work system principle in Figure 2.3, "Please the customers." The basis of customer satisfaction is the complete **customer experience**, the customer's entire involvement with the product starting with defining the requirements and acquiring the product. Table 6.3 shows that the customer experience for a pure product is somewhat different from that for a pure service. In each case it starts with determining requirements and acquiring the product or service. The third stage is different because the customer uses the product after obtaining it but receives benefit from the service without receiving a tangible product. For durable products such as software or machines there is also a maintenance stage and possibly a retirement stage.

Each of the five stages in the customer experience can be viewed as a separate subsystem that produces benefits for the customer. Figure 6.6 identifies some of the opportunities for using e-business approaches to improve the customer satisfaction at each of the five stages. For example, the discussion of Otisline showed how information could

TABLE 6.3

Comparing the Customer Experience for a Pure Product versus a Pure Service

The customer experience for a pure product has up to five stages; for a pure service, it has just three stages.

Customer experience for either a pure product or a pure service

Requirements: establishing what the customer wants, matching these requirements to the available alternatives, and, in some cases, customizing the product to fit the requirements

Acquisition: determining the customer's acquisition cost, determining product availability, and performing purchase or acquisition transactions

Customer experience for a pure product	Customer experience for a pure service
Usage: the customer's usage of the product, typically viewed in relation to the customer's processes	*Execution:* performing the service to provide the benefits
Maintenance: the customer's efforts to maintain durable products used over extended periods of time	*(No maintenance stage)*
Retirement: whatever must be done to get rid of the product or its remnants once it is no longer useful to the customer	*(No retirement stage)*

FIGURE 6.6

Opportunities to increase customer benefits across the stages of the customer experience

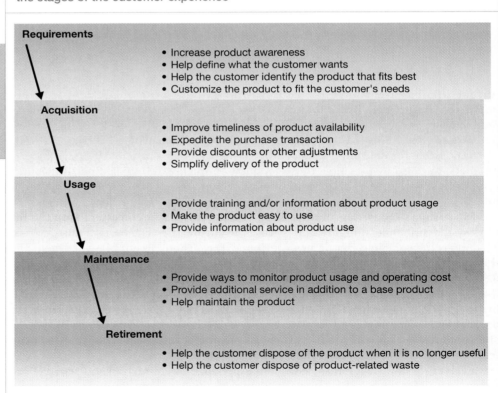

Requirements
- Increase product awareness
- Help define what the customer wants
- Help the customer identify the product that fits best
- Customize the product to fit the customer's needs

Acquisition
- Improve timeliness of product availability
- Expedite the purchase transaction
- Provide discounts or other adjustments
- Simplify delivery of the product

Usage
- Provide training and/or information about product usage
- Make the product easy to use
- Provide information about product use

Maintenance
- Provide ways to monitor product usage and operating cost
- Provide additional service in addition to a base product
- Help maintain the product

Retirement
- Help the customer dispose of the product when it is no longer useful
- Help the customer dispose of product-related waste

Each stage in the customer experience provides a number of possible ways to improve customer satisfaction.

be used more effectively as part of elevator service. That discussion emphasized the usage and maintenance stages in the customer experience. The discussion also mentioned new E*Direct capabilities for calculating requirements and tracking the order; in other words, uses of the Web to improve customer satisfaction with the requirements and acquisition stages.

The idea of the customer experience applies to both external and internal customers. It is used most frequently when thinking about external customers because a firm's success is directly related to how well it satisfies its external customers. Its use in thinking about internal customers is also warranted, however, because it reminds work system participants that inwardly directed systems such as payroll, health benefits, and expense reimbursements also have customers with a legitimate desire to feel satisfied in their complete experience with these systems. We will look at several typical e-business applications across the customer experience.

Determining Requirements

The process of determining requirements varies from product to product, depending on how the product is sold and whether it can be customized. Opportunities to apply e-business approaches in this area include helping the customer learn about the product, evaluate product options, and possibly customize the product before acquiring it.

Learning about Product Options and Benefits   The Web makes it surprisingly easy to explain a product to a customer. Instead of talking to someone on the phone or requesting a paper sales brochure, the potential customer only has to log on to the right Web site to find the same types of information that might otherwise arrive days later.

There are many ways for the Web site to go beyond "brochureware." If the customer can specify a clear requirement, an information system can search for satisfactory options and may be able to rank them in terms of the customer's relative preferences related to cost, convenience, and other factors. This is what happens when an online travel site helps a traveler find a particular flight. Real estate agents use similar methods to identify homes or apartments that meet a client's needs and ability to pay.

It is also possible to provide pictures and animated demos that graphically demonstrate product features and benefits. Even more powerful is an interactive demo that allows the potential customer to try out different product options (see Figure 6.7). For example, the Lands' End Web site allows a customer to enter a few physical characteristics to get a preliminary idea of what an item of clothing might look like when it is worn. This simulation is very rough, but if more detailed information could be provided in the future and stored in a personal information database, it would be possible to get a much better idea of what clothing and other fashion items might look like when used by the customer. An indication of what might be possible in the future is a body measurement system being developed that uses white-light scanning to capture an accurate 3D cloud of points that could be fed into a CAD system to create a pattern for a garment that will really fit. Linking the stored output of this type of scanner into a retailer's Web site could generate an accurate representation of what a particular size and cut would look like on the customer.[11]

The Web provides many new options for fashion and cosmetics industries, which have used information technology for matching products to customer needs for over a decade. In early applications, Elizabeth Arden and Shiseido augmented their department store sales techniques by allowing cosmetologists to use computers to try out different makeup combinations electronically. Today this can be done on the Web by performing a "virtual makeover" starting with a digital photo submitted to a cosmetics site such as eMakeover.com, MakeoverStudio.com, and EZface.com. A practical limitation of this approach is that only 8% of households have a digital camera or scanner that can be used. In addition, delays and frustration one doesn't find at a cosmetics counter stem from the effort of taking an adequately clear photo, e-mailing it the site, having the site reproduce skin tone realistically, and wondering whether monitor settings are introducing bias.[12]

FIGURE 6.7

A Web site that helps determine customer requirements

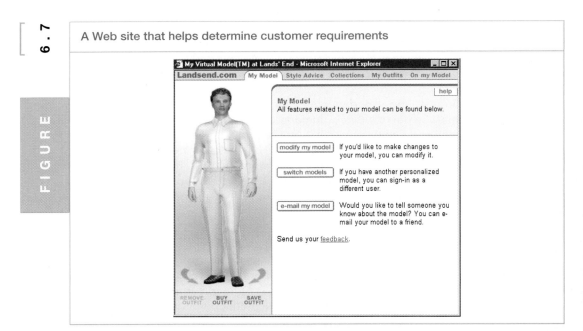

Lands' End's Web site uses a few personal characteristics to provide a rough hint of what the customer might look like in its clothes.

Exercising Customization Choices   As was mentioned earlier, one way to satisfy each customer's unique requirements is to customize the product so that it actually fits the customer's needs. This starts with finding the product options that fit best. Next is customization, the creation or modification of a product based on a specific customer's needs, thereby increasing the product's value for that customer. Information products are especially amenable to customization because information is so fluid. Figure 6.8 shows an example of greeting card customization. This started with selecting among standard components but also allowed the customer to introduce a totally personal message. The customized cards initially cost around $3.50, almost twice the cost of most greeting cards. Like any other competitive action however, customization is not guaranteed to succeed. By 1997 Hallmark had removed all of its 2,700 Touchscreen Greetings machines and its competitor American Greetings had removed most of its 10,000 Creatacard kiosks.[13] An intriguing idea had flopped due to a combination of the price, the time requirement, and the customer's interests and abilities. During the next few years, the ability to customize and send free electronic greeting cards became common on the Web.

Customization is becoming an important competitive issue for many physical products as well. With the ability to link CAD systems to computer-aided manufacturing (CAM) systems that control machines using CAD specifications, it is becoming more practical to tailor anything from clothes to machines based on the customer's requirements or wishes. This approach has been used extensively by the prefabricated housing industry in Japan. These businesses are set up to use mass customization by standardizing production even though the product is customized. Customers for prefabricated homes meet with salespeople to design their homes on a computer screen using representations of thousands of standardized parts. The completed designs are transmitted to a factory that produces the building's structural components on an assembly line. It takes one day for a crane and seven workers to put up the walls and roof of a two-story house. Finishing the job takes another 30 to 60 days.[14]

Acquiring the Product

After determining the requirements, the next step is acquiring the product. From a customer's viewpoint this involves finding the best price, performing a purchase transac-

Direct customer participation in customizing an information product

Hallmark Cards installed 2,700 computerized kiosks that customers could use to create customized greeting cards via touch-screen inputs. This method of creating customized cards failed commercially, in part because the customized cards were almost twice as expensive as most other greeting cards.

tion, and taking delivery. The supplier's view of pricing, especially dynamic pricing, will be discussed later.

Finding a Good Price   The Web provides a number of different methods for finding a good price for a retail product. Some informational sites provide direct comparisons between prices at different vendors. Figure 6.9 gives an example taken from an e-commerce case study. In that particular situation, a combined purchase of the product in the price comparison and another product went awry because the online merchant failed to deliver.[15] Various Web-based auctions (such as those at eBay mentioned in Chapter 4) provide another way to find a good price, assuming that the customer is willing to put in the effort and accept the delays and uncertainty of auction bidding. Yet another model is provided by Priceline.com, which allows the customer to offer a price for a round-trip airline ticket between two locations on particular dates. The customer submits a credit card number and is obligated to accept any ticket on a major airline that Priceline obtains on those dates, with certain exceptions.

With all the comparative pricing information that is available on the Web it might seem surprising that consumers don't do very much price shopping. A study by the market research firm NFO Interactive found that only about half of those polled who had made an online purchase in the prior six months even knew about the price-comparison services, and only 28% of those who knew about them used them even occasionally.[16]

Performing Purchase Transactions   Secure methods for making credit card purchases over the Web have been developed and will be explained in Chapter 13, which

FIGURE 6.9

Price comparisons on the Web

	Merchant	Price	State	Phone	Approx. Shipping	In Stock	Last Updated	Int'l Sales
1	BuyCom.com	$135.95	CA	888.880.1030	See Site	Yes	12-21-98	No
2	CMPExpress.com	$136.99	PA	800.950.2671	See Site	35840	12-21-98	Yes
3	PC Save	$142.99	**	888.498.9884	See Site	Yes	12-20-98	No
4	firstsource.com	$145.74	CA	800.858.9866	Two Day (best way) $9.95+	36867	12-19-98	No
5	IC-Direct.com	$147.38	MS	888.281.8007	$8.00	Yes	11-24-98	Yes
6	Neutron, Inc.	$148.66	PA	800.813.4218	See Site	Yes	12-20-98	No
7	1stMicro	$148.66	FL	800.680.1112	See Site	36528	12-19-98	Yes
8	Computer Warehouse	$148.85	CA	800.511.6071	See Site	Yes	12-19-98	No
9	HardwareStreet.com	$148.99	NV	888.447.4406	$5.70	20314	12-18-98	Yes
10	Necx.com	$149.95	MA	800.808.3375	UPS GND: $6.95	Yes	12-21-98	No
---	------	-----	----	------	------	-----	------	----
21	CDW	$158.62	IL	800.726.4239	$3.99	See Site	12-19-98	Yes
22	Libi Industries, Inc.	$159.95	NY	800.886.5424	See Site	Yes	12-19-98	Yes
23	PC Mall	$159.99	**	800.863.3282	See Site	46916	12-18-98	Yes
24	Computability	$159.99	WI	800.554.2184	$4.99	47278	12-21-98	Yes
25	MicroWarehouse	$169.95	NJ	800.397.8508	$9.95+ 1 Day	Yes	12-18-98	Yes
26	CompSource	$170.13	OH	800.413.7361	$8.00	Yes	12-21-98	No
27	Soft4U.com	$170.66	CA	877.276.3848	$3.00	Yes	12-10-98	Yes
28	Egghead.com	$170.99	WA	800.344.4323	See Site	Yes	12-21-98	No
29	Software Online	$199.00	ON	905.637.8890	See Site	See Site	12-18-98	No

These price comparisons for a software product were published in an e-commerce case study.

will also mention several examples of credit card numbers stolen from poorly secured e-commerce sites. One of the possible ways to reduce the likelihood of this type of problem is to use electronic cash that operates like a smart card in a Web-based environment. A person wishing to use digital cash would transfer money to a bank, which would transfer a corresponding amount to a **digital purse** that plays the role of a smart card in that person's computer. This is similar to the "vault" mentioned in the E-Stamp case at the end of Chapter 3. A user wishing to pay a small amount for accessing information or playing a game on the Web simply would transfer digital cash from the digital purse to the online merchant. Unlike a credit or debit card payment, the payment transaction would be completed when the electronic transfer occurs. No record of who paid for what would be necessary because the information completing the purchase would be delivered immediately and because the amounts would be small, perhaps even fractions of a penny.

In other situations, the purchase transaction involves much more than just a credit card or electronic cash transaction. For example, health care is an industry in which the purchase transactions for medical care and pharmaceuticals have become incredibly burdensome due to the checking and record keeping required for insurance reimbursement. There is a great deal of room for Web-based methods of simplifying these purchase transactions and eliminating the paperwork.

Another step toward facilitating purchasing transactions is to allow suppliers to control their customers' inventories, thereby making a supplier-customer relationship into more of a partnership with specific performance goals for both parties. These partnerships have been used in a number of industries. For example, Procter & Gamble manages Wal-Mart's inventory of diapers this way, just as Baxter International manages inventories for its hospital supply customers based on performance targets and risk-sharing arrangements.

Taking Delivery   Delivery has turned out to be a central issue in e-commerce. Regardless of how well the previous steps operate, the customer is not happy if the product does not arrive or is delayed. According to a Boston Consulting Group study, 19% of online customers said the delivery of their orders either took longer than they expected or never occurred.[17] As a result, many stopped shopping online; others simply refused to do more business with the offending retailer. Delivery delays are often attributed to the parcel carrier, but mishaps frequently occur before an order leaves the warehouse, which is why e-commerce sites are now putting much more emphasis on inventory control and order fulfillment systems.

E-business approaches have made it possible to exert much tighter control of order fulfillment processes, with order entry systems tightly linked to picking and packing processes that are sometimes operated by completely different companies. Once the delivery process begins, FedEx and United Parcel Service can now track packages as they pass checkpoints on the way to their destination. This reassures the customer and reduces the likelihood of lost packages.

Many additional delivery options emerge when the item being delivered is information as opposed to physical objects. Information can often be delivered immediately over a data network, thereby avoiding the delays and extra work of printing it, packaging it, and delivering the physical package to the destination the next day, at the earliest. The U.S. Internal Revenue Service (IRS) has taken many strides in this area. Until several years ago, for example, the way to order an infrequently used U.S. tax form was to call the IRS, stay on hold until someone answered, request the form, and then wait five days or more until it arrived. The new approach is much faster. Simply log onto the IRS Web site, download the form, and print it. Many organizations have used the Web in a similar way because this method of information distribution is faster and cheaper for all concerned. Similar processes are also used frequently for downloading software.

Using the Product or Receiving the Service

Making products more useful and easier to use is another way to apply e-business approaches. This can be done in three ways: incorporating electronic enhancements into products, providing better service, and providing the customer with accessible information or knowledge about the product.

Electronically Enhanced Products   Electronically enhanced products of many types are becoming commonplace. The inclusion of wireless communication capabilities is becoming increasingly widespread. For example, personal digital assistants will soon be able to link with PCs for data uploads and downloads without requiring a physical connection. Information systems are becoming increasingly important components of a wide range of products. Figure 6.1 illustrated that automobiles now contain a number of information systems. The same applies for buildings, which use computerized control systems to reduce maintenance and security personnel by checking the temperature of each floor, the location of every elevator, and the status of all doors (locked or unlocked). Automatic switches turn the lights on when people enter offices and off 12 minutes after they leave. Security systems record the electronic ID card used whenever someone enters a secured area. Extreme examples of electronically enhanced products are some current jet fighters that simply can't be flown by an unaided human being. The pilot determines the direction and speed of these jets, and a real-time information system in the background performs adjustments that make sure that the jet remains stable enough to be controllable.

WEB CHECK [✓]

Log onto the IRS Web site at www.irs.ustreas.gov and download Form 1040, a version of which U.S. taxpayers must submit every year. Explain whether and how the Web site itself should be modified to facilitate these downloads.

Providing Better Service   Leading companies in many industries attempt to differentiate themselves by providing an extra measure of service for their customers. Consider the way national car rental firms such as Avis use information systems to provide high-quality service. From a busy traveler's viewpoint, every minute spent in the process of renting or returning a car is a waste of valuable time. In the early days of car rentals, the rental and return processes involved waiting in line and filling out paper forms. Hertz, Avis, and some of their competitors have minimized the waiting and paperwork in these business processes. Figure 6.10 shows the handheld terminal a service representative uses to record a car's mileage reading and gas-tank level. The hand-held terminal uses a radio link to a computer network to transmit the check-in information and receive the billing information in return. For customers who presented a credit card when they rented the car, it can then print out a final receipt without requiring the customer to set foot in an office again. This process enhances productivity while ensuring the quality and responsiveness customers want.

Providing Product Information or Knowledge   Another way to enhance a product is to provide better information or knowledge about the product itself. For example, because people frequently misplace owner manuals for household items, finding another way to provide such information would have many advantages. Even when manuals are available, many owner and user manuals are difficult to use because they are presented in broad context and they can't adjust to the user's knowledge or to the situation the user faces. Many manufacturers address these shortcomings by providing telephone hotlines staffed by human operators. More recently, firms have begun experimenting with using Internet "chat rooms," in which customers can exchange typed messages with trained customer service representatives. One consulting study estimated that servicing customers this way could cost as little as $0.25 per transaction, compared with $1.25 for each phone transaction.[18]

The Web has made an enormous impact in providing self-service access to product-related information and knowledge. For example, Cisco Systems has made its help desk information available through the Web. The reasoning is simple: If our help desk peo-

FIGURE   6.10

Handheld terminal used to speed the process of returning rental cars

The system Hertz uses for checking in returned cars has competitive significance because user convenience is one of the ways Hertz differentiates itself from its competition.

ple use this information our customers should also be able to use it. Most other companies haven't gone quite so far, but the benefits of self-service for providing product information are enormous.

Maintaining and Retiring the Product

Product maintenance is an important determinant of whether a customer's experience with a product is favorable. Products prone to excessive downtime or catastrophic failure simply don't provide the value the customer expects. Information systems can be used to support maintenance and repair processes in a variety of ways, including providing maintenance information, linking to machines from remote sites, and even performing product upgrades automatically.

Supporting Maintenance and Repair Processes   Good information systems are an essential part of an effective field service operation. The Otis Elevator case at the beginning of the chapter described a system that supported field service through communication, data storage, and data analysis. The communication role of the system was to ensure that technicians were contacted immediately whenever an elevator problem occurred. The informational role was to provide a complete history of service calls to all elevators. This information could be used to identify long-term service problems and to monitor the emergency response process.

Product maintenance systems also serve many other functions. Some provide direct linkages to computerized parts inventories. These systems help field technicians find the parts they need and help them estimate when repairs will be completed; other systems provide direct guidance for repair people. Figure 6.11 shows a picture of a mechanic using one of these systems developed for Ford to analyze electrical problems. The system scans computer chips built into the car. If the mechanic doesn't find the problem, the customer can borrow a five-pound recorder and turn it on when the problem reappears.

Using Remote Monitoring   Use of information technology to observe a building, business operation, person, or computer from a distance is called **remote monitoring**. An everyday example of remote monitoring is the service burglar alarm companies provide using sensors that detect events such as a door opening, a motion, and a sudden impact such as breaking glass. On detecting any of these events, the automatic system notifies operators in a central location, who then try to decide whether it is a false alarm by phoning the premises or studying the signals from the sensors.

Many manufacturers of electronic equipment such as telephone switching systems and computers provide remote monitoring services as an add-on following an equipment purchase. Typically, these remote monitoring systems poll each machine nightly to try to identify electronic components that have failed or are going bad. Doing this frequently minimizes emergency calls when the customer's operations are disrupted by a hardware failure. This also makes it less likely that the customer will even notice equipment failures. In addition, these systems make it possible to perform some repairs by transmitting machine instructions over a network, thereby reducing the cost of service calls.

Retiring Obsolete Products and Upgrading to New Versions   The continual sequence of upgrades required with software and many other information products demonstrates how e-business can be used in the final part of the customer experience, namely, retiring products whose useful life is over, removing them, and upgrading to current versions. The programs that perform these upgrades have stringent requirements because they could cause great inconvenience if they disable the old version and fail to perform the complete upgrade. At some point, e-business may even play a role in retiring physical products. For example, an owner registry for products such as appliances and wall-to-wall carpets might play some role in removing and recycling obsolete products. Whether this type of use will develop remains to be seen.

FIGURE 6.11

Ford's Service Bay Diagnostic System

Ford Motor Company's Service Bay Diagnostic System is designed to help mechanics with two of the most frustrating service department occurrences—intermittent problems and hard-to-find problems.

REALITY CHECK ✓

The Customer's Experience Related to a Product

This section described a five-stage customer experience.

1. Describe the customer experience for several products you are familiar with.

2. Explain ways in which changes in the customer experience for these might increase customer satisfaction.

CUSTOMER'S CRITERIA FOR EVALUATING PRODUCTS AND SERVICES

Customers think about product performance in terms of a variety of performance variables. Table 6.4 identifies five product performance variables that can be used to evaluate any stage in the customer experience. The table also lists typical performance measures for each, plus common ways information systems are used to improve the product. Other possible criteria, such as image and aesthetics, are not included because information systems usually affect them only indirectly.

Notice that these variables often interact, sometimes by working together and sometimes by working in opposite directions. For example, cost and reliability issues overlap because poor reliability generates unwanted costs for the customer. Likewise,

TABLE   6.4

Common Roles of Information Systems in Improving the Product of a Work System

Product performance variable	Typical measures	Common information system roles
Cost	• Purchase price • Cost of ownership • Amount of time and attention required	• Reduce internal cost of business process or increase productivity, making it easier to charge or allocate lower prices to customers • Improve product performance in ways that reduce the customer's internal costs
Quality	• Defect rate per time interval or per quantity of output • Rate of warranty returns • Perceived quality according to customer	• Insure the product is produced more consistently • Make it easier to customize the product for the customer • Build information systems into the product to make it more usable or maintainable
Responsiveness	• Time to respond to customer request • Helpfulness of response	• Improve the speed of response • Systematize communication with customers • Increase flexibility to make it easier to respond to what the customer wants
Reliability	• Average time to failure • Failure rate per time interval • Compliance to customer commitment dates	• Make the business process more consistent • Make the business process more secure • Build features into the product that make it more reliable on its own right
Conformance to standards and regulations	• Existence of nonconformance • Rate of complaints about non-conformance	• Clarify the standards and regulations so that it is easier to determine whether they are being followed • Systematize work to make the output more consistent

responsiveness, reliability, and conformance are sometimes viewed as partially overlapping aspects of quality. In other cases, product performance variables such as responsiveness and reliability may push in opposite directions because the product variations needed to increase responsiveness might diminish reliability. Despite the overlaps and contradictions, it is useful to consider ways in which each of these variables helps clarify the customer's view of how good the product is and how it might be improved. At least a few of the five product performance variables could be irrelevant in any particular situation, but each performance variable should be considered, if for no other reason than to assure yourself that it is not important in a given situation. We will look at each of the performance variables in turn.

Cost

Cost is a prime determinant of customer satisfaction. When considering **cost**, we are not thinking about it in a strict accounting sense but as what the internal or external customer must give up in order to obtain, use, and maintain the product of a work system. Often called the **total cost of ownership (TCO)**, this includes money plus time, effort, and attention that could be used for other purposes. This view of cost illustrates how the product of any work system involves cost to the internal or external customer even when no money is transferred.

There are many e-business approaches for reducing costs felt by internal or external customers. These start with reducing the cost of acquiring or using the product, such as the way ATMs eliminate the time and effort of standing on line during bank hours or the way MCI increased its market in the 1990s by offering special "friends and family" rates. Information systems can also be incorporated into the product to make it more efficient, such as the way computers control combustion in car engines. Information systems can also provide more usable billing data to promote efficiency, such as by analyzing telephone bills and telling customers what services and pricing options would minimize their future bills if the same usage patterns continue.

Insurance transaction data is also especially valuable in controlling costs. Instead of treating its claims data as a secret, Travelers Insurance analyzes the data for its customers. When the manufacturer Allied-Signal noticed a rise in some of its self-insured workman's compensation claims, data from Travelers pinpointed a large number of hand injuries by maintenance workers. Allied-Signal halved these injuries through better training and the use of gloves.[19]

Quality

The concept of quality has been interpreted many different ways and spans many aspects of performance. Even though product quality is often linked to the consistency of the process that produced the product, we will view quality as a criterion by which the customer evaluates the product. The coverage of business processes in Chapter 3 treated consistency, productivity, and cycle time as aspects of process performance.

For our purposes, **quality** refers to the customer's perception that the product has desired features and that these features are in line with the product's costs. As in the example of increasingly computerized automobiles, incorporation of information systems into physical products sometimes provides capabilities and aesthetic features associated with quality. For information products, the perception of quality is related to accessibility and usefulness, such as the way graphical user interfaces made it easier for nonprogrammers to extract data from databases. For services, the perception of quality is related to whether the service seems complete and whether it is delivered attentively. For example, one of the complaints about some HMOs is that doctors are so swamped they cannot provide high-quality service.

Responsiveness

With regard to customer satisfaction, **responsiveness** means taking timely action based on what the customer wants, such as when a sales clerk uses a company-wide inventory system to find an out-of-stock item at another store and has it shipped to the customer's home. As another example, many architectural firms now use computer-aided design systems to provide simulated walk-throughs of proposed buildings; this sometimes enables them to make immediate modifications based on customer feedback. The highest levels of responsiveness often require creating or modifying a product or service based on a specific customer's needs, thereby increasing its value for that customer.

Responsiveness involves more than just speed. Even in today's fast-paced business world, convenience and personalized service are often more important than speed. As an example, AT&T Universal Card Services gave an employee a $6,000 award for suggesting that AT&T should give the customer a choice between a 10:00 A.M. delivery or a 3:00 P.M. delivery when a credit card is lost. Providing a choice instead of automatically delivering new replacement cards early the next day had the potential of increasing customer satisfaction and reducing costs for AT&T because a 3:00 P.M. delivery would be cheaper.[20]

Computerizing a work system may increase or decrease responsiveness, either by design or by accident. As managed care takes hold in medicine, for example, more medical decisions, such as how many sessions of psychotherapy to allow, are being constrained (and hence made less responsive) by partially computerized systems based on statistical data. As an example of responsiveness decreasing by accident, consider what happened when a Bay Area restaurant began using handheld terminals for taking orders. The terminals had many benefits, but they provided no way for waiters to record special customer requests, such as putting the sauce on the side. Service was faster and more reliable, but not as responsive to the customer.

Reliability

The **reliability** of a work system's product refers to the likelihood that it will not fail when the customer wants to use it. Although computerizing work systems often creates an additional layer of structure that increases reliability, there is no way to guarantee that computers are programmed correctly or that communication networks will always stay up. On April 13, 1998, a breakdown in AT&T's high-speed data networks affected thousands of customers, such as Wal-Mart, about half of whose 2,400 stores experienced difficulties processing credit card purchases or updating inventories. AT&T had spent billions of dollars modernizing its networks and often boasted that they were "self-healing." In this case, however, the "self-healing" features that reroute data traffic when a cable is cut were useless because the major switches that perform the routing were down, apparently due to a software problem.[21] Eight years earlier, a previously unobserved bug in software used by AT&T's long distance telephone network prevented completion of 44% of the 148 million long distance calls on the network between 2:30 P.M. and 11:30 P.M. on January 15, 1990. That disruption left national sales offices and other large-scale telephone users unable to operate and led many corporations to consider using MCI and Sprint as backup suppliers of telephone service.[22]

One of the paradoxes of reliability is that measures taken to increase reliability are often the cause of failure. An ironic example is a power failure at an air traffic control center serving Chicago's O'Hare Airport. Thousands of airline passengers were delayed for hours because a contractor accidentally caused a short circuit while testing a system for preventing power failures. This was the second time in the same year that installation of an "uninterruptible power system" interrupted power at an air traffic center.[23]

Conformance to Standards and Regulations

Adherence to standards and regulations imposed by external bodies such as major customers, industry groups, or the government is a crucial issue for the product of many work systems. We will call performance in this area **conformance to standards and regulations**. Unlike cost and quality, conformance does not play a direct role in the return on investment, yet it is the driving force behind the way many work systems operate. The most obvious examples of conformance issues occur in work systems that gather and analyze information related to paying taxes; nonconformance in these systems results in fines or even jail terms. In other cases, nonconformance with industry standards such as the shape of electric plugs, the width of a typical doorway, or the dimensions of a piece of paper is unacceptable because it would cause incompatibility with many other products used by the same customers.

Standards are precisely stated, widely publicized rules governing the size, shape, and operating characteristics of products or processes. The existence of an American standard for the size of copy paper (8 1/2 by 11 inches) means that any paper supplier can provide paper fitting any copy machine or laser printer built for the American market. Different standards can coexist, as illustrated by the fact that Europe and Asia use different standard sizes for paper, and that people in America and continental Europe drive on the right side of the road while people in England and Japan drive on the left side. The chapters on information technology will explain why "competing standards" is a major competitive issue in the computer and telecommunications industries. The enormous growth and market power of Microsoft and Intel attest to the importance of controlling technical standards—in this case, the standards for personal computer operating systems and microprocessors.[24]

Where standards are either negotiated voluntarily or determined by the way things evolve in business or society, **regulations** are rules based on laws administered by federal, state, or local governments. International bodies such as the European Union also generate regulations. Regulations require businesses to operate in particular ways and to submit tax forms and tax payments consistent with specific rules. Depending on the size of the business, regulations may require additional information about hiring practices, energy utilization, waste disposal, and other topics. One of the most far-reaching system-related regulations in current business is the conversion from national currencies to a new European currency called the euro. This conversion requires banks, corporations, and government agencies to overhaul their financial information systems. Invoices, tax calculations, and bank statements all have to be changed from marks or francs to euros.

Electronic data interchange (EDI) systems (mentioned in Chapter 5) exemplify the way conformance to standards applies across the customer experience. Before EDI, large companies spent exorbitant amounts of money to process each invoice because of paperwork and inconsistent data formats. In many cases, these companies told their suppliers that reducing paperwork costs was so important that the use of EDI was a requirement for doing business regardless of the particular features of the product being purchased. This forced changes in the smaller companies' internal information systems to permit linkage into the standardized EDI systems the large companies were establishing. In effect, EDI became an essential part of the product the large companies were buying.

R E A L I T Y C H E C K [✓]

Evaluating Product Performance

This section has discussed a number of product performance variables.

1. Identify two work systems, one with internal customers and one with external customers. Identify the product performance variables that seem most important and least important in this situation. Explain how you might measure those variables.

2. Assume someone actually measured each variable. Estimate the numerical value the person would find currently and compare the likely value if the product were improved as much as seems conceivable.

DIVERSE CONCERNS OF DIFFERENT CUSTOMERS

It is difficult to please customers without knowing who they are, either as individuals or as members of a definable group. An immediate complication for any internally or externally directed work system is that there may be a variety of customers with different needs, interests, and capabilities. In other words, their view of products and services may be different, their customer experience may be different, and their criteria for evaluating the product may be different.

In practice, pleasing customers reduces to deciding which customers to try to please and to what extent. For example, a toy retailer's sales system should appeal to the children who use the toys and the adults who purchase them. Customers of a college textbook publisher's sales and distribution system include not only the students who buy the books, but also the professors who select the books, and the professional societies that may set the curriculum. In these cases, the customers include the people who receive and use the product as well as the people who select it or pay for it. In other cases such as corporate intranets used for distributing documents, messages, and providing simple transaction capabilities, the customers may be employees at various organizational levels, in various functional areas, and in different locations.

Responding to different needs of different customers may require producing different types of products directed at different types of customers. For example, a typical e-commerce Web site has at least three types of customers: customers who are purchasing something, customers who want to obtain information about the vendor and the products being sold, and internal customers who use the information by-products of each sale. These information by-products include the transaction data that is essential for inventory management, financial accounting, and tax remittances. They also include the trail of mouse-clicks that can be used for marketing analysis and Web site improvement. An effective e-commerce site should meet all three needs.

There is also a difference between mandatory and voluntary customers. Typical B2C e-commerce customers are voluntary customers because they can choose whether to shop online and whether to buy anything. In other situations, the customers have little choice. The Internal Revenue Service might view taxpayers as its customers, but the penalty for not paying taxes and not filling out tax forms properly can be severe.

Thus far we have surveyed the basic ideas for describing the essence of products and services that a work system produces in addition to the customer experience and the customer's criteria for evaluating a product. These ideas are basically the same regardless of whether the product or service is directed at internal or external customers. With this background, we will now turn to the competitive uses of information systems in producing, extending, or servicing products for external customers. The last part of the chapter will discuss challenges related to e-commerce, but first we need to look at ideas about competitive use of information systems. These ideas were widely applicable before e-commerce emerged but remain applicable today.

INFORMATION SYSTEMS AND COMPETITIVE ADVANTAGE

Organizations compete based on their value chains, the series of processes that create products and services external customers pay for. **Competitive advantage** occurs when a firm's value chain generates superior product and service features, quality, availability, lower cost, or other things customers care about. Competitive advantage comes from many sources. Some companies have a natural competitive advantage (for example, a steel mill that has lower transportation costs because it is near a good source of iron ore and coal). Others must create competitive advantage through superior product design, marketing, customer service, or distribution channels.

Whether and how a firm can use information systems competitively depends on the firm's strategy. Although competitive situations vary widely, most companies adopt some combination of three idealized strategies described by Porter.[25] A firm using a **cost leadership strategy** competes on lower costs. A firm using this strategy can reduce its own costs, its supplier's costs, or its customer's costs, or it can raise its competitor's costs. A firm using a **product differentiation strategy** provides more value than competitors or eliminates the competitor's differentiation. A firm using a **focus strategy** sells its product or service into a restricted market niche with limited competition. Although viewing strategy in terms of these idealized models is sometimes useful, a growing consensus is that most companies have to focus on both cost and differentiation in order to succeed in today's business climate.

Mission-Critical Information Systems

Today, after so much attention has been devoted to e-commerce and dot.coms, the idea that an information system might be strategic seems obvious. Although some information systems clearly have strategic importance, a number of important points emerge when looking at the concept of strategic information systems. Among other things, this helps in seeing that a Web site may or may not be strategic, depending on a firm's business model and competitive stance in its industry. We will start with the difference between mission-critical information systems, which exist in almost every large firm, and strategic information systems, which are not as common.

Today many information systems are so infused throughout entire organizations that many have become essential for a business to operate. Even if these systems provide no competitive differentiation whatsoever, they are often considered **mission-critical information systems** because their failure prevents or delays basic business activities such as selling to customers, processing orders, and manufacturing. The importance of mission-critical systems was reflected in a 62% plunge in the stock of Oxford Health Plans after an unanticipated quarterly loss in 1997. Oxford attributed the loss to problems with upgrades in basic systems for billing and reimbursement. Many bills had been sent out late over the course of eight months, and some customers balked when Oxford tried to collect back payments. Oxford had fallen hundreds of millions of dollars behind in payments to hospitals and doctors and had been forced to advance money to them without verifying they were obeying Oxford's cost-saving rules.[26] Had Oxford implemented the information system upgrades successfully, it wouldn't have fallen so far behind in its billing, it would have been able to make all its payments, and it would have avoided a devastating quarter. In 1999 and 2000 a poorly executed reorganization at Xerox led to similar problems when it consolidated 53 customer administration centers (finance, billing, call centers) in Europe to one location, and 36 centers in the U.S. to three. "The result was chaos. The invoices and shipping orders piled up; Xerox sales reps had to spend up to 40% of their time getting the orders right and answering billing questions. Instead of cutting expenses, the transition ended up costing Xerox money and customer goodwill."[27]

Strategic Information Systems

In contrast to the many mission-critical information systems most organizations rely on, a small number of **strategic information systems** are designed to play a major role in an organization's competitive strategy. These systems typically increase the customer's perceived value by customizing products, augmenting products thorough information and services, eliminating delays, improving reliability, making products easier to use, bypassing intermediaries, or reducing transaction times. Otisline is one of many examples of this type of system.

Many examples of e-commerce throughout this book initially represented strategic systems but were soon copied by others. To introduce the long-term dynamics of strategic information systems, we will look at classic examples from Merrill Lynch and McKesson.

Merrill Lynch's Cash Management Account was introduced in 1977 as a way to combine three previously distinct investment services: credit using a margin account; cash withdrawal using a check or Visa card; and automatic investment of cash in a money market. The Cash Management Account was aimed at customers who were tired of the confusion and inefficiency of having too many different accounts in too many different places. Combining these services required a state-of-the-art transaction processing system. Building the information system and developing the other business activities required for this type of financial product was so complex that Merrill Lynch enjoyed a monopoly for four years. It had gained over 450,000 new customers by the time its competitors could respond with a me-too product of a type that is now commonplace and easier to create because the underlying technology has improved.

McKesson, a distributor of pharmaceuticals, used what was initially an innovative system to help its customers simultaneously achieve two seemingly contradictory goals, reducing inventory costs and avoiding stock-outs. Pharmacies traditionally ordered inventory from distributors in a way that was inefficient and error-prone. A pharmacy employee checked the pharmacy's inventory, recorded amounts needed, and mailed orders to distributors, who responded days later. Delays in all the steps and errors in transcribing information several times forced pharmacies to tie up money in large inventories. To minimize these problems, McKesson's system allows pharmacies to record their orders using a handheld, calculator-like terminal. Bar code labels on shelves make it unnecessary even to write product names. Orders recorded on the terminal are transmitted over phone lines to McKesson's computer system and entered automatically. McKesson attained a competitive edge by reducing its internal costs, reducing customers' internal costs, and providing better customer service. The benefits for McKesson included a reduction in order entry clerks from 700 to 15. From 1975 to 1987, McKesson's sales increased 424%, whereas its operating expenses increased only 86%.[28, 29]

Competitive Advantage Creates Competitive Necessity

The Merrill Lynch and McKesson systems were both attempts to attain competitive advantage through product differentiation. Both were so successful that they created new expectations and changed the basis of competition in their respective industries. With the bar raised, competitors either had to create a different type of differentiation or had to build similar systems to eliminate the differentiation these strategic systems originally created. The me-too systems were built not for competitive advantage but because particular features or capabilities had become a de facto requirement to participate in the market. The ultimate result of many strategic information systems is that the capabilities in the system become a **competitive necessity** and are no longer a source of competitive advantage because all the major competitors do something similar.

The banking industry relied on computers for decades before electronic banking created new ways to provide service. A first step in electronic banking for consumers was the advent of automatic teller machines (ATMs) popularized by Citibank in the late 1970s. Thanks to ATMs, Citibank tripled its depositors from 1978 to 1987, increasing its local consumer market share from 4.5% to 13%.[30, 31] As happened in the Merrill Lynch case, the competition responded. Other banks banded together to produce their own network, the New York Cash Exchange, or NYCE, which began operations in 1985, and which Citibank eventually joined. More recently, several national ATM networks permit customers to withdraw money from ATMs in all major cities in the United States and some cities abroad.

Similar events occurred in response to Internet-based e-commerce initiatives. For example, American Airlines, Continental, Delta, Northwest, and United looked at online travel sites and asked themselves why they should pay commissions to unnecessary intermediaries. They created a project to set up a joint site called Orbitz. General Motors, Ford, DaimlerChrysler, and Renault/Nissan did the same thing when they founded an automotive industry site called Covisint. These partnerships face many competitive, practical, and legal issues, and their future involves many unknowns.[32]

These examples show that even if a strategic information system is initially successful, there is no guarantee it will provide **sustainable competitive advantage**. If one firm can build a system, there is usually no reason why another firm or group of firms cannot copy the idea. The main challenge to sustainability is how long any single system or capability will provide competitive advantage before it is copied, equaled, or even surpassed by competitors. The most sustainable sources of competitive advantage are the firm's culture, its personnel, its major business processes, and its special resources such as patents or land that cannot be copied. The fact that competitive advantage through information systems may be temporary does not invalidate this approach, however. During the four years Merrill Lynch's competitors struggled to catch up, Merrill Lynch expanded its customer base and could look to new opportunities while its competitors were matching its existing capabilities. The same phenomenon occurred for early e-commerce leaders such as America Online (AOL), Yahoo!, and eBay.

R E A L I T Y C H E C K ✓

Using Information Systems for Competitive Advantage

This section noted that many information systems are mission-critical, but that some might be called strategic information systems because they are part of a firm's strategy.

1. Identify three mission-critical information systems in organizations you are familiar with and explain why you believe these systems are mission-critical.

2. Explain why you do or do not believe these can also be considered strategic information systems.

CHALLENGES AS COMMERCE BECOMES E-COMMERCE

Chapter 1 defined **e-commerce** as using the Internet and other communication technology for marketing, selling, and servicing products and services. Aspects of e-commerce include informing a customer of a product's existence, providing in-depth product information, establishing the customer's requirements, performing the purchase transaction, delivering software or information electronically, and providing customer service electronically.

Figure 6.12 uses the work system framework to identify a number of challenges faced by firms trying to exploit e-commerce. This section looks at a number of these

FIGURE 6.12

Challenges of e-commerce from a supplier's or merchant's viewpoint

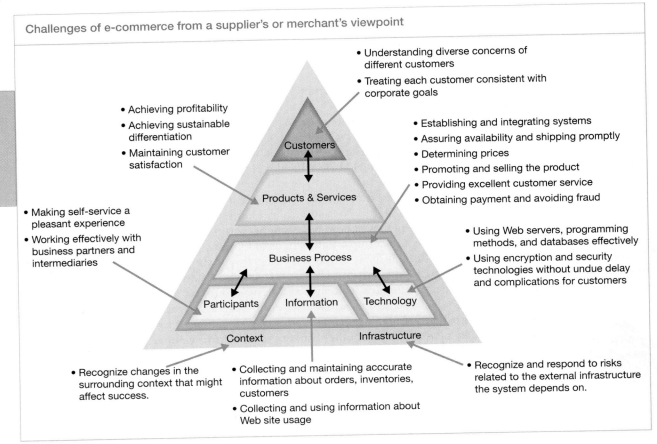

challenges. It starts from the inside with topics such as establishing and integrating systems and setting prices. It then moves toward the customer with topics such as attracting customers, providing an effective self-service environment, providing excellent customer service, and achieving profitability and sustainable differentiation.

Establishing and Integrating Systems

Although e-commerce sometimes has a glitzy external appearance, internally it is basically a systems business. Like any business it requires competitive products and prices, but it succeeds only if the firm has reliable systems in place to market the product, take orders, deliver the product, and provide customer service, including returns of faulty shipments.

This book has already discussed many concepts and system types that apply equally in e-commerce and traditional commerce. The entire discussion of the supply chain and value chain in Chapter 1 is certainly applicable in both areas, as are the systems analysis concepts in Chapter 2, the business process concepts in Chapter 3, the database and information concepts in Chapter 4, and many of the system types described in Chapter 5. For example, many of the concepts of customer relationship management (CRM) apply to e-commerce even though the specifics need to be adapted to an online environment instead of a traditional sales environment. In this case much of the data collection occurs automatically through Web site interactions, but the resulting ability to analyze customer actions, needs, and profitability follows a similar pattern.

Clicks and Bricks   There has been a substantial amount of conjecture about the comparative advantages and disadvantages of pure Internet start-ups versus Internet initiatives of previously existing firms. Well over half of the volume of e-commerce occurs not through pure Internet start-ups, but through established firms that had established products and markets before moving to e-commerce as one of several distribution channels. Adding a new distribution channel was a major challenge for most of these firms. Some started with a completely separate e-commerce operation that had its own inventory replenishment and order fulfillment systems. Others tried to use existing systems to support both their traditional channels and e-commerce. Each approach had initial advantages and disadvantages for getting started with e-commerce, but from a customer's viewpoint the idea of separation between one firm's traditional channels versus that same firm's e-commerce effort had disadvantages and no advantages unless the customer would enjoy a price difference.

A strategy of using e-commerce while maintaining store- or office-based channels is sometimes called **clicks and bricks**. David Pottruck, co-CEO of Charles Schwab & Co., coined this phrase in 1999 to describe the discount brokerage's successful efforts to coordinate all its services so that customers can trade stock online, in person at its walk-in retail branches, or by telephone, either using an automated touch-tone system or talking to a call center representative. Pottruck predicted that future business success would hinge not on pitting brick-and-mortar companies against online-only efforts, but in successfully integrating the two. After all, Pottruck observed, "We're all embedded in the real world."[33] Barnes & Noble, the largest U.S. book chain, moved to a similar strategy when it decided to provide Internet service counters at its superstores so that store customers could order books or other products through its Web arm, Barnesandnoble.com. Shoppers would be able to pay by cash, check, or credit card and would be able to pick up their orders at the stores or have them delivered. Customers would also be able to return books and CDs purchased from the Web site to any Barnes & Noble store.[34]

Assuring Availability and Shipping Promptly   The ability to sell a product over the Internet does not matter very much unless it is possible to deliver the product as well. During the 1999 holiday season a number of Internet merchants lost credibility and customer goodwill because they ran out of stock or couldn't deliver. This even became an issue for the Federal Trade Commission, which fined CDnow, Macys.com, Toysrus.com, and four other companies a total of $1.5 million as a result of poor delivery performance during the 1999 season. In November 2000 the FTC warned more than 100 online merchants not to make unrealistic "quick ship claims" to entice customers to their sites during the 2000 season. The FTC's rule is that a merchant unable to fulfill a good-faith claim must notify the customer of the delay within the original shipping time, must provide a revised shipping date, and must give them a right to cancel the transaction and receive a full and prompt refund.[35]

Maintaining Security and Avoiding Fraud   System issues in e-commerce span the entire relationship with the customer. In addition to systems for attracting customers, replenishing inventories, and fulfilling orders, e-commerce sites need systematic methods for maintaining security and avoiding fraud. Maintaining security includes making sure that no one steals credit card numbers or other customer information from the databases supporting the site. It also includes making sure that no one infiltrates the company's Web server and "hijacks" the site, which has actually happened a number of times. Avoiding fraud is a major issue from the merchant's viewpoint because the rate of using stolen credit card numbers is ten times greater in online transactions than in face-to-face transactions.

[**L O O K   A H E A D**]

Chapter 13, "E-Business Security and Control," starts with a case about Visa's fraud avoidance advice to merchants. It also discusses digital signatures and other methods for avoiding fraud in e-commerce transactions.

Setting Prices

Ready access to pricing information by both customers and competitors has made pricing a more challenging issue than it was in the past, when many merchants knew that most of their customers had little ability to compare prices in an organized way. For example, in the past someone buying a car might go from dealer to dealer trying to figure out the logic of a variety of prices for whatever cars happened to be on the car lot when they visited. Today, someone wanting to buy a P44 Ford Mustang 2-door, 5-speed convertible could look at www.edmunds.com and find the invoice price to the dealer, the manufacturer's suggested retail price (MSRP), and the approximate market value in

WEB CHECK ✓

Look at www.edmunds.com to find how much your car or a car you would like to have would cost in your area. Compare this information with prices offered in a local newspaper or elsewhere on the Web by a dealer.

a local area. The same Web site also provides information about the price of customer options along with an outline of the methods that automobile salespeople often use to influence customers and convince them they are being offered a good price. This information does not guarantee getting a good deal, but using it as a starting point reduces the chances that dealers will be able to benefit from ignorance of their customers.

Shopbots (shopping robots) may also increase the challenge for merchants. Current shopbots are programs that search for the best price on a particular product or bid for particular items at auctions. An interesting issue with shopbots is that some major online retailers have programmed their sites to reject shopbot inquiries needed to make the comparisons.[36] Whether and how this technology will develop remains to be seen. Some researchers are looking forward to a time when these "autonomous agents," as they are known to their programmers, will bid at dozens of auctions simultaneously and will bid not just for one product, but for several related goods, such as a combination of paper, ink, binders, and printing press time. Capabilities such as these might cause major changes in B2B and B2C marketplaces. Shopbot competitions have become part of the research in this area. For example, in one competition shopbots were asked to arrange round-trip air tickets to Boston along with hotel accommodations, tickets to a Red Sox game, and so on. The winner from AT&T achieved the lowest total price among twenty entrants.[37]

Market Segmentation   Although customers have much more information than they ever had, merchants have much greater ability to use information to set prices that maximize their profits. An important way to do this is to divide the market into different customer groups, each of which is willing to pay different amounts for different types or levels of service. Airline yield management systems are the heavyweight champions of market segmentation. Unlike products that retain their value from day to day, a seat on a specific flight has value until flight time and no value thereafter. **Yield management** systems try to maximize revenue by selling the same service (a seat on a flight) to different customers at different prices. Because vacation travelers can usually plan their trips longer in advance than business travelers, there is a natural segmentation in the market. Exploiting this segmentation, these systems charge higher prices for tickets purchased at the last minute and try to fill the planes by giving lower prices to vacationers who can reserve weeks in advance but wouldn't fly at higher prices. The economic challenge for these systems is to avoid two types of errors: selling too many cheap seats that last-minute travelers would have purchased at high prices and having too few cheap seats, resulting in empty seats on flights. These systems also have other challenges, however, such as maintaining customer satisfaction when people sitting next to each other on a flight have paid vastly different amounts for what they see as the same thing.

Dynamic Pricing   A merchant's prices for most retail products such as packaged goods typically remain relatively stable over the course of days or weeks. In contrast, stock prices change minute-to-minute just as the bid price for an item at an auction may change. The way that Web pages are assembled electronically makes it possible for e-commerce applications to change prices continually based on demand or other situational variables. Thus far this has worked for market-oriented pricing, as happens in stock markets or energy spot markets, but has not been successful for consumer goods. For example, Amazon.com had a rocky experience with dynamic pricing when it did an experiment to see how the pricing of DVDs would affect their sales. The experiment included 68 DVD titles and ran for five days, with the discounts from 20% to 40% offered to different customers. Many shoppers complained that they paid more than other shoppers for the same item. In response to the complaints, Amazon refunded an average of $3.10 to 6,896 customers who had bought DVDs at higher prices than those paid by other shoppers during the same period.[38]

Auctions and Marketplaces   Auctions and marketplaces present another side of pricing in e-commerce, because in these environments the merchant or seller can only set a minimum price and must allow an interaction among bidders to determine the actual selling price. Pricing models[39] that are increasingly practical through the Internet include:

Marketplace with optional minimum or maximum prices: As in online stock sales or purchases, the seller or buyer can request a transaction at the current market value. The seller can also set a minimum price and the buyer can set a maximum price for the sale. Ideally the broker representing the buyer or seller in the transaction will try to buy below the buyer's maximum price or sell above the seller's minimum.

Auction: The seller accepts bids for an item during a particular time span. When the time is over the highest bidder purchases the item for the bid amount plus any commission to the auction firm.

Reverse auction: The seller sets a very high price for the item and reduces the price periodically until the first bidder submits a bid and thereby agrees to purchase the item at that price.

Barter: This is a negotiated, nonmonetary exchange of goods and services between two individuals.

The question for the e-commerce merchant is whether any of these auction or market-based methods would provide benefits when compared to the type of seller-determined pricing that is common in retail stores. A fascinating aspect of e-commerce is that it has brought many new ways to use pricing models that have existed for centuries.

Attracting Customers

E-commerce has expanded upon traditional ways to attract customers and has provided new ways to promote products and services. Web sites provide company and product information that would otherwise be difficult to obtain. E-mail provides an ability to contact individual customers. Search engines and informational sites can help customers to learn about the existence of products and merchants they might have never found. The Internet also provides many ways to support a traditional sales force through convenient availability of product information and comparisons with competitive products.

The simplest method for attracting customers involves links from other Web sites. Advertising on those sites can sometimes achieve the same goals as direct marketing because Web site usage often mirrors personal interests and concerns. For example, individuals who happen to use a Web page related to a special interest such as auto loans, tropical fish, or Star Trek would probably be interested in sites selling related products and services. **Banner ads**, Web advertisements containing a link to another site, are often used for this type of marketing (see Figure 6.13). For example, an automobile information site might have banner ads leading to other sites that offer financing or insurance. With banner ads, the advertiser pays to place the ad and therefore takes all of the risk. "Cost per link" is an intermediate approach in which a Web site includes links to other sites and is paid a small commission each time someone clicks

Use of banner ads

FIGURE 6.13

Gateway has placed a banner ad on the Britannica.com Web site in the hope that some encyclopedia users would be interested in buying a Gateway personal computer.

on the link, regardless of whether something is purchased at the other site. In another approach for attracting customers, Amazon.com pioneered **affiliate programs** in which a Web site's owners benefit from sales resulting from links to other sites where products can be purchased. For an item bought through Amazon.com the reward for the initiating site is a commission of up to 15% of the list price.[40]

Another way to entice customers to visit an e-commerce site is to be sure it is registered with search engines so that a search engine used by a potential customer will be able to find it. A number of Web sites provide a service of registering other Web sites with the major search engines and Web directories. Merely being registered does not guarantee that a search engine will notice a particular site or will give it an appropriate priority when attempting to answer a query for which millions of sites might be pertinent. Consequently, Web site developers need to pay attention to the different ways major search engines perform their searches and calculate priorities. Some focus more on the title of the homepage. Some pay more attention to "keyword" and "description" meta tags included in the HTML defining the home page. (Meta tags help search engines find the page but do not affect the Web page's appearance.) Others use the content of the home page. Many Web merchants never dreamt they would have to be involved in this type of topic, yet it is one of many factors that may affect e-commerce success.

Providing an Effective Self-Service Environment

A major innovation in e-commerce is the shift toward self-service in determining requirements, performing acquisition transactions, and obtaining information about how to use and maintain the product. Providing an effective self-service environment poses two distinct challenges. On the one hand, self-service is effective only if the product characteristics permit self-service and if the Web site and other electronic links are genuinely easy to use. On the other hand, self-service raises potential threats to firms that serve as intermediaries because self-service may displace them from their position in the value chain.

The Message from Abandoned Shopping Carts   The challenge of maintaining an effective self-service experience is crucial because self-service fails if it is just too much trouble for the customer. An indicator of the limits of self-service is that shoppers abandon their online shopping carts at a rate between 25% (Andersen Consulting) and 78% (Bizrate.com). Although eliminating the trip to the mall, online shopping is sometimes so full of annoying surprises and confusing directions that shoppers often just bail out. According to a consultant to start-ups, "For every one thing I buy online, there are probably two times that I don't. There's the shipping costs or too much information is required or there are too many clicks." Another consultant noted that a physical shopping cart goes with you and you can see how much you will spend, whereas this is rarely available online.[41]

Presenting the Company and Product on the Web Site   The shopping cart is just one part of the overall experience of using an e-commerce Web site. Overall, the chance of making a sale is much higher if the Web site quickly and accurately explains what products are being offered, why the customer should want these products, how to buy them, and why it is plausible that the company will stand behind them.

Many observers have identified desirable characteristics of e-commerce sites. Since e-commerce products range from fashion apparel for teenagers through electronic components selected by purchasing agents, characteristics that are important for some types of sites are not as significant for other sites, and some recommendations are in conflict. Here are some typical suggestions combined from a number of sources:

1. *Keep it simple*: Unnecessary complexity is a turn-off. Keep individual pages short. Avoid animation unrelated to content.
2. *Be consistent*: An e-commerce site is like a brand and should have a consistent appearance and tone. Also, use Web standards, such as a blue color for links a user has not yet used and red or purple for links a user has already used.

3. *Provide clear, but unobtrusive navigation:* It should be easy for users to find what they want, but their attention should go to the content, not the navigation tools. Provide effective internal search capabilities that are genuinely useful.

4. *Organize around the customer:* Make sure it is easy and obvious how each major group of customers should use the site.

5. *Make the shopping experience effective:* Many sites have confusing methods for dealing with shopping carts, price calculations, and details of the purchase transaction.

6. *Minimize unnecessary inputs from the user:* Don't ask the user to register before demonstrating the benefits of registering.

7. *Avoid excessive download times:* Users with 56K modems are likely to leave the site if they have to wait too long for downloads of images.

8. *Make the site visually appealing:* Use colors and graphical design in a way that encourages users to stay.

9. *Design for common screen sizes:* Even though the designer may have a 21-inch monitor, most users do not.

10. *Keep the site updated:* Links to obsolete or nonexistent sites are annoying and indicate a lack of interest by the merchant.

Personalizing the Web Experience   A different way to look at these and other suggestions is to think about the use of an e-commerce Web site as a work system in which the customer is the main participant. This customer/participant's evaluation of the overall experience would be more favorable if each of the suggestions were followed. The evaluation would also be more favorable if the site appeared to remember previous visits by this user and adjusted each Web page to make it unnecessary to re-enter pertinent data. Ideally, each Web page the customer sees should be personalized based on the history of what the customer has done in the past.

The fact that the Web site's server compiles each Web page on the fly makes it easier to provide this type of personalization. The server starts from a template for each page, a set of options for the page, and a history of the customer's past usage of the site. For this to work the server must know the identity of the user, or at least the identity of the computer. Box 6.1 explains how "cookies" afford a modicum of customization in Web interactions. A highly controversial by-product of this form of customization is the possibility of using cookies to collect data about Web use by individuals.

Threats to Intermediaries   Although self-service creates a series of challenges for any e-commerce merchant, it creates a more fundamental challenge for intermediaries such as travel agents, insurance brokers, loan brokers, stockbrokers, and brokers of food and mechanical parts. The threat to these intermediaries is that their customers will bypass them by obtaining information and meeting their purchasing needs through new, online channels. Consider the way readily available information about airplane flight schedules and prices threaten travel agents and other intermediaries who make a living by accessing and filtering information for customers. An increasing number of travelers see little advantage in working through a travel agency if its services involve little more than providing the same information and purchase options that online travel services provide. As with other e-commerce examples, a traveler's choice between a traditional travel agency and an electronic one depends on whether World Wide Web access is readily available, whether it would be quicker to use the human travel agent, and whether the price or seat availability might be better with either choice. Some travel agencies are still thriving, however, because their business approach is to provide special services that are more convenient and more valuable than what one can find on the Web.

In addition to threats, e-commerce also poses opportunities for intermediaries, some of whom use e-commerce to create new channels, thereby providing better service than a customer could otherwise obtain. The Charles Schwab case at the beginning of Chapter 3 shows how one intermediary, a discount stock brokerage, evolved and benefited from the ability to provide data to customers and perform transactions.

LOOK AHEAD

The DoubleClick case at the beginning of Chapter 7 describes how the use of cookies has raised controversies related to privacy.

BOX 6.1   HOW "COOKIES" MAKE WEB SITES MORE EFFECTIVE

Assume that an e-commerce Web site is being designed so that a user doesn't have to start from scratch and repeat the same name and address and preference information with each new order. Assume that an Internet advertiser wants to rotate the banner ads a Web user sees so that the user doesn't tune out totally after seeing the same ad over and over. Assume that a subscription-based news service wants a user to be able to use its site without the inconvenience of logging in each time with the same username and password. All of these goals can be addressed using cookies.

A **cookie** is a small text file that a Web browser such as Netscape or Internet Explorer stores in a folder on a Web user's PC. The information in a cookie consists of name-value pairs. For example, a cookie deposited by a Web site might contain a user ID and a string of characters such as B34AYX2V7H. A cookie with more extensive information might contain additional name-value pairs that identify user preferences, the time of the most recent session, and other information. Since a cookie is a text file rather than an executable file it cannot contain a virus. You can probably see the cookies on your PC by looking at the folder C:\WINDOWS\Cookies. The name of each cookie identifies the Web site or server that it came from. Web browsers allow a Web site to deposit a cookie and modify it, but do not allow one Web site to access cookies deposited by other Web sites.

Cookies make it possible apply a user's history with the Web site to tailor the site's appearance and the options offered to the user. Either the history information is stored in the cookie itself or the user ID in the cookie makes it possible for the server to find the history information within the server's database. The reason for using cookies in this way is that the Internet's HTTP protocol controls the current session but contains no memory of any other session.[42, 43, 44]

Cookies are controversial because they create the possibility of tracking Web usage in ways that may compromise individual privacy. The DoubleClick case at the beginning of Chapter 7 deals with this question. Web browsers contain options about whether or not to accept cookies, but the choice of not accepting them makes the use of many Web sites less convenient.

Providing Excellent Customer Service

The main principles of good customer service include knowing who the customer is and being aware of the customer's status and past interactions with the firm. Good customer service also requires being able to handle customer requests, questions, and complaints quickly and efficiently. A classic example of an IT-based innovation in this area involves USAA, a major insurance company based in San Antonio, Texas. It once stored most of its customer contact information on paper in a warehouse, which meant that finding a particular document, such as a letter from a customer, often took a day or more. However, in the 1980s USAA began working with IBM on what was then an innovative IT application that eliminated the paper altogether. Using this system, all incoming mail containing more than a check is scanned and stored electronically. Upon receiving a phone call and entering a customer's account number at a terminal, any customer service agent can have immediate access to all the recent transactions and correspondence with the customer. This allowed USAA to complete over 90% of all requests and transactions at the first point of contact with customers, without talking to multiple agents or waiting until the files can be located.[45] More recently, companies with technically complex products have improved customer service by making more of their product information available on the Web to help customers find what they need.

Is Customer Service Getting Worse?   Given this example and others like it, it is ironic that use of technology is sometimes blamed for bad customer service. Customer service satisfaction has dropped overall since 1994 according to the American Consumer Satisfaction Index compiled at the University of Michigan. "American consumers are unhappier with the service they are receiving in nearly every sector of the economy measured by the index, including the computer industry, hotels, airlines, telephone companies and automobile manufacturers. There are many causes, but one that is widely recognized is technology itself. Phone systems and Web sites that are supposed to help can turn into infuriating mazes."[46]

Internal cost is a major issue with customer service. For example, Fidelity Investments receives over 700,000 calls daily. Over three quarters of these calls go to automated systems and cost less than a dollar each, including system development. In contrast, calls answered by human operators cost $13 each. Fidelity even identified 25,000 customers who make an excessive number of calls and asked them to use the Web or automated services.[47]

Due to cost considerations many companies have made a conscious decision not to provide excellent service for their less profitable customers. This is the theme of the cover article in the October 23, 2000 *Business Week*. Its title was, "Why Service Stinks: Companies know just how good a customer you are—and unless you're a high roller they would rather lose you than take the time to fix your problem." The article started by describing how a customer service representative at an electric utility could not get anyone at First Union to listen to his complaints when he found mysterious charges on his monthly account statement. Although frustrated, he knew what was going on because where he works the top 350 business customers are served by six people, the next 700 are served by six people, the next 30,000 have him and one other rep, and 300,000 residential customers have an 800 number.[48]

Rationing Customer Service Resources   Armed with better information about the profitability of each group of customers, many companies are rationing their service resources consistent with profitability. For example, Sears offers big spenders on its credit card a preferred two-hour time slot for deliveries compared to four hours for everyone else. When United Airlines cancels a flight, it rebooks frequent fliers, first class, full-fare, economy class, and discount ticket holders in that order. According to a United spokesman, "We're going to reward the people who are most loyal to us, and also recognize customers who pay more."[49]

The e-commerce challenge related to customer service is therefore a combination of providing service that satisfies customers and doing it in a cost-effective way. Using technology such as automated phone response systems and Web sites can help in many cases, but it if the systems are too cumbersome to use they leave a distinct impression that the firm is trying to get the customer off its back instead of solving the problem.

A number of approaches have been used to provide some amount of direct human attention while retaining the cost and convenience advantages of using the Web. As mentioned earlier, Dell Computer makes it convenient to fill out an order on the Web and then discuss it with a sales representative who therefore does not have to start from scratch. Several variations on e-mail have been used for communicating directly with existing customers. Some firms are adding new capabilities that give more choices such as "text chat" in which a customer service representative communicates with the customer in what appears to be a one-to-one chat room environment. One of the benefits of this method is that a service rep can handle three to five chat sessions at a time, as compared to only one phone call. Some of the dangers are overloaded agents or technology glitches that can make the experience slow and cumbersome for the customer.[50]

Achieving Profitability and Sustainable Differentiation

After several years of rapid growth, extensive venture capital investments, and inflated stock prices, e-commerce firms and many other technology firms suffered a painful fall in 2000. Suddenly sentiment changed. E-commerce companies that had been scrambling to establish first-mover advantage by attracting early e-commerce customers with money-losing offers and extensive advertising suddenly found themselves under severe pressure to show a profit. Some unprofitable companies could not find further financing and had to shut down. Some resorted to layoffs and other draconian measures to stay alive. Others merged or were acquired.

Over the last several years comparatively few e-commerce firms demonstrated that they had "captured" customers who would return again and again to maintain the kind of

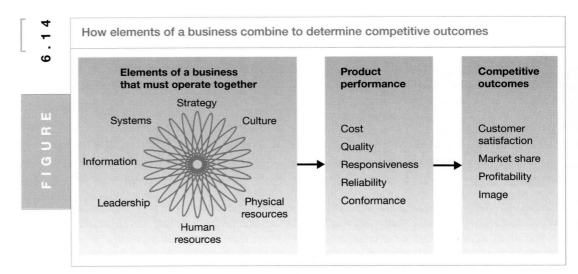

How elements of a business combine to determine competitive outcomes

Information, systems, and many other elements combine to generate the controllable product performance results that are the basis of competition.

revenue stream needed for profitability. Among those who succeeded in this regard were companies mentioned in the opening cases of the first four chapters, Dell Computer, Amazon, Charles Schwab, and eBay. (Amazon was not profitable, but it did have high revenues and a loyal customer base.) Another firm that succeeded in this regard was America Online (AOL), which raised prices after recognizing that the convenience of not changing personal e-mail addresses would outweigh the annoyance of paying several more dollars a month. Companies providing Internet infrastructure, programming tools, and other services with high switching costs were among the Internet firms that showed the highest likelihood of sustainable success, even though stock prices for these firms also dropped after March 2000, especially if they faced new competition.

Not a Magic Bullet   The widespread acceptance of the Internet and e-commerce clearly indicates that e-commerce has already become an important part of commerce. Some firms have early leads, but it is not obvious whether these leads are sustainable. As current firms compete for leadership and "old economy" firms set up new distribution channels, it is increasingly apparent that e-business and e-commerce are not magic bullets, but rather, increasingly commonplace methods that are being incorporated into the operations of most companies.

Figure 6.14 represents a business as an engine that contains a number of connected elements: strategy, leadership, culture, people, physical resources, systems, and information. Although it might seem obvious that these elements should be aligned, top managers often reflect on how difficult it is and how many years it takes to attain the degree of alignment that maintains competitive performance in terms of cost, quality, responsiveness, reliability, and conformance with regulations and standards. This book emphasizes the part of Figure 6.14 involving information and systems, but it always recognizes that information systems are one of many components of business success.

R E A L I T Y C H E C K   ✓

Challenges as Commerce Becomes E-Commerce

This section identified a number of important challenges faced by e-commerce merchants.

1. Identify three examples of electronic commerce in which you have participated.

2. In each example, explain what you see as some of the major challenges the merchants faced and identify any areas where they seemed to need improvement.

CHAPTER CONCLUSION

SUMMARY

What three dimensions can be used to describe and look for improvements in the products and services produced by a work system?

A work system's product is a combination of information, physical things, and service the customer receives. The three dimensions are product versus service, information versus physical things, and commodity versus customized.

What are the unique characteristics of information products and service products?

Information is intangible, copyable, nonconsumable, transportable, and manipulable. These characteristics have major ramifications in many areas such as publishing, which has taken on a new meaning in the world of electronic documents. Services are typically produced and consumed simultaneously, with the customer receiving value from actions rather than from possessing and using information or physical things. Service through supplier-customer encounters occurs through interactions between customers and providers who are strangers. Service through a supplier-customer relationship occurs when a customer has repetitive contact with a particular provider and when the customer and provider get to know each other personally.

What are the stages in an idealized customer experience related to a product or service?

The customer experience is a customer's entire involvement with the product: defining the requirements and acquiring the product, using the product, maintaining it, and retiring it. Each step in the cycle provides opportunities to increase customer satisfaction in terms of performance variables such as cost, quality, responsiveness, reliability, and conformance to standards and regulations.

How are information systems related to competitive advantage?

Competitive advantage occurs when a product's value chain generates superior product performance. Most firms have information systems that are mission-critical because their failure would prevent or delay basic business activities such as selling to customers, processing orders, and manufacturing. In contrast, strategic information systems are designed to play a major role in an organization's competitive strategy. These systems typically increase the customer's perceived value by providing information and services with products, customizing products, eliminating delays, improving reliability, making products easier to use, bypassing intermediaries, or reducing transaction times.

Why is it difficult to achieve sustainable competitive advantage through information systems?

Even if a strategic information system is initially successful, there is usually no reason why competitors cannot copy the idea. This is why information systems that temporarily provide competitive advantage often become a competitive necessity for all major players. The most sustainable sources of competitive advantage are the firm's culture, its personnel, its major business processes, and its special resources such as patents or land that cannot be copied.

What are some of the challenges of electronic commerce?

E-commerce is using the Internet and other communication technology for marketing, selling, and servicing products and services. Challenges of e-commerce include establishing and integrating systems, setting prices, attracting customers, providing an effective self-service environment, providing excellent customer service, and achieving profitability and sustainable differentiation.

KEY TERMS

information product
physical product
service product
digital rights management (DRM)
free version of a product
supplier-customer encounter
supplier-customer relationship
smart product
interactive product
programmable product
customer experience
digital purse
remote monitoring

cost
total cost of ownership (TCO)
quality
responsiveness
reliability
conformance to standards and
    regulations
standards
regulations
competitive advantage
cost leadership strategy
product differentiation strategy
focus strategy

mission-critical information
    system
strategic information system
competitive necessity
sustainable competitive advantage
e-commerce
clicks and bricks
shopbot
yield management
banner ad
affiliate programs
cookie

REVIEW QUESTIONS

1. What does the story of Encyclopedia Britannica reveal about the nature of products?

2. What are some of the special characteristics of information products and why are these characteristics important?

3. What is digital rights management?

4. Explain the logic of the free version of an information product.

5. Why is the distinction between personal, impersonal, and automated services important?

6. Compare different approaches to customization and adaptability.

7. How is the customer experience for products different from the customer experience for services?

8. What performance variables other than cost are customers often concerned with?

9. What are Porter's three basic competitive strategies?

10. Differentiate between a mission-critical information system and a strategic information system.

11. Explain the relationship between competitive advantage and competitive necessity.

12. How is the idea of clicks and bricks related to e-commerce?

13. In what ways is price determination more difficult with today's e-commerce than it might have been in the past?

14. What are shopbots?

15. What are some of the different pricing models that are practical to use through the Internet?

16. What is an affiliate program in e-commerce?

17. What are typical guidelines for good Web sites?

18. How do cookies work?

19. Why might a company decide to provide better customer service for some customers than for others?

DISCUSSION QUESTIONS

1. Auctiva introduced a free service that allows sellers who use multiple auction sites to consolidate their listings onto Auctiva's Web site. This enables buyers to view items simultaneously on several auction sites. The largest auction site, eBay, maintains that copying listings from eBay without permission constituted "trespass" and "misappropriation" of eBay property. In the past it sued others that copied its listings, and now it terminated auctions of merchants who linked their eBay auctions to Auctiva.[51] How is this related to the characteristics of information products? How does it represent a challenge to e-commerce?

2. One response to the privacy concerns raised by database marketing is the proposal that individuals should own all data about themselves and should be able to sell that data to others. This leads to the idea of a "consensual database," in which a consumer might receive coupons, samples, or even money in exchange for yielding the rights to a personal transaction history. Identify some of the practical and ethical issues related to consensual databases and explain whether you believe that this form of marketing database could become widespread.

3. In France it is illegal to sell goods that evoke violent actions or racist sentiments. In May 2000 a French judge ordered Yahoo! to block all French access to over 1,000 items of Nazi paraphernalia on its auction site. Yahoo! appealed, saying that it cannot identify French Internet users. A law professor said it was appropriate for France to assert jurisdiction because French law was being broken.[52] Explain how this situation represents a challenge to e-commerce. What parallel situations might occur in which Internet sales in other countries would break U.S. law?

4. Use the customer's parts of the value chain to identify a number of ways an automobile manufacturer's information systems could provide extra value for its customers.

5. In 1999, the pharmaceutical industry spending on product promotion was $13.7 billion, 87% of which was aimed at health professionals who could prescribe drugs. By keeping detailed histories of prescriptions filled at pharmacies, companies in the industry can develop "prescriber profiles" that reveal prescription patterns for specific doctors. One doctor said he was invited to an expensive dinner and offered a $250 "honorarium" to provide feedback about a particular drug. He declined and complained that drug companies keep asking him "How can we change your prescribing, what would it take, do you want to serve as a consultant?" Explain whether you believe this use of prescription information is ethical. If so, explain why. If not, explain the appropriate limits of using this type of information.[53]

C A S E   Ernst & Young: Providing Consulting through the Web

In May 1998 Ernst & Young announced that its online consulting service called Ernie had been nominated for a Computerworld Smithsonian Award. Each year, this award program honors visionary uses of information technology that produce positive social, economic, and educational change. Ernie was started in 1996 as an Internet-based consulting service for medium-sized companies that can benefit from the knowledge of consultants but cannot afford the high prices experienced consultants charge for extended engagements. Companies that used this service paid $6,000 per year for access to information on the Ernie Web site plus the ability to direct questions to E&Y consultants via e-mail.

Ernie provided client benefits by using information technology instead of much more expensive face-to-face meetings. After logging on using a company's password, the person needing help accessed an extensive collection of Frequently Asked Questions (FAQs) in many areas. If the FAQs didn't provide the answer, the user could direct the question to human experts by filling in a computerized form. In addition to the user's question itself, the form requested the general topic area (such as organizational change), general background information about the user's firm, and the selection of one of eight categories the Web site offered (accounting, corporate finance, human resources, information technology, personal finance, process improvement, tax, and other). The forms were routed to appropriate Ernst & Young consultants using its corporate intranet and a one- to two-page response came back via e-mail within two days. Users could ask as many follow-up questions as they want.

The information directly accessible through www.ernie.ey.com could be used without the direct involvement of consultants. In addition to FAQs, in mid-1998 it included five "Ernie SuperTools." Ernie Diagnostix for supply chain provided a way to compare a firm's supply chain with those of top-performing companies in an E&Y database. Ernie Software Selection Advisor provided an eight-step approach for selecting the right enterprise-wide software package. A technology selection tool provided a way of determining technology needs and taking advantage of E&Y's buying power. Ernie Business Analysis provided a way to commission an in-depth report to analyze competitors, markets, and industry trends. A link to the Gartner Group's self-paced courses provided a way for end users, managers, and programmers to learn recent software applications. A 1998 extension called Ernie MediaWatch also linked Ernie to seven prominent trade magazines, including *HRfocus*, *Management Review*, *Real Estate Forum*, and *Management Accounting*. Linking to these magazines provides additional expertise and perspective that otherwise might not be as readily accessible.[54]

Responding to predictions that Ernie would cannibalize E&Y's traditional consulting business, in 1998 the firm's director of Internet service delivery said the firm had not viewed this as an important issue. "Bringing a team of consultants onsite remains the best way to implement large computer systems or to bring large-scale change to an organization. . . . The pace of change is so fast today

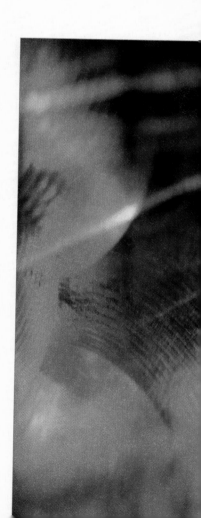

that there is a need for immediate support to help navigate the waters of change. That need hasn't always been there. Organizations used to have time to adapt to change. Now they don't. They need help today, and traditional consulting can't offer that kind of help. So Ernie is serving an entirely new market—the market for decision support."[55]

Several years later, in early 2000, the international consulting company Cap Gemini acquired Ernst & Young's consulting unit and www.ernie.ey.com was no longer visible on the Web. Ernst & Young brought out a new online service called Ernst & Young Online Tax Advisor. The Tax Advisor provided specific, actionable advice related to specific client questions and charged by the question. A dedicated group of subject matter experts answered the questions. The maximum fee per inquiry was $2,500, with the average around $1,200. The client could get a feeling for the fee for an inquiry by looking at a list of previous inquiries and the fees charged. By 2000, Tax Advisor had handled over 15,000 questions.[56]

QUESTIONS

1. What are the advantages and disadvantages of the direct service business model upon which Ernie and Tax Advisor are built?

2. The previous chapter discussed knowledge management systems and decision support systems. How are these ideas related to Ernie and Tax Advisor?

3. Explain why online services such as these are or are not a competitive threat to traditional consultants.

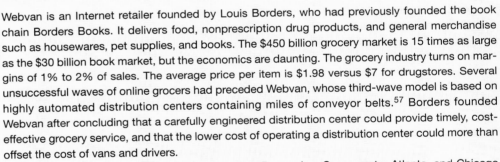

C A S E   Webvan: Can an Internet Grocer Make a Profit?

Webvan is an Internet retailer founded by Louis Borders, who had previously founded the book chain Borders Books. It delivers food, nonprescription drug products, and general merchandise such as housewares, pet supplies, and books. The $450 billion grocery market is 15 times as large as the $30 billion book market, but the economics are daunting. The grocery industry turns on margins of 1% to 2% of sales. The average price per item is $1.98 versus $7 for drugstores. Several unsuccessful waves of online grocers had preceded Webvan, whose third-wave model is based on highly automated distribution centers containing miles of conveyor belts.[57] Borders founded Webvan after concluding that a carefully engineered distribution center could provide timely, cost-effective grocery service, and that the lower cost of operating a distribution center could more than offset the cost of vans and drivers.

Webvan's first operations in the San Francisco Bay region, Sacramento, Atlanta, and Chicago allow customers to order the same popular grocery products that they can order from a Safeway or other large grocery store. (During 2000, Webvan merged with Homegrocer.com and added sites in other cities.) Webvan charges approximately the same prices as typical grocery stores and provides approximately the same quality. Webvan customers submit orders using its "Webstore." When the order is received, Webvan's order fulfillment process occurs in a large, highly automated distribution center designed to package the items in a specially designed tote, move the order to a refrigerated Webvan delivery truck, and complete delivery within a time window committed to the customer at the time of the order. This approach automatically tracks every item purchased and therefore creates much more accurate customer profile data than is available through customer loyalty cards and other methods used by typical groceries.

The Webstore is divided into 11 intuitively organized categories and allows the customer to find items quickly and efficiently by drilling down from general to more specific categories, such as moving from produce to fruits to bananas. To add to shopping convenience Webvan encourages customers to keep an online list of nonperishable items they purchase regularly. Customers can add items to a shopping cart or save them in a shopping list. The shopping cart is always visible and instantly updates and calculates the order total while the customer shops. Customers schedule their delivery by selecting a time from a grid of 30-minute alternatives on the same day or within the next several days. Deliveries from the Oakland facility occur from 7:00 A.M. to 10:00 P.M. every day of the week. Customers must be at home to accept delivery of perishable or frozen items or regulated products such as alcohol and tobacco.[58]

Through Q3 of 2000 Webvan had not yet become profitable even in its initial San Francisco facility. Following its merger with Homegrocer.com its revenues for Q3 were $87 million but its loss was $120 million. The company delivered an average of 2,350 orders each day, with an average order size of $105. To achieve break-even, it would need 3,300 to 3,500 orders per day. To achieve that goal, the company's best customers would have to shop on average 3.8 times each quarter, up from the current average of three times a quarter. Webvan planned to improve its Web site and offer preferred deliveries, coupons, and online promotions to its best customers in an effort to achieve that goal.[59]

Webvan had an innovative business model, but on November 20, 2000, the Monday before Thanksgiving, it had some of the same inventory problems that other grocers have. It ran out of pumpkin-pie filling, some gravy products, and turkey stuffing. When customers tried to order those goods, a message popped up saying they were out of stock. The torrent of shoppers also caused some longer-than-normal delays in turning pages on the site. According to Internet research firm PC Data, Webvan's total traffic on the previous Saturday more than doubled from the week before. The number of shoppers jumped from 144,000 unique users to 294,000.[60] After Webvan went public in late 1999 share prices went as high as $34, but by mid-February 2001 the price had fallen below $0.34 per share, a 99% drop from the peak.

QUESTIONS

1. From a customer's viewpoint, what are the advantages and disadvantages of using Webvan instead of a typical grocery store?

2. From Webvan's viewpoint, what seem to be its advantages and disadvantages compared to a typical grocery store?

3. Which aspects of Webvan's business (its inventory management, Web site, delivery fleet, pricing, etc.) do you believe will be its most important differentiator compared to online and traditional competition?

4. Assume that Webvan becomes very successful or becomes very unsuccessful. Identify other areas where e-commerce might be applied widely and explain what Webvan's success or lack of success would say about their possibilities.

Human and Ethical Issues

chapter7

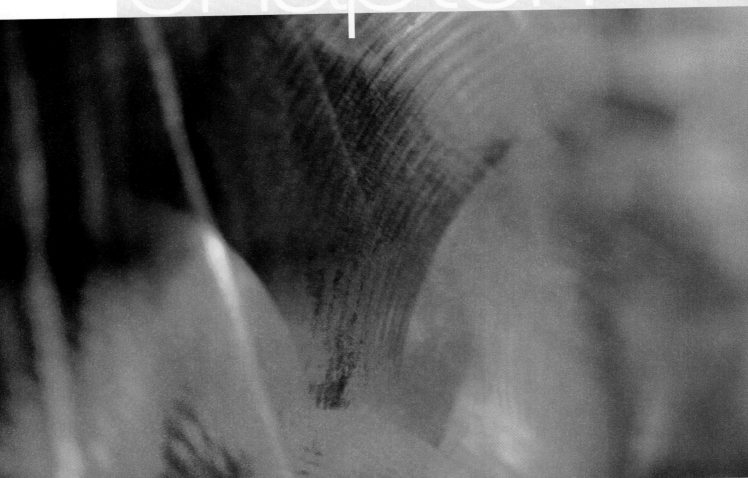

STUDY QUESTIONS

- What kinds of dilemmas result from impacts of information systems on people?
- What is the difference between machine-centered design and human-centered design?
- What are the characteristics of healthy work, and how do information systems affect these characteristics?
- How is computer-mediated work different from other types of work?
- What are the different ways to explain resistance to change?
- What are ethical theories, and how are they related to information systems?
- What are the major ethical issues related to information systems?

OUTLINE

Technology and People
    Human-Centered Design versus Machine-
      Centered Design
    User Friendliness
    Technology as a Metaphor and Influence

**Positive and Negative Impacts on People
at Work**
    Health and Safety
    Autonomy and Power
    Use of Valued Skills
    Meaningfulness of Work
    Social Relationships

**Dependence on People for Information
System Success**
    Skills and Knowledge
    Involvement and Commitment
    Resistance to Change
    Unanticipated Innovations

Systems and Ethics
    Ethical versus Legal Issues
    Ethical Theories
    Privacy
    Accuracy
    Property
    Access

Balancing Positive and Negative Impacts

Chapter Conclusion
    Summary
    Key Terms
    Review Questions
    Discussion Questions
    Cases

Human and Ethical Issues

OPENING CASE

DOUBLECLICK: COLLECTING DATA ABOUT WEB USAGE

DoubleClick is an Internet advertising agency that encountered a firestorm of complaints after its June 1999 acquisition of Abacus Direct, a repository of names, addresses, and buying habits collected from almost 1,800 merchants and about 90 million households.

DoubleClick's business is based on capabilities related to banner advertisements a Web user often sees at the top and on the sides of Web pages. DoubleClick controls the banner advertisements in the following manner across its network that links to 1,500 sites. If BMW wanted to place a banner ad on a luxury car Web site, that Web site would provide a link that allows DoubleClick to display the BMW ad whenever a particular Web page is viewed. If the user clicks on the ad, DoubleClick sends the user to the appropriate BMW Web page and also deposits or updates a DoubleClick cookie on the user's computer. (Box 6.1 explained how cookies work and why they are used.) If a DoubleClick cookie already existed on the user's computer, DoubleClick would therefore know at least one other site that the user

had visited. Since DoubleClick places banner ads for over 1,000 Web merchants, it can use its database to generate anonymous profiles that show correlations between visiting one site and visiting other sites. DoubleClick aggregates these profiles in a variety of ways to help specific companies understand their customers and markets.

These anonymous profiles generally were not considered a major threat to individual privacy because the basic identifier in the cookies linked to each profile refers to the computer rather than the individual user. DoubleClick's purchase of Abacus was considered a much greater threat to privacy because Abacus had a large database that included names and addresses taken from magazine subscriptions and other sales activities. This database would give DoubleClick a way to link many of its profiles to information about specific individuals. Now it could have a single database containing a person's name, address, details of all of the gardening supplies or sweaters they've bought from catalogs, and a log of every Web site they've visited that's part of DoubleClick's network. This would have great commercial value, at least in theory, because the personal information plus the Web usage information could be used to direct highly targeted promotions and advertisements at people whose past purchases and Web activity revealed interests in particular types of products. Privacy advocates complained and the U.S. Federal Trade Commission began a probe into the matter. DoubleClick retreated and said it would not link its Web data with profiles that identified individuals. On March 2, 2000 DoubleClick's CEO Kevin O'Connor said, "I made a big mistake. It was wrong to try to match that information in the absence of government or industry standards, so until there's agreement on it, we will not." O'Connor also said, "It became very clear that the overwhelming point of contention was under what circumstances could a name be associated with anonymous Web activity. Now we're just happy to get this behind us and move on."[1, 2]

The spring and summer of 2000 did not treat DoubleClick kindly. The privacy backlash meant that it could not make the most of the Abacus database of consumer shopping information. Its quarterly report for Q3 of 2000 also disclosed delays and business slowdowns in Abacus Direct's core business. By late October DoubleClick's stock price had plummeted to $12 from a 52-week high of $135.[3]

WEB CHECK [✓]

Look at DoubleClick's Web site and see how it explains what it does, and why it does or does not infringe on privacy.

DEBATE TOPIC

Current Web site privacy is typically based on an opt-out model whose default mode is that the user will allow personal data to be collected and used. Should the default model be changed to an opt-in model in which there will be no transmission of personal data to other organizations unless the individual agrees explicitly to that use?

The introduction of new technologies often has both positive and negative impacts far beyond the immediate problem they were supposed to solve. Technological change is not neutral because it can be used for good or bad ends, because the positive and negative impacts are often intertwined, and because many of the impacts are not anticipated.[4] The story of DoubleClick illustrates these ideas. Any merchant would like to know about its customers' buying habits and media habits, yet a database that combined information from DoubleClick's Web advertising network and Abacus Direct's consumer database would create a threat to personal privacy.

As information systems become more pervasive in today's businesses, managers need to think about the way systems depend on people and the way they affect people. Dependence on people starts with the system development process and extends to reliance on the knowledge and skills needed to use an information system effectively. Impacts on people occur in many areas. In some cases, systems affect them because they are participants; in others, because they are customers; in yet others, because they are being monitored. This chapter explores these issues and emphasizes the management dilemmas posed by today's technical capabilities. A theme throughout is that the social and psychological impacts on people are not caused by technology itself, but rather, by the way technology is used.

TECHNOLOGY AND PEOPLE

IT-enabled systems are much more than IT applied to a business process. This is why the pictorial version of the work system framework (refer back to Figure 2.2) contains a link between participants and the business process. Using a two-headed arrow for this link also says that the business process affects the participants and that their abilities, interests, and skills determine whether the business process is practical.

W O R K   S Y S T E M   S N A P S H O T
Using DoubleClick to Track Customers

CUSTOMERS
- Web merchants trying to
  understand their customers

PRODUCTS & SERVICES
- Click-throughs that bring customers from
  the banner ad to the Web merchant's site
- Data about Web usage patterns

BUSINESS PROCESS
Major steps related to setting up the DoubleClick service:
- Create a business arrangement governing the way
  the banner ads will be displayed
- Create the appropriate banner ads
- Transmit the banner ads to DoubleClick's servers

Major steps related to understanding customers:
- Obtain data directly from users of the merchant's Web site
- Obtain Web usage pattern data from DoubleClick
- Analyze the data

PARTICIPANTS	INFORMATION	TECHNOLOGY

• Internal analysts
• Web site users
• Marketing analysts
	• Data from users of the
	  merchant's Web site
	• Web usage patterns related
	  to this site and other sites
		• Web user's personal computer
		• DoubleClick's servers
		• Software for data analysis

Human-Centered Design versus Machine-Centered Design

For a work system to operate well, the division of labor between people and machines should take into account the particular strengths and weaknesses of both people and machines. Table 7.1 summarizes these strengths and weaknesses. It shows that people are especially good at tasks involving understanding, imagination, and the ability to see a situation as a whole. Machines are especially good at repetitive tasks involving endurance, consistency, speed, and execution of unambiguous instructions.

The challenge in the division of labor between people and machines is to give each the tasks for which they are best suited and to design business processes that exploit their respective strengths and weaknesses. This is easier said than done. This chapter includes a number of examples of problems that occurred when work systems treated people somewhat like machines.

The contrast between human-centered design and machine-centered design is useful in thinking about the design of technologies and work systems. In **human-centered design**, the technology or business process is designed to make participants' work as effective and satisfying as possible. In **machine-centered design**, the technology or process is designed to simplify what the machine must do, and people are expected to adjust to the machine's weaknesses and limitations. Machine-centered design has been the tradition in many computerized systems, although there has been much progress in the last two decades. An assumption within this tradition is that technology users will read and understand manuals, regardless of how arbitrary and illogical a system may seem. Another assumption is that people will follow procedures, regardless of how confusing or contradictory they are.

When accidents occur, this type of thinking leads to the conclusion that the user is the problem, rather than the technology or the system. Perrow's study of major accidents in power plants, aircraft, and other complex systems found that 60% to 80% of

TABLE 7.1

Human versus Machine Strengths and Weaknesses

Characteristic	People	Machines
Endurance	• Become tired and bored • Need variety • Need to stop to rest and eat	• Never become tired or bored • Don't need variety • Need to stop for servicing
Consistency	• Often somewhat inconsistent even when doing highly structured tasks	• Operate totally consistent with their programmed instructions
Speed	• Comparatively slow in storing, retrieving, and manipulating data	• Enormously fast in storing, retrieving, and manipulating data
Memory	• Often forget things • Time required for remembering is unpredictable • Able to retrieve information based on associations not programmed in advance	• Storage and retrieval times are predictable • In most cases can retrieve data based only on associations programmed in advance
Ability to perform programmed tasks	• Can perform highly structured work, but may find it boring and unsatisfying	• Can only perform totally structured tasks (which may be parts of larger tasks that are not totally structured)
Understanding	• Capable of understanding the meaning of work • Want to understand the meaning of work	• Incapable of understanding the meaning of work • Only capable of following unambiguous instructions
Imagination	• Can invent new ideas and associations • Can draw conclusions from data without using formulas	• Basically unable to invent ideas • In a few limited areas, can draw conclusions by combining specific facts in preprogrammed ways
Ability to see the whole	• Can recognize things as wholes in addition to recognizing details	• Recognize details and combine them into recognizable wholes only through appropriate programming

the accidents were blamed on **operator error,** mistaken or incorrect action by systems participants who operate equipment or use information within systems.[5] For example, the commission investigating the partial meltdown at the Three Mile Island nuclear plant in Pennsylvania concluded that operator error caused the problem. Given the nature of human limitations, poor system design creating a high likelihood of operator error might have been blamed equally.

As an everyday example of machine-centered versus human-centered design, consider the way typical telephone calls are completed.[6] One person dials a number, a telephone rings in another location, and someone picks up the phone. This method is comparatively simple for the machine because it rings the same way regardless of whether the caller is a spouse, an acquaintance, a colleague from work, or someone trying to sell magazine subscriptions. From the user's viewpoint, there might be better ways to announce calls, such as by including with the ring a five-second message identifying the caller and purpose of the call. Perhaps simpler, the system might ring differently for emergencies, family matters, calls by acquaintances, or uninvited sales calls. Although each alternative system has both advantages and disadvantages, the point is that the simplest system for the machine might not be best for the participants, customers, and stakeholders.

User Friendliness

Although often no more than a slogan, genuine user friendliness is an important outcome of human-centered design. Anything a person uses, ranging from everyday objects such as utensils and vacuum cleaners to technically advanced products such as computers and copiers, should be user friendly. User friendliness involves more than just cosmetic issues. Something is **user friendly** if most users can use it easily with minimal start-up time and training, and if it contains features most users find useful.

User-friendly information systems are more productive because users waste less time and effort struggling with system features that get in the way of doing work.

Unfortunately, computers and computerized systems have often been more user hostile than user friendly. A technology is **user hostile** when it is difficult to use or makes users feel inept. Early computers were truly user hostile, because they were non-interactive and could be programmed only in languages appropriate for professional programmers. Advances in computer languages, interactive computing, and graphical interfaces were driven in part by the desire for user friendly computing.

Features and characteristics of computer systems can be designed to make them more user friendly or less user friendly. Genuinely user-friendly computer systems help the user focus on the business problem rather than on the computerized tool being used to help solve the problem. In contrast, user-hostile systems force the user to use codes and procedures that seem arbitrary and absorb effort that should go into doing useful work. Aspects of user friendliness are related to the nature of what the user must learn and remember, the nature of applications, the nature of application programs, and the nature of the user interface.

Nature of What the User Must Learn and Remember   A user-friendly computer system is intuitively simple and interacts with the user in readily understood terms, never forcing the user to learn or pay attention to seemingly arbitrary or irrelevant details. Consequently, the user must understand basic principles but does not have to remember the precise spelling or grammar for commands. Multiple applications have similar organization and appearance and are therefore easier to learn. If the computer system operates this way, the user manual is basically a reference. The users can figure out how the computer system works mostly by playing with and modifying examples.

Nature of the Applications   A user-friendly computer system provides easy ways to access and reuse work done earlier by the user or by others who built templates as starting points for users. Computer system flexibility fits task flexibility, permitting the user to do the task in whatever way the user finds easiest. The computer system is designed to minimize errors by users and to make it easy to fix any user errors that occur.

Nature of the Interface   In a user-friendly computer system, input methods are tailored to the task at hand. Different methods are combined to make the work efficient. The menus are well structured, easy to understand, and consistent with menus in other applications. Ideally, the computer system adjusts to what the user knows. Novices see and use only basic features. Experts are not forced to interact the same way as novices. The user can name files or other objects with whatever names make sense instead of being constrained by seemingly arbitrary technical restrictions such as the now outdated limitation of filenames to eight characters.

Technology as a Metaphor and Influence

Combining the ancient Greek roots for man (anthro) and form (morpho), the word **anthropomorphize** means to ascribe human attributes to an animal or object. One often hears statements such as: the computer *knows* the client's age, the computer *chooses* the best move in a chess game, or the computer *understands* the difference between discount prices and regular prices. Although basically a way to say the computer has stored certain data or performs certain preprogrammed processing, taken literally terms such as *knows* and *understands* are extreme exaggerations of what computers can currently do. (See more on this in Chapter 9.)

"The computer *knows*" may seem a trivial concern, but what about "the computer *made a mistake*"? People who say that seem to experience computers as autonomous entities that can act on their own behalf and are therefore blamable. When things go wrong, these individuals might blame the computer instead of their company's policies or their fellow workers.[7]

Although there may not be a fancy word for it, the reverse of anthropomorphizing is using computer functions and attributes to describe people. Some psychiatrists have observed patients who work with computers all day and end up describing themselves and their relationships using computer terminology. These patients sometimes prefer computers to human company. Computers provide immediate, unambiguous responses and provide a tiny world a user can control. The world of people, with its slow responses, ambiguous messages, and disagreements, is messier, more difficult to control, and in some ways less safe for these patients.

Extensive use of certain computerized systems may even affect the way people perceive the world. Noting that over 30 million American homes had Nintendo, a book about Nintendo[8] cited surveys showing that the Nintendo character Super Mario was more recognized by American children than Mickey Mouse. Childhood entertainment had once been imbued with Mickey's message, "We play fair and we work hard and we're in harmony." Mario's message imparts different values: "Kill or be killed. Time is running out. You are on your own." In 2000 the Federal Trade Commission's report on a yearlong study deplored "the pervasive and aggressive marketing" of violent entertainment to children. Though careful not to blame violent entertainment for the violence in society, the FTC chairman said that exposure to violent materials was "a valid cause for concern." He said, "Exposure does seem to correlate with aggressive attitudes, insensitivity to violence and an exaggerated view of how much violence occurs in the world."[9]

The chapter has opened by identifying some of the relationships between technology and people. It is clear so far that computerized systems have meaning and impact far beyond basic functions such as storing and retrieving information. The next section goes into more depth by looking at positive and negative impacts on people at work.

R E A L I T Y C H E C K [✓]

Technology and People

This section discussed the relationship between technology and people in terms of human-centered versus machine-centered design, user friendliness, and technology as a metaphor and influence.

1. Considering several technologies you use or have seen used, identify several features you see as especially human-centered or user friendly, and compare these to features that are machine-centered or user hostile.

2. Considering computers, cars, or other machines, give examples of anthropomorphizing that you have encountered and explain why you do or do not believe this is a problem.

POSITIVE AND NEGATIVE IMPACTS ON PEOPLE AT WORK

The impacts of information systems on individuals vary widely. For some, new technology has brought professional and personal gains. For others, it has meant obsolescence and frustration. For some, work has become easier or more enjoyable. For others, it has become more difficult and sometimes intolerable. We will explore personal impacts by identifying characteristics of a healthy job and then looking at related impacts of information systems.

IT applications have changed the nature of the workplace. Tasks ranging from taking orders to analyzing business plans are done using computers rather than paper and pencil. Where people once relied on the corporate office or factory as their workplace, much more of the work is being done wherever and whenever it is most convenient. **Telecommuting**, using telecommunications technology as a substitute for travel, is one part of a trend of bringing the work to the workers rather than the workers to the work. In the same general vein, the phrase "any place, any time" increasingly summarizes the customer's expectation that businesses will provide what the customer wants, when and where the customer wants it.

Characteristics of a Healthy Job	
Job characteristic	**Meaning to you as an employee**
Skills	You can use and increase your skills.
Meaningfulness	You understand and respect the importance of your work and understand how it fits into the organization's work.
Autonomy	You can control your work. You are not made to feel childish by the methods of supervision.
Social relations	Your job includes collaboration and communication with others.
Psychological demands	Your job includes a mix of routine demands and new but reasonable demands. You have some control over what demands to accept.
Personal rights	You feel that you have appropriate personal rights at work and have reasonable ways to settle grievances.
Integration with life outside work	The job does not interfere excessively with your ability to participate in family and community life.

TABLE 7.2

Table 7.2 summarizes the characteristics of a healthy job. People in healthy jobs use their skills in meaningful work, enjoy autonomy and social relations with others, have personal rights including some control over the demands of the job, and can have enough time and energy to participate in family and community life.[10] Based on these characteristics, the least healthy types of work are those with continual pressure to perform but little personal control. Examples include assembly-line workers, clerks who process business transactions, and telephone operators. These are jobs with rigid hours and procedures, threats of layoff, little learning of new skills, and difficulty in taking a break or time off for personal needs. Stereotypical high-stress jobs such as manager, electrical engineer, and architect are healthier because professionals have more control over their work.

Health and Safety

Researchers have found relationships between psychological well-being at work and physical health. People with active jobs involving initiative, discretion, and advancement have the lowest heart attack rates, even though these jobs often involve stress. People in high-stress jobs at the bottom of the job ladder have the highest rate of heart attacks. Even when such risk factors as age, race, education, and smoking are considered, those in the bottom 10% of the job ladder are in the top 10% for illness. These workers have four to five times greater risk of heart attack than those at the top 10% of the ladder, whose jobs give them a high sense of control.[11] The same type of pattern applies in the middle of the socioeconomic distribution. A study that followed 7,400 men and women with civil service jobs in London found that those in low-grade positions with little control over their responsibilities were at a 50% higher risk of developing heart disease than those in higher-level jobs. The author of the study concluded, "Our research suggests that illness in the workplace is to some extent a management issue. . . . The way work is organized appears to make an important link between socioeconomic status and heart attack."[12]

Information systems can have an impact on health because they are part of the job environment. The impact is positive if the system contributes to a person's feelings of initiative, discretion, advancement, and control. It is negative if the system reduces these feelings by diminishing skills, meaningfulness of work, autonomy, and social relations. We will see examples in both directions.

Even though they may have generally healthier jobs, some professionals and managers believe their stress level has increased due to **information overload**. They believe information technology has contributed to this overload, and that routine use of v-mail, e-mail, fax, and personal computers has not been liberating at all. To the contrary, they feel unremitting work pressure because the technology brings work faster, and people expect immediate responses. The Nobel Prize winner Herbert Simon described this phenomenon eloquently: "What information consumes is rather obvious: it consumes the attention of its recipients. Hence, a wealth of information creates a poverty of attention and a need to allocate that attention efficiently among the overabundance of information sources that might consume it."[13]

Using Video Display Terminals at Work   An additional aspect of information systems that has come into question is the effect of personal computers on intensive users. These individuals often suffer higher stress levels and related physical problems than other workers in the same businesses. This stress has been attributed to a combination of lack of control, feelings of being monitored, lack of social contact, and physical discomforts such as eyestrain and physical tension. A study comparing clericals who worked on video display terminals (VDTs), clericals who did not work on VDTs, and professionals who worked on VDTs revealed that clericals working on VDTs had the highest stress. They had to follow rigid work procedures and had little control over what they did. They felt that machines were controlling them. In contrast, the professionals who used VDTs experienced the least stress. They were newspaper reporters who found satisfaction in their work and had flexibility in meeting deadlines.[14]

Impacts specifically related to the physical relationship between people and their work environments are studied in the field of **ergonomics**. Many VDT operators suffer eyestrain, backache, and muscle tension (see Figure 7.1). Some also suffer **repetitive strain injury** (RSI) such as carpal tunnel syndrome, which causes severe pain due to nerve irritation in the wrist. Figure 7.2 shows one of the modified keyboards that attempts to reduce these risks. The voice recognition systems mentioned in the chapter about computers may address this problem for at least some of the people who could dictate more and type less.

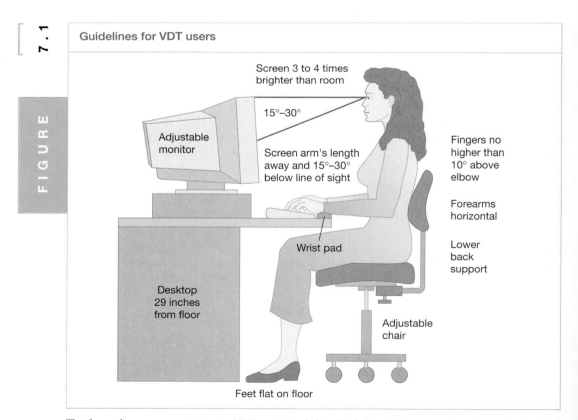

FIGURE 7.1

Guidelines for VDT users

Screen 3 to 4 times brighter than room

15°–30°

Adjustable monitor

Screen arm's length away and 15°–30° below line of sight

Fingers no higher than 10° above elbow

Forearms horizontal

Lower back support

Wrist pad

Desktop 29 inches from floor

Adjustable chair

Feet flat on floor

This figure shows a person sitting at a VDT, practicing habits that help minimize eyestrain, reduce radiation exposure, avoid carpal tunnel syndrome, and reduce back pain.

FIGURE 7.2

Adapting the keyboard to the person

This is one of several ergonomically designed keyboards that try to reduce repetitive use injuries by permitting the typist's hands to remain in a more natural position.

A number of studies have raised concerns about the effects of electromagnetic emissions from VDTs. In one with a sample size too small for statistical significance, pregnant women who spent 20 or more hours per week working at VDTs were twice as likely as non-VDT users to suffer a miscarriage during the first trimester of pregnancy. Reviewing these findings and many others, a World Health Organization (WHO) report concluded that "psychosocial factors are at least as important as the physical ergonomics of workstations and the work environment in influencing health and well-being of workers."[15] A more recent study of the effect of stress on female lawyers supported the general thrust of the WHO findings. This study found that female lawyers who worked more than 45 hours per week were five times as likely to experience great stress at work and three times as likely to suffer miscarriages as female lawyers who worked fewer than 35 hours per week.[16]

Autonomy and Power

Autonomy in a job is the degree of discretion individuals or groups have in planning, regulating, and controlling their own work. **Power** is the ability to get other people to do things. Information systems can cause increases or decreases in either area.

Information systems may increase autonomy whenever the individual can control the use of the tools. For example, a data analysis system might permit totally independent analysis work by a manager who previously had to ask for assistance to analyze data. Likewise, professionals such as engineers and lawyers can use information systems to do work themselves that previously would have required more collaboration and negotiation with others (see Figure 7.3).

In contrast, many information systems are designed to reduce autonomy. The need for limited autonomy is widely accepted in transaction processing and record keeping. Systems in these areas are designed to assure that everyone involved in a repetitive process, such as taking orders or producing paychecks, uses the same rules for processing the same data in the same format. If individuals could process transactions

FIGURE 7.3

Increasing autonomy through tools

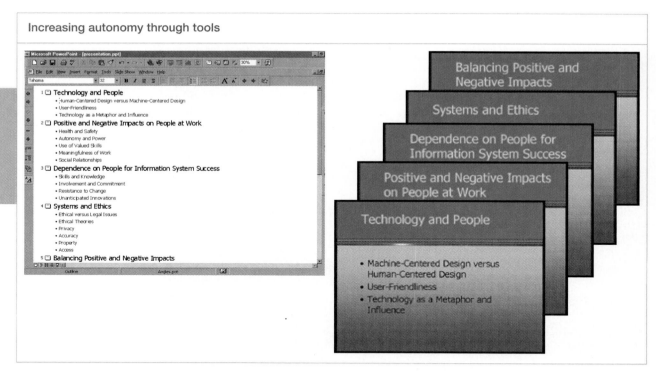

A presentation software package automatically converts this chapter's outline into the format and appearance of a professional-looking presentation. Using convenient tools like this makes business professionals more independent.

however they wanted to, tracking systems and accounting systems would quickly degenerate into chaos.

In other situations, a competition-driven push toward consistency and cost-cutting is leading toward increased electronic surveillance, especially where computerized systems are used continually as part of work. Over a decade ago, a survey found that 6 million American workers were being monitored electronically.[17] For jobs using telephones intensively, this means someone may be listening in. For jobs involving sales transactions or anything else that can be tracked, every completion of a unit of work may be recorded and available for analysis by someone at a remote location. For data entry jobs, every keystroke may be monitored and statistics taken for speed and accuracy of work, and even time spent on breaks.

As a case in point, a small company called WinVista developed software that monitors a personal computer and records every file that is opened, every Web site that is visited, and every e-mail message that is sent. The original version of this software was developed by two brothers who wanted to help their mother avoid more trouble with carpal tunnel syndrome by reminding her to take a break every 5,000 keystrokes. Although this software can be used to identify people who spend too much time playing games, it can also be used to improve work practices. For example, Metropolitan Life tested the software on insurance agents who use up to 50 different programs. The goal was to see how the best agents use programs and then to pass that wisdom on to other agents.[18]

Information systems that monitor workers closely and decrease autonomy are often experienced as threats. Consequently, systems that increase employee monitoring may lead to resistance and may result in turnover of personnel, especially if autonomy is traditional in the work setting. In the trucking industry, for example, many formerly independent drivers are now among the most closely monitored U.S. workers. A decade ago truckers were able to set their own schedules as long as they occasionally called a dispatcher from a pay telephone. Today, over half of trucking firms have computers on board each rig, and many trucks have antennas used to monitor the truck's exact location. The trucks themselves have engines programmed for efficient gear shifting, optimum idling times, and top speed. Truck drivers are happy to use cellular phones instead of lining up at pay phones, but some object to the monitoring and the limits on how they drive. Some have taken evasive action such as blocking their truck's satellite dishes or parking under a wide overpass to escape surveillance from the sky.[19] The monitoring will be even closer if the National Transportation Safety Board's planned recommendation about the use of "black box" recorders in all commercial trucks is adopted. The director of the NTSB said these recorders would allow investigators to more accurately reconstruct accidents involving truckers by providing such information as speed, rate of acceleration, and whether the driver appropriately applied the brakes. They would also accurately record the number of hours a truck driver is behind the wheel. Currently, a driver is allowed to drive 10 hours in a 15-hour period. Drivers now keep a paper log of the number of hours they are on the road, but these paper logs are susceptible to manipulation. An attorney representing trucking companies also complained, saying that the data might be misused in trials related to truck accidents.[20]

Capabilities to monitor minute details of work may create the temptation to misuse the available information, but the way the information is used determines whether system participants feel as though "big brother" is watching. For example, recording conversations by telemarketers can help resolve disputes with customers even if it is never used for day-to-day monitoring of individuals. Similarly, random samples of calls can be used for training rather than for punishment. Given the natural tendency to wonder whether such systems are being misused, it is especially important for managers to explain whether they will be used for monitoring work, and if so, how they will be used.

Just as information systems can affect autonomy, they can also affect power by redistributing information, changing responsibilities, and shifting the balance of power in an organization. Across the entire organizational spectrum, information systems have increased the power of people who operate largely on facts and technical competence, and have reduced the ability of people to give orders based on the power of their position. The availability of information across business functions has also made it easier to resolve conflicts based on facts rather than on opinions and power.

Information systems have had an important impact in reducing the power of many middle managers. Higher-level executives can often use their MIS or EIS directly to get some of the information they once received from middle managers. In addition, they can use communication systems such as e-mail and v-mail to bypass middle mangers and go directly to the individuals who know the most about a particular situation or issue. Middle managers therefore may see information systems squeezing them from below and above.

Use of Valued Skills

Information systems may have either positive or negative effects on people's skills. As a simple example, consider what happens when you rely on a pocket calculator to do arithmetic. Although you usually get the right answer more quickly, your ability to do arithmetic without the calculator deteriorates through disuse. The calculator has the positive effect of helping you calculate more quickly and the negative effect of allowing your skills to decline.

New information systems have enhanced the skills in a wide range of jobs. MIS and EIS have provided information to managers that helps them learn how to manage based on analyzing facts rather than just on intuition. DSS and functional area systems such as CAD have helped professionals analyze data, define alternatives, and solve problems in new ways.

Introducing information systems has also had the opposite effect in some cases, especially when the system automated the judgment and discretion in the work. Such systems redefined jobs by replacing the individual's autonomy and authority with computer-enforced consistency and control. Now a less skilled person could do the same task, and previous skills had less value. Reducing the value of skills previously needed to do specific types of work is called **de-skilling**.

Tasks most susceptible to de-skilling call for repetition, endurance, and speed, rather than flexibility, creativity, and judgment. Such tasks are highly structured and can be described in terms of procedures. These tasks could involve processing data or could involve physical actions such as spray painting a new car. In some specific cases, de-skilling has occurred with the partial automation of decision processes once thought of as requiring years of experience. For example, managers of an insurance company once believed it took five years to become a reasonably good group health insurance underwriter. (An underwriter determines rates for insurance premiums.) The mystery in training new underwriters disappeared when a new system automated standard underwriting calculations. Although the system's purpose was to provide better customer service and reduce the stress of year-end peak loads, it also de-skilled the job. New underwriters could be productive on simple cases within months, and the knowledge of the more experienced underwriters was less valued.[21]

Automating significant job components also tends to reduce people's skills by encouraging mental disengagement and "peripheralization," a feeling that one is at the periphery of the action. Consider the way automatic flight control systems built into new airliners (see Figure 7.4) allow pilots to almost become spectators. Many aviation experts wonder whether pilots of highly automated planes will be able to react quickly enough in emergencies. The quandary of how much control to put into automatic systems came up when an airliner with highly automatic systems crashed while flying low at an airshow in June 1988, killing three people and injuring 50. Although the automatic system was suspect, it is also possible that pilot error caused the crash and that the automatic system prevented a worse crash by keeping the wings level after the plane hit a group of trees.[22] Regardless of how much training pilots receive in realistic flight simulators on the ground, there is also the question of whether this practice is enough. For example, the survivors of a 1989 DC-10 crash in Sioux City, Iowa, owe their lives to an experienced crew that managed to guide the plane to an airport despite an engine explosion that destroyed all of the plane's steering equipment.

FIGURE 7.4

Cockpit of a Boeing 777 airliner

Flying a modern jet requires a great deal of skill and experience, even though some aspects of a pilot's job have been automated.

Information systems may require that workers learn new skills. For professionals, the skills may involve new analytical methods or new ways to obtain information. For nonprofessional workers, the necessary skill may simply be literacy. Many companies have installed flexible manufacturing systems to permit the same manufacturing line to produce different products. In many cases, companies found that their workers were not literate enough to read the instructions for product changes or new machine set-ups. In some cases, the employees were foreigners who couldn't read English. In others, the employees were good workers who had not learned to read in school. In response to this problem, many companies now provide literacy training for employees.[23]

Meaningfulness of Work

Information systems can affect the meaningfulness of work in several ways. First, the information system can be set up to either expand or limit the scope, variety, and significance in the user's job. In addition, the mere fact that work takes place through the medium of a computer may affect the way people experience their work.

Variety and Scope of Work   The range of different types of things people do at work is called **task variety**. Most people desire variety in their work environments and get bored if the work becomes too routine and repetitive. **Task scope** is the size of the task relative to the overall purpose of the organization. Installing a single door lock on an automobile assembly line is a task with minimal scope. Assembling the entire door is a task of larger scope. Information systems can either increase or decrease the variety and scope of work.

Information systems reduce variety if they force the worker to focus on a small aspect of work. Consider what happened with the implementation of a computer-based dental claims system at an insurance company. With the previous paper-oriented system, the benefits analyst pulled information about each account from a set of paper files, checked contract limitations, completed the necessary paperwork, and returned the account information to the files. Analysts were often hired based on their prior knowledge of dental procedures, and they frequently discussed cases with their supervisors and other analysts. With the new computerized system, much of the information was on the computer, which also ran programs that assured claims were processed in a standard way. The analysts spent more time entering claim data into computers and less time using their knowledge and judgment. Claims analysts who previously knew a lot about each account started saying things like: "I don't know half the things I used to. I feel that I have lost it—the computer knows more. I am pushing buttons. I'm not on top of things as I used to be."[24] Within a year the system had increased productivity 30% to 40%, but at the cost of job satisfaction for the analysts.

The Nature of Computer-Mediated Work   The fact that work is done through a computer may affect its meaningfulness to participants. Work done using computers, rather than through direct physical contact with the object of the task, is often called **computer-mediated work**.[25] Box 7.1 identifies different types of computer-mediated work and emphasizes the relationship between how work is done and how people experience their work.

There are many situations in which working through a computer affects the way workers experience their work. The **abstractness of work** is a related issue because computer-mediated work doesn't involve direct physical contact with the object of the task.[26] This work is designed to focus on symbols on a computer screen rather than a more tangible reality. Consider the example of a bank auditor. With a new system, he had less need to travel to the branches, talk with people, and examine financial paperwork. Although some tasks were quicker, he felt it was more difficult to define what information he needed. With nothing in front of him except numbers, he had a limited basis for figuring out what the numbers meant. The job had become abstract and for better or worse didn't feel like the kind of auditing he had done before.[27]

DIFFERENT TYPES OF COMPUTER-MEDIATED WORK

The fact that work is done through a computer affects the way people experience their work and exercise their skills. The meaning of working through a computer is somewhat different in different types of computer-mediated work.

Computer-mediated production work: The worker enters instructions into a terminal attached to a robot or numerically controlled machine. Instead of the person holding tools and doing the work, the machine does the work based on instructions the person enters. The person becomes more like a programmer and less like a machinist.

Computer-mediated office work or record keeping: The worker uses a computer to record and retrieve data instead of writing on paper. The work takes place through a keyboard and display screen. Since so much of the work goes through the computer, there is less reason to get up, walk over to a file cabinet, or even open a drawer. The computer becomes the only important physical object.

Computer-mediated intellectual work: The worker uses a computer as a tool for creating ideas, performing analysis, or doing other intellectual work. Computers allow analysis and manipulation of information in new and different ways. But computerized systems may also constrain both the form of the work and the ability to change to a different method after a major investment in one way of doing things.

Computer-mediated control or supervision: The worker receives instructions through a computer or is monitored based on the rate or accuracy of inputs into a computer. The nature of interactions with supervisors changes. The instructions come from the computer, and it is less necessary to interact with other people to find out what to do. The feedback is based more on data the computer recorded and less on the supervisor's direct observation.

Social Relationships

Social interaction at work is an important part of many people's lives that work systems can affect. In some cases computerized systems may create new possibilities for interaction by automating repetitive paperwork and calculations, thereby giving people more time to work on the issues that require interaction with others. Furthermore, communication systems such as e-mail and v-mail support additional contact between people separated geographically or organizationally.

Impacts of computerized systems on social relationships may also be negative, however. Jobs that require sitting at VDTs all day doing repetitive work tend to reduce social interaction. Even though the people in Figure 7.5 are in an open office setting, their work processes make the workstations their primary information source and work tool, and minimize interaction with their peers. People working in this type of environment may feel the lack of social contact and become alienated. Trends toward downsizing and telecommuting amplify isolation and alienation because they reduce the number of people working in organizations and permit these people to work from their homes.

Extensive use of computers can also have an impact on home life. The first large-scale study of the societal impact of the Internet found that its availability is leading many Americans "to spend less time with friends and family, less time shopping in stores and more time working at home after hours." The study surveyed 4,113 adults in 2,869 households, and looked most closely at the 20% who spent at least five hours a week online. According to the principal investigator, "the more hours people spend on the Internet the less time they spend with real human beings."[28] Not surprisingly, some Internet enthusiasts argued that e-mail and other forms of online community make it easier to increase human connection to friends and family members who are not living in the same household.

Impacts on the social side of work

The physical layout and the nature of this work forces employees to sit at their terminals while having little interaction with their peers.

The chapter started by discussing human interface issues such as human-centered design and user friendliness, and then described five areas in which information systems can have positive or negative impacts on people at work. The next section comes from the reverse viewpoint and looks at the impact of people on work system success.

R E A L I T Y C H E C K ☑

Positive and Negative Impacts on People at Work

Positive and negative impacts on people occur in areas such as health and safety, autonomy and power, use of valued skills, meaningfulness of work, and social relationships.

1. Explain whether you or others you know have ever felt positive or negative impacts of information systems in any of these areas.

2. For the examples you identify, describe the extent to which you think the impact was the type of issue managers should be concerned with.

DEPENDENCE ON PEOPLE FOR INFORMATION SYSTEM SUCCESS

The most brilliant state-of-the-art information system is a waste of time and effort unless people in the organization accept it and use it. Many information systems never work successfully in the organization even though the software operates correctly on the computer. This section looks at several areas in which system success depends on people.

Skills and Knowledge

Anyone who has learned how to use a computer recognizes that information systems operate successfully only if participants have the necessary skills and knowledge. These start with literacy and include knowledge about how to use computers for specific tasks and how to interpret information in the system. In what is often called an Information Age, it is troubling that industry surveys repeatedly conclude that a large percentage of workers lack important basic skills. In a 1997 survey of 4,500 manufacturers, 60% said their workers lacked basic math skills, 55% noted deficiencies in writing and comprehension skills, and 48% said their workers lacked "the ability to read and translate drawings, diagrams, and flow charts."[29]

Some companies have addressed skill and knowledge deficits by designing systems requiring minimal skills from employees. To attain consistent results with a labor force of 500,000 teenagers, McDonald's reduces work to procedures requiring little or no judgment. The system for producing golden brown french fries in consistent portions monitors the boiling grease and beeps to tell the worker to remove the fries. The worker then uses a special fry scoop designed to produce 400 to 420 servings per 100-pound bag of potatoes and make the fries fall into the package attractively. A former employee said he quit because he felt like a robot. Timers controlled every step of his work on the hamburger grill to produce consistent burgers in 90 seconds. He said, "You don't need a face, you don't need a brain. You need to have two hands and two legs and move them as fast as you can. That's the whole system. I wouldn't go back there again for anything."[30]

The McDonald's system represents an extreme, but it helps in seeing the range of system design choices. Many transaction processing systems are highly structured but still call on employees to exercise judgment. MIS, EIS, and DSS all call for knowledge in interpreting the data. Specialized information systems for professional work such as designing buildings or analyzing financial statements require a higher level of knowledge because the business process is much less structured.

System design is clearly important to work system participants, ranging from the teenagers working at McDonald's to professionals and managers doing highly skilled work. Because participants care about the ways work systems affect them, their acceptance of a system or resistance to it is a key determinant of its success. This acceptance or resistance is often tied to involvement and commitment while the system is being designed and implemented.

Involvement and Commitment

Using information system modifications to improve a work system requires changing that work system and overcoming the inertia of current ways of doing things. **Social inertia** is the tendency of organizations to continue doing things in the same way and, therefore, to resist change. Unless a business problem is both evident and painful, overcoming inertia often takes a lot of work. For some projects, more time and effort is spent in overcoming inertia than in the computer-related parts of information system development.

The main force against social inertia is involvement and commitment by participants and their managers. Low levels of involvement and commitment make it more likely that the information system will never reach its full potential or will fail altogether. If commitment is low, even an information system that has been implemented somewhat successfully may be used for a while and then gradually abandoned, soon making it seem that the project never happened.

Table 7.3 shows some of the possible levels of **user involvement** in an information system development project, ranging from noninvolvement to active ongoing participation in the project team. Noninvolvement occurs if the users are unable to participate or if the system is to be imposed on them and they are not invited to participate in its development. Noninvolvement may sound like a recipe for disaster, but it sometimes works, such as when a software package developed elsewhere is the most practical basis for a new information system and when the implementation of that package is well explained. Involvement through advice or sign-off uses a small amount of users' time to provide input that influences priorities and features and therefore reduces political problems.

TABLE 7.3

Alternative Levels of User Involvement in System Development

These levels of involvement go from the lowest to the highest level.[31]

Level of involvement	Description of involvement at this level
Noninvolvement	Users are unwilling to participate, unable to contribute, or are not invited to participate.
Involvement by advice	User advice is solicited through interviews or questionnaires, but others make decisions about which features are included in the system.
Involvement by sign-off	Users approve the results produced by the project team, but are not actively involved in analyzing or designing the system.
Involvement by design team membership	Users participate actively in design activities, such as interviews of other users and creation of functional specifications and external specifications.
Involvement by project team membership, management, and project ownership	Users participate throughout the entire project, including initiation, development, implementation, and operation; a user representative manages the project; the user organization owns the project.

Unfortunately, limited involvement often leads to overlooking system shortcomings and organizational issues that fuller participation would catch. The highest levels of involvement require ongoing participation by users in the project team. In some cases a user representative manages the project to make sure that it genuinely solves the problem. Higher levels of involvement make it more possible to address issues such as mutually inconsistent requests from different users, different needs that cannot all be supported due to resource constraints, and requested features or capabilities that the analysts believe are too difficult or expensive to provide.

The importance of involvement and commitment are clear from attempts to implement the same information system in four unrelated life insurance firms, Sun Alliance Insurance Group in the United Kingdom, National Mutual in Australia, and Prudential and Lutheran Brotherhood in the United States. All sold a full line of life insurance products and had a geographically diverse field sales force with a central home office. All attempted to implement an information system developed by Applied Expert Systems to perform comprehensive financial planning in areas such as cash management, risk management, income protection, general insurance, education funding, and retirement planning. The system used an extensive questionnaire to obtain data and produced a professional-looking personal financial profile and agent's report. It was designed to create a better client relationship based on a thorough understanding of client needs and seemed promising because early pilot projects in four organizations showed that profiling might increase the total premium per sales call between 10% and 30%. There were disadvantages, however, starting with the need for an extra sales call to obtain the client data. The profiles often suggested buying disability insurance, because people are more likely to become disabled than to die in the short term. Life insurance salespeople often disliked suggesting disability insurance, however, because the premiums are high and because the underwriting process for disability insurance causes delays. The move to profiling also changed the way information was controlled. Both new and experienced agents traditionally controlled their own client files, but with profiling, all the detailed client data was fed to the home office.

Figure 7.6 shows the number of profiles done per month in the four organizations. The pilot project peaked and then died out at National Mutual and Lutheran Brotherhood. In contrast, the use of profiling increased steadily at Sun Alliance and Prudential. Both firms that abandoned profiling implemented it through an approach that began with lead users and progressively widened availability to other participants. In these cases the system was presented to the sales force much like a new insurance product that they could sell if they so desired. The initiative was championed by someone

Importance of involvement and commitment during implementation

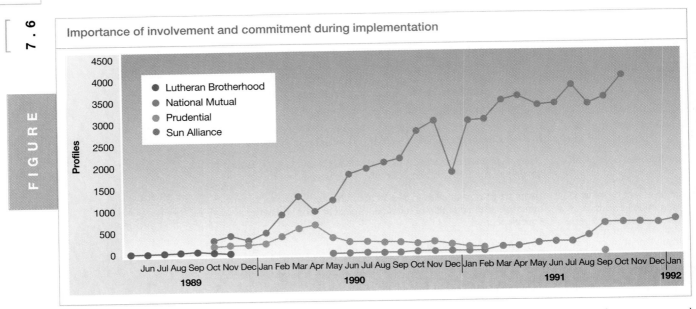

These are the levels of utilization for similar expert systems installed at unrelated insurance companies. After several years, the system was used widely by two companies even though its use was discontinued at two others.

from headquarters who tried to persuade the sales force that the technology could help them. In the two firms where profiling succeeded, it became a central concept in training new agents and in the way the organization intended to operate. The implementation was done on a focused, office-by-office basis, with a senior manager taking a major role in training and implementation. In these cases, the involvement and commitment of both managers and agents contributed strongly to the system's growing use.[32]

The differing results at these four companies show that a system's success is determined partially by its features and partially by the development and implementation process itself. The likelihood of success drops if this process cannot overcome the inertia of current business processes or if the implementation itself causes resistance.

Resistance to Change

Even with a lot of effort to make the change process successful, many systems encounter significant resistance from potential users and others. **Resistance to change** is any action or inaction that obstructs a change process. Resistance may come in many forms, ranging from public debate about the merits of the system to outright sabotage. Public debate can be expressed through direct statements about system shortcomings or reasons why the system is unnecessary or undesirable. Sabotage can occur through submission of incorrect data or other forms of conscious misuse.

Between the extremes of public debate and sabotage are many less overt forms of resistance including benign neglect, resource diversion, inappropriate staffing, and problem expansion.[33] A person resisting the system through *benign neglect* would say nothing against the system but would take no positive action to improve its chances of success. A person resisting through *resource diversion* would say nothing against the system but would divert to other projects the resources it needs. Resistance through *inappropriate staffing* involves assigning people to the project who lack the background and authority to do a good job. A final form of resistance is *problem expansion*. This is done by trying to delay and confuse the project effort by claiming that other departments need to be involved in the analysis because the system addresses problems related to their work.

Resistance is a complex phenomenon because it often comes from a combination of motives. It can be a highly rational response motivated by a desire to help the organization. For example, a manager might believe a new system is useless and might try to

TABLE   7.4

Common Explanations of Resistance to Information Systems

Caused by people	Caused by the system	Caused by interactions
Perhaps the resisting users are not smart enough to understand the system's advantages.	Perhaps the system is too difficult to learn in a reasonable amount of time or too difficult to use effectively.	Perhaps the system is wrong for these particular users.
Perhaps users are involved in a political fight unrelated to the system.	Perhaps the system is causing a political problem for some of the users.	Perhaps the system will change the political distribution of power in the organization.
Perhaps users are lazy and want to continue doing things the outmoded way they have always worked.	Perhaps the system doesn't solve enough of the problem to make the change worthwhile.	Perhaps the system will help some users but harm others by increasing their workloads or devaluing their skills.
Perhaps users' complaints about missing or poorly designed features are an excuse for not plunging in.	Perhaps the system is poorly designed.	Perhaps the system needs to be enhanced to make it more effective for these users.
Perhaps users are overly perfectionistic in their expectations.	Perhaps the system doesn't solve the problem well.	Perhaps the system doesn't meet expectations and needs to be improved.

get others to come to agree. In contrast, resistance can have selfish or vindictive motives. For example, a manager might feel that the system will undermine personal ambitions or improve the prospects of personal rivals.

It is useful to think about resistance by looking for multiple causes. One approach is to say that resistance can be caused by people, or by the system, or by interactions between the characteristics of the people and the characteristics of the system.[34] Table 7.4 shows five typical person-related explanations of resistance. Next to each of these is a corresponding system-related explanation and an interaction-related explanation. The table illustrates how different individuals might cite different reasons for resistance to a particular information system. Highly committed members of the project team might view resistance as caused by the action or inaction of people. Users who didn't want the system might view resistance as caused by the system's characteristics. An unbiased observer might be more likely to cite all three reasons shown in the table.

Awareness of the different causes of resistance is helpful in anticipating implementation problems that may arise in a project. Table 7.4 implies that anyone who holds only one view of the causes of resistance may be missing important ways to improve the situation. Regardless of personal beliefs about which causes are foremost in any situation, considering the range of causes may lead to better implementation strategies.

Unanticipated Innovations

A final aspect of the impact of people on information systems is the unending stream of unanticipated uses. Some may be beneficial, others may just be unexpected, and yet others may create new problems. Since this chapter is full of examples of surprising uses and impacts, we will not discuss the topic further at this point.

R E A L I T Y C H E C K ✓

Dependence on People for Information System Success

People-related determinants of system success include skills and knowledge, involvement and commitment, resistance to change, and unanticipated innovations.

1. Identify situations you know about in which involvement and commitment had important impacts on the success or failure of a project or activity.

2. Think of an example of resistance to change in which you were the person resisting the change. Explain how you resisted the change and how you justified your position.

SYSTEMS AND ETHICS

Ethics is a branch of philosophy dealing with principles of right and wrong behavior related to other people. Ethics is a key concern for everyone involved with information and systems because of the many ways one's actions in this area can affect other people.

Ethical versus Legal Issues

Table 7.6 summarizes important distinctions between ethical issues and legal issues. Laws are a society's official statements defining proper behavior and governmental actions in response to improper behavior. Laws related to arbitrary societal rules such as "drive on the right side of the street" exist only for societal convenience and are unrelated to ethical issues. Other laws such as "don't commit robbery" grow out of the society's ethical sense of right and wrong in dealing with people. Laws cover some, but not all ethical issues. They typically cover only ethical issues that can be described clearly, have impact on society, and are governed by commonly accepted ethical principles.

Ethical dilemmas are difficult choices related to ethical issues that may or may not be covered by laws. Here are examples of ethical dilemmas that occur every day in business and society.

- The supervisor of five telephone attendants has received numerous complaints lately and is considering secretly listening in on the attendants' phone conversations to monitor their service. Is this right or wrong?
- A software engineer working for a city government prints a file while debugging a computer program and notices that a large number of unpaid parking tickets have been canceled for several individuals, one of whom is an elected official. Is it right or wrong to publicize this?
- A manager under severe competitive pressure is thinking about installing a new computerized system that will eliminate the jobs of five people who will probably be unable to get equally good jobs anywhere else. Is this right or wrong?
- A programmer in a software firm is dissatisfied with the way a new information system has been tested and is considering telling his manager's boss that the system should not be distributed to customers, even though it has no obvious bugs.

These situations all pose ethical dilemmas related to the impact of one person's actions on others, whether or not laws could be used to decide what to do. None of these dilemmas involves either conscious lawbreaking or malicious acts such as trying to hurt someone, steal something, or damage something mischievously. If malicious acts were involved, the perpetrator would be less likely to think about ethical dilemmas and more likely to think about the chances of being caught and the nature of punishment. In each case, the person faced with the dilemma is trying to figure out what principles and values to apply in deciding what to do.

TABLE 7.5

Distinctions between Ethical Issues and Legal Issues		
	Ethics	**Laws and regulations**
What is the basis?	Customs and beliefs about how people should treat each other	A combination of: • society's consensus about ethics • practical issues about what can be enforced • historical precedents from existing laws
Who is the judge?	Individuals	Judges appointed or elected through a governmental process
What is the price of nonconformance?	Criticism or ostracism	Legal penalties such as fines or jail sentences
Does the principle have geographical boundaries?	May differ from society to society or region to region	May differ from society to society or region to region

Ethical Theories

Over thousands of years, philosophers have proposed a range of **ethical theories,** principles that can be used as the basis for deciding what to do in ethical dilemmas. Some of these theories are based on the potential consequences of the action whereas others are based on the way people should be treated. Here are simplified statements of three common ethical theories.

- *Maximize the overall good.* This theory says that people should choose to act in ways that maximize the overall good of society. As the examples in the preceding section illustrate, it is often difficult to decide what will maximize the overall good. Consider the manager who is trying to decide whether to install a system that will displace five people. That action may be part of the only practical strategy for the company's survival. On the other hand, there may be alternative approaches such as changing people's jobs but maintaining their salaries and working conditions.

- *Maximize personal good.* This theory says people should make choices that maximize their own personal outcomes. In business situations, this theory can be translated into a theory of employer rights whereby an employer has the right to treat any employee at the job site in any way the employer wants, limited only by the law. In the telephone attendant example, the supervisor might use this theory to justify listening in on the phone conversations, even though other methods of supervision might work equally as well.

- *Treat others well.* This theory resembles the biblical rule of acting toward others as you would have them act toward you. It differs from the other two theories because it focuses on the actions one might take rather than the consequences of those actions. For example, someone following this theory might feel it is never appropriate to lie, whereas someone trying to maximize the overall good might feel that lying could be justified depending on the likely consequences. In business situations, the ethical theory of treating others well is translated into theories of employee rights based on personal respect, healthy working conditions, fair wages, and employment continuity.

Regardless of how the ethical principles are stated, ethical dilemmas such as the preceding are difficult to resolve. Over time, societies and organizations gradually develop negotiated guidelines for what constitutes ethical behavior in those environments and what happens when the guidelines are broken. Rapid technological change in today's world creates many ethical dilemmas with minimal precedent. This is one of the reasons major professional societies involved in information systems have issued codes of ethics for their members.

Now that several typical ethical dilemmas have been listed and several ethical theories have been introduced, it is important to identify some of the major ethical issues that people working in information systems face. These ethical issues are organized under the headings of privacy, accuracy, property, and access (summarized by the acronym PAPA[35]).

Privacy

Information systems can have impacts on two types of privacy, physical privacy and information privacy. **Physical privacy** is the ability of an individual to avoid unwanted intrusions into personal time, space, and property. **Information privacy** is the ability of an individual to determine when, how, and to what extent personal information is communicated to others.

Physical Privacy   Information technologies provide numerous opportunities to intrude on others. Computer-generated phone calls interrupt dinner to invite you to buy things you don't want or to give to a charity you may not support. Your fax machine runs out of paper due to a long, unsolicited fax. You receive junk mail you don't want. You receive electronic junk mail you don't want. (Sending such electronic junk mail is called **spamming** and is a controversial topic on the Internet.) Computer-generated "personalized" letters have no person at the other end. High-decibel speaker systems operate at such high volume that "one loud rock concert can leave patients with permanent tinnitus (ringing in the ears), and legions of frequent concertgoers now suffer high-frequency hearing loss," according to the director of audiology at the University of California at San Francisco.[36]

A variety of state and federal laws and regulations protect physical privacy. For example, the Telephone Consumers Protection Act of 1991 prohibits "any telephone call to any residential telephone line using an artificial or prerecorded voice to deliver a message without the prior express consent of the called party, unless the call is initiated for emergency purposes." This law was disputed in court by owners of small businesses such as the A-Aa-1-Lucky Leprechaun chimney-sweeping company in Keizer, Oregon. It had purchased a $1,800 system that dials telephone numbers, delivers a recorded sales pitch, and lets potential customers leave messages. Such calls are an intrusion for many households, but the business owners maintained this type of system is the key to their survival. In 1993 a court granted a preliminary injunction preventing the Federal Communications Commission from enforcing the 1991 ban. The judge wrote that the law might not make much of a dent in the volume of unsolicited telemarketing calls, and it could wipe out Lucky Leprechaun.[37]

The optional caller ID feature in current telephone systems raises many questions about physical and information privacy. Phones with **caller ID** display the caller's telephone number on a special unit attached to a telephone. This feature is useful for telemarketing and customer service because the caller's telephone number can trigger the retrieval of account information such as the latest bill and outstanding balance. Use of caller ID may also reduce nuisance calls because the person receiving the call will know the source. Caller ID is controversial because it raises questions about who should be favored, the caller or the person called. The person called would like to eliminate some telephone calls or respond more appropriately to others. But a caller with an unlisted telephone doesn't want that number exposed unnecessarily, and a person who anonymously calls a business to get price information doesn't want to become part of that business's mailing list automatically. In 1992 a Pennsylvania court ruled that caller ID was a form of illegal wiretapping.[38] At the same time many other states permitted it subject to various limitations and caller options.

Pacific Bell offers a $6.50 per month caller ID option that displays both the caller's phone number and the name in which the phone is registered, regardless of whether the caller's phone number is unlisted (a $0.30 per month option). It also offers a free option of complete or selective "caller ID blocking," which prevents the number and name from being displayed on a caller ID unit. Pacific Bell advised people not to use complete caller ID blocking because these calls will not be accepted by phones with caller ID equipment that contains a feature called "block the blocker." What would Alexander Graham Bell think about the way his invention developed?

A 1998 *Wall Street Journal* article described a different, less complex side of the phone intrusion issue. According to a market research survey, around two-thirds of homes have answering machines and around half of these are used to screen calls. Contrary to previous social norms, increasing numbers of people simply don't answer their telephone at all until they know who is calling.[39]

Information Privacy   Most Americans feel that they should not be monitored without consent, that they should not have to divulge personal information, and that personal information they provide should be treated confidentially. Whereas most Americans think of privacy as a right, no specific provision in the United States Constitution guarantees the right to privacy. A century ago, innovations related to "instantaneous photographs" and newspapers led to the first influential article about privacy.[40] The issue then was the right to be free from unwarranted publicity regarding private affairs. Just over 100 years later concerns about privacy became front-page news when Britain's Princess Diana died after her car crashed while being chased by photographers.

Even with more awareness of privacy, concepts about privacy are by no means universal. For example, the idea of privacy was so much less prominent in Japan's traditionally group-oriented culture that a word equivalent to privacy didn't exist in the Japanese language.[41] At the other extreme, Article 18 of Spain's 1978 Constitution codifies a concept of privacy exceeding what one expects from American newspapers and television, especially in regard to public figures. It establishes a right to privacy, saying: "Rights to honor, personal and family privacy, and one's own image are guaranteed. . . . The law shall limit the use of known information for the sake of guaranteeing honor and personal and family privacy of citizens and the full exercise of their rights."[42]

Widespread use of computers and computerized databases makes privacy a much broader issue than in the past. Each of us leaves a trail of computerized data every time we use a credit card, write a check, use medical insurance, or subscribe to a magazine. Data from various sources can be combined to create a very detailed picture of how you live, with whom you associate, what your interests are, and how you handle money.

Several legal actions related to e-commerce firms in bankruptcy demonstrate how information collected for one purpose may be used for vastly different purposes. In May 2000, Toysmart.com shut down and during its bankruptcy proceedings solicited bids for assets including 250,000 customer names, addresses, and credit card numbers. The Federal Trade Commission intervened, saying that Toysmart's proposed sale of its customer list violated its own assurances to customers that their registered information would "never be shared with a third party." An interim settlement said that Toysmart could sell its customer list only if the buyer abided by the terms of the privacy policy of Toysmart's Web site. The following month a federal judge set aside these conditions saying that the deal with the regulators could be considered only when an actual buyer for Toysmart's assets emerges.[43, 44] Possibly as a response to the Toysmart situation, the following month Amazon.com sent an e-mail message to 20 million customers announcing a revised privacy policy that includes: "As we continue to develop our business, we might sell or buy stores or assets. In such transactions, customer information generally is one of the transferred business assets. Also, in the unlikely event that Amazon.com, Inc., or substantially all of its assets are acquired, customer information will of course be one of the transferred assets."[45]

Credit information firms such as Experian (formerly TRW), Equifax, and Trans Union have credit histories on 190 million Americans. A summary fact sheet about any one of these individuals can be obtained in several seconds by merchants and landlords all over the United States. Many other publicly accessible databases contain information about financial transactions, media preferences, driving records, political affiliations, insurance claims, and much more. For example, for $5 New York State sells a driver's personal data including height and weight, driving record, license revocations, vehicle ownership, accidents, and police reports.[46] These databases are used for many different purposes and are very valuable to people who need to make business decisions such as granting loans, renting apartments, and hiring employees.

There is considerable question about how much and which information about an individual should be available through a computerized information service. It is hard to know what personal information exists in these databases, whether it is correct, or who is actually using that information. It is also not clear what information is held in government databases and whether that information is more or less threatening than information in private databases. Finally, regardless of the true purpose of an information system, there is no way to guarantee the information in the system will be protected from someone intending to use it for an illegal or simply inappropriate purpose. The Web page for one firm in the personal information business advertises the availability of many types of personal information. Prices quoted in a separate letter to private investigators included $80 for long-distance phone records and $400 for ten years of medical treatment history. Some personal data can be pieced together through publicly available sources such as driver data. Investigators obtain other data illegally by misrepresenting themselves. For example, an investigator might call a credit card company with a tale about a wife who left ten days ago with a credit card. The investigator would claim he did not want to report the card stolen, but did want to know whether his wife was generating huge bills. An investigator who had served time in prison for perpetrating this type of fraud said this method of obtaining recent transactions usually worked for him.[47]

To demonstrate how easy it is to obtain private information about individuals, the author Jeffrey Rothfeder obtained fiscal histories, phone numbers, and consumer preferences of Dan Rather, Arsenio Hall, Dan Quayle, and others. Before publishing this information in his book *Privacy for Sale* he wrote a letter to Rather, who hit the roof, saying Rothfeder's actions were akin to breaking into his home, stealing his diary, and publishing it. Publication of the book was delayed two months, and Rothfeder said that Rather's angry response reinforced the book's point that privacy really matters.[48]

Many other examples show how trails of computerized data have jeopardized common expectations of privacy. For example, as revenge against a magazine columnist who had written an article critical of computer hackers, a computer hacker broke into a national credit database and posted the columnist's credit card number on a national bulletin board. During the confirmation hearing of Supreme Court nominee Robert Bork, a list of the videotapes that he or his household had rented from a video store was printed in a Washington newspaper. When he rented those videotapes as a private citizen, he probably did not believe that the record of the rentals would become public information. Congress reacted swiftly with the Video Privacy Protection Act of 1988, but this involved only one of many types of transaction data that could be used to breach personal privacy.

Code of Fair Information Practices   Many aspects of physical privacy and information privacy have generated a discussion and debate. The following are five principles proposed within the U.S. government in 1973 as the beginnings of a Code of Fair Information Practices related primarily to databases.

1. There must be no personal record-keeping systems whose very existence is secret.
2. There must be a way for an individual to find out what information about him or her is on record and how it is being used.
3. There must be a way for an individual to correct or amend a record of identifiable information about him or her.
4. There must be a way for an individual to prevent information about him or her that was obtained for one purpose from being used or made available for other purposes without his or her consent.
5. Any organization creating, maintaining, using, or disseminating records of identifiable personal data must assure the reliability of the data for their intended use and must take reasonable precaution to prevent misuse of the data.

These principles are equally applicable to record-keeping systems in the government and in the private sector. With the collection of data by computerized systems whenever anyone uses a credit card, gets on an airplane, or even rents a video, implementing and enforcing this code would be an enormous undertaking. In many ways governments are no more sensitive to privacy issues than are other organizations. For example, 34 states sell driver's license information including name, address, height, weight, age, vision, social security number, and type of car. Buyers include private investigators, who pay a few dollars for an individual lookup, and direct marketers, who receive complete databases to build targeted mailing lists based on personal characteristics.[49] Most people who apply for driver's licenses wouldn't imagine their personal information is made available this way. Nor would most people who submit a change of address card to the U.S. Post Office dream that this information is sold to organizations that use lists of recent movers for targeted marketing.

The availability of the World Wide Web to children has generated a facet of this problem that the Fair Information Practices committee probably didn't anticipate. "As millions of kids go online, marketers are in hot pursuit. Eager to reach an enthusiastic audience more open to pitches than an adult buried in junk mail, companies often entertain tykes online with games and contests. To play, these sites require children to fill out questionnaires about themselves and their families and friends, valuable data to be sorted and stored in marketing databases." For example, the Mars, Inc., site asked kids to search out fake M&M candy by supplying names and e-mail addresses of their friends. A spokesman for Mars said the search was "just part of the fun" and that the company didn't keep the names or e-mail addresses.[50] Regardless of how the information is used, it is legitimate to ask whether children benefit from being trained to divulge private information in this way. A rule to address this type of situation went into effect in April 2000 based on the Children's Online Privacy Protection Act of 1998. The rule bars Web sites from collecting personal information from children under 13 without verifiable parental consent.[51]

R E A L I T Y C H E C K [✓]

Privacy

This section discussed various aspects of privacy and the way computerized information systems may compromise your privacy. Explain what you think is acceptable in the following questions related to privacy:

1. To what extent should your medical records be available to your boss?

2. To what extent should your financial records such as credit card and car payments be available to anyone who pays for them?

3. To what extent should your conversations at work be monitored by your employer?

4. To what extent should you be able to avoid unwanted intrusions such as phone solicitations during dinner and electronic junk mail?

5. To what extent should there be limits on the types of information others can collect about you without telling you they are doing so?

Accuracy

Chapter 4 introduced the issue of information accuracy and indicated that it involved much more than questions about data errors. Figure 4.18 showed why managers should expect some degree of bias in analysis, proposals, and suggestions. Although some bias exists in any explanation from a personal viewpoint, bias becomes an ethical issue when relevant information is knowingly suppressed or misrepresented. This is a recurring ethical issue throughout business, government, and society. Here are several health-related examples reported in the news within one month.

- *Suppression of information:* Executives of Philip Morris admitted before a congressional committee that publication of a company study of the addictiveness of cigarettes had been suppressed.[52]
- *Misrepresentation of information:* The Agriculture Department gave the milk industry a dispensation allowing them to use the "low fat" label for milk with 2% fat even though all other products with the same percentage of fat do not qualify.[53]
- *Acceptance of misleading information because it fits the rules:* A watchdog agency demonstrated that the "smoking machines" used by the government to identify cigarettes as "low in tar and nicotine" actually "puff" the cigarettes in a way that absorbs much less tar and nicotine than an average smoker would absorb. This discrepancy, which exaggerates the benefits of smoking low-tar cigarettes, was known for years, but no one did anything about it.[54]

One case involves suppression of information and the other two involve varying degrees of misrepresentation. At the heart of all three are ethical issues about accuracy, regardless of whether computerized systems are involved.

Storage of personal data in computerized systems brings an additional dimension to the accuracy issue because of harm that may occur when data in these databases is incorrect. Every year, people come forward with horror stories about not being able to rent an apartment because of a past dispute with an unfair landlord or because a data entry error became a virtually indelible mark against them in a database. A clerical error at the U.S. Treasury Department demonstrates the types of problems that can result from incorrect data. The error deleted the social security number of Edna Rissmiller, a 79-year-old widow. Soon thereafter her pharmacy refused to honor her insurance card and the government re-collected a $672 pension check from her bank account. Her son William found it difficult to reestablish that she was alive. Her bank told him that as far as they were concerned, she was dead until he could prove otherwise.[55]

An increasingly important part of the data inaccuracy problem is **identity theft**, in which a criminal obtains a victim's social security number and other credit information and then uses the victim's name to commit fraud. In 1999 the Social Security Administration received over 30,000 complaints of misuse of social security numbers. The identity thief might even obtain the social security number using the Web. For example, a site called docusearch.com says it will retrieve a person's social security number in one day for $49. Its director said he gets the numbers from "various sources." Aside from the commercial losses suffered by merchants, identity theft creates an incorrect credit history for the person whose information is stolen. In one example, more than three dozen individuals working at Ligand Pharmaceuticals in San Diego discovered that their identities were being used to obtain credit cards, buy merchandise, open cellular phone accounts, and rent apartments. On being warned by First USA that someone was using her name for fraudulent credit card charges, one victim who was hoping to obtain a car loan around that time contacted the three major credit-reporting agencies. They said her records couldn't be cleaned up without a report from First USA, and it took 16 weeks to generate the report. Subsequently, she did some of her own detective work after an inquiry from a San Francisco real estate agent. This helped the police apprehend a suspect who had worked at Ligand and who had a box of personal records of Ligand employees in her car when she was arrested.[56]

R E A L I T Y C H E C K ☑

Accuracy

Many computerized databases contain inaccurate information about individuals that may cause them inconvenience and harm.

1. Explain why you do or do not think there should be a legal requirement for accuracy in public databases containing information about individuals. If the requirement existed, what do you think it should be?

2. If you were in charge of a database of financial and medical information about individuals, what do you think you might do to assess the accuracy of the data?

Property

Imagine that you were in a video rental store and saw someone steal a blank videotape. Imagine that the same person rented a videotape of a film and copied it. Both situations involve theft, but the nature of the theft seems different to many people. In the first case, the person stole a physical object. In the second case, the person stole the information recorded on the physical object. Although the information is more valuable than the physical object, many people act as though copying the information is not theft.

As children, we come to understand the concept of property and ownership by recognizing our own bodies, our own clothes, and our own toys. This concept of ownership involves physical things. If someone takes a child's toy, the child no longer has it. If the child has one toy and would like another like it, there is no instantaneous way to duplicate it. The world of computerized information products does not follow these commonsense features of the physical world. Someone can copy a movie, a piece of music, a computer program, or a database without changing it. The original owner still has the original even if a million copies were made, and a million unauthorized copies may be made, as the entertainment and software industries certainly know. By some estimates up to 97% of the software used in Thailand has been copied illegally, compared to as much as 40% in the United States. Estimates of pirated software in Europe range from 80% in Spain to 25% in the United Kingdom.[57]

Outright piracy is a clear case, but the widespread existence of electronic information on different electronic media has many difficult legal and ethical questions related to property rights for information. Databases, music, and video can all be stored, transmitted, and reformatted in a variety of ways. Techniques such as desktop publishing are making it increasingly easy to produce information by modifying other information, thereby leaving issues about rights to intellectual property even more blurred. Web-based commerce has raised legal issues concerning property rights in many areas. Consider some examples:

Copying and modification of creative work: Napster and other Web-based file-sharing systems highlight many issues related to copying of creative work. This type of copying is a threat to artists who make recordings that are sold by recording companies. If someone stores the recording online and makes it available to anyone for free, people who copy it are much less likely to buy it. The compelling logic that this is tantamount to theft of intellectual property is why a number of major media companies sued Napster for massive copyright infringement. For more about Napster, see the opening case in Chapter 8.

Posting of decryption software on the Web: Eight leading Hollywood studios sued Eric Corley, editor and publisher of *2600: The Hacker Quarterly* for posting software on his Web site that allows users to bypass the security system of DVD movie disks, thus paving the way to unauthorized viewing, copying, and online transmission of movies. A federal judge found that this was a violation of the 1998 Digital Millennium Copyright Act.[58, 59]

Cybersquatting: **Cybersquatting** is registering a Web domain name in order to sell it later to a company or person who wants to use it. Cybersquatting on a domain name based on a common term such as baby, television, or mortgage raises no particular legal or ethical issues, but what about when someone totally unassociated with the World Wrestling Federation registered www.worldwrestlingfederation. com? The Federation had long maintained a site at www.wwf.com, dating back to when domain names were limited to only 22 characters. It took its complaint to the World Intellectual Property Organization, which ruled that the address holder had acted in bad faith, hoping only to profit from reselling the name, and gave the name to the Federation. Of 1,000 cases that have gone before the four arbitration and mediation centers approved to resolve such disputes, three quarters have been won by trademark owners.[60]

Unauthorized "framing" of material on the Web: One Web site can contain a link to a second Web site, but it shouldn't be able to "frame" information from the second Web site so that it appears to belong to the first site. An important detail of framing is that it is possible to frame just part of a Web page. This makes it possible to display another site's information while cutting off its banner advertising and replacing it with other advertising. The contentiousness of the framing issue was clear when a small company called TotalNews, Inc. built a Web site that links to 1,100 other news sites, mostly through framing. An attorney for the *Washington Post* complained, "It's a completely parasitic Web site." An attorney for TotalNews countered, "They're just paranoid."[61] The *Times of London* went further by notifying a different site called News Index that it violated the paper's copyright by listing *Times* stories in its index and maintaining hypertext links back to stories at the *Times* site. The News Index disputed the charge, saying that the site's indexing, summaries, and links fall within "fair use."[62]

Hiring employees to obtain trade secrets of former employers: In October 1998, Wal-Mart sued Amazon.com and Drugstore.com for systematically recruiting 15 former Wal-Mart employees in order to steal trade secrets. The trade secrets were Wal-Mart's information systems for tracking purchases and inventories. These systems are widely viewed as a key component of Wal-Mart's competitive success.[63] In a settlement in April 1999, the work assignments of nine of the employees were restricted, but no injunction was issued prohibiting further hiring of Wal-Mart employees.[64]

Intellectual property is different from other forms of property and has therefore become a specialty in the legal profession. In general, property is usually defined as an exclusive right to own and dispose of a thing. When the thing is an automobile, the ideas of ownership and disposal are reasonably clear. When it comes to information or knowledge, neither ownership nor disposal is as straightforward as with other forms of property. The preceding examples illustrate this question: Who owns the appearance of a product or the knowledge in the mind of the engineer or the musical sounds produced by the drummer and then recorded and modified by someone else? How would anyone know if the information in these cases were stolen? If a car is stolen and then found, it is usually possible to verify that it is the same car. What about the knowledge or the sounds, especially if they are used in a slightly different context and therefore modified or extended in some way?

Ownership rights for intellectual property have traditionally been protected in the United States by copyright, patent, and trade secret laws. Copyright laws protect the literary expression of an idea, not the idea itself, for the life of the author plus 50 years. Patent laws protect for 17 years inventions or discoveries having distinguishing features that are innovative, useful, and not obvious. Both copyrights and patents require public disclosure of the intellectual property that is being protected. Trade secrets are protected by contracts designed to ensure confidentiality. All of these tools have serious practical shortcomings at a time when new intellectual property products can be developed in months rather than years.

Many thousands of software patents have been awarded, and several patented information systems were mentioned earlier in this book. These include Merrill Lynch's cash management account (U.S. Patent #4,346,442 dated August 24, 1982) and Mrs. Fields Cookies' staff scheduling system (U.S. Patent #5,111,391, dated May 5, 1992). The latter was titled "system and method for making staff schedules as a function of available resources as well as employee skill level, availability, and priority."[65] Scheduling employees is a common problem in most businesses and is used commonly as an example in operations research textbooks. Even if Mrs. Fields uses a truly unique technique, there are important practical questions about how anyone trying to develop a method for scheduling employees would know about this patent and how Mrs. Fields would enforce it. Although the U.S. Patent and Trademark Office had made it more difficult to patent software-related inventions, a July 29, 1994 ruling by the U.S Court of Appeals for the Federal Circuit seemed to open the floodgates for new patents. That ruling declared that a general-purpose computer run by software can be patented because the program essentially creates a new machine.

The advent of e-commerce has led to a number of controversial business methods patents. Amazon.com sued Barnes & Noble in October 1999 for infringing on its patent for One-Click shopping, the efficient method Amazon.com had invented for handling online shopping carts. Amazon won a temporary injunction against Barnes & Noble and the case was awaiting trial a year later. In another case, Priceline sued Microsoft for copying its name-your-own-price system on Microsoft's Expedia travel Web site. Priceline's patent was for a business method of allowing a customer to use the Web to offer a price for an airline ticket instead of just accepting the price listed by a Web site. Many observers argued that potential purchasers have made offers to merchants for centuries and that the mere fact that this happens over the Web should not be the basis of a patent. Microsoft itself had received 352 patents in 1999 alone, but said through a spokesman, "We respect intellectual property rights, but we don't respect some companies abusing the system."[66]

R E A L I T Y C H E C K ✓

Property

The special characteristics of information raise a number of issues about property. Explain what you think is acceptable in the following questions related to information as property:

1. To what extent should an engineer be allowed to take any of his or her original work for a company upon leaving for another job?

2. To what extent should an executive who moves to another company be prevented from discussing the affairs of the company she left? Is there any practical way of doing this?

3. Under what circumstances should you be allowed to store or copy a magazine article, a book, a computer program, a taped rendition of a song, a football game broadcast on television, a videotaped movie?

Access

A citizen in an information society needs at least three things: intellectual skills to deal with information, access to information technology, and access to information. Although access to information and information technology has exploded in recent decades, the explosion has not been uniform. Some people have much greater access and others have much less, with impacts ranging from power in organizations to employment opportunities and job satisfaction.

Intellectual Skills   Consider the workers in a factory under great competitive pressure to automate using numerically controlled machines. Skilled machinists who may not have much formal education may be doing high-quality work based on 20 years of experience working with the previous generation of tools. To run the new machines, these workers would have to do a form of programming, and they may lack the necessary literacy and abstract reasoning ability.

Access to Information Technology   Access is also important for handicapped workers (see Figure 7.7). Both general-purpose and specially adapted technology have helped people with vision, hearing, mobility, or dexterity impairments do a wide range of jobs that might have been difficult or unattainable for them. For example, voice recognition tools make it possible for people who cannot handle a mouse or keyboard to work effectively with computers. Although certainly far from perfect, voice recognition can also help people with hearing problems by capturing spoken words and converting them into text.

Cost-effective technologies that compensate for visual limitations include screen magnification, Braille printers, optical character recognition, speech recognition, and high-speed voice synthesizers. Although these new technologies have increased access for the visually handicapped, the graphical interfaces used in current software were a step backward for them. The problem is that the use of icons and mouse clicks relies on vision much more heavily than the use of text-based screen displays, which can be read aloud using a voice synthesizer.

The release of GUI-based Windows 95 became a serious vocational threat to blind and visually impaired computer users. Subsequent development of screen readers was a step forward in many situations. A **screen reader** is a software program that allows a blind person to use text on the screen and identify some graphics such as buttons on a toolbar or desktop icons by means of a speech synthesizer. Special keyboard

Extending technology to increase access

(a)

(b)

(c)

These photos represent the many ways information technology can be used to aid people who have problems with muscular control, vision, or hearing. (a) Commercially available voice recognition capabilities that reached a new plateau of power in 1998 permit a user to enter data via dictation and to speak commands such as "print" and "copy" instead of typing them or pointing with a mouse. This allows a person with physical limitations to use a computer productively without touching it. (b) The Kurzweil reading machine uses synthesized speech to read texts to people with visual impairments. After working with a Kurzweil music synthesizer, the rock star Stevie Wonder encouraged Ray Kurzweil to build a reading machine. Years later, Stevie Wonder stayed up all night listening when he received the first release of the product. (c) This photo shows Stephen Hawking, one of the world's greatest physicists, whose use of a special data entry device and a voice synthesizer helps him participate in scientific research despite suffering from an advanced case of ALS, "Lou Gehrig's disease," which causes muscular degeneration.

commands provided with the screen reader make it unnecessary to use a mouse.[67] Unfortunately, the existence of screen readers does not mean that all Web sites use them effectively. In November 1999 the National Federation of the Blind filed suit against America Online charging that its Internet service is inaccessible to the blind and violates the Americans with Disabilities Act. The suit charged that AOL, unlike other Internet service providers, had designed its service in a way that made it incompatible with screen readers. For screen access to work, the software must provide text labels for all graphics; permit keyboard access to all functions; and rely upon standard Windows controls such as dialog boxes, list boxes, and edit boxes. The suit said that AOL software uses unlabeled graphics, commands that can be activated only by using a mouse, and custom controls painted on the computer screen. Screen-access programs can't read an unlabeled graphic. AOL replied that the next version would have the screen reader capabilities.[68]

Access to Information   Ethical issues related to information access cut in many directions. Because people need information to participate in economic life, the extensive use of computerized information sources such as the Web raises questions about whether technical progress will divide the haves and have-nots in society even further. Coming from a totally different direction, the existence of pornography on the Web raises questions about whether and how information access should be restricted or controlled. A final question concerns the kind of access individuals should have to information about themselves. The three main credit bureaus will sell an individual his or her own credit report. Why shouldn't people have guaranteed, immediate, free access to information about themselves that resides in commercial databases, such as credit history databases and medical databases? The nature of the ethical issues we have discussed is that there are no easy answers, but it is very important to recognize the questions.

R E A L I T Y C H E C K ✓

Access

This section explained that access to information and information technology is an ethical issue in an information age. Explain the degree to which you agree with the following.

1. Businesses should not build internal systems that might exclude potential participants due to deficits in mobility, vision, or hearing.

2. Universities should not use educational materials that might exclude potential participants due to deficits in mobility, vision, or hearing or due to lack of access to technology such as personal computers and networks.

BALANCING POSITIVE AND NEGATIVE IMPACTS

Many readers probably came to this book thinking that technology was the main topic when one thinks about information systems. The work system framework introduced in Chapters 1 and 2 emphasized that people play key roles as participants and customers. This chapter goes further by showing that information systems have impacts on people and raise human issues and ethical dilemmas.

As in many business situations, decisions about information systems often involve conflicts between positive impacts in some areas and negative impacts in others. Table 7.6 shows how many of the systems mentioned in this chapter had impacts of both types. You and your business colleagues may well decide that a system is appropriate, even if it will have negative impacts on some people. This issue should be understood and dealt with rather than ignored.

The examples in this chapter concerning negative impacts on people inside or outside an organization should also remind you to be skeptical in evaluating claims about the success and benefits of a system. A new system that ostensibly improves quality or responsiveness perceived by business process customers may nonetheless have negative impacts on job satisfaction, loyalty, and length of service of people within the organization. It may also raise ethical concerns related to privacy, accuracy, property, or access. Decisions about information systems clearly involve many factors other than technology.

TABLE 7.6

Positive and Negative Impacts of Innovations Mentioned in This Chapter

Innovation	Positive impacts	Negative impacts
Tracking personal usage of Web sites	Better understanding of customers	Threat to personal privacy
Software that monitors use of corporate networks	Identifies people who spend too much time playing games; identifies best users of particular software	Promotes feeling that Big Brother is always watching
Computerized systems for monitoring truck usage	Increased efficiency through better use of equipment and time	Reduced feeling of autonomy; feeling of being spied upon and distrusted
Computerized systems for insurance underwriting	Better service to customers; shorter training time; better work conditions	De-skilling of experienced underwriters
Use of auto pilots in airplanes	Greater safety and consistency in many situations	Mental disengagement of pilots; de-skilling
Automation of data processing for insurance claims	Greater productivity in claim processing	Decreased social interaction at work; feelings of alienation
Auditing through a computer system	Less need to travel to branches because the computer provides information	Increasing abstractness of work; difficulty relating numbers to reality
Highly structured work in fast-food restaurants	Making it likely that somewhat unskilled workers will produce consistent results	Feeling that the work requires participants to act like machines
Development of national credit-rating services	Better information for decisions related to granting credit, renting apartments, and hiring employees	Possibility of incorrect decisions based on incorrect information in the database; possibility that information will be retrieved and used illegally
Use of profiling in insurance sales	Creates a better understanding of client needs; informs client about need for disability insurance	Makes the sales process lengthier and more complex
Proliferation of electronic information on various media	Ability to disseminate and use that information more effectively	New opportunities to steal that information and use it illegally
National database of new hires	Helps track down parents who fail to pay child support	Jeopardizes privacy of millions of workers who have no child support obligations

CHAPTER CONCLUSION

What kinds of dilemmas result from impacts of information systems on people?

Information systems can have positive or negative effects on people inside and outside of the organization. Positive impacts involve empowering people to do their work well by making work more enjoyable and by helping people grow professionally. Negative impacts involve eliminating jobs, de-skilling jobs, making jobs less satisfying, creating greater job stress, or reducing personal privacy.

What is the difference between machine-centered design and human-centered design?

In machine-centered design, the technology or process is designed to simplify what the machine must do, and people are expected to adjust to the machine's weaknesses and limitations. In human-centered design, the technology or business process is designed to make participants' work as effective and satisfying as possible.

What are the characteristics of healthy work, and how do information systems affect these characteristics?

People in healthy jobs use their skills in meaningful work, enjoy autonomy and social relations with others, have personal rights including some control over the demands of the job, and have enough time and energy to participate in family and community life. Especially unhealthy jobs are those with continual pressure to perform but little personal control. Information systems can provide tools and information that make jobs healthy, or they can contribute to work patterns and control methods that make work unhealthy.

How is computer-mediated work different from other types of work?

Computer-mediated work is work done through computers. This kind of work is more abstract than most other types of work because it does not involve direct physical contact with the object of the task. At least part of a worker's reality consists of symbols on a computer screen rather than the more tangible physical world.

What are the different ways to explain resistance to change?

Resistance to change is any action or inaction that obstructs a change process. Resistance comes from a combination of motives. It can be a highly rational response motivated by a desire to help the organization, or it can have selfish or vindictive motives. Resistance to change can be explained as determined by people, determined by the system, or determined by interactions between the people and the system.

What are ethical theories, and how are they related to information systems?

Ethics is a branch of philosophy dealing with principles of right and wrong behavior related to other people. Ethics is related to information and systems because of the many ways one's actions in this area can affect others. Ethical theories are principles that can be used as the basis for deciding what to do in ethical dilemmas. Stated simply, three ethical theories related to information systems are: maximize the overall good, maximize personal good, and treat others well.

What are the major ethical issues related to information systems?

The major ethical issues related to information systems can be broken down under the topics of privacy, accuracy, property, and access. Privacy falls into two categories, physical privacy and information privacy. Issues related to accuracy involve incorrect conclusions drawn from incorrect data. Issues related to property start with the ease of copying data on electronic media and include the inability of existing laws to protect intellectual property. Issues related to access include access to information and access to technology.

KEY TERMS

machine-centered design
human-centered design
operator error
user friendly
user hostile
anthropomorphize
telecommuting
information overload
ergonomics
repetitive strain injury (RSI)

autonomy
power
de-skilling
task variety
task scope
computer-mediated work
abstractness of work
social inertia
user involvement
resistance to change

ethics
ethical dilemmas
ethical theories
physical privacy
information privacy
spamming
caller ID
identity theft
cybersquatting
screen reader

REVIEW QUESTIONS

1. What is the difference between machine-centered design and human-centered design?

2. Compare the strengths and weaknesses of people versus machines.

3. What characteristics make computerized systems user friendly or user hostile?

4. What are the characteristics of a healthy job, and how are information systems related to these characteristics?

5. What characteristics of work determine whether people who use VDTs find their work stressful?

6. How can information systems affect a person's autonomy?

7. What is de-skilling? Explain whether information systems necessarily lead to de-skilling of their users.

8. What are some of the impacts of information systems on the meaningfulness of work?

9. Explain why user involvement in system development is related to implementation success.

10. What are the different forms of resistance to systems?

11. What is the difference between ethical issues and legal issues?

12. Compare three common ethical theories.

13. What is the difference between physical privacy and information privacy?

14. What are some of the issues related to the storage of personal information in databases?

15. Why would it be difficult to enforce a national code of fair information practices?

16. Why is the accuracy of information in publicly available databases an important problem?

17. How is intellectual property different from other types of property in terms of the ethical issues it raises?

18. In what ways is access an ethical issue?

1. Recognizing that two-thirds of all trucking accidents are caused by fatigue, alcohol, and drugs, the Federal Highway Administration funded Evaluation Systems, Inc., to develop a computerized driver-monitor system. At a set time, the driver pulls off the road and takes a simulated driving test that gives the driver orders such as turn left or turn on the lights. The results are transmitted via satellite to a central computer that compares them to the driver's baseline results. If the driver fails, a retest is given. If the driver fails again, the computer orders a rest and can prevent the truck from restarting until the driver passes the test.[69] Identify any human and ethical issues in this situation. Explain whether you do or do not believe this system should be used.

2. When Dr. Donald Miller closed his Taylors, South Carolina, family practice in 1991, he auctioned off the patient records for his 10,000 patients to the highest bidder, an auto junk dealer who paid $4,000. The dealer sold photocopies to some former patients for $25 each and eventually resold the records for $6,000 to a new doctor who moved into town.[70] Explain why ethical, economic, and practical considerations should or shouldn't have called for different actions.

3. The e-mail administrator for Epson computer company in Torrance, California, trained 700 employees to create and send e-mail messages to coworkers. She assured them that e-mail communications would be totally private but later discovered that her boss was copying and reading employees' e-mail. When she was fired after complaining, she sued her former employer on behalf of the employees whose e-mail had been opened. Epson argued that state privacy statutes make no mention of e-mail. The judge agreed and dismissed the case.[71] What ethical issues do this case and the legal finding raise?

4. A Georgia furniture store targeted residents of upscale neighborhoods in Atlanta suburbs with offers of free credit and a 25% discount on initial purchases but did not offer the same rates to residents of less prosperous adjoining suburbs.[72] Explain why this use of database marketing does or does not raise ethical issues. Would your answer be different if you knew that the targeted neighborhoods were primarily white and the nontargeted neighborhoods were primarily black?

5. The legal scholars Arthur Miller and Alan Westin have suggested that information privacy problems could be solved by giving individuals property rights in all personal information about themselves.[73] They, and not the credit bureaus, private firms, and government organizations, would own all information related to themselves. Identify legal, ethical, and practical issues that this approach raises.

The U.S. Congress passed the Personal Responsibility and Work Opportunity Reconciliation Act of 1996 as part of an effort to change many aspects of the welfare system. One of its many provisions called for the creation of a National Directory of New Hires containing the name, address, social security number, and wages for each of the 60 million people hired into a full- or part-time job in the United States by all but the smallest employers. Several states already had state directories that had been quite useful. In Missouri, for example, child support collections had increased 17% in 1996 after the state required reporting of new hires even though its state directory did not cover people who had moved to different states. Welfare officials predicted that matching the federal and state directories would produce billions of dollars in child support payments. Under the new law, the directory would be available to state welfare and child support agencies. The Internal Revenue Service (IRS), Social Security Administration (SSA), and Justice Departments would also have access for some purposes.[74]

Some privacy advocates voiced alarm about the new database, noting that most new hires have no child support obligations whatsoever. Including information about them in this database would be a threat to their privacy because so many agencies would have access to this information and because data in this type of database has not been totally secure in the past. This type of risk had been publicized in 1992, when an 18-month federal investigation found a ring of "information brokers" who allegedly bribed SSA workers to steal personal information. The going rate to obtain a ten-year earnings history within three to five days was apparently $175, of which $25 went for the bribe to the SSA worker. Buyers of the information apparently included private investigators, prospective employers, lawyers, and insurance companies.[75] In 1994 more than 420 IRS employees received some form of discipline for illegally browsing through tax returns of friends, relatives, and neighbors. Since that time the IRS has increased its training on privacy issues and has installed automatic systems to monitor data access by its employees. In 1997 the IRS Commissioner asked Congress for legislation that would add criminal penalties to the law that prohibits IRS employees from snooping into taxpayer records. This request followed shortly after a Federal appeals court reversed the 1995 conviction of an IRS employee who was also a Ku Klux Klan member. That employee had been convicted of using his computer terminal to look through tax records of other white supremacists he suspected of being informers for the FBI. The conviction was overturned because the prosecution failed to prove that the former employee had done anything with the information he collected.[76]

QUESTIONS

1. Explain why you do or do not believe that creating this database and making it accessible unnecessarily infringes on the privacy of new hires who have no child support obligations.

2. Explain the ethical dilemmas and legal issues this case raises.

3. Assume that the agencies with access to this information put in place procedures and database controls designed to minimize the probability of unauthorized access and use of the information. Explain how those procedures might work and how those procedures would not interfere unreasonably with getting work done in the agencies.

CASE   Visionics: Applying Facial Recognition Software in Driver Registration

On April 15, 1998 Polaroid Corporation signed an agreement with Visionics Corporation to integrate Visionics' FaceIt facial recognition software into Polaroid's secure identification products for Departments of Motor Vehicles (DMVs). Integrating facial recognition software into the processing of driver's license applications should help combat identity fraud by making it extremely difficult for anyone to obtain multiple driver's licenses under assumed names.

Polaroid's press release stated that "computerized facial recognition works from a standard DMV photograph and does not require the collection of any additional information, making it convenient and non-invasive for the applicant. FaceIt extracts a 'face print' from the photograph, similar to a fingerprint, which is unique to the individual. This print is resistant to changes in lighting, skin tone, eyeglasses, facial expression and hairstyle. When a new license application is submitted, the face print extracted from the digital photograph will be used to search the DMV database of millions of faces for potential duplication. The speed of the FaceIt search engine makes it possible to process thousands of images in less time than it would take a DMV agent to scroll through and verify an individual's address or the spelling of their name in a computerized driver license record."[77]

According to the FaceIt Web site,[78] the product utilizes a mathematical technique called local feature analysis that "represents faces in terms of statistically derived features from specific regions of the face. These features are used as building blocks that make it possible to quickly map an individual's identity to a complex mathematical formula." Using this type of transformation for a new photo and for every picture in a photo database makes it possible to display quickly the closest matches in order of similarity. The mathematical "faceprint" can be compressed to 84 bytes. It is resistant to changes in lighting, skin tone, eyeglasses, facial expression, and hair and is robust with respect to pose variations, up to 35 degrees in all directions.

A number of other current or potential applications of facial recognition are mentioned on the FaceIt Web site. One of these is access control for PCs. A computer equipped with a video camera can lock a PC after a period of inactivity and start it again only after the user looks at the camera and is recognized by the software. The mathematical representation of the user's face can even be used as part of the key for encrypting information stored by the computer. Face recognition could be used in a similar way to control access to ATMs, thereby reducing the chances that stolen cards can be used or even eliminating the need for the cards. In time and attendance applications, facial recognition can make it unnecessary for employees to punch in and punch out. In a video surveillance application, a version of FaceIt can search live video of a crowd to find faces of individuals on a watch list. This might be used in an airport to identify known terrorists or in a department store to identify previously convicted shoplifters within minutes of their arrival. It might also be used to identify missing children.

QUESTIONS

1. The chapter emphasized that technology often has positive and negative effects. Identify some of the negative effects of this technology or explain why its effects are all positive.

2. Explain why you do or do not believe it may be necessary to create laws related to the proper use of this technology and the information it generates.

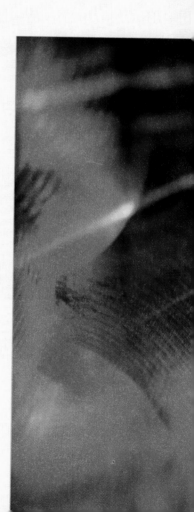

Computers in a Networked World

chapter8

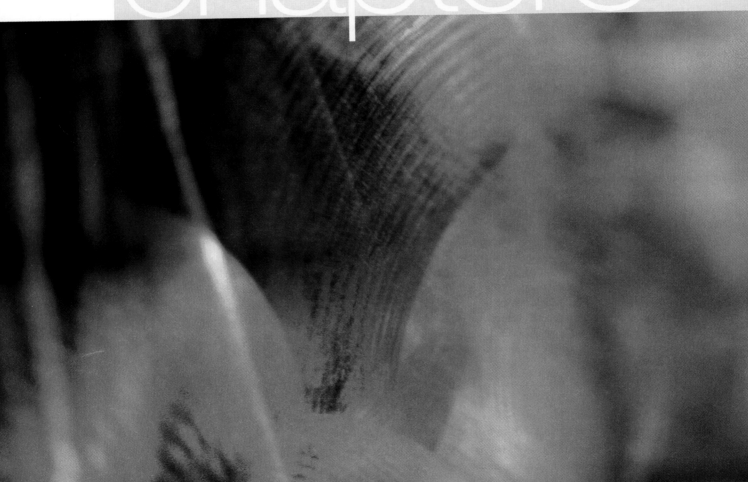

STUDY QUESTIONS

- Identify performance variables for computer technology.
- What are typical measures of performance for computer technology?
- What are the basic components of a computer system?
- What are the different types of computers?
- What are the organizational approaches to computing?
- How is client/server computing different from centralized computing?
- How is it possible for computers to process data of any type?
- What are the different approaches for increasing data manipulation speeds?
- What are the different forms of data input, storage, and output?

OUTLINE

Performance Variables for Information Technology
Functional Capabilities and Limitations
Ease of Use
Compatibility
Maintainability

Units of Measure for Technology Operation
Measuring Amounts of Data
Measuring Time
Measuring the Rate of Data Transfer
Measuring Clock Speed and Transmission Frequency
Measuring the Speed of Executing Instructions
Technology Performance from a Business Viewpoint

Overview of Computer Systems
Basic Model of a Computer System
Types of Computers

Four Approaches to Computing in Organizations
Centralized Computing
Personal Computing
Distributed Computing
Network Computing
Client/Server and Beyond

How Computers Manipulate Data
Converting Any Type of Information to Bits
Machine Language
Impact of Miniaturization and Integration on Performance
Other Approaches for Improving Performance

Data Input: Capturing Data
Keyboards and Pointing Devices
Optical Character Recognition
Capturing Pictures, Sounds, and Video

Storing and Retrieving Data
Paper and Micrographics
Magnetic Tapes and Disks
Optical Disks
Flash Memory
Smart Cards

Data Output: Displaying Data
Screen Outputs
Paper Outputs
Audio Outputs

Chapter Conclusion
Summary
Key Terms
Review Questions
Discussion Questions
Cases

OPENING CASE

NAPSTER.COM: USING THE WEB TO CHANGE THE RULES OF AN INDUSTRY

Napster.com came from nowhere to threaten the basic premises on which the recording industry operates.[1,2,3] After listening to a friend talk about wanting to be able to download songs from someone else's computer, a Northeastern University freshman named Shawn Fanning had an idea. Lots of people stored songs on their computers, often in the form of MP3 files whose compressed format stored one minute of near-CD quality sound in about a megabyte of storage. He created an online directory that listed these songs plus software for using the directory to download music from a computer whose owner leaves it running as a download site. This idea led to the creation of Napster.com, whose name came from Fanning's childhood nickname.

Napster.com created an overnight sensation. Suddenly music lovers could obtain music for free and without going to a record store. All they had to do was to log onto Napster.com and find what they wanted in the directory. Nap-

ster's user list zoomed to 20 million and soon the computer networks at many colleges were jammed with music downloads, a far cry from their initial purpose. Networks at some universities were so overwhelmed that the universities installed filters to prevent transmission of MP3 files.

The recording industry went to court, claiming that Napster's services were no more than a method for illegal copyright infringement. Much of the MP3 music had been copied from commercial CDs and reformatted as MP3 files. The original recordings were copyrighted, meaning that no one had the legal right to make and distribute copies. Napster's view was that it merely allowed users to share music, but in July 2000, a federal judge ruled that Napster contributed to copyright infringement in violation of the 1992 Audio Home Recording Act, which gave consumers a right to make digital copies of music for personal use. The court's injunction stopped the downloading of music that had been ripped from

CDs and agreed with the music industry's view that Napster is designed to facilitate music piracy. As the court case unfolded, Napster hustled to turn its audience of millions of users into a profitable business. In addition to providing the disputed capabilities, its site provided noncontroversial services such as downloading songs submitted voluntarily by little known artists in the hopes that their reputations would grow as listeners learned about their work.

Legal issues aside, the recording industry faced the prospect of vastly reduced revenues because much of the music they sold was now available for free. Many observers believed that regardless of how the case was settled the cat was out of the bag and the recording industry would have to come up with a different business model. Some suggested that a major recording company should try to exploit Napster's name recognition and user list by purchasing it and using it as the distribution channel for a subscription service. In late 2000 the CEO of Bertlesmann announced a deal in which Bertlesmann would loan cash-starved Napster $50 million to develop technology and services that would get users to pay for music instead of downloading it for free. While waiting to see how Napster would respond, Bertlesmann continued pursuing an industry lawsuit for blatant copyright infringement.[4]

On March 5, 2001, Napster responded to a court order by beginning to block a list of files submitted by a lawyer for Metallica and Dr. Dre. The blocking only operated on specific file names, and an intentional or unintentional misspelling such as "Fade 2 Black" instead of "Fade to Black" would not be detected. On March 6, 2001, a federal judge told the recording industry plaintiffs to notify Napster of the title of each song they want removed, the name of the recording artist and the names of the Napster files on which each appears. Napster would then have three days to comply by removing each of the files identified. The ruling acknowledged that "it would be difficult for plaintiffs to identity all infringing files on the Napster system given the transitory nature of its operation."[5]

WEB CHECK [✓]

Check the napster.com Web site and see what types of services it is providing, and at what price. If it is a free service, identify impacts on the property rights of artists and recording companies. If it has become a for-pay service, discuss how Napster pays artists and recording companies for using their material.

DEBATE TOPIC

Will the information-copying capabilities provided by Napster and similar Web businesses have a negative impact on innovations in software, video, and other information-based products that take great efforts to produce?

apster is not the first Internet-related company to leap to prominence in a short amount of time. Netscape, the company that produced the first readily available Web browser, was founded in April 1994. The Web wasn't even on the radar screen of most businesses, yet within six years either the Netscape browser or Microsoft's Internet Explorer were being used by millions of people who use the Web for work or pleasure. Napster was such a surprise because it used the Web in an unanticipated way. Instead of allowing users to search a music company or distributor's Web site to identify items to buy, it allowed users to search personal computers offering downloads at no charge. With this service one person could buy a CD-ROM and could transfer its songs to a thousand people who would pay nothing to the record company or musicians.

Aside from legal and ethical issues, the Napster case raises questions about the nature of computers and computer networks. On a technical level, Napster used the Internet to allow its users to locate and retrieve files stored on someone else's computer. In effect, the boundary between a user's computer and someone else's computer was being blurred because Napster made it possible to view a computer as a part of a much larger network for transferring audio files.

In today's highly networked world, an understanding of computers includes the computers themselves, software, and the networks they are a part of. Topics related to computers, software, and networks are presented in the following order:

Chapter 8, "Computers in a Networked World," focuses on computers, organizational approaches to computing, and computer peripherals. After identifying mea-

WORK   SYSTEM   SNAPSHOT

Napster.com provides a new way to obtain recorded music

CUSTOMERS
- People who want to download music for free

PRODUCTS & SERVICES
- Download of particular songs or other music

BUSINESS PROCESS
- Decide what music to obtain
- Use Napster's music directory to find a computer where this
  music is available for downloading
- Use Napster's software to link to that computer and perform
  the download

PARTICIPANTS	INFORMATION	TECHNOLOGY
• People who want to download music for free • People willing to store music on a computer and make it available to others	• Songs (in MP3 format) • Directory of songs stored in different computers	• Napster's software • Personal computers storing the music and receiving the download • The Internet (infrastructure)

sures of performance for computer technologies, it mentions different types of computers and looks at four organizational approaches for deploying computer systems. It also discusses the coding of information, trends toward even faster computing, and a variety of technologies for data input, storage, and output.

Chapter 9, "Software, Programming, and Artificial Intelligence," discusses software and programming by building on the discussion of databases and DBMS in Chapter 4. It presents basic concepts about programming and then looks at programming languages, other advances in programming, and operating systems. It links these topics to artificial intelligence issues that illustrate the current limits of software and programming.

Chapter 10, "Networks and Telecommunications," looks at networks and telecommunications, with special emphasis on different types of networks, different media for transmitting data, the role of standards, and the importance of telecommunications policy.

Chapter 13, "E-Business Security and Control," explains technical and organizational approaches for reducing threats from accidents and computer crime. The technical approaches emphasize preventing intrusions, encrypting data, and e-commerce techniques for validating transactions.

In combination, these chapters introduce technical background that business professionals need to participate effectively in efforts to exploit the potential of e-business. Part of this is always about how businesses can operate more efficiently and serve their customers better, but another part is usually about the capabilities and limitations of technology. Business professionals do not have to be technology experts, but they should have enough familiarity with basic concepts to think effectively about functions served by IT and to appreciate the nature of technical alternatives that might be considered.

PERFORMANCE VARIABLES FOR INFORMATION TECHNOLOGY

Table 8.1 shows that technology performance variables cluster under four headings: functional capabilities and limitations, ease of use, compatibility, and maintainability.

TABLE 8.1

Performance Variables for IT

GROUP OF PERFORMANCE VARIABLES	TYPICAL ISSUE RAISED WHEN USING THIS TERM TO DESCRIBE A PARTICULAR TECHNOLOGY
Functional capabilities and limitations	**What types of processing is the technology supposed to perform and what capabilities does it have?**
• Capacity	How much information can it store or process?
• Speed	How fast can it process data or instructions?
• Price-performance	How many dollars does it cost per amount of information stored or for a given calculation speed?
• Reliability	How long will it likely continue operating without errors or unplanned interruptions?
• Operating conditions	How much space does it take up? How much does it weigh? What temperature does it require? How much electricity does it use?
Ease of use	**How easy is it to use this technology?**
• Quality of user interface	How intuitive and easy to learn is the method for instructing the technology to perform its task?
• Ease of becoming proficient	How much effort is required to become proficient in using the technology?
• Portability	How easy is it for the user to move the technology in the course of doing work?
Compatibility	**How easy is it to get this technology to work with other complementary technologies?**
• Conformance to standards	To what extent does the technology conform to accepted industry standards?
• Interoperability	To what extent does the technology use the same internal coding and external interfaces as other technology it must operate with or substitute for?
Maintainability	**How easy is it to keep the technology operating over time?**
• Modularity	Is it divided into modules that can be snapped together when building systems? Can these modules be replaced by equivalent modules if necessary?
• Scalability	Is it possible to significantly increase or decrease capacity without major disruptions?
• Flexibility	Is it possible to change important aspects of system operation without major disruptions?

Notice that some of the terms used for IT performance are also used at other times for process or product performance.

Functional Capabilities and Limitations

The **functional capabilities** of a particular type of information technology identify the types of processing it is supposed to perform and the degree of capability it has. Functional capabilities are often measured as capacity or speed, using terms such as number of instructions executed per second, amount of data that can be stored, and rate of data transfer. Another aspect of technology performance is reliability, the likelihood that the technology will continue operating without errors or unplanned interruptions. A final aspect of functional capabilities is operating conditions, which include issues such as how much something weighs, how much space it takes, and how much electricity it uses. Although these questions may not seem to be technological issues, they often determine whether a particular technology, such as the laptop computer, is effective in a particular situation.

Because the productivity of a business process depends partially on the cost of the technology and other resources it uses, it is always important to think of performance in terms of **price-performance,** the relationship between the price of technology and the performance it provides. (The more general term is cost-effectiveness, the relationship between what something costs and how much it accomplishes.) For example, competition among personal computer manufacturers throughout the 1990s generated major improvements in both performance and price-performance. Computers became faster and more powerful (performance) at the same time that the price for any given level of processing power plummeted (price-performance). Similar improvements have occurred in all areas of computing for four decades.

Ease of Use

Ease of use includes ease of learning how to use the technology, ease of setting it up, ease of becoming proficient, and ease of using it directly. Everyday experience with audio equipment such as a Walkman or a CD player shows that features that contribute to ease of use include size, portability, user interface, and compatibility with technology standards such as the dimensions of the tape cassette. These same aspects of ease of use apply for business technology such as telephones and computers.

Compatibility

Compatibility is important because most information technology is genuinely useful only in combination with other information technology. **Compatibility** is the extent to which the characteristics and features of a particular technology fit with those of other technologies that are also used in the situation. You know the importance of compatibility and conformance to standards if you have ever wanted to plug a hair dryer built for the American market into a typical wall socket in Europe or Asia. The plug's shape is not compatible with the outlet's shape, and the hair dryer won't operate unless you have a special adapter. IT compatibility issues range from "technical" details, such as internal machine languages and data coding methods, to mundane issues such as the size of paper in copy machines and the shape of plugs.

Compatibility issues arise at several different levels. At one level, maintenance of two devices or programs is simpler if both of them operate according to the same standards even if they do not have to work together. At another level, the question is whether the two devices or programs can be used together, even if they use different brands of hardware or different computer languages. This type of compatibility is called **interoperability**. An essential feature of Internet technology is the way it applies standards to permit convenient usage through a wide variety of otherwise incompatible computers and networks.

Maintainability

Maintainability is the ease with which users or technical specialists can keep the technology running and upgrade it to suit the changing needs of the situation. It is easier to maintain technology if the components are designed for **modularity**, separation into a set of components that can be developed, tested, and understood independently and then plugged into other related components to create a system or device. Dividing systems into modules makes them easier to build and understand because solving many small problems is usually easier than solving one big problem. The modules work together based on the way the outputs of one become the inputs of others. **Scalability**, the ability to significantly increase or decrease capacity without major disruptions, is another important aspect of maintainability because upgrading capacity beyond certain limits often requires a complete change in the technology. For example it is possible to hitch a trailer behind most cars, but if the trailer is too big the car can't drive safely and it is necessary to switch to a truck.

UNITS OF MEASURE FOR TECHNOLOGY OPERATION

An unavoidable part of the basic vocabulary for discussing computers and peripherals is the units of measure used to describe amounts of data and rates of processing. These terms involve things such as the amount of information (number of bits and bytes), time (milliseconds and microseconds), speed of processing (MIPS, FLOPS, bits per second), and frequencies. Familiarity with these technical terms is useful because

[R E M I N D E R]

The discussion of user friendliness in Chapter 7 explains major issues related to ease of use.

people use them to talk about computer and telecommunications devices just as they talk about cars using number of passengers, gas tank capacity, number of cylinders, miles per hour, and miles per gallon.

Measuring Amounts of Data

A key characteristic of any computer is how much data it stores and processes. Amounts of data are described using the terms *bit, byte, kilobyte, megabyte, gigabyte,* and *terabyte*. A **bit** is a binary digit, namely, a 0 or 1. This chapter will show how any number, letter, or even picture or sound can be represented as a set of bits. A **byte** is 8 bits, whose 256 different possible combinations are sufficient to represent 256 different characters, including all ten digits (0, 1, 2, 3, . . .), all 26 uppercase and 26 lowercase letters (a, b, c, . . .), and all the common special characters (:, ;, @, #, $, . . .). The storage of computers is described in kilobytes, megabytes, gigabytes, and terabytes.

kilobyte (KB)	approximately 10^3 (one thousand) bytes
megabyte (MB)	approximately 10^6 (one million) bytes
gigabyte (GB)	approximately 10^9 (one billion) bytes
terabyte (TB)	approximately 10^{12} (one trillion) bytes

The term *kilobyte* is slightly inaccurate because it usually refers to 2^{10} bytes, which is actually 1,024 bytes. Similarly, megabyte is really 2^{20} bytes or 1,048,576 bytes, and the same pattern applies for gigabyte and terabyte. The random access memory (RAM) in the first PCs was described in kilobytes, such as 16 KB or 64 KB. Now it is described in megabytes, such as 128 MB or 256 MB. Typical computer diskettes can store 1.4 MB. Typical capacities for hard disks in early personal computers were 10 MB or 40 MB. Hard disk capacities in today's inexpensive personal computers often exceed 10 GB.

Measuring Time

Because computers operate at speeds that are difficult to imagine, the typical time units for discussing their operation are fractions of seconds.

millisecond	10^{-3} (one thousandth of a) second
microsecond	10^{-6} (one millionth of a) second
nanosecond	10^{-9} (one billionth of a) second
picosecond	10^{-12} (one trillionth of a) second

Hard disks for PCs can access data in 7 to 10 milliseconds. Computers can execute machine language instructions in fractions of a microsecond. The switching speed of a semiconductor circuit is around 200 picoseconds, although switching speeds of 2 picoseconds have been produced in research labs.

Measuring the Rate of Data Transfer

Data transmission is measured in **bits per second** (**bps**) or in thousands or millions of bits per second (kbps or mbps). The speed of data transfer over telephone lines and fiber optics depends partly on the medium and partly on the speed of the devices that encode and decode the message. Typical modems on PCs operate at 56 kpbs, although cable modems can operate at 1.5 mbps. Data travel over fiber optic cable at 100 mbps or more. The engineering term **baud** is sometimes used instead of bits per second. Baud refers to the rate of signal changes per second. If a device can send only off-on signals, its bits per second rate equals its baud rate. Higher speed devices that transmit individual signals with gradations finer than just 0 versus 1 can send messages whose bits per second rate is higher than their baud rate.

Measuring Clock Speed and Transmission Frequency

Hertz is a measure of frequency. The internal clocks in most personal computers operate between 700 MHz and 1.5 GHz. Data transmissions are broadcast at different frequencies. For example, AM radio is broadcast in the range around 1 MHz, FM radio is around 100 MHz, and satellite transmissions are around 10 GHz. Although clock speed is strongly related to computer speed, many other factors such as the computer's internal machine language affect a computer's data processing speed.

Hertz (Hz)	1 cycle per second
kilohertz (KHz)	10^3 cycles per second
megahertz (MHz)	10^6 cycles per second
gigahertz (GHz)	10^9 cycles per second

Measuring the Speed of Executing Instructions

The terms *MIPS, FLOPS, megaflops,* and *gigaflops* are used to describe the speed of executing instructions. **MIPS** is an abbreviation for one *million instructions per second.* It typically is used in a context such as, "This microprocessor can operate at 500 MIPS." The term **FLOPS** stands for *floating point operations per second.* Floating point operations are the addition, subtraction, multiplication, and division of decimal numbers. FLOPS are a better measure than MIPS for talking about the computing power of computers used to do complex scientific calculations. Millions, billions, and trillions of FLOPS are called megaflops, gigaflops, and teraflops, respectively.

Although they are indicators of a computer's speed, MIPS and FLOPS tell only part of the story because the effective speed of a computer system also depends on other factors, such as internal data transfer speed and disk speed. Different types of computers also accomplish different amounts of work while operating at the same speed because they use different internal computer languages and process data in different-sized chunks.

Technology Performance from a Business Viewpoint

Business professionals not directly involved with the IT industry often find the onslaught of product announcements and technical jargon overwhelming. What are they to make of all these announcements and all the new technical terminology? For example, how should they decide whether it would be worthwhile to switch from a 333 MHz Pentium II to a 1.5 GHz Pentium IV?

From a business professional's viewpoint, it is important to separate two issues: (1) What does the organization want to accomplish? (2) What combination of currently available hardware and software provides the necessary capabilities, and at what cost? A given technological advance may support business capabilities that would otherwise be impractical or impossible. Alternatively, an advance may simply reduce costs compared to other methods for performing similar functions. Another possibility is that the more advanced technology will have no effect whatsoever because another part of the system is the limiting factor in overall performance. For example, the upgrade to a more powerful microprocessor might have no discernable impact on simple word processing but might make it possible to use voice recognition software that cannot operate effectively on a slow machine. Even when marveling at the incredible technical progress that has occurred, it is always worthwhile to remember that technology is just one part of a larger work system that also includes business processes, information, and human participants.

R E A L I T Y C H E C K

Performance Variables for Information Technology

The text cites a number of performance variables related to functional capabilities, ease of use, compatibility, and maintainability.

1. Explain how each of these characteristics does or does not apply to information technology you are familiar with, such as a personal computer or a home audio system.

2. Identify which of these characteristics seemed important the last time you or someone you know made a purchase related to using this technology.

OVERVIEW OF COMPUTER SYSTEMS

A **computer** is a device that can execute previously stored instructions. Because the instructions for performing a particular task are called a **program**, computers are programmable devices. A **computer system** consists of computers and other devices that capture, transmit, store, retrieve, manipulate, and display data by executing programs. Table 1.5 in Chapter 1 defined each of these functions and showed some of the devices or technologies used to perform each of them. The physical devices in a computer system are its **hardware**. The programs are its **software**. Later in this chapter we will look in more detail at devices for capturing, storing, retrieving, and displaying information. Chapter 10, "Networks and Telecommunications," will discuss data transmission.

Basic Model of a Computer System

In the late 1940s, John von Neumann and his colleagues published a description of the internal architecture of an idealized electronic computer. Most computers from that time until today are based on extensions of this architecture, which involves a unit that performs calculations, a unit that controls the sequence of operations, a memory that holds data and programs, and input and output units. The earliest computers used vacuum tubes to store data. The basic component for storing data and programs while they are being used by today's computers is a zero-one semiconductor switch called a transistor, first invented at Bell Labs in 1948. Further breakthroughs such as the ability to embed an entire circuit on a chip (the integrated circuit) and the first microprocessor design did not arrive until 1958 and 1971, respectively.

Figure 8.1 illustrates a typical personal computer system. In today's personal computers, one or more microprocessors chips made of silicon dioxide decode and execute programs, thereby serving as the computer's **central processing unit (CPU)**. Microprocessors are linked to another type of semiconductor chip, **random access memory (RAM)**, which stores instructions and data the microprocessor executes or works on. The term random access implies that the microprocessor can directly address and access any data location in the RAM. A related term encountered frequently in discussions of computers is **read only memory (ROM)**. Programs stored in this permanent memory cannot be changed. They control internal computer activities such as the way the computer boots up when it is turned on.

Input devices used for entering instructions and data into computers start with a keyboard and mouse. Other input devices include scanners, voice input devices, electronic cameras, touch screens, and electronic tablets. An **output device** displays data to people. The output devices for computers start with a monitor and printer, and can also include speakers for sound output. **Storage devices** hold programs and data for future processing. Typical storage devices for computers include hard disks, floppy disk (diskette) drives, and other devices such as zip drives that are used for backups and transferring data between non-networked computers. Because input, output, and storage devices are usually considered to be options separate from the computer itself, they are often called **peripherals**.

Types of Computers

The original concept of computation, storage, input, and output has developed into many types of computers. This section focuses on computers whose users see them as computers rather than as components of other machines. A computer that is an internal component of another machine is called an **embedded computer**. Machines ranging from airplanes to television sets and automatic coffee makers contain embedded computers. Embedded computers used for controlling chemical and mechanical processes in industry are essential components of information systems for factory automation.

Nonembedded computers are classified based on a combination of power, speed, and ability to control or link to other computers or terminals. A reasonable first cut at

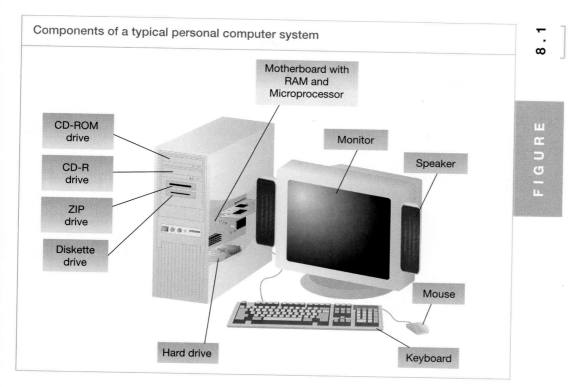

Components of a typical personal computer system

FIGURE 8.1

computer categories includes personal computer, workstation, midrange computer, mainframe, and supercomputer. Although these categories have merged somewhat and have become less meaningful, they are still part of everyday terminology and they help in visualizing new options related to networked computer systems.

A **personal computer (PC)** is a single-user computer that sits on a desktop or can be carried around by the user. **Laptop** and **notebook computers** are portable PCs that fit into a briefcase but contain enough computing power and disk storage to support a business professional's personal requirements for word processing, spreadsheets, and storage of documents. **Personal digital assistants (PDAs)** and **palmtop computers** are small, handheld devices with enough computing power to store personal information such as address and phone lists, to-do lists, and current documents. PDAs typically synchronize data with a PC using a cable or wireless transmission and provide a pen-like stylus for making choices and entering simple printed data (see Figure 8.2). A **workstation** is a powerful single-user computer used for computing-intensive work such as complex data analysis, graphic design, and engineering. Workstations often come with large screens needed to work with complex images. Although the first PCs could run only simple word processors, spreadsheets, and specialized applications, technical advances in hardware and software permit current PCs to perform tasks previously reserved for workstations.

Current PCs and laptops are typically advertised in terms of their processing power, storage, and input and output devices. Processing power is summarized by the type of microprocessor, and by the amount of RAM and hard disk memory. For example, the headline on a typical ad might mention a desktop computer with a 1.5 GHz Pentium IV microprocessor, 256 MB of RAM, and a 20 GB hard drive. Input and output features include the type of display and size of the screen, the speed of the modem, the speed of the CD-ROM drive, and the type of sound card. Other technical features such as internal data transfer rates are also mentioned frequently because they affect the computer's speed in processing instructions and moving data.

Midrange computers and mainframes typically perform processing for a large number of users working at terminals. **Midrange computers** (previously called minicomputers) are centralized computers typically shared by a department for processing

FIGURE 8.2

Portable computers

(a)

(b)

(a) This laptop computer contains more processing power than a top-end desktop computer had only several years earlier. (b) This pen computer is used for data input where a keyboard would not work. PDAs provide a palm-sized version of related capabilities.

transactions, accessing corporate databases, and generating reports. **Mainframe** computers are even more powerful; they typically are linked to hundreds or even thousands of terminals for processing high volumes of online transactions and generating reports from large databases. Mainframe systems contain extensive data storage capabilities. The tape library might contain thousands of tapes, and the computer center could include hundreds of hard disk units containing enormous databases. Printed outputs could be produced on high-speed printers at centralized locations or on low-speed printers at end-user locations. Mainframes are usually housed in environmentally controlled and physically secure computer rooms. **Supercomputers** were initially thought of as computers designed for exceptionally high-volume, high-speed calculation, rather than transaction processing. Such computers have been used for complex analysis problems such as simulations of the weather or the flow of air around a wing. More recent applications include banking, manufacturing, and data mining applications.

Twenty years ago the CPUs of mainframe computers operated at a much higher MIPS rate than minicomputers, which were much faster than the early PCs. By the 1990s, these computer categories started to break down, hastened by the fact that the cost per MIPS for PCs is far lower than for mainframes. Improvements in raw computing power do not mean that PCs can replace centralized computers, however. Using PCs for applications that formerly ran on mainframes requires that they be linked together in a network. Midrange computers and mainframes are designed to accept inputs from many simultaneous users. PCs cannot support this type of application, regardless of whether they can perform an individual user's numerical calculations at the speed of a larger computer.

The trend toward computer networks has spawned a newer category of computers that overlaps with all the others. **Servers** are specialized computers linked to other computers on a network in order to perform specific types of tasks requested through those computers. Low-end servers are basically powerful PCs configured to perform specific tasks, such as finding data in a database, controlling printing, or controlling

FIGURE 8.3

A server farm that supports high-volume Web operations

This is an example of a server farm at a large scale Web-hosting facility.

electronic mail. High-end servers perform similar functions for larger networks or larger databases and often compete with midrange computers or even mainframes. For example, in September 2000, Hewlett-Packard's announcement of its Superdome product line said that a single server might contain 16, 32, or 64 CPUs operating at 552 MHz, up to 128 GB of memory per cabinet, and up to 192 input/output ports. (Figure 8.3 shows a "server farm" used to support high-volume Web operations.) Many observers believe that mainframe computers gradually will evolve into database servers that control and update large databases. In October 2000 IBM rebranded its entire line of mainframe computers as "e-servers" in order to simplify the brand image of the product choices it provides. IBM's president said, "This is clearly the largest announcement out of IBM for the last two or three years."[6]

You will understand more about the role of servers after the following discussion of approaches to computing in organizations, including client/server.

FOUR APPROACHES TO COMPUTING IN ORGANIZATIONS

Computer systems should be deployed in a way that mirrors business processes. If people work individually and rarely share their work products, computer systems should provide effective tools for individual work. If people work as a group, computer systems should make it easier to share work. If the organization relies on a central database for orders, reservations, or inventory, computer systems should provide access to the database.

Figure 8.4 shows four alternative approaches to computing in organizations. First comes **centralized computing**, in which all the processing for multiple users is done by a large central computer. In **personal computing**, users have their own machines and rarely share data or resources. In **distributed computing**, users may have their own computers and the organization uses a network to share data and resources. In **network computing**, some of the computing is done on each user's computer, but the processing is controlled centrally. Each approach raises its own management issues

FIGURE 8.4

Four approaches to computing in organizations

Approach to computing	Basic idea of the approach	Advantages	Disadvantages
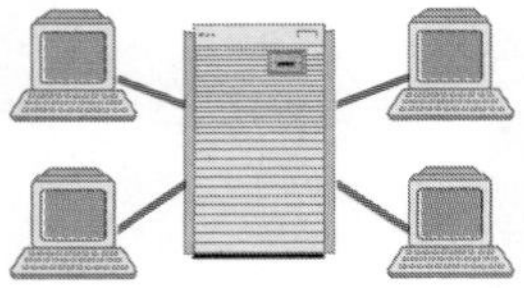	In **centralized computing**, terminals are attached to a central computer that performs all the computations and controls all the peripherals, such as printers.	• Greater security because all processing is controlled at a central location	• Central computer must perform computing and must do work to control the remote terminals • Total reliance on the central computer; if it goes down, so does the entire system
	In **personal computing**, individual microcomputers are used for individual work but are not linked in a network.	• Greater flexibility for individual users doing inherently individual work • Less impact from what others are doing using a computer	• Difficulty sharing the work individuals do • Duplication of underutilized hardware and software
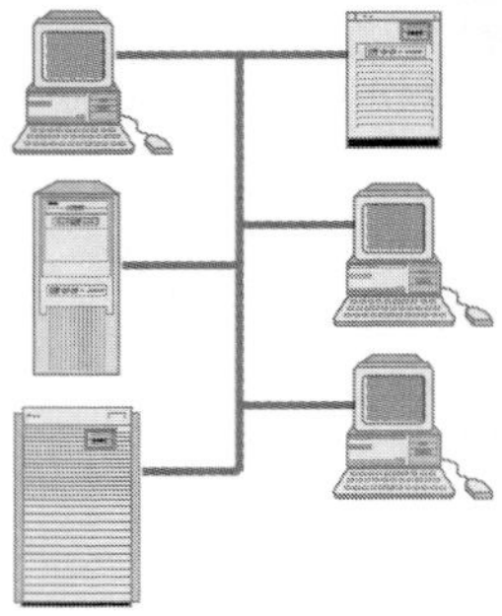	In **distributed computing**, multiple workstations are linked to share data and computing resources. The data and resources may be at the local site or may be elsewhere.	• Greater ability to share work, information, and resources • Ability to continue doing some useful work even if part of the network is down	• Complex to administer • Security more difficult because computing and data are so spread out
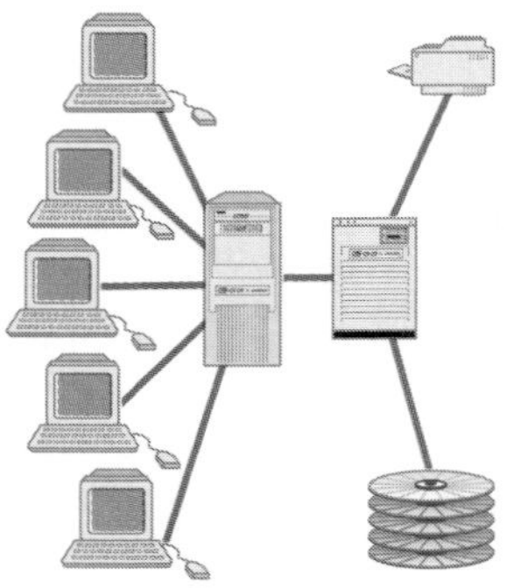	In **network computing**, multiple network computers are linked to a central server that controls their operation and that provides links to other servers.	• Greater ability to share work, information, and resources • Easier to administer than distributed computing	• Reliance on a central server • Limited processing ability at user's computer

With the first computer systems, centralized computing was the only option. Personal computing arose as an alternative providing more flexibility to individual users. Distributed computing uses a network to share data and resources. Network computing tries to combine the benefits of centralized computing with the flexibility and responsiveness of distributed computing.

concerning the effective and efficient use of data and equipment. Although the four approaches are introduced separately here, they may be combined in many ways in practice.

Centralized Computing

This approach involves a single mainframe or midrange computer that performs the processing for multiple users. The first computerized systems for business transaction processing operated in batch mode and used punched cards for data input and storage. Later, online transaction processing permitted multiple users at terminals to perform transactions simultaneously. In this original form of online transaction processing, every input went directly from the terminals to the central computer, and it controlled all outputs to the users. The terminals in these systems were eventually called **dumb terminals** because they could not actually process information and served only as an input/output mechanism linking users with the central computer.

Using centralized computing to service multiple users has many shortcomings. First, the computer has to perform two types of work: It has to do the computing for the users, and it has to manage the status and progress of work being done for each online user. The operating system software that keeps track of the jobs uses a lot of the CPU's processing power. As a result, a substantial percentage of the available computing resources goes toward controlling the job stream rather than accomplishing the work the users want. A second shortcoming is total reliance on the central computer. No work can be done using the dumb terminal if the computer or the telecommunications line goes down. A third shortcoming is the tight schedules and controls required to balance the computer's workload to avoid peak-load problems when people across the organization want to use it simultaneously. These procedures support the processing scheduled in advance but limit users' flexibility in doing their own work.

Despite these problems of centralized computing, centralized functions are needed for many business operations. For example, order entry functions in many businesses such as airlines, distributors, and large manufacturers require online access to central databases by geographically dispersed users. Centralized computing has evolved in many ways to perform these functions while reducing the problems of totally centralized processing by moving some of the processing to other computers on the network. In addition, various forms of redundancy have been built in to improve overall system reliability.

Personal Computing

Computer system deployment changed dramatically in the late 1970s when personal computers first provided computing to individuals and small businesses at an affordable price. In the 1980s, worldwide shipments of personal computers exceeded the shipments of the large-scale systems that had previously dominated the market. The basic idea of personal computing is that a computer should be available as a tool for individual work at any time. This approach is particularly effective for inherently individual work such as word processing, spreadsheets, presentations, personal calendars, and simple graphic design work. It also succeeds for small companies whose limited record keeping fits on a PC.

Major advances have occurred in areas where the first PCs were especially weak, such as awkward user interfaces, limited software capabilities, and data and software storage only on diskettes. A **graphical user interface (GUI)** allowed the use of a mouse or other pointing device to express commands by selecting icons or entries on pull-down menus. This advance provided a more user-friendly interface by eliminating the need to memorize command languages, filenames, and other details that previously made personal computing difficult for nonprogrammers. Storage of data and programs on hard disks made it easier to start programs, access data, and work with several programs at the same time. As the power of microprocessors increased, software such as spreadsheets and word processors could provide many more capabilities and operate much faster. PCs can support several activities at once; for example, they permit a user to print out a large document while doing other work on the computer. Portable laptop computers provided additional convenience because they run on rechargeable batteries and can be used even if an electric plug is unavailable for several hours. Overall, personal computing made computer usage practical and affordable on a much wider scale.

Distributed Computing

Despite all these advances, personal computing is a limited approach because people in organizations work together. Even departments that enthusiastically embraced PCs soon felt the need for individuals to share information and computing resources. The information included databases, phone messages, memos, and work in progress such as drafts of documents. The resources included computers, printers, fax machines, and external databases.

In distributed computing, individuals do their own work on PCs or workstations and use a telecommunications network to link to other devices. Distributed computing improves coordination, helps in sharing data, messages, and work products, and permits sharing of resources such as printers. Data, messages, and work products are shared in two ways. First, an individual may send a message or file to other computers on the network. Second, an individual may access data residing on a hard disk attached to a different computer on the network. For example, an insurance adjuster using a portable computer can upload the day's data from a central database. Later, an insurance pricing analyst might access the claims database through another part of the network. The sharing of printers is accomplished by designating a computer on the network as a print server and sending print jobs to that computer.

Unfortunately the advantages of distributed computing come with a price: the need for controls and administration that make it more complex than personal computing. The need for greater controls is apparent from the fact that a given user on a network may want to share some files but restrict access to others. For example, a supervisor may wish to share work-related files with subordinates but keep employee salary review files private. (Similarly, a Napster user would want to allow access to songs but not access to personal information.) Restricting access to specific files makes it necessary to state explicitly who can access which files. It is also critical to enforce standards to facilitate access to data controlled by someone else. The result is a more restricted environment than personal computing, but one in which a group of people can work more effectively. The degree to which computing should be distributed depends on trade-offs between data transmission costs, user convenience, maintainability, and security.

Network Computing

One response to the complexity of distributed computing is to step back and ask whether networks of powerful PCs are unnecessarily expensive to maintain. In 1997 the Gartner Group estimated that the total cost of ownership for a networked PC in a large organization was $9,785. Of this surprisingly large amount, the desktop equipment accounted for only $1,850, and technical support and administration, end-user operations, and network costs totaled $2,011, $3,464, and $2,460, respectively.[7] More recent surveys of the total cost of ownership have produced similar results. A major part of the hardware and support costs comes from users changing configurations, installing nonstandard applications, and plugging in cards, thereby making every machine unique and greatly complicating troubleshooting and maintenance. Some users also cause expensive crises by downloading programs infected with viruses.

Network computing is an approach that addresses these problems by trying to combine the traditional benefits of centralization with the flexibility and responsiveness of distributed computing. This approach is based on networks of stripped-down personal computers sometimes called **network computers** (**NCs**) or **thin clients**. The NCs do not contain hard disks, and therefore cannot store programs or data. The programs and data are all stored on centralized servers that download to the NCs whatever programs and data they may need at a particular time. Because NCs are designed to be controlled through a network and do not have a hard disk, they are designed to run under special operating systems designed for NCs, rather than under typical desktop operating systems. Aside from using cheaper computers, centralizing the data and the programs eliminates much activity related to updating software versions and assuring data security and consistency. Key disadvantages of network computing are its reliance on centralized control and the relative immaturity of software designed to support this approach.

The initial debate about PCs versus NCs was surprisingly vehement. In some ways the NC seemed a manager's dream: a closed box with no slots for inserting messy diskettes or CD-ROMs, a way to eliminate some of the costly individualism of the PC environment, and a way to prevent workers from installing their favorite software. "What's a floppy disk?" asked Scott McNealy, CEO of Sun Microsystems. "It's a way to steal company secrets." Bill Gates, CEO of Microsoft, responded to NC promoters by saying they were trying to "portray PCs as an evil." He said the campaign against PCs espouses "grinch management," a shortsighted effort to take tools away from workers and control their behavior.[8] The initial versions of NCs were not commercial successes, in part because the cost of PCs dropped. Several forms of thin clients exist now and are being used for some corporate applications. Regardless of whether NCs replace PCs in corporate networks, the reasons for considering the NCs in the first place will likely lead to improvements in both software and administrative procedures that will reduce some of the excessive costs of administering and supporting networked PCs.

Client/Server and Beyond

The previous section introduced four ways to deploy computers in organizations. Because there is both speculation and controversy about the relative advantages of different forms of distributed computing and network computing, we will look at this in more detail. We start with the client/server concept, which was developed as part of the original architecture of the Internet, and which remains the basis of this important tool.

In **client/server architecture**, different devices (or processes) on the network are treated as clients or servers. The client devices send requests for service, such as printing or retrieval of data, to specific server devices that perform the requested processing. For example, the client devices might consist of ten workstations within a department, and server devices might be a laser printer and a specialized computer, called a **file server**, dedicated to retrieving data from a database. In many networks, the file server is a powerful computer containing special data retrieval and network management capabilities. Some networks use other types of specialized servers such as print servers that execute requests for printing, mail servers that handle electronic mail, and communication servers that link the network to other external networks.

Although the computers themselves are often called servers, the client/server model is really about software and is actually a programming model. Within this model, a server is a program that fulfills requests it receives from other programs called client programs. The client programs and server programs may or may not run on the same physical machine. When you use the Web, your browser is the client program. It conveys requests to server programs called Web servers or application servers that may be running on computers almost anywhere in the world. The Web servers or application servers receive the request you enter into your browser, interpret it, compile the appropriate response, and send it back to your browser program (the client).

In effect, client/server computing is a way to modularize the work performed by computers. Figure 8.5 shows the difference between client/server and centralized mainframe computing in terms of the division of labor in handling the user interface, application program logic, and database access. Instead of having a mainframe computer control everything from the displays on user terminals through the application

FIGURE 8.5

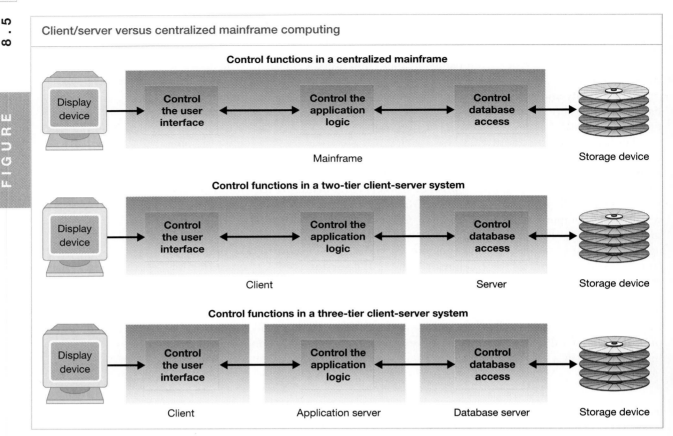

Client/server versus centralized mainframe computing

With the centralized mainframe approach, the central computer controls the user interface, the application logic, and database access. Permitting the same program to control aspects of all three elements makes it much more difficult to change the software over time. With a two-tier client/server, the application programs and user interface are controlled by the client workstation, and database access is controlled by the server. With a three-tier approach, application logic is controlled by an application server that links to both the client and a database server.

logic and database updates, client/server divides these functions between specialized client and server components. There are actually many different forms of client/server computing depending on factors such as the volume of transactions, whether the application is mission-critical, and whether the application is localized or enterprise-wide. The two-tier client/server approach shown in the figure is typically used in simpler situations. The three-tier approach is preferred for mission-critical, enterprise-wide systems that require stringent controls.

The advantages of client/server computing include user convenience, technical scalability, and greater ability to accommodate and maintain hardware and software from different vendors. User convenience starts with having a powerful PC that can serve personal computing needs but can also link into a network. Attaching a PC to a network instead of using a dumb terminal also means that the graphical user interface and the validation of data no longer have to be controlled by an overworked central computer. Scalability is enhanced because it is easier and less disruptive to add or enhance individual client or server devices instead of modifying a centralized system.

A client/server approach may accommodate hardware and software from different vendors with reasonable ease because the interfaces between each vendor's products and the other parts of the network are becoming more like off-the-shelf products. For example, a client device might request particular customer data from a network without "knowing" the type of database management system the server uses to store the data. The query simply goes to the right server, which contains off-the-shelf software that can interpret the query for the type of database it is using.

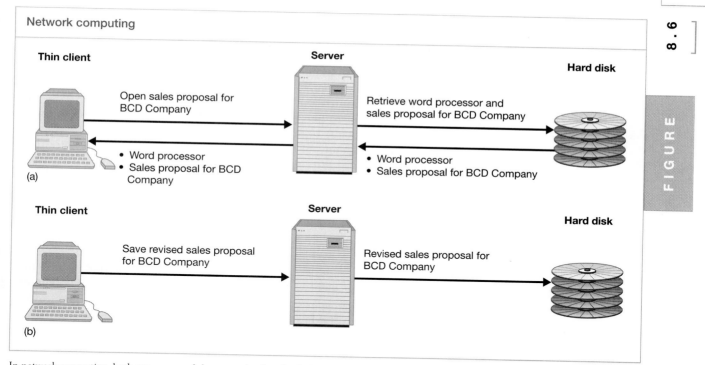

Network computing

Thin client

Server

Hard disk

Open sales proposal for
BCD Company

Retrieve word processor and
sales proposal for BCD Company

- Word processor
- Sales proposal for BCD
  Company

- Word processor
- Sales proposal for BCD Company

(a)

Thin client

Server

Hard disk

Save revised sales proposal
for BCD Company

Revised sales proposal for
BCD Company

(b)

FIGURE 8.6

In network computing, both programs and data must be downloaded from a server to the "thin client." (a) The downloading of an existing sales proposal and a word processor to the client. (b) The revised document is saved through the server.

Network computing can be viewed as a variant of client/server that puts more of the processing in the server. The client computer in this approach is called a thin client because it does not store programs or data. Figure 8.6 shows how network computing applies client/server principles without storing programs or data on the client. The user logs on and wants to modify a word processing document. The server downloads the document along with the word processor. If the work reaches the point where additional programs or data are needed, the client detects this need, automatically conveys that request to the server, and receives the required programs or data. The user completes the document and stores it on a hard disk attached to the server. The user turns off the computer and the program modules that were used are erased from the client.

Middleware The common requirement for using different types of hardware and software on the same network generated a need for new programming methods. These methods divide programming tools between client tools, such as methods for creating graphical user interfaces and validating data inputs, and server tools, such as database management systems. Between the client tools and server tools is another category of tools called middleware. **Middleware** controls communication between clients and servers and performs whatever translation is necessary to make a client's request understandable to the server. There are several types of middleware. Distributed database middleware provides a common, high-level programming interface, such as structured query language (SQL), that packages information so that it can be used by multiple applications. In contrast, message-oriented middleware facilitates interaction with other applications and operating systems by sending data or requests in the form of messages.

Despite its advantages, client/server computing also has disadvantages. Many early adopters of client/server computing found that it increases data and system administration efforts. In addition, the interfaces and middleware translations between modular components consume computing time and therefore may slow down the network.

The separation between clients and servers also requires using rapidly changing programming methods that are unfamiliar to many programmers.

Peer-to-Peer   Peer-to-peer architecture is an important alternative to client/server for small computer networks. In **peer-to-peer**, each workstation can communicate directly with every other workstation on the network without going through a specialized server. In effect, each computer on the network can play the role of a server for the others on the network. Peer-to-peer is appropriate when the network users mostly do their own work but occasionally need to exchange data. In these cases, it may be more efficient to keep data and copies of the software at each workstation to avoid the delays of downloading data and software each time a user gets started. Peer-to-peer has potential problems, however, in security and consistency. For example, with data at someone else's workstation, the data may be difficult to retrieve when that person is out of the office and the workstation is shut off.

Napster used the Internet's client/server architecture to simulate an enormous peer-to-peer network of personal computers. Its approach is not actually peer-to-peer because the computer requesting a file goes through Napster's centralized directory. Subsequent developments in programs such as Gnutella created actual peer-to-peer networks on the Internet because the search does not go through a central computer.

Although the various forms of client/server, network computing, and peer-to-peer differ from traditional mainframe computing in the way they divide computing and data transmission tasks, they still require human infrastructure to perform many of the same centralized chores required in mainframe computing. Someone must set up the network and maintain it. Someone must make sure that the data files are defined properly, that the network provides adequate performance, and that it is secure from misuse. If the network delivers the software to the workstations, someone must make sure that the software is updated appropriately and that users know when it is updated. The combination of new administrative burdens and unfamiliar and sometimes immature programming technology have led many industry observers to question exaggerated claims about the benefits of these newer technologies, regardless of the fact that they put a high-MIPS microprocessor close to the user.

R E A L I T Y C H E C K   [✓]

Approaches to Computing in Organizations

This section identifies four approaches to computing in organizations: centralized computing, personal computing, distributed computing, and network computing.

1.   Identify times (if any) when you have used a computer system of each type.

2.   Referring back to the performance variables in Table 8.1, explain how each approach felt different from a user's viewpoint. If you have used only one or several, explain how you think the others might feel different to a user.

HOW COMPUTERS MANIPULATE DATA

With this background on types of computers and organizational approaches to computing, we can now take a deeper look at what actually happens inside a computer system. We will introduce a series of computer-oriented topics, each of which will help you appreciate something about the way computers are used in business. Understanding the coding of data will help you understand why a single picture may be worth 10,000 words but may use 100 times as much storage in a computer system. Similarly, it will help you see why video conferencing requires far greater data transmission capabilities than e-mail. The discussion of the semiconductors inside the computer helps you understand why it has been possible to shrink computer sizes and make computers portable.

Converting any Type of Information to Bits

According to the famed technologist Danny Hillis, "The Internet will become the universal system for the delivery of information, and every communications and media company, as well as every government agency, will need to adapt to the new digital reality: all information can be made into bits, and bits are going to find their way to the consumers that want them."[9] To understand what Hillis means, you need to understand the way any type of data including numbers, text, pictures, and sounds can be coded for processing by machines. This is not just a technical detail because it helps in understanding the capabilities and limits of current computers.

Binary Representation of Numbers   Before a computer can process data, the data must be converted into a form the computer can process. This section will show how any type of data (numbers, text, images, and sounds) can be represented as organized set of bits (0's and 1's). Representing data as a series of bits is especially efficient because digital computers are built from components that switch between off-on (0-1) states.

Consistent with their off-on internal components, computers perform calculations using the base 2, or binary, number system. Figure 8.7 shows binary addition and multiplication tables to illustrate the advantage of using binary representation for the internal operations within a computer. The addition and multiplication tables involve only four entries instead of 100 entries that would be required for base 10 tables. The small number of entries in the binary tables simplifies the internal circuitry inside the computer. Because people work with base 10 numbers, computers automatically convert these numbers into binary form before they perform calculations. They then change the results back into base 10 for use by people. Figure 8.8 explains how to convert a number from our everyday base 10 number system into binary.

Binary Representation of Text   The memory in most computers is organized in groups of eight bits. Eight bits, or one byte, is enough to uniquely identify 256 different characters (digits, uppercase and lowercase letters, punctuation marks, and special characters such as $ or @). The 256 possible configurations of a single byte can represent all characters used in English and most other languages that have alphabets. However, 256 different characters are not sufficient for coding the thousands of different Chinese characters, or kanji.

The industry requirement for standard ways of coding data comes from the frequent need to move data between different brands of computers even if their internal operation is inconsistent. **ASCII** is one of several standard codes for representing letters, digits, and special characters on computer systems. ASCII stands for American Standard Code for Information Interchange. Table 8.2 shows how ASCII-8 represents

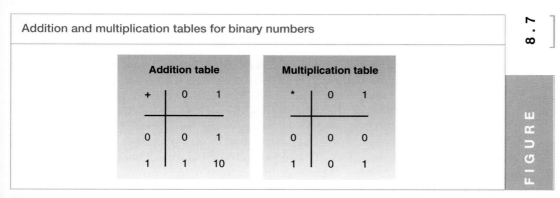

Addition and multiplication tables for binary numbers

FIGURE 8.7

Addition and multiplication tables for binary numbers have only four entries and only several possible values. Expressing these tables within a computer's circuitry is much simpler than implementing base 10 tables that would have to include 100 situations.

Expressing numbers in base 2

The location of each digit in a base 10 number determines that digit's value. For example, the base 10 number 3,597 can be expressed in powers of 10 as follows:

$$
3597 = \begin{array}{rcl} 3 & * & 1{,}000 \\ + 5 & * & 100 \\ + 9 & * & 10 \\ + 7 & * & 1 \end{array} \quad = \quad \begin{array}{rcl} 3 & * & 10^3 \\ + 5 & * & 10^2 \\ + 9 & * & 10^1 \\ + 7 & * & 10^0 \end{array}
$$

Base 10 uses the 10 digits 0 through 9. In contrast, base 2 uses only two digits, 0 and 1. The location of digits in base 2 has the same effect as the location of digits in base 10, except that each position represents powers of 2 rather than 10. For example, the base 2 number 10111 (which is equivalent to the base 10 number 23) represents the following combination of powers of 2:

$$
10111 = \begin{array}{rcl} 1 & * & 2^4 \\ + 0 & * & 2^3 \\ + 1 & * & 2^2 \\ + 1 & * & 2^1 \\ + 1 & * & 2^0 \end{array} \quad = \quad \begin{array}{rcl} 1 & * & 16 \\ + 0 & * & 8 \\ + 1 & * & 4 \\ + 1 & * & 2 \\ + 1 & * & 1 \end{array} \quad = \quad \begin{array}{l} 16 \ (\text{in base 10}) \\ + 0 \\ + 4 \\ + 2 \\ + 1 \\ \hline 23 \ (\text{in base 10}) \end{array}
$$

It is possible to express any base 10 number as an equivalent base 2 number by breaking it up into successive powers of 2. The base 10 example (3,597) is equivalent to the base 2 number 111000001101.

This figure shows how to convert from base 10 numbers to binary numbers and vice versa.

letters and digits as sequences of 0's and 1's. Unicode is a superset of the ASCII character set that uses two bytes for each character rather than one and is therefore able to handle 65,536 combinations rather than just 256. It is important in the global market because it encompasses the alphabets of most of the world's languages.

Numerical Representation of Sounds and Pictures   Images and sounds can also be represented as a series of numbers and therefore as a series of 0's and 1's. The process of generating these numbers is called **digitizing,** and the result is called a digital representation of the image or sound. Figure 8.9 shows how an image can be digitized by dividing it into tiny squares and assigning a number to each square representing the shade in the square. Imagine that a 1-by-1-inch image is covered with a 200-by-200 grid that isolates tiny picture elements, or **pixels.** Each pixel is coded on a scale ranging from absolutely white to absolutely dark. With the 200-by-200 grid, the 1-inch square image would be represented by 40,000 numbers, which could then be stored in a computer or transmitted. Representations of this type are actually approximations. The denser the grid, the more precise the representation, as was demonstrated by Figure 4.17. Four times as many numbers would be required to represent a color image, because color images can be represented as a combination of four colors such as red, blue, yellow, and black. The second part of Figure 8.9 shows that sounds can also be digitized by dividing their waveforms into tiny increments and coding each of these numerically.

The fact that any type of data can be represented as a series of bits means that a computer system can manipulate and transmit any type of data. Just as it can add numbers, it can change the shade of part of an image or can store and transmit audio

TABLE 8.2

ASCII-8 Code for Data

Digit	ASCII representation	Letter	ASCII representation
0	0011 0000		
1	0011 0001	A	0100 0001
2	0011 0010	B	0100 0010
3	0011 0011	C	0100 0011
4	0011 0100	D	0100 0100
5	0011 0101	E	0100 0101
6	0011 0110	F	0100 0110
7	0011 0111	G	0100 0111
8	0011 1000	H	0100 1000
9	0011 1001	I	0100 1001

data. Until the 1980s, computer systems rarely processed images and sounds because inadequate price-performance made it too expensive to handle the amount of data required for useful applications. Although most business data processing still involves numbers and text, image and audio applications have become commonplace. Image applications include creating engineering drawings, storing correspondence from customers, and displaying graphical information for decision makers. Audio applications include voice mail, controlling computers by voice commands, and even entering numerical or textual data by voice.

Data Compression   Digitizing images and video generates an enormous number of numbers. Consider a black-and-white 8×10 photograph digitized at the resolution of 200 dots per inch. Because each square inch contains 40,000 dots and the photograph contains 80 square inches, the digitized image would contain 3,200,000 numbers, more than enough numbers to represent every letter in every word in this book. A picture

FIGURE 8.9

Digitizing images and sounds

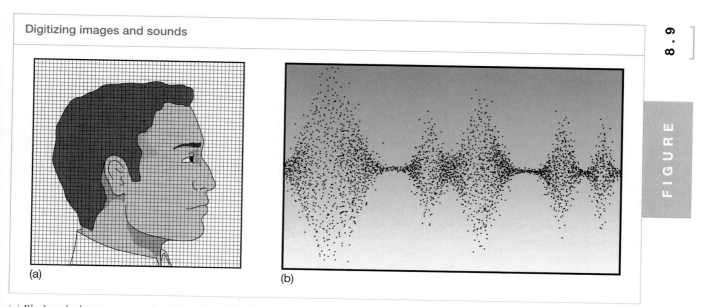

(a) Black-and-white images can be digitized by subdividing them using a fine grid and then assigning a number to each point on the grid. The number for each point represents its value on a scale from absolutely white to absolute black. The fineness of the grid (in lines per inch) determines the precision of the digitized image. (b) Sounds can be digitized by dividing their waveforms into tiny increments and coding each increment. The picture shows how voice waveforms can be represented.

may be worth ten thousand words, but it may require many times the computer resources for storage and transmission.

Data compression is one of the ways to increase the storage and transmission capability of computer and communication hardware without upgrading the hardware. Data compression is the coding of data to remove types of redundancies that can be detected easily. The basic idea is to use computational techniques to compress data whenever it is stored or transmitted, and to decompress it whenever it is used. There are two groups of compression methods. **Lossless compression** is used for typical business data and text. It can shrink programs and word processing documents to roughly half their normal size, making it possible to squeeze more data into the same floppy disk or hard disk. Given that it applies to business data and text, the corresponding decompression process must recreate an exact bit-for-bit duplicate of the original data. In contrast, **lossy compression**, which actually loses some data, can be used for audio, video, and some image applications in which minor degradations in data quality are much less important than drastic reductions in file size. Lossy compression of 90% or more for video signals helps make video conferencing possible. The sources of the reduction include taking fewer frames per second, transmitting only the parts of the picture that change from frame to frame, and identifying and coding special patterns within individual frames, such as areas of unchanging color.

Compression standards that many PC users have heard of include JPEG and MP3. JPEG uses mathematical transformations to perform lossy compression of images at a ratio of up to 20-to-1. MPEG encompasses several methods used for compressing video. It includes MPEG-1, which is used for CD-ROMs, MPEG-2, which is used for television, and MPEG-3 (also called MP3), which compresses CD-quality audio by a ratio of 12-to-1. Napster was developed to share MP3 audio files.

Data Encryption　A special type of coding is sometimes used to prevent unauthorized or illegal use of data that can be stolen or intercepted while being stored or transmitted. **Encryption** is the process of coding data to make it meaningless to any unauthorized user. The encrypted data is meaningful only to someone who can use a special decoding process for converting the data back to the original form. Encrypting data is essential for performing financial transactions on the Internet and for transferring money electronically between financial institutions. It is also important to pay-television operators who don't want their signals used for free. Some people encrypt data on their own PCs to prevent unwarranted access.

An example of a simple encryption scheme is to replace each letter in a word by the letter five positions after it in the alphabet. With this scheme, the word *encryption* would appear as *jshwduynts*. Because a scheme like this would be easy to figure out, real encryption schemes are much more complicated and typically involve complex manipulations of bit patterns.

Machine Language

Computers are devices that can execute previously stored instructions. Although the details of computer circuitry are immensely complicated, the basic idea of executing previously stored instructions is quite simple. Instructions a computer can execute directly are expressed in **machine language**, the computer's internal programming language. Different brands of computers may use different machine languages because their CPUs contain different microprocessors. For example, a server produced by Sun might use a Sparc chip, whereas IBM-style PCs from both IBM and Dell might use a Pentium microprocessor. The difference in machine languages implies that software written in the machine language of a particular type of chip will not run on a different type of chip.

The details of a machine have many important ramifications for a computer's internal efficiency. For example, the number of internal locations that can be referenced directly has important implications for the effective speed of the processor that executes machine language instructions. The Intel Pentium line of microprocessors uses

[L O O K A H E A D]

Encryption techniques including private key and public key encryption will be explained in Chapter 13, "E-Business Security and Control."

[L O O K A H E A D]

Box 9.1 in Chapter 9 will show a hypothetical example of a highly simplified machine language as part of an explanation of different generations of programming languages.

32-bit addressing, meaning that it can address over 16 million (2^{32}) locations directly. Previous 8-bit or 16-bit processors could address only 64 (2^8) or 4,096 (2^{16}) locations directly. Because machine language programs are often much larger than this, computers with 8- or 16-bit addressing had to do extra work to keep track of data in memory locations that they could not address directly. In addition to making it even harder to program these computers, limited address spaces slowed these computers down compared to what they might otherwise do. In 1993 Digital Equipment Corporation released a 64-bit microprocessor called the Alpha Chip, but it did not achieve commercial success. The generation of microprocessors following the Pentium is being designed with 64-bit addressing.

Impact of Miniaturization and Integration on Performance

A driving force for many new computer uses is the incredible rate of improvement in computer performance that has continued for decades. We will look at this topic in more depth by focusing on four approaches: making processors faster and more powerful, improving the instruction set, using specialized processors, and programming computers so that the processors operate in parallel. A fifth approach, distributing computing functions across a network, has already been introduced. That approach is based on the idea of separating the computer system into specialized modules that perform particular tasks such as finding data in the database, interacting with users, or controlling printing.

Faster and More Powerful Processors   Developments in miniaturization and speed of computing devices have changed computers from room-sized machines to machines the size of a notepad. The first computers represented data using off-on switches that were wired together. Today's computers would not be possible without the **integrated circuit** that was first developed in 1958. The concept of the integrated circuit was that an entire electronic circuit could be embedded into a single piece of silicon called a **chip.** The **microprocessor** was another key development because it integrated control logic and memory on a single chip. Extensions of this 1971 invention led to the development of personal computers and are the heart of current computers. Table 8.3 looks at the successive generations of microprocessor chips produced by Intel to date, showing advances in memory and speed, plus what those advances meant for PC users.

In general, advances in computers have been related to advances in the miniaturization and integration of semiconductor chips. Miniaturization and integration increase speed and reduce the power consumption of circuits by making the individual devices smaller, putting more devices on one chip, and packing them more tightly. Improvements in performance occur because the electrons travel a much shorter path and because off-on switching times decrease.

This miniaturization is accomplished through a complex manufacturing process that etches circuits on thin slices of silicon called wafers. Later, these wafers are cut into individual chips and put into small plastic packages. Figure 8.10 shows how this sequence produces a chip that might appear in a personal computer. The lines on that chip are actually metallic channels through which the electrons move. Table 8.3 shows that the first Intel microprocessor had a line width of 10 microns, over 50 times wider than the .18-micron line width of a Pentium III and IV. (A **micron** is one millionth of a meter. By comparison, bacteria and human hair are about 8 microns wide and 80 microns wide, respectively.) In November 2000 Intel announced it had completed development of a .13-micron technology for a new generation of chips,[14] although there is some question about how long advances in this direction can continue without bumping into fundamental limits related to the wavelength of the light beams used to create the circuits. At some point a switch to a new type of manufacturing equipment using ultraviolet light or x-rays instead of visible light may be necessary.

Faster and more powerful processors combined with similar improvements in hard disk storage have led to vast increases in the power of the software that computers can execute. The first spreadsheet program, VisiCalc, was released in 1980 and occupied

TABLE 8.3

Advances in Intel's Microprocessor

Successive generations of microprocessors from Intel, the industry leader, show the advances that occurred in the 1980s and 1990s.[10,11,12] Each new processor could run more complex software for PC users.

Processor #	Release date	Number of Transistors	Line width	Addressing	Initial MIPS	What this meant to a PC user
4004	1971	2,300	10 micron	4 bit	0.06	The first microprocessor, developed for a desktop calculator.
8080	1974	3,500	6 micron	8 bit	0.06	Ran the first personal computer, the Altair, which was assembled by hobbyists.
8086/8088	1978	29,000	3 micron	16 bit	0.3 MIPS	Chip for the first IBM PCs. Ran MS-DOS, the most common operating system for early PCs.
286	1982	134,000	1.5 micron	16 bit	0.9 MIPS	Ran early versions of Microsoft Windows, but with poor performance.
386	1985	275,000	1.5 micron	16 bit	5 MIPS	Ran subsequent versions of Microsoft Windows, with adequate performance.
486	1989	1.3 million	1.0 micron	32 bit	20 MIPS	Runs Microsoft Windows 95 with good performance.
Pentium	1993	3.2 million	.35–.80 micron	32 bit	100 MIPS	Used for desktop computers and laptops.
Pentium Pro	1995	5.5 million	.35 micron	32 bit	200 MIPS	Better processing of multimedia data for engineering workstations; packaged with a speed-enhancing memory cache chip; primarily for servers and multiprocessor workstations.
Pentium II	1997	7.5 million	.25 micron	32 bit	300 MIPS	Designed to process video, audio, and graphics data efficiently; primarily for high-end desktops and multiprocessor workstations.
Pentium III	1999	10–28 million	.18 micron	32 bit	500–1,000 MIPS	Better support for advanced imaging, 3D, streaming audio and video, and speech recognition applications.
Pentium IV	2000	42 million	.18 micron	32 bit	Over 1,500 MIPS	More powerful processing for 3D graphics, audio, and streaming video.
Itanium	2000	25 million	.18 micron	64 bit		For the server market.
Micro 2011 (prediction by Andrew Grove)[13]	2011 (est.)	1 billion			100,000 MIPS	Not known.

29 kilobytes of memory on an Apple II computer. The first Apple operating system consisted of six files totaling 216 kilobytes. These numbers are a tiny fraction of the multimegabyte space requirements for current applications and operating systems. For example, the Mac OS X, the new Apple operating system distributed for beta testing in 2000, required 1.5 gigabytes of hard disk space and was expected to require 64 megabytes of RAM, several hundred times the requirements for the original version.[15]

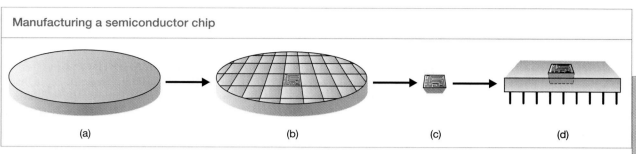

Manufacturing a semiconductor chip

(a)   (b)   (c)   (d)

FIGURE 8.10

The manufacturing process starts with a pure silicon wafer the size of a salad plate (a). The manufacturing process creates complex circuit patterns on separate areas of the wafer (b). The wafer is cut into separate chips, also called die (c), which are mounted into plastic packages (d) that are inserted into circuit boards.

Major improvements in the cost-effectiveness of all computing equipment have also come from integrating functions of many separate chips into a single chip. An IBM PC/AT built in 1984 using an Intel 286 microprocessor contained around 100 chips. One of the first chip sets built for clones of the PC/AT consisted of only six chips. A much more powerful single-chip version cost $25 in 1990.[16] During the 1990s additional chips were required to support the use of graphics, audio, and video. Exemplifying the continuing trend toward integrating multiple chips, National Semiconductor's second generation of its Geode product line provided a single chip that consolidated Pentium-class CPU functions plus graphics, memory interface, audio, networking, and other functions needed for TV set-top boxes, Internet appliances, and certain types of thin clients for networks. The chips cost between $30 and $50.[17]

Other Approaches for Improving Performance

Miniaturization and integration have greatly increased the performance of microprocessors and other computer components, but a number of other approaches have also provided a significant performance boost. These approaches include improved instruction sets, specialized processors, and parallel processing.

Improved Instruction Set   Another approach to increasing speed is to change the types of instructions the individual processors perform. The **RISC** (reduced instruction set computer) microprocessor was developed to increase speed by using a simpler processor that operated faster. The concept of RISC was originally developed by IBM but was not commercialized at first for fear it would compete with IBM's existing technologies. Instead RISC was first exploited in the 1980s by other manufacturers. By 1989, RISC chips were helping increase computer speeds at an annual rate of 70%. In 1993 Digital Equipment Corporation used RISC technology in its 64-bit Alpha chip, which could operate up to 300 MIPS and was later acquired by Intel. As the RISC advances were occurring, **CISC** (complex instruction set) microprocessors were also attaining performance improvements such as those shown in Table 8.3. Many of the advances in RISC architecture have influenced the design of CISC chips such as the Pentium III and Pentium IV.

Specialized Processor   The chips recognized most widely by the general public are microprocessors that control PCs and dynamic RAMs that serve as memory. A second way to increase speed is to use specialized chips designed to perform a particular type of processing very efficiently. **ASICs** (application specific integrated circuits) are chips tailored to a particular application such as controlling a machine or a videogame. **DSPs** (digital signal processors) are specialized, single-purpose microprocessors devoted to processing voice or video signals. These chips are used in electronic musical equipment, voice mail systems, and video applications. A typical application is reducing audio distortion in cell phones. Doing this with regular microprocessors would be slower and wouldn't provide the level of performance needed. In a different area, several companies have developed special-purpose microprocessors optimized for running the Java programming language (discussed in Chapter 9) in conjunction with devices ranging from advanced cellular phones and pagers to Internet televisions and laptop computers.

Parallel Processing   As if progress due to miniaturization were not enough, many advances have also occurred by rethinking basic methods computers use in their internal processing. In **parallel processing**, a larger computation or query is divided into smaller computations or queries performed simultaneously. This idea is inconsistent with the traditional von Neumann architecture of general-purpose computers, which dictates that the computer fetches and performs one instruction at a time. Various forms of parallel processing have been used to build servers that contain multiple processors, thereby increasing the throughput of a single server instead of buying multiple servers.

Parallel processing has been used in a number of ways, but it works only if programmers can figure out how to decompose the problems they are solving into subproblems that can be solved in parallel. Its first use was for complex scientific and engineering calculations that involved predicting weather patterns, studying fluid mechanics, and performing detailed simulations of physical systems. An important current use is in engineering workstations that generate photo-realistic images from detailed engineering specifications. Some of these systems simultaneously create an outline of the drawing, color it, shade it, and rotate it. Performing these tasks simultaneously allows speed and picture quality that would be impossible if everything were done in sequence.

Business applications of parallel processing typically are based on querying and analyzing different parts of a huge database simultaneously. For example, Internet search engines can use parallel processing by converting a single query into several separate queries that can be performed simultaneously. A number of large companies have also started using parallel processing in data mining efforts aimed at finding and understanding otherwise obscure patterns in their own operational data.

Parallel processing may also have important applications in attempts to get computers to mimic intelligent behavior. Some artificial intelligence researchers see the human mind as a complex network of parallel processes. Although human consciousness focuses on one train of thought at a time, many other processes are going on in parallel in the background. These range from maintaining proper heart rate to filtering out background stimuli so that we don't get overloaded by all of the things happening around us.

R E A L I T Y C H E C K

Increasing Computer Performance

The text discusses several approaches for increasing computer performance.

1. At a time when PCs can operate as fast as mainframes of the past, explain why you do or do not think computer performance is an important issue for users and managers.

2. Identify several situations in which inadequate computer system performance or improved computer system performance affected you directly.

The remainder of this chapter will discuss devices and media used for capturing, storing and retrieving, and displaying data. Chapter 10 will extend this picture by discussing data transmission.

DATA INPUT: CAPTURING DATA

Input devices used to enter data into computer systems range from keyboards and bar code readers to devices for voice and handwriting recognition. Before looking at specific devices, it is worthwhile to ask what characteristics an ideal input device should have. Like any other device, it should be inexpensive, reliable, accurate, and convenient to use. An ideal input device would also have characteristics unique to input devices. It should capture data automatically at its source and shouldn't require human intervention that might cause delays or introduce errors. For example, it should be unnecessary for people to record data in one form (such as handwriting) and then transcribe into another form (by typing it). In addition, an ideal input device should do whatever is possible to ensure accuracy of the data. This section looks at several forms of data input involving keyboards and pointing devices, character recognition, and inputting images and sounds.

Keyboards and Pointing Devices

Although many Americans take keyboards for granted, even this familiar technology raises many issues, starting with the shape and layout of current keyboards. People who designed the first typewriters experimented with many different layouts before standardizing on what is called the "qwerty" keyboard (because of the order of letters in the third row). Ironically, this layout of keys was developed to force people to type more slowly, thereby reducing the incidence of jammed keys in the mechanical typewriters of the time. Typewriters are no longer mechanical, but the qwerty keyboard has remained the standard for English keyboards.

Other languages that use different alphabets require different keyboards, but the whole idea of the keyboard breaks down for Chinese and Japanese whose ancient writing system uses thousands of symbols called kanji, each representing an idea rather than an alphabetic character. Because it takes a long time to learn thousands of symbols, Japanese is written in two ways. Within the first few years at school, children learn approximately 100 kana, phonetic characters in two alphabets called hirigana and katakana. But since adults in business settings rarely use kana, computer usage requires a way to deal with kanji.[18] Figure 8.11(a) shows a Japanese word processor that takes input in the form of kana and searches for the equivalent kanji. Difficulty dealing with kanji is a key reason why Japanese offices were much slower than U.S. offices in adopting computers. Computers became more widespread in Japanese offices as direct input of handwritten kanji became easier.

The basic idea of the keyboard has also been adapted to make it more effective for particular situations. Modified cash registers such as those used in McDonald's make it unnecessary for the cashier to remember the price of an item (see Figure 8.11(b)). Instead, the cashier presses a key that represents a particular type of hamburger or drink. Portable computers and touchtone phones made it possible to enter data from work locations without being anchored to a bulky VDT. Because the touchtone phone has no visual display, data input through a touchtone phone is a response to audio prompts from the computer system.

The last adaptation of the keyboard is to eliminate the keys altogether. The touch screen made it possible to enter data by pointing to a spot on a screen (see Figure 8.11(c)). Pointing on a touch screen is less precise than pointing with a mouse and is therefore limited to applications where pointing to areas of the screen suffices.

The mouse and other pointing devices made it possible to point with more precision. The mouse was an important breakthrough for expressing commands to a computer. Before it was developed, users had to type commands such as "Print Cust_File." This was difficult because users had to know the commands, syntax, and filenames, and had to spell everything correctly. With the mouse, touch screen, or screen designed for input using an electronic pen, a user can simply point to select the command and the file. Pointing is an excellent way to make computers easier to use, but it is not a way to enter large amounts of data. This is where the keyboard remains far more effective.

Optical Character Recognition

Several types of input technology are based on recognizing characters or special markings. **Magnetic ink character recognition (MICR)** was developed by banks as an early technology of this type. With MICR, account numbers are written on checks and deposit

FIGURE 8.11

Data input examples

(a)

(b)

(c)

(a) Using a keyboard to enter Japanese kanji characters is awkward. The first step is to type a word or sentence phonetically using either the English alphabet or a combination of two alphabetical forms of Japanese writing called hiragana and katakana. The computer uses a dictionary to find the equivalent kanji. Since two different kanji characters can sound the same (like "red" and "read" in English), the user must occasionally stop to select among such alternatives. (b) This specialized cash register permits the cashier to ring up a restaurant purchase without having to enter or even remember the price of each item. (c) This touch screen is used to buy airline tickets. This form of input is effective in applications involving user choices rather than extensive data entry.

slips in a standard location and format using magnetic ink that can be recognized by special input devices. This technology expedites the clearing of checks and deposits.

Optical character recognition (OCR) applies a similar idea to capture machine-generated or hand-printed numbers or text. OCR involves two steps: capturing an image and then deciphering it. The deciphering step is a software function that consists of finding the individual characters, subdividing them into the equivalent of pixels, and identifying each character by comparison with previously stored patterns.

Although OCR started with collecting data from forms filled in carefully by hand, bar coding to identify prelabeled objects is the most important current OCR application. As you can see by looking at the bar code label on a grocery product, bar coding represents characters by using bars in a standard format. Bar code readers come in several forms. Some are stationary and scan the bar code as the object moves by. Others are more like wands that scan across a stationary object. Bar codes are often integrated into point-of-sale terminals used in department stores to record sales and track inventory. By making it unnecessary for people to read and copy data, bar-coding applications decrease data entry effort and increase accuracy.

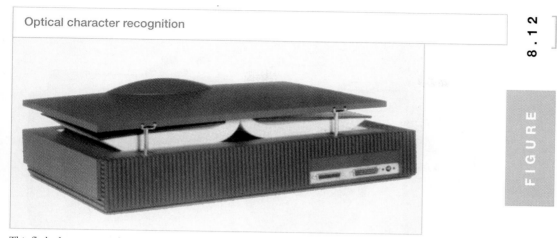

Optical character recognition

FIGURE 8.12

This flatbed scanner can be used to capture images and text in the form of a static picture. Converting the text into characters in a word processing document requires OCR software.

OCR for hand printing can be used with paper input forms or electronic tablets. For OCR to work with hand printing, either the person must be trained to write letters in a prespecified format or the computer must be trained to recognize an individual's printing. Existing OCR systems are not efficient for inputting large amounts of text and cannot decipher cursive handwriting accurately. OCR can also be used for inputting previously typed or typeset characters. Inexpensive scanners with OCR software can capture previously typed text with high accuracy (see Figure 8.12), although someone still needs to check the recovered text for errors.

Capturing Pictures, Sounds, and Video

Earlier this chapter showed how every type of data can be digitized and can therefore be handled by a computer. Two approaches are used for inputting image and audio data into computer systems. One approach consists of simply recording or copying the data in a computer-readable form. This is what happens when a scanner captures an image and stores it in a computer system. Digital cameras perform a similar function (see Figure 8.13). The other approach is to capture image or audio data and then, as part of the input process, do something to interpret what it means. This approach is used with voice recognition systems.

Voice recognition matches the sound patterns of spoken words with previously stored sound patterns. Work situations in which voice input is important include input while the speaker's hands are busy; input while mobility is required; and input while the user's eyes are occupied. Typical users are people looking through a microscope and not wanting to look away each time they make a note, or aircraft engine inspectors, who can use a wireless microphone and a limited vocabulary to issue orders, read serial numbers, or retrieve maintenance records. Voice recognition is also becoming important in customer service applications in which the customer's options are simple enough to identify with a single word or phrase that can be recognized easily by comparing the speaker's sound pattern to a previously stored sound pattern. This is why many automated telephone response systems permit the user to enter a number manually or speak the number.

Dictation of documents presents a much more difficult challenge for voice recognition because the spoken words are not limited to predictable responses to questions. A 1999 benchmark by *PC Magazine* found that voice recognition capabilities of inexpensive commercial products had increased greatly in the last few years due to a combination of software improvements and speedier computer chips. The best performing voice recognition software in their tests had accuracies of 96% to 98% after being

FIGURE 8.13

A digital camera for input to a computer system

Front view

Back view

This digital camera takes electronic pictures that can be downloaded to a computer. The resolution of the images and the capacity of its flash memory card determine how many images a digital camera can store.

"trained" to the user's voice pattern by the user's reading of prespecified selections. *PC Magazine* concluded that mainstream productivity would require 99% accuracy, but that these products were closing in on that accuracy level.[19]

There has been speculation about whether keyboards will be bypassed in favor of direct voice input or handwritten input in many applications over the next several decades. Although no one knows what will happen, this type of development would have major impacts on managerial, professional, and clerical work. Bypassing keyboards may also be crucial for expanding computer use in China and Japan, whose use of kanji was mentioned earlier. Surprisingly, the complexity of these characters may help computers recognize them. Because the strokes in kanji characters are typically written in a particular order, handwriting-recognition devices have been developed that use the order of the strokes as information for deciphering the characters.

R E A L I T Y C H E C K

Data Input

The text identifies a number of data input technologies.

1. Identify times (if any) when you have entered data into a computer system. Explain why the process seemed as efficient as possible, or alternatively, how it probably could have been improved.

2. Explain how you think you will input data or interact with computers in your career.

STORING AND RETRIEVING DATA

An ideal storage device should be able to store and retrieve any data immediately and in a minimum amount of space. Space used and storage and retrieval times are useful indicators for comparing storage technologies. This section looks at several forms of data storage: paper, micrographics, magnetic storage, optical storage, flash memories, and smart cards.

Paper and Micrographics

Paper is a 2,000-year-old medium for storing data. Although paper is easy for people to use when they are reading or annotating a document, it has many shortcomings. For one thing, it is so bulky that many large businesses have rooms full of paper records and documents. Finding a specific document in a personal file cabinet can take seconds or minutes. Finding a document in a firm's paper archives can take hours, days, or weeks, if it can be found at all (see Figure 8.14(a)). Another shortcoming is that paper is not conveniently computer readable even though OCR scanners can capture text from paper documents.

Punched cards were an innovation from the U.S. census of 1890. This innovation led to machines for sorting and tabulating cards, and these were the products of International Business Machines (IBM) long before the invention of computers. Punched cards were the primary medium for storing programs and for storing data in the first computerized business systems (see Figure 8.14(b)).

Computer output microfilm is a solution to the bulkiness of paper that reduces pages of output to tiny images stored on film. A hand-sized card called a microfiche can store the equivalent of hundreds of pages of computer output. Although microfilm greatly reduces the amount of physical space required to store data, it is not conveniently computer readable, which makes it useful only for rarely accessed data. Finding

Data storage examples

(a)

(b)

(c)

(d)

FIGURE 8.14

(a) In 1990 Connecticut Mutual Life Insurance used this warehouse, which was the size of a football field, to store paper files. Vans stuffed with paper shuttled between the office and warehouse hourly. Simple changes in an insurance policy could take a week. (b) Early business data processing was based on punched cards. The pattern of holes punched in each column represented the letter or number at the top of the column. A mechanical card reader sensed the holes. The typed line at the top of the card was for the convenience of the person looking at the card. (c) The first hard disks for PCs contained 10 or 40 megabytes of data. This hard disk is only 3.5 inches in diameter, but can hold 20 gigabytes. (d) The CD-R and CD-RW disks in the picture hold 650 megabytes, the equivalent of over 450 diskettes.

a particular item of information using a microfilm or microfiche reader takes several minutes at best. Furthermore, microfilm cannot be changed once it is produced.

Magnetic Tapes and Disks

The shortcomings of paper media led to the development of media based on the magnetization or demagnetization of tiny locations on an iron oxide surface. The first of these was the **magnetic tape**, a plastic tape on which data could be stored using numerical codes. The ability to magnetize and demagnetize a tiny region of a magnetic tape without punching a hole means that the data on the tape could be modified by writing over it in a process similar to recording over an audiotape or videotape. Like entertainment audiotapes and videotapes, tapes for storing computer data are sequential devices whose data are read in their order of location on the tape. The fact that tapes must be read sequentially greatly limits the types of processing for which they can be used, but they are well suited for backup due to their speed and reliability.

Data can also be stored magnetically on a **hard disk**, which is a rotating device that stores data using magnetization and demagnetization methods like those for magnetic tapes. Like diskettes, hard disks store data in concentric circles called tracks. Unlike diskettes, many hard disks have multiple platters. While in use, a hard disk rotates continually. Whenever a program requires data, it passes the request to the operating system, which determines the location of the data on the disk and instructs a disk arm to look for the data at that point. The disk arm moves a read head into position over the correct track and performs the read. The data are read when the rotation brings the required location under the read head. Hard disks are also called direct access storage devices (DASDs). The special advantage of hard disks over tapes is their ability to access data immediately instead of having to read sequentially through all previous data on the device.

A major disadvantage of hard disks is that they rely on continuous rotation at thousands of revolutions per minute with a read head just 15-millionths of an inch above the disk. Occasionally the read head crashes into the disk, destroying both the data and the disk. This is one of the reasons why it is especially important to make frequent backup copies of any important data stored on a hard disk. One response to this problem in large-scale data processing is the use of **redundant arrays of independent disks (RAID)**. With this approach, the same data is stored on several different disks. If one happens to crash, the other will almost always have the same data. Furthermore, RAID can increase access speed because the work of accessing data can be shared across several disks.

Rotating disks come in a variety of sizes. Pocket-sized 3.5-inch diskettes commonly hold 1.4 megabytes of data. Inexpensive removable disks providing between 100 megabytes and 2 gigabytes of backup storage have created another important option for data storage and backup. For example, a rewriteable 100-megabyte zip disk that costs less than $10 holds the same amount of data as 70 diskettes. This technology permits business professionals to carry much of their frequently used data on a single portable disk even when they are not carrying a laptop.

Continual improvements in hard disks have created the same type of exponential performance increase and cost decrease that chip improvements have created. The average capacity of hard disks sold in 1990 was around 60 megabytes. By 2000 this increased to around 10 gigabytes, well over a 100-fold increase in 10 years. During this period the price of hard disk storage decreased by a similar ratio, making it possible to buy a gigabyte of disk storage for less than $20 (see Figure 8.14(c)). The combination of vastly increased RAM and hard disk capacities has made it practical to use PC software with vastly more powerful features and capabilities than the early PC software that had to reside entirely on a single diskette or within limited hard disk storage.

Optical Disks

Optical disk technology involves the use of a laser beam to store or retrieve data as microscopic spots on a disk. The first optical disks came out in 1978 and competed with videotapes in the home entertainment market. Audio compact disks came out in 1982 and revolutionized the record business in the late 1980s since a single 5.25-inch disk could hold 74 minutes of music, more than would fit on both sides of a vinyl LP record.

The **CD-ROM** applied optical storage for business processing. CD-ROMs are 650-megabyte optical disks that can be read but not written on. They emerged in 1985 for publishing databases, directories, and encyclopedias. CD-ROMs are useful for distributing large files of computer-readable data ranging from software programs to technical manuals. They cost less than $1 to produce and therefore deliver data much more cheaply than diskettes. The initial CD-ROM drives operated at 150 Kbps, but the more current drives operate many times faster. For example a 48X drive operates 48 times as fast as the initial standard. The **DVD** (digital versatile disk) is a newer optical technology that uses disks of the same size to hold 4.7 gigabytes of data, enough to store a two-hour movie. DVDs have become common as an alternative to videotapes, which need to be rewound and which have lower visual clarity. DVD drives that also read CD-ROMs are an increasingly popular option on personal computers, although most software is still distributed on CD-ROMs.

CD-ROMs were initially limited because the user could not change the data after it was recorded. This "read-only" limitation was eliminated with the development of CD-R and CD-RW disks. Recordable **CD-R** disks along with a CD-R drive make it possible for anyone to store data on a CD-ROM just as they might store data on a diskette. Their 650-megabyte capacity is sufficient to store many of the documents that a typical business professional uses. Instead of using and keeping track of a tray full of 1.4 megabyte diskettes, a business professional can store the equivalent of over 450 diskettes on a single CD-R. These disks cannot be rewritten, however, and therefore must be discarded when a new version of the data is produced. Rewriteable **CD-RW** disks use a somewhat different technology to produce CD-ROMs using media that can be rewritten up to 1,000 times. Unfortunately the different technology creates a different degree of reflectivity, which means that many CD-ROM and CD-R drives cannot read CD-RW disks.

Flash Memory

Hard disks and optical disks can store an enormous amount of information, but both involve mechanical devices with moving parts. This results in shortcomings such as moving parts that can break, and consumption of energy necessary to spin the disk and move the read/write mechanism. In contrast, the RAMs within the computer itself are semiconductor devices without moving parts. Unfortunately, RAMs have the problem of losing information when the computer is turned off.

A **flash memory** is a semiconductor device that stores and modifies information while the computer is operating, and retains information when the computer is turned off. Currently flash memory chips are used in battery-powered products such as electronic cameras, cellular phones, and notebook computers. Flash memory is still much more expensive per bit than both RAM and hard disk memory, but it illustrates yet another direction in which storage technology is developing.

Smart Cards

Smart cards, such as prepaid phone cards, copy cards, and electronic meal tickets, are plastic cards containing an embedded chip that stores coded information that can be updated as the card is used. They therefore differ from standard credit cards and debit cards that contain identifying information that does not change once the card is created. Today's smart cards typically are used via simple vending machines that deduct the amount of a purchase from the stored amount on the card and add that amount to an account that is receiving the payment. Smart cards can also be used to store medical information, pictures, and other more detailed information about an individual or object. Some smart cards can be programmed to do a number of things automatically, such as self-destruct if an incorrect password is entered too many times.

REALITYCHECK

Data Storage and Retrieval

The text says that most managers and professionals can carry around most of the computerized information they need on a single zip disk or CD-R.

1. Explain why you do or do not believe that everything you have ever written and every test you have ever taken could be stored on a single portable disk.

2. Assume that someone develops a cheap electronic scanner that can capture an entire page in one second and can store it on a high-capacity portable disk. Explain how this would or would not affect you at school or work.

DATA OUTPUT: DISPLAYING DATA

Output devices display information for users. Aside from being inexpensive and reliable, ideal output devices should make it as it easy as possible to display information in the most useful form. Early printers and terminals were limited because they were anchored to fixed locations and because they could not produce good graphical output. Advances in the last decade made it much cheaper to incorporate graphics, images, voice, other sounds, and video. This section looks at output devices in the following categories: screen outputs, paper outputs, and audio outputs.

Screen Outputs

The most common device for desktop output on screens is the VDT monitor, like the ones most PCs use. Improvements in monitors over the years include higher resolution (more dots per inch), larger screen size, graphical outputs rather than just numbers and text, and color displays rather than just black and white. All of these improvements have made monitors easier to use and have permitted them to display better information to users. VDTs have shortcomings, however, such as being bulky and taking up a lot of space on a desk. Extensive use often leads to eyestrain. In addition, they give off electromagnetic radiation that may be a health hazard, at least for people whose desks are behind the monitors.

A great deal of work has been done to produce flat screens such as those used with laptop computers (see Figure 8.15(a)). By 2000, the tiny black-and-white screens of early laptops had been replaced by 12- to 15-inch (diagonal) color screens that were much larger and much easier on the eyes. Flat screens for desktops are available but are substantially more expensive than VDT monitors with similar screen sizes. Flat screens are also used in factories where a wall-mounted screen is more convenient than a desktop device. Screen display technology is important not only for the future of computer displays but also for television screens.

Specialized displays of many other types have also been used. "Heads-up" displays originally developed for military applications have been used in some automobiles to project auto control panel information in front of the driver instead of forcing the driver to look down. In a more advanced version of this idea, Figure 8.15(b) shows a head-mounted display developed by Boeing to help workers performing complex wiring tasks in airplane manufacturing. This display uses semireflective lenses that permit the worker to see a wiring diagram (transmitted from a computer) superimposed on top of the circuit being wired.

Paper Outputs

Many different types of printers are available for paper outputs from computer systems (see Figure 8.15(c)). The first computer systems used impact printers, which create marks on paper by hitting a print head against a ribbon. Nonimpact printers include

Data output examples

FIGURE

8.15

(a)

(b)

(c)

(a) This flat panel display is more expensive than a VDT display but uses much less space. (b) Boeing developed this head-mounted display to help the production worker by projecting a wiring diagram onto the visual field of the circuit the worker is wiring. (You can see the projected wiring diagram in the lenses.) The image changes when the worker turns or proceeds to a new task. (c) Unlike the small printers found in most offices, this plotter can print complex engineering drawings on large sheets of paper.

inkjet printers and laser printers. Inkjet printers "spit" ink onto the paper. Laser printers create marks on paper by focusing laser beams on black particles of toner. Prices of printers have dropped so much that ink jet printers are sometimes almost given away for free because the primary profit is in the ink cartridges. Color printing is also available with inexpensive ink jet printers, although color printing is sometimes slow and surprisingly expensive because of the amount of ink that it uses.

Audio Outputs

Audio outputs are starting to appear more prominently in many business computer systems. In voice mail systems and many systems for obtaining standardized data such as bank balances, prerecorded prompting messages help the user specify what information is needed. In one specific application, Bell Canada uses voice synthesis to read locations of broken phone equipment to repair people and to tell them how to fix the equipment. Gradual refinements in speech synthesis have resulted in more natural-sounding synthesized speech, making future applications more likely. Anyone who uses the Web to download songs knows that the transmission of audio files via the Web is common. This also has business applications, such as disseminating news bulletins, stock analyst reports, and corporate information.

This chapter has covered a variety of methods used for data input, storage, and output. Some, such as magnetic tapes, hard disks, and impact printers, have been used for decades. Others, such as voice recognition, are less common today but will have wider impact in the future. Although technological progress will continue, it is difficult to predict which technologies will be adopted widely enough to change the way people work.

CHAPTER CONCLUSION

SUMMARY

Identify technology performance variables related to functional characteristics, ease of use, compatibility, and maintenance.

Technology performance variables related to functional capabilities include capacity, speed, price-performance, reliability, and operating conditions. Variables related to ease of use include the quality of the user interface, ease of becoming proficient, and portability. Compatibility is related to conformance to standards and interoperability. Maintainability is related to modularity, scalability, and flexibility.

What are typical measures of performance for computer technology?

Measures of amounts of data include byte, kilobyte, megabyte, gigabyte, and terabyte. Measures of time include millisecond, microsecond, nanosecond, and picosecond. Clock speed is measured in terms of cycles per second as Hertz, kilohertz, megahertz, and gigahertz. Speed of execution is measured in terms of millions of instructions per second (MIPS) and floating point operations per second (FLOPS).

What are the basic components of a computer system?

A computer system consists of computers and other devices that capture, transmit, store, retrieve, manipulate, and display data by executing programs. The physical devices in a computer system are its hardware, and the programs are its software. Aside from the computer itself, a computer system also includes peripherals for input, output, and storage.

What are the different types of computers?

Embedded computers are internal components of other machines. Categories of nonembedded computers include personal computers, workstations, midrange computers, mainframes, and supercomputers. The newer category of server crosses many of the older classifications. Personal computers include desktop computers, portable laptop computers, and personal digital assistants.

What are the organizational approaches to computing?

The organizational approaches to computing are centralized computing, personal computing, distributed computing, and network computing. In centralized computing, all the processing for multiple users is done by a large central computer. In personal computing, users have their own machines and rarely share data or resources. In distributed computing, users have their own computers and use a network to share data and resources. Network computing treats network computers as "thin clients" and links them to central servers in order to combine the benefits of centralized computing with the flexibility and responsiveness of distributed computing.

How is client/server computing different from centralized computing?

In client/server computing, different devices on a network are treated as clients or servers. The client devices send requests for service, such as printing or retrieval of data, to specific server devices that perform the requested processing. Client/server differs from centralized computing in terms of the division of labor in handling the user interface, application program logic, and database access. Instead of having a central computer control everything from the displays on user terminals through the application logic and the updating of the database, client/server divides these functions between specialized client and server components.

How is it possible for computers to process data of any type?

Digital computers are built from components that switch between off-on (0-1) states. Because eight bits, or one byte, is enough to uniquely identify 256 different characters, numerical data and text can be represented as a series of 0's and 1's. Pictures and sounds can be represented as 0's and 1's by breaking them into tiny elements and assigning a numerical value to each element.

What are the different approaches for increasing data manipulation speeds?

The approaches include miniaturization, improving the instruction set, using special-purpose processors, and using parallel processing. Miniaturization has been accomplished by changing the manufacturing processes to pack more individual devices into more highly integrated circuits. Improving the instruction set increases speed by combining individual instructions more effectively. Special-purpose processors are tailored to specific tasks. In parallel processing, a large computation is divided into smaller computations that are performed simultaneously.

What are the different forms of data input?

Keyboards are the dominant input device for business data processing but are used when a person has already captured (or just created) the data and is now entering the data into the computer as a separate step. Character recognition techniques such as optical character recognition and bar coding reduce the handling of data being entered into a computer system. Scanners capture images. Voice recognition systems bypass keyboard input, but are not as accurate.

What are the different forms of data storage?

The principal forms of data storage include paper, micrographics, magnetic storage, and optical storage. Micrographic devices replace paper by storing miniature pictures of document pages on microfilm. Magnetic tapes and disks store data through the magnetization and demagnetization of tiny regions on an iron oxide surface. Magnetic tapes must be used sequentially, whereas disks can be used for direct access. Optical disks come in a variety of read-only, write-once, or rewriteable forms. Flash memories use chips that retain data when the computer is turned off.

What are the different forms of data output?

The most common device for interactive output on screens is the VDT monitor, although flat screens have been used for portable computers and factory applications and are becoming affordable for desktop applications. Many types of printers and plotters are used for paper outputs. Audio outputs are used both for prerecorded messages and for synthesized interaction with computer system users.

KEY TERMS

functional capabilities
price-performance
ease of use
compatibility
interoperability
maintainability
modularity
scalability
bit
byte
bits per second (bps)
baud
MIPS
FLOPS
computer
program
computer system
hardware
software
central processing unit (CPU)
random access memory (RAM)
read only memory (ROM)
input device
output device
storage device
peripherals

embedded computer
personal computer (PC)
laptop computer
notebook computer
personal digital assistant (PDA)
palmtop computer
workstation
midrange computer
mainframe
supercomputer
server
centralized computing
personal computing
distributed computing
network computing
dumb terminal
graphical user interface (GUI)
network computer (NC)
thin client
client/server architecture
file server
middleware
peer-to-peer
ASCII
digitizing
pixel

lossless compression
lossy compression
encryption
machine language
32-bit addressing
integrated circuit
chip
microprocessor
micron
RISC
CISC
ASIC
DSP
parallel processing
MICR
OCR
voice recognition
computer output microfilm
magnetic tape
hard disk
RAID
CD-ROM
DVD
CD-R
CD-RW
flash memory

1. What are the basic units of measure for computing?

2. What is the von Neumann architecture and why is it important?

3. Identify the difference between an embedded computer and a nonembedded computer.

4. What is a server?

5. Describe the difference between centralized computing, personal computing, distributed computing, and network computing.

6. Why does distributed computing require more controls and administration than personal computing?

7. What is client/server architecture, and what does it accomplish?

8. Explain the role of middleware in client/server architecture.

9. How is peer-to-peer architecture different from client/server?

10. Why are base 2 numbers important in computing, and how is it possible to convert a base 10 number to base 2?

11. Define digitizing and explain what determines how closely a digitized picture resembles the original.

12. Why does high-resolution storage of a one-page picture involve more data than storing several hundred pages of text?

13. What are data compression and data encryption and why are they important?

14. Describe the difference between 8-bit, 16-bit, 32-bit, and 64-bit addressing and why this is important.

15. Explain the difference between RISC and CISC microprocessors and why this is important.

16. What is parallel processing and why is it potentially useful for studying artificial intelligence?

17. Describe optical character recognition and how it operates.

18. How does voice recognition operate?

19. What are the advantages and disadvantages of optical disks?

1. This chapter mentioned information technology performance variables in four areas: functional capabilities and limitations, ease of use, compatibility, and maintainability. Assume you have a five-year-old PC and are considering buying a new one. Explain how each group of performance variables is or is not pertinent to your purchase decision.

2. Responding to Japan's 95% market share in flat panel displays, the U.S. government announced a nearly $1 billion "flat panel display initiative" providing incentives for American manufacturers to achieve full-scale manufacturing. According to the president of the U.S. Display Consortium, flat panel screens will be used in everything from autos to fighter planes, and on "every exit ramp on the Information Highway."[20] Explain why you agree or disagree that it is important for the United States (or any other leading industrial power) to have a significant share of this market.

3. Assume that computerized voice recognition is widespread. Identify some of the possible applications of this technology. How do you think it might affect you personally? How would it affect people you know?

4. Assume that a hand-printing pad and hand-drawing pad became standard components of both desktop and portable PCs. Would this have any effect on you? Identify some ways it might affect work practices in specific jobs.

5. It is now possible to carry around all of the text data you have generated in your life on a single CD-R. This includes your medical records, finances, homework assignments, papers, and so on. It also has enough room to store data you need for your current work, such as the syllabus for all your courses, scanned images for papers, and so on. Assuming this technology was available for free, what would you be able to do differently?

6. Estimate how many megabytes would be required to store this entire book. (Your answer will depend on your assumptions.) In making your estimate, consider the fact that the book contains both text and graphics. Based on your results for this book, estimate the number of bytes required to store all the books in a 600,000-volume college library. How many 650 megabyte CD-ROMs would this require?

Transmeta Corporation: Building a New Chip for Mobile Computing

Transmeta Corporation was founded in 1995 to build a new type of computer chip directed at mobile applications that rely on battery power to run laptop computers and other portable devices. The company said nothing about its product until an unveiling on January 19, 2000. By October 2000, NEC, Sony, and Fujitsu had all launched notebook computers based on its Crusoe chip. Sony said it will use the processor in its new Vaio PictureBook C1VN notebook, and Transmeta claimed that Crusoe should nearly double the battery life of the new model.[21] Its November 2000 IPO was greeted favorably on Wall Street even though just a few days earlier IBM had announced a decision not to use Transmeta's Crusoe chip in the new IBM ThinkPad 2400.

Transmeta's Crusoe product is actually a family of processors. The TM3200 is designed to provide a full day of Web browsing on a single battery charge for mobile Internet devices weighing one to two pounds. The TM5400 and TM5600 are designed to solve the problems of poor battery life and sub-par performance in the ultra-light (weighing less than four pounds) mobile PCs. Performing at 700 MHz, TM5400/5600-based laptops can last up to eight hours on battery power when running everyday office applications, and three to four hours running heavy-duty multimedia applications like DVD movies.[22]

Major challenges in designing Transmeta's Crusoe chip centered on reducing the chip's power consumption while still supporting applications that ran on Intel's 86xx line of processors (which include the Pentiums). Transmeta applied a unique design that shifted the balance of work between hardware and software. According to Transmeta, "The hardware component is a very simple, high-performance, low-power VLIW (Very Long Instruction Word) engine with an instruction set that bears no resemblance to that of x86 processors. Instead, it is the surrounding software layer that gives programs the impression that they are running on x86 hardware. This innovative software layer is called the Code Morphing software because it dynamically 'morphs' (that is, translates) x86 instructions into the hardware engine's native instruction set. . . . This unique approach to executing x86 code eliminates millions of transistors, replacing them with software. The current implementation of the Crusoe processor uses roughly one-quarter of the logic transistors required for an all-hardware design of similar performance."[23] Because the hardware is fully decoupled from the x86 instruction set architecture, it is possible to improve the hardware over time without affecting legacy software. The Crusoe chips require a bootable ROM chip on the computer's motherboard. This ROM chip holds the Code Morphing software and loads the Code Morphing software into memory; Crusoe runs it before doing anything else. With the right Code Morphing software, the Crusoe will not only translate x86 instructions, but any other instruction set. With this scheme it could also run Linux, Windows, BeOS, or another operating system.[24]

As the first Transmeta chips were being incorporated into portable products there was some controversy about the importance of the power saving afforded by the Crusoe chip. Transmeta claimed that "the chip consumes around one watt of power when running, compared with an Intel Pentium's 15 to 20 watts. This means it uses significantly less battery power, and enables lightweight notebooks to work for up to eight hours. In standby mode, the chip consumes around 20 milliwatts of power." A Toshiba product manager was not greatly impressed, saying that the chip does give an increase in battery life but that the back light on a subnotebook computer also consumes a lot of power. He thought the battery life advantage in this market would be no more than 30% to 40%.[25] After IBM decided not to go ahead with the Crusoe for its new product, a spokeswoman said, "The IBM 480 notebook has a battery life of 4.5 hours and it was hoped that Crusoe would extend this to eight hours. However, Crusoe only managed 5.5 hours in IBM's benchmarking tests." A Gartner Group consultant said, "The main issue is performance. The chip uses emulation or 'code morphing' and therefore does not give the same performance as you get with Intel. . . . The reason IBM moved away from the chip is that either there was not enough power or there was not enough performance."[26] There was no guarantee that the Crusoe chip or Transmeta would succeed, especially since Intel and other companies were developing chips for the same market.

Continued

QUESTIONS

1. Why might portable computing and desktop computing call for different types of microprocessors?

2. Review the performance variables in Table 8.1. In which areas did the Transmeta chip try to excel?

3. Review the approaches mentioned in this chapter for attaining higher levels of computer performance. Which approaches did the Transmeta apply in its Crusoe chip?

4. Look at Transmeta's Web site. To what extent is it possible for a nonengineer to evaluate the real benefits of Transmeta's product?

C A S E | **Gemstar International: Will Its E-Book Reader Provide Enough Benefits?**

Although it is possible to access enormous amounts of information using computers, the human factors of using paper media such as traditional books, magazines, and newspapers are attractive in many ways. For example, given a choice of reading articles in a paper magazine or reading exactly the same articles on a computer screen, most people would view this as no contest and would choose the paper magazine. A student lugging six heavy textbooks in a backpack might have second thoughts, however, and anyone looking at the amount of paper that is produced and discarded might wonder whether there is a way to enjoy the beneficial features of paper publications without the bulk, inflexibility, and waste.

Gemstar's solution is an e-book reader, a portable electronic screen display about the size of a book, but able to store 4,000 pages of text. It can be used to download electronic books through a personal Gemstar eBook account, an online retailer, or a bookstore. Gemstar purchased two companies that had developed previous e-book readers (NuvoMedia and Softbook) and then upgraded their products and brought out two new products for the holiday season of 2000. The black-and-white REB1100 cost around $300 and the larger, full-color REB1200 cost around $700. Many observers were surprised that these readers were so expensive, especially with the limited amount of available content, but Gemstar's CEO said that an e-book would probably cost around $100 by 2001 and by 2003 might be given away as a free premium for making book purchases.[27]

E-book readers are useless if there is no content, but content was starting to become available. Gemstar signed up major publishers including Penguin Publishing, Simon & Schuster, Time Warner Trade Publishing, Random House, HarperCollins, and others. Along with the launch of Gemstar's new e-book readers, six titles by popular authors such as Patricia Cornwell, Ken Follett, and Robert Ludlum were released in e-book format prior to print release and were exclusive to Gemstar for 90 days.[28] Earlier in the year the horror author Stephen King had published the most successful e-book thus far, a 66-page novella called *Riding the Bullet* that was priced at $2.95. It had sold more than 500,000 copies but there was the question of how many people actually read the book since it was protected by encryption technology that prevented people from mailing, copying, or printing it.[29] Another development that indicated e-books might be at a take-off phase was an announcement by Random House that it would pay authors a 50% royalty for books sold and delivered electronically. This is much higher than a typical royalty, but Random House felt it was justified since there would be no inventory and transportation costs.

Other companies were looking further into the future and wanted to combine the efficiency of electronic distribution with the human factors of paper books. Xerox invented electronic paper in the form of a thin piece of transparent plastic that contains millions of small beads that act somewhat like toner particles in an office copier. Each half-white and half-black bead is enclosed in an oil-filled cavity and is free to rotate within its cavity. Electronic paper is electrically writeable and erasable and can be reused thousands of times. When voltage is applied to the surface of the sheet, the beads rotate to display either their black sides or white sides. Images of pictures and text are created when a pattern of voltages is sent to the paper. The image will remain until the voltage pattern changes.[30] The initial version has only two colors, but Xerox is working on adding additional color capacity.[31]

E Ink, a spin-off from MIT's Media Lab, developed a type of electronic ink that can be printed onto nearly any surface. Within the ink are "millions of microcapsules, each one containing white particles suspended in a dark dye. When an electric field is applied, the white particles move to one end of the microcapsule where they become visible. This makes the surface appear white at that spot. An opposite electric field pulls the particles to the other end of the microcapsules where they are hidden by the dye. This makes the surface appear dark at that spot. To form an electronic display, the ink is printed onto a sheet of plastic film that is laminated to a layer of circuitry. The circuitry forms a pattern of pixels that can then be controlled by a standard display driver." E Ink's initial products are industrial displays, but one of its long-term goals is to produce high-resolution displays so thin and flexible that they can be bound into an electronic book.[32]

QUESTIONS

1. An e-book reader is like a personal computer in some ways but not others. Identify the similarities and differences in function and form.

2. Review the technology performance variables in Table 8.1 and identify some of the performance issues and measures of performance that are pertinent to e-book reader technology. Consider the same question for a personal computer and identify performance issues and measures of performance that are pertinent to either e-book readers or personal computers, but not both.

3. Assume that e-book readers were available for $100. What would determine how widely they would be adopted and whether 25% of new books purchased would be purchased in electronic form?

4. Assume that electronic paper or electronic ink could be used in electronic readers that had movable pages and were the approximate size and shape of this textbook. Would that provide important benefits beyond the much simpler e-book reader?

Software, Programming, and Artificial Intelligence

chapter9

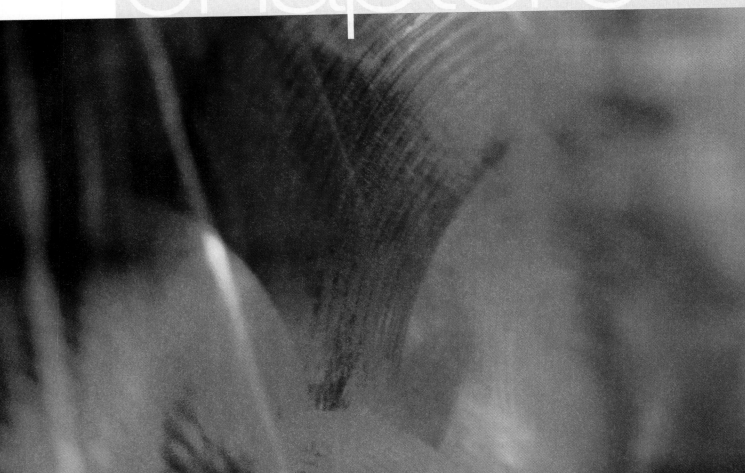

STUDY QUESTIONS

- What are the different types of software?
- How is programming like a translation process?
- What aspects of programming do not depend on the programming language used?
- What are the four generations of programming languages?
- What are some of the other important developments in programming?
- What are operating systems, and why should managers and users care about them?
- What is the most basic limitation of programming?

O U T L I N E

Thinking about the Current Limits of Software

Types of Software
    Application Software
    System Software

Programming Viewed as a Business Process
    Programming as a Translation Process
    Organizing Ideas
    Testing Programs
    The Changing Nature of Programming
    The Trend toward Object-Oriented
      Programming

Four Generations of Programming Languages
    Machine Languages
    Assembly Languages
    Higher Level Languages
    Fourth Generation Languages

Other Major Developments in Programming
    Special-Purpose Languages
    Spreadsheets
    Computer-Aided Software Engineering Systems

Operating Systems
    Operating Systems for Personal Computers
    Operating Systems for Multiuser Computer
      Systems
    Why Operating Systems Are Important

Steps toward Making Computers "Intelligent"

Chapter Conclusion
    Summary
    Key Terms
    Review Questions
    Discussion Questions
    Cases

Software, Programming, and Artificial Intelligence

O P E N I N G   C A S E

MICROSOFT: PROGRAMMING SOFTWARE FOR A NEW RELEASE

Microsoft has become one of the world's most valuable corporations by writing software used in over 100 million computers. Each software product goes through numerous updates and is released in different versions. In the planning stage for each release, Microsoft identifies the new capabilities that customers request plus those that it wants to include for its own strategic reasons. It divides the new features for the planned release into three parts in order of priority. If it runs out of time on the release, it eliminates the lower priority items.

Microsoft's programming process tries to maintain overall discipline and project control while permitting small teams to do their own work independently. It does this by assigning specific portions of each release to small teams consisting of three to eight programmers and the same number of testers. Permitting each team to operate independently maintains the team's sense of responsibility and permits it to exercise creativity in the way it does its work. The teams attempt to meet goals for providing specific capabilities, but do not start with the type of detailed specification that would be necessary if the software was designed to control mission-critical processes such as the operation of the space shuttle. Around 30% of each release is often the result of discoveries about unanticipated connections and relationships.

The method for maintaining overall control of the project is sometimes described as "synch and stabilize" because it tries to synchronize what people are doing as individuals and as members of parallel teams, while it also tries to stabilize the product in increments as the project continues. At the heart of this approach is a "daily build," a daily test of whether the most recently debugged version of all the separate modules of the product still operate together and still produce correct results for examples that the previous release could handle correctly. One of the few rules developers must follow is that they have to transmit their latest tested version by a particular time in the day so that the project team can assemble and recompile the latest completed version of all components, and can therefore create a new "build" of the product that can be tested. Any code that prevents the build from compiling must be fixed immediately. As the release date approaches, the list of known bugs is carefully monitored.[1] Many releases are distributed with known bugs, but these can often be corrected with program patches that can be downloaded through the Internet.

WEB CHECK [✓]

Look at Microsoft's Web site to see how it handles the distribution of bug fixes. Focus on the extent to which Microsoft addresses the needs of both corporate IT staffs and home computer users.

[**LOOK AHEAD**]

Chapter 12, "Building and Maintaining Information Systems," will explain the complete life cycle of a system, including implementing it in an organization and maintaining it. It will show that Microsoft's "synch and stabilize" is not a standard textbook method.

DEBATE TOPIC

Microsoft's business success is based in part on an unethical practice of distributing imperfect software.

microsoft uses its "synch and stabilize" method to organize its programming efforts. This chapter provides background for understanding this story in more depth and for understanding what can and cannot be done using today's programming methods. It introduces basic concepts about software including different types of software, the process of programming and debugging, different programming languages, other advances in software, and operating systems. These are basic topics about software and programming that business professionals need to understand in order to work knowledgeably with information system developers and to appreciate what today's computers can and cannot do. The chapter's major theme is the unending development of tools and techniques that make it easier to instruct computers to perform important business tasks.

THINKING ABOUT THE CURRENT LIMITS OF SOFTWARE

Just as it happened with computer hardware, computer software has seen an incredible progression of innovations. Today's software instructs computers to do what seemed like science fiction just 40 years ago, such as recording every item sold by an international corporation, permitting nonprogrammers to create complex spreadsheets, creating complex animations used in computer games, producing realistic visual representations from engineering specifications, and retrieving data from servers around the world.

In addition to introducing software vocabulary and concepts that business professionals should be familiar with, this chapter also tries to provide perspective about what is and is not possible with today's programming methods. Consider the story of Deep Blue, the IBM computer that defeated Garry Kasparov, the world chess champion, in a six-game match in 1997. Although chess is considered a hallmark of strategy and intellect, Deep Blue used a largely brute force approach. With its 512 microprocessors operating in parallel, it could evaluate 200 million board positions per second. It performed these evaluations by scanning the board for hundreds of factors such as pawn structure or the position of the king, and then combining these factors into a score for each move it considered. The machine's victory over the world chess champion led to speculation in many directions. Some believed that this was an important breakthrough for machine intelligence and indicated great promise for the kinds of problems that would be susceptible to software in the future. Others thought this merely demonstrated a great deal of concentrated effort on a situation that is limited by explicit rules of a type that do not exist in important real-world problems.

To think about the genuine implications of Deep Blue's victory, it is worthwhile to look at a far more difficult programming problem that has been studied for over thirty

WORK SYSTEM SNAPSHOT
Microsoft programs software for a new release

CUSTOMERS
- Customers who purchase Microsoft's software
- Microsoft itself, because it must create a basis for new releases and because the software reflects its strategy

PRODUCTS & SERVICES
- New release of a software product
- Internal documentation as the basis for the bug fixes and for the next release

BUSINESS PROCESS
- Identify features customers want and features Microsoft wants for strategic reasons
- Decide which features to include in a release
- Divide the work among small teams and break each team's work into three phases
- Program and test features in each module
- Perform a daily build to make sure all parts of the product work together
- Decide which features to delay to subsequent releases
- Test the entire release
- Package and distribute the new release

PARTICIPANTS	INFORMATION	TECHNOLOGY
• Programmers and testers	• Features to be included in the release • Programs • Examples for testing • Project plan	(Not mentioned in the case) • Programming languages • Debugging techniques • Computers used in programming and testing

years but has not been solved. This is the problem of programming a computer to understand and respond to questions about stories that four-year-old children can understand, such as:

> Billy was invited to Sally's party. He asked his mother if she would like a kite. She said that Sally already had a kite and would return it.

Here's the irony. People have programmed a computer to defeat the world chess champion, but no one knows how to program a computer to understand a simple story that children understand easily. The difficulty with the story is that many aspects of the situation are unstated or implied. We assume that Billy and Sally are young children (but not infants) and that Billy thinks Sally would like a kite as a birthday present. The word *she* in the second sentence refers to Sally because it is unlikely that Billy would be asking his mother if she (his mother) would like a kite, especially since the previous sentence referred to Sally's party. Even though the word *gift* did not appear in the story, we assume the kite is to be a gift because we know that children usually bring gifts to birthday parties. Apparently Billy's mother believes he understands that if Sally already had a kite she wouldn't want another. (If Sally already had a $100 bill, however, she probably would want another, especially as she got older.)

It was possible to program Deep Blue because the programming team had deep knowledge of chess and because the world of chess was completely described by explicit rules. We cannot yet program computers to understand everyday life because no one knows how to identify all the factors and describe how they interact. Between these two extremes is the real-world data processing that can be programmed using the tools and techniques that will now be explained. After discussing standard software topics such as the types of software, the process of programming, and the succession of ever more powerful programming languages, this chapter will return briefly to the question of artificial intelligence to add a few more comments about the current limits of software and programming.

TYPES OF SOFTWARE

The software in a computer system consists of programs—coded instructions created by programmers or users to tell the computer system what to do.

Figure 9.1 illustrates the division of labor between the two basic types of software, application software and system software. **Application software** defines the tasks the computer should perform, and expresses that processing from a user or business perspective. **System software** performs the background work that makes it possible for application software to run on computer hardware. It controls the internal operation of the computer system and serves as an intermediary between the application software and the computer hardware. In general, software should be designed to focus the user's attention on business activities and to minimize attention users devote to system software and computer details.

Application Software

Application software can be divided into two types, general-purpose application software and situation-specific application software. General-purpose application software

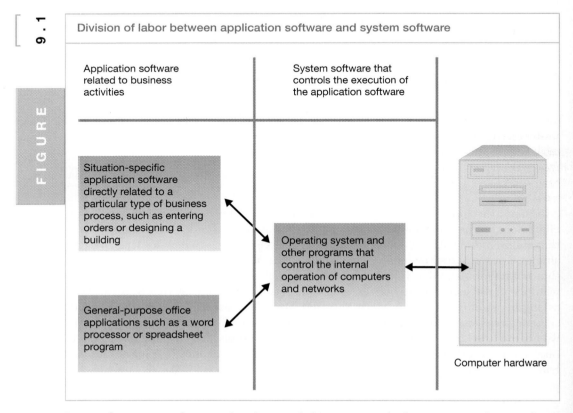

FIGURE 9.1

Division of labor between application software and system software

Application software related to business activities

System software that controls the execution of the application software

Situation-specific application software directly related to a particular type of business process, such as entering orders or designing a building

General-purpose office applications such as a word processor or spreadsheet program

Operating system and other programs that control the internal operation of computers and networks

Computer hardware

System software serves as the intermediary that controls the way computer hardware executes application software.

is sometimes called **end-user software**. It includes word processors, spreadsheet programs, presentation programs, and relatively simple DBMSs that end users can apply directly. These general-purpose tools are designed for use by end users without assistance from professional programmers. They are used in two ways: (1) simply to get work done, such as writing a memo or performing a calculation; and (2) to automate repetitive business tasks such as calculations related to monthly budgeting. End-user software typically is used to develop comparatively simple information systems that don't require a professional level of programming knowledge and expertise. It sometimes permits end users to access and analyze data downloaded from large, complex systems developed by programmers. Users and managers are affected personally by end-user software because it is a fundamental tool for getting their work done efficiently. Firms that adopt this software especially well may enjoy some competitive advantage in internal efficiency.

Situation-specific application software organizes data for particular uses and structures or automates parts of specific business processes. For example, in a sales department it might include programs for forecasting sales, controlling purchase transactions, maintaining customer data, and sending bills to customers. This software may be built by a firm's programmers or may be purchased from an application software vendor. In either case, it is developed by analyzing specific work systems, deciding how they might be improved, and writing programs that improve work system operation by providing better information or by structuring or automating part of the desired process.

Situation-specific application software is designed to support business strategies and tactics. Compared to general-purpose application software, it has more potential for competitive impact because it is more tightly linked to business processes that the organization uses to differentiate itself from its competitors. Effective use of the other types of software is still important, however, because it supports the organization's internal effectiveness and efficiency.

System Software

System software performs the background work that makes it possible for application software to run on computer hardware. System software is produced by programmers who are expert in the computer system's internal operation. Examples of system software include operating systems and compilers. Software such as Web browsers might be viewed as application software because they are used directly by end users and also as system software because they make it possible for other application software to run on the user's computer.

An operating system controls the execution of programs, the flow of data and programs within the computer system, and the use of computer system resources, such as disk space. Examples include the various versions of UNIX, Windows, and the Macintosh operating system. System software also includes programming languages and tools that programmers use when creating and maintaining the software within information systems. Examples of these tools include compilers, industrial-strength DBMSs, and computer-aided software engineering (CASE) systems. Compilers translate programs written in languages such as COBOL or C++ into instructions that can be executed by computers. Data communication software controls the transmission of data among devices and computer systems. Other system software includes utilities for sorting and merging files and performing background functions related to maintaining computer systems.

Decisions about system software affect managers and users in several ways. Because programs are written to run under a particular operating system on a particular type of computer, the choice of an operating system affects the portability of programs and the ability to use purchased software. Programming languages and tools affect managers and users in an indirect way because they can help programmers produce more benefits for an organization with the same level of effort. The ultimate impact is a combination of better information systems and lower costs.

PROGRAMMING VIEWED AS A BUSINESS PROCESS

Programming is the process of creating instructions that a machine will execute later. This is done by organizing and communicating ideas in a form a machine can recognize. Setting a telephone to forward calls to another extension is a simplistic form of programming. Setting up a spreadsheet to calculate budget alternatives is a more complex form. Building large transaction processing systems is a much more complex form. These instances all involve generating instructions that a machine will execute.

Since programming is a business process, programming performance can be evaluated using the performance variables introduced in Chapter 2 (refer back to Table 2.6). For example, the programs that are the product of the programming process can be evaluated in terms of cost to the customer (including learning time), quality, responsiveness, reliability, and conformance. The programming process itself can be evaluated in terms of activity rate, output rate, consistency, productivity, cycle time, downtime, and security.

Infrastructure and context issues are important to consider for programming because it is part of the larger process of building and maintaining information systems. Steps that precede programming include analyzing the problem, getting agreement on how the system should operate, and designing the computer system. Steps after programming include training users, implementing the information system in the organization, and maintaining it over time.

[L O O K   A H E A D]

The last three chapters of this book discuss topics related to information system planning and the entire system life cycle in an organization.

Programming as a Translation Process

Computers are programmed by writing computer programs. A **computer program** is a set of instructions in a programming language that specifies the data processing to be performed by a computer. Figure 9.2 shows that writing programs is part of the process of translating what a user wants to accomplish into instructions that can be executed by a computer. Writing the programs expresses the user's ideas in a programming language. In most cases, these computer programs cannot be executed directly by the computer; instead, they must be translated into machine language. This additional step is performed automatically by other programs written by experts in the programming language.

The rules and limitations of the programming language affect both the programs expressing the user's ideas and the automatic translation process. The rules determine what kinds of statements and commands can be used in the programs, as well as the exact grammar for using them. Programs that perform the same processing but are written in different languages use different commands and different grammar. The automatic translation step uses the rules of the language as a guide in deciphering the programs. One reason programming languages contain so many seemingly arbitrary rules is to make this automatic translation practical.

Organizing Ideas

Regardless of the programming language used, programming involves careful organization of ideas. **Successive decomposition** (also called stepwise refinement) is the technique programmers typically use for organizing ideas. This "divide and conquer" strategy is consistent with the way process modeling divides business processes into successively

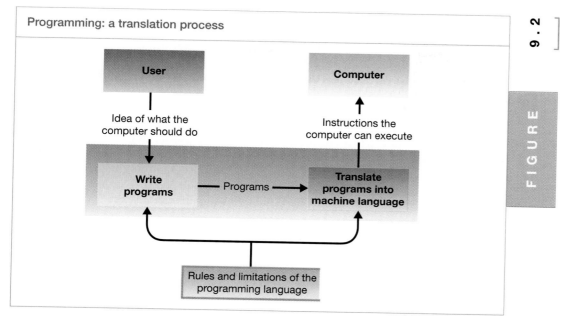

9.2 FIGURE

Programming is a process of translating a user's idea of what a computer should do into a set of instructions that a computer can execute.

smaller subprocesses (see Chapter 3). This strategy is an essential skill for programmers, who need to keep track of the various parts of complex problems. When successive decomposition is applied to programming, programs are divided into small subprograms sometimes called **modules**. Modules are self-contained subsystems that produce predictable outputs from known inputs. Figure 9.3 illustrates how a program can be divided into a set of subprograms, which can be divided further. Decomposition into modules makes the logic of a program more apparent by separating the details of the modules from the overall logical flow.

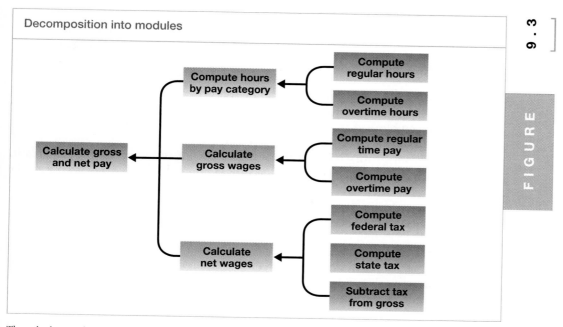

9.3 FIGURE

The calculation of gross and net pay in a payroll system can be decomposed into several levels of subprograms. On the first level, the calculation is expressed as three smaller subprograms. Each of these is then divided into several modules, each of which could be specified in more detail to show the precise logic. (Note that the data flows between modules are not included in the diagram.)

Successive decomposition allows programmers to solve a problem with a module and then reuse that solution in new situations. This avoids reinventing program logic that has already been developed. For example, suppose that you want a computer to list every customer whose payments are delinquent. The same module that finds the next customer might also be used in a different program that sends a promotional mailing to specific categories of customers.

Even though most programming languages contain methods for successive decomposition, undisciplined programming still produces poorly organized programs. Such programs are difficult to test and to maintain. Over 20 years ago these problems led to the development of **structured programming**, a disciplined style of programming based on the successive decomposition. Structured programming has achieved wide acceptance because it results in programs that are much easier to create, understand, test, and maintain. Such programs have the following characteristics:

- The program code is divided into functional constituent parts called modules.
- The modules can be tested separately and reused in different applications.
- The modules are related to each other hierarchically.
- A main module at the top of the hierarchy controls program execution.
- Each module should have only one entry point and only one exit point.
- Each module should operate depending only on the input data and not on any information remembered from the last time it was used.
- The logical flow within any module should be specified using only three basic control structures shown in Figure 9.4: sequence, selection, and iteration. The use of GO TO statements that jump forward or backward in a program should be minimized or eliminated because a nonsequential flow tends to be confusing.
- Each module should be small enough to be understood easily.

Organization of ideas and structured programming are not just issues for professional programmers. Programs written by business professionals without programming training are often poorly structured. An estimated 20% to 40% of all spreadsheets contain errors. One reason for this is that spreadsheet software does little to encourage or enforce proper structure. Another is that many of the people programming the spreadsheets neither understand nor use proper testing procedures.[2]

Testing Programs

Testing is the process of determining whether a program or system operates in the desired manner. A flaw in a program that causes it to produce incorrect or inappropriate results is called a **bug.** The process of finding and correcting bugs is called **debugging.** The two types of bugs are syntax errors and logic errors.

Syntax errors involve incorrect use of the programming language. The SQL translation of the user's query in Figure 4.8 in Chapter 4 demonstrates the meaning of syntax. The second line of the translation uses the term *select* because that command has a specific meaning in SQL. Conceivable English alternatives such as *find* or *look for* would be syntax errors because these terms are not recognized as commands in SQL and would be rejected. The syntax of programming languages has been a major stumbling block preventing nonprogrammers from developing information systems. Current user interfaces eliminate parts of this problem by permitting users to select from a list of commands instead of assuming that users will remember command names.

Logic errors are bugs that cause a program to perform incorrect processing even though the program is syntactically correct. For example, it may calculate the tax on the entire purchase when it is supposed to exclude food items. Programs that seem correct individually may also fail due to mutual inconsistencies when they are used together with other programs. Another possible logic error is that the program performs the intended processing but the initial intention when the program was designed was incorrect or too limited. In software firms, this problem has become a standing joke: Customer service people explain to customers that the way a particular program operates is a "feature," not a "bug." This means that the program operates the way it was

FIGURE 9.4

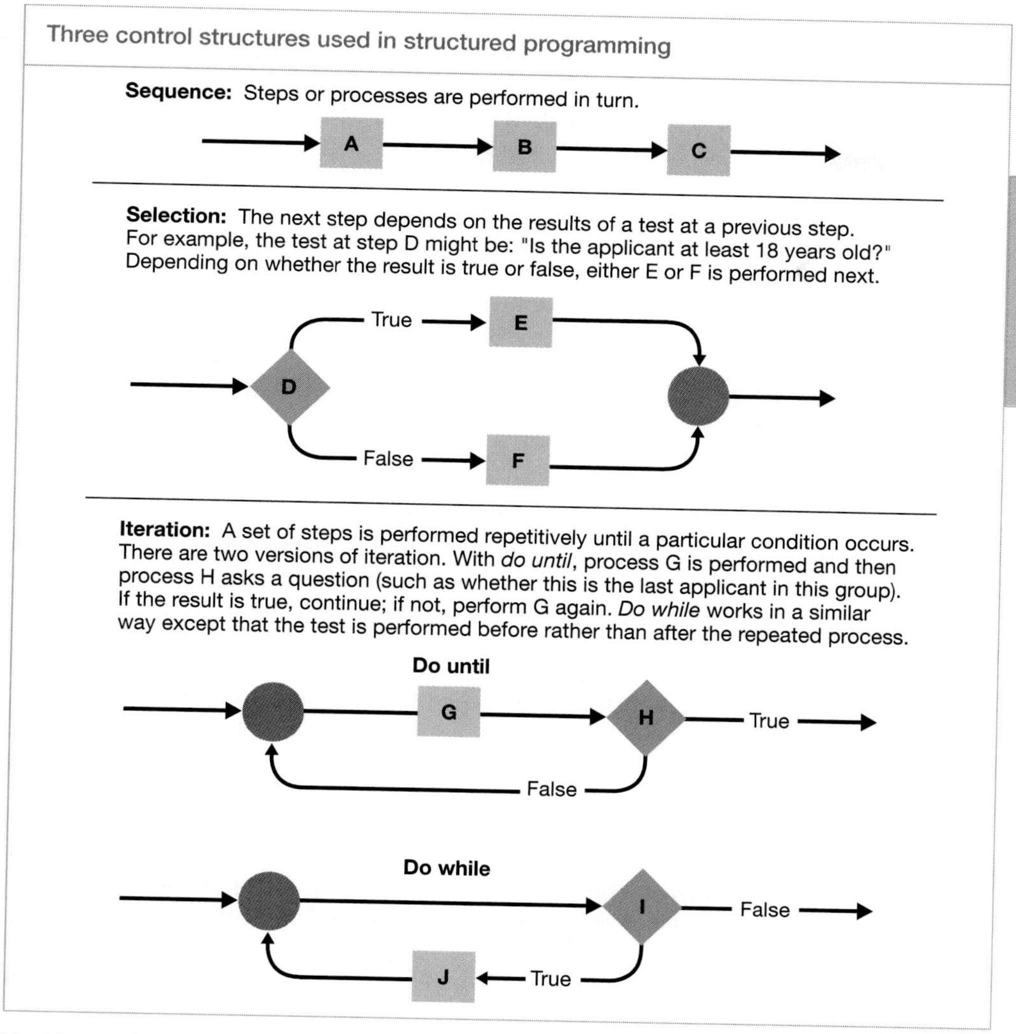

Three control structures used in structured programming

Sequence: Steps or processes are performed in turn.

Selection: The next step depends on the results of a test at a previous step. For example, the test at step D might be: "Is the applicant at least 18 years old?" Depending on whether the result is true or false, either E or F is performed next.

Iteration: A set of steps is performed repetitively until a particular condition occurs. There are two versions of iteration. With *do until*, process G is performed and then process H asks a question (such as whether this is the last applicant in this group). If the result is true, continue; if not, perform G again. *Do while* works in a similar way except that the test is performed before rather than after the repeated process.

Do until

Do while

To make sure that computer programs are understandable and easy to maintain, structured programming calls for consistent use of only three control structures within programs.

supposed to operate, and the way the manual says it should operate, whether or not the user believes this makes sense.

Most programs initially contain bugs and inappropriate features regardless of how carefully they are first written. Business programs rarely work correctly the first time. The larger the program and the larger the number of interactions with other programs, the higher the likelihood of bugs. Furthermore, some bugs go undetected until after the program has been used in practice for weeks or months. Finding such bugs in important public computer systems has become like a sport in some computer science departments. In 13 months spanning 1996 and 1997, university students hunting for bugs in available software found at least six. These included a way to booby-trap a Web page so that it would delete the files of anyone visiting it, a flaw in a Web browser's privacy protection for credit card transactions, a way to use Internet software to make unauthorized bank transfers, and a flaw in the encryption code that the U.S. government permitted companies to export at that time.[3]

Software bugs are an especially severe problem in situations where a single erroneous calculation could cause disaster. One of the most expensive bugs to date caused a European Space Agency's Ariane 5 rocket to destroy itself when it went off course while transporting a pair of three-ton communication satellites into orbit in 1996. The bug existed in guidance system software that converted the sideways velocity of the rocket from a 64-bit format to a 16-bit format. The velocity number was too large to fit into 16 bits and caused an overflow error, which shut down the guidance system. A redundant backup version of the guidance system took over, but it failed in the same way milliseconds later because it was running the same software. The software should have checked before creating an overflow, but the guidance code had been written for the Ariane 4, which was not as fast as an Ariane 5.[4] A similar overflow problem at the Bank of New York had been widely publicized in 1985 when it prevented the bank from balancing its books at the end of a day in which it traded $23 billion in securities. The Bank had to pay $5 million interest to borrow that amount for one day because a 16-bit field overflowed the first time the bank performed more than 65,536 (2^{16}) transactions in a day.

Good practice in real-world programming includes the development of a test plan for debugging the program and the system it is part of. The debugging of an individual program is sometimes called **unit testing**, which is usually done by testing a program under a wide range of conditions. For example, inputs that are transformed or that participate in program logic are set to typical values and to their high and low values in different tests. Tests using the high and low values often reveal bugs because the errors in the results they generate are often more obvious than errors in results calculated from typical values. In contrast to unit testing, **system testing** determines whether the entire computer system operates as intended. System testing is more complicated than unit testing because the number of possible combinations of conditions is much larger. Since it is extremely difficult to prove that even a simple program is correct, testing of programs and systems is a key area of computer science research.

In the world of commercial software there is often an additional round of testing in which a software product is released to selected users who volunteer to report flaws they find through initial usage in real-world situations. This is called **beta testing**. Microsoft and other large software companies do a substantial amount of beta testing before finalizing each major release of their products.

Surprisingly, it is often difficult to debug your own work because you are too familiar with the program's intent. Programmers testing their own work often test for what they think it is supposed to accomplish and decide that the program is correct, but they never test for situations or conditions they have overlooked. To avoid such omissions, many programming groups have someone else test a program after a round of unit testing by the programmer. Taking this form of collaboration a step further, some have experienced higher productivity and lower defect rates using a method called pair programming in which two programmers work side-by-side at one computer, continuously collaborating on the same design.[5]

[**L O O K A H E A D**]

Pair programming is mentioned in the Chrysler case at the end of this chapter.

R E A L I T Y C H E C K ✓

Programming Viewed as a Business Process

Basic ideas about programming include organizing ideas and testing programs.

1. What techniques do you use to test spreadsheets or other programs you write? Explain why you believe those techniques would or would not be adequate if the problem you were solving involved 20 times as many variables and relationships.

2. Explain how you feel about this statement: "I don't know whether my bank programmed its systems correctly, but I just have to trust those systems and assume that my checking account is being handled correctly."

The Changing Nature of Programming

The principle guiding progress in software is that people should be able to express themselves in a form that is easy and natural for them and that allows them to focus on their business problem and not on the details of representing the problem for the computer. Figure 9.5 identifies some of the major advances that were enabled by the hardware progress in Chapter 8; these advances have permitted greater focus on the business

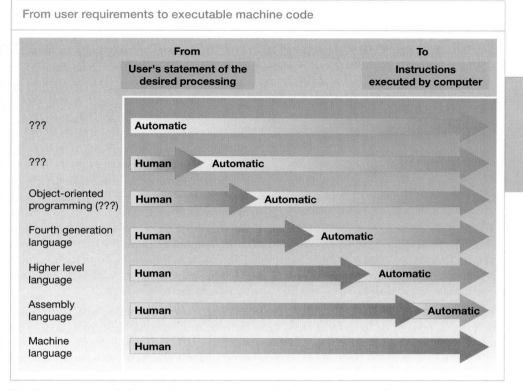

FIGURE 9.5

From user requirements to executable machine code

This figure summarizes the history of programming as a set of milestones in translating from what a user wants into instructions that can be executed by a computer. With each step, more of the translation is done automatically and less is done by a person. Where object-oriented programming belongs in this progression remains to be seen, since it is very powerful but has been applied mainly in the context of current higher level languages. The question marks at the top of the figure indicate future developments whose form and content are unknown.

problem. The figure illustrates that these software advances have changed the balance of responsibilities between humans and computers. With the first machine languages, programmers performed 100% of the translation from the idea of what users wanted to accomplish into machine-executable code and kept track of minute, computer-related details about how programs operated. With each successive development, more of the translation is done automatically. The figure illustrates that we don't know whether programming methods will ever advance to the point where people can just say what they want and have it programmed automatically. The natural language that we use in everyday speech will remain ineffective for this purpose for the foreseeable future because it is so unstructured, and, as was illustrated by the story of Billy and Sally at the beginning of the chapter, so much is left unsaid.

Before discussing specific developments in programming it is useful to recognize some of the major trends supporting the automation summarized in Figure 9.5. In combination, these trends are changing the nature of programming by reducing the number of steps between specifying how the information system should help users and getting it to operate correctly on the computer.

Greater Nonprocedurality   People can increasingly express *what* should be accomplished instead of *how* it should be done by a computer. A program that specifies the procedures for how something should be done is described as **procedural.** One that specifies what should be accomplished, but not the procedures for doing it, is **nonprocedural.** For example the query "Which sales territories exceeded their forecast by more than 10% last month?" explains what the user wants, but not how the computer should answer the question. Greater nonprocedurality helps people specify the required processing in the terms in which they think about the problem. With greater nonprocedurality, programming is more directly linked to analysis, which is often done with diagrams such as data flow diagrams for process modeling (refer to Chapter 3) and entity-relationship diagrams for data modeling (refer to Chapter 4). As a result, less programming effort is needed to express the user's ideas in a programming language, and it is less necessary for people to make choices about computer-related details unrelated to the business problem.

Greater Modularity and Reusability   As discussed earlier, modularity is a form of division of labor in which systems are designed as a set of self-contained modules that work together, with the output of one module serving as the input of another. Modularity makes it easier to design and test systems because each function is isolated in one place. An important example of modularity is the separation between graphical interfaces that present information to users and database programs that find the data in databases. Early systems might have placed both functions in the same program, making it much harder to maintain. As software becomes more modular, it becomes less necessary for programmers to write programs from scratch. With the trend toward **reusability**, they are encouraged to reuse the work of others by cobbling together and modifying pre-existing modules. Typical reusable modules include programs that control windows on a screen, open and close files, find data in databases, or perform repetitive calculations. For reusability to be practical, programs must be created as carefully chosen modules and stored in a module library that makes reuse easy.

Greater Machine and Data Independence   Trends toward open systems and modularity have reinforced long-term trends toward machine and data independence. With greater **machine independence**, programs are increasingly written in ways that permit them to be executed on a variety of operating systems and machines from different vendors. This is a key advantage of the Java programming language, which is used extensively for Internet applications. With greater **data independence**, programs are increasingly written in ways that make it possible to change the physical storage of the data without changing the program. Enterprise applications with appropriate middleware have achieved a degree of data independence by making it possible to switch database software at the server without changing the application software at the client.

Tighter Links between Analysis and Programming   Although students often view programming as an end in itself, businesses see programming as part of a larger process of building and maintaining information systems (summarized in Figure 9.2). That larger process includes analyzing the problem, comparing alternatives, designing the new business process, designing the technical system, coding the system, testing it, implementing it in the organization, and maintaining it over time. Each of the advances in Figure 9.5 moves toward linking analysis and programming by eliminating steps between the expression of what people want (analysis) and the instructions for the computer (programming). A number of commercial products have been developed that attempt to systematize this linkage. These **computer-aided software engineering (CASE)** systems differ in detail and scope, but they typically include process and data modeling, a comprehensive data dictionary, methods for designing the technical structure of programs and databases, and modules for creating user interfaces and reports.

As these four trends take hold even further, entire technical systems will become more self-explanatory because the programs will be less procedural, more modular, more machine and data independent, and more tightly linked to the analysis. This will make it easier for people other than the original programmers to understand what individual programs and entire systems accomplish. Programmers should find it easier to modify programs when this becomes necessary. The four trends may seem very abstract at first blush, but they are basic ideas underlying much of the progress that has occurred in programming languages and techniques. One of the places where these trends are converging is in the increasing application of object-oriented programming.

The Trend toward Object-Oriented Programming

Some software developers believe that major advances in programming are being created through applications of a programming philosophy called object-oriented programming (often abbreviated OOP). This general approach was invented in the 1960s with the simulation language Simula67 but did not become popular until the 1990s. Although OOP may seem to be an extension of the structured programming techniques mentioned earlier, there is more to it than that because it is a fundamentally different way of thinking about programming.

Object-oriented programming (OOP) treats data and programs in a way that may seem strange to someone who has programmed using the traditional languages that will be explained in the next section. Figure 9.6 illustrates the major OOP concepts. OOP starts with *objects* and *classes*. Objects are the things about which data exist. Associated with an object are both data and actions related to the object that can be performed on the data. For example, an object might be a document written using a word processor. Any particular document is a member of a *class* of objects called "document." Associated with that class of objects are *actions* that can be taken, such as opening it, closing it, saving it, or deleting it. These actions all have *methods* for performing the action. The classes exist in hierarchies and a class *inherits* the attributes and actions of the classes that precede it in a hierarchy. This implies that a document within the sub-class "memo" would have all attributes and actions related to documents as well as additional attributes and actions related specifically to memos.

In object-oriented programming all actions are controlled by *messages* passed between objects. For example, the object "user" could send a message to the object "Memo to A. Jones" telling it to open itself. If there are ten different types of documents and one standard way to open a document, that method for opening documents would be attached to the object class "document" and inherited by all ten types of document. To open a document of any type, it would only be necessary to send an "open" message along with any additional data required to perform this action. For example, the additional data might be the identification of the object sending the message because the method for opening documents might check whether the message came from an object permitted to open this document.

Although it may seem strange to tell a document to open itself, treating things in terms of objects, classes, actions, inheritance, and messages encourages modularity and reusability. The most visible applications of object-oriented programming to date have been in graphical user interfaces, which can be described in terms of particular types of objects such as windows, menus, fields, and buttons. These same classes of objects apply regardless of whether the application is a billing system or a spreadsheet. It is therefore possible to program many methods only once and then reuse them for many different applications. Because the user interface and data handling make up a large part of many applications, OOP saves programming effort, simplifies overall system design, and creates more consistent-looking applications. Objects and object orientation are becoming increasingly important across the information systems landscape. Object orientation is starting to transform the way programmers work and is increasingly common in applications, especially Web-based applications. We will see in the next section that object orientation is an important feature of newer programming languages such as C++ and Java.

R E A L I T Y C H E C K ✓

Object-Oriented Programming

Object-oriented programming is a fundamentally different way of thinking about the programming process.

1. Assume you were a programmer who had not used this technique but had many years of experience in traditional programming. Do you think you would be enthusiastic about OOP?

2. Assume you were an IT manager who recently heard about the advantages of OOP. How would you decide whether to pursue it in your organization?

FIGURE 9.6

Major concepts of object-oriented programming

Classes and objects: Objects are the things about which data exists. Objects of the same type are grouped together into classes. Classes can include subclasses. In this example, speadsheets and memos are objects in the class *Documents*.

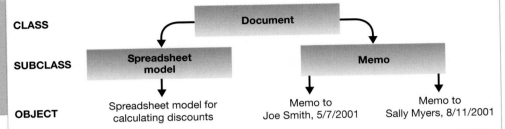

Inheritance and methods: The objects within a class inherit the methods associated with the class. The methods are functions that can be performed on the objects in the class. In this example, associated with the class Documents are a series of methods such as opening, closing, saving, and printing. All of these are inherited by the objects in the subclasses.

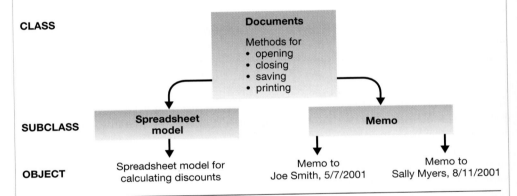

Message passing: The only way to communicate between objects is to send an explicit message.

Polymorphism: The same message can be sent to objects in distinct yet similar classes to start an action that may be handled in a different way depending on the characteristics of the classes. Although some aspects of printing are the same in this example, such as identifying a printer, other aspects are different, such as the need for a method for splitting the spreadsheet across columns and pages.

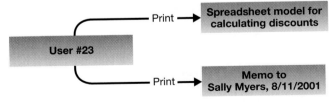

The major concepts of object-oriented programming include classes, objects, inheritance, methods, message passing, and polymorphism. Building these ideas into the analysis and programming of an information system makes it easier to develop and maintain.

FOUR GENERATIONS OF PROGRAMMING LANGUAGES

The progression from machine language to fourth generation languages and beyond is often called the **generations of programming languages**. We will summarize this progression to explain the directions in which progress is continuing to occur. Although business professionals do not work with machine language directly, starting from this point provides useful background for understanding the advances that are continuing today.

Machine Languages

The internal programming language for a particular chip is called its **machine language**. Although the first programmers had to write programs in machine language, today's application programmers no longer have to do so. Box 9.1 presents a hypothetical example that compares a highly simplified machine language with an assembly language. In this example, the instructions are performing the calculation

$$A = (B - C) * D + (E * F)$$

The machine language instructions in the box look nothing like the formula. Instructions in this hypothetical machine language consist of a numerical operation code and the location of the data item that is being added, subtracted, or multiplied. For example, the second instruction in the program is "37 – 202," which says "Add the contents of location 202 to the contents of the accumulator." Each instruction is in a physical location inside the computer; each data item is in a physical location that must be referenced explicitly by the program.

Writing programs in machine language is extremely difficult because it forces programmers to make many explicit choices they do not care about, such as the physical location of the data and machine language instructions. The code itself is also so inexpressive that it is difficult to understand what another person's machine language program is trying to do. Even the original programmer may find complex programs difficult to understand. Machine language programs are also difficult to modify or expand. Changes as seemingly simple as inserting several lines of code may require many corrections in location references. Major changes in data configurations or program flows are a programming nightmare. In addition, the lack of machine independence makes it necessary to rewrite a program for it to accomplish the same processing on a different type of machine. Although machine language is essential for the internal operation of the machine, it is an inordinately difficult medium for business programmers to use.

Assembly Languages

Early programmers developed an ingenious solution to the shortcomings of machine language. The solution was to write programs using assembly language and then have the computer automatically translate those programs into machine language instructions. Box 9.1 illustrates that **assembly language** allows the programmer to write the program using the names of the variables (such as A, B, C) rather than the location of the data in the computer (201, 202, 203 in the machine language example). Working with the names of variables avoids the problems of physical references required in machine language programming and makes programs easier to write and maintain.

Programs called assemblers and loaders were developed to work together in translating the programmer's assembly language program into a machine language program. This translation includes a number of things. It converts all mnemonic operation codes (such as *add* and *sub* in Box 9.1) into the equivalent machine language codes (such as 37 and 46). More important to programmers, the translation identifies all variables in the program and assigns a machine location to each of them. When the program runs on the computer, a machine location is assigned for each translated instruction. Assemblers also perform other important functions such as identifying syntax errors and certain logical errors. For example, if a program statement says ADD X, but X does not yet have a value, the assembler identifies X as an "undefined variable."

BOX 9.1 COMPARISON OF MACHINE LANGUAGE AND ASSEMBLY LANGUAGE

A programmer wants the computer to calculate the value of the variable A using the formula

$$A = (B - C) * D + (E * F)$$

On the left is a set of instructions expressing this calculation in a hypothetical machine language. On the right is an equivalent set of instructions in a hypothetical assembly language. For example, the operation code "sub" in the third assembly language instruction is equivalent to the operation code 46 in the third machine language instruction. Although programming in assembly language is easier than programming in machine language, it is still much harder than just stating the formula.

Machine language

To program in this machine language, one must specify the location of each instruction, the numerical operation code, and the location of the operand (the data item the instruction uses).

LI = location of instruction

OC = operation code

LO = location of operand

Assembly language

To program in this assembly language, one must specify the operation code and the name of the variable. Notice how the programmer had to make up a temporary variable that was not part of the business problem.

OC = operation code

VAR = variable name

Machine language instruction			Meaning of instruction	Assembly language instruction		Meaning of instruction
LI	OC	LO		OC	VAR	
101	19	—	Clear accumulator	cle	—	Clear accumulator
102	37	202	Add contents of location 202 to contents of accumulator	add	B	Add B to contents of accumulator
103	46	203	Subtract contents of location 203 from contents of accumulator	sub	C	Subtract C from contents of accumulator
104	52	204	Multiply contents of accumulator by contents of location 204	mpy	D	Multiply contents of accumulator by D
105	24	207	Store contents of accumulator in location 207	sto	T	Store contents of accumulator as a temporary variable T
106	19	—	Clear accumulator	cle	—	Clear accumulator
107	37	205	Add contents of location 205 to contents of accumulator	add	E	Add E to contents of accumulator
108	52	206	Multiply contents of accumulator by contents of location 206	mpy	F	Multiply contents of accumulator by F
109	37	207	Add contents of location 207 to contents of accumulator	add	T	Add T to contents of accumulator
110	24	201	Store contents of accumulator in location 201	sto	A	Store contents of accumulator in A

Despite the improvements embodied in assembly language, programming in assembly language retained many of the major drawbacks of programming in machine language. It remained a laborious, highly detailed, and error-prone activity. In addition, because assembly language is so directly related to the machine it runs on, transferring a program to a different machine language remained tedious and error-prone. The next step was to provide a better tool than assembly language.

Higher Level Languages

The shortcomings of assembly language programming led to the first **higher level languages** in the late 1950s. Also called third generation languages (3GLs), their purpose was to permit people to program at a higher level. In the assembly language example, the programmer is thinking about how to calculate A from the variables B, C, D, E, and F. Ideally, the programmer should be able to give the formula instead of having to break the calculation into ten tiny steps. Higher level languages permit concise statements of this type.

A program called a **compiler** translates higher level language programs into machine language. For example, a compiler allows a programmer simply to write the equation in the example and translates the equation into machine language. In this type of translation process, the original program is called the **source code**, and the equivalent machine language program is called the **object code** (which is not related to "object" in OOP). The object code is used each time the application is executed. When it is necessary to change the program, the changes are made in the source code, which is then translated into new object code. These procedures make it unnecessary to translate the source code each time an application is executed. In addition to allowing programmers to express arithmetic statements directly, compilers and other system software also provide automatic mechanisms for handling input, output, and data formatting. These mechanisms permit the programmer to use a command such as *PRINT*, which automatically is translated into hundreds of machine language instructions that take care of all the details required for the computer to retrieve the data. These details are related to the internal operation of the computer and its interface with the printer and are of no interest to the application programmer, who simply wants certain data printed.

Interpreters perform a similar function in a different way. An **interpreter** for a higher level language translates and executes each successive line of a program. The interpreted programs remain in source code, and object code is not generated for later use. Interpreted programs often run more slowly than compiled programs because the compiler can optimize the translation instead of being required to translate and execute each line. Compilers have major advantages when repetitive use and speed are important, but the use of interpreters makes it easier to debug programs and is fast enough in many situations. The Java language used for many Internet applications is an interpreted language.

The same higher level language needs different compilers or interpreters for different types of computers because different microprocessors use different machine languages. This is an important issue related to the portability of programs between different types of computers. Ideally most application programs should be machine independent, and therefore able to operate on any computer with sufficient capacity. Although many higher level languages were designed with machine independence in mind, compilers for the same language on different machines often have some inconsistencies. Consequently, programs written in a higher level language on one type of computer may not run properly on another type of computer. Such programs must be retested on the second computer and may have to be modified before they can be used.

Many higher level languages have been developed, but only a few have attained widespread use, including COBOL, FORTRAN, PL/I, BASIC, Pascal, Ada, C, C++, and Java. All of these were developed initially with a particular set of capabilities but have been modified and expanded through subsequent versions on different computers. Box 9.2 explains more about these languages.

Figure 9.7 compares three programming languages by showing how each can express the same simplistic program. COBOL is the traditional language for most business data processing. BASIC was created as a simple language for teaching programming but has developed into Visual BASIC, which is often used in programs for personal computers. C++ is a newer language used frequently for developing new, industrial-strength software. To a nonprogrammer, the differences between these languages may appear superficial, but each important language has certain features that make it especially useful for a particular purpose. For example, the COBOL program contains a mandatory data division for defining the format of the data in the program. Capabilities related to data definition and the formatting of inputs and outputs are one

BOX 9.2 **HIGHER LEVEL PROGRAMMING LANGUAGES**

FORTRAN (FORmula TRANslator) was introduced by IBM in 1957 as the first higher level language. It was developed for scientific programming focusing predominantly on calculations and with relatively simple input and output requirements. Initially, it had few structured features.

COBOL (COmmon Business Oriented Language) was developed in 1959 by a committee whose goal was to produce a higher level language for business data processing. These applications required extensive control of inputs and outputs but relatively simple calculations. Improved versions of COBOL came out in 1968, 1974, and 1985. In attempting to make COBOL programs self-explanatory, COBOL's designers permitted lengthy names of variables and subroutines and used sentence-like grammar. This design made programs extremely verbose but easier to maintain than FORTRAN programs. COBOL is the language used most commonly in existing business data processing systems, although it is used less frequently for newer systems. It is a good tool for organizing programming ideas through successive decomposition and contains some features supporting structured programming.

PL/I was introduced by IBM in 1964 as a single language that could be used for both business data processing and scientific calculations. It is extremely complicated because it incorporates and extends most of the capabilities of both FORTRAN and COBOL. PL/I did not replace COBOL because businesses were not convinced it was worth the expense to rewrite their existing COBOL programs.

BASIC (Beginner's All-purpose Symbolic Instruction Code) is an interpreted language developed at Dartmouth in 1965 as a simple language for teaching introductory programming. Students learning BASIC could write small programs within an hour instead of days or weeks. The early versions of BASIC were very limited. For example, the names of variables could be only one or two characters long in the early versions.

Visual BASIC, starting with a first version in 1981, added numerous features to BASIC, especially the ability to create graphical user interfaces quickly and simply by dragging and dropping prebuilt objects into the right location on the screen. It is used for designing programs that run on personal computers and contains the ability to use functionality from Microsoft applications such as Word and Excel.

PASCAL was developed by Niklaus Wirth in 1971 as a tool for teaching and enforcing structured programming. It has become widely used as a teaching tool in computer science departments and is also used widely instead of BASIC. Its input-output capabilities are too limited for most business data processing.

Ada is a language developed by the Department of Defense in 1980 to try to standardize data processing for its information systems and to make programs more reusable to reduce programming costs. It is a structured language that encourages modular design and facilitates testing and reusing code. The latest version, Ada 95, was the first internationally standardized object-oriented language.

C was introduced by Bell Laboratories in 1972 to combine some of the low-level machine control capabilities of assemblers with the data structures and control structures of higher level languages. It is designed to be machine independent and is used to write programs that can be used on different types of computers. The UNIX operating system is written in C so that it, too, can be portable. C is used extensively for infrastructure programs and new software development.

C++ is a superset of C that is more effective for application-level software. It provides capabilities related to object-oriented programming and is used by software firms to develop many of their new commercial applications. It is used extensively for client/server applications.

Java was developed in 1995 as a general-purpose, object-oriented, application-development language for producing programs that operate in a distributed environment involving many different platforms. Java source code is compiled into a format called bytecode that can be executed by a Java interpreter. Compiled Java code can run on most computers because Java interpreters and runtime environments called "Java virtual machines" exist for most operating systems. The first programs written in Java ran much more slowly than comparable programs that are optimized for a particular CPU. Subsequent improvements in compiler methods have greatly reduced this problem. Programmers knowledgeable in C++ can become productive quickly in Java because the languages have similar constructs and Java leaves out many of the error-prone features of C and C++ that force programmers to manage low-end tasks like memory management. Eliminating these features greatly reduces the number of bugs in programs and makes Java programs easier to develop and maintain.

Comparison of programs in COBOL, Basic, and C++

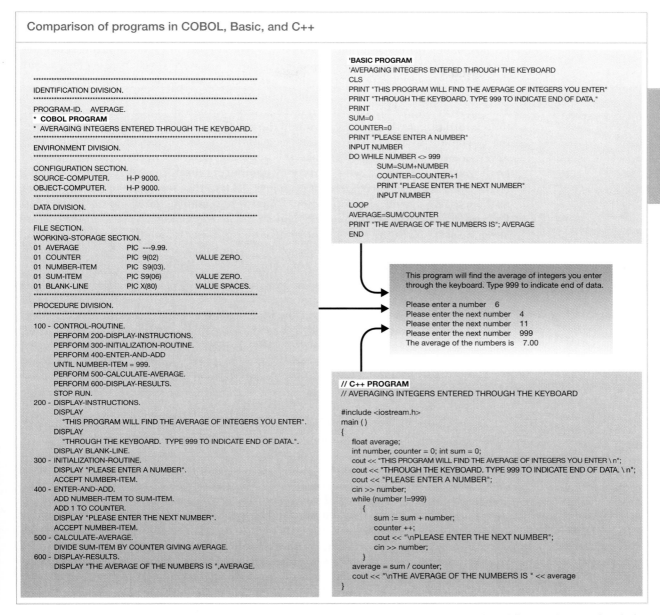

These three programs produce the same results (in slightly different format) and therefore illustrate some of the differences between three higher level programming languages. This simple example actually uses poor programming techniques because 999 could be both a code and a number to be included in the averaging.

of the major reasons COBOL is the most common programming language for business data processing.

The language Java, an object-oriented language similar to C++ in appearance but with a different object model, requires a few additional comments because it has received so much publicity due to its emerging role in distributed computer systems. The original Java development in 1995 was an offshoot of an unsuccessful project at Sun Microsystems aimed at controlling the user interface for home appliances. The team created Java when it redirected itself toward creating a standard, machine-independent language for distributed applications on the Internet. Java source code is compiled into a format called bytecode that can be executed by a Java interpreter. Compiled Java code can run on most computers because Java interpreters and run-time environments called "Java virtual machines" exist for most operating systems. Small Java applications called **applets** can be downloaded from a Web server and run on Java-compatible Web browsers such as Netscape Navigator or Internet Explorer.[6] Java has become increasingly popular in enterprise computing systems. As a general-purpose language Java is applicable in many types of distributed computing other than Internet applications. For example, IBM's Lotus software division used Java to produce eSuite, a set of office applications designed for use on network computers.

The attempt to make Java a computing standard generated important commercial and political issues. Microsoft sent a letter to ISO, the International Organization for Standardization, saying that Sun wanted the benefit of an ISO standard but was unwilling to commit to an open process for developing the technology in the future.[7] In its advertisements IBM seemed to take the opposing view, saying, "since most business environments contain a wide variety of computing platforms, Java is just common sense. So is the idea of 100 percent pure Java—a Java that is not corrupted by offshoots and operating system dependencies."[8] Just a few months later, however, Hewlett-Packard accused Sun of keeping too tight a rein on developing new versions of Java and announced its own Java variant for noncomputer devices such as printers.[9] The continuing development and acceptance of Java is not only a question for programmers, but also a major strategic issue for competition in the computer industry.

Fourth Generation Languages

Third generation languages are basically tools for professional programmers. The high level of programming skill needed to use these languages for business applications makes their direct use by business professionals impractical. Using these languages is arduous and time-consuming even for professional programmers, and the amount of work for professional programmers has always exceeded programmer availability. These factors encouraged the development of new ways to make programmers more productive and to permit nonprogrammers to do programming work.

Fourth generation languages (4GLs) are a loosely defined group of programming languages that make programming less procedural than third generation languages. The term *4GL* is closely associated with query languages and report generators for retrieving data from databases, although 4GLs can also perform transactions using data in databases. Many 4GLs are subsets of larger products, such as DBMSs or integrated systems for designing and building business applications.

Query languages are special-purpose languages used to provide immediate, online answers to questions such as, "Which five customers in New Jersey had the highest purchases last month?" **Report generators** are special-purpose languages used to answer questions or to program reports that will be used repeatedly. The SQL in Figure 4.8 in Chapter 4 was an example of a query language that permits queries stated in a less procedural form than would be necessary in a typical 3GL. The query specification in the example identifies the desired output but doesn't say exactly how the computer should find the data. Similarly, the heading and body of the output are formatted by default. Typical report specifications in a 4GL report generator once looked like a set of text statements, but have moved to more of a graphical approach with the user specifying options using a mouse.

The benefits of 4GLs extend to both programmers and end users. Programmers need less time and effort to specify the required processing. Writing the same reporting program in COBOL might take ten times as long because of all the details that must be incorporated into COBOL programs. End users benefit because 4GLs provide a way to obtain information without requiring the direct help of a programmer. The use of 4GLs for queries and report generation reduces the pressure on programmers to write reporting programs to support immediate information needs.

Although 4GLs have been adopted widely because of their advantages, they did not replace COBOL and other 3GLs for a variety of reasons. The existing investment in over 100 billion lines of COBOL code made rewriting all of these programs an enormous task with a questionable payoff, especially because it would involve a major training effort in addition to the program revisions. The capabilities of 4GLs were also too limited for a great deal of new development because they could not handle complex formats and logic and because they did not address many of the issues related to client/server computing.

The four generations of programming languages define an important stream of developments that make programming less procedural and permit the user to be more concerned with the desired processing or outputs rather than the specific method used for performing the processing. No fifth generation of languages is used in business today.

R E A L I T Y C H E C K ✓

Programming Languages

The generations of programming languages illustrate progress in four directions: greater nonprocedurality, greater modularity and reusability, greater machine and data independence, and tighter links between analysis and programming.

1. Assuming you are a business professional whose job is not directly related to software development, explain why these trends might or might not matter to you.

2. As a spreadsheet user now and in the future, explain what these trends might mean to you.

OTHER MAJOR DEVELOPMENTS IN PROGRAMMING

Although the four generations of programming languages represent an important stream of developments, they certainly don't encompass all that has happened. We will now look at other significant developments, including special-purpose languages, spreadsheets, and CASE systems. We discussed object-oriented programming earlier because of the change in programming philosophy that it signifies.

Special-Purpose Languages

General-purpose programming languages have an important shortcoming. They contain no ideas about the area of business or type of problem the programmer is working on. For example, even through COBOL may be used to program an inventory system or a financial system, it contains no specific ideas about inventory or finance. If you were a programmer analyzing the cash flow from a complex real estate investment, you would prefer to use a programming language that contained financial ideas, such as net present value and return on investment. You might save more time and make fewer errors if the language contained specific ideas about real estate investments.

Modeling languages, special-purpose languages for developing models, are used extensively in decision support systems. Unlike general-purpose languages, they contain specific capabilities that make it easy to build models. Many modeling languages contain financial functions. Some contain special ways of organizing data in two- or three-dimensional arrays for easy analysis. Others include methods for drawing a picture of a model and using that picture to check the consistency of the equations in the model. Figure 9.8 shows the way the modeling language Extend can be used to create a model for analyzing the operations of a car wash. Each of the building blocks was produced in advance and stored in a module library. The programmer created this model by selecting and modifying the building blocks.

Spreadsheets

Like the 3GLs, the first modeling languages were effective only if used by programming professionals. Model building became much more practical for nonprogrammers with the advent of computerized spreadsheets. Excel and other spreadsheet programs are a special type of modeling language that only can be used to describe problems that fit into a spreadsheet format. Spreadsheet programs are used widely because many types

FIGURE **9.8**

Graphical representation of a simulation

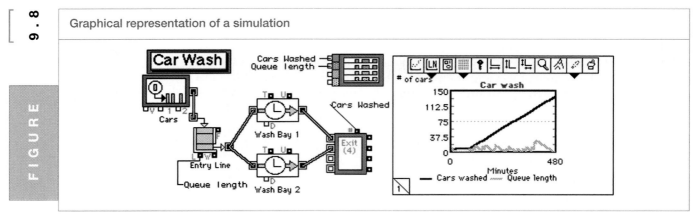

This is the graphical representation of a simulation developed using the Extend simulation system. The simulation was created by linking existing modules provided by the software vendor and specifying values of variables within those modules, such as speeds or capacities. Running this type of simulation many times generates statistics about average waiting times and other factors pertinent to improving the process.

of business calculations can be structured as spreadsheets and because the familiar spreadsheet format makes it unnecessary to struggle with a new way of thinking about problems. Spreadsheet software also provides an easy way for users to work with a model. Instead of forcing the users to name every variable, the spreadsheet permits users to recognize what each variable means based on the cell it occupies in the grid. Focusing on the cells and their specific locations also provides a virtually automatic way of formatting the outputs for printing, making it unnecessary to master a separate report generator.

Although these factors contribute to the popularity of spreadsheets, they sometimes result in spreadsheets that are inflexible and difficult to maintain. It is difficult to look at spreadsheet outputs in different ways because the location of the cells is static. Users attempting to reorganize rows and columns run the risk of introducing errors. Figure 9.9 shows how the pivot table function in Excel made spreadsheets more flexible while maintaining the benefits of the spreadsheet approach.

Programming errors are a pervasive issue with spreadsheet models for several reasons. First, many of the people who build spreadsheet models are not trained in debugging techniques and therefore do not know how to check a model for accuracy. In addition, spreadsheet software permits a very casual style of model building that does little to encourage the characteristics of structured programming. A study by Coopers and Lybrand found that over 90% of spreadsheets with more than 150 rows contained at least one significant mistake.[10] A widely publicized problem in debugging a spreadsheet model occurred when Fidelity's huge Magellan fund forecast a $4.32 per share capital gains distribution in November 1994 but distributed nothing. A clerical worker had put the wrong sign in front of a $1.2 billion ledger entry, creating an incorrect $2.3 billion gain in place of the real $0.1 billion loss. This probably affected the financial decisions of some Fidelity customers who may have sold to avoid the distribution.[11]

Computer-Aided Software Engineering Systems

Computer-aided software engineering (CASE) is the use of computerized tools to improve the efficiency, accuracy, and completeness of the process of analyzing, designing, developing, and maintaining an information system. CASE is based on the idea of improving quality and productivity by approaching system analysis and development in a highly structured and disciplined way. CASE products sold by different vendors overlap in many ways but also contain certain unique features.

Users of CASE products avoid reinventing methods that have been developed carefully and integrated into a consistent package. Ideally, CASE products increase coordination and reduce confusion by enforcing standard methods used by the entire organization. They establish effective methods for storing and using the data generated

Using a pivot table to make spreadsheets more flexible

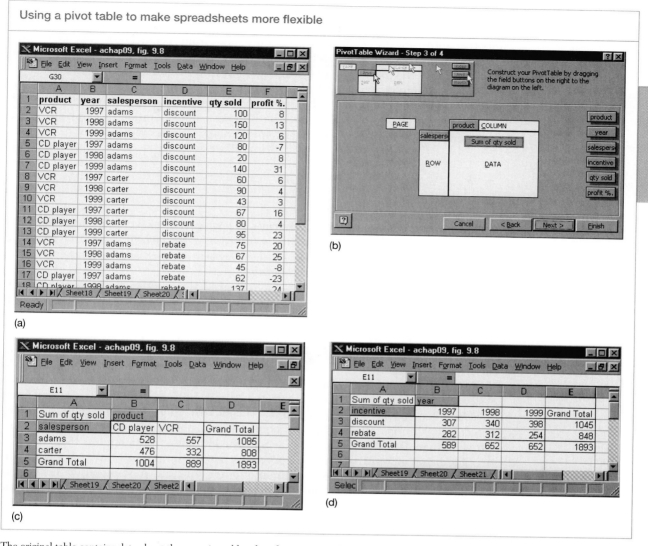

(a)

(b)

(c)

(d)

The original table contains data about the quantity sold and profit percentage for different salespeople, different products, different years, and different incentives. The pivot table feature in Excel makes it possible to look at different slices of this data, such as sales by salesperson and product, or sales by sales incentive and year. To convert from one view to another, the user switches the order and placement of the icons representing the various dimensions.

during systems analysis, design, and development. They also automatically check for inconsistencies and errors such as inconsistent data names or formats. They also make maintenance more efficient because the programs are constructed based on the same structures and standards.

CASE is sometimes divided into upper-CASE versus lower-CASE. **Upper-CASE** refers to tools used by business and IT professionals to describe business processes and the data needed by those processes. Upper-CASE techniques mentioned earlier in this text include data flow diagrams for process modeling (refer back to Chapter 3), and entity-relationship diagrams for data modeling (refer back to Chapter 4). **Lower-CASE** is a set of tools used by programmers to facilitate the programming process. Screen generators simplify programming of data input screens by making it easy to place headings, instructions, comments, and the actual data entry fields anywhere on the screen with minimal effort compared to what is required in traditional programming. DBMSs for personal computers all contain this type of capability, which was barely available for professional mainframe programmers just a decade ago. Report generators, which are often 4GLs, make it easy to program simple listings and reports based on the fact that reports typically contain headings, subheadings, totals, and subtotals of prespecified size and format in particular locations on the page. Some CASE products contain code generators that automatically generate computer programs from specifications that are not in a programming language. Code generators require a completely structured specification of exactly how the information system should operate. Code generators convert those specifications into programs written in COBOL or other languages. CASE systems may contain many other tools and techniques that make system development more efficient, including the maintenance of subroutine libraries, the generation of data for testing, debugging techniques, and techniques for controlling changes in programs.

R E A L I T Y C H E C K ✓

Developments in Programming

This section mentioned a number of examples illustrating progress in programming. Despite that progress, many people still have trouble instructing VCRs to record television programs.

1. Based on the trends and examples, speculate about the way spreadsheet users may create spreadsheet models five years from now.

2. Based on the trends and the examples, speculate about the user interfaces for VCRs, microwave ovens, and other home equipment five years from now.

OPERATING SYSTEMS

Thus far, the chapter has focused primarily on programming application software designed to support the user's or organization's processes and activities. It also explained how compilers translate programs into object code that a machine can execute. This section will look at operating systems, a type of system software (rather than application software) that affects business professionals by controlling the computers they use.

Operating systems are complex programs that control the operation of computers and networks by controlling (1) execution of other programs running on the computer, (2) communication with peripheral devices including terminals, and (3) use of disk space and other computer system resources. Box 9.3 identifies some of today's most widely used operating systems. When centralized computing was the norm, it was easier to generalize about operating system functions. Today, different operating systems are designed for different computing situations including desktop computing, networked multiuser computing, centralized mainframe computing, real-time control of industrial processes, and robotics. Each computing situation calls for different operating system functions. For example, the type of operating system that controls a client/server network has to deal with different issues than an operating system that controls an individual PC. To make things more complicated, operating systems are often intertwined with other layers of software including DBMSs, communication software, and middleware.

Operating systems differ in size and complexity. The first operating systems for personal computers, such as MS-DOS and CP/M, were written by just a few programmers. As operating systems took on new functions, the amount of development work multiplied. Microsoft's Windows NT, an operating system for networked computers, cost over $150 million to develop with a team of 200 programmers. It contained 4.3 million lines of code when it was first released in 1993, and has been developed much further since that time.[12] The discussion of operating system functions will start with the simplest case, personal computers.

Operating Systems for Personal Computers

The purpose of a PC's operating system is to make it possible for you to use application programs such as spreadsheets, word processors, or drawing programs. It accomplishes this by performing a variety of functions related to controlling the user interface, controlling access to data, controlling jobs in progress, and allocating resources.

The most widely used operating systems today are various versions of the Windows desktop operating system, Windows NT, the Mac OS, and Unix. The sequence of the following listing emphasizes the relationships between these and several other operating systems.

UNIX: This multiuser operating system was developed at Bell Labs in 1969 to allow mainframe computers to communicate with several other computers or terminals to let users share data and programs. It was eventually given to universities for free because AT&T was not allowed to sell software at that time. UNIX is the original operating system. The UNIX family of operating systems includes Linux, Solaris, Ultrix, AIX, A/UX, Xenix, and others, and it is widely used for mainframe computers, midrange computers, and workstations. Its important benefits include a high degree of reliability and scalability. Inconsistencies between different dialects of UNIX cause problems in software portability. UNIX has a reputation of being unfriendly to users, who once had to learn numerous character-based UNIX commands, although a number of graphical interfaces have now been developed.

Linux: This is a UNIX-like operating system given away for free via Web downloads, although a number of companies have been formed to provide Linux-related services. It got its name from its original author, Linus Torvalds, who wrote the first version in 1991 when he was 21 years old. Within eight years it was running on over ten million computers. Linux became popular for sophisticated users because it is compact and capable of running on different computer platforms. It is not owned by a company; instead, Torvalds heads a committee that decides which features should be added and makes sure each new version is debugged. Linux source code is open, meaning that anyone can look at the source code to understand what it does. The combination of open source code and a compact, well-designed kernel make Linux especially adaptable for applications in different areas. By the end of 2000, it was being used on servers and modified for use in game machines, Internet appliances, handheld devices, mainframes, supercomputers, phones, and digital VCRs.[13]

MS-DOS: The abbreviation stands for Microsoft Disk Operating System. An earlier version of this operating system called QDOS was purchased by Microsoft, improved, and then licensed to IBM for use with its first PCs. IBM licensed the operating system instead of building its own because it wanted to avoid delays in coming to market with a PC. In retrospect most observers believe this was a strategic mistake because it yielded to Microsoft control of a crucial element of all PCs. MS-DOS had many shortcomings in function, including the lack of a graphical user interface, the restriction of programs to 640K of memory, and the lack of multitasking. It was a 16-bit operating system used for 16-bit PCs. The first versions of Windows (through 3.1) were overlays that were superimposed on top of MS-DOS to provide a graphical interface. Subsequent versions replaced MS-DOS.

MAC OS: The Macintosh operating system was the first operating system that provided a convenient graphical user interface for personal computers. During the 1990s, many Macintosh enthusiasts bemoaned the widely held belief that the Macintosh interface was far better than the Microsoft Windows interface even though Windows PCs held around 90% of the market. Many observers believe Apple made a strategic mistake by being unwilling to license the operating system to other manufacturers (with several temporary exceptions) and by keeping prices high in comparison with IBM PCs.

Windows 95, Windows 98, Windows ME (Millennium Edition): These are the comparatively recent 32-bit versions of Microsoft's desktop operating system. Each of these versions provides a graphical user interface and a wide range of capabilities including multitasking, networking, and various degrees of plug and play for peripherals. Each succeeding version has more capabilities related to Web usage, application with a variety of peripherals, and handling of video. Unfortunately, many users have complained that Windows 95 and Windows 98 tend to be unstable and crash too frequently.

Windows NT and Windows 2000: Windows NT is a 32-bit operating system that contains both client and server capabilities. It was built by Microsoft and originally released in 1993. It controls both the client and the server and competes with Novell Netware in the market for network operating systems. Windows 2000 replaces Windows NT and provides more powerful capabilities for networking and memory management.

OS/2 and OS/2 WARP: IBM built this operating system for personal computers. It provides robust 32-bit capabilities and supports multitasking and networking. It was to be an alternative to Windows 3.1 and Windows 95, but is used primarily by IBM corporate customers. By 2000, IBM's Web site described both client and server capabilities.

Palm Operating System and Windows CE: These are competing operating systems for personal digital assistants (PDAs) such as the Palm Pilot and Handspring's Visor. These operating systems are much simpler than a full Windows operating system because the PDAs they control have far fewer capabilities than PCs.

Regardless of whether the PC operating system is a version of Windows, the Macintosh operating system, or even UNIX, the following operating system functions affect a PC user:

Controlling the user interface: When you turn on a personal computer, the operating system displays start-up information along with menus, icons, or other indications of the choices you can exercise. As you use the computer, the appearance of what you see on the screen is controlled by the operating system or by the interaction between the operating system and whatever application program is being used.

Controlling tasks in progress: When you select an application or document to open, the operating system recognizes your inputs and performs the action you request. If you print something, the operating system controls the printer interface and reports problems, such as when the printer is out of paper. By supporting **multitasking**, operating systems permit the user to operate two or more programs concurrently on the same computer. For example, they permit a user to switch back and forth between a spreadsheet and a word processor without turning off one application in order to use the other. See Box 9.4 for some of the current limits on multitasking.

Controlling access to data: When you access previously stored data through an application program, the operating system uses internal directories and other internal information to find and retrieve the data. Some operating systems can update one document automatically based on data changes in another document; for example, automatically updating a word processed report when changes are made in a spreadsheet, part of which is included in the report. The operating system can also ask for a password before permitting use of a restricted file.

Allocating resources: The operating system allocates memory while the computer is running. When you want to save a document or spreadsheet, the operating system decides where to store the data in the storage device. It makes sure that each file stored does not accidentally overlay files stored previously. If it is necessary to break the data into several blocks in different places on the storage device, the operating system keeps track of the different blocks. When you delete files, the operating system frees up the space so that it can be used again.

BOX 9.4   CURRENT LIMITS ON MULTITASKING

While revising this chapter for this edition, I sent an e-mail message to the *Wall Street Journal*'s "Personal Technology" columnist Walter S. Mossberg. Here is the message I sent and a summary of the response printed in the "Mossberg's Mailbox" column, *Wall Street Journal*, October 5, 2000, page B10. In evaluating the response, remember that the first PC operating systems did not allow multitasking at all.

Q. I am writing this on a one-year-old Dell PC with a 500 MHz Pentium III chip, 256 MB of RAM, a 27 GB hard disk, and Windows 98. As I write this, all I'm running is Outlook Express, along with one window of Internet Explorer. Yet Windows informs me that my "system resources" are only 55% free. If I were to open Microsoft Word and additional browser windows, the available system resources would drop to very low levels. Sometimes I even receive a warning that the computer doesn't have enough resources to open a new document. What are system resources? Doesn't my vast 256 megabytes of memory help with this?

A. Regardless of how much memory your PC has, Windows will only allow a limited number of programs to run simultaneously and a limited number of open windows. The bottleneck is "System Resources," a chunk of memory Windows allocates to each program or window that is open. This is severely restricted, and can fill up long before memory is taxed to capacity. This aggravates users like you who invested in extra memory to avoid running out of capacity.

Operating Systems for Multiuser Computer Systems

Operating systems for mainframe computers and servers with multiple processors perform the same functions in much more complex situations. Instead of taking care of a single user, they run many jobs simultaneously for different users, taking into account the priority of different jobs. Some of the jobs involve online interaction with users. Other jobs are run in a background mode with the user detached. These operating systems make sure that the users, their data, and their various jobs do not interfere with each other. They also maintain computer system security.

Operating systems for multiuser computer systems monitor the current status of the system and decide when to start jobs. This is necessary because computer systems have a finite computing capacity, a specific number of peripherals of each type, and a finite capacity for communicating with the peripherals. The operating system considers resource availability when it allocates resources to jobs. For example, before starting a job that requires a tape drive, it allocates a specific tape drive to that job, and it delays the job if all tape drives are currently allocated to other jobs. Likewise, before permitting an online user to log on, it decides whether the capacity is available for that user. When multiple processors are involved, the operating system must also make sure that work being done by one processor does not interfere with work being done by another.

In networked computer systems, the **network operating system** establishes the links between the nodes, monitors the network's operation, and controls recovery processes when nodes go down or the entire network goes down. The network operating system must work in conjunction with the operating systems for the individual workstations on the network. This adds to the complexity of establishing and maintaining computer networks because the two operating systems (for the workstation and for the network) and the application software all must be compatible. This may also affect computer system performance by creating noticeable delays compared to doing individual work on a personal computer.

A number of different multiuser operating systems are used today. Older operating systems still used for mainframe and minicomputer applications from the 1970s and 1980s include IBM's MVS and Digital's (now part of Compaq) VMS, both of which were upgraded substantially in 1995. Starting in the mid-1980s there was a shift away from these mainframe operating systems and toward a widely used multiuser operating system called UNIX, which was developed at AT&T's Bell Labs before the time of PCs. It was eventually given to universities for free because AT&T was not allowed to sell software at that time. Based on this history, it is not surprising that most Internet backbone computers run UNIX, which was written in the programming language C and was designed as a portable operating system. Although UNIX is used widely in networks of up to 1,000 users, early hopes that it would become a universal operating system working uniformly on all computers have not been realized. Currently used dialects of UNIX include IBM's AIX, HP/UX, Sun's Solaris, Digital's UNIX, SCO's UNIX, and several others. In 1993 Microsoft sold the first release of the Windows NT operating system, which contains both server and client components. By 1997 it could support corporate networks with up to 200 users. It overlaps with Novell's NetWare in the network operating system market and competes with the various forms of UNIX for new multiuser applications. Many observers believe that the client side of Windows NT will eventually evolve into a product that will replace Microsoft's sequence of client/desktop operating systems, Windows 95, Windows 98, and Windows Me.

Why Operating Systems Are Important

Operating systems are a crucial component of any computer system because they can lock in some applications and lock out others. Current application programs and end-user software are written to run under a particular operating system. A program written to run under one operating system may not run under another operating system. Anyone who has attempted to switch between a *wintel* PC (which uses Windows on an Intel microprocessor) and an Apple Macintosh PC understands that switching to a different operating system often entails the expense of abandoning or modifying much existing software. Until the mid-1990s, even Microsoft Word documents or Excel spreadsheets produced on one platform could not be used on the other. A substantial degree of interoperability is now available because the file formats have been synchronized. However, this still doesn't solve the problem of what to do about backward compatibility when successive releases of application software use inconsistent formats.

Department of Justice (DOJ) actions against Microsoft between 1997 and 2000 showed that operating systems even raise antitrust issues. In 1995 Microsoft signed a consent decree with the DOJ prohibiting it from tying the sale of one product to another. Microsoft changed its licensing contracts as a result. The DOJ filed suit against Microsoft on October 20, 1997, saying that it had breached the consent decree by requiring PC makers to ship Internet Explorer, Microsoft's Internet browser, as a condition of licensing the industry-standard Windows 95 operating system. The government suit said that Windows 95 and Internet Explorer are separate products and that Microsoft was using its near monopoly to restrict competition in the Internet browser market. In Microsoft's view the company had the right to define what went into its own products, and therefore had the right to declare the operating system and the browser an integrated product.[14] In June 2000, U.S. District Judge Thomas Penfield Jackson cited a pattern of anticompetitive practices and ruled against Microsoft. He ordered Microsoft to submit a plan for splitting itself into an operating systems business and an applications business. As expected, Microsoft appealed the judgment. Whether and how this dispute will eventually affect the balance of power between Microsoft and other industry players such as IBM and Sun remains to be seen.

R E A L I T Y C H E C K ✓

Operating Systems

This section discusses some of the functions of operating systems for personal computers, such as controlling the user interface, controlling access to data, allocating resources, and controlling jobs in progress.

1. Which operating systems have you used on a personal computer? What appeared to be the relationship between the operating system and the applications you ran, such as spreadsheets or word processing?

2. What aspects of the operating system could probably be improved? For example, was it extremely easy to learn, and did it do everything for you that you imagine an operating system could do?

Steps toward Making Computers "Intelligent"

Programming advances to date have been impressive, to say the least, but there is still a long way to go. Figure 9.2 illustrated that programming is about translating a vision of what is to be accomplished into instructions a machine can execute. Figure 9.5 showed that although this translation is increasingly automatic, programming languages still must be used. To round out the coverage of software and programming it is useful to return to the question of "computer intelligence" as a way to visualize the current limits of software and programming.

Questions about artificially created intelligence existed long before the first computers were developed. With the advent of the computer, researchers saw greater possibilities of making progress toward intelligent machines. A great deal of progress occurred. For example:

- Computers have played chess at a grandmaster level.
- Computers have solved mathematical problems that challenge expert mathematicians.
- Computers have constructed accurate three-dimensional representations from two-dimensional satellite photos.
- Computers have controlled guided missiles and airplanes.

Although these examples are impressive, and might have seemed like science fiction 40 years ago, people today would question whether they are examples of intelligence. This leads to an interesting question: How can we decide that a computerized system is intelligent?

In 1950, the English mathematician Alan Turing suggested the following test: An interrogator should use a computer terminal to ask questions to something—a person or machine—that is in another room. If the interrogator cannot tell from the typed responses whether a person or a machine is answering the questions, the machine would be judged intelligent. Turing's test does not ask whether the machine can perform impressive tasks using preprogrammed mathematical procedures. It asks whether a machine could answer questions well enough to be indistinguishable from a person.

Efforts to make computers more "intelligent" are often grouped under the general heading of artificial intelligence (AI), which first achieved prominence at a small conference of AI pioneers at Dartmouth in 1956. **Artificial intelligence** is the field of research related to the demonstration of intelligence by machines. This includes, but is not limited to, the ability to think, see, learn, understand, and use common sense.

Chapter 5 briefly discussed five areas in which AI research that once seemed "far out" eventually led to important practical applications in business. (Other important applications in areas such as machine vision and robotics were not mentioned.) Table 9.1 summarizes the AI issue and approach to intelligence that eventually led to useful results in each of these five areas and in natural language processing, which will be discussed here. All of the AI applications in Table 9.1 are related in some way to the general issue of interpreting or using ambiguous or incomplete information.

Although AI research has led to important practical applications, the general topic of machine intelligence has spawned a great deal of hype, confusion, and speculation. As illustrated in Figure 9.10, people sometimes exaggerate computer intelligence and think of computers as gigantic brains. People often say a computer "knows" something, when they really mean that the computer program has access to that information. People often give undeserved credit or blame to computers, almost implying that the computer was responsible for something that happened in business or government. People often generalize about computer intelligence from isolated examples. People often use the terms "smart" or "intelligent" to describe computer systems even though they don't come close to showing many types of intelligence that the least intelligent human employee shows every day.

TABLE 9.1

Comparison of Practical Applications of AI Research

Type of AI application	AI issue	Approach to intelligence
Natural language processing	Understanding language	Use dictionaries, grammatical analysis, statistical techniques, and situation-specific knowledge if available.
Expert system	Understanding and reasoning about specific types of situations	Capture and apply an expert's understanding of a problem domain through a set of rules about reasoning within that domain.
Neural network	Learning how to make a specific type of decision	Use statistical methods to "learn" how to make good decisions by weighting various aspects of a problem situation.
Fuzzy logic	Reduce reliance on ineffective and sometimes useless yes/no distinctions	Perform reasoning by weighting multiple rules that can be posed using overlapping categories.
Case-based reasoning	Reasoning based on similarity of cases	Compare past cases to find and apply the ones with the greatest bearing on a current situation.
Intelligent agents	Finding desired information by exploring across a network	Generate automated processes that operate autonomously.

FIGURE   9.10

Images and headlines about machine intelligence

(a)

(b)

The two pictures illustrate the two questions underlying this section: What does artificial intelligence mean, and what are its current limits? (a) People sometimes think of computers as giant brains. Election day 1952 was one of the first situations in which computer intelligence was widely reported. Hours before the newscasters were willing to predict the outcome, a computer projected that Eisenhower would win. This was publicized as a demonstration of computer intelligence even though the projection was based on statistical formulas that are covered in undergraduate statistics courses today and can be used on any personal computer. (b) People may subconsciously believe part of the dream of human-like robots. This dream may inspire an image of computers that fuels some of the confusion about what computers can do today.

The most basic limitation of both current programming methods and "computer intelligence" is that no one knows how to program **common sense**, which is a shared understanding of how things work in everyday life. Even when programmers include every rule, exception, and special case that they can think of, something may still be missing. The resulting programs may respond incorrectly or even disastrously when they encounter unanticipated or poorly understood situations or interactions of factors. In contrast, people usually exercise common sense about what they do and do not understand. When an unanticipated situation arises, they can recognize it as such and respond accordingly.

Figure 9.11 shows that programming greater intelligence into computers involves moving in two directions, increasing the scope of the information processed, and increasing the degree of understanding of the information. Although the Deep Blue example at the beginning of the chapter has been trumpeted as a demonstration of computer intelligence, Figure 9.11 would categorize this accomplishment as "following unambiguous instructions" related to "several predefined types of information about one type of situation." Deep Blue might seem intelligent if it were evaluated on its ability to create chess moves better than most human chess players. It would not seem intelligent if it were judged on how well it could converse about its strategy. The success with Deep Blue is impressive, but the problem itself is not nearly as far along the scales in Figure 9.11 as the problem of trying to interpret the little three-sentence story about Billy and Sally at the beginning of the chapter. Interpreting that story would involve using "many types of information about many types of situations" in order to "understand a situation and use common sense."

Our current inability to program common sense is one of the reasons for the question marks in Figure 9.5. The figure shows how programming methods have improved greatly over the years by allowing programmers to focus less on how the machine per-

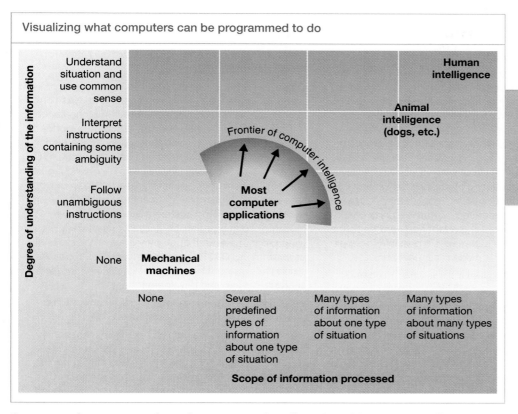

Visualizing what computers can be programmed to do

FIGURE 9.11

Computers are being incorporated into what were previously totally mechanical devices such as coffee makers and automobile brakes. Techniques for interpreting information such as voice and handwriting are being extended. More applications are being developed that handle many types of data. Despite these developments, computerized systems do not yet demonstrate common sense or understanding.

forms its work and more on expressing the desired result. At each stage programmers have been able to operate at a higher level of abstraction, but current programmers must still use programming languages that are unambiguous. It therefore might seem that natural language would complete the progression in Figure 9.5 because the translation from the user's ideas to machine language would be 100% automatic. Moving to this level would require computers to understand **natural language**, the spoken or written language used by people to communicate with each other.

Research on natural language has generated important accomplishments. Grammar checkers and voice recognition programs have been developed and are used in some situations even though they have significant limitations. Database query programs use situation-specific data dictionaries to convert natural language queries into SQL queries. Automatic translation programs convert technical manuals and other noncolloquial documents into other languages. Information extraction services scan news articles to select the articles that might be useful to people interested in specific areas. All of these applications have attained usefulness even though none are perfect and their outputs require careful checking by people.

Natural language seems unlikely as a programming language for building application systems in the near future even if the entire vocabulary could be defined with a dictionary. Statements in everyday natural language are often ambiguous and poorly structured. Even if the sentences are clear, in combination they are often inconsistent or illogical. Furthermore, people often misunderstand each other even though they share understandings about how the world operates. These problems of ambiguity, interpretation, and inconsistency would overwhelm any current attempts to program application systems using natural language because computers do not currently understand how the world operates. At minimum, the lack of an unambiguous set of requirements would make it impossible to test the resulting business application to ensure it operates correctly.

CHAPTER CONCLUSION

What are the different types of software?

Application software, which defines the tasks the computer should perform and expresses that processing from a user or business perspective, can be divided into two types. General-purpose application software is sometimes called end-user software. It includes word processors, spreadsheet programs, presentation programs, and relatively simple DBMSs that end users can apply directly in performing common tasks such as writing memos or performing calculations. Situation-specific application software processes data to structure or automate parts of specific business processes. System software performs the background work that makes it possible for application software to run on computer hardware.

How is programming like a translation process?

Programming is the process of creating instructions that a machine will execute later. Programming requires that a person organize and communicate ideas in a format that a machine can use. The use of programming languages automates part of the translation process. A programmer writes a program that expresses what the person wants. An assembler or compiler automatically translates that program into machine language instructions the machine can execute.

What aspects of programming do not depend on the programming language used?

Regardless of the programming language used, programmers have to organize their ideas and test them. The most common technique for organizing ideas is successive decomposition, the process of breaking up a problem into smaller and smaller subproblems. Testing is required for all programs to find and correct bugs.

What are the four generations of programming languages?

The generations are machine language, assembly language, higher level language, and fourth generation language (4GL). Each succeeding generation is less procedural and permits programmers to use concepts more related to the business situation.

What are some of the other important developments in programming?

Object-oriented programming treats data and programs as if they are tightly intertwined, and uses concepts such as object, class, method, and inheritance to make programs more reusable. Other important developments include special-purpose languages for specific types of problems, spreadsheets, and CASE systems. Special-purpose programming languages contain ideas about specific areas of business or types of analysis, such as financial calculations or queuing models. Spreadsheets are a special type of modeling language that permit millions of people to write programs even though they are not professional programmers. CASE systems establish methods for storing and using the data generated during systems analysis, design, and development.

What are operating systems, and why should managers and users care about them?

Operating systems are complex programs that control the operation of computers and networks by controlling (1) the execution of other programs running on the computer, (2) communication with peripheral devices including terminals, and (3) the use of disk space and other computer system resources. Managers and users should care about operating systems because they regulate the efficiency of the computer system and because the choice of an operating system can lock in some applications and lock out others.

What is the most basic limitation of programming?

This limitation is that no one knows how to program common sense, which is a shared understanding of how things work in everyday life. Even when programmers include every rule, exception, and special case that they can think of, something may still be missing. The resulting programs may respond incorrectly or even disastrously when they encounter unanticipated or poorly understood situations or interactions of factors.

application software
system software
end-user software
system development software
programming
computer program
successive decomposition
modules
structured programming
testing
bug
debugging
syntax error
logic error
unit testing
system testing

beta testing
procedural
nonprocedural
reusability
machine independence
data independence
computer-aided software
    engineering (CASE)
object-oriented programming
    (OOP)
generations of programming
    languages
machine language
assembly language
higher level language
compiler

source code
object code
interpreter
applet
fourth generation language (4GL)
query language
report generator
modeling language
upper-CASE
lower-CASE
operating system
multitasking
network operating system
artificial intelligence
common sense
natural language

1. What is the difference between application software and system software?

2. Explain the significance of viewing programming as a business process.

3. In what sense is programming a translation process?

4. Why is successive decomposition important in programming?

5. Why is it necessary to test software?

6. Compare the two types of errors that can be found by debugging a program.

7. What is the difference between procedural and nonprocedural programming languages?

8. Define machine independence, and explain why it is important.

9. Why is it important to have tighter links between analysis and programming?

10. Identify the basic ideas of object-oriented programming.

11. Explain the difference between machine language, assembly language, higher level languages, and fourth generation languages.

12. What prevents companies from abandoning COBOL in favor of 4GLs?

13. What are CASE systems?

14. Which operating system functions affect personal computer users?

15. Why would it be especially difficult to program in natural language?

16. Why can't current computerized systems understand stories for four-year-olds?

1. Someone has proposed that the job of programmer will be obsolete in 20 years, when users will be able to converse with computers in natural language. Explain why you agree or disagree.

2. Give examples of programming you perform in everyday life. Is anything notably easy or hard about this programming? How might programming in these areas become more complex?

3. Why is it comparatively easy to get an answer to a question such as, "List all customers whose current account balance is greater than $1,000," but much more difficult to answer a question such as, "List all of the customers we need to call to 'remind' them to pay their bills."?

4. Read the following, answer the questions, and then explain how your answer is related to the ideas in the chapter: Imagine that it is the year 2015. You have just come home after a hard day at work, and you are hungry. As it does every day, the home robot you purchased last year at a clearance sale says, "Good evening. I hope you have had a good day. Is there anything I can do for you?" On this particular evening, you would really like to have spaghetti and meatballs for dinner. How do you think you would communicate your request to the robot? How would the robot interpret and execute your request?

5. CHIPS, the Clearing House for Interbank Payments, transfers more than $1 trillion among 120 participating banks. System developers faced a unique problem when a system upgrade was needed. They could test the programs in a simulated mode, and could do trial installations on Saturdays, but could not test this entire, mission-critical system before putting it into operation because the banks did not have dual hardware and software. Fortunately nothing went wrong when they installed the changes on August 17, 1992, because there was no fallback.[15] Use ideas in this chapter to explain the practical and ethical issues raised by this example.

6. Do any of the examples in this book represent what you consider to be machine intelligence? If so, what are the examples and why do you believe these are examples of machine intelligence? If not, explain what you think machine intelligence might be, and give several hypothetical examples that illustrate this type of intelligence.

C A S E

Chrysler: Using "Extreme Programming" to Improve Quality and Minimize Defects

Programming is often viewed as a solitary occupation involving isolated programmers who work in their own cubicles, type mysterious computer code, and occasionally emerge to get pizza. This might be the image, but some programming groups are increasingly aware of psychological and social dimensions in programming and testing. An early book on this topic, called *The Psychology of Computer Programming*,[16] urged "egoless" programming practices that aim for high-quality, well-tested programs rather than verifying the brilliance of an individual programmer's method for solving a problem. Team methods such as those used by Microsoft in the opening case extend these ideas. An additional step in this direction is extreme programming (XP), an emerging software development methodology in which all the code is written with a partner. XP's requirements gathering, resource allocation, and design practices are a radical departure from most accepted methodologies.[17]

XP is designed for small, colocated programming groups. XP's management strategies focus on communication and user involvement. Releases should be as small as possible and should emphasize the features most valuable to the business. XP uses stories and scenarios in planning. This makes the need to consider both business and development roles much more explicit. XP's development strategy starts with a 40-hour work week, recognizing the fact that overworked programmers make more mistakes. It also calls for pair programming, in which two programmers work side-by-side at one computer, continuously collaborating on the same design. XP's notions of collective ownership and continuous integration depart radically from typical methods that regulate the way code is produced and modified. XP programming practices related to design, coding, and testing are more in line with typical methods.[18] Less typical is the idea of refactoring, the ongoing redesign of software to improve its responsiveness to change.

The most prominent XP project reported through early 2000 is the Chrysler Comprehensive Compensation system (the C3 project), which was initiated in the mid-1990s and converted to an XP project in 1997. Originally, the C3 project was conceived as an object-oriented programming project using the GemStone object-oriented database system. It was transformed into a pilot of XP practices after the original project was deemed unreclaimable, but succeeded with the help of several consultants who were OOP experts and XP proponents. (Eight people replaced 26 after an initial failure.[19]) The initial requirements were to handle the monthly payroll of some 10,000 salaried employees. The system consists of approximately 2,000 classes and 30,000 methods and was ready within a reasonable tolerance period of the planned schedule. According to one of the project leaders, success on the C3 project did not translate into near term XP use on other Chrysler IT projects.[20]

The planning started with a complete pass through the system to try to identify different ways it would be used. These separate cases were called stories and these were summarized in 135 4×6 cards with a name and a paragraph of description. During the six weeks of creating the stories, the developers were building prototypes of parts that they thought would be difficult technically. The stories were then prioritized in relation to meeting business goals. The developers sorted the stories by whether they understood enough to produce the required programs. The schedule was developed by estimating the work related to each card and then sorting the cards again based on priority and risk. Laying the cards out on the table helped everyone understand the scope of the project. The cards were then divided into ten piles, each representing three calendar weeks. This process convinced the users and developers that the resulting schedule was reasonable.[21]

The C3 system went into production almost on schedule and was operational through 2000. The C3 project later encountered some difficulties due to communication problems between the development team and the two sets of management stakeholders (the IS department, which was the customer, and the payroll department, which was the user). This is ironic since communication between the customer and the team lies at the heart of XP's approach.[22] According to a series of Web postings from the extreme programming community, the C3 system was terminated in early 2000 after changes in personnel and management. The postings combined appreciation of all that

had been learned, regrets that C3 was terminated before its final phase, and observations about organizational politics.[23]

In late 2000 an apparently informal survey conducted by IBM's Developer Works staff and reported on its Web site asked the following question: "What are your thoughts on extreme programming?" The comments from the survey broke out as follows:[24]

> 51%: I've tried it and loved it.
>
> 25%: It's a good idea but it could never work.
>
> 16%: It's a bad idea—it could never work.
>
> 8%: I've tried it and hated it.

QUESTIONS

1. How do the ideas in the chapter help in understanding this case?

2. Is there any way to know whether the success of extreme programming in this case was directly related to the method itself versus the situation or the people in the situation?

3. Explain why you do or do not believe extreme programming is primarily suited for object-oriented programming.

4. Someone told you that Chris is a great programmer. What does that mean in a world of typical programming practice? What does it mean in an XP environment?

CASE — Cycorp: Building a Knowledge Base to Support Commonsense Reasoning

Developing techniques for capturing commonsense knowledge and building it into computerized systems is one of the greatest challenges of computer science. Capturing and codifying common sense is difficult because the rules of thumb used in everyday life to understand language and to interpret the world are almost never published explicitly in books or dictionaries. Here are some examples:

- You have to be awake to eat.
- You can usually see people's noses, but not their hearts.
- You cannot remember events that have not happened yet.
- Once people die they stay dead.
- If you cut a lump of peanut butter in half, each half is also a lump of peanut butter; but if you cut a table in half, neither half is a table.
- A glass filled with milk will be right-side-up, not upside-down.

The CYC project began in 1984 at the Microelectronics and Computer Technology Corporation (MCC) in Austin, Texas, with the goal of codifying this type of knowledge.

Cycorp, Inc., a 1995 spin-off of MCC, was founded to continue the development of CYC technology. In 2000, Cycorp, Inc. had approximately 70 employees and a number of corporate sponsors who hoped to apply CYC technology in a variety of ways. The Cycorp Web page describes the CYC product family as "an immense, multi-contextual knowledge base, an efficient inference engine, a set of interface tools, and a number of special-purpose application modules running on Unix, Windows NT, and other platforms. The knowledge base is built upon a core of over 1,000,000 hand-entered assertions (or 'rules') designed to capture a large portion of what we normally consider consensus knowledge about the world."[25] If successful, CYC will help "break the 'software brittleness bottleneck' once and for all by constructing a foundation of basic common sense knowledge. This will provide a 'deep' layer of understanding that can be used by other programs to make them more flexible." Applications of CYC that are available or in development are in areas such as natural language processing, extracting information from databases, searching for examples in captioned databases (such as news photos or film clips), creating application-specific thesauruses, and retrieving information from the Web.

CYC technology includes a knowledge base, a representation language, an inference engine, interface tools, and modules designed for specific applications. The knowledge base is a formalized representation of commonsense knowledge including facts, rules of thumb, and methods for reasoning about the objects and events of everyday life. It consists of a vocabulary of terms and a "sea of assertions" about those terms. The assertions are related to causality, time, space, events, substances, intention, contradiction, belief, emotions, planning, and other aspects of human existence. New assertions are added continually. The knowledge base currently contains hundreds of thousands of assertions and is divided into hundreds of "microtheories," each of which is a set of assertions sharing a common set of assumptions. Various microtheories are focused on a particular domain of knowledge, a particular level of detail, a particular interval in time, and so on. Use of microtheories makes it possible to reconcile and resolve assertions from separate contexts that are both applicable to a situation, but may yield contradictory inferences. For example, in the context of total darkness you cannot see anything, and this seems to contradict the assertion that you can usually see people's noses. The CYC inference engine performs logical deductions using a variety of logical techniques. The vast size of the knowledge base requires that special inference techniques be developed, such as using microtheories to optimize the inference process by restricting search domains. Special-purpose inference modules were developed for a few specific classes of inference. One such module handles reasoning concerning set membership or disjointness. Others handle equality reasoning, temporal reasoning, and mathematical reasoning.[26, 27]

In 1999 an interviewer asked Doug Lenat, CYC's original developer, whether CYC would be able to learn things on its own. He responded: "We're already able to see isolated cases where CYC is learning things on its own. Some of the things it learns reflect the incompleteness of its knowledge and are just funny. For example, CYC at one point concluded that everyone born before 1900 was famous, because all the people that it knew about and who lived in earlier times were famous people. There are similar sorts of errors. But what we're seeing is not so much something that sits quietly on its own and makes discoveries but rather something that uses the knowledge it has to accelerate its own education."[28]

QUESTIONS

1. How is CYC related (or not related) to basic programming concepts such as computer programs, successive decomposition, structured programming, debugging, syntax error, logic error, and reusability?

2. Explain how CYC might be used for data mining or for finding photos in an image database.

Networks and Telecommunications

chapter10

STUDY QUESTIONS

- What aspects of the convergence of computing and communications are important for understanding telecommunications?
- Compare a typical home network with a LAN or WAN.
- What are the steps in the basic telecommunications model?
- Why is the difference between analog and digital important?
- What is the difference between circuit switching and packet switching?
- Compare different forms of wired and wireless transmission.
- Why are telecommunications standards important?
- What is IP telephony and what challenges does it raise?
- How is telecommunications policy related to issues faced by managers?

OUTLINE

Applying Telecommunications in Business
Vital Role of Telecommunications
in E-Business
Convergence of Computing
and Communications
Making Sense of the Terminology and Details

Types of Networks
A Typical Home Network
A Local Area Network in a Business
A Telephone Network
The Internet (from a User's Viewpoint)
A Wide Area Network

**Functions and Components of
Telecommunications Networks**
Generating and Receiving Data
Transmitting Analog versus Digital Data
Directing Data from Source to Destination

Transmitting Data through Wired and
Wireless Media
Telecommunications Standards
More about Network Technology
More about LANs
More about WANs
Wireless Networking
IP Telephony
Telecommunications Policy
Chapter Conclusion
Summary
Key Terms
Review Questions
Discussion Questions
Cases

Networks and Telecommunications

OPENING CASE

FEDEX APPLIES TELECOMMUNICATIONS IN
PACKAGE DELIVERY

FedEx grew to be a multibillion-dollar company by providing reliable overnight delivery of high-priority, time-sensitive packages and documents. Its 590 airplanes, 40,000 trucks, and 137,000 people deliver over 2.9 million packages a day. After the parcels are picked up at the customer's site or dropped off at a FedEx location, they are rushed to the local airport and flown to a FedEx hub where they are sorted by destination, loaded on planes, and shipped to the destination airport. Packages designated for overnight delivery are delivered to their destination within 24 hours.

To maintain a high degree of reliability in its shipping process, FedEx tracks each package through each step on its path from the shipper to the recipient. When the driver picks up the package, it is logged immediately using Supertracker, a portable, handheld computer containing a bar code reader for capturing the bar code identification on the package and a keyboard for entering additional information such as the destination's zip code. Upon returning to the truck, the driver inserts the Supertracker into a small

computer that transmits the data by radio waves to the local dispatch center, which has a link to the corporate database. Within five minutes of initial pickup, the FedEx database contains the package's identification, location, destination, and route. The location data is updated automatically (using the package's bar code) as the package moves through each step on its way to the destination. Although package pickup and delivery involve a series of steps in different places, the combination of telecommunications and computing permits FedEx to know the location of every package at any time and to make sure that procedures are followed throughout. Any deviation would become obvious quickly.

Package-tracking information is used in many ways. Information about pickups and deliveries is the basis of customer billing. Detailed tracking information supports customer service by permitting customer service agents to tell customers where their packages are. Customers can access the FedEx Web site to obtain the same information.

As a method for managing their own internal operations, FedEx developed a service quality index based on 12 types of events that disappoint customers, including late delivery, damaged or lost packages, and complaints. Even a delivery at 10:31 for a package promised for 10:30 is considered a problem. So that they will learn from past problems and mistakes, people throughout the company receive daily feedback reports identifying problems that occurred the previous day.[1]

As other major package delivery and shipping companies built similar systems, FedEx decided to expand from a package delivery company to a fully integrated corporate partner that picks up, transports, warehouses, and delivers all of a company's finished goods from the factory to the customer's receiving dock—with status data available every step of the way. For example, when orders are sent from Omaha Steaks' central computer to its warehouses, a FedEx tracking label is generated automatically. Omaha Steaks delivers the warehouse-fulfilled orders by truck to a FedEx hub, and FedEx delivers the steaks to the customer. As the result of a five-year project, FedEx performs most of the warehousing and distribution for National Semiconductor, which manufactures most of its products in

Asia and ships them to a FedEx distribution warehouse in Singapore. National Semiconductor's mainframe sends a daily batch of orders over a dedicated line directly to a FedEx inventory-management computer in Memphis. FedEx sends the orders to its warehouse in Singapore, where they are packaged and shipped. This system reduced the average customer delivery cycle from four weeks to seven days, and reduced distribution costs from 2.9% of sales to 1.2%.[2]

FedEx has also tried to extend its reach though a set of what it calls e-business tools that include, in FedEx terms, eShipping tools, eCommerce tools, eCommerce Builder, and FedEx Global Developer Program. The eShipping tools include a number of ways to initiate and track shipments directly from a desktop, such as creating FedEx shipping labels, tracking package status, and finding drop-off locations and rates. The eCommerce tools include capabilities related to controlling shipping and managing returns from customers. The eCommerce Builder provides methods for building and managing a small online store. The Global Developer Program provides methods for integrating shipping and tracking capabilities directly into a merchant's Web site.[3]

WEB CHECK [✓]

Compare the Web sites of FedEx and UPS to see whether there is any apparent difference in the services that are available, especially the customer's ability to know a package's location.

DEBATE TOPIC

Manufacturing and marketing firms that rely on quick, reliable delivery of consumer products and spare parts should plan to transfer most of these delivery functions to logistics firms such as FedEx and UPS that have built processes and information systems needed for quick, reliable delivery.

Initially, FedEx's service was about delivering packages. Gradually, an international information system supported by a telecommunications network became an important part of the package delivery service because this system kept track of each package at all times. Later, the telecommunications network became an essential part of FedEx's expansion into a corporate logistics business that required a highly distributed but tightly controlled information system.

As FedEx moved in these directions it had to make many decisions about how to transmit information within its worldwide computer network and from pick-up points and other tracking locations into its computer network. In making these decisions it had to evaluate alternatives related to topics such as:

- Which data transmission methods and technologies should be used? For example, where will it be appropriate to use wire-based versus wireless transmission?
- Should the data move through public communication networks or private FedEx channels?

W O R K   S Y S T E M   S N A P S H O T

FedEx applies telecommunications in package delivery

CUSTOMERS

- Individuals and companies who want packages shipped
- FedEx's billing department

PRODUCTS & SERVICES

- Quick, reliable shipment of packages from shipper to destination
- Excellent customer service such as the ability to report where any package is at any time

BUSINESS PROCESS

- Identify the package when it is picked up
- Determine package routing
- Move the package through checkpoints, recording its location at each step
- Provide tracking information to customer service representatives and to customers using the FedEx Web site
- Provide information for billing

PARTICIPANTS	**INFORMATION**	**TECHNOLOGY**
• Pickup and delivery drivers • Workers in the sorting centers • Customer service representatives	• Identification of the package • Routing of the package • Location of the package • Customer information	• Handheld terminal • Radio link to central computer system • Bar code readers in sorting centers • Central computer system

- Where and to what extent should data transmission systems be integrated with FedEx's voice transmission systems?
- How should the integrity and security of the data be protected during transmission?

This chapter provides background needed to visualize the issues and alternatives for these choices. The previous two chapters discussed computer systems and software but said little about telecommunications concepts or technology. This chapter will cover topics that business professionals need to be aware of simply to read a current business magazine such as *Business Week* or *Forbes*.

APPLYING TELECOMMUNICATIONS IN BUSINESS

Telecommunications is the transmission of data between devices in different locations. Typical initial experiences with telecommunications include watching television, listening to the radio, and using the telephone. In these cases, the data transmitted are sounds and images. Telecommunications applications in business include transmission of data of every type. The term **data communications** often refers to telecommunications involving computerized data, but not voice.

In essence, the purpose of telecommunications is to reduce or eliminate time delays and other impacts of geographical separation. Telecommunications reduces the effect of geographical separation when people talk on a telephone and eliminates time delays when a customer links into a supplier's computer system to order products. It provides both benefits when a network consolidates results from a company's branch offices.

Vital Role of Telecommunications in E-Business

Only 25 years ago, most business people often thought of telecommunications as telephone calls and paid little attention to it. Today, telecommunications is a requirement for business effectiveness and success. E-commerce simply can't exist without using telecommunications. In many businesses, national or international networks are a competitive necessity for typical e-business activities such as tracking inventories, taking customer orders, verifying product availability, and granting credit. Telecommunications systems have improved the effectiveness of sales and customer service work by creating immediate access to data. They have also changed the nature of internal communication within geographically dispersed organizations.

Telecommunications can be a strategic business issue even if the organization resides in a single building. Consider the importance of the voice and data networks within a hospital. This infrastructure makes it possible to communicate doctors' orders, lab results, and other vital information needed to coordinate patient care. Despite this, hospital administrators often focus on other issues and plan inadequately for the infrastructure needed to improve services for patients and doctors.

One way to visualize the importance of telecommunications in business is to look at the value chain and identify common telecommunications applications that have competitive significance. Table 10.1 lists applications in both primary and background activities along the value chain. Telecommunications reduces delays and eliminates unnecessary work in all these applications.

The telecommunications applications in Table 10.1 might be used across many high-tech and low-tech industries. In contrast, a number of increasingly important business models depend directly on telecommunications. Among these are the following:

- E-retailers: These companies sell other companies' products over the Internet.
- E-marketplaces: These companies use the Internet to create marketplaces for buyers and sellers.
- Internet content providers: These companies provide information that is made available and possibly sold on the Internet.
- **Internet service providers (ISPs):** These companies provide links and computer processing consumers and firms need in order to use the Internet. They also provide Web-hosting services that operate Web sites for other companies.
- **Application service providers (ASPs):** These companies operate business application software on their own servers for other companies. Use of an ASP makes it unnecessary to own, operate, and maintain the more sophisticated hardware and software needed to perform these functions.
- Telephone and cable companies: These companies install, operate, and maintain telephone, cable, and other communications equipment.
- Telecommunications equipment manufacturers: These companies produce telecommunications hardware used to operate networks and to perform end-user tasks.
- Internet and telecommunications software firms: These companies provide software and data processing services used by firms that create and operate Web sites.

Convergence of Computing and Communications

Before discussing telecommunications concepts and technologies, it is useful to mention four aspects of the convergence of computing and communications, a widely discussed trend introduced in Chapter 1.

Reliance of Telecommunications on Computers The earliest telephone systems included human operators who established telephone connections by plugging wires into a switchboard. Later, electromechanical switches automated this work by establishing the connections mechanically. Today, computers make the long distance connections electronically. Computers also monitor the traffic on the network and balance the loads on different parts of the network by determining which path across the network each telephone call will take. Several widely publicized failures of long distance telephone systems during the 1990s were caused by bugs in computer programs that controlled these networks.

Role of Telecommunications in Computing During the first decades of computer use, people thought of computing as something that occurs when using a single computer.

Examples of Telecommunications Applications Supporting E-Business

TABLE 10.1

Value chain activity	Typical telecommunications applications supporting e-business
Product Development	• Share data with other departments and with customers to make sure the product meets market needs and is manufacturable. • Work together with others who have simultaneous access to the same computerized data and drawings.
Production	• Transmit orders to suppliers' computer systems for immediate action. • Receive orders from customers for immediate action. • Transmit customer specifications to automated machines in the factory. • Collect quality data across the manufacturing process to analyze quality.
Sales	• Provide prices and production data to customers. • Obtain data from headquarters while traveling or visiting customers. • Transmit orders to the factory. • Permit customers to enter orders directly. • Transmit credit card purchase data for quick credit approval.
Delivery	• Receive delivery orders. • Track merchandise in the delivery process. • Confirm receipt of order.
Customer Service	• Receive requests for service from customers. • Transmit data to customers to help them use the product or fix problems. • Dispatch repair crews.
Management	• Consolidate data from across the organization. • Maintain personal communication with people throughout the organization.
Finance	• Transfer funds to suppliers. • Receive funds from customers. • Complete transactions related to financing of the organization.

More recently, the convergence of computing and communications has made distributed processing more practical, with the data stored anywhere and the computing occurring anywhere. In the FedEx example, handheld computers performed some of the processing but then hooked into a computer in the truck, which transmitted data to a central database where other processing occurred. In this type of distributed system, users often do not care about the location of the computers and data as long as they can do their work conveniently. The organization cares, however, because the location of computing and data affects costs, security, control of the data, and many other important issues. Figure 10.1 illustrates how distributed computing is increasing the overlap between what people think of as computing and what they think of as telecommunications.

New Options in Wired and Wireless Transmission   Figure 10.2 shows how progress in wired and wireless transmission is creating a wide range of telecommunications options. In metropolitan areas, wireless transmission of radio and television broadcasts has been challenged by cable broadcasting, which can provide more choices and higher quality reception. At the same time, direct satellite broadcasting is creating a new wireless option. Similarly, the first telephone networks transmitted conversations only through copper wire. The inconvenience of transferring data through wire has led to the emergence of portable telephones and data transmission through satellites. At the same time, however, fiber optic cable has greatly increased the amount of data that can be transmitted by wired transmission.

New Combinations of Data and Computing   In Chapter 1, Figure 1.10 showed some of the new combinations of data and computing that have emerged by combining certain elements of telephone, telegraph, broadcasting, and data processing. For example,

FIGURE   10.1

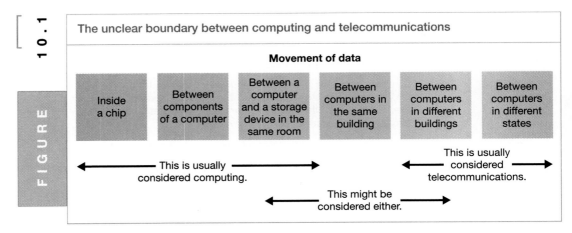

The unclear boundary between computing and telecommunications

This figure shows that there is no precise boundary between computing and telecommunications.

electronic mail takes some of the function of a telegraph but uses a computer to generate and receive the message. Voice mail uses a computer to control recording and retrieval of the voice message that might have been missed. Video conferencing applies the idea of video from television broadcasting to expand what would have been a telephone conversation. Many new combinations of data and computing can be expected in the future.

Making Sense of the Terminology and Details

Like computer systems, telecommunications systems present us with a large number of technical terms and choices. Although many business professionals may think they don't care about such things, these technical choices do determine what types of telecommunications applications are possible, and at what cost. You need an introduction to telecommunications technology because business professionals with no understanding of the types of networks or technical options have difficulty contributing to discussions of how a telecommunications infrastructure can be used effectively and economically to support an organization's mission.

FIGURE   10.2

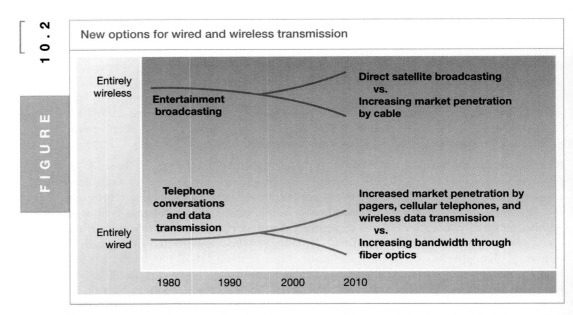

New options for wired and wireless transmission

Local wireless entertainment broadcasting is being superseded by transmission through cable at the same time cable is seeing new competition from satellite television. Correspondingly, telephone conversations increasingly are transmitted using wireless methods, while fiber optics vastly increases data transmission bandwidth. (The diagram is meant to show the direction of change rather than absolute amounts.)

Recognizing both the need to understand telecommunications basics and the need to avoid a deluge of terminology, this chapter proceeds by introducing five types of networks and then providing a simple model of telecommunications that applies to every one of these networks, even though they differ drastically in scale and intent. With the examples and the model as background this chapter then discusses some of the major options for different parts of the model.

The reason for the various choices and types of equipment is the same as the reason for different types of computer system equipment. Recall how Table 8.1 identified technology performance variables under the general headings of functional capabilities, ease of use, compatibility, and maintainability. All of the issues identified in that table apply to telecommunications just as they apply to computers, peripherals, and software. Table 10.2 shows examples of telecommunications

TABLE 10.2

Performance Variables and Related Telecommunications Choices	
PERFORMANCE VARIABLES	**EXAMPLES OF TELECOMMUNICATIONS CHOICES RELATED TO EACH PERFORMANCE VARIABLE**
Functional capabilities and limitations	
Capacity	• Each transmission medium operates in a particular capacity range in terms of data transmission speeds and distances covered. • Multiplexers increase the effective capacity of a data channel by combining multiple transmissions and separating them out when they are received.
Speed	• The promise of the Information Superhighway is limited by practical constraints on data transfer rates and capacity. • Transmitting voice communications through a satellite introduces a noticeable delay in response.
Price-performance	• Fiber optic cable has far more data-carrying capacity than twisted pair or coaxial cable, but is more expensive. • Cellular phones are more convenient than fixed-location phones, but are more expensive.
Reliability	• Networks sometimes fail altogether, calling for alternative routes and other forms of backup. • Electronic and optical signals degrade as they move through a physical medium, motivating the use of digital transmission and calling for the use of repeaters to boost the signal. • Data networks can use encryption to prevent unauthorized access.
Operating conditions	• Clouds, rain, and buildings interfere with some wireless transmissions. • Weight and portability of cellular phones affect their use. • Telephone switches require uninterrupted electric supply.
Ease of use	
Quality of user interface	• Digital transmission provides clearer transmission than analog transmission.
Ease of becoming proficient	• Proficiency with basic telephone capabilities systems is almost immediate, but many users never learn the more advanced features, such as transferring phone calls.
Portability	• Portable technology such as cell phones and PDAs are convenient for many purposes.
Security	
Ease of interception	• Analog cellular calls are comparatively easy to intercept.
Cost of security	• Encryption requires additional calculation capabilities built into telecommunications devices.
Compatibility	
Conformance to standards	• Telecommunications operates based on many *de facto* and *de jure* standards.
Interoperability	• Multiple inconsistent standards exist in computer networking, such as OSI, SNA, and TCP/IP.
Maintainability	
Modularity	• Data networks are modularized so messages can follow the routing that is least busy at any time.
Scalability	• PBXs can handle particular numbers of lines and then need to be upgraded.
Flexibility	• There is often a need to upgrade or downsize networks.

choices related to these performance variables plus security, which is a special concern for telecommunications.

Many telecommunications decisions are difficult because these goals pull in opposite directions. For example, increasing a network's compatibility with external standards may increase its maintainability but decrease its functional capabilities by making it slower. Increasing a network's ease of use by simplifying aspects of its operation may make it incompatible with standards and may have positive or negative impacts on its functional capabilities. As we introduce the technical aspects of telecommunications networks, it is important to remember that the purpose of each option is to improve some combination of functional capabilities, ease of use, security, compatibility, and maintainability.

R E A L I T Y C H E C K [✓]

Convergence of Computing and Telecommunications

The text mentions four aspects of the convergence of computing and telecommunications: the dependence of telecommunications on computers, the dependence of distributed computer systems on telecommunications, the changing roles of wired and wireless transmission, and new ways of combining computing and telecommunications.

1. Think about ways you have used computers and telecommunications in your everyday life. What aspects of this convergence have you felt personally?

2. Some people think that televisions will be more like computers in the future. What could this mean and how is it related to the convergence of computing and telecommunications?

TYPES OF NETWORKS

The simplest way to introduce the specifics of networks and telecommunications is to look at common examples such as:

- A typical home network linking two PCs and a printer and providing Internet access
- A local area network (LAN) in a small business
- A telephone network (from a business user's viewpoint)
- The Internet (from a home user's viewpoint)
- A wide area network (such as the FedEx network)

The examples are simplified to introduce particular points that will be developed later in the chapter.

A Typical Home Network

The home network in Figure 10.3 is one of the simplest common networks. As home usage of computers increased, the demand to link home computers also increased. After all, why have two separate printers and why pay for two separate Internet connections? Furthermore, linking the computers makes it more convenient to share files and other computing resources.

Figure 10.3 identifies components of a home network that uses a cable modem, but it does not show all technical options that are possible even for this simple network. For example, the PCs might be linked using specialized cables for data, phone lines, or a wireless network. Similarly, Internet access might occur through a high-speed digital subscriber line (DSL) or even a dial-up modem instead of using a cable modem linked to a cable originally installed for cable television. Issues in selecting options such as these will be discussed later.

A Local Area Network in a Business

Local area networks (LANs) connect personal computers and other equipment within a local area, such as a floor of a building. A home network is a simple example.

FIGURE 10.3

A typical home network

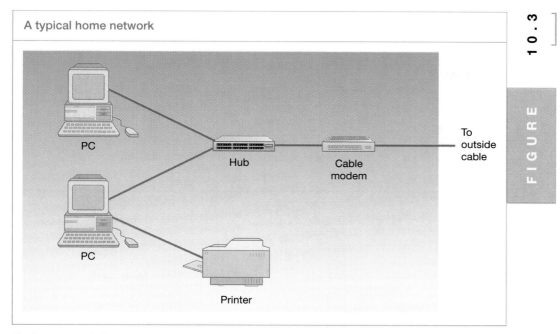

This home network allows two personal computers to share files, to access the Internet using a single cable modem, and to share a printer.

LANs are used widely in small businesses and in departments of larger businesses. They help people share equipment, data, and software, and help them work together more effectively. They may also link to wide area networks (described later).

Chapter 8 introduced distributed computing, which permits users to have many of the benefits of both centralized computing and personal computing. LANs provide access to more computing power, data, and resources than would be practical if each user needed an individual copy of everything. They provide the benefits of personal computing, such as not being forced to do personal work through a central computer that can get bogged down when many users share its capacity. They also provide a number of ways to make an organization more efficient and effective through sharing equipment, sharing personal files, sending messages, sharing databases, and administering software effectively.

Sharing equipment: As shown in Figure 10.4, LANs can link multiple workstations to one laser printer, fax machine, or modem. This makes a single piece of equipment available to multiple users and avoids unnecessary equipment purchases.

Sharing personal files: LAN users can select personal files that they want coworkers to see, such as engineering drawings, department plans, contracts, or drafts of memos. Coworkers can look at these files without delays for printing paper copies.

Sending messages: LANs can be used to transmit and manage electronic mail. They can also be used as a conduit for audio and video conferencing.

Sharing databases: LANs can be used for accessing shared databases. The LAN in Figure 10.4 is set up for this purpose because it contains a file server for retrieving data requested by the workstations. The file server accesses shared databases, such as the firm's customer list and telephone directory. When a workstation needs data in a shared database, it sends a request message to the file server, which performs the retrieval from the disk and sends the data to the requesting workstation. This arrangement avoids maintaining redundant copies of data. In addition to not wasting storage, having only one version of the database avoids problems with inconsistent data.

Administering software: Instead of storing separate copies of spreadsheet or word processing software at each workstation, the file server can send a temporary copy

FIGURE 10.4

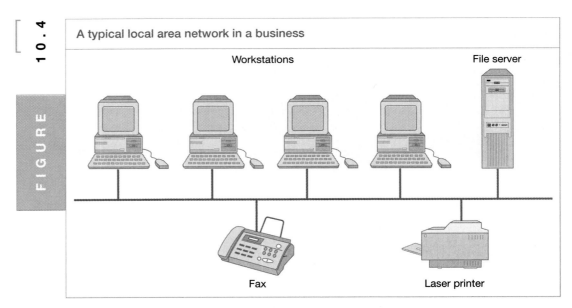

A typical local area network in a business

Workstations — File server

Fax — Laser printer

This LAN permits the users at workstations to share a laser printer and a fax machine, and to receive e-mail and share files. It also allows them to access a database through a file server.

to a workstation that needs the software. Handling software this way assures that everyone uses only the latest version of the software. Upgrading to a new software version involves only one replacement instead of finding and replacing each copy. This approach also reduces the number of copies of the software that must be purchased. For example, if no more than 10 out of 25 people on a LAN typically use a spreadsheet at the same time, the firm can purchase a license for 10 copies instead of 25, and can use the LAN to monitor the number of copies in use.

Like many other forms of wired telecommunications, LANs are becoming wireless for some applications (see Figure 10.5). Although the advantages of not having to string the wires are obvious, there are some disadvantages, such as limits on data transmission speed, problems in maintaining signal quality, and concerns about electromagnetic radiation in the workplace.

A Telephone Network

Figure 10.6 shows a telephone network from a business user's viewpoint. Assume that a user is placing a long distance phone call across the United States. The signal goes to the corporate private branch exchange (PBX), and from there to a local telephone company switching station, and then to a long distance switching station that sends the signal across long distance phone lines toward the location of the receiver. Closer to the destination, the signal causes the recipient's phone to ring after going through a long distance switching station, a local telephone company switching station, and a corporate PBX. The link designated as the "last mile" is an area of major concern for telephone and cable companies. **The last mile** is a general term for the communication link between a high-speed public communication network and the consumer's home or the corporate user's office. In terms of cost per bit transmitted, the last mile is much more expensive than the rest of the network because of the need to install and service equipment at the user's site.

As with the LAN example, there are many technical alternatives in designing a telephone network. The original phone networks were completely wire-based. Today a single phone call might go through several different wired technologies (such as twisted pair copper wire and fiber optic cable) and also might go through wireless technologies including cellular and satellite transmission. Traditional forms of telephony are based on creating a temporary circuit between two telephones that could be anywhere. As we

Handheld terminal linked to a wireless LAN

FIGURE 10.5

This handheld terminal transmits data about packages to a computer within a LAN.

A telephone network (from a business user's viewpoint)

FIGURE 10.6

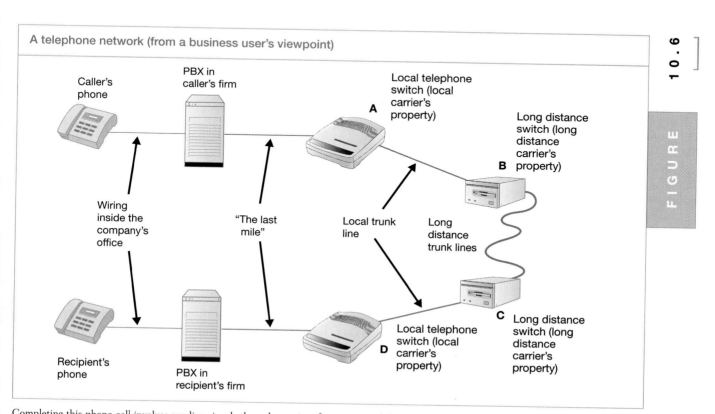

Completing this phone call involves sending signals through a series of computerized devices owned by the company, the local telephone carrier, and the long distance carrier. Transmission between the nodes might involve a variety of wired and wireless technologies.

F I G U R E

10.7

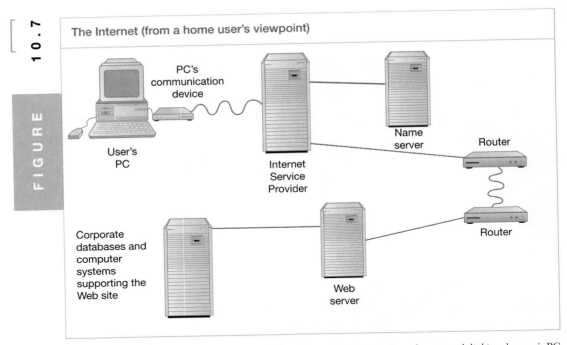

The Internet (from a home user's viewpoint)

From a home user's viewpoint, the Internet provides access to Web pages through a network linking the user's PC with an Internet service provider, which transmits messages to the routers that send these messages to the appropriate Web servers.

discuss later, another possibility is to route the voice signals through the Internet without creating the temporary circuit.

The Internet (from a User's Viewpoint)

Figure 10.7 provides a simplified user's viewpoint of how the Internet operates. The communication device attached to the PC could be a typical PC modem, a cable modem, or a DSL modem (compared later). User inputs go from the PC's communication device to the user's Internet service provider (ISP). The ISP links to a name server to retrieve the numerical equivalent of an address entered by the user. It also transmits messages from the user's browser to the routers that control the flow of messages through the Internet. Those routers send requests for Web pages or information to the appropriate Web server, which may or may not link directly to the corporate computer systems and databases that support the Web site. The picture would be similar for a corporate user, except that the link to the ISP would typically go through a corporate LAN.

A Wide Area Network

Wide area networks (WANs) are telecommunications networks that span a wide geographical area such as a state or country (see Figure 10.8). WANs are used for many different purposes. Some are designed as a communications backbone for a large distributed organization. For example, large national banks typically have WANs that connect thousands of employees in hundreds of branches. Other WANs, such as FedEx's package-tracking network, focus on a particular transaction processing application, such as taking orders, making reservations, or tracking packages. Many WANs transfer and consolidate corporate data, such as daily transaction summaries from branches. HP used a WAN to manage its 90,000 desktop PCs by permitting all HP users to download new desktop applications from centrally controlled servers, thereby ensuring that PC configurations and software releases were uniform throughout the organization.[4] FedEx's package-tracking network illustrates that a WAN may include both wired and wireless data transmission.

[R E M I N D E R]

Figure 4.13 explained the steps in retrieving a Web page.

A WAN that includes several LANs

FIGURE 10.8

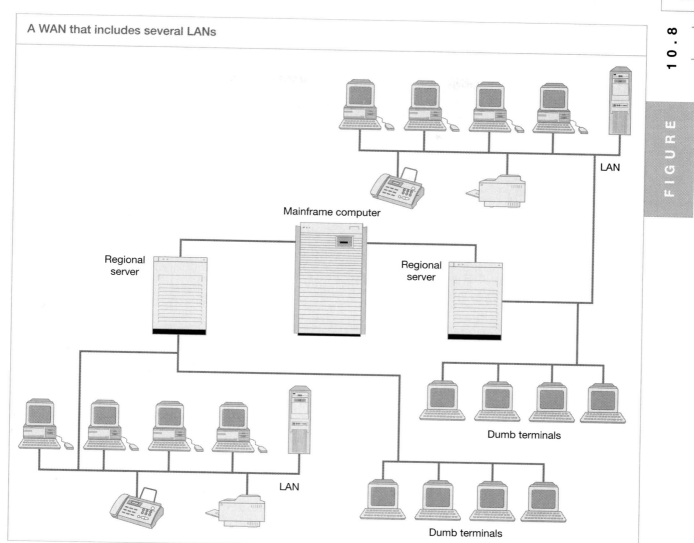

This WAN includes several LANs, each of which links to the rest of the network through regional servers.

FUNCTIONS AND COMPONENTS OF TELECOMMUNICATIONS NETWORKS

A **network** is a set of devices plus communications channels linked to transmit data between the devices. Each device in a network is called a **node**. The nodes of a network can include many types of devices, such as telephones, terminals, secondary storage devices, and computers. The nodes can be a few feet apart or thousands of miles apart. The data transmitted from one node to another are often divided into small chunks called *messages*. The overall amount of data transmission on a network is often called the *traffic* on the network.

Connectivity, the critical objective of telecommunications, is the ability to transmit data between devices at different locations. Although connectivity refers to machine linkages, it allows people in different parts of an organization to communicate with each other, and to share and coordinate their work. Connectivity therefore supports business processes but has a technical side that managers must appreciate.

Figure 10.9 shows the basic functions of a telecommunications network along with the network components that perform those functions. This general model applies to a telephone network just as it applies to a LAN or to the Internet. Table 10.3 lists some

FIGURE 10.9

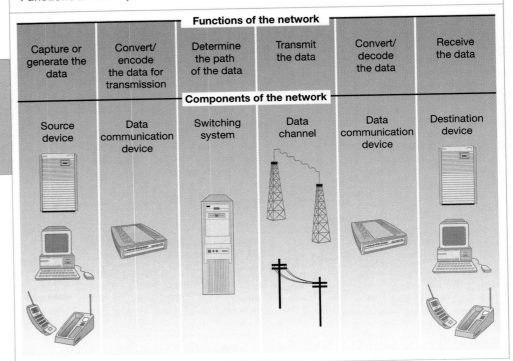

Functions and components of a telecommunications network

Functions of the network					
Capture or generate the data	Convert/ encode the data for transmission	Determine the path of the data	Transmit the data	Convert/ decode the data	Receive the data

Components of the network					
Source device	Data communication device	Switching system	Data channel	Data communication device	Destination device

Network components can be understood in terms of the various functions a network performs. Notice that some of the functions can be performed at several different times by different equipment in different places during the same transmission.

of the terminology associated with each step and mentions a few of the questions associated with each step. An initial summary will introduce each step in the model. The subsequent sections look at each step in more detail.

The first step in telecommunications is capturing or generating the data to be moved to another device. For example, a telephone caller generates data by speaking, just as an ATM user generates data by keying it into the ATM terminal. A salesperson may generate data by using a push button telephone as a terminal. A computer may generate data for an overnight transfer of transactions to headquarters by copying the day's computerized transaction log.

However the data is generated, it must be converted from the original form into a form for transmission. This process is called **encoding**. In a telephone conversation, the telephone mouthpiece encodes sounds into electrical impulses. In transmitting a picture by fax, the original image is encoded when it is digitized by a scanner built into the fax machine. In a system for transferring funds electronically from one bank to another, the encoding uses encryption to make the signal meaningless to anyone who might intercept it for unauthorized use.

Next comes the process of directing a signal from its source to its destination. This process is called **switching** and is comparable to the process of switching a train from one railroad track to another. Telephone systems require switching decisions because the data may follow alternative paths from its source to its destination. Switching is automatic in most current telephone systems. A computer assigns each outgoing telephone call to one of the firm's outgoing lines. An instant later, a computer or mechanical device in a telephone company switching station chooses among alternative physical paths to establish the circuit between the parties on the call.

A path along which data are transmitted is called a **channel**. Both wired and wireless channels are used frequently. Telephone systems once used only copper wire channels. Fiber optic cable made of ultrapure glass is now an alternative for networks with high

TABLE 10.3

Summary of Hardware or Other Terminology Associated with Each Step in the Telecommunications Model

Step	Hardware or other terminology often associated with the step
Capture or create the data	Hardware that might be used: • Computers: PCs, laptops, PDAs, servers, mainframes • Telephones: wired telephones, cell phones • Sensors: real-time data collection devices for monitoring Questions: • Generate the data in analog or digital form? • Compress the data? • Encrypt the data?
Convert/encode the data for transmission	Hardware that might be used: • Dial-up modem, cable modem, DSL modem • Network interface card (link between cable modem and PC) • Multiplexer (combines messages for efficient transmission) • Front-end processor (links from a mainframe to a network) Questions: • Transmit the data in analog or digital form? • What type of compression? • What type of encryption?
Determine the path the data will take	Hardware that might be used: • Hub (links computers within a LAN) • Routers (for LANs, WANs, and for the Internet) • Bridges (to link incompatible networks) • Gateways (to link compatible networks) Questions: • What is the current state of the devices this message might encounter? • What is this message's destination? • What is the most efficient path from this point to the destination?
Transmit the data	Hardware that might be used: • Wired channels: fiber optic cable, coaxial cable, twisted pair telephone cable • Wireless channels: microwave, satellite, local • Repeaters (boost the signal at intermediate nodes) Questions: • Transmit the data in analog or digital form? • Compress the data? • Encrypt the data?
Convert/decode the data	Hardware that might be used: • (See hardware for convert/encode for transmission) Questions: • Method for detecting and correcting erroneous bits? • Method for organizing data packets in the right order?
Receive the data for use	Hardware that might be used: • (See hardware for capture and generate data) Questions: • Is the information received in the most effective form?

data volume. Air or space is the channel for wireless transmission, which eliminates some of the restrictions of wires. Telephone systems use wireless channels for many types of transmissions. A cordless telephone in a house covers a small local area, whereas transmission through a communications satellite uses a channel covering 22,300 miles of space in each direction. Many applications use several different channels. For example, a single telephone call may be transmitted through several wired and wireless channels.

On arrival at the destination, the data must be converted from the coded form back to the original. This conversion is called **decoding**. In a telephone conversation, the telephone handset decodes the data back into audible sounds. In electronic funds transfer, the decoding process reverses the encryption step that preceded data transmission.

Finally, the decoded data are received, restored to the original form. This form may be a reproduction of the original sounds for a telephone conversation, a reproduction

FIGURE 10.10

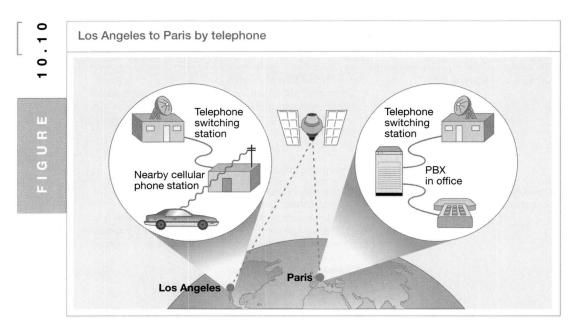

Los Angeles to Paris by telephone

This diagram shows one of many possible routings for a telephone call between Los Angeles and Paris.

of the original document for fax transmission, or identical data for transmission of computer data.

To apply the telecommunications model to a specific situation, consider a telephone call from a person in a car on a freeway in Los Angeles to a person in an office in Paris. Figure 10.10 shows the steps of creating, encoding, switching, transmitting, decoding, and receiving data. Notice how several switching and transmission steps are included in this process.

Figure 10.9 showed the functions directly involved in moving data, but it left out a crucial background function. **Network management** is the process of monitoring the network's operations, detecting and repairing faults, and balancing traffic so that the network handles its workload efficiently. Every large network requires major efforts in network management. Figure 10.11 shows the network management center used by AT&T for its long distance lines.

The steps in the telecommunications model rely on technology for generating signals at precise frequencies and moving and receiving those signals with minimal data loss. Although users and managers needn't be involved in complicated technical details, they do need to recognize common telecommunications choices related to the basic functions. Next, each of the functions and components is covered in more detail, focusing on the types of things users and managers should know. The discussion is divided into four sections: generating and receiving data, encoding and decoding data, switching, and transmitting data.

Generating and Receiving Data

Telecommunications systems can use many types of telephones, terminals, secondary storage devices, computers, and other devices for generating and receiving data. In some systems, the data are generated by a handheld terminal and transmitted to a computer elsewhere. In a paging system, the data are generated by a person using a pager and received by a person using a beeper. In a large building's automatic air conditioning system, a computer receives readings from sensors and then generates commands that are sent to the cooling equipment.

The variety of terminals in telecommunications systems is expanding continually. The discussion of distributed computing in Chapter 8 traced the progression from dumb terminals to networked PCs and workstations. Regardless of whether some of

FIGURE 10.11

AT&T's long distance control center

AT&T's Network Operations Center balances resource utilization on AT&T's long distance network, which includes 114 interconnected switching centers in the United States.

the processing is done at the terminal, the data are transmitted to a computer called the host computer. The **host computer** controls the database, checks the inputs for validity, and either accepts the transaction or sends error messages back to the terminal, touch-tone telephone, or whatever other device is used to enter the data.

Many types of special-purpose terminals are used in telecommunications applications. The special-purpose terminals for ATMs permit only numerical inputs. Those used to check credit cards before granting credit also contain a slot through which the credit card is passed for identification. Handheld terminals play a key role in applications where stationary terminals are too awkward. For example, car rental company employees use them while inspecting returned cars to enter the mileage and gasoline level. The terminals may transmit the data to the office for generating an invoice or may print a receipt themselves using a tiny printer.

An entire computer is sometimes used as communication gear for originating and receiving network messages. A **front-end processor** is a computer that handles network communication for another computer such as a mainframe that processes the data. The division of labor between the two computers improves the efficiency of the overall system. The front-end processor is set up to send and receive network communications efficiently, whereas the mainframe is set up to update the transaction database efficiently.

Thus, the equipment that generates or receives a message on a network can range from a telephone, to a tiny special-purpose terminal, to a computer. Once the data is present, the next step is to encode or decode the data for transmission.

Transmitting Analog versus Digital Data

Data transmission requires that data be encoded as electrical or optical signals, transmitted, and later decoded. The basic choices in encoding and decoding data are related to two factors:

1. Whether the original data are naturally analog or digital. Sounds, images, and video are naturally analog because they are continuous and depend on their shape

for their meaning. Numbers, text, and other characters used in written language are naturally digital because they are discontinuous, separable codes with a specific meaning.

2. Whether the data are transmitted in analog or digital form. Transmitting data using **analog signals** means that the signal varies continuously in a wave pattern mimicking the shape of the original data. Transmitting data using **digital signals** means that the signal is represented as a series of 0's and 1's.

To see the importance of analog versus digital we will look at the four possibilities summarized in Table 10.4.

Analog Data, Analog Signal   Figure 10.12 summarizes the physical method for analog encoding and decoding. The starting point is a **carrier signal** recognized by both the sending and receiving equipment. As shown in the figure, the carrier signal literally carries the encoded data and is itself a wave that swings back and forth in steady cycles. A typical telephone handset encodes sounds using the type of process shown in the figure. The handset at the receiving end decodes the signal by subtracting out the carrier signal.

[R E M I N D E R]

Figure 8.9 demonstrates how pictures and sounds can be digitized.

Analog Data, Digital Signal   Using a digital signal to transmit analog data such as an image or sound requires that the data be digitized. The digitized image or sound is only an approximation of the original. The quality of the image or sound received depends on the precision of the digitizing process.

Digital Data, Analog Signal   To transmit computer-generated digital data over a standard analog telephone line, a **modem** (*m*odulator/*dem*odulator) is used at each end

TABLE 10.4

Transmitting Analog or Digital Data Encoded in Analog or Digital Form		
	Transmission using an analog signal	**Transmission using a digital signal**
Original data in analog form, such as sounds, images, and video	*Method:* superimpose the "shape" of the data on a carrier signal; receive the signal and subtract out the carrier wave to reconstruct the original signal	*Method:* digitize the sounds or images to approximate them using a stream of 0's and 1's; receive the stream of 0's and 1's and reconstruct the approximation
	Examples: transmit voice using traditional telephone lines or radio broadcasting; use a fax to digitize a picture and then transmit it over a typical analog telephone line; transmit video in traditional television broadcasting	*Examples:* transmit voice using a digital telephone line, transmit voice via satellite, transmit television using cable
	Advantages: basic idea of the early telecommunications applications	*Advantages:* can manipulate the data more effectively and can have mixed forms of data as new transmission services emerge
	Shortcomings: signal degrades as it moves through the channel; can boost its power, but cannot restore its shape	*Shortcomings:* greater processing requirements at the nodes and greater data transmission capacity required of the network
Original data in digital form, such as numbers and text	*Method:* superimpose a stream of 0's and 1's on a carrier signal; receive the signal and subtract out the carrier wave to reconstruct the original signal	*Method:* transmit a stream of 0's and 1's by sending them through the channel as a series of pulses
	Examples: use a modem to transmit data from one computer to another via analog telephone line	*Examples:* transmit computerized data in a local area network; transmit a Web page from a Web server to a PC
	Advantages: permits using typical telephone lines to transmit computerized data	*Advantages:* low error rate
	Shortcomings: not as efficient as simply sending the 0's and 1's down the channel; limited by base frequency of the analog signal	*Shortcomings:* cannot use existing analog telephone lines for these applications

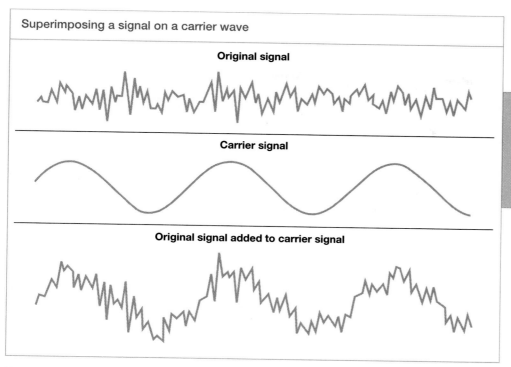

Superimposing a signal on a carrier wave

Original signal

Carrier signal

Original signal added to carrier signal

To encode sounds for analog transmission, their wave pattern is added to a carrier signal. The receiver decodes the message by subtracting out the carrier signal.

of the transmission. The sending modem superimposes the pattern of 0's or 1's on the carrier signal. The receiving modem subtracts out the carrier signal to reconstruct the original pattern of 0's and 1's. Different modems send signals at different speeds, which are measured in bits per second (bps) or baud. (Chapter 8 explained that the term *baud* is sometimes used instead of bits per second because some devices can transmit individual signals with gradations finer than just 0 versus 1.) Early dial-up modems operated as slowly as 300 bps, although current dial-up modems for PCs commonly operate at 56 Kbps. Limited modem speed is often frustrating when using the World Wide Web from home computers. **Cable modems** are more expensive, but they are also much faster, and provide up to1.5 Mbps Internet access through cable television connections. Another advantage of cable modems is that they are always on and usually have no delays for dialing the ISP's telephone number.

Digital Data, Digital Signal   With digital signals, the data are not superimposed on a carrier wave. Instead, they are just sent down the channel as a series of electrical or optical on/off pulses. In digital transmission, modems are replaced by other electronic devices that transmit the data in a precise pattern and recognize the data at the other end. Responding to the threat of Internet access though cable television providers, major regional telephone companies have begun to provide **digital subscriber line (DSL)** technology in 1.5 Mbps digital modems for use with existing copper phone lines. DSL is also called asymmetric digital subscriber line or ADSL.

As with cable modems, DSL modems are always on. With DSL a user can make a telephone call and access the Internet simultaneously because DSL reserves frequencies below 4KHz for telephone service and higher frequencies for data. Since each DSL subscriber has a dedicated line to a telephone central office, DSL has an advantage over cable service, which may slow down because the same cable is shared by neighbors. DSL quality degrades rapidly as a function of distance, however, and currently users must be within a three-mile radius of a telephone company central office.[5] Newer DSL technologies may increase this distance. By late 2000, around one million consumers and smaller businesses had high-speed Internet access, but the Gartner

Group forecasted that revenues in this area would be approximately eight times higher by 2004. Cable had a head start with about 88% of the market, but competition between cable and DSL providers remained intense.[6] Unfortunately customer satisfaction was often disappointing due to installation delays and unreliable service.

Significance of Analog versus Digital Transmission Table 10.4 shows that the difference between analog and digital is more than just a technical point. The choice of type of data and type of transmission signal affects the quality of the data received, the cost of the transmission system, and the receiver's ability to manipulate the data as part of the decoding process.

The first telecommunications applications encoded analog data such as voice and video using analog encoding methods. Analog encoding of discontinuous, coded data such as numbers and text would have been necessary to transmit computer-generated data using typical analog telephone lines. Digital encoding was the natural way to transmit computer-generated data, but it required digital transmission media. Continuous data can be transmitted using digital transmission media after being digitized.

The differences between analog and digital representations of data affect the quality of the transmission. The quality of analog data depends on preserving the precise shape of the waveform as it moves through a wire or through space. If the signal degrades gradually during transmission, there is no way to regenerate it. It is possible to boost the signal using a device called a repeater, but it is not possible to correct any distortions in its shape. With digital data, reconstructing the signal using a device called a regenerator requires only the ability to differentiate between the 0's and the 1's and make them sharper. Digital coding also provides many ways to use special bits for error checking and correction.

One of the most important differences between analog and digital data is that digital data can be manipulated readily. This issue underlies the struggle during the 1990s about standards for **high definition television (HDTV)**, a new standard for broadcasting and receiving television signals. If the standard were totally analog, as some competitors suggested, the result would be clearer pictures than the previous standard allowed. The ultimate decision was to use an all-digital standard, resulting in both clearer pictures and greater ability to manipulate the data. It would be possible to give the user new types of choices that would make a television more of a controllable, interactive medium. For example, at some point it might be possible to let the viewer of a televised baseball game select on the vantage point for viewing it. This would be possible because the data transmitted for the game would include views from different positions and software within the television would select one of the views.

Directing Data from Source to Destination

After the signal is encoded, it must move from the source to the destination. For special applications involving high data volumes, a firm may find it cost-effective to lease a **dedicated line**, a telephone line used exclusively by that firm for transmitting voice or computerized data between two locations.

In contrast, public telephone networks are shared among all users and can be used for typical telephone communication as well as computerized data. These networks often have alternative paths from a source to a destination and contain switching systems that decide what path each message will take. Figure 10.10 showed the switching steps that might occur to connect a telephone call from a car in Los Angeles to an office in Paris. Ideally, it should seem to the caller that there are only two steps: dialing the call and speaking to the person in Paris a few seconds later. The switching process therefore should be transparent to the user, even though there might be a number of data transmission steps with separate switching decisions between them.

A **switch** is a special-purpose computer that directs incoming messages along a path and therefore performs switching in a network. Some types of switches control transmission across national telephone networks, whereas others control the distribution of telephone calls within a building. The first type of switch routes long distance telephone calls through long distance trunk lines that cross the country. When a particular line gets very busy or is out of operation, these switches automatically assign telephone calls to other lines. Likewise, local telephone switching stations use switches to create the temporary circuits for telephone calls.

A **private branch exchange (PBX)** is a special-purpose computer that distributes calls within a customer site. In its simplest form, a PBX automates functions formerly performed by switchboard operators who plugged wires into a grid. All incoming calls go to the PBX, which connects them to the correct extension if the caller knows it, or possibly after asking the caller to select from options describing typical reasons for the call. Outgoing calls also go through the PBX, which automatically assigns each call to an available outside telephone line. Using a PBX permits a company with 50 telephones to have only five or ten outside lines, depending on how frequently employees use the telephone. If all of the outside lines are in use, someone trying to make a call has to wait until a line becomes free. Likewise, incoming callers will get a busy signal if all the incoming lines are occupied. PBXs may also provide other features directed at making communication more convenient and cost-effective, such as call waiting, call forwarding, voice mail, and automatic selection of the cheapest carrier for outgoing long distance calls.

Circuit Switching versus Packet Switching   Different switching methods are used in different situations. **Circuit switching** is the switching method traditionally used in telephone networks and for other situations when the network must guarantee a minimum level of real-time service. With a telephone call, for example, a caller expects a very short delay in order to carry on a conversation with the other person. Circuit switching sets up a temporary circuit between the source and destination, with resources reserved in the network to provide high-quality service. When the telephone call or other transmission is terminated, the temporary circuit is also terminated. Switching for a local telephone call usually occurs in a local telephone switching facility. Switching for a long distance call can involve several steps, depending on how many different physical links are established in the temporary circuit.

Although a switching process has always been required for telephone calls, switching technology has become much faster and more highly automated over the years (refer back to Figure 1.13). In the first telephone systems, all telephone calls required a manual switching step at a local telephone office. At that time, some forecasters estimated that the number of telephone operators who could be hired would limit the maximum number of possible telephone calls. Today, most central telephone offices in the United States use digital switching equipment, although the loop from the central office to the home or office is usually analog.

When data are transmitted infrequently from a large number of nodes, **packet switching** typically is used. Data transfer on the Internet is based on packet switching. In this process, a temporary circuit is not established. Instead, as shown in Figure 10.13, the message is divided into a series of segments or packets, each of which contains the destination address and control instructions in addition to all or part of the data in the message. The Internet routers use the address information in each packet to send it on an efficient path toward its destination, although different packets carrying part of the same message may follow different paths. The message is reassembled when all of the packets reach the destination. Maximum packet sizes vary from 64 bytes to 4,096 bytes, with 1,024 bytes as the default on Ethernet LANs. Thus, a small message can fit into a single packet, whereas larger ones are divided into separate packets.

Packet switching provides better sharing of resources and is simpler and less costly when supporting a large number of users. Packet switching has the advantage of allowing multiple users to share the same transmission facilities because packets from different users can be interspersed on the same line. This is consistent with what can also be done for nonpacketized analog or digital data by **multiplexers**, devices that collect signals from

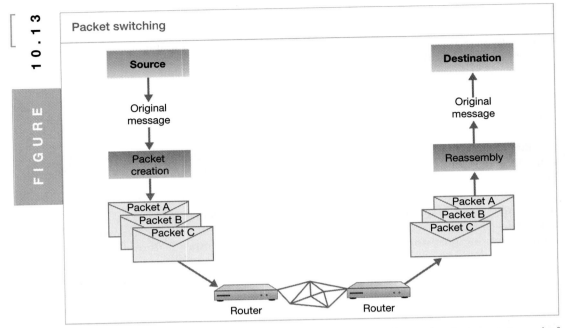

FIGURE 10.13

Packet switching

In the diagram, the original message is 3,000 bytes long. It is divided into three packets for transmission, each of which is separately routed across the Internet. The packets might follow a variety of paths. When the packets arrive at the destination the original message is reassembled.

multiple terminals and interweave these signals so that they can be transmitted more economically on a single high-speed channel. A mirror image of the interweaving process is used to separate the messages during decoding.

The disadvantages of packet switching stem from the process of creating packets, directing them through a series of routers during transmission, and then reassembling them at the destination. The resulting delays for computing done at different points in the network are inconsequential for most data communication, but make it difficult to provide a good signal when the continuous, real-time data is required, as happens with telephone calls and video conferencing. It is more difficult to guarantee a given level of real-time service with packet switching. The possibilities of using the packet-switched Internet as a replacement for traditional telephone networks will be discussed later.

Transmitting Data through Wired and Wireless Media

Transmission of data from a source to a destination may use a variety of wired and wireless methods. In wired transmission, a signal moves through a "wire" such as a telephone wire, coaxial cable, or fiber optic cable; in contrast, wireless transmission moves the signal through air or space. Different types of wireless transmission use different wave frequencies and require different types of receivers. Common categories of wireless transmission include radio and television broadcasting, microwave, radar, and satellite transmissions.

As was illustrated in Figure 10.2, wired and wireless transmission have changed places in many applications such as television broadcasting. In addition to the fact that it can provide more channels, cable television is becoming more popular in some areas because it can deliver a stronger and more reliable signal than broadcast television. In contrast, telephones started with wired transmission and are becoming wireless. Wireless telephones are popular because they can perform the functions of fixed telephones without the inconvenience of being anchored to one location.

Although data transmission involves many technical issues, business professionals should recognize several important characteristics of data transmission systems. For analog transmission, **bandwidth** was originally defined as the difference between the highest

Data Rates Related to Different Telecommunications Technologies	
Data rate	**Telecommunications channel or device**
6 to 30 Kbps	Wireless network services for mobile workers
28.8 or 56 Kbps	Data transfer through a typical modem for a PC
64 Kbps	Uncompressed, digitized voice
112 Kbps	Basic rate ISDN for twisted pair wire using 2 data channels
1.5 Mbps	T-1 phone line, commonly used for transferring business data between company sites; also, primary rate ISDN for twisted pair wire using 23 data channels
1.5 Mbps	Cable modems and ADSL modems
10 Mbps	Ethernet standard for a local area network using coaxial cable
100 Mbps	Fast ethernet; also, FDDI (Fiber Distributed Data Interface) standard for local area networks using fiber optic cable
155 Mbps	Data switch using asynchronous transfer mode (ATM) technology
1 Gbps	Gigabit ethernet
2.3 to 9.2 Mbps	Transmission to a large satellite terminal
12 to 274 Mbps	Microwave transmission at frequencies between 2 GHz and 18 GHz[7]
2.5 Gbps	Typical data rate for a single strand of fiber optic cable
3.28 terabits per second	Data rate in Bell Labs demo of terabit transmission for long distance using 300 kilometers of experimental fiber optic cable[8]

TABLE 10.5

and lowest frequency that can be transmitted. This term is still used in relation to digital transmission, but it is usually thought of as the capacity of the channel stated in megabits or gigabits per second. In practice, networks with higher bandwidths can transmit more data. For example, voice transmission requires a bandwidth of about 4 KHz, whereas television requires a bandwidth of about 6 MHz, over 1,000 times as great. This is why television cannot be transmitted on a voice-grade telephone line. Cable television is practical because fiber optic cable has enough bandwidth to transmit television signals for many different channels at the same time. To demonstrate the range of capacities and requirements in current telecommunications, Table 10.5 lists data rates for a variety of technologies discussed in this chapter. Table 10.6 shows the historical improvement in data rates. The starting point is a century earlier than the starting point for computers, but the recent rate of improvement is as fast or faster than that of computers.

Bandwidth limitations are a major obstacle reducing the practicality of what has been called the **information superhighway,** the idea that every citizen should have virtually unlimited access to information in electronic form via the Internet. A simple example illustrates the problem: Assume you want to download a 600-page novel using a 56 Kbps modem. If the novel contained no pictures but had 300 words per page and an average of six characters per word (including spaces), the transmission time would be 2.5 minutes (compared with about 5.6 seconds for a 1.5 Mbps DSL connection). If the information superhighway were to provide video on demand, its bandwidth would have to be staggering. Chapter 8 explained why a single high-resolution picture might contain as many bits and therefore might take as much transmission time as the text of the entire novel. Video involves 10 to 30 images per second and a single copy of the movie *Jurassic Park* contains about 100 billion bytes of data. Even when compressed 25-to-1 by removing redundant background information that doesn't change from frame to frame, this is still four billion bytes.[9] Assuming you wanted to download the movie onto a hard disk, the data transmission time at 56 Kbps would be 555,555 seconds, or about 6.4 days (compared to 5.8 hours for a 1.5 Mbps DSL connection).

TABLE 10.6

Historical Improvements in Data Rates[10]

Year	Data rate	Technology
1844	5 bps	Telegraph
1876	2 Kbps	Telephone
1915	30 Kbps	Transcontinental copper telephone cables
1940	7.6 Mbps	Coaxial telephone cable carrying 480 voice calls
1956	1.3 Mbps	Transatlantic telephone cable carrying 36 voice calls
1962	0.8 Mbps	Telstar, the first communications satellite, carrying 12 voice calls
1983	45 Mbps	First fiber trunk line between New York and Washington, DC
1996	2.5 Gbps	Phone companies install new, much faster fiber optic equipment for long distance lines
2000	3,280 Gbps	Data rate in Bell Labs demo of terabit transmission for long distance using 300 kilometers of experimental fiber optic cable

Although no one intends to download movies using 56 Kbps modems, the example shows that the promise of the information superhighway must be tempered by the limits of what is practical with current technology. Even if faster modems were available, there is still the question of how high-speed signals would be transmitted into homes and small businesses. As mentioned earlier, this is frequently called the last mile problem because installing a high-speed data line for every home and business would be enormously expensive even if the local telephone infrastructure provided a high bandwidth phone line in the street. On the other hand, every telecommunications company recognizes this issue, and the next five years will see tremendous competition to provide adequate last mile capabilities for most users.

Data loss is another important characteristic of data transmission systems. **Data loss** occurs during transmission when the physical properties of the data channel or the presence of other signals weakens or distorts the signal. Causes of data loss include *noise* (due to movement of electrons in the transmission medium), *crosstalk* (interference between signals in an adjacent channel), *echo* (reflections of signals), and *attenuation* (due to distance). Telecommunications channels use devices called repeaters to amplify the signal before too much of it is lost. Because both wired and wireless systems may transmit many different signals at the same time, preventing mutual interference between signals is essential. For example, interference between signals limits the number of television and radio stations that can broadcast within a metropolitan area. Using too many frequencies within the range of frequencies set aside for radio and television broadcasting would cause distortion.

Next, we will look at available choices in wired and wireless transmission.

Wired Transmission   Wired transmission requires that wires and cables be manufactured, installed, and protected from damage. Wires and cables take up space, can be messy to install, and get in the way. However, wire can transmit vast amounts of data with high quality and little interference from other signals. Three types of wire media are illustrated in Figure 10.14.

Copper telephone wire is often called **twisted pair** because it consists of a pair of copper wires that are twisted to help minimize distortion of the signal by other telephone lines bundled into the same sheath of cable. Copper wire is used for voice transmission and for low-volume data transmission. These wires are the slowest medium for data transmission but can be used over long distances. Using typical switching and transmission methods, the maximum data rate for copper telephone wire is up to 64 Kbps. The main advantage of copper wire is that so much wire is already in place in businesses and in telephone networks. But it also has disadvantages. It transmits data slowly and is heavier and bulkier than fiber optic cable. Unless current encryption

Three types of wired media

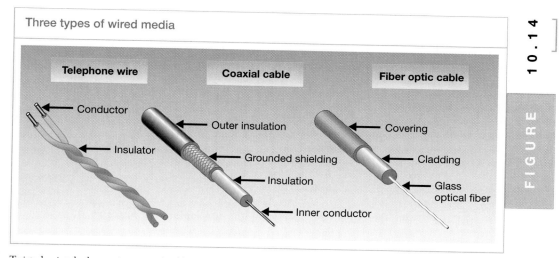

FIGURE 10.14

Twisted pair telephone wire, coaxial cable, and fiber optic cable have different physical configurations because the "wire" for transmitting the data in each case has different physical characteristics.

methods are used it is vulnerable to unauthorized intrusion because messages traveling through telephone wire generate electrical emissions that can be sensed.

Coaxial cable consists of a copper data transmission wire surrounded by insulation, electrically grounded shielding, and a protective outer insulator. It is used in local area networks and for other data transmission covering less than ten miles. Its advantages include data transmission speed of ten million or more bits per second, little distortion from external signals, and easy modification of networks without disrupting service.

Fiber optic cable contains an ultrapure glass core, a layer of "cladding," and a plastic covering. Unlike copper wire, fiber optic cable carries data in the form of light. Its data transfer rate of 100 million bits per second or more is much higher than the rates attainable with copper wire because the frequency of light is much higher than the frequencies used with copper wire. A single strand of optical fiber can carry 8,000 telephone conversations, and there are many strands of fiber in a single cable. Fiber optic cable carries most of the long distance traffic in the United States. Fiber optic cable has other advantages. It is 20 times lighter than copper wire, very difficult to tap into, and has comparatively little data loss because the glass fiber is ultrapure. Recent advances have increased the capacity of fiber even further through wave division multiplexing, in which different colors of light can be used to transmit 100 separate channels simultaneously through a single strand of fiber. Fiber also has some disadvantages, however. The use of light frequencies in fiber optics transmission requires expensive, high-speed encoding and decoding. Fiber optic cable is also difficult to splice because the glass itself is only as thick as a hair. Consequently, although fiber optic transmission is cost-effective for high-volume applications, it is too expensive for many low-volume applications.

Wireless Transmission   Wireless transmission does not need a fixed physical connection because it sends signals through air or space. All wireless transmission uses a particular frequency in the electromagnetic spectrum, regardless of whether the transmission is a television program, a cellular telephone call, or computerized data (see Figure 10.15). To prevent different uses of wireless transmission from interfering with each other, governments allocate specific frequency ranges to specific uses. Within those ranges, the governments allocate specific frequencies to individual users, including radio and television broadcasters and businesses that use certain frequencies for data communications.

Figure 10.16 shows four common types of wireless transmission. The differences in scale and complexity among these four applications are enormous. Building and

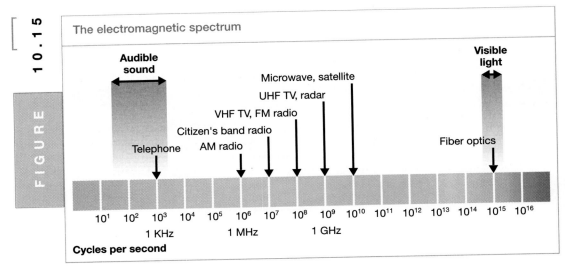

FIGURE 10.15

Various parts of the electromagnetic spectrum have been allocated for different uses.

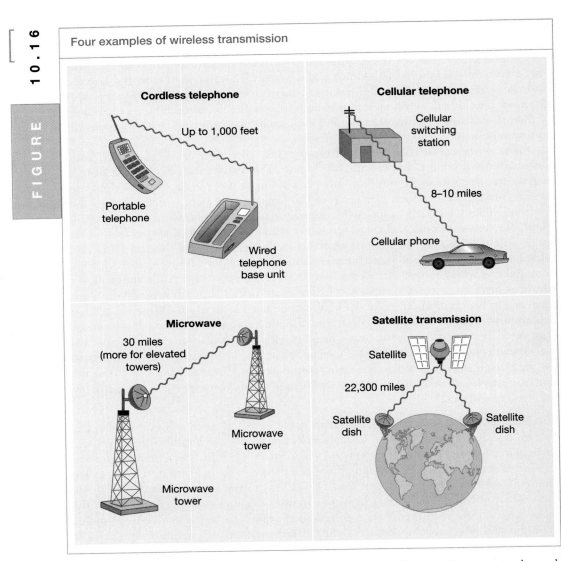

FIGURE 10.16

Wireless transmission ranges from cordless telephones within buildings to satellite transmission covering thousands of miles.

launching a communications satellite costs over $100 million, whereas cordless telephones are an inexpensive consumer item.

Cordless and cellular phones both achieve portability by moving from wired to wireless channels. Cordless phones for a home transmit to a base unit within a small radius, such as 100 feet. Cell phones transmit signals to a grid of cellular stations that are linked to the wire-based telephone network. Cell phones originally operated only within metropolitan areas with nearby cellular stations, but many cellular networks have now expanded outside these areas. The convenience of cell phones is offset in the United States by high per minute rates charged for both outgoing and incoming calls. The regulatory decision to charge for incoming calls is one of the reasons why many cell phone users leave their phones off except when they expect a call. In contrast, Europe has attained much higher cell phone usage because cell phone rates are lower and because only outgoing calls are charged, regardless of whether the phone is wired or wireless.

Although not as visible in everyday life, microwave transmission was the earliest of the four types of wireless transmission in Figure 10.15 to attain common use. It has been used for several decades to transmit both voice and data. Because earth-based microwave transmission is restricted to line of sight, microwave towers must be placed no more than 30 miles apart unless they are located on mountains or tall buildings. The line of sight restriction limits the use of microwave transmission within city centers. Microwave transmission can also be disrupted by atmospheric conditions and is comparatively easy to intercept.

Telecommunications satellites move in geostationary orbits that remain 22,300 miles above the same part of the earth. At this altitude, the satellite can send signals to earth stations up to 11,000 miles apart. These satellites can carry 40,000 simultaneous telephone calls or 200 television channels. Satellite communication has many advantages. Because it doesn't use a wire channel and doesn't need earth-bound relay towers, it can be used in remote areas. Unlike undersea telephone cables, satellite earth stations can be placed near the people who use them and are therefore easier to maintain and repair. Unlike wired transmission, the cost of satellite communication is the same regardless of the distance between the sender and receiver on earth.

The widespread use of satellite communication became more practical in the late 1980s as the cost and size of transmission equipment decreased. **Very small aperture terminals (VSATs)** can even transmit and receive data from computer terminals. VSATs are used widely in both data communication and broadcasting. For example, oil drilling companies can use VSATs to transmit data from drilling platforms for analysis at headquarters. Large retailers such as Wal-Mart and K-Mart use VSATs to transmit daily sales data. Unfortunately, only a finite number of satellites can operate in the 22,300-mile-high geostationary orbits. The problem is not that the satellites will collide, but rather that their signals will interfere with each other.

Wireless communication provides telecommunications opportunities for emerging nations, remote rural areas, and other regions where it is impractical or inefficient to build and maintain a wire-based infrastructure. Even where a wire-based infrastructure exists, cell phones have provided an important option. In Thailand, for example, the wait for installing a regular phone in the early 1990s was over a year, whereas cell phones were more readily available. Many believe Thailand's economic expansion in the early 1990s depended in part on the communication afforded by cell phones.[11]

The functions and components of a telecommunications network have been covered so far. The functions include generating, encoding, switching, transmitting, decoding, and receiving data. The components include a variety of computers and terminals, communications gear, switching systems, and data channels. The next sections look at telecommunications standards and additional aspects of network technology.

R E A L I T Y C H E C K   ✓

Basic Telecommunications Model

The basic telecommunications model includes creating data, encoding data, determining the data path, transmitting data, decoding data, and receiving data.

1. Thinking about every way you have used telecommunications, which of these steps have required your active involvement and which have basically been invisible to you?

2. Explain why and how you think this should (or should not) change in the next five years.

TELECOMMUNICATIONS STANDARDS

Technological standards have been a crucial issue ever since the industrial revolution called for interchangeable parts. Abraham Lincoln illustrated this point in the fall of 1863 when he signed a bill standardizing railroad gauges at 4 feet 8 1/2 inches between the rails, rather than the 5-foot measure that permitted bigger loads. This was bad engineering but made sense politically at the time because most of the 5-foot track that was going to have to be torn up was in the South.[12]

Standards are an equally crucial issue today because they make it practical to build networks containing hardware from different vendors (see Figure 10.17). Standards involve important trade-offs. They may disallow certain features or capabilities that are valuable in a particular situation but are inconsistent with the standard. Standards may also contradict the features vendors have built into their own proprietary products. This strikes at fundamental competitive issues because vendors often rely on their own proprietary data architectures as strategies to lock out competitors. The enormous market value of Microsoft and Intel demonstrates the huge potential rewards for controlling standards.

Standards can be divided into de facto standards and de jure standards. **De facto standards** are standards established by the fact that a product dominates a particular market. Examples of de facto standards in personal computing include the Windows and Mac operating systems and the machine language of Pentium microprocessors. **De jure standards** are standards defined by industry groups or by the government. Many de facto standards become de jure standards when analyzed and ratified by industry standards associations.

The **OSI** (Open Systems Interface) **reference model**, a framework for defining standards, is useful for appreciating the complex nature of networking standards. It was created to guide the development of standards for communications between networked systems, regardless of technology, vendor, or country of origin. These standards cover all aspects of network operations and management. Developed by an industry consortium

FIGURE 10.17

Standards that are visible in hardware

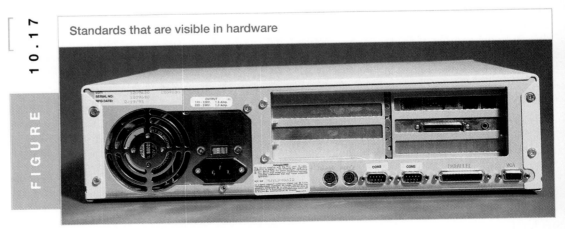

This rear view of a personal computer shows standard plug configurations. Conformance to accepted standards permits the use of many different brands of peripherals.

called the International Standards Organization, the OSI reference model identifies issues that specific standards should address. At each level the standards themselves are expressed through **protocols**, which are precisely defined rules, codes, and procedures for linking devices or transmitting data between devices. The various protocols needed to implement the OSI reference model cover topics such as establishing, maintaining, and terminating connections; routing information packets; controlling errors; disassembly and reassembly of messages; and multiplexing and demultiplexing of messages.

The OSI model divides a network's operation into seven layers, each having well-defined and limited responsibilities. Each layer receives data from an adjacent layer, performs specific processing tasks, and passes the data up or down to the next level of the hierarchy. At the bottom, level 1 is concerned with the physical attachment of devices and looks at issues such as what type of plug to use. Intermediate levels are concerned with the formatting of messages, methods of transmission, and error correction. At the top, level 7 is concerned with the logic of the application itself. Breaking network operation into these layers makes it easier to identify and solve problems, and it simplifies adding enhanced capabilities because they can be installed a layer at a time. Figure 10.18 explains the seven levels of the OSI reference model in more detail.

Although the Internet is based on a different five-layer model, the OSI layers are useful in identifying some of the important standards that have made it possible for millions of users to access Web sites around the world. At the physical layer, the standards that define fiber optic transmission were the key. At the data link layer, extensions of the original bps standards related to Ethernet for LANs and frame relay technology

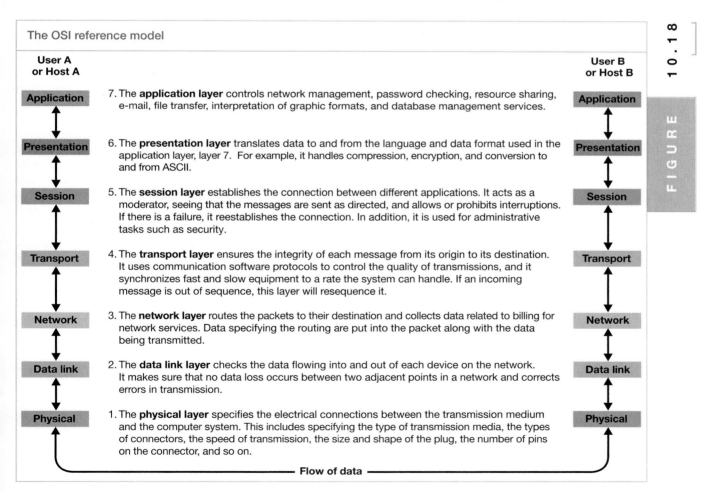

The OSI reference model

User A or Host A ... **User B or Host B**

7. The **application layer** controls network management, password checking, resource sharing, e-mail, file transfer, interpretation of graphic formats, and database management services.

6. The **presentation layer** translates data to and from the language and data format used in the application layer, layer 7. For example, it handles compression, encryption, and conversion to and from ASCII.

5. The **session layer** establishes the connection between different applications. It acts as a moderator, seeing that the messages are sent as directed, and allows or prohibits interruptions. If there is a failure, it reestablishes the connection. In addition, it is used for administrative tasks such as security.

4. The **transport layer** ensures the integrity of each message from its origin to its destination. It uses communication software protocols to control the quality of transmissions, and it synchronizes fast and slow equipment to a rate the system can handle. If an incoming message is out of sequence, this layer will resequence it.

3. The **network layer** routes the packets to their destination and collects data related to billing for network services. Data specifying the routing are put into the packet along with the data being transmitted.

2. The **data link layer** checks the data flowing into and out of each device on the network. It makes sure that no data loss occurs between two adjacent points in a network and corrects errors in transmission.

1. The **physical layer** specifies the electrical connections between the transmission medium and the computer system. This includes specifying the type of transmission media, the types of connectors, the speed of transmission, the size and shape of the plug, the number of pins on the connector, and so on.

— **Flow of data** —

FIGURE 10.18

The OSI reference model divides network operation and management into seven layers. Layers 1 through 4 are responsible for moving data from one place to another, whereas 5 through 7 handle the exchange of data between application programs. Communicating between two programs running on two different computers requires going through each step in some way.

TABLE 10.7

TCP/IP Protocols and Extensions Related to the Application Layer
Network and e-mail users frequently encounter the TCP/IP protocols and extensions, including the following: • Telnet: a protocol that supports access to remote computers. It makes it seem as though the user's terminal is attached to the remote host. • File Transfer Protocol (FTP): a protocol that permits transfer of files between computers on a network. • Post Office Protocol (POP): a protocol for storing e-mail and downloading it when a user logs on. • Simple Mail Transfer Protocol (SMTP): electronic mail protocol permitting e-mail between computers. • Multipurpose Internet Mail Extensions (MIME): extensions to SMTP permitting transfer of messages containing additional data types. • Hypertext Transport Protocol (HTTP): protocol for sharing hypertext information on the World Wide Web.

for WANs were essential in making transmission of images effective. At the network layer, **TCP/IP** (Transmission Control Protocol/Internet Protocol) defines the way data packets are constructed and addresses are specified. TCP/IP was developed in the late 1960s and early 1970s to permit information sharing between different computers running incompatible operating systems. At the application level, HTML and the **HTTP** (Hypertext Transfer Protocol) became key standards for coding and for displaying pages on the World Wide Web. The skyrocketing acceptance of the World Wide Web led software developers in other areas of computing to begin using HTTP for file transfers and transmission of Java applets.[13] Other frequently encountered protocols and extensions related to the application layer are listed Table 10.7.

The fact that TCP/IP, HTTP, and HTML were developed as open standards meant that their use in commercial applications would not be constrained by the commercial interests of a particular corporation. The story of the Internet illustrates the potential benefits of **open standards**, published standards that are owned by no one and can be used by anyone. In contrast, **proprietary standards** are owned by a corporation and licensed to others. As discussed in Chapter 9, the growing use of the Linux operating system kernel in operating systems for many different types of devices is also an example of how open standards promote broader usage.

Issues about which standard to adopt have had a major impact on the emergence of the digital phone market and on society's long-term ability to achieve connectivity. In this market, different vendors are using incompatible technologies called time-division multiple access (TDMA), code-division multiple access (CDMA), and global system for mobile communication (GSM). All can process calls digitally and can be used for data transmission, but they operate quite differently. **TDMA** multiplexes conversations for one to three users using the same frequency and then reassembles the original signals quickly enough to give the illusion of continuous sound. **CDMA** breaks conversations into segments that travel on different frequencies and are later reassembled. **GSM** is a variant on TDMA that dominates Europe's wireless market. TDMA is the older and more stable technology, but CDMA has the potential to transmit more conversations on a limited number of frequencies. These "technical details" will have direct bearing on which competitors can offer the best price/service trade-off.

MORE ABOUT NETWORK TECHNOLOGY

The previous sections identified different types of networks and provided a model for understanding the steps and basic options for transmitting data from one node to another. This section goes deeper into several aspects of network technology.

More about LANs

LANs perform the same operations that any network performs. They route messages from source to destination, ensure the destination nodes are ready to accept the messages, and monitor network utilization. Network operating systems and protocols control the flow of data between the devices on the network and handle requests for data. Control of a LAN includes preventing a node from sending a message until the network is ready to process it correctly and taking care of situations where a node is not ready to receive a message because it is busy.

LANs (and other networks) may be configured in a number of ways. A network topology is the pattern of connections between the devices on a network. There are many possible network topologies, each with its own advantages and disadvantages. Table 10.8 shows three representative network topologies: the star, ring, and bus.

LANs use a variety of methods for their internal communication; one of the most common is **token passing,** which is used in ring topologies. A token is a bit pattern that circulates between nodes. To transmit data, a node appends the data to the token. When the token arrives at the destination node, it adds a notation that the data has been received, and the token continues back to the sending node. The sending node removes the packet and the token continues circulating.

Most LANs use either twisted pair telephone wire or coaxial cable. Fiber optic cable is used rarely for LANs because it is more expensive. LANs use two types of data transmission: baseband and broadband. Most LANs are baseband networks. In **baseband**

Representative Network Topologies   TABLE **10.8**

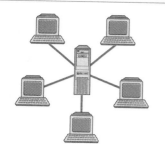

In a **star topology**, all messages go through a central node that serves as a switch, receiving messages and forwarding them to a destination node. Because every node is attached to the central node, a star network requires at most two links for a message to move from one node to another. A star network typically uses circuit switching and can integrate voice and data traffic. It provides good control because all messages go through the same node. It is also easy to expand without disrupting ongoing processing. However, a star network may have reliability problems because the entire network is down whenever the central node is down. The expansion of a star network is limited by the processing power of the central node. In addition, the cost of linking every node to the central node becomes excessive as the number of nodes grows and if the nodes are far from the hub.

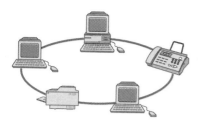

In a **ring topology**, the nodes are linked directly without a central server, which means that messages between nodes must be retransmitted by all nodes between the source and destination. Unlike a star network, the network control and processing are distributed to each node on the network. If any node is disabled, messages must be routed around that node to keep the network operating. Adding or subtracting a node while the network is in operation requires special effort to keep the network running.

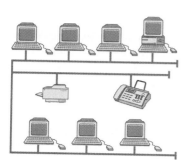

A **bus topology** attaches each node to a central channel called a *bus.* Each device on the network can access any other device directly by using its address on the bus. All messages are "heard" by every device on the network, but only the addressed device responds to a message. Bus topologies are easy to expand because the addition or loss of a node has no direct effect on any other node. As with a ring, control is distributed among the nodes. Network performance degrades as traffic increases, however, because each message requires the attention of each node. LANs commonly use bus or ring topologies. Ethernet is a common baseband network that uses a bus topology.

networks, the entire capacity of the cable is used to transmit a single digitally coded signal. Ethernet is a common baseband network that uses coaxial cable and traditionally has operated at 10 Mbps or 100 Mbps, although gigabit Ethernet is now available. In **broadband** networks, the capacity of the cable is divided into separate frequencies to permit it to carry several signals at the same time.

It is often necessary to link several sections of the same LAN, or to link a LAN to another network. For example, a LAN with 100 users might run more efficiently if it were divided into several distinct LANs that are linked. Links between LANs and between LANs and other networks are accomplished using routers, bridges, and gateways, all of which are a combination of hardware and software. A **router** links two parts of the same LAN or two compatible LANs by looking at each message and directing it to a node on the other network, if appropriate. Routers permit two LANs to operate like one from a user's viewpoint, thereby making it simpler for someone in a department to send data to someone in another department. Routers also direct packets on routes across WANs. A **bridge** links two networks by converting the addressing data from one into addressing data in the appropriate protocol for the other. A router may also select among alternative paths for each message, thereby balancing the traffic on the network. A **gateway** permits communication between computers on incompatible networks. It does this by translating the data format of an incoming message into the data format of the destination network.

More about WANs

Today's WANs can be applied for e-commerce, internal distribution of company data, e-mail, and many other purposes. The Internet can be viewed as an enormous WAN. Some WANs operate primarily through wires; others used by mobile salespeople and field support personal use wireless transmission to provide database access and e-mail. Some WANs are only for computerized data; others process data and voice in the same network. Some WANs link directly to workstations or terminals; others operate through LANs that perform local data processing and link to the WAN for data needed or provided beyond the local environment. This section will discuss several points about WANs that were not mentioned earlier.

Virtual Private Networks   WANs are often implemented in the form of a **virtual private network (VPN)**, a private network configured within a public network. Telephone companies have provided nonswitched leased lines for decades by dedicating portions of their high-capacity trunk lines to links between specific company sites. VPNs go a step further by supporting communication to any point within the private network but not supporting communication outside. This type of VPN service costs more than a pure leased line approach, but a telephone company manages the network. An example of a multifirm VPN is the Automotive Network Exchange, which lets thousands of companies in the auto supply chain swap CAD files, e-mail, and other information. This VPN may eventually link as many as 40,000 companies involved in manufacturing, financing, and insuring cars and trucks.[14] Today there is tremendous interest in building VPNs that use the Internet to provide a secure and encrypted connection between two points. These VPNs are run by Internet service providers (ISPs), who are responsible for maintaining bandwidth, network availability, and security.

Value Added Networks (VANs)   Due to their size, complexity, and response time requirements, WANs must be managed by telecommunications experts. Work can grind to a halt or costs can expand if WANs are set up inefficiently or used inappropriately. The difficulty of keeping networks operating is one of several reasons for using VANs. **Value added networks (VANs)** are public data networks that "add value" by transmitting data and by providing access to commercial databases and software. VANs are complex technical systems that use packet switching so they can be accessible from many different types of workstations. VAN services are usually sold by subscription, with users paying for the amount of data they move. They transmit computerized data between remote sites and therefore offer a service similar to what the telephone networks do for telephone calls. They are often used in electronic data interchange (EDI) systems because they reduce the complexity of connecting to the disparate EDI systems of various trading partners. In this application they collect forms in an electronic mailbox, translate and forward them to recipients, and guarantee they will reach their destinations intact. Other common VAN services include electronic mail, access to stock market data and other public databases, and access to electronic banking and other transaction processing services.

VANs are used for a number of reasons. They are a cost-effective solution for companies that need data communication services but don't want to invest in setting up their own private networks. They are commonly used by companies that lack the technical expertise to maintain a network. Even small companies can enjoy the benefits of data communications by using VANs and leaving the technical details to the vendors. VANs permit companies to use part of a network instead of paying a large fixed cost for their own underutilized network. VANs also provide for easier expansion because they are set up to use their capacity efficiently and to bring in new capacity if necessary. Finally, VANs can provide convenient access to data that would not otherwise be available.

The widespread acceptance of the Internet is creating an alternative to VANs for many applications that do not involve huge amounts of data. For example, Cummins Engine plans to keep its EDI system for its major customers, such as automobile companies. Their data-intensive orders require several hours of data transmission time even with a high-speed line. At the same time, Cummins lets small customers and suppliers use the Internet for low-volume transactions. Similarly, Boise Cascade uses EDI with its major customers, even though it saved $1 million in one year by allowing 1,300 smaller trading partners to post electronic orders using the World Wide Web instead of submitting paper and fax forms that require expensive manual processing.[15]

Public Switched Data Network Technologies   In the past, companies had to use dedicated, leased telephone lines to operate WANs. They are now moving toward **public switched data networks (PSDNs)**, in which their data flows through a public network managed by a telecommunications carrier. Today's most widely used public switched data network technologies are ISDN, X.25, frame relay, and ATM. ISDN is circuit switched and all of the others are packet switched.[16]

ISDN (integrated service digital network) is a set of standards originally designed to provide additional telephone capabilities without scrapping existing copper telephone lines. By providing integrated service, ISDN offers consistent ways to handle voice and computer data in telephone networks. As a digital network, ISDN provides for digital transmission of both voice and computer data on the same copper telephone lines that were used previously for analog transmission. The higher volume ISDN service, called the primary rate interface (PRI), uses multiple 64 Kbps channels for linking computers, local area networks, and PBXs into a telephone network at up to 1.5 Mbps. This ISDN service permits telephone wire to serve as cabling for small network applications. ISDN's basic rate interface (BRI) provides two voice or data channels that operate at 64 Kbps. A firm switching to ISDN for its telephone service must install totally digital telephone gear, thereby replacing all analog on-premises telephone equipment, even including the telephone handsets.

X.25 was used in the first commercial packet switched networks. It was designed to incorporate error detection and correction at each switch that a packet encounters. The resulting delays meant that it often operated at 9.6 bps or even less. It is not adequate for current data transmission systems if an alternative is available.[17]

Frame relay, currently the most popular PSDN technology, is form of packet switching that operates more quickly than X.25 because it does not perform error correction. Frame relay can operate at 1 to 2 Mbps, which is sufficient for most current corporate needs.

Asynchronous transfer mode (ATM) has the same acronym as automatic teller machine but means something entirely different. It is a form of high-bandwidth switching that provides connectivity between a variety of networks including LANs and WANs that use different technologies and therefore operate at different speeds. ATM attempts to combine the features of circuit switching with the robustness and efficiency of packet switching. It was designed to make it possible to use the same network for both data and voice and is highly scalable. Typical speeds for current ATM units are 25 Mbps, 155 Mbps, or 622 Mbps. Although ATM is still quite expensive, some observers believe it is the most likely technology to provide a common architecture for public, private, and on-premises networks in the future.

Wireless Networking

As with other types of networks, important developments have also occurred in wireless networks of all types. The FedEx package-tracking system described at the beginning of this chapter is an example of a WAN that uses wireless technology to transmit information to a central database as soon as the package is picked up. In another example, about 7,000 Sears technicians use a wireless data network for more than 130 million wireless messages annually.[18] In a typical use, a technician can locate a required part in the company's inventory, order it, and tell the customer when it will be available. This reduces the separation between the office and the field and thereby improves the efficiency of field service and sales work. It also permits a local office to send new instructions to a service technician driving to a service call that is now unnecessary because the customer fixed the problem. Although the promise of wireless network services was not attained in the 1990s due to a combination of high cost and low data rates (between 6 and 30 Kbps),[19] these services are attaining wider use as the technology improves.

Wireless Internet access provides a special challenge for mobile workers who carry personal digital assistants (PDAs) such as Palm Pilots and Handspring Visors. These devices have tiny screens and cannot display the types of Web pages that are effective on desktop computers. In 1997 a consortium of electronics companies developed a standard technology framework for the wireless Internet called **wireless application protocol (WAP)**. WAP allows some of the content on the Internet to be accessed readily from a mobile phone, but it fails to capture the flavor of the World Wide Web because it is totally text-based. By mid-2000 WAP was being used only sparingly due to a combination of "quirky handset designs, incompatible technology, and an unforgiving programming language." Internet sites had to be reprogrammed for WAP and many sites were not compatible with particular handsets. Unlike what a company would do for a typical Web site, a company setting up a WAP site had to program it in wireless markup language (WML) and test it with all the available handsets and gateways.[20] WAP played no role in the wireless Internet's biggest success story to date, NTT DoCoMo's i-Mode service, which was built using IP and a subset of HTML. It has more than eight million subscribers in Japan.[21]

Bluetooth represents a completely different type of networking issue—the challenge of supporting wireless communication between electronic devices such as cell phones and PCs within a home or business office. **Bluetooth** is a short-range wireless technology that operates up to 1 Mbps within a distance of 10 meters. Its backers predicted that it could turn cell phones into electronic wallets by zapping information to vending machines. Similarly, it could perform wireless uploads and downloads between PCs and PDAs or between PCs and MP3 players. Despite its allure, Bluetooth is still expensive for use in a wireless computer mouse or keyboard, and probably won't become an established technology until 2003, according to the Gartner Group.[22, 23]

IP Telephony

Voice over the Internet, often called **Internet telephony** or **IP telephony**, has received a great deal of attention and deserves special comment. The idea of IP telephony is to use Internet technology for voice conversations, with people on each end of the conversation using a headphone or traditional telephone handset. IP telephony could greatly reduce the costs of long distance calls by allowing the caller to bypass the charges imposed by long distance telephone carriers. After all, if it is possible to access a Web site anywhere in the world, why isn't it possible to hold a phone conversation through the Web?

Figure 10.13 illustrates the technical challenge. The Internet operates through packet switching. If IP telephony is to work, spoken words must be converted into packets that are individually routed across the Internet and then reassembled quickly and accurately enough that the person on the other end can respond in a typical conversation mode. IP technology was designed to packetize and route messages in situations that do not have stringent timing requirements. Alternatives to traditional circuit switching may provide many benefits, but it is not obvious why reliance on the Internet will attain the best trade-off between cost and quality. The first attempts at IP telephony required both the caller and the recipient to install special software, but produced service whose quality was inadequate for typical commercial uses. Both large telephone companies and small start-ups are working on better forms of Internet telephony. One approach is to link through the Internet, thereby avoiding even local access charges, but to transmit the bulk of the conversation on a private data network. Another approach is to bypass the Internet altogether and simply use a private packet switched network as a telephone network. By April 2000, approximately 2% of all phone calls were going through the Internet.[24]

TELECOMMUNICATIONS POLICY

This chapter closes with a brief discussion of telecommunications policy. This is a topic whose impacts range from personal concerns, such as what telephone service will be available at what price, through regulatory issues, such as who will be allowed to broadcast on which radio frequencies.

Figure 10.19 shows a framework for thinking about telecommunications policy in terms of issues and stakeholders. The issues include questions such as what products and services will be available at what prices, what level of access will be guaranteed to

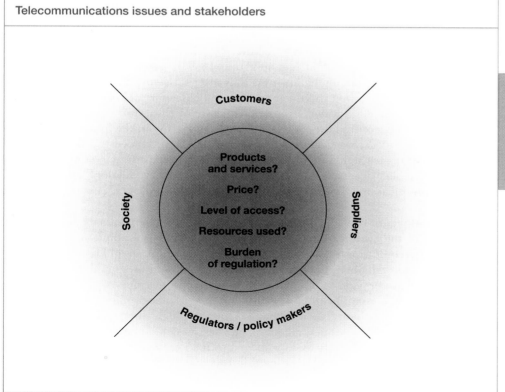

Telecommunications issues and stakeholders

FIGURE 10.19

Customers, suppliers, regulators and policy makers, and society as a whole are all stakeholders in telecommunications issues such as what products and services will be provided at what price, what level of access will be guaranteed, what societal resources will be used, and how much burden regulation will cause.

whom, what societal resources will be allocated to telecommunications in what ways, and how will telecommunications be regulated for efficiency and effectiveness. The stakeholders in most of these matters include telecommunications suppliers, customers, regulators or policy makers, and society in general. Telecommunications policy is a complex area because the issues cut so many ways.

Until 1984, AT&T was a telephone monopoly servicing most of the telephones and telephone networks in the United States. A consent decree between AT&T and the Justice Department in 1984 broke up AT&T's telephone monopoly, leaving a long distance company (AT&T) and seven regional operating companies that handle local telephone calls. Often called the Baby Bells, the regional operating companies originally included Ameritech, Bell Atlantic, BellSouth, Nynex, Pacific Telesis, Southwestern Bell, and US West, although mergers have left just four descendants of the original seven. The consent decree prevented the Baby Bells from selling equipment, carrying long distance calls, and manufacturing telephone equipment. Subsequent rulings permitted them to enter new lines of business including some information services, but these services couldn't manipulate the data they transmit. Their potential competitors in information services include cable television companies, newspapers, companies that provide VANs, long distance carriers such as MCI, Sprint, and the new AT&T, and most recently, companies that provide information services over the Internet. The broad span of companies and potential products and services raises many complex issues, some of which are summarized next.

Why should the government permit some companies, but not others, to sell products in a particular line of business?   Permitting the original telephone monopoly avoided duplication of telephone systems and made the original investment in telephone systems less risky. The limitations on the Baby Bells were designed to prevent them from using their local telephone monopolies to block access to long distance carriers and to freeze out local competition from smaller companies. This rationale was consistent with U.S. antitrust laws but left questions about economic efficiency, customer satisfaction, taxation, and even national security. The Telecommunications Act of 1996 allowed local telephone, long distance, and cable companies to compete against each other, thereby eliminating many of the restrictions in the 1984 consent decree that had split up AT&T. It permitted the Baby Bells to enter the long distance telephone business only after satisfying a 14-point checklist of conditions guaranteeing that their competitors will have fair access to residential customers. In 1998 a federal judge struck down some of these provisions by declaring that they unfairly prevented the Baby Bells from competing in the long distance business. The judge ruled that Congress had essentially pronounced the Bells guilty of antitrust violations without a trial, in violation of the Constitution.[25] The ruling was highly controversial, especially since the Baby Bells had actually lobbied in favor of the Telecommunications Act because they believed it would open new opportunities for them.

Another aspect of the overall situation is that direct descendants of the old AT&T are only part of the current telecommunications picture. For example, if cable television companies could run fiber optic cable into a house, why should or shouldn't they be able to provide telephone service? Similarly, why should or shouldn't a telephone company be able to provide cable television or other information? Who should be able to provide wireless communication services, and under what conditions?

The telecommunications world is both dynamic and highly uncertain because all the players have many options for new alliances, new services, and new types of competition, and because everything they try to do is judged by both regulators and the marketplace. The Internet has proved a major wild card in this area, especially with the promise of Internet telephony. This is a threat to the lucrative market for long distance and international calls because it creates a way to provide services that completely bypass existing carriers. Some forms of IP telephony bypass billing systems altogether, and other forms bill for maintaining reasonable quality, but compete based on low prices.

What should be the rationale for regulating telecommunications and setting prices? The rapid change in the telecommunications world has created many questions about the rationale for regulation. An example mentioned earlier is the rule that cell phone users should be charged for both incoming and outgoing calls. This provides protection for the existing infrastructure investments owned by the descendents of the Bell System, but it also raises prices for 80 million U.S. cell phone users and is an obstacle to the level of cell phone usage that has occurred in Europe. The United States is certainly not the only country facing issues such as these. In 1999 the daytime phone rate of ten yen (US$0.08) per three minutes was often viewed as an obstacle to the future of e-commerce in Japan. Masayoshi Son, President of the Japanese e-business conglomerate Softbank, warned, "The Japanese Internet industry will lag behind the U.S. by 5 to 10 years if the rates remain at their current level."[26]

The Internet itself has also raised many regulatory issues. In late 2000 the Federal Communication Commission (FCC) agreed to start determining whether and how to regulate a cable company that offers Internet access. Any resulting regulations could affect an ongoing battle between ISPs and cable companies and could shape how millions of consumers receive high-speed Internet service.[27] Around the same time, the FCC was considering a proposed merger between AOL and Time-Warner and questioning whether it should force AOL to make its popular instant messaging capabilities open to other messaging services. At that time, users of AOL services could send messages only to other AOL users, and not to users of rival services, such as Microsoft's Messenger. An underlying technical issue was how AOL should help its instant messaging rivals correlate usernames with IP addresses in order to achieve openness between their systems. AOL voiced concerns about consumer privacy and security.[28]

The way the FCC has analyzed telecommunications issues leads some observers to complain that U.S. telecommunications policy is being determined by antitrust policy rather than by national telecommunications needs. In other countries where antitrust is not an issue, monopoly telephone companies are able to plan their products and services based on their view of what is needed for telecommunications and national security.

Who should be able to use specific public resources, such as radio frequencies? This question shows how public issues and interests intersect with technology. Because there are only a finite number of usable frequencies, the electromagnetic spectrum shown in Figure 10.15 can be considered a scarce resource that has been allocated by governments. Such allocations are always controversial. There is no widely accepted right way to decide that a particular radio station or wireless service provider should own a particular frequency in a region. In the past these frequencies were granted outright. In the mid-1990s, the government auctioned around 200 megahertz that it still controlled. An important issue at that time was how or whether to protect the interests of small, innovative businesses that larger rivals easily could outbid. Several years later the question was whether or how to bail out several companies that had overpaid. On an international scale, many Third World nations have complained that the industrialized world has too much control over the frequencies used for satellite communication. They argue that these frequencies are a finite resource that is allocated unfairly today.

To what extent is universal access possible and to what extent should it be guaranteed? Access to telecommunications is important in today's society, but is it a right that should be guaranteed to any citizen? Assuming that the government wants to promote universal access, how can it do this and still encourage competition, technical progress, and personal initiative? Issues related to these issues include who will pay for universal access and whether most people want access to anything other than entertainment. Access to information and technology was one of the ethical issues discussed in Chapter 7. In a society sensitive to differences between haves and have-nots, access to new telephone, text, and video services is an important political and practical issue as well.

Business professionals don't confront issues such as these every day, but they need to be aware that their ability to use telecommunications will be shaped by a dynamic and unpredictable interplay of technology, business strategy, and government policy.

R E A L I T Y C H E C K [✓]

Telecommunications Policy

The text mentions a number of impacts of telecommunications policy.

1. Explain why you do or do not believe telecommunications policy has affected you in your everyday life.

2. What human and ethical issues arise in discussions of telecommunications policy?

CHAPTER CONCLUSION

What aspects of the convergence of computing and communications are important for understanding telecommunications?

Communications capabilities have become essential to many computer systems, especially with the trend toward distributed computing. Roles of computers in telecommunications include making long distance connections, monitoring the traffic on the network, and balancing the loads on different parts of the network by determining which path across the network each telephone call or data packet will take.

Compare a typical home network with a LAN or WAN.

A typical home network is a simple LAN that allows several PCs to share a printer and access the Internet using a single modem and single account with an Internet service provider. Local area networks (LANs) connect computers and other equipment within a local area, such as a floor of a building. They help people share equipment, data, and software. Wide area networks (WANs) link geographically separated locations. Some WANs are used as a communications backbone for a large organization; others focus on a particular application, such as taking orders or making reservations.

What are the steps in the basic telecommunications model?

Telecommunications is the movement of data between devices in different locations. Telecommunications starts with generating the data. The encoding step converts data from an original form into a form for transmission. The switching step directs the signal from its source to its destination. Data can be transmitted using a variety of wire or wireless channels. Upon arriving at the destination, data are decoded into the original form.

Why is the difference between analog and digital important?

Data transmission requires that data be encoded as electrical or optical signals, transmitted, and later decoded. The data may be naturally analog or digital. The data may be transmitted as analog or digital signals. This gives four possibilities, each of which has advantages and disadvantages in terms of price-performance.

What is the difference between circuit switching and packet switching?

Circuit switching sets up a temporary circuit between the source and destination. When the telephone call or other transmission is terminated, the temporary circuit is also terminated. With packet switching the message is divided into a series of segments or packets, each of which contains the destination address and control instructions in addition to all or part of the data in the message. The packets move through the network separately and the original message is reassembled at the destination. Packet switching provides better sharing of resources and is simpler and less costly when supporting a large number of users, but it is more difficult to guarantee a given level of real-time service with packet switching.

Compare different forms of wired and wireless transmission.

Wired transmission requires that the wires be installed and protected from damage. This is difficult in remote geographical areas and in locations where wires would take up too much space. Although a great deal of copper wire is already in place, it transmits data slowly, is heavy and bulky, and generates electrical emissions that can be intercepted. Coaxial cable is much faster but can be tapped into easily. Fiber optic cable can transmit vast quantities of data, is very light, and generates no electrical emissions, but is comparatively expensive. Wireless transmission is the only effective method for many applications, but it can be intercepted and can be disrupted by physical objects or atmospheric conditions.

Why are telecommunications standards important?

Telecommunications standards make it practical to build networks containing hardware from different vendors. However, they may disallow valuable capabilities that are inconsistent with the standard. Standards may also contradict the features vendors have built into proprietary products. This strikes at fundamental competitive issues because vendors often rely on their own proprietary data architectures as strategies to lock out competitors.

What is IP telephony and what challenges does it raise?

IP telephony is the use of Internet technology for voice conversations, with people on each end of the conversation using a headphone or traditional telephone handset. IP telephony could greatly reduce the costs of long distance calls by allowing the caller to bypass the charges imposed by long distance telephone carriers. Widespread adoption of IP telephony would have a great impact on telephone companies. Technical challenges in this area are related to the fact that IP technology was designed to packetize and route messages in situations that do not have stringent timing requirements.

How is telecommunications policy related to issues faced by managers?

Telecommunications policy is one determinant of who owns telecommunications networks, what products come to market, and who can sell these products. The issues in this area range from economic efficiency and customer satisfaction to national security. The allocation of broadcasting frequencies, both nationally and internationally, is a question that has major impacts on business and security interests.

KEY TERMS

telecommunications
data communications
Internet service provider (ISP)
Application service provider (ASP)
local area network (LAN)
the last mile
wide area network (WAN)
network
node
connectivity
encoding
switching
channel
decoding
network management
host computer
front-end processor
analog signals
digital signals
carrier signal
modem
cable modem
digital subscriber line (DSL)
high definition television (HDTV)

dedicated line
switch
private branch exchange (PBX)
circuit switching
packet switching
multiplexer
bandwidth
information superhighway
data loss
twisted pair
coaxial cable
fiber optic cable
very small aperture terminal (VSAT)
de facto standards
de jure standards
OSI reference model
protocol
TCP/IP
HTTP
open standards
proprietary standards
TDMA
CDMA
GSM

star topology
ring topology
bus topology
token passing
baseband
broadband
router
bridge
gateway
virtual private network (VPN)
value added network (VAN)
public switched data network
    (PSDN)
ISDN (integrated service digital
    network)
X.25
frame relay
asynchronous transfer mode
    (ATM)
wireless application protocol
    (WAP)
Bluetooth
Internet telephony (IP telephony)

1. Identify some of the ways telecommunications affects e-business activities.

2. What is a LAN and what are common uses of LANs?

3. Summarize how a telephone network operates when it uses circuit switching.

4. Explain the role of an Internet service provider.

5. Identify and define the telecommunications functions included in the basic telecommunications model.

6. Describe the difference between analog and digital signals.

7. What is the difference between a cable modem and a DSL modem?

8. What is the difference between circuit switching and packet switching?

9. Why would it take a long time to transmit a movie over a telephone line?

10. Explain some of the performance differences between twisted pair, coaxial cable, and fiber optic cable.

11. What are the advantages and disadvantages of communication via satellite?

12. Define the difference between de facto and de jure standards.

13. What is the OSI reference model and what do its layers represent?

14. Identify important differences between star, ring, and bus topologies.

15. What is a VAN and what are the advantages and disadvantages of using VANs?

16. Why is Internet telephony an important challenge to established telephone companies?

17. What are some of the current limitations of wireless networking?

18. Discuss some of the issues in telecommunications policy.

1. According to 1994 data from the International Telecommunications Union, 71% of the world's phone lines were in countries with 15% of the world's population. In Latin America only 7% of the population had access to a phone line, and only 1% had access in most of Asia and Africa.[29] Explain whether disparities in telephone access have an unfair impact on global competition. What might the less developed countries do about this situation?

2. You have just seen two commercials. In one, an executive has received an important message by cell phone while driving. In the other, an executive relaxing under an umbrella on an isolated beach is using a portable computer to have a video conference with people in the Paris home office. Use ideas about data transmission to compare the situations and to explain what would make the second situation feasible.

3. Assume that the U.S. Congress totally deregulated telecommunications. Based on ideas in this chapter, identify five major impacts this development might have.

4. Assume that typical houses will have home networks that link to several computers, all the telephones in the house, all the televisions, and possibly other appliances. These networks will connect to an Internet service provider through a cable modem. How might this arrangement matter to a typical household? To your household in particular?

5. What kinds of telecommunications capabilities would be required for a large multinational food company to provide any employee with instant access to any data in the entire company? What types of data-handling capabilities would this require? Aside from technical capabilities to transmit data, explain why you do or do not believe this is practical.

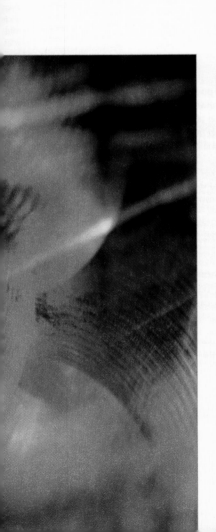

CASE NTT DoCoMo—Pioneering the Wireless Internet via Cell Phone

"DoCoMo (meaning 'anywhere' in Japanese) is a NTT subsidiary and Japan's biggest mobile service provider, with over 31 million subscribers as of June 2000. In February 1999, NTT DoCoMo launched its i-mode service. Within one year it had over four million subscribers, and within another six months it had eight million and had overtaken other Japanese Internet service providers (ISPs) that provide service to the desktop. DoCoMo's i-mode is the only network in the world that now allows subscribers continuous access to the Internet via mobile telephone. The service lets users send and receive e-mail, exchange photographs, do online shopping and banking, obtain financial information, download personalized ringing melodies for their phones, and navigate among more than 7,000 specially formatted Web sites."[30] Additional content such as news and games is offered on a subscription basis in the range of $1 to $3 per month.

Since i-mode service is used through cell phones with tiny screens, the types of interaction and graphical displays expected by World Wide Web users are not possible. I-mode was built using IP and a subset of HTML.[31] The initial version operated at only 9.6 Kbps, slower than the 56 Kbps modems that often seem very slow for downloading Internet graphics. The 9.6 Kbps data rate was initially adequate, however, because most of the data was text. NTT DoCoMo announced that it would come out with a 384 Kbps service in Spring 2001. The fact that the connection is also online makes it unnecessary to log on and much easier to use instant messaging, a feature that teenagers love, but that is gradually creeping into business environments as well.

I-mode's pricing model is totally different from the fixed-rate U.S. model or a time-metered European model. I-mode charges are based on the number of packets of data sent per month (as of April 2000, around $0.003 per packet). The more requests for Web pages or e-mails that a user sends, the higher the total charge. I-mode users pay a $3 flat monthly fee for unlimited access to mobile data services. Additional charges are applied on a per-packet basis. Another source of revenue for DoCoMo is billing services. For example, when Bandai charges for its cartoon character downloads, the charges appear on the user's mobile phone bill and the provider pays DoCoMo a 9% gross commission. Although pay-per-use content accounts for only 20% of all i-mode content, 70% of i-mode users subscribe to these services, generating an additional $1 per customer per month in billing and collection commissions for DoCoMo.[32]

I-Mode is so popular in Japan that the primary method of Internet access in Japan could soon be through mobile phones and other portable devices. DoCoMo announced that Internet access would be an option on every phone it sells. In March 2000 the number of mobile phone users in Japan exceeded the amount of fixed phone line subscriptions (56.9 million mobile phone users vs. 55.5 fixed phone users). Factors that encourage i-mode use include the limited amounts of space to put computers in a Japanese home, the high price of dial-up Internet access, and the fact that PC use in general is not as widespread in Japan as in the United States.[33]

NTT DoCoMo has looked at ways to penetrate the U.S. market. Some observers are skeptical about whether i-mode would succeed elsewhere. They note that Japan may be a unique market, with unique characteristics that may not exist elsewhere, such as a huge audience interested in using the Internet, culturally specific content, and a huge commuting population. According to one analyst, "Successful mobile applications are highly specific to cultures and national demographics. What flies in Japan won't necessarily fly in the States or Europe" . . . "People [in the U.S.] think text is boring—especially coming from the graphics-rich PC world. Until we get color graphics, mobile access won't become something that people, on an emotional level, think 'I've got to have.'"[34]

QUESTIONS

1. How does this case demonstrate the importance of data transmission rates in business? Does it imply that people in Japan are willing to accept lower data rates than people in the U.S.?

2. Assume that NTT DoCoMo succeeds in penetrating the U.S. market with its i-mode service. What difference would that make in work or play for business people? For teenagers?

3. Some people say that the Internet fosters globalization by providing worldwide access to the Web. Discuss arguments for and against this statement.

Exodus Communications: Growth Directions for a Large Internet Service Provider

Founded in 1994, Exodus Communications helped create the complex Web hosting business and has attained a market value of over $10 billion. The company offers sophisticated system and network management, along with professional services to support performance for customers' Web sites. Exodus manages its network infrastructure via a worldwide network of Internet Data Centers (IDCs) located in North America, Europe, and Asia Pacific. Exodus has 22 data centers around the world and is building another 14. Its customers include eBay, Yahoo!, Merrill Lynch, British Airways, and Johnson & Johnson.

When Ellen Hancock, its CEO, joined the company before its IPO in 1998, 80% of its customer base was Internet start-ups and 20% were in the "enterprise" category. By 2000, 49% of the customer base was in the enterprise category. In the same time frame, it had grown from no consultants to 660 as managed services increased from 8% to 34% of its business. During this transition, Exodus bought two computer security companies and had moved into a number of new services.[35]

An example of the types of service demands that Exodus encounters occurred when the Webmasters of RollingStone.com, the Web site of *Rolling Stone* magazine, had difficulty trying to solve a slow response time problem just a day before the publication of a multimedia cover story on Britney Spears. This would obviously cause a spike in demand that would exacerbate the response time problem. Since Exodus was hosting and maintaining the site, its engineers helped in solving the problem, which involved incorrect configuration data that caused the server to use 10 to 15 seconds to refresh domain name data every few minutes instead of daily.[36]

Approximately 400 of its customers (12% of its customer base of 3,300 companies) are application service providers (ASPs) that run application software for other firms using remote servers linked to a WAN so that those firms no longer have to install and maintain the software. Exodus charges for service based on usage, and this fits well with an ASP charging scheme. Its ASP customers range from start-ups to established software firms such as PeopleSoft and Oracle's BusinessOnline.[37] According to Ellen Hancock, "It's very hard to say what you're not doing, but we've spent a lot of time trying to do that. We say we're not going to know applications. We're not in that business. We just support the ASP. . . . We have no notion of competing with Oracle on e-commerce. We do not intend to ever understand HR [human resources] apps. That's a whole different skill base, and we don't have it."[38]

Both Exodus and its rival Digex seem to be evolving into "managed service providers," but using different paths. In late 2000, Digex unveiled a customer self-service portal called myDigex.com that gives them the ability to manage and provision their own services, such as performance statistics, site/server layouts, asset management, billing, and help desk issues. In addition, it gives access to service-level agreements and Digex support staff. In contrast, the new but not yet named services Exodus announced included remote monitoring, storage management, and performance monitoring. According to one industry analyst, "These guys are happy to host, and they're willing to manage your servers, but they're unwilling to raise the level of responsibility to something that is application-specific or customer-specific."[39]

QUESTIONS

1. Visit www.exodus.net and look at its summary descriptions of the various services it provides (such as security services, storage services, and content distribution and caching). What is the challenge in providing Web hosting services? What could be some of the measures of performance for this type of service?

2. Why should a large, technically sophisticated company like Merrill Lynch buy Web hosting services from Exodus Communications?

3. According to the case study, Exodus Communications is an ISP for ASPs, but currently says it is not interested in moving into that market based on its current skills. What are the possible advantages and disadvantages of moving into the ASP market as it learns more about how to support this type of activity?

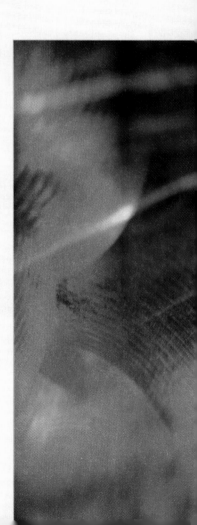

Information Systems Planning

chapter11

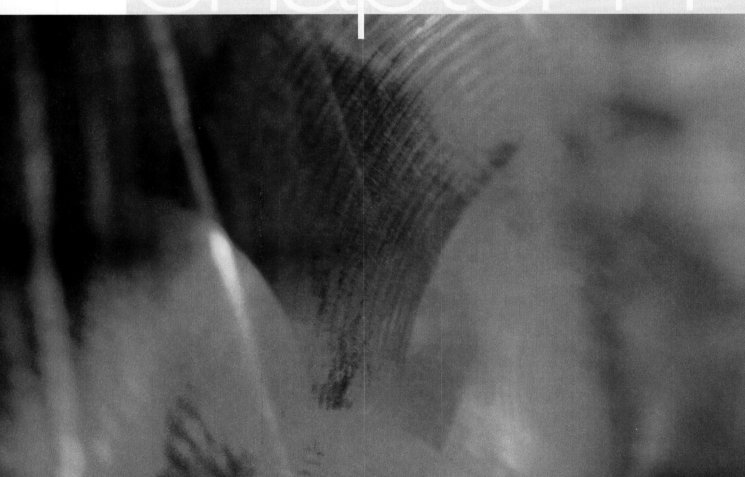

STUDY QUESTIONS

- What is an information system plan?
- Why do users and managers have to participate in information system planning and development?
- How is information system planning linked to business planning?
- What are some of the strategic issues in information system planning?
- What are the key issues in balancing centralized versus decentralized processing and control?
- How is cost/benefit analysis used in making investment decisions about information systems?
- What are the basic elements of project management for information system projects?

OUTLINE

The Process of Information System Planning
    What Is an Information System Plan?
    Challenges in IS Planning
    Principles for IS Planning
    Planning Role of the IS and User Departments
    Allocating Resources between New and Old
      Information Systems
    Project Roles of IS Professionals

Strategic Alignment of Business and IT
    Consistency with Business Priorities
    Reengineering and Downsizing
    Enterprise-wide and Interorganizational
      Systems
    Information System Architecture
    Centralization versus Decentralization
    Describing a Business-Driven IT Infrastructure
    Outsourcing
    International Issues

Selecting Systems to Invest In
    Cost/Benefit Analysis
    Risks
    Financial Comparisons

Project Management Issues
    Division of Labor between the IS Department
      and Users
    Keeping the Project on Schedule

Systems Analysis Revisited
    Information Sources for Analyzing Systems
    Performing Interviews

Chapter Conclusion
    Summary
    Key Terms
    Review Questions
    Discussion Questions
    Cases

Information Systems Planning

OPENING CASE

KMART PLANS A NEW INFORMATION SYSTEM THRUST

On September 1, 2000, three months after becoming Kmart's CEO, Chuck Conway announced the arrival of Randy L. Allen as Kmart's fourth chief information officer (CIO) in five years. Conway's announcement said Ms. Allen was "an expert on supply chain effectiveness, product development, merchandising, logistics, information technology and vendor/retailer relationships," and that she would be "instrumental as we implement new technology, systems, business processes and strategies that will enable Kmart to achieve world-class execution that benefits Kmart customers nationwide." With a two-year, $1.4-billion plan to revamp IT systems and improve execution and store performance, she would have far more resources than the previous CIOs.[1]

In a subsequent announcement Conway described Kmart's plans "to beef up its supply-chain and Web store-front operations, standardize and automate its ordering and fulfillment processes and make sure products get to stores when they're supposed to." He cited "a supply chain with no coordination, accountability or effective means of tracking inventory." The lack of integrated supply chain proc-esses meant that customers went to stores looking for advertised goods that weren't available. Kmart also needed better ways to forecast customer demand for its goods and improve its transportation operations.[2] One article called Kmart's supply chain "disastrous," and said it was "outdated and full of bottlenecks and inefficiencies that resonate throughout the company. Merchandise planners can't get a good handle on what's selling, leaving Kmart with too many items on clearance racks and not enough of what shoppers want. Meanwhile, store clerks are tied up with paperwork in the back room instead of waiting on customers."[3]

During the previous five years Kmart had lagged far behind its rivals in terms of growth and stock price. Since 1996 its sales had increased 14%, while those of Wal-Mart and Target had increased 77% and 46%, respectively. Kmart's inefficient supply chain contributed to the problem. It turns over its inventory 4.1 times a year, compared to 7 times a year for Wal-Mart and Target. If Kmart could turn over its inventory as fast as Wal-Mart, it would have $11 billion more in cash at its disposal and would be able to use some of that for advertising, improving stores, or paying down debt.[4] Despite these problems, however, Kmart did have advantages in some areas, including "a strong lineup of private-label brands such as Route 66 casual clothing and Sesame Street children's clothing. The biggest private-label star, Martha Stewart, sold $1 billion worth of merchandise through Kmart" in 1999.[5]

Part of Kmart's strategy was an e-commerce initiative through its partially owned subsidiary BlueLight.com,

named after Kmart's "blue light" specials. BlueLight offered free Internet access to anyone who registered and 1.5 million did so in just a few months. Most were low- and middle-income shoppers who learned about the service at their local Kmart, and 40% were new to the Internet. The site had exclusive marketing deals to sell Martha Stewart housewares. BlueLight.com's planned enhancements included integration between the site's order management functions and in-store kiosks, thereby permitting store service representatives to accept returns, even for products not offered in physical stores.[6, 7]

WEB CHECK [✓]

Compare the Bluelight.com site with Walmart.com and decide whether there would be any compelling reason to shop at one or the other.

DEBATE TOPIC

The Kmart Web site might be the source of new sales, but it is a very minor part of Kmart's operations and is not nearly as important as having an effective inventory system and good products to sell.

t he issue motivating this case is whether and how extending e-business capabilities through improved information systems would revive Kmart's competitive position. Inadequate supply chain and inventory systems were clearly an obstacle to the company's ability to serve its customers and maintain low prices.

In the background behind the story was a series of IS planning issues including aligning information systems with business strategies, deciding what projects to do, and deciding who should work on those projects. Notice from the work system snapshot that the case did not explain the planning process. The main point of this chapter is to explain the issues underlying this type of planning process.

This is the first of three chapters about building and maintaining information systems. Aspects of these topics, such as the phases of building and maintaining systems, were introduced early in Chapter 1 and will now be explained in more depth. This chapter covers information system planning at both the strategic and project levels. It introduces many of the IS planning issues that every firm should address in some way. Regardless of whether the firm has one employee or 100,000, it is still necessary to decide what will be done, who will do it, when they will do it, how it will be done, and what are the desired results. Chapter 12 covers alternative approaches for building and maintaining information systems. Chapter 13 covers e-business security and control.

The work system framework can be used throughout these chapters to visualize the work systems that are discussed and to think about alternative ways of doing the work. For example, there are a variety of IS planning methods, but there is often a question about whether the payoff is worth the time and effort expended. Moreover, there are many ways to create financial justifications of IS investments, but participants often wonder whether these justifications have much bearing on actual decisions. There are also various ways to build systems, each with its own advantages and disadvantages. And there are many methods for controlling and protecting systems, each with its own costs, benefits, and risks. Approaching Chapters 11, 12, and 13 with the work system framework in the back of your mind will help you use the ideas when you participate in planning, building, or managing systems.

A final comment is necessary about the use of the abbreviations *IT* and *IS*. This is a book about information systems (IS) that use information technology (IT), but many

WORK SYSTEM SNAPSHOT

Kmart develops a plan for the future

CUSTOMERS
- Kmart's employees
- Kmart's current and potential stockholders

PRODUCT SERVICES
- Corporate plan that includes an information system plan

BUSINESS PROCESS

Major steps (not mentioned in the case):
- Identify current competitive strengths and weaknesses
- Analyze recent operational results
- Identify strategic and operational alternatives
- Produce a plan with a high likelihood of meeting company goals consistent with its resources

PARTICIPANTS	INFORMATION	TECHNOLOGY
• Top management and functional area managers at Kmart	• Operating results for Kmart and competitors • Projected market conditions • Agreements and understandings about company capabilities	• Office automation software (not mentioned in the case) • Planning models (not mentioned in the case)

journalists and business and technical professionals write or say things that imply information systems exist under the general umbrella of IT. To give a flavor for how people often talk about this area, this chapter usually refers to the IS department and IS plan, but then to IT professionals and IT resources.

THE PROCESS OF INFORMATION SYSTEM PLANNING

The work of planning, building, and managing information systems can be viewed in work system terms and can be described, evaluated, and improved just like any other work system. The same issues apply, such as identifying the customer and product of the business process and attaining alignment between the business process, participants, information, technology, and the results expected by the customer.

What Is an Information System Plan?

Planning is the process of deciding what will be done, who will do it, when they will do it, how it will be done, and what are the desired results. Table 11.1 shows that information systems planning requires addressing these questions at several levels. At the strategic level, the questions are about the firm's overall priorities and goals for information systems, and the technical and organizational approaches that will be used. At the project level, the questions boil down to two types of concerns: first, what specific capabilities are required in each system, and second, who will do what and when will they do it to produce the specific results needed in a specific project, such as building a new sales-tracking system or retraining users of a customer service system that has been changed.

Information system planning should be an integral part of business planning. Business planning is the process of identifying the firm's goals, objectives, and priorities,

TABLE 11.1

Planning Questions for Information Systems		
Issue	**Strategic level**	**Project level**
Who?	• What are the responsibilities of the IS department and the user departments? • Which vendors will perform major functions that are outsourced?	• Who will work on each project? • Who will decide how the business process should operate? • Who will manage and support the information system after it is in operation?
What?	• What are the major things that the IS department must do so that the firm can accomplish its goals?	• What specific capabilities are required in the information system? • What will be the individual steps in each project?
When?	• What are the major completion dates that the firm can rely upon?	• When will the individual steps in each project be completed?
How?	• What technology will be used to do the work? • What technology should be available so that the work can be done more effectively? • What capabilities must the firm have to compete in the future?	• How will system development techniques be used to produce the desired results? • How will the IS department and user departments work together on the project?
Desired results?	• How will business processes change in terms of detailed operation and controllable results?	• What will be the deliverable results from each step in each project?

and developing action plans for accomplishing those goals and objectives. **Information systems planning** is the part of business planning concerned with deploying the firm's information systems resources, including people, hardware, and software. Figure 11.1 illustrates the similarity between information system planning and planning in various functional areas. The goals, objectives, and priorities of the business should drive all the plans. Furthermore, although each plan is produced by specialists in a particular department, all the plans should support the same strategy and goals. From this viewpoint, the unique aspect of the IS plan is that it concentrates on IS projects.

Challenges in IS Planning

The specific steps and procedures for creating an IS plan vary from company to company, depending on factors such as the way the company manages its various planning and control cycles and the extent to which IT professionals are centralized or dispersed into the business units. Often missing from explanations of IS procedures, policies, and standards is the way the procedures and policies address the major challenges in IS planning.

Difficulty Foreseeing and Assessing Opportunities   It is sometimes said that IS strategies become apparent only after they have been accomplished. Consider what happened with the Sabre reservation system, which is often considered a major factor in American Airlines' competitive success during the 1980s and 1990s. That system was not designed initially as a major competitive strategy. Rather, it evolved through four distinct stages over 30 years. It began in the early 1960s as a response to American Airlines' inability to use manual methods to monitor its inventory of available seats. Although a technical achievement for the time, it was a far cry from the powerful system later accused of presenting biased displays to travel agents so they would see and select American Airlines flights for their clients.[8] A similar story applies for the order entry and inventory control system American Hospital Supply (later acquired by Baxter International) built for its customers in hospital supply departments. From its start as a simple way to keep track of orders, it evolved into a major competitive tool by providing such complete service that customers found it expensive to switch to other suppliers. But competitors eventually offered similar systems, leading to frustrating situations in which a hospital might have to use different systems, including different terminals, for different vendors. Starting in 1988 Baxter moved to an EDI-based system called

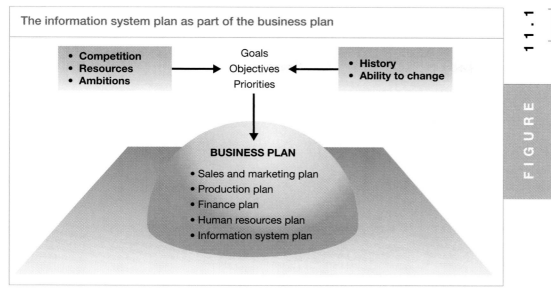

The information system plan as part of the business plan

- **Competition**
- **Resources**
- **Ambitions**

Goals
Objectives
Priorities

- **History**
- **Ability to change**

BUSINESS PLAN

- Sales and marketing plan
- Production plan
- Finance plan
- Human resources plan
- Information system plan

F I G U R E   1 1 . 1

The plan for each functional area (and for information systems) should be based on the firm's goals, objectives, and priorities. The individual plans in each of the areas are part of the business plan and should be consistent with it and support it.

ValueLink, which permitted it to provide just-in-time delivery not just to hospital loading docks, but to nursing stations and supply closets. A proprietary order entry system for Baxter's own product line had changed into a service system, allowing Baxter to manage a hospital's inventory of products from multiple suppliers (see Figure 11.2).[9]

The point of both examples is that it is usually difficult to foresee the way information system innovations will develop. As with many complex products, users typically identify new uses and possible improvements that the inventor never imagined. Consequently, IS plans should be reviewed periodically and systems should be designed to be flexible and extendible.

Difficulty Assuring Consistency with Organizational Plans and Objectives   A fundamental problem with IS planning is that individual departments within companies have their own priorities and business practices and often have difficulty working toward a mutually beneficial plan. This issue is especially significant if a large organization attempts to develop an IS architecture and infrastructure that spans departmental boundaries. Even if mutual benefits seem likely, the process of developing the plans takes a lot of time and effort and the rewards may be distributed unevenly.

Difficulty Building Systems   Large information systems are complex creations that often take years to build, and involve many organizational, political, and technical trade-offs. In many system development efforts, only a small cadre truly understands what the system is trying to do and how it will operate both organizationally and technically. It is not surprising that even major business organizations such as American Airlines, Bank of America, Chemical Bank, and the London Stock Exchange have suffered costly project failures. For every failure reported in the press, many smaller failures are never reported, and for every unreported failure there have been many semifailures, systems that were developed and installed but never came close to accomplishing their goals. The difficulty of building systems is one of the reasons information system investments require management attention.

Difficulty Maintaining Information System Performance   Each of elements of the Work system framework points to things that can go wrong with information systems. Regardless of whether the system performs as it was designed, the customer may be dissatisfied for a variety of reasons. The products and services produced by the information

FIGURE 11.2

Evolving from an ordering system to a service partnership

The early predecessor of Baxter International's ValueLink system was a computerized order entry system. With ValueLink, Baxter shares risk in managing a hospital's inventory of supplies.

system may not have the cost, quality, responsiveness, reliability, and conformance expected by its customers. The business processes within the system may lag in productivity, flexibility, or security. Participants can cause problems through anything from inattention to criminality. The information in the system can cause problems due to anything from occasional inaccuracy to fraud. Furthermore, the technology can impede or stop the business process by degrading or failing. Each of these problems can be anticipated to some extent and a preventive response can be planned, but at the cost of more effort, more attention, more expense, and less flexibility.

Difficulty Collaborating with IT Professionals   Business professionals and IT professionals sometimes talk past each other as if they come from different worlds. Anyone who has dealt with lawyers, doctors, or math teachers recognizes the resulting frustrations. Specialists may have trouble translating their specialized knowledge and world view into terms nonspecialists genuinely understand. Nonspecialists may feel they can't speak the lingo and can't even explain their concerns, no less engage in a genuine dialogue about alternatives. Even if they trust the specialists, they are left with a queasy feeling of operating too much on trust and too little on mutual understanding.

Attaining a genuine dialogue is important because the business professionals and the IT professionals each bring knowledge and understanding essential for system success. Many IT professionals have worked on different types of information systems and may be able to suggest approaches the business professionals would not have imagined. They know what is easy and difficult to do with computers. They know how to analyze, design, program, and debug computerized systems. They know what it takes to make an information system maintainable over time. Business professionals have the most direct experience of the business problem but may not have much experience articulating the problem systematically. Even if they can use spreadsheets and data analysis tools proficiently, they may not appreciate the problems of building maintainable systems for supporting business processes. Quite justifiably, they often want a quick solution to their business problems and lack patience for the delays required to build robust systems.

Principles for IS Planning

A series of management principles applies to IS planning and to the topics covered in the next two chapters as well.

Support the Firm's Business Strategy with Appropriate Technical Architecture, Standards, and Policies
Finding the right balance between centralized and decentralized decision-making is crucial. If people or departments plan, build, and manage their own systems according to their own whims, opportunities for coordination and economies of scale are lost. In large companies, immense amounts of time and effort have been wasted trying to bridge technical gaps and inconsistencies between multiple systems that all do roughly the same thing, such as generate paychecks or keep track of purchases. If central authorities make too many decisions about systems, some of the best knowledge about differing local needs and conditions will be ignored. Individuals or departments with genuinely different needs will then have to do extra work to get around the shortcomings of whatever was decided centrally.

Although different firms have come to different conclusions about the balance between centralization and decentralization, most have concluded that some issues should be decided centrally. The key issues involve tools for building and maintaining systems, the general architecture for information, and technical standards such as what personal computers and operating systems to use. In today's world of rapid organizational change, consistent decisions in these areas make it much easier to keep information systems operating effectively even as the business reorganizes.

Evaluate Technology as a Component of a Larger System
Specific hardware and software products should always be evaluated in their own right and as a component of an overall system. Consider what a highway engineer said about the rebuilding of certain highway overpasses after the 1994 San Fernando Valley earthquake: "When we strengthen some of the older structures using the newest highway technology, what we are basically doing in many cases is moving the likely point of failure from one place to another." In a similar way, having the latest microprocessor may not change system performance at all if the system continues using old software whose internal design cannot exploit the newer technology. Similarly, the latest hardware and software may have little impact if the training and support for participants is inadequate or if the right data is not available.

Recognize Life Cycle Costs, Not Just Acquisition Costs
The discussion of a customer's view of a product in Chapter 6 was based on the way a customer perceives costs and benefits across the entire cycle of learning about a product, customizing it, using it, and maintaining it. A similar cycle applies for information systems, and the costs of any information system typically far exceed the cost of the hardware and software. For example, the discussion of network computers in Chapter 8 explained that a typical company's PC-related costs include not only the cost of computers, but also the costs of installing computers and using them effectively. These costs are related to linking the computer to a network, buying software, training users, and providing support for users.

[L O O K   A H E A D]

Chapter 12 will explain several alternative system life cycles in depth.

Design Information Systems to Be Maintainable   Anyone who has ever tried to remodel a house recognizes the value of designing information systems to be maintainable. The difficulty of doing the home improvements depends on what you find when you tear open the wall. The work is much easier if you have an accurate blueprint or wiring diagram telling you where to look and what to expect. Information system users whose main computer experience is with their own spreadsheets often misunderstand why it takes so long to build and implement information systems. Unlike spreadsheet models developed for temporary, personal use in analyzing a current situation, many information systems must last for years and must be maintainable long after the original system builders have moved to other jobs. This requires that the systems be constructed and documented carefully, and that the documentation be updated whenever the system is changed. In general, it is also easier to maintain systems if the parts are simpler and are designed using modular components that operate consistent with accepted industry standards.

Recognize the Human Side of Technology Use   A point made repeatedly throughout this book is that people are part of the system. A technically spectacular system may still fail if its human participants are unwilling or unable to play their part effectively. Similarly, even technically primitive systems are often successful when supported and understood by active participants. The human side of technology use is one of the reasons the process of designing systems and implementing them in organizations requires involvement and commitment by system participants and their management. Processes for planning, building, and managing systems should be designed accordingly.

Support and Control the Technical System   Important as the human side of the system is, the technical side should also be supported and controlled. Information systems need care and maintenance in much the same way as cars or houses. If care and maintenance are ignored, systems gradually degrade and become more prone to failure from overloaded databases, incorrect data, faulty documentation, or human error. This leads to the question of who should do maintenance work. The trend toward decentralization and outsourcing leaves less of this work in the hands of centralized groups. These groups often have greater technical depth than individual functional departments and greater company allegiance than outsourcing vendors who have their own external business agendas. Consequently, the support and control of technical systems is just as much a planning issue as deciding what new information systems to build.

Planning Role of the IS and User Departments

A firm's IS department is usually responsible for producing the IS plan in conjunction with the user departments, such as marketing and finance. As happens in other departments, managers in the IS department start the planning process by reviewing their progress on the existing plan. They look at special problems, such as systems approaching technical obsolescence. They confer with managers in the user departments to learn about user priorities and needs for system improvements, new systems, and user support. IS department managers also look at the needs of their own department such as training, hiring, and personnel development.

Many questions and issues arise in producing and reviewing an initial IS plan. Users are often frustrated by how long it takes to build new systems and how much effort it takes to make what might seem like small changes to existing systems. The IS department often feels frustrated by its inability to keep up with many of the business's pressing problems.

It is especially important to allocate resources carefully because most firms don't come close to having the IT resources needed to develop all of the information systems that people in the company say they need. It is not unusual for a central IS department to have more than a two-year backlog of committed projects, with many other requests simply turned down or never submitted formally because of the minimal chance that they would be acted upon.

Chief Information Officer   Recognizing the importance of information systems in corporate success, some firms have designated the head of the IS department the **chief information officer** (**CIO**), just as the head of finance is the CFO and the chief executive of the company is the CEO. By leading the IS function, the CIO has special responsibility for making sure that the IS plan supports the firm's business plan and provides long-term direction for the firm's system-related efforts.

The role of CIO calls for a rare mix of business skills and technical knowledge. CIOs too focused on computer technology may have trouble being accepted as business professionals working for the overall good of the firm. CIOs too focused on general business issues may have trouble resolving the technical issues in creating a practical plan for adopting new technologies essential for future business practices. Throughout the 1990s, career turmoil among CIOs was so common that some claimed CIO stood for "career is over." Regardless of whether individuals succeeded in filling an ambitious role, the strategic nature of IS leadership is increasingly clear.

User Roles in IS Planning   Even though the IS department compiles the IS plan, members of user departments also have important planning responsibilities. Because information systems exist to help them do their work, they have to ensure that the right systems are developed and are used effectively and efficiently. Members of user departments participate in IS planning in various roles including sponsor, champion, and steering committee member.

- **Sponsors** are senior managers who recognize the importance of an information system and make sure resources are allocated for building and maintaining the system. In addition to funding, the crucial resource is people from the user department who would be doing their regular work if they were not working on the information system project. For example, an accounting manager might spend months as the user representative in a project building a new accounting information system.
- **Champions** are individuals who recognize the importance of an information system and exert effort to make sure that others share that recognition. Champions may not have direct control of resources for the system, even though they promote its success.
- **IS steering committees** meet to make sure the IS effort reflects business priorities. These committees typically include knowledgeable representatives from user groups plus members of the IS department. Responsibilities of these committees range from identifying problems to reviewing system proposals and long-term IS plans.

Because IS planning efforts inevitably face questions about resources for maintaining existing systems versus resources for building new systems, we will look at this issue next.

Allocating Resources between New and Old Information Systems

An IS plan allocates resources such as budgets and programmer time between different possible uses of those resources. Major uses of those resources include maintaining existing systems, developing new systems, supporting users, and trying out new ideas and techniques.

Maintaining Existing Information Systems and Supporting Users   Keeping existing information systems operating efficiently and effectively as business conditions change often absorbs 60% to 80% of the planned work in an IS plan. This work can be split into three categories: user-support, system enhancements, and bug fixes.

User-support projects include helping users with applications developed by the IS department, with applications purchased from outside vendors, and with performing individual work on personal computers. The individual work typically involves personal use of tools such as spreadsheets, word processors, and presentation software. Given the ongoing nature of user-support projects, many firms have staffed separate groups devoted to helping users develop and maintain their own applications, especially applications that extract data from corporate databases. Ideally these groups should reduce costs and increase effectiveness by standardizing on a few types of hardware and software, offering training programs for users, and helping users analyze and solve their own problems.

Enhancements are improvements in an existing system's function without changing its fundamental concepts or operation. Work system participants who care about what the information system does are often able to suggest many desired enhancements. The list of suggestions usually grows as users come to recognize the current system's limitations and think up new ways to use it to greater advantage. Many IS departments could assign every programmer to enhancements and barely make a dent in the list of suggestions from their users.

Bug fixes are projects directed at correcting bugs in existing systems. Bugs are flaws in systems that cause them to produce incorrect or inappropriate results. All large information systems (and most small ones) contain bugs. The planning issue is to decide how much effort should go into fixing them. Because important bugs may be discovered during the period covered by the plan, IS plans should reserve time and effort for bug fixes even though the specific bugs to be fixed may not be known in advance.

Bugs are usually divided into priority-based categories. Bugs that prevent people from doing their work or prevent departments from operating effectively receive the highest priority and usually preempt other scheduled work. Bugs that cause minor problems for users typically are fixed when convenient. Minor bugs having little impact on users' ability to do their work may never be fixed.

New Development, Infrastructure, and Other Projects   Resources not assigned to maintaining existing information systems and supporting users can be allocated to a variety of other projects, including new-application development, IT infrastructure projects, and research projects.

Major new-application projects provide new types of capabilities for users rather than small improvements in existing application systems. New-application projects can be divided further into projects that require new technology, knowledge, and methods, versus systems for which existing knowledge and methods suffice. Projects that require new technology, knowledge, or methods are usually riskier than those applying currently used approaches. To reduce the likelihood of high-visibility failures, only a limited number of high-risk projects should be undertaken at any time.

IT infrastructure projects install and maintain the hardware, software, and human support organizations that are used by application systems. The configuration and implementation of ERP systems (introduced in Chapter 5) is typically a huge infrastructure project that affects many users directly. Other types of infrastructure projects that affect users directly include installing and maintaining computers, telecommunications networks, and messaging systems. Also important but not as visible to users are infrastructure projects emphasizing system development tools.

Research projects evaluate new methods or technology to determine how they might be used. The research may involve finding out about the existence of new tools and trying them out. When a new technology seems applicable, the firm typically does a **pilot project**, a limited, experimental application to get experience with the new technology. Pilot projects are usually done with users who are particularly interested and wish to be innovators. Although these projects use a small percentage of a firm's IS resources, they are important because they help bring about innovation and change.

Just looking at the different types of projects helps you see that IS planning involves much more than just making a list of the new systems to be developed. Many IS professionals feel frustrated that so little of their effort can go into new development.

Project Roles of IS Professionals

IS projects vary greatly in size and complexity. In small system development projects, a single person or several people may play all the necessary roles without defining them explicitly. For example, if a small business buys and uses an accounting package, a user or IS professional may purchase it from a computer store, install it on a personal computer, train other users, and consult the vendor's customer support staff for questions. Various roles may be combined into a single person's job responsibilities in this way.

In large projects involving hundreds or even thousands of people, many distinct roles are assigned to individuals. Box 11.1 briefly defines common roles in typical major projects, such as developing online transaction processing systems used for day-to-day operation of large companies. Teams of analysts, programmers, and, possibly, programmer-analysts produce the application software. Technical writers produce the user documentation. Computer operators keep the computer systems running and make sure the reports are produced at the right times. The system manager makes sure that the computer system itself is maintained. The user support staff makes sure that the users are trained and are receiving benefits.

Many of the same roles apply even if the project involves acquiring and installing an ERP system or application package sold by a software vendor. For example, systems analysts still need to determine the requirements, and the user support staff still has to train the users. Programming may also be required to tailor the purchased software to the firm's needs or to link the resulting data to the firm's other internal systems.

This introduction to IS planning started by saying that planning is the process of deciding what will be done, who will do it, when they will do it, how it will be done, and what are the desired results. Thus far we have seen some of the roles in IS planning and the types of projects the plan includes. With this background we can now look at the strategic issues and project-level issues that must be faced while developing the plan.

[L O O K   A H E A D]

Chapter 12 will explain the process of selecting and implementing a software package.

ROLES OF INFORMATION SYSTEM PROFESSIONALS IN BUILDING AND MAINTAINING INFORMATION SYSTEMS

BOX 11.1

Large system development projects involve many roles such as the following.

- *Project managers* manage the people doing the work to make sure that project goals are accomplished. Among other things, project managers develop schedules, monitor work for completeness and quality, and help in resolving conflicts and questions that arise. Project managers in IS departments typically started as programmers or systems analysts and showed they could take responsibility for larger parts of projects.

- *Application programmers* convert a general understanding or written description of a business problem into a set of programs that accomplish the required computer processing. Their jobs include designing the programs and database, coding and testing the programs, and producing the related program documentation.

- *Systems analysts* perform the analysis to decide how a new or updated system can help solve a business problem or exploit a business opportunity. They communicate part of the results to programmers who write the programs.

- *Programmer-analysts* play the role of both programmer and analyst in situations where it is more effective to combine these roles.

- *Technical writers* produce user documentation and training material.

- *Computer operators* make sure that a computer is running, that tapes and removable disks are loaded and unloaded, and that jobs such as backups and database reconfigurations are performed on time.

- *Database administrators* control the definition of all items in a shared database and monitor the performance of the database.

- *System managers* manage computer installations and make sure that the hardware is configured properly and that the operators do their jobs.

- *Systems programmers* write programs related to the operating system and internal operation of the computer system. This is a more specialized job than programmer, which generally refers to someone who produces programs related to business applications.

- *User-support staffs* help the users use the system by providing training, answering questions, and collecting change requests.

STRATEGIC ALIGNMENT OF BUSINESS AND IT

Strategic alignment of the business effort and IT effort is the central issue in IS planning. Figure 11.3 combines ideas from two[10, 11] of the many strategic alignment models. It differs from most of these models because it illustrates two distinct rationales that strategic alignment should balance simultaneously. The primary rationale (indicated by the darker arrows) is that the business needs, opportunities, and strategy should determine both how the firm and its processes are organized and how its information systems should operate. In turn, both the firm's processes and organization and its IT needs, opportunities, and strategy should dictate the form and operation of the IT infrastructure. Because IT infrastructure takes a long time to change, however, a series of restrictions pushes in the opposite direction. A firm's IT infrastructure is a key determinant and limiting factor in how the firm can actually operate. It is also a determinant of needs for changing IT as well as being a limiting factor in how much can be accomplished at what pace. In turn, business organization and processes and IT needs are both limiting factors that constrain a business's realistic opportunities and strategic options.

This section surveys some of the strategic issues related to alignment between business and IT. It starts on the business side of Figure 11.3. First it looks at critical success factors, which are used to foster strategic alignment by identifying information needed for the business to succeed. It continues by discussing IT-related ideas often used as the rationale for changing business processes and organizations. These ideas include reengineering, downsizing, and the trend toward enterprise information systems and interorganizational systems. Moving to the IT side of the figure, the next topic is IS architecture and its relationship to centralization versus decentralization. The topic of strategic alignment is addressed directly through a method for articulating business-driven infrastructure requirements. Outsourcing is then discussed as a central issue in a firm's overall IT strategy. A final topic is international IT issues.

Consistency with Business Priorities

Since information systems exist to support work systems that carry out a company's plans, it might seem obvious that a company's IS plan should be linked to its business plan. Obvious or not, this has not always happened. Only 36% of the CEOs interviewed in a 1989 survey[12] believed that the deployment of IS resources in their firm supported their company's business plan. With the extensive attention IT has received in the 1990s, many companies are now more careful that IS plans truly reflect business needs.

Critical success factors (CSFs) is an idea that leads to strategic alignment by highlighting the way better information might help the firm achieve its business goals. **Critical success factors** are the things that must go right for a business to succeed. The first step in the CSF method is to identify the firm's primary mission and the objectives that define satisfactory overall performance. Next, executives identify the CSFs.

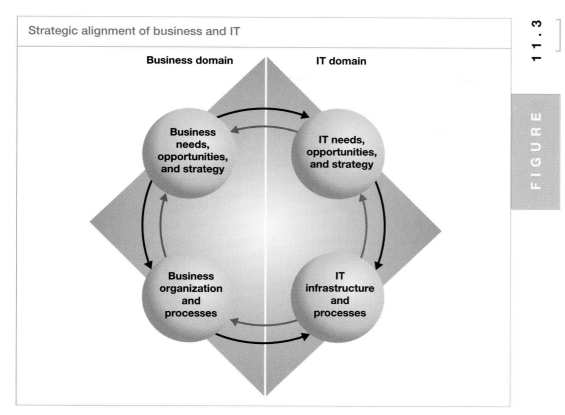

FIGURE 11.3

Strategic alignment of business and IT

Business domain   **IT domain**

Business needs, opportunities, and strategy

IT needs, opportunities, and strategy

Business organization and processes

IT infrastructure and processes

The dark arrows represent business requirements as the starting point for strategic alignment between business and IT. The light arrows illustrate a completely opposite set of linkages that start with strengths and shortcomings in the IT domain.

Most businesses have relatively few of them, and these typically come from sources such as the structure of the industry, the firm's competitive strategy, its industry position or geographic location, environmental factors surrounding the firm, and temporary operating problems or opportunities.[13] CSFs for one firm included improving customer relationships, improving supplier relationships, making the best use of inventory, and using capital and human resources efficiently and effectively. The third step is to identify the pertinent indicators or measures of performance for each CSF. For example, customer relations might be measured in terms of trends in customers lost, new customers, the ratio of customer inquiries to customer orders, or on-time delivery. The fourth step is to decide which measures are most important and then make sure that IS plans provide means for collecting and using this information.

The benefits of using the CSF method start with a shared understanding of what is critical to a company. This aids executive communication about important company issues and influences priorities for system development. Although the CSF method provides a useful framework in many situations, like any technique it should be applied with care, and has some important weaknesses. It is more effective when used with senior managers rather than middle managers who focus more on their own areas and are less aware of the organization's overall CSFs. Furthermore, some managers who focus on day-to-day operations rather than planning may have difficulty dealing with the conceptual nature of CSFs.[14] Finally, since CSFs focus on issues in specific areas of business, they may not be very helpful in making investment decisions about IT infrastructure shared between different areas.

Reengineering and Downsizing

Reengineering is a highly publicized idea that became an umbrella term for a variety of internal corporate initiatives in the early 1990s. Michael Hammer, the consultant who popularized the term, initially said that **business process reengineering (BPR)** is "the fundamental rethinking and radical redesign of business processes to achieve dramatic improvements in critical measures of performance, such as cost, quality, service, and speed."[15] Highly publicized examples such as Ford's accounts payables system (mentioned in Chapter 3) made reengineering a guiding motto for projects aimed at changing key business processes such as the way insurance companies handle claims and the way manufacturers design products.

A basic tenet of reengineering is that nothing about an organization or business process is sacred. The way things are done today may reflect nothing more than many years of trying to do things the same way even though the business environment and customers changed. Therefore, the business process of tomorrow may be completely different. Common outcomes of BPR include combining several jobs into one, permitting workers to make more decisions themselves, defining different versions of processes for simple cases versus complex ones, minimizing situations when one person checks someone else's work, and reorganizing jobs to give individuals more understanding and more responsibility.[16] Many reengineering efforts also result in significant staff reductions.

The promise of BPR captured the imagination of American managers in the early 1990s, and many impressive successes were announced. But it was also seen in many quarters as a slogan or umbrella term under which any important project might be explained and as a convenient excuse for layoffs. For example *Fortune* quoted a telephone company executive who said, "If you want to get something funded around here—anything, even a new chair for your office—call it reengineering on your request for expenditure."[17] The author Paul Strassmann was even more skeptical—"There's nothing new or original about business process reengineering. It's just a lot of old industrial methods, recycled and repackaged to seem like the latest in management science. . . . Reengineering excels more in its packaging than in its substance. Its purpose is to make the purging of past staffing gluttony more palatable."[18]

Because of the radical restructuring it calls for, most firms attempting major BPR projects have found them difficult and risky. The President of SIM, the leading organization for IS executives, expressed part of the problem as follows: "One way to judge if you are reengineering: The first time you bring it up, if no one screams, 'Are you crazy?' then it is not a reengineering project." The same article cited a report coauthored by Michael Hammer speculating that the failure rate for reengineering projects is likely on the order of 70%.[19] A 1994 survey of 350 executives by the consulting firm Arthur D. Little concluded that more than 85% of the respondents were dissatisfied with the results, and 60% encountered unanticipated problems or unintended side effects related to turf battles, lack of management buy-in, and inadequate implementation skills. By the late 1990s even the original gurus of the area had rethought their message and concluded that the main point was an emphasis on improving processes rather than radical change for its own sake.

One of the reasons reengineering became controversial was its common association with **downsizing**, the effort to increase corporate efficiency by changing processes in order to reduce the number of people a firm employs. Some corporate initiatives that were presented as reengineering projects seemed to the participants much more like employee elimination projects. Downsizing was sometimes recast as *rightsizing*, but that didn't placate many of the employees who were laid off or who had to do their own previous work plus that of others who were laid off. The combined push for reengineering and downsizing raised many questions about loyalty and incentives. After all, why should someone be loyal to a company that is not loyal to its employees? An issue like this may seem far afield from how IT can help firms reengineer processes, but it is pertinent to planning decisions because the ultimate success of reengineering, downsizing, or any other major change depends on both the business and economic rationale and the ability of the organization to implement the changes successfully.

Enterprise-wide and Interorganizational Systems

The enterprise systems (also called ERP systems) introduced in Chapter 5 provide integrated databases and consistent data formats that support an organization's core information systems for order fulfillment, manufacturing, inventory, distribution, human resources, and financial accounting. Many large organizations have struggled with this type of integration issue because incompatibilities between information systems designed to solve local problems that existed years ago make it much more difficult to attain world-class performance today. ERP vendors such as SAP, Baan, Peoplesoft, J.D. Edwards, and Oracle flourished in the late 1990s by promoting ambitious expectations for short cycle times, fast response, unified action within the firm, and efficient data exchange with customers and suppliers. Later these companies encountered business problems as many ERP implementations bogged down due to their organizational scope and complexity.

The Owens Corning case at the end of Chapter 5 illustrates the level of effort needed for analyzing basic business processes and identifying the ERP options that fit best for both enterprise-wide and local reasons. Owens Corning assigned 250 people to its ERP team, an enormous expense of time and energy. Just as there are ERP success stories, there are also horror stories of companies going far over budget on these projects. For example, a failed ERP implementation contributed to the bankruptcy of Foxmeyer Drug. The requirement for extensive involvement and coordination across so many functions implies that this type of investment requires strong agreement and commitment by top management. Accepting this requirement, CEO George Fisher participated in the executive council for Kodak's $500 million SAP implementation. Actually it was a reimplementation because the first attempt had failed. This council made sure the options chosen followed company priorities rather than divisional priorities. In another example, Dell Computer scuttled an SAP implementation that was designed to integrate many parts of the business. Dell decided to use only part of the software because using such highly integrated systems would make it difficult for Dell to respond to the rapid changes in the PC marketplace.[20]

Interorganizational information systems reflect the customer- and supplier-facing side of the integration issues addressed by ERP. These systems transmit information between different firms as part of on-going business processes involving suppliers and their customers, such as designing custom products, entering orders, transmitting invoices, making payments, and servicing the product. Large companies have used electronic data interchange (EDI) for entering orders, sending confirmations, transmitting bills, and transferring funds for several decades. Many of these systems were developed by industry-specific trade groups for the mutual convenience of industry members, who naturally wanted to focus their efforts on whatever the industry was producing, be it automobiles or chemicals, instead of wasting resources on deciphering standard information coded inconsistently in paperwork from various suppliers or customers. More recent developments of this type are the B2B marketplaces introduced in Chapter 1 and the extranets described in Chapter 5. For example, extranets use Internet technology in private networks that provide information to customers, such as detailed product descriptions, frequently asked questions about different products, maintenance information, warranties, and how to contact customer service and sales offices. Much of this information was formerly difficult for customers to access because paper versions of it at the customer site became scattered and outdated.

One of the most complex areas in which interorganizational information systems are applied is the integration between ERP packages and supply chain management. For example, Farmland Industries, a $9 billion agricultural cooperative in Missouri purchases everything from grain to livestock for more than 1,400 independent farm cooperatives, which in turn sell these supplies to local farmers. Farmland has implemented SAP's ERP product, but the local cooperatives still use their own point-of-sale, accounting, and inventory management systems. Maximizing the benefits to all concerned would involve greater integration across the entire supply chain.[21]

Interorganizational systems are also part of the increasing adoption of **virtual organization** approaches, in which major aspects of core processes such as design, production, and delivery are outsourced to other organizations that specialize in these areas. Virtual organizations exist by agreement of their members and sometimes need immediate access to shared information in order to operate efficiently, such as when a delivery firm takes over the warehousing and distribution of spare parts for a computer manufacturer. Without good interorganizational information systems, the term *virtual organization* is no more than a slogan in such situations.

Thus far we have looked at aspects of strategic alignment that fit on the business side of Figure 11.3. Next we will look at the IT side by looking at IS architecture, centralization and decentralization in deploying IT, business-driven IT infrastructure, and outsourcing of IT-related activities.

Information System Architecture

The term *architecture* was introduced in Chapter 2. A firm's **information system architecture** is the basic blueprint showing how the firm's data processing systems, telecommunications networks, and data are integrated. It is a highly summarized answer to the following questions:

- What data are collected?
- Where and how are the data collected?
- How are the data transmitted?
- Where are the data stored?
- What applications use the data, and how are these applications related as an overall system?

Just creating an organized list of IT assets sometimes shows major problems in IS architecture. For example, in 1993 General Motors had 27 e-mail systems, ten word processing programs, five spreadsheet programs, and seven business graphics packages. GM's director of desktop computing said, "We probably had one of every system that had ever been made." GM decided to standardize to eliminate this low-value variability. Three years later every PC user at GM worked on the same configuration: Windows 3.1, Microsoft Office, and Lotus Notes running on high-end Compaq PCs. No software outside the standard configuration was even allowed on the computers without special approval.[22]

Legacy systems are a part of IS architecture that sometimes make it more difficult to improve the work systems they support. **Legacy systems** are old, and often technically obsolete, information systems that still exist in many firms because they perform essential data processing such as accounting and customer billing. Many of these systems were initially built in the 1960s or 1970s and still use programming methods that are 20 years out of date even after numerous enhancements. The many past changes to these systems are often poorly documented, and the people who made the changes have often left for other jobs. The difficulty of operating and upgrading these older information systems is one of the reasons companies adopted SAP and other enterprise software packages. Unfortunately for IS staffs, obtaining funding to overhaul technically fragile legacy systems is often difficult because the benefits are indirect and largely related to greater flexibility and reliability in the future. Other large projects that could use the same funds often generate greater immediate business benefits. Legacy systems frequently remain in place until a business-driven rationale emerges, such as the need for enterprise-wide integration, the need to serve customers more effectively, or, as was paramount in the late 1990s, the risk of system failure due to Y2K problems.

The choice of a computing platform is another important part of IS architecture. The term **platform** is used to describe the basic type of computer, operating system, and network that an information system uses. The choice of a platform has long-term ramifications because most application software is programmed for a particular platform. This implies, for example, that software written to operate on servers that use the Windows NT operating system will have to be reprogrammed and retested before they can run on servers that use the UNIX operating system. Sharing information and applications while using different platforms is often a waste of resources and can become a nightmare if incompatibilities are serious. Consolidating from multiple platforms to a unified platform to make the infrastructure more efficient is rarely a prized project. The benefits are in the background and are often less visible to users than direct benefits from application enhancements. Consequently, the choice of a platform for large shared applications has long-term implications and should be considered carefully.

Although IS architecture may seem like a technical issue, it should reflect a strategic, managerial view of how an organization operates. IS architecture may be a constraint to a firm's business strategy because it determines the practical range of business and product strategies the firm can employ. Consider a bank whose new business strategy is based on combining checking accounts, savings accounts, credit cards, and loans into a simplified account relationship. This strategy can be used only if customer IDs for each of the separate products can be grouped into single combined accounts. In addition, the bank can provide 24-hour response to customer queries only if all the data is in an immediately accessible database rather than on paper files at branches. The wrong IS architecture would doom the business strategy.

Centralization versus Decentralization

A central issue in any IS architecture is the balance between centralization and decentralization. As with many other organizational endeavors, overcentralization results in overly rigid systems that cannot handle local variations. Similarly, excessive decentralization creates systems that may solve local problems but may not conform or interface well enough to solve problems that cross departments. Decisions involving centralization and decentralization often hinge on debates about efficiency (using the least resources to produce a given output) and effectiveness (producing the right output). Centralization is often more efficient because it eliminates redundant resources and effort. Assuming that decentralization is technically feasible, it is often more effective because it allows people to make the right decisions for their own local situations. Key factors in centralization and decentralization include location of the hardware, location of data, standards, and ownership and management control (see Table 11.2).

Location of Hardware and Data   Computer hardware owned and managed within a corporation can exist at any or all of the following levels: corporate headquarters, regional processing centers, site processing centers (for individual factories or offices), department processors, work group processors, and individual work stations. The most centralized approach is to have all of the computers in a centralized computer center, with telecommunications links to terminals at other locations. The least centralized

TABLE 11.2

Centralization versus Decentralization

	Highly centralized	Intermediate	Highly decentralized
Hardware configuration	Central computer, remote terminals	Distributed network linking local data centers	Independent local data centers, personal computers
Data location	Centralized database	Central database plus local databases	Local databases
Hardware and software choices	Central decisions	Central guidelines, local choices	Local choices
Ownership and control	Central information systems group	Central services, system ownership by user departments	User departments
Organizational affiliation of IS staff	Central IS group	Highly technical IS roles affiliated with central group, less technical roles in user organization	Most IS roles affiliated with user organization (except infrastructure and planning)

FIGURE 11.4

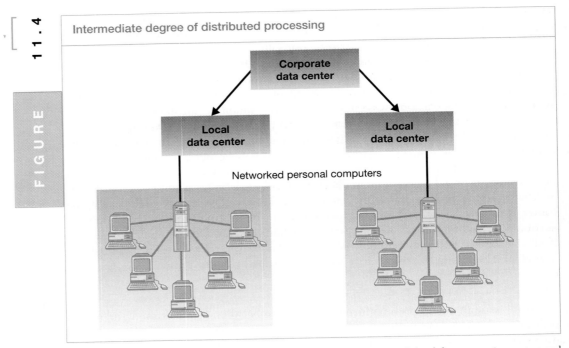

Intermediate degree of distributed processing

Most large firms use intermediate degrees of centralized data processing, with local data processing centers and personal computers for individuals or offices.

approach is to provide employees with their own personal computers and allow them to perform and control their own data processing. Figure 11.4 shows how most large firms use intermediate configurations that combine a centralized data processing facility with local data processing centers and networked personal computers for individuals or offices. Centralized locations process data that must be shared across the company or that can be processed most efficiently in a centralized way. Local data centers process data that should be shared within a division or geographical location but are not needed elsewhere in the company. The personal computers are used for individual data processing.

Choices in distributing data range from maintaining all the data at a centralized location through allowing individuals to maintain their own data locally. Intermediate configurations employ a centralized database for data that must be accessed across the organization, plus local or individual databases for data pertinent only to an office or individual. Centralized databases are used for corporate accounting, corporate inventories, and other data that must be controlled at the corporate level and accessed broadly. Firms frequently compromise between convenience and accessibility of local data and control and maintainability of centralized data. They do this through various forms of database replication or through downloads that make locally relevant data available to local users even if transactions update the central database. Many large companies have extensive telecommunications networks for moving data to and from centralized databases.

Standards, Ownership, and Guidelines for Action   Establishing corporate standards is essential for efficiency, even if the hardware and data are physically decentralized. Corporate standards determine which hardware and software can be purchased and what procedures to use in deploying information systems. Standards for hardware and data make it easier for people to share their work. They are also necessary for economies of scale in purchasing equipment, training personnel, and using data. Without standards, individuals and departments can make independent decisions about which hardware and software to buy, often resulting in incompatible systems. The existence of incompatible systems may not affect individuals doing their own individual work, but is grossly inefficient when data or models must be shared by many users. Having standards doesn't guarantee that systems will be consistent but does increase the chances of realizing economies of scale.

Regardless of where hardware and data reside, the question of ownership is always an issue. For example, who should own a division's sales-forecasting system: the marketing department or the IS department? With a centralized approach, a central IS department owns and controls all information systems and a request to change a system would go to that department. With a decentralized approach, whatever group uses the information system should own it. Permitting decentralized ownership of information systems leads to greater responsiveness to change requests but may result in systems that are not well controlled. For example, a company using a decentralized approach found that one of its important information systems had absolutely no documentation. The developer, a flamboyant individual who liked helping users but hated writing documentation, had left the company. Had the system been under central control, it probably would be documented but might not have had as many of the features users wanted.

Whether or not a central IS group owns the information systems, there are still important reasons to have general guidelines for building and administering these systems. At minimum such guidelines reduce the organizational inefficiency of learning how to install, interface, and manage unnecessary variations on the same basic technologies. But the guidelines can go further by specifying the way the organization's systems should be justified and built. For example, the guidelines might say that a formal cost/benefit analysis must be done for any system beyond a particular size, or that data should be captured when first created. To support interoperability even when different types of hardware or software are used, the guidelines can cover things such as eliminating redundant data definitions, defining uniform transmission standards, separating data definitions from the programs that use them, and establishing uniform programming environments.

Issues concerning location, ownership, and control of resources are by no means unique to information systems. Questions about centralization versus decentralization occur in all business functions whether or not computerized systems are involved. In sales, the question is often whether several product divisions will share the same sales force or distribution channels. In production, it is whether product divisions will share factories and research labs. In each case, the decision incorporates historical precedent in the company, economies of scale from centralization, advantages of focus from decentralization, and other personal, political, and economic issues.

Issues about centralization or decentralization are often even more complicated for information systems because the technology itself adds a layer of professional expertise, details, inertia, and confusion. Each approach has its advantages. Centralization may enhance the IS department's effectiveness and long-term potential. It also increases the ability to maintain standards for quality, consistency, and maintainability. Decentralization may avoid bureaucracy and lengthy system development backlogs. Decentralization also makes it possible to try things out locally and grow in smaller increments, and to continue processing work even when a central computer is down.

Position of the IS Staff   The division of labor between user and IS departments is based on a combination of organizational history and practical trade-offs. With a highly centralized approach, the programmers, analysts, and support personnel are in the IS department. This maintains professional affiliations with systems activities and may lead to greater professional depth in their discipline. But it may also separate them from the users and reduce responsiveness to user needs. In a decentralized approach, the programmers and analysts are in the user department, which tends to generate greater loyalty to the user department and greater understanding of the application. It also reduces their affiliation with other professionals in their field, however, and may ultimately reduce their technical depth. Table 11.3 lists some of the commonly cited differences between IS professionals and typical IS users. Like most generalizations about groups of people, there are many counterexamples to the differences listed in the table. No individual should be treated on the basis of a stereotype.

TABLE 11.3

Commonly Cited Differences between IS Professionals and Typical Users

Type of difference	Tendency of IS staff	Tendency of user department
Professional orientation	Allegiance to profession	Allegiance to firm
Language	Language of computers	Language of business
Interests and basis of recognition	Technical elegance	Practical solutions produced quickly
Project goals	Long-term maintainability	Practical solutions produced quickly
Work style and content	Analytical work related to computers	Work through people

The balance between centralizing and decentralizing the IS staff may affect the success of information systems. With too much centralization, users often feel that they don't receive enough support and that the IS department doesn't appreciate their needs. With too much decentralization, servicing of small requests may be fine but there is less of the centralized focus and planning needed to achieve economies of scale and to develop strategic information systems.

Describing a Business-Driven IT Infrastructure

A firm's **IT infrastructure** is the shared technical and human resources used to build, operate, and maintain information systems included in the firm's IS architecture. Figure 11.5 summarizes the elements of the IT infrastructure that supports a firm's value chain. IT infrastructure is a long-term investment shared across various departments and applications. Operating a firm's IT infrastructure often consumes more than 50% of its IT budget.[23] Any feasible IS plan must include provisions for operating and upgrading this infrastructure to support changing business needs.

Because many aspects of IT infrastructure involve technical issues that seem far removed from business issues, it is often difficult for executives to participate effectively in discussions about the long-term strategy for IT infrastructure. A promising method proposed by Broadbent and Weill is called the **management by maxim** framework, which begins by considering "the company's strategic context, synergies among business units, and the extent to which a firm wants to exploit those synergies. The strategic statements or business maxims are derived from the strategic context and identify the firm's future direction. From the business maxims, business and IT man-

FIGURE 11.5

Typical elements of IT infrastructure

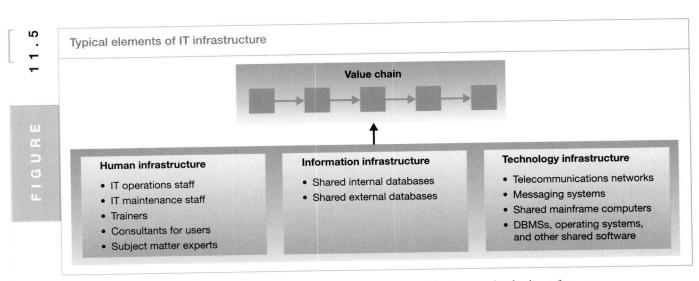

IT infrastructure that supports the value chain includes human infrastructure, shared databases, and technology infrastructure.

agers together identify IT maxims, which express the company's need to access and use information and the technology resources required."[24]

Table 11.4 illustrates this approach by looking at a hypothetical chain of hardware stores and identifying its business maxims in six aspects of business strategy along related IT maxims in five aspects of IT strategy. If the business maxims were to change, the IT maxims would change accordingly. For example, if this chain saw no synergies through analyzing the transaction information from its various stores, it would not put as much effort into the overnight consolidation and data mining efforts. Similarly, if the stores themselves would benefit from closer cooperation, the IT maxims might say something about using IT to improve store-to-store communication.

Firms that have performed this type of analysis, regardless of whether they called it management by maxim, have arrived at vastly different IT strategies based on different business needs. Amcor, a large Australian firm that makes packaging, corrugated boxes, plastic containers, and cans, chose a highly decentralized IT strategy because its various business units had unique cultures and rarely shared customers. Its IT strategy was to focus on local accountability and minimize central mandates. In contrast, the auto and motorcycle manufacturer Honda saw itself as "a global network with 83 production facilities in 39 countries that supply Honda products" around the world. It enhanced its communications network to improve its parts system for all products.[25] In another case, the health-care supplier Johnson & Johnson saw that it needed to create stronger partnerships with its large customers because the health-care industry was changing. Its customers wanted to deal with a limited number of vendors, but J&J was organized as over 100 separate product divisions, each of which dealt with customers through its own marketing and sales arms. J&J's IT infrastructure in 1995 was not

Business and IT Maxims for a Hypothetical Chain of Hardware Stores		**T A B L E 11.4**
Business maxims	**IT maxims**	

Business maxims	**IT maxims**
Cost focus	*Expectations for IT investments*
• Low-cost retailer for consumers.	• IT investments provide common infrastructure and systems to minimize these concerns for the local stores.
Value differentiation perceived by customer	
• Low prices supported by reasonably good service.	*Data access and use*
• Reliable availability of medium-to low-priced hardware and building supplies.	• All sales data available to central purchasing nightly.
• Major distributor for particular suppliers and brands.	• Local access to local customer and prospect list, plus corporate access for data mining and analysis.
Flexibility and agility	*Hardware and software resources*
• Stay focused in hardware market, expand slowly into related products for kitchens and gardens.	• Support consistent, automatic processing of repetitive transactions.
• Detect and exploit trendy new products.	• Standardize on minimum number of platforms to minimize cost of support.
Growth	*Communications capabilities and services*
• Gradually expand across the United States and Canada.	• Support nightly consolidation of daily sales transactions to help identify product and pricing trends.
• Grow revenues using targeted discounts to bring back customers for repeat purchases.	• Support EDI to minimize transaction costs.
Human resources	*Architecture and standards approach*
• Staff stores with people who enjoy home-remodeling projects.	• Control IT architecture and standards centrally to minimize cost.
• Maintain pleasant work environment but assume high turnover in store personnel due to relatively low salaries.	
Management orientation	
• Maximize ability of local stores to satisfy needs of local markets.	
• Support stores with standardized systems and information, but permit local autonomy in decision-making.	
• Share information about hot products and trends.	

designed to support a unified external view of J&J due to inconsistent connectivity and data standards across the divisions. These inconsistencies made it more difficult to exchange data and generated a great deal of duplicated effort. J&J decided to move toward greater connectivity and data standardization through common financial, purchasing, order entry, accounts payable, payroll, and human resources systems.[26]

Outsourcing

Another key issue in attaining strategic alignment is the extent to which IT infrastructure, programming, training, support, and other IT-related activities will be outsourced. When used in general conversation, the term **outsourcing** denotes any product or service that is purchased from another firm. For example, all major auto companies outsource manufacturing of many components. Likewise, many firms outsource company cafeterias to food service companies. In general, companies outsource the products and services they do not want to produce or are unable to produce themselves. Competitive pressures of the 1990s have increased outsourcing across all industries by forcing companies to focus on what they do best, such as manufacturing at the lowest cost or providing excellent customer service in retailing.

Outsourcing of computer hardware, telecommunications services, and systems software such as operating systems and DBMSs is a long-standing practice in IS departments. These departments also purchase end-user software such as spreadsheets and word processors because there is no reason to reinvent tools a software company specializing in these products can provide much more cheaply. Although these examples involve products and services bought from other firms, this is not the type of IT outsourcing that has become controversial.

The controversial side of IT outsourcing involves hiring outside organizations to perform functions often performed by IS departments. Business application software was one of the first areas for this type of outsourcing, with many firms purchasing commercial software for common functions such as keeping track of inventory, purchase orders, and customer orders. Buying commercially available application software makes sense when there is nothing unique or competitively significant about the way the firm wants to perform the business function. Firms attempting to attain competitive advantage from a unique way of performing a business function typically cannot buy readily available commercial software to support the function because any other company could also buy it.

Maintaining computer centers and telecommunications networks is another common area for outsourcing. Companies deciding whether to do this look for reasons why they can perform these functions more efficiently and effectively than firms whose main business is in this area. By performing these functions for many customers, outsourcing vendors may have more experience doing the work and greater ability to negotiate quantity discounts with hardware and software vendors. They may also be more able to pick up the slack if key staff members at a particular site leave.

The **application service provider** (ASP) is a newer type of outsourcing vendor that has recently gained notoriety. ASPs operate a firm's application software on remote servers on a wide area network. The advantage is that the firm no longer has to install and maintain the software. The disadvantage is that the firm has less control over essential software and data, and may have difficulty transferring to another ASP if the current one proves unsatisfactory. Oshkosh B'Gosh, Inc. encountered an example of the type of problem that can occur when the communication link between its online store and the company hosting its Web site went down. Oshkosh had an outsourcing contract with Pandesic LLC, which had subcontracted with Digex to host the Web site. A fourth party, Oshkosh's telecommunications carrier, needed to get into Digex's site to repair the equipment. According to Oshkosh's CIO, "It was like the Three Stooges and Keystone Cops combined, . . . But we were not laughing at the time."[27] Initial results for many ASPs were disappointing due to a combination of inadequate software and service capabilities plus common concerns about outsourcing mission-critical processing to young firms using a somewhat untested approach.[28] Whether ASPs will become more successful remains to be seen.

Taken to an extreme, outsourcing of IT activities would mean having a very small IS department limited to developing IS plans and negotiating with outsourcing vendors. This is risky due to the reliance on an outside firm to perform essential functions including building and maintaining application systems. Because the outsourcing vendor would have so much of the knowledge about the company's information systems, the company might end up lacking the staff and vision needed to create competitively significant systems. If the outsourcing vendor encountered business problems of its own, the company's basic data processing could be thrown into chaos. Even without a calamity, a long-term outsourcing contract might spawn other problems by not anticipating evolving business requirements.

There is a common belief that IT operations should be outsourced wherever they do not provide strategic advantage, but several studies questioned this belief because it led to problems and disappointments in the majority of the cases observed. Outsourcing vendors were not necessarily more efficient than internal IS groups, which could often achieve similar results. Five- or ten-year contracts were signed in situations in which business conditions and availability of technology could not be predicted more than a few years in advance. Outsourcing vendors had their own separate profit motives and business issues. Companies considering outsourcing should have been more skeptical of slogans describing outsourcing vendors as "partners" and should have written outsourcing contracts with greater care. Regardless of whether an IT operation was strategic or a commodity, a company's overarching objective should have focused on maximizing flexibility and control so that it could pursue the best options as conditions changed. The overall conclusion was that managers should not make a one-time decision to outsource, but should structure outsourcing contracts in a way that permitted competition to provide the best IT services over time.[29, 30]

International Issues

A final aspect of strategic alignment involves international issues that have become more important as business has become more international and as more information systems cross national boundaries. Some of these systems are internal management and control systems of multinational companies. Others are links between companies in one country and customers, suppliers, and agents elsewhere. The significance of these systems is growing because they provide a way to reduce the limitations of time and geography.

International issues start with a basic fact that things just work differently in different places, especially when different histories, cultures, and languages are involved. These differences appear at many different levels and make it necessary to retest basic assumptions about how things work. Shirts may button differently, paper may be a different size, doors may open differently, people may drive on the other side of the street, and, as shown in Figure 11.6, the power plug of a computer made in one country may not fit another country's wall sockets. Many other international technology incompatibilities are hidden from view. For example, a cell phone that works in the United States will not work in Europe because the coding of signals is different.

American and French electrical plugs

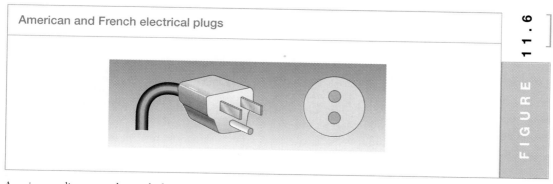

FIGURE 11.6

American appliances need special adapters in order to use French electrical outlets.

Technical incompatibilities in hardware, software, and data standards often make it difficult to transfer or share software between countries. An example is the international differences in the formats of numbers and dates. The date 6/8/99 means June 8, 1999 in the United States and August 6, 1999 in Europe. The same date would be written 99/6/8 in Japan. This simple discrepancy necessitated changes in hundreds of programs when the software company Consilium first installed its manufacturing system at Siemens in Germany. Companies in Italy face a different incompatibility problem with the European Union's conversion to the euro. Italy's national currency, the lira, is expressed in whole numbers only. Since programs written for the lira may therefore use integer fields for monetary amounts instead of decimal fields, the move to the euro requires testing or revision of all those programs.[31]

Social and political issues cause many types of confusion and inefficiency in systems used in more than one country. These problems start with incomplete personal communication caused by speaking different languages. At a deeper level, differences in laws, work rules, accounting practices, and general expectations of workers may make information system practices from one country impractical in another. For example, labor agreements in different countries might differ on whether information can be recorded that indicates how well or how quickly a particular worker performed a particular work step. National culture is another issue. For example, red is generally a symbol of good luck in China, but writing text in red might be confusing in China because it is often reserved for notes ending a romantic relationship. Similarly, when DHL set up new account numbers in China, none could begin with four because the spoken word sounds a lot like the word for death.[32]

Telecommunications is an area where regulation, economics, and quality are especially intertwined. In the United States, telecommunications is highly competitive and there is a tradition of high quality, customer orientation, and rapid service. In many other countries, telecommunications is controlled by government monopolies that are less customer-oriented and may take a year or more to install a telephone. On the other hand, Europe and other parts of the world are ahead of the United States in cell phone applications because standards are more consistent and because U.S. regulations make cell phone calls comparatively expensive. Regulation and economics also affect the way the Internet is used. Per-minute phone charges in Europe make Internet usage more expensive than it is in the United States. On the other hand, in Japan around half of all Internet users used wireless connections, and most of these involved a cellular phone service called i-mode. NTT DoCoMo's plan for 2001 included offering five types of wireless Internet access devices that might further blur the line between cell phones and computers.[33]

Economic issues in international information systems are obvious to any international traveler who has noticed how much more a phone call costs when it goes from Europe to the United States rather than in the reverse direction. A number of "callback services" have been formed just to exploit this imbalance. Callers from Europe can dial a U.S. number and hang up. This triggers a telephone switch that returns the call and provides a U.S. dial tone. The caller from Europe enters the desired telephone number and is connected. Because the bill at the end of the month is calculated at U.S. rates, it may be 50% to 70% lower than it would have been at European rates. Needless to say, many national telephone monopolies are not pleased with these callback systems. The Kenyan government took out newspaper ads warning callback users they could be prosecuted. Japanese telephone companies pressed regulators for a ban on this service.[34] In 1997 France and Germany, which impose value added taxes of 21% and 15% on all goods and services including telephone calls, announced plans to start imposing sales taxes on callback services. The U.S.-based callback services doubted the taxes could be collected because the service would be provided from the U.S.[35]

A final international issue is the laws some countries have passed concerning the handling of data linked to individuals, especially in transborder data flows. For example, France once stopped Fiat from transferring its French personnel records to Italy because privacy laws there did not meet French regulations.[36] More recently, the

European Union (the United Kingdom, France, Germany, Spain, Italy, among others) adopted a privacy policy for trade throughout Europe. Starting in late 1998, European citizens were guaranteed rights including the right of access to their data, the right to know where the data originated, the right to have inaccurate data rectified, and the right to withhold permission to use their data for direct marketing. Article 25 of the directive prohibits European countries from sending personal information to countries that do not maintain adequate privacy standards. Because the United States has few privacy guarantees of the types covered, U.S. companies selling to European customers would be prohibited from using direct marketing practices that are legal in the U.S.

The EU guidelines conflict directly with the practice of many U.S.-based Web sites. In what was described as a "privacy truce" in mid-2000, U.S. sites can gain "safe harbor" from EU legal action by telling visitors what information is being collected, what it will be used for, and with whom it will be shared. Consumers must also be able to choose whether their information will be shared with a third party. They also have the right to view and, if necessary, correct their personal data. These guidelines are not just about U.S. sites. Following strict Italian laws, the Italian Data Protection Commission temporarily shut down Libero, a free Internet service for consumers, which relied on targeted ads for revenue. The Commission determined that Libero sought too much data in its required registration form without explaining why, and this was a violation of privacy laws. Libero agreed to overhaul its policies.[37]

R E A L I T Y   C H E C K ✓

Strategic Issues for IS Planning

This section discussed a series of strategic issues for IS planning.

1. Consider any major purchase you or your family have made in the last few years. For example, it could be a car, a computer, or a college education. Explain the extent to which that purchase did or didn't fit into a strategic plan.

2. Explain why strategic planning is or isn't relevant for the decision you identified.

SELECTING SYSTEMS TO INVEST IN

The decision to build an information system is an investment decision, as is the decision about which capabilities to include in the system. The strategic issues from the previous section provide guidelines for these investments, such as building systems that support the business plan, the IS architecture, and the company's approach to distributed processing and outsourcing.

Although these ideas provide some guidance and eliminate some options, there is no ideal formula for deciding which systems and capabilities to invest in. Many IS departments could double and still not have enough people to do all the work users would like. In practice, many IS departments allocate a percentage of their available time to different project categories, such as enhancements, major new systems, and user support. But within each category they still need to decide which systems to work on and what capabilities to provide. Cost/benefit analysis may help with these decisions.

Cost/Benefit Analysis

Cost/benefit analysis is the process of evaluating proposed projects by comparing estimated benefits and costs. Cost/benefit analysis should occur only after the proposed project has been analyzed and designed in enough depth to clarify key issues in each aspect of a current or proposed system.

Cost/benefit analysis requires that estimated benefits and costs be expressed in dollars. If the benefits are substantially greater than the costs, the project may be worth pursuing. Cost/benefit analysis can be used in several ways. First, it is a planning tool to help in deciding whether the new system is a worthwhile investment compared to other possible uses of resources. In addition, it may be used as an auditing tool to determine whether a project actually met its goals.

Although the idea of comparing estimated benefits with estimated costs sounds logical, it has limitations. It is most appropriate when the system's purpose is improving efficiency. If its purpose is providing management information, transforming the organization, or upgrading the IS infrastructure, predicting either the benefits or the costs is more difficult. Furthermore, because cost/benefit analyses are usually done to justify someone's request for resources, the numbers in a cost/benefit study may be biased and may ignore or understate foreseeable project risks. Key issues for cost/benefit analysis include the difference between tangible and intangible benefits, the tendency to underestimate costs, and the effect of the timing of costs and benefits.

Tangible and Intangible Benefits   Benefits are often classified as either tangible or intangible. **Tangible benefits** can be measured directly to evaluate system performance. Examples include reduction in the time per phone call, improvement in response time, reduction in the amount of disk storage used, and reduction in the error rate. Notice that tangible benefits may or may not be measured in monetary terms. However, using a cost/benefit framework requires translating performance improvements into monetary terms so that benefits and costs can be compared.

Intangible benefits affect performance but are difficult to measure because they refer to comparatively vague concepts. Examples of intangible benefits include better coordination, better supervision, better morale, better information for decision-making, ability to evaluate more alternatives, ability to respond quickly to unexpected situations, and organizational learning. Although all of these goals are worthwhile, it is often difficult to measure how well they have been accomplished. Even if it is possible to measure intangible benefits, it is difficult to express them in monetary terms that can be compared with costs. All too often, project costs are tangible and benefits are intangible. Though hard to quantify, intangible benefits are important and shouldn't be ignored. Many of the benefits of information systems are intangible.

Tendency to Understate Costs   A common flaw of cost/benefit studies is the understatement of costs. Incomplete cost analysis often includes the cost of hardware, software, and programming but omits other costs related to problem analysis, training, and ongoing operation of the system.

Table 11.5 separates some of the more apparent costs of information systems from some of the costs that are easy to overlook. Notice how the time and effort of user management and staff is easy to overlook in each of the four phases of an information system (refer back to Figure 1.7). This is because their salary and overhead are already accounted for in other budgets related to the work they normally do. For many systems, training, implementation, and troubleshooting absorb so much time and effort that their cost far exceeds the original cost of the hardware and software.

Timing of Costs and Benefits   The cost and benefit streams from an information system project occur at different times. The timing of costs and benefits in the customer service system in Figure 11.7 is typical in that many costs precede any benefits. The shape of the cost curve reflects different staffing levels at different points in the system-building process. The figure shows that the benefits start in month 6 and increase to a high level when implementation is complete. If these estimated cost and benefit streams actually are accomplished, the cumulative net benefit of having the system will become positive during month 11. If development takes longer than planned or if the benefits accrue more slowly than originally anticipated, net benefit becomes positive later.

The cost of any information system includes the cost of buying the hardware, building or buying the software, and the cost of ownership. The **total cost of ownership (TCO)** includes the cost of implementing, operating, and maintaining it. For many information systems, the cost of only the implementation is much higher than

TABLE   11.5

IS Costs That Are Easy to Overlook

Cost/benefit analysis is often used to justify system projects. Effective use of this technique depends on estimating both the obvious costs and the costs that may be hidden.

Phase	Costs easily assigned to a project	Costs that are easy to overlook
Initiation	• Salary and overhead for IS staff • Cost of communication and travel related to the project • Consulting fees (if any)	• Salary and overhead of user staff and management involved in the analysis • Other work that is displaced in favor of work on the project
Development	• Salary and overhead for IS staff • Equipment purchase and installation costs • Purchase (if any) of system or application software	• Salary and overhead of user staff and management involved in the analysis • Site modifications such as wiring offices
Implementation	• Salary and overhead for IS staff and trainers • Cost of communication and travel related to the project	• Salary and overhead of user staff and management involved in the implementation • Disruption of work during implementation process • Salary of users during training and initial usage
Operation and maintenance	• Salary and overhead for IS staff • Software license fees (if any) • Depreciation of hardware	• Salary and overhead of user staff and management involved with system maintenance activities

FIGURE   11.7

Estimated benefit and cost streams

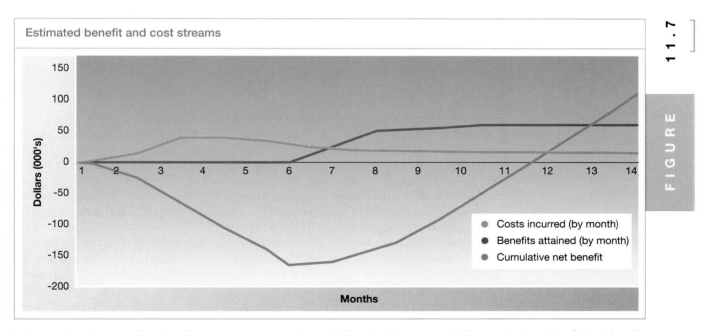

In these estimated costs and benefits of a new system, costs are incurred before benefits are attained. The cumulative net benefit (total benefits minus total costs) is negative until month 11 even though the benefits start in month 6. Monthly costs decrease after the system goes into operation but continue for the life of the system. This estimate includes minimal maintenance. Costs will be higher if more maintenance is needed.

the cost of the original development because training and conversion require work by all of the users. Total cost of ownership is therefore a key performance variable for any information system.

Risks

A surprisingly large percentage of information system projects either fail to attain their goals or attain them only after the expenditure of more time and effort than was initially anticipated. Common disappointments include:

- Desired benefits are not achieved.
- The project is completed late or over budget.
- The system's technical performance is inadequate.
- User acceptance is low.
- Shifting priorities reduce the project's importance.

Since information system development is a risky endeavor, decisions about which projects to attempt should consider these risks. To anticipate the risks inherent in a proposed system, it is possible to compare the proposed system to a situation with minimum risk:

> The system is to be produced by a single implementer for a single user, who anticipates using the system for a very definite purpose that can be specified in advance with great precision. Including the person who will maintain it, all other parties affected by the system understand and accept in advance its impact on them. All parties have prior experience with this type of system, the system receives adequate support, and its technical design is feasible and cost effective.[38]

The further a system development situation deviates from this ideal situation, the greater the inherent risks. This does not mean that only low-risk systems should be developed. Companies developing only low-risk information systems are not learning much in this area and probably are not implementing competitively significant information systems. The appropriate use of comparisons with this ideal situation is to identify areas of risk and then determine implementation strategies for managing those risks.

Financial Comparisons

IS steering committees often select among proposed IS projects by reviewing formal proposals and deciding how to allocate resources among them. The proposals usually include a formal justification stated in terms of the likely monetary costs and benefits. Expressing costs and benefits in dollars provides a useful way to compare and rank projects, even though dollar benefits are hard to estimate for projects involving major changes of business processes or IS infrastructure. Going through a formal justification process also eliminates some projects because their sponsors cannot devise a plausible justification that satisfies cost/benefit criteria.

Common criteria used for comparing and ranking projects include net present value, internal rate of return, and payback. These three measures take into account the cost and benefit streams that go into a cost/benefit analysis. All three are thoroughly explained in introductory finance courses.

Net present value (NPV) is the estimated amount of money the project is worth to the firm, taking into account the cost and benefit streams and the time value of money. The ratio between the value of a dollar today and a dollar a year from now is reflected by the *discount rate* applied. NPV is calculated by taking the difference between benefits and costs in each period, discounting to the present, and adding up the resulting terms. Given two otherwise equally beneficial projects, one would prefer the project with the higher NPV. However, NPV favors larger projects (with higher benefits and costs). The NPV of mediocre large projects can exceed that of very good small ones.

Internal rate of return (IRR) is a way to convert NPV into a form that makes projects more directly comparable. A project's internal rate of return is the interest rate one would have to receive on its cost stream to produce the same ultimate return as the project. IRR is computed by treating the discount rate in the NPV formula as a variable, setting NPV to 0, and solving for the discount rate. Many organizations use internal rate of return as a *hurdle rate* by funding only projects whose IRR is at least 12% or 15%.

Payback period is that length of time until the project's net benefit becomes positive. Given two projects with roughly equivalent long-term benefits, the one with a shorter payback period is preferred. A shorter payback period reduces the risk that the project will miss its targets. Different companies place different amounts of weight on payback. The governance model used by Cisco Systems calls for a positive return within six months and completion within one year for projects that come out of a functional manager's budget (as opposed to infrastructure projects whose benefits will cross many groups).[39]

The division head of a large bank that often missed system deadlines decided to use payback as a primary criterion for selecting projects. Until system development performance improved, no systems with a payback of over six months would be approved. The division could not even consider very large projects involving significant change, but its development efforts were brought under control.

A problem common to NPV, IRR, and payback is that they assume the final decision is made at a point in time using only the information available at that time. A newer technique called **real options** takes into account the fact that many information system projects have a high level of uncertainty along with opportunities to obtain additional information after the project begins. Instead of pushing toward a yes or no decision for the entire project, real options calculations work through a decision tree of possibilities and recognize that projects or subprojects can be deferred, modified, expanded, or abandoned based on initial accomplishments and problems.[40]

Although NPV, IRR, and payback can serve as useful controls on resource allocations, use of these criteria is ineffective when they are applied to the wrong projects. They are most applicable for projects with easily estimated benefits and costs, such as projects that automate part of a well-understood process. Because major changes often generate unanticipated benefits and costs, the financial return on highly innovative systems is often hard to estimate. Managers realize that proposals for these projects are based on unreliable guesses and that purely financial criteria may provide insufficient insight for choosing among them. It is also worth noting that strict adherence to guidelines such as requiring an estimated rate of return over 15% may eliminate innovative projects that are worth the risk. Viewing this as a problem, American Express set aside a substantial sum for innovative high-risk projects. One of the resulting projects was the Authorizer's Assistant, a highly publicized expert system that improved the decisions of agents who approve large or unusual purchases. Although not undertaken based on NPV or IRR, it paid for itself many times over.[41]

R E A L I T Y C H E C K ✓

Cost/Benefit Analysis

This section discussed costs, benefits and risks, and financial criteria that can be used to compare projects.

1. Consider any major purchase you or your family have made in the last few years, such as a car, a computer, or a college education. Identify the costs, benefits, and risks of several alternatives you considered or should have considered.

2. Explain why cost/benefit analysis would or wouldn't have been helpful in that decision.

PROJECT MANAGEMENT ISSUES

A project plan outlines initial answers to the *who*, *what*, *how*, and *when* questions summarized in Table 11.1. Answering these questions before starting a project helps organize the work and helps keep it on track. A project plan is especially important in IS projects because unanticipated technical and organizational problems often arise. At minimum, having a plan helps in identifying surprises and evaluating their impact. This section will look at two types of issues related to project plans, division of labor between the IS department and users, and challenges of staying on schedule. The next chapter will look at alternative approaches for building information systems.

Division of Labor between the IS Department and Users

There are many ways to allocate IS personnel and responsibilities between the IS department and user departments. Mixed results with projects totally led by IS departments have encouraged giving user departments responsibility for the information systems they use. Even many technical roles for these systems have been moved into user departments.

As an example, Figure 11.8 shows how a food company divides work between the user departments and the IS department. The shaded and unshaded areas in the figure show that jobs closer to the application and user tend to be in the user department, whereas those closer to the machine and technology tend to be in the IS department. The location of jobs shown in Figure 11.8 is actually a change from the way this company operated previously, when programmer-analysts and systems analysts were in the IS department. These jobs were moved into the user departments to increase responsiveness to user needs.

However the work is divided, people in both the IS department and the user department should recognize staffing issues mentioned in the section on centralization

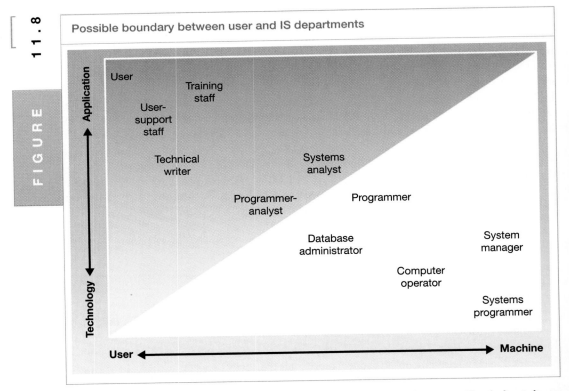

FIGURE 11.8

Possible boundary between user and IS departments

Many of the jobs in this figure could be in either the user department or the IS department. The shading indicates one possible way to divide the work. Jobs in the shaded area are assigned to the user department, and the others are assigned to the IS department.

versus decentralization. These issues make it all the more important to keep projects on schedule.

Keeping the Project on Schedule

IS projects have an unfortunate tradition of exceeding budgets and missing schedules. For example, a 1995 survey mentioned in Chapter 1 obtained information from 365 respondents about 8,380 projects. Only 16.2% of the projects were completed within schedule and budget and produced all of the features initially specified. Around 52.7% went over budget, over the time estimate, or produced fewer features. An amazing 31.1% of the projects were cancelled before completion.[42] Project participants and users can help avoid these problems by appreciating the need for project goals, deliverables, and schedules, and by recognizing some of the special challenges in these projects.

Goals, Deliverables, Schedules   Effective project management requires clear, measurable goals. A **project goal** is a result that should occur if the project is carried out successfully. For example, a project's goal might include staying within a $250,000 budget; project completion by June 30, 2002; average order confirmation time of 15 minutes; and average customer satisfaction rating of 4.7 six months after system installation. The first two goals involve the process of building the information system; the last two involve the organization's operation after system installation. Each goal is specific enough to measure. Without such goals, it is impossible to evaluate project completion or success.

In addition to their own unique goals, IS projects share commonsense goals in the back of any project manager's mind: creating the right system, creating it efficiently, making sure it works properly, and making sure it can be maintained and enhanced. Although these goals might seem obvious, too many system development efforts create the wrong system, create it inefficiently, fail to make sure it works properly, or create it in a form that is difficult to maintain. Information systems miss the mark frequently enough that the picture in Figure 11.9 has become a cliché.

The essence of project management is controlling tasks that occur in a particular sequence and have an expected duration. Dividing a project into steps, or subprojects, clarifies what needs to be done and helps the people doing the project understand exactly what they have to do and how their work fits into the overall project. This approach also supports a project management process of monitoring progress and recognizing problems early enough to make midcourse corrections.

Each step in an IS project produces one or more deliverables. **Deliverables** are tangible work products, such as documents, plans, or computer programs. Specifying the deliverables expected with each step is a way to make sure the work is progressing. The steps simply aren't finished until deliverables are completed. In combination, the deliverables in IS projects provide a running history of what was done, when it was done, and why it was done. The deliverables for each step in a project form the basis for work done in subsequent steps.

The deliverables are produced according to a schedule. A **project schedule** is a terse project description identifying the timing of major steps and who will do the work. Many project management tools have been developed to record and update schedules and track progress versus schedules. Most IS projects use **Gantt charts,** illustrated in Figure 11.10. Gantt charts represent a schedule visually by displaying tasks along with their planned and actual start and completion times and resource requirements. The tasks may or may not overlap in time and may or may not have mutual dependencies. Resource requirements may be stated in terms of person-months, dollars, or time allocations for specific individuals.

Gantt charts are excellent tools for communicating with project groups, identifying problems, and deciding what corrective action to take. A quick glance at a Gantt chart shows whether a project is ahead of or behind schedule. In team meetings, Gantt charts are effective in reviewing progress, identifying problems, and explaining why

FIGURE

11.9

Why is it hard to develop the right system?

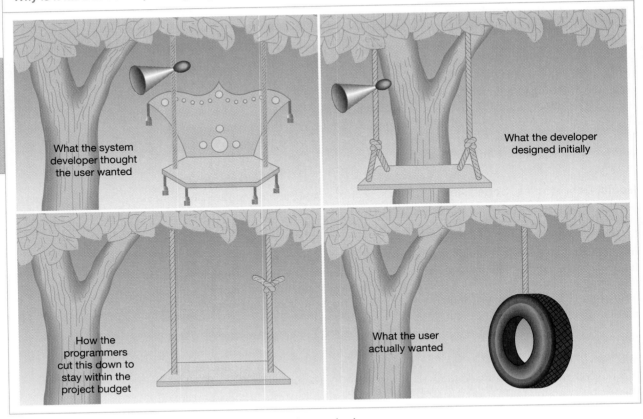

This figure illustrates a dilemma that has frustrated a generation of system developers.

FIGURE

11.10

Gantt chart

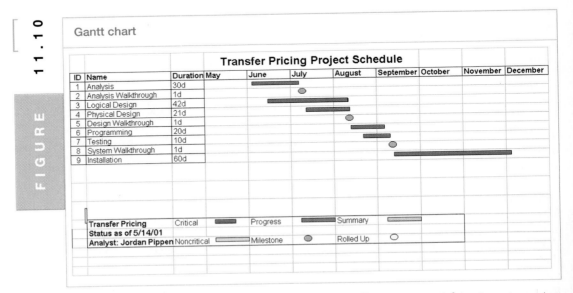

This Gantt chart shows the planned sequence and timing of the different steps in an information system project. Among other things, it shows that physical design will start about halfway through logical design, that programming will start just before a design walkthrough, and that installation will take almost three months.

resources must be shifted. Gantt charts and similar management techniques depend on the quality of schedule data. If the tasks are stated vaguely, it is difficult to say when they are completed. If people are reluctant to report problems or if they say tasks requiring more polishing are "almost complete," the Gantt chart will display and amplify misleading data.

Managing IS projects involves balancing system scope and quality against schedule performance. Participants are often overoptimistic about how long the work will take, especially because these projects often hit unanticipated complexities. Possible responses to problems and slippages include maintaining the project's scope and schedule, changing the project's scope, changing the schedule, or adding more resources. Maintaining an unrealistic schedule causes morale problems and staff turnover. Reducing the scope may create a feasible project that doesn't solve the user's problem; extending the schedule may cause unacceptable delays. Making up for delays and other problems is often difficult because of the learning required if the staff is expanded. Losing a key individual from an IS project is an especially difficult problem due to the loss of knowledge.

Challenges in Information System Projects   Many of the challenges of project management mirror those of any other form of management: assigning the right people to the right jobs, getting people to do high-quality work, getting people to report their progress realistically, and resolving issues and disputes. Especially important in project-oriented work are estimating project scope and duration, minimizing rework on completed steps, and recovering from delays.

Estimating project scope and duration: It is difficult to estimate the scope and duration of projects for a number of reasons, including uncertain project scope, changes in scope, individual differences in productivity, and the way work is distributed in projects. The first phase of an IS project is basically research to understand the true nature of the problem and to identify a cost-effective solution. Consequently, project scope is only partially known when the first project estimates are made. Even after this research is finished, important details involving both the business situation and the technical solution may remain poorly understood. Projects also change in scope because the business situation changes or because the users learn that their original understanding of the situation was off the mark. Both of these issues often cause **requirements creep**, continual increases in project scope that make project completion a moving target. A survey of 160 IS professionals found that 80% believed requirements creep "always or frequently" affected schedule performance.[43]

Vast productivity differences between individuals doing IS work cause additional estimating problems. An often-cited study of programming productivity factors found that a mediocre team developing software often takes over four times as long as a superior team.[44] Even when the development team is known in advance, such wide productivity differences make it difficult to estimate what any individual will accomplish.

The combination of estimation difficulties, requirements creep, and individual differences often results in difficult practical and ethical dilemmas, starting with the common reluctance to pass on bad news to managers. People who are evaluated on the basis of meeting schedules are tempted to underplay problems that endanger schedules, even if this means that the result of the work will be less useful.

Minimizing rework on completed steps: Although some steps of an IS project may be performed simultaneously, many steps build on the outputs of previous steps. Ideally, it should not be necessary to return to previous steps to correct errors and omissions that become apparent later. In reality, each succeeding step tests the feasibility of conclusions from previous steps. Conclusions or outputs from previous steps may have to be changed because more is understood now or because the previous work contained errors. Consequently, there is often some rework even though a project is described as a sequence of successive steps.

Recovering from delays: The most natural unit for estimating the size of system development projects and tracking their progress is the *person-week* or *person-month*. A manager therefore might describe a new application as a 20 person-month project, meaning anything from 1 person for 20 months to 20 people for 1 month. If this 20 person-month project falls behind schedule by the equivalent of 5 person-months, it might seem possible to bring in the equivalent of 5 additional person-months of work to get back on schedule. This tactic often fails for IS projects, even if it might work for other projects.

In the early 1970s, Fred Brooks summarized the difficulty of getting IS projects back on schedule by coining the term the **mythical man-month.**[45] (The more current term *person-month* is used here.) Brooks deemed the man-month (person-month) mythical because it implied people are interchangeable and can be added to a project at any time. In fact, people are interchangeable only in projects that require little knowledge, communication, or learning.

To coordinate effectively with other project members, participants in each step of an IS project should understand its goals and strategy, the plan for doing the work, and the technology used. A great deal of effort must go into training and communication. Bringing a new worker into a project requires a knowledgeable worker to spend less time doing productive work while bringing the new worker up to speed. Adding many new workers to an ongoing project can temporarily halt progress. The mythical person-month is therefore one of the reasons it is so important to keep projects on schedule. The amount of communication and coordination time absorbed by large project teams is also a reason to avoid allowing a project to get too large too soon.

R E A L I T Y C H E C K ✓

Project Management

This section discussed project management issues related to division of labor between users and technical specialists and keeping the project on schedule.

1. Consider a significant project you or your acquaintances have been involved in during the last few years. Identify any important issues related to the division of labor or related to keeping the project on schedule.

2. Explain any special issues that were unrelated to division of labor or keeping the project on schedule.

SYSTEMS ANALYSIS REVISITED

Chapter 2 defined systems analysis as a general process of defining a problem, gathering pertinent information, developing alternative solutions, and choosing among those solutions. By covering many different facets of information systems, this book's main purpose is to help you understand how to analyze these systems from a business professional's viewpoint. This is why tools such as the work system framework, data flow diagrams, and entity-relationship diagrams were introduced in the first few chapters. This last section looks at the process of gathering information during systems analysis. The discussion is equally applicable to IS planning and to building and maintaining information systems (covered in the next chapter).

Information Sources for Analyzing Systems

Common sources of information for analyzing information systems include interviews, documentation of existing systems, inputs and outputs of existing systems, on-site observation, questionnaires, and examination of similar systems.

> *Interviews:* Interviewing users and their managers is probably the most obvious method for gathering information about a system. After all, who should understand the situation better than the people who will use the system?

> *Inputs, outputs, and documentation of existing systems:* An existing information system's input screens and output reports can give a good idea of what data are avail-

able and what data people use. System documentation often helps explain why the system exists, what business problems it solves, and how it solves them. However, documentation may be so detail-oriented that it doesn't explain the purpose of system features. Also, if the system has been modified many times, it is likely that the documentation will be inaccurate.

On-site observation: One of the best ways to understand how a system operates is to go to the site and observe it for several days, or even weeks. If possible, an analyst should even try to perform the job the system will support. Analysts who never observe the current system in action often misunderstand the problem they are trying to solve.

Questionnaires: Questionnaires can be used to gather information from users, managers, and other stakeholders in the project. This method is especially useful when there are many geographically dispersed stakeholders, making it impractical to interview everyone. Although questionnaires sometimes capture ideas that would otherwise be missed, people often fill them out in a perfunctory way because they are busy with other things and feel uninvolved in the project.

Benchmarking: **Benchmarking** is the analysis of similar systems in other companies to provide both perspective and new ideas about the situation being analyzed. Many companies use this approach in their total quality management (TQM) efforts. In addition to new ideas, interviewing users of similar systems may produce insights about why particular system features are effective or ineffective.

Each of these methods provides a way to obtain information needed when analyzing a system. Using different methods is important because systems analysts often discover that things said in interviews are inconsistent with what they find when they observe systems in action. We will look at the interviewing process in more detail because interviews are used so commonly.

Performing Interviews

Although talking to users might seem like a simple task, a surprising number of problems may reduce interview effectiveness. Table 11.6 summarizes some of these, which include missing viewpoints, superficial information, and distorted information. Minimizing these problems involves careful preparation, execution, and follow-up,

---

Common Problems Encountered by Analysts Interviewing Users

Analysts encounter a number of problems while interviewing information system users, but many problems can be prevented by paying attention to typical causes.

Problem	Typical cause	Preventive action
Missing viewpoints	Users unwilling or unable to participate	Make involvement of key users a condition for doing the project
	Stakeholders who are not invited to participate	Include all groups affected by the system
Superficial information	Lack of preparation by the analyst	Learn about the business setting; prepare before the interview
	User's assumption that only minor changes are possible	Don't just ask for the user's wish list; understand the reason for the user's problem rather than just the suggested solution
Distorted information	User responses based on user aims other than the system, such as political position in the organization	Obtain multiple viewpoints to confirm data and conclusions
		Be sure users know the purpose of the interview
	Analyst misunderstanding or biasing the user's response	Learn about the business setting
		Prepare before the interview

including an insistence on understanding the situation rather than just making a list of what the users apparently want.

Careful preparation for an interview includes gathering background information before the interview and going to the interview with a clear goal and a list of key questions. Conducting an interview without a clear goal, such as understanding a user's problems or understanding a user's information requirements, wastes time and leads to garbled conclusions. Having a list of questions helps you focus the discussion and helps the respondent understand the interview's purpose. Although the discussion may move to unanticipated topics that are important, starting with a list of questions helps keep the interview on track and helps you recognize important observations. Prior knowledge of the organizational setting, business process, and other aspects of the situation helps you understand what the user means. It also avoids giving the user the impression of wasting time explaining things you should know. Being prepared keeps you focused on receiving information and helps you avoid putting words in the user's mouth.

Although interviews differ in content and feeling, there are common rules of thumb for interviewing:

- Make sure that the interviewee knows the reason for the interview. In too many cases the interviewee is unclear about the purpose and may withhold information or cooperation as a result.
- Ask **open-ended questions**, which invite the interviewee to provide more information than a yes or no. For example, ask, "How do you use the customer file?" rather than a yes-no question such as "Is the customer file useful?"
- Validate responses by restating them and by comparing different people's responses. Different people often disagree about problems, causes, and priorities. The greater the disagreement, the more difficult it will be to design and implement a successful system.
- Pay attention to body language (both yours and the interviewee's). Uninterested or antagonistic interviewees often project a different feeling from those who genuinely want the project to succeed.
- Close the interview by reviewing some of the main points covered, thanking the respondent, and requesting permission to call back if you need clarification or additional information.

Follow-up after an interview is also important. Avoid the strong temptation to file your notes and go on to other work without analyzing what was said. In complex projects, it may even be worthwhile to rewrite your notes. If you neglect doing this, weeks later you may not understand much about what was said or why. Reviewing your notes also encourages you to follow up on unclear responses or on questions you hadn't raised during the interview. It is much better to ask more questions than to develop an information system based on misunderstandings.

These guidelines for gathering information are useful in IS planning, in system development projects (discussed in the next chapter), and in many other areas of business. The guidelines help project participants stay focused and help them avoid unnecessary difficulties in projects that already have many challenges.

CHAPTER CONCLUSION

S U M M A R Y

What is an information system plan?

A plan is a statement of what will be done, who will do it, when they will do it, how it will be done, and what are the desired results. At the strategic level, IS plans focus on priorities and goals for information systems and the technical and organizational approaches that will be used. At the project level, they focus on specific capabilities required in each system and on who will do what and when will they do it to produce specific results.

Why do users and managers have to participate in information system planning and development?

Even though the IS department compiles the IS plan, members of user departments have to ensure that the right systems are developed, are used efficiently and effectively, and have the desired impact.

How is information system planning linked to business planning?

IS planning is the part of business planning concerned with deploying the firm's IS resources. Like plans in all business functions, the IS plan should support the strategy and goals in the business plan and should be linked to the plans in the functional areas.

What are some of the strategic issues in information system planning?

The issues most directly related to business activities include attaining consistency with business priorities, supporting the redesign of business processes called for by reengineering and downsizing, and attaining the right level of internal and external integration by deploying enterprise-wide and interorganizational systems. Strategic issues more related to how IT is deployed include designing an appropriate IS architecture, finding the right balance between centralization and decentralization in the IT effort, defining a business-driven IT infrastructure, and outsourcing the right IT functions.

What are the key issues in balancing centralized versus decentralized processing and control?

The key issues focus on the extent to which information system location, ownership, and control should be dispersed to different parts of the organization. Excessive centralization often results in rigid systems that cannot handle local variations. Excessive decentralization often solves local problems but often does not solve problems that cross departments and misses opportunities for economies of scale.

How is cost/benefit analysis used in making investment decisions about information systems?

Cost/benefit analysis is the process of evaluating proposed systems by comparing their estimated benefits with their estimated costs, both expressed in dollars over a time horizon. Key issues for cost/benefit analysis include the difference between tangible and intangible benefits, the tendency to underestimate costs, and the effect of the timing of costs and benefits. Decisions about which projects to attempt should also consider risks and comparisons with other proposed projects.

What are the basic elements of project management for information system projects?

Like any business project, IS projects have goals, deliverables and schedules, and roles and responsibilities. The essence of project management is controlling tasks that occur in a particular sequence and have an expected duration. Dividing a project into steps with specific deliverables clarifies what needs to be done and helps the people doing the project understand exactly what they have to do and how their work fits into the overall project.

K E Y   T E R M S

information systems planning
chief information officer (CIO)
sponsor
champion
IS steering committee
user-support project
enhancement
bug fix
pilot project
critical success factor (CSF)
business process reengineering (BPR)
downsizing

interorganizational information systems
virtual organization
information system architecture
legacy system
platform
IT infrastructure
management by maxim
outsourcing
application service provider (ASP)
cost/benefit analysis
tangible benefits
intangible benefits

total cost of ownership (TCO)
net present value (NPV)
internal rate of return (IRR)
payback
real options
project goal
deliverables
project schedule
Gantt chart
requirements creep
mythical man-month
benchmarking
open-ended question

REVIEW QUESTIONS

1.   Describe the difference between strategic-level and project-level plans for information systems.

2.   What is IS planning and how should it be related to other planning in a business?

3.   Identify important user roles in information systems planning.

4.   How much of a typical IS group's work typically is involved with keeping existing systems operating, and what types of projects does this include?

5.   Identify some of the roles of IS professionals in building and maintaining information systems.

6.   What are critical success factors, and how are they used in IS planning?

7.   Explain why business process reengineering is a controversial topic.

8.   How are interorganizational information systems related to virtual organizations?

9.   What is the significance of legacy systems and platforms in IS architecture?

10.   How is the idea of management by maxim related to the strategic alignment of IT infrastructure?

11.   In relation to centralization versus decentralization, what are the major issues involving standards and ownership?

12.   Why is outsourcing controversial?

13.   What is an application service provider?

14.   Describe some of the problems that often arise when information systems span two countries or are moved from one country to another.

15.   Explain the difference between tangible and intangible information system benefits.

16.   Why is the timing of costs and benefits important in evaluating proposed information systems, and how does it affect financial measures such as NPV, IRR, and payback?

17.   Describe the characteristics of information system projects with minimal risks.

18.   Why are goals, deliverables, and schedules important in project management?

19.   What limits the effectiveness of Gantt charts and other project management methods?

20.   Explain the idea of the "mythical man-month."

21.   Describe some guidelines for interviewing during information system projects.

DISCUSSION QUESTIONS

1.   Assume that you had been an IS manager at XYZ Corp. for the past 12 years and have just been informed that the outsourcing contract signed yesterday transferred all major IS operations to a leading outsourcing vendor. As part of the deal, you and your staff are to become employees of the vendor, which has different salary scales, different benefits, and a different culture. Ignoring any laws that might apply to this, what economic or ethical responsibilities did XYZ Corp. have toward you and your colleagues as it negotiated this contract?

2.   A noted software expert has stated that "the introduction of new CASE tools may cause a short-term productivity problem that will impact the current project. . . . Most organizations have found that productivity typically declines for the first 3 to 6 months after the introduction of CASE tools, and sometimes by as much as 25% during the first year."[46] Explain how this phenomenon is related to IS planning topics covered in this chapter.

3.   To improve customer responsiveness in its consumer banking group in the early 1980s, Citibank decided to "decentralize its information process capabilities quickly to as low a level of responsibility and control as possible. . . . Instead of increasing responsiveness, Citibank soon found itself drowning in a sea of systems,

unable to collect, store, disseminate, or analyze vital information." Citibank quickly recentralized its information management processes.[47] Explain how Citibank's experience is related to issues covered in this chapter.

4. "When a company budgets $1 million to develop a new software system it is, in fact, committing to spend more than $4 million over the next five years. Each dollar spent on systems development generates, on average, 20 cents for operations and 40 cents for maintenance. Thus, the $1 million expenditure automatically generates a follow-on cost of $600,000 a year to support the initial investment."[48] Explain whether this quotation seems surprising to you and how it is related to topics covered in this chapter.

5. This chapter's coverage of information system planning mostly takes the viewpoint of a large firm. Which topics in the chapter seem equally applicable to a small firm? Which topics seem less applicable?

6. You are nearing the end of a seven-month system development project. Last week, the leader of one of your teams estimated his group was 95% finished. This week, he says he may have been a bit optimistic and his team is probably only 85% finished. He asks you to assign two more programmers to his team to help him finish. What ideas from the chapter would you think about before responding?

C A S E **Economist Intelligence Unit: Launching a Web-Based Business Intelligence Service**

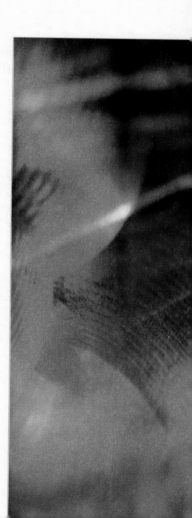

The Economist Group grew out of *The Economist*, a weekly newspaper of international news and business founded in Great Britain in 1843. It currently comprises *The Economist*, Economist enterprises, the Economist Intelligence Unit, *CFO Magazine*, the *Journal of Commerce*, and specialist magazines. Converted to dollars, its revenue for the fiscal year ending in 2000 was around $330 million and its loss before taxes was around $74 million, compared to profits of $46 million, $35 million, and $38 million in the previous three years.[49]

The Economist Intelligence Unit was founded in 1946 and directed toward companies establishing and managing operations across national borders anywhere in the world. It provides objective and timely analysis and forecasts of the political, economic, and business environment in 195 countries. EIU is a worldwide operation with offices in London, Vienna, New York, Hong Kong, Singapore, and Cambridge (USA). The intelligence is based on regular contributions from a global network of more than 500 information specialists. EIU's electronic publishing division provides the EIU's full database of country, regional, and industry information through a range of electronic media including CD-ROM, Lotus Notes, online databases, news services, and customized network feeds to corporate intranets. Business executives can access the EIU's full-text reports directly over the Internet at www.eiu.com, which was launched in February 1996 as a way to make the existing content more conveniently accessible.[50]

In May 1998, the EIU launched ViewsWire, www.viewswire.com, which describes itself as "a pioneering web-based intelligence service from the Economist Intelligence Unit. It delivers timely analysis on key economic, political and business developments around the world. Each day, the ViewsWire supplies 100–150 analytical articles on any of 195 countries." Unlike a traditional news service, "it provides views—not news—from the Economist Intelligence Unit and the rest of The Economist Group. The aim is to give the content the analytical depth needed to make informed decisions about doing business around the world. [It] also includes carefully selected analysis from other respected sources to ensure a full perspective on international business conditions. As a complete decision-support tool for global executives, [it] supports navigation by country, by subject and by a powerful search facility, which includes the option to set up a range of personal profiles." Pricing is based on the number of authorized users. The sliding scale for the Global EIU ViewsWire network goes from $8,650 for one user to $102,050 for over 100,000 users. The pricing for the regional network goes from $3,900 to $46,000.[51]

"To successfully produce ViewsWire required the EIU to reengineer how it organized information internally and how it coordinated that process across more than 500 editors and analysts in more than 100 countries, working in a variety of different formats and timelines." The previously existing culture had been organized around producing news articles on strict deadlines. The mandate of publishing a total of 100–150 new articles every day previously required a quota of submissions from reporters and editors. Now they had to change their emphasis and had to be on alert to provide analysis and forecasts in response to fast-changing events. Editors had to learn to break out of publishing time frames to adopt more of a daily focus in their work. They would also have to learn to use more internal resources within the Group instead of only turning to their typical sources for reports. Users had to learn things as well, especially how to drill down into the EIU database to find information they needed.[52]

QUESTIONS

1. Visit www.eiu.com and www.viewswire.com. What are some of the roles that information systems probably play in providing these services?

2. Figure 11.1 identifies the information system plan as part of a business plan. Based on the case and the Web sites identify some of the ways the information system plan for EIU should be related to its plans for sales, production, finance, and human resources.

3. Assume that you were involved in the planning process for EIU. Give examples of business maxims and IT maxims that are implied by the case and by what you see at the two Web sites.

4. The case says nothing about how the information systems are built and maintained. Assume that EIU wanted to outsource part of the process of building, operating, and maintaining these information systems. How should EIU decide which functions to outsource? Which functions seem most amenable to outsourcing?

CASE **Cemex: Incorporating IT into a Cement Company's Strategy**

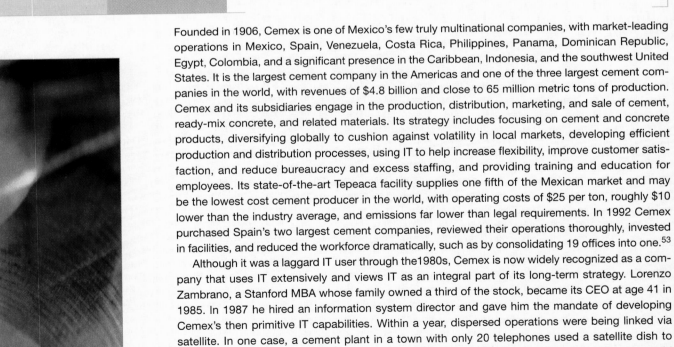

Founded in 1906, Cemex is one of Mexico's few truly multinational companies, with market-leading operations in Mexico, Spain, Venezuela, Costa Rica, Philippines, Panama, Dominican Republic, Egypt, Colombia, and a significant presence in the Caribbean, Indonesia, and the southwest United States. It is the largest cement company in the Americas and one of the three largest cement companies in the world, with revenues of $4.8 billion and close to 65 million metric tons of production. Cemex and its subsidiaries engage in the production, distribution, marketing, and sale of cement, ready-mix concrete, and related materials. Its strategy includes focusing on cement and concrete products, diversifying globally to cushion against volatility in local markets, developing efficient production and distribution processes, using IT to help increase flexibility, improve customer satisfaction, and reduce bureaucracy and excess staffing, and providing training and education for employees. Its state-of-the-art Tepeaca facility supplies one fifth of the Mexican market and may be the lowest cost cement producer in the world, with operating costs of $25 per ton, roughly $10 lower than the industry average, and emissions far lower than legal requirements. In 1992 Cemex purchased Spain's two largest cement companies, reviewed their operations thoroughly, invested in facilities, and reduced the workforce dramatically, such as by consolidating 19 offices into one.[53]

Although it was a laggard IT user through the1980s, Cemex is now widely recognized as a company that uses IT extensively and views IT as an integral part of its long-term strategy. Lorenzo Zambrano, a Stanford MBA whose family owned a third of the stock, became its CEO at age 41 in 1985. In 1987 he hired an information system director and gave him the mandate of developing Cemex's then primitive IT capabilities. Within a year, dispersed operations were being linked via satellite. In one case, a cement plant in a town with only 20 telephones used a satellite dish to transmit voice and data, thus bypassing Mexico's chaotic phone system. By 1998, managers could use the satellite-based communications network to monitor operations and market conditions all over the world and to communicate using voice, video, Lotus Notes, and other technologies.[54]

Application areas that demonstrate the importance of IT include management information and control of operations. Cemex managers can immediately link to any of the 18 plants in Mexico and immediately access the status of each cement kiln, recent production data, and even the deployment of trucks dispatched by different cement and concrete distribution centers. Financial statements are available two days after the end of the fiscal month, an endeavor that used to take a whole month. Eliminating these lengthy delays in evaluating production, costs, and sales volume helps in running a lean, low-cost operation by making it possible for management to take action quickly instead of waiting almost two months to just receive the data in some cases.[55]

Use of IT in controlling operations occurs at many points. Cemex's ready-mix delivery trucks are equipped with dashboard computers that allow tracking using global positioning satellite technology. A central dispatcher in a region constantly reroutes the trucks as customers cancel, delay, or speed up orders. "In 1995, because of traffic gridlock, capricious weather, and labor disruptions at the construction site, Cemex could promise delivery no more precisely than within three hours of the scheduled delivery time. Such conditions often forced customers to cancel, reschedule, or change half of their orders. Today, at its largest operations in Mexico and Venezuela, Cemex is committed to delivering ready-mix shipments within 20 minutes of the scheduled time. The reason for this dramatic improvement in customer service is its dynamic synchronization of operations, which has increased the productivity of the company's trucks by 35%. The result is significant savings in fuel, maintenance, and payroll costs, and a considerable increase in customer goodwill.[56]

A Cemex news release in September 2000 announced "the launch of CxNetworks, a new subsidiary that will build a network of e-businesses, as an integral element of its overall e-enabling strategy. CxNetworks will leverage Cemex's assets onto the Internet and extend the reach of the company into marketplaces that complement its core business. . . . CxNetworks will initially focus on three business areas: the development of online construction marketplaces, the creation of an Internet-based marketplace for the purchase of indirect goods and services, and the expansion of Cemtec—Cemex's information technology and Internet consulting services company—into new markets. . . . CxNetworks is in the process of developing and will soon launch a series of online construction marketplaces with a variety of local partners in South America, Europe, the United States, and Mexico. These businesses will offer an array of construction products, including cement, as well as online services and information to small and large contractors, builders, and other construction industry participants."[57]

QUESTIONS

1. Based on the case, identify what seem to be some of Cemex's business and IT maxims.

2. What issues related to centralization and decentralization seem to apply in this case?

3. Review this chapter's discussion of international issues and explain which of those issues, if any, apply to this case.

4. People sometimes encourage businesses to "Stick close to your knitting," meaning that they should focus on the customers, products, and processes where they have competitive advantage. Explain why you do or do not believe Cemex's e-business initiative follows this advice.

Building and Maintaining Information Systems

chapter12

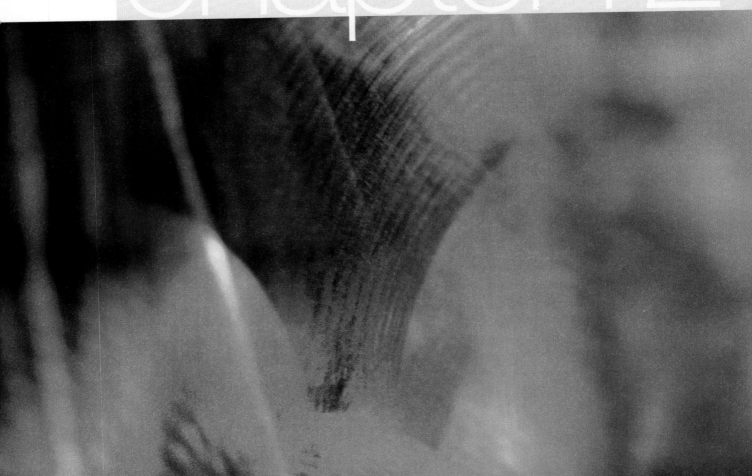

STUDY QUESTIONS

- What are the four phases of information system projects?
- What types of issues are addressed by the different system development processes?
- How does the traditional system life cycle solve the control problem of keeping a project on track?
- What are the advantages and disadvantages of prototypes?
- What are the advantages and disadvantages of application packages?
- What are the advantages and disadvantages of end-user development?
- How is it possible to combine system development approaches into a system's life cycle?

OUTLINE

Phases of Any Information System
Initiation
Development
Implementation
Operation and Maintenance

Overview of Alternative Approaches for Building Information Systems

Traditional System Life Cycle
Initiation
Development
Implementation
Operation and Maintenance

Prototypes
Phases
Advantages and Disadvantages

Application Packages
Phases
Advantages and Disadvantages

End-User Development
Phases
Supporting the Users
Advantages and Disadvantages

Deciding Which Combination of Methods to Use
Comparing Advantages and Disadvantages
Combining System Development Approaches

Chapter Conclusion
Summary
Key Terms
Review Questions
Discussion Questions
Cases

Building and Maintaining
Information Systems

OPENING CASE

YAHOO! STORE: BUILDING YOUR OWN ONLINE STORE

One of many parts of the Yahoo.com portal is a shopping section that contains a large number of online stores. Some of these stores are Web sites of large e-retailers that have paid to be included within Yahoo!'s shopping section. Other stores represent small retailers that have no technical staff or ability to program a Web site using typical programming tools. Instead, they have used a capability called Yahoo! Store to create and maintain their own online stores by using their Web browsers to submit information describing their stores. The process of building an online store starts with compiling standard types of information (mentioned below) that specify the contents of the store. Once the information is entered the merchant tests the online store to make sure that it is operating correctly. At that point the store is published onto the Yahoo! Shopping Web site. Yahoo! Store users pay a flat rate depending on the size of the store. A small store with up to 50 items costs $100 per month. For a larger store, the first 1,000 items costs $300 per month and each additional 1,000 items costs $100 per

month. There is no transaction fee, startup cost, or minimum time commitment.[1]

It is possible to create a store without doing programming because Yahoo! Store uses a standard structure for all stores. Every store has a front page that introduces the store and identifies the store's sections—the major groupings of items that it sells. Clicking on one of the sections listed on the front page takes a shopper to a page devoted to that section. The section page lists all of the items within that section. Clicking on an item takes the shopper to a page that shows a picture of the item, describes it in words, and gives its price. Clicking on "add to shopping cart" adds the item to an online shopping cart within Yahoo! Shopping. The shopper can make the purchase through Yahoo! Shopping and the order will appear on the merchant's order list. In addition to sections, items, prices, and images, the online merchant must also provide other standard information. It must provide applicable tax rates; it must identify the payment choices for the customers; it must describe the delivery terms. It also should provide contact information for the customers.

Because the entire structure is standardized, Yahoo! Store can provide management information beyond just the orders themselves. For example, it can show the number of times each page was viewed and the number of sales and revenue for each item. To help analyze the value of clickable advertisements on other Web sites, it can summarize the visits, orders, and revenue derived from each referring URL. As the online store is used, the merchant is able to modify it by changing the inputs related to sections, items, prices, and so on. The merchant makes the desired change in a test area, tests the result to make sure that it is right, and then publishes it as the updated online store.[2]

WEB CHECK [✓]

Look at the Yahoo! Shopping site and find several stores built by apparently small e-retailers you haven't encountered. To what extent does a standard store format seem to fit these retailers?

DEBATE TOPIC [

With Yahoo! Store's capabilities to create an online store, it is unnecessary for small online merchants to know anything about computer technology other than how to run a browser.

you might wonder why a chapter about building and maintaining information systems starts with a case in which programmers play no direct role. The use of Yahoo! Store to create an online store illustrates one of many possible ways to build and maintain an information system. In this particular case the information system is an online store that fits within tightly defined parameters required by the overall structure of the Yahoo! shopping site. The reason for selecting the Yahoo! Store case is the strong trend toward building information systems by configuring application software built by vendors. Business professionals need to understand this type of process, but it is best understood in relation to other processes, including those for building an information system from scratch.

The work system snapshot for the Yahoo! Store case points out that the creation of the store fits within the process for building and maintaining systems initially introduced in Figure 1.7. The *initiation* phase is deciding to build the online site using Yahoo! Store. The *development* phase is about creating the store. The *implementation* phase is putting the store into operation. This includes many background activities that customers never see directly, such as how to handle orders and replenish inventory. Before implementation, the merchant has only the technical capability of operating the store. After implementation, the store is actually open for business. This leads to the *operation and maintenance* phase, during which the merchant keeps the store in operation, fills orders, replenishes inventory, and updates the site as appropriate. As with any other information system, the life cycle of an online store involves much more than doing the computer work necessary to get something running on a computer. The online store will have no impact whatsoever until customers use it.

This chapter's purpose is to explain different ways to build and maintain information systems in organizations. Business professionals need to understand options related to software and system development processes because many IS projects encounter serious problems that ultimately affect business results. For example, a survey of 300 large companies by KPMG Peat Marwick, a big five accounting firm, discovered that 65% had at least one project that went grossly over budget, was extremely late, and ultimately produced results of little value. Peat Marwick called such a project a **runaway**, as in a "runaway train."[3] Chapter 1 mentioned other studies by consulting companies that revealed similar problems.

This chapter starts by reviewing the four phases of any information system originally introduced in Chapter 1 (see Figure 1.7). These phases can be used as a least common denominator for discussing and comparing alternative methods for building and maintaining information systems. With this background, the chapter summarizes

WORK SYSTEM SNAPSHOT
Building an online store using Yahoo! Store

CUSTOMERS
- Potential shoppers at the store being built

PRODUCTS & SERVICES
- A Web-based store open for business and operating effectively

BUSINESS PROCESS

Initiation
- Decide to build an online store and use the capabilities of Yahoo! Store

Development
- Learn how to create a store using Yahoo!'s capabilities
- Compile all the necessary information about store identity, products, prices, and payment options
- Enter the information into the Yahoo! Store program
- Test that the store works as desired

Implementation
- Train the merchant's staff in procedures for handling orders, replenishing inventory, monitoring the Web site, etc.
- Go live by publishing the Web site as part of Yahoo! Shopping
- Monitor usage and sales

Operation and Maintenance
- Keep the online store in operation
- Perform offline functions such as filling orders and replenishing inventory
- Update the online store with new products and prices
- Monitor improvements in Yahoo! Store capabilities and decide whether to use new capabilities

PARTICIPANTS
- Online merchant and any staff involved in creating and maintaining the store

INFORMATION
- Instructions for creating a Yahoo! Store
- Information about products and prices
- Operational information about Web site usage

TECHNOLOGY
- Yahoo! Store software for creating and maintaining a store
- Personal computer
- Yahoo! Store servers and software for operating the store

and compares four alternative models for performing the four phases. These alternative approaches include the traditional system life cycle, prototypes, application packages, and end-user development. The Yahoo! Store approach is most similar to using an application package. Because each approach has advantages and disadvantages, project managers need to decide on the combination of these approaches that makes the most sense in any particular situation based on priorities, capabilities, and resources.

As you read this chapter, remember that building an information system is a business process. Like other business processes the way it is designed ultimately affects its internal performance and the product it produces for customers. Product performance can be evaluated in terms of cost to the customer, quality, responsiveness, reliability, and conformance. Internal process performance can be evaluated in terms of activity rate, output rate, consistency, productivity, cycle time, downtime, and security.

In addition, please recognize that understanding this process requires attention to the difference between the information system that is being built and the work system that is being improved. The terms *system*, *work system*, and *information system* will be used carefully throughout the chapter. Since repeated references to "the information system and the work system it supports" would be tedious, the term *system* is used alone when the distinction between the information system and the work system is unnecessary for the point being made or when the term applies to both simultaneously, such as "the new system was ineffective."

PHASES OF ANY INFORMATION SYSTEM

The starting point for building or improving an information system is the recognition of a business problem or opportunity and the belief that a better information system might create benefits by improving the operation of a work system. Next comes the refinement of that idea into a specific statement of what the work system should accomplish, how the improved information system should help, and what parts of the information system will be automated. Analysts or designers decide how to create computer programs that accomplish the automated functions on specific hardware. The technical staff either writes the programs or acquires them. The organization acquires whatever hardware is needed. The programs are tested to ensure the correct functions are performed in the correct manner. A team implements the information system in the organization through a process involving user training and conversion from the previous information system. The information system then goes into operation and is modified as necessary for further improvements in the work system. Eventually the work system or the information system may be absorbed into other systems or terminated.

Regardless of whether the software is produced by the IS department, the user department, or by an outside vendor, this general process can be summarized in terms of four phases: initiation, development, implementation, and operation and maintenance (see Figure 12.1). This model serves as a least common denominator for understanding and comparing different types of business processes used for building and maintaining systems. Figure 12.1 shows how the end product of one phase is the starting point of the next. It also shows some of the reasons for returning to a previous phase even though the four phases ideally occur in sequence.

FIGURE 12.1

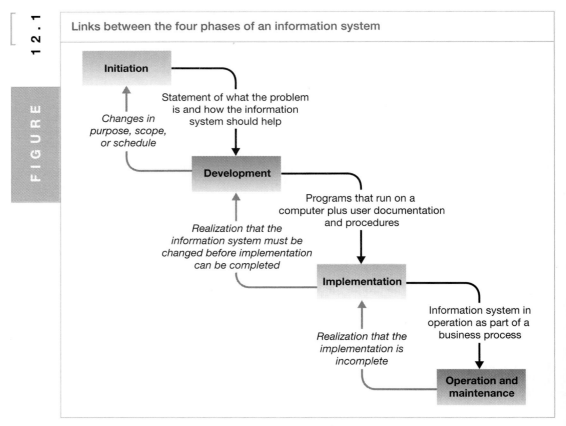

Links between the four phases of an information system

This diagram shows how the end product of each of the first three phases of an information system is the starting point of the next phase. It uses italics to show why it is sometimes necessary to return to a previous phase. The products of the first three phases differ slightly from those in Figure 1.7 (Chapter 1) because that diagram referred to the phases of any work system, not just an information system.

Common Issues and Problems in Each Phase of an Information System		**12.1**
Phase	**Common issues and problems**	
Initiation	• Can we agree on the purposes and goals of the proposed system? • Are the requirements unnecessarily elaborate and expensive?	
Development	• Can we assure that the system genuinely solves the user's problems? • Can we assure that users will participate effectively in the design process?	
Implementation	• Can we convert effectively and painlessly from the old system to the new system? • Can we solve political issues related to changes in power relationships?	
Operation and maintenance	• Can we keep system performance and uptime at acceptable levels? • Can we correct bugs and enhance the system to keep it focused on current business problems?	

The seeds of success or failure can often be seen in relation to the phases of an information system. Table 12.1 summarizes problems and issues that must be dealt with in order for each phase to succeed.

Before we explain the terms *development* and *implementation*, notice that authors from different disciplines use these terms in different ways. In this book, the term *development* refers to the phase concerned with designing, programming, and testing the computerized parts of an information system. This is the second of four phases for any successful information system. Consistent with common usage, the verb *develop* is also used here in a general sense, as in "Company ABC developed a sales system." For programmers, the term *implementation* often refers to the process of designing and programming a computer system. Since this is a book for business professionals, the word *implementation* is used in the way they typically use it—namely, to refer to making the information system and the improved work system operational in the organization. Defined this way, implementation is the third phase of the system life cycle.

Initiation

Initiation is the process of defining the need to change an existing work system, identifying the people who should be involved in deciding what to do, and describing in general terms how the work system should operate differently and how any information system that supports it should operate differently. This phase may occur in response to recognized problems, such as data that cannot be found and used effectively, or high error rates in data. In other cases, it is part of a planning process in which the organization is searching for ways to improve and innovate, even if current systems pose no overt problems. This phase concludes with a verbal or written agreement about the directions in which the work system and information system should change, plus a shared understanding that the proposed changes are technically and organizationally feasible.

A key outcome of this phase is an understanding of a proposed information system's purposes and goals. Errors in this phase may result in information systems that operate on the computer but don't support the organization's goals. Because it is possible to change a system after it goes into operation, design errors in the initiation phase may not be fatal to the project. However, they are especially expensive because the subsequent effort in developing both the information system and the work system are based on these errors. Figure 12.2 demonstrates the importance of identifying design errors early in a system development process by showing how the cost of design errors escalates the later they are discovered.

Some system projects never go beyond the initiation phase. For example, the analysis in this phase may show that the likely costs outweigh the likely benefits, or that the system is technically or organizationally impractical. Other system efforts are abandoned because people cannot agree on system goals or because too few people in the

FIGURE 12.2

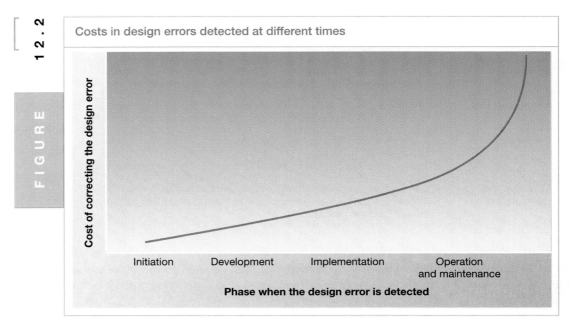

Costs in design errors detected at different times

The later a design error is detected, the more expensive it is to correct because so much rework and retesting is required.

organization care about the problem the system addresses. Although no one wants to invest time and effort in a project and then stop it, stopping a project at this phase is far better than pouring time and effort into something that will probably fail.

Development

Development is the process of building or acquiring and configuring hardware, software, and other resources needed to perform both the required IT-related functions and the required functions not related to IT. This phase starts by deciding exactly how the computerized and manual parts of the work system will operate. It then goes on to acquire the needed resources. If the hardware isn't already in place, development includes purchasing and installing the hardware. If the software isn't in place, it includes purchasing the software, producing it from scratch, or modifying existing software. Regardless of how the hardware and software are acquired, this phase includes creating documentation explaining how both the work system and the information system are supposed to operate. The development phase concludes with thorough testing of the entire information system to identify and correct misunderstandings and programming errors. Completion of development does not mean "the system works." Rather, it only means that the computerized parts of the work system operate on a computer. Whether or not the "system works" will be determined by how it is actually used in the organization.

A key goal of the development phase is assuring that work system and information system features really solve problems the users want solved. This is sometimes difficult because many users are unable to describe exactly how a better information system might help them. They also may not see that system modifications could help them in some ways but might become a hindrance in other ways. Another key goal is to perform the technical work in a way that makes it easier to modify the information system as new needs arise.

The rate of major difficulty and even outright project failure during the development phase is surprisingly high. The previous chapter mentioned a large survey in which only 16.2% of development projects were completed within schedule and budget and produced all of the features initially specified. Around 52.7% went over budget, over the time estimate, or produced fewer features. An amazing 31.1% of the projects were cancelled before completion.[4] In general, the larger and more complicated the project is, the more likely that it will encounter problems at this phase. Particularly difficult are projects that require inputs from many stakeholders in business situations in which new information and new priorities are emerging continually. Projects of this type often encounter a combination of unreasonable expectations, insufficient resources, technological risk, and inadequate project methodology and staff.

Some development failures also occur due to insufficient specification and testing. A very visible example of this type occurred in 1999 when a $125 million spacecraft sent to study the climate of Mars was lost because it was off course by 60 miles after a 416-million-mile journey from Earth. Although the full details were still under investigation, it was known the Jet Propulsion Laboratory's computer models for calculating position and speed had been programmed using the metric system but that Lockheed had provided data on the rocket thrusters using the English system. The thrusters had been used over months for making fine adjustments, and no one had noticed the discrepancy until the Orbiter reached the vicinity of Mars. Researchers hoping to gain important climate knowledge from data that would have been collected were devastated by a system development error involving one of the most basic principles of high school physics.[5]

Implementation

Implementation is the process of making a new or improved work system operational in the organization. This phase starts from the point when the software runs on the computer and has been tested. Activities in implementation include planning, user training, conversion to the new information system and work system, and follow-up to make sure the entire system is operating effectively. The implementation phase may involve a major change in the way organizations or individuals operate. Conversion from the old to the new must be planned and executed carefully to prevent errors or even chaos. For information systems that keep track of transactions such as invoices and customer orders, the conversion process requires some users to do double work during a pilot test, operating simultaneously with the old and new systems. Running two information systems in parallel helps identify unanticipated problems that might require information system or work system modifications before implementation is complete.

Political issues related to power and control within the organization often become visible during implementation. For example, implementing an integrated sales and production system might make computerized production scheduling data directly accessible to a sales department. Ideally, this data should help sales and production work together. However, it might also permit sales to exert new pressure on production, which previously had sole access to the data. The new system's cooperative rationale might be replaced with a win-lose feeling. Such issues should be identified and discussed as early as possible.

Many information system projects that survive the development phase limp through an ineffective implementation and never generate the planned benefits. For example, CompuSys (disguised name of a computer manufacturer) had developed a successful system for verifying existing sales orders to be sure they were complete and consistent before shipping the computer to the customer. CompuSys decided to extend this approach to generate error-free configurations before even quoting prices to the customer. An information system was built over several years with participation of sales reps and eventually produced more accurate configurations than average sales reps could produce. A survey showed that 75% of the reps had tried the information system, but only 25% were using it, and that dropped to 10% within three years. An expensive revamping resulted in a much more effective user interface but no change in usage patterns because sales reps had little motivation to use it. They were evaluated and paid

[**L O O K   A H E A D**]

The NIBCO case at the end of the chapter illustrates implementation issues that come with ERP systems.

based on sales revenues, not on correct configurations. Furthermore, they actually felt disincentives because this information system was not completely linked to a pricing information system and therefore made it more difficult to complete the paperwork for a sale. Building the new information system without considering the participants' incentives wasted a lot of time and money.[6]

Regardless of who is to blame, this example hints at many of the elements of disappointing implementations: inconsistent priorities, incomplete communication between the developers and the users, and inadequate follow-up to make sure the information system is used effectively. Many types of systems have encountered related problems. For example, groupware and other forms of networking are often sold based on the claim that they help people work together. But the benefits are only modest in many cases unless people consciously strive to change the way they work together. Implementation problems such as these are sometimes cited as an important reason for what is sometimes called the "productivity paradox," in which companies with higher levels of IT investment often have no better competitive success than comparable companies with lower levels of IT investment.

Operation and Maintenance

Operation and maintenance is the ongoing operation of the work system and the information system, plus efforts directed at enhancing either system and correcting bugs. At minimum, this requires that someone be in charge of ensuring that the work system is operating well, that the information system is providing the anticipated benefits, and that the work system and information system will be modified again if the business situation calls for it.

People tend to overlook the significance of this phase. To the IS staff, building new information systems often seems more challenging and creative than keeping old ones effective as needs change. Perceiving this phase as less creative, users may assume that upgrades should be easy. In fact, the operation and maintenance phase is often challenging. For example, consider the response time and uptime requirements of information systems companies rely on for taking customer orders or managing factories. Once an information system is in operation, users expect it to work. Downtime and bugs must be dealt with immediately, which requires the ability to diagnose and correct problems under time pressure.

Furthermore, the longer an information system has been in operation, the harder it is to change. Original developers who understood it best may have different jobs; documentation becomes outdated; infrequently used parts of the system fall into disrepair. Programmers become justifiably wary of changing the system because a change in one place is more likely to cause a bug elsewhere. In turn, work system participants are less likely to get the changes they want and start to complain about the IS department's unresponsiveness and the information system's ineffectiveness. Ideally, the business process chosen for building an information system should minimize these problems.

R E A L I T Y C H E C K [✓]

Project Phases

This section explained the four phases of an information system project and explained why it is sometimes necessary to return to a phase that was previously considered complete.

1. Think of a project or team effort that you or your family members have been involved in. Explain how well each of the four phases applied in that project.

2. Explain which of the issues in Table 12.2 are most related to important aspects of your project. (Because your project might not have involved an information system, you may have to restate the issues.)

Differences between Four System Life Cycle Approaches		
Life cycle approach	**Issue addressed**	**Summary of method**
Traditional system life cycle	Control	Go through a fixed sequence of steps with sign-offs after each step and careful documentation.
Prototype	Knowledge	Quickly develop a working model of the system; use the model to gain experience and decide how the final system should operate.
Application packages	Resources and timing	Purchase application software from a vendor; customize the software if necessary.
End-user development	Responsiveness	Provide tools and support that make it practical for end users to develop their own information systems.

TABLE 12.2

OVERVIEW OF ALTERNATIVE APPROACHES FOR BUILDING INFORMATION SYSTEMS

Different business processes are used to perform the individual phases depending on the type of system, the problem it attempts to solve, and the situation in which it will operate. In some situations, the requirements are clear and easily agreed upon; in others, no one may be able to describe the requirements clearly until they have a prototype to try out. In some cases, existing technology will be used; in others, new technology must be mastered and used for the first time in the organization. In yet other situations, buying application software from a vendor may be a better choice than building it from scratch.

This chapter summarizes and compares four alternative models for performing the four phases of building and maintaining an information system. These alternative approaches are summarized in Table 12.2 and explained in the sections that follow. The approach used in any particular situation should combine appropriate elements of these models and possibly others.

The **traditional system life cycle** uses a prescribed sequence of steps and deliverables to move reliably from user requirements to an information system in operation. These deliverables are related because each subsequent step builds on the conclusions of previous steps. The traditional system life cycle tries to solve a *control* problem by keeping the project on track. This type of process became popular in response to numerous system development efforts that went out of control and either failed to produce an information system at all or produced a system that did not solve the users' problem effectively. Accordingly, the traditional system life cycle establishes tight controls to guarantee that technical and organizational issues are addressed at each step. The controls are project deliverables ensuring that each step is completed in turn and documented carefully. Box 12.1 explains how the **capability maturity model (CMM)** tracks the extent to which an IT organization uses this type of life cycle in its development work. Notice that that model focuses on building software rather than on the larger problem of creating or modifying work systems in an organization.

A **prototype** information system is a working model of an information system built to learn about its true requirements. Firms build prototypes to solve a *knowledge* problem of not knowing exactly what the system should do to address an important issue. In this situation, the user needs some way to get a feeling for how the system should operate. Accordingly, a prototype is built quickly to help the user understand the problem and determine how an information system might help in solving it. Many Web sites are developed using what is basically a prototyping approach—get the site running, try out it, and fix it.

An **application package** consists of commercially available software that addresses a specific type of business application, such as sales tracking, general ledger,

The capability maturity model was developed by the Software Engineering Institute to track the extent to which an IT organization uses predictable, manageable processes for building information systems. By using record keeping and assessment tools based on this model, an IT organization can determine how its processes compare to a theoretical ideal and can see how quickly it is moving toward that ideal. As with many such detailed tracking methods, there is controversy about whether the extensive record keeping is worth the effort. For example, the model's training and record-keeping requirements may slow down IT work for several years. Whether or not the model is adopted fully, it provides a useful way to think about why information system projects often miss their targets for functionality, schedule, or budget. The model rates the organization's practices on a five point scale.[7]

Level 1—initial	Processes are ad hoc and sometimes chaotic. Because few processes are defined, successful projects often depend on heroic individual effort.
Level 2—repeatable	Basic project management processes are used to track cost, schedule, and functionality. The discipline exists to repeat previous success with similar projects.
Level 3—defined	Both management and technical processes are documented and integrated into a standard software process for the organization. Projects use an approved, tailored version of the standard software processes.
Level 4 —managed	Detailed measures of the software process and product quality are collected and that information is used to understand both the product and the process in quantitative terms.
Level 5—optimizing	Continuous process improvement is facilitated by quantitative feedback from the process and by doing pilot studies of innovative ideas and technologies.

Approximately 60% of U.S. IT organizations operate at level 1 and around 25% are at level 2. This means that only around 15% have attained a degree of stability that gives credibility to schedules and project plans. Only 2% have attained level 4 or 5.[8]

or inventory control. Firms acquire application packages to solve a *resource and timing* problem by using commercially available software that performs most of the functions desired. The IS department installs and operates this software instead of building customized software from scratch. This approach reduces the delays in developing custom software, reduces risks due to technical uncertainties and possible changes in the business problem, and reduces the resources needed to solve the problem.

End-user development is the development of information systems by work system participants (end users) rather than IS professionals. Firms apply end-user development to solve a *responsiveness* problem involving the inability of IS departments to keep up with individuals' changing information needs. The idea is to allow end users to produce their own information systems without requiring development by programmers. This is accomplished by giving end users spreadsheets, database programs, report generators, analytical packages, and other tools that can be used by nonprogrammers. End-user development is effective only for information systems that are small enough that an IT professional is not needed for design, programming, testing, and documentation.

We will now explain each of the four alternatives in more detail.

TRADITIONAL SYSTEM LIFE CYCLE

The goal of the traditional system life cycle is to keep the project under control and assure that the information system produced satisfies well-formulated requirements. The traditional system life cycle divides the project into a series of steps, each of which has distinct deliverables, such as documents or computer programs. These deliverables are related because each subsequent step builds on the conclusions of previous steps. Some deliverables are oriented toward the technical staff, whereas others are directed toward or produced by users and managers. The latter ensure that users and their management are included in the system development process.

Although there is general agreement about what needs to be done in the traditional system life cycle, different authors name the individual steps and related deliverables differently. Many versions of the traditional system life cycle emphasize the building of software and deemphasize what happens in the organization before and after software development. Because this book is directed at business professionals, its version of the traditional system life cycle emphasizes implementation and operation in the organization in addition to software development.

Initiation

The initiation phase may begin in many different ways. A user may work with the IS staff to produce a written request to study a particular business problem. The IS staff may discover an opportunity to use information systems beneficially and then try to interest users. A top manager may notice a business problem and ask the head of IS to look into it. A computer crash or other operational problem may reveal a major problem that can be patched temporarily but requires a larger project to fix it completely. Regardless of how this phase begins, its goal is to analyze the scope and feasibility of a proposed system and to develop a project plan. This involves two steps, the feasibility study and project planning, which produce the functional specification and a project plan.

The **feasibility study** is a user-oriented overview of the proposed information system's purpose and feasibility. A system's feasibility is typically considered from economic, technical, and organizational viewpoints.

Economic feasibility involves questions such as whether the firm can afford to build the information system, whether its benefits should substantially exceed its costs, and whether the project has higher priority than other projects that might use the same resources.

Technical feasibility involves questions such as whether the technology needed for the information system exists and whether the firm has enough experience using that technology.

Organizational feasibility involves questions such as whether the information system has enough support to be implemented successfully, whether it brings an excessive amount of change, and whether the organization is changing too rapidly to absorb it.

If the information system appears to be feasible, the initiation phase produces a functional specification and a project plan. The **functional specification** explains the importance of the business problem; summarizes changes in business processes; and estimates the project's benefits, costs, and risks. The **project plan** breaks the project into subprojects with start and completion times. It also identifies staffing, resource requirements, and dependencies between project steps.

The functional specification is approved by both user and IS personnel. It clarifies the purpose and scope of the proposed project by describing the business processes that will be affected and how they will be performed using the system. Functional specifications once consisted primarily of prose. With the advent of diagramming tools such as data flow diagrams and entity-relationship diagrams (Chapters 3 and 4), functional specifications have become much easier to read and understand. These visual representations help explain how the work systems will be improved and what general role the computerized parts of the system will play. Functional specifications typically do not explain exactly what data, reports, or data entry screens will be included. This more detailed description is produced in the development phase.

Development

The development phase creates computer programs (with accompanying user and programmer documentation) plus installed hardware that accomplish the data processing described in the functional specification. This is done through a process of successive refinement in which the functional requirements are translated into computer programs and hardware requirements. The purpose of the various steps and deliverables in the development phase is to ensure that the system accomplishes the goals explained in the functional specification. These steps are summarized in Figure 12.3.

The first step in the development phase is the **detailed requirements analysis**, which produces a user-oriented description of exactly what the information system will do. This step is usually performed by a team including user representatives and the IS department. It produces a document called the **external specification**. Building on the functional specification, the external specification shows the data input screens and major reports and explains the calculations that will be automated. It shows what information system users will see, rather than explaining exactly how the computer will perform the required processing. Users reviewing this document focus on whether they understand the data input screens, reports, and calculations, and whether these will support the desired business process. By approving the external specification, the

FIGURE 12.3

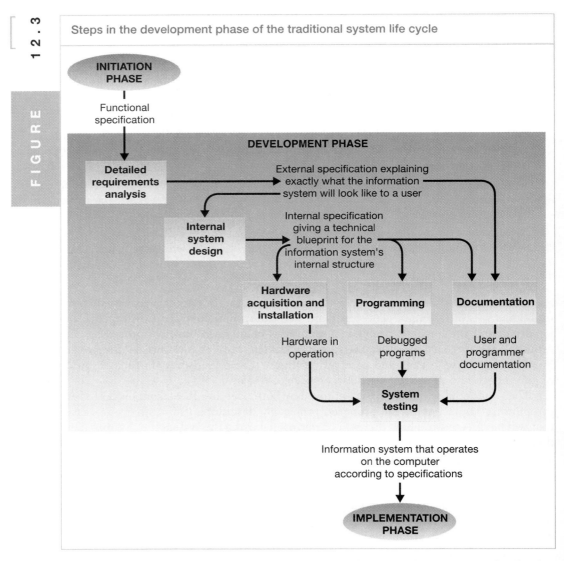

Steps in the development phase of the traditional system life cycle

The development phase of the traditional system life cycle starts with the detailed requirements analysis based on the functional specification from the initiation phase. The resulting external specification is used for the system's internal design, which outlines the structure of the programs and specifies hardware requirements. System testing occurs on completion of hardware installation, programming, and documentation. The development phase ends with an information system that operates on the computer according to the specifications.

users and IS staff signify their belief that the information system will accomplish what they want.

The next step is **internal system design**, in which the technical staff decides how the data processing will be configured on the computer. This step produces the **internal specification**, a technical blueprint for the information system. It documents the computer environment in which the system will operate, the detailed structure and content of the database, and the inputs and outputs of all programs and subsystems. Users do not sign off on the internal specification because it addresses technical system design issues. Instead, the IS staff signs off that the internal specification accomplishes the functions called for in the external specification the users have approved.

Thus far the discussion has focused on software. Because the software will work only if there is hardware for it to run on, an essential step in the development phase is **hardware acquisition and installation**. For some information systems, this is not an issue because it is a foregone conclusion that existing hardware will be used. Other systems require a careful analysis to decide which hardware to acquire, how to acquire it most economically, where to put it, and how to install it by the time it is needed. Factors considered in hardware acquisition decisions include compatibility with existing hardware and software, price, customer service, and compatibility with long-term company plans. Computer hardware can be purchased or rented through a variety of financing arrangements, each with its own tax consequences. A firm's finance department usually makes the financing arrangements for significant hardware purchases. Especially if new computer hardware requires a new computer room, lead times for building the room, installing the electricity and air conditioning, and installing the computer may be important factors in the project plan.

In firms with large IS staffs, users rarely get involved with the acquisition, installation, and operation of computer hardware. Much as with telephone systems, users expect the hardware to be available when needed and complain furiously whenever it goes down. This is one reason computer hardware managers sometimes consider their jobs thankless.

Programming is the creation of the computer code that performs the calculations, collects the data, and generates the reports. It can usually proceed while the hardware is being acquired and installed. Programming includes the coding, testing, and documentation of each program identified in the internal specification. Coding, writing instructions in a computer language, is what most people think of as programming. The testing done during the programming step is often called **unit testing**, because it treats the programs in isolation. The documentation of each program starts with the explanation from the internal specification and includes comments about technical assumptions made in writing the program, plus any subtle, nonobvious processing done by the program.

A number of improvements in programming methods have made programming faster and more reliable. Structured programming (explained in Chapter 9) is often used to make the programs more consistent, easier to understand, and less error prone. Fourth generation languages (4GLs) also expedite programming for some systems. However, as should be clear from all of the steps leading up to coding and following coding, coding often accounts for less than 20% of the work in building a system. This is one of the reasons 4GLs and other improved programming tools do not drastically shrink the system life cycle for large systems, even when they reduce programming time.

Documentation is another activity that can proceed in parallel with programming and hardware acquisition. Both user and technical documentation is completed from the material that already exists. The functional specification and external specification are the basis for the user documentation, and the internal specification and program documentation are the basis for the programmer documentation. With the adoption of CASE tools described in Chapter 9, more of the documentation is basically a compilation of data and diagrams already stored on a computer. Additional user documentation is usually required, however, because different users need to know different things depending on their roles. People who perform data entry tasks need to understand the data entry procedures and what the data mean; people who use data from the system need to understand what the data mean and how to retrieve and analyze data, but do not need to know much about data entry details.

After the individual programs have been tested, the entire information system must be tested to ensure that the programs operate together to accomplish the desired functions. This is called the **system testing**, or integration testing. System testing frequently uncovers inconsistencies among programs as well as inconsistencies in the original internal specification. These must be reconciled and the programs changed and retested. One of the reasons for Microsoft's "synch and stabilize" method (mentioned at the beginning of Chapter 9) is to eliminate the surprises and extensive rework that might occur if system testing showed that programs were incompatible. Although system testing may seem an obvious requirement, inadequate system testing has led to serious problems. For example, a new trust-accounting system put into operation prematurely by Bank of America on March 1, 1987 lost data and fell months behind in generating statements for customers. By January 1988, 100 institutional customers with $4 billion in assets moved to other banks, several top executives resigned, and 2.5 million lines of code were scrapped.[9] More recently, in 1999 many of Whirlpool's dealers complained of unreliable shipments after Whirlpool went live with new ERP applications over Labor Day weekend. An SAP consultant had warned them that several transactions needed about a week of reprogramming but Whirlpool and its consultants decided to go ahead with the launch. Things were fine with 1,000 users, but when the number of users hit 4,000 Whirlpool dealers noticed that appliance shipments were not arriving on time. The problems were fixed by November 1999, but not after inconvenience to dealers and lost sales for Whirlpool.[10]

An important part of testing is the creation of a **testing plan**, a precise statement of exactly how the information system will be tested. This plan includes the data that will be used for testing. Creating a testing plan serves many purposes. It encourages careful thought about how the system will be tested. In addition, having a thorough plan increases the likelihood that most foreseeable contingencies will be considered and that the testing will catch more of the bugs in the system.

It should be clear that the development phase for a large information system is a complex undertaking, quite different from sitting down at a personal computer and developing a small spreadsheet model. Explicitly separating out all the steps in the development phase helps to ensure that the information system accomplishes the desired functions and is debugged. Such an elaborate approach is needed because the system is a tool of an organization rather than an individual. An individual producing a spreadsheet is often trying to solve a current problem, not intending to use the spreadsheet next month, much less intending that someone else will need to decipher and use it next year. In contrast, the traditional system life cycle assumes that the system may survive for years, may be used by people who were not involved in its development, and may be changed repeatedly during that time by people other than the original developers. The steps in the traditional life cycle try to make the long-term existence of the information system as efficient and error-free as possible.

Implementation

Implementation is the process of putting a system into operation in an organization. Figure 12.4 shows that it starts with the end product of the development phase, namely, a set of computer programs that run correctly on the computer, plus accompanying documentation. This phase begins with **implementation planning**, the process of creating plans for training, conversion, and acceptance testing. The training plan explains how and when the users will be trained. The conversion plan explains how and when the organization will convert to new business processes. The acceptance testing plan describes the process and criteria for verifying that the information system works properly in supporting the improved work system.

FIGURE 12.4

Steps in the implementation phase of the traditional system life cycle

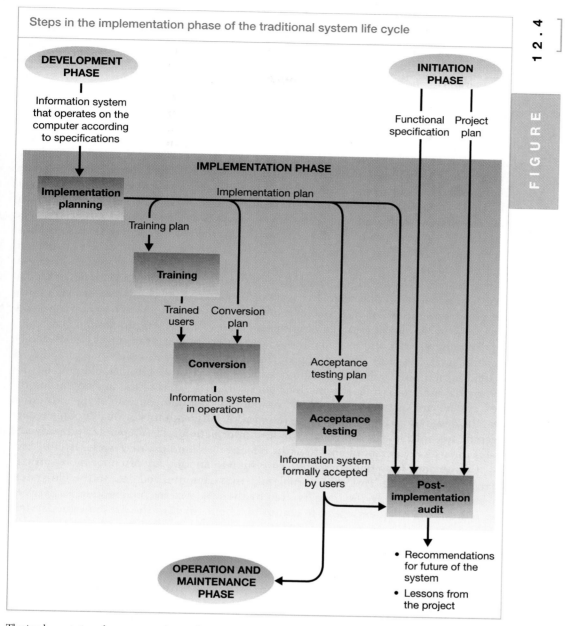

The implementation phase starts with an information system that operates on the computer, but not in the organization. Implementation planning creates the plan for training the users, converting to the new business processes, and gaining formal acceptance by the users.

Training is the process of ensuring that system participants know what they need to know about both the work system and the information system. The training format depends on user backgrounds and the purpose and features of both the work system and the information system. Users with no computer experience may require special training. Training for frequently used transaction processing systems differs from training for data analysis systems that are used occasionally. Information systems performing diverse functions require more extensive training than systems used repetitively for a few functions. Training manuals and presentations help in the implementation by explaining what will be different with the new work system and new information system. After the previous methods have receded into history, other types of training material are more appropriate.

Following the training comes the carefully planned process of **conversion** from the old business processes to new ones using the new information system. Conversion is often called *cutover* or *changeover*. It can be accomplished in several ways, depending on the nature of the work and the characteristics of the old and new systems. It is possible simply to choose a date, shut off the old information system, and turn on the new one while hoping that the work system will operate as intended. This is risky, though, because it doesn't verify that the information system will operate properly and that the users understand how to use it.

Consider the following example: The State of California installed an optical disk system to streamline the process of doing title searches (establishing ownership and identifying indebtedness on a property) for borrowers who wished to purchase property. Previously, there was a two- to three-week delay between the borrower's loan request and the bank's receipt of a confirmation that the title was clear. The new system was to reduce this delay to two days. Both the vendor and several state officials recommended that the old manual system remain in full operation during the conversion in case of problems. However, the Secretary of Finance rejected the request for an additional $2.4 million, and the manual system was simply shut down when the optical disk system came up. Unfortunately, software bugs plagued the new system, and the resulting logjam of 50,000 loan requests delayed title searches for up to 10 weeks. The new system was shut down for repair, and the old manual system reinstated. The Assistant Secretary of State stated that some banks almost went out of business because of the slow turnaround.[11]

To minimize risk and wasted effort, most conversions occur in stages, which can be done in several ways. A **phased approach** uses the new information system and work system for a limited subset of the processing while continuing to use old methods for the rest of the processing. If something goes wrong, the part of the business using the new system can switch back to the old system. The simultaneous use of the old system and the new system is called **running in parallel.** Although this involves double record keeping for a while, it verifies that the new information system operates properly and helps the users understand how to use it effectively within the new work system.

Conversions from one computerized system to another are often far more difficult than users anticipate. Part of the problem is that computerized data in the old system must be converted into the formats used by the new system. Inconsistencies between the two systems frequently lead to confusion about whether the data in either system are correct. Furthermore, programs that convert the data from one system to another may have their own bugs, thereby adding to confusion and delays.

Conversion requires careful planning because even minor problems can be blown out of proportion by people who don't want the new system and use the problems as an opportunity to complain. For these reasons, it is often wise to do a **pilot implementation** with a small group of users who are enthusiastic about the system improvements. Ideally, their enthusiasm will motivate them to make the effort to learn about the changes and to forgive minor problems. After a pilot implementation demonstrates that the new information system works, it is usually much easier to motivate everyone else (including the skeptics) to start using it.

Acceptance testing is testing of the information system by the users as it goes into operation. Acceptance testing is important because the information system may not fit, regardless of what was approved and signed off in the external specification. The business situation may have changed; the external specification may reflect misunderstandings; the development process may have introduced errors; or the implementation may have revealed unforeseen problems. For all these reasons, it makes sense to include an explicit step of deciding whether the information system is accepted for ongoing use. If it doesn't fit user needs, for whatever reason, installing it without changes may lead to major problems and may harm the organization instead of helping. Acceptance testing also solidifies user commitment because it gets people in the user organization to state publicly that the system works.

The **post-implementation audit** is the last step in the implementation phase, even though it occurs after the new system has been in operation for a number of months.

Its purpose is to determine whether the project has met its objectives for costs and benefits and to make recommendations for the future. This audit is also an opportunity to identify what the organization can learn from the way the project was carried out.

Operation and Maintenance

The operation and maintenance phase starts after the users have accepted the new system. This phase can be divided into two activities: (1) ongoing operation and support and (2) maintenance. Unlike the other steps in the life cycle, these steps continue throughout the system's useful life. The end of a system's life cycle is its absorption into another system or its termination.

Ongoing operation and support is the process of ensuring that the technical system components continue to operate correctly and that the users use the system effectively. This process is similar to the process of making sure a car or building operates well. It works best when a person or group has the direct responsibility for keeping the information system operating. This responsibility is often split, with the technical staff taking care of computer operations and a member of the user organization ensuring that users understand the system and use it effectively.

Day-to-day computer operations typically include scheduled events such as generating summary reports for management and backups of the database. The **operations manual** specifies when these jobs should be done. For transaction processing systems essential to the operation of the business, a member of the technical staff also monitors computer-generated statistics about response times, program run times, disk space utilization, and similar factors to ensure the programs are running efficiently. When the database becomes too full, or when response times start to increase, the technical configuration of the information system must be changed. This is done by allocating more disk space, unloading (backing up onto tape or discarding) data that are not current, or changing job schedules.

Maintenance is the process of modifying the information system over time. As users gain experience with a system, they discover its shortcomings and usually suggest improvements. The shortcomings may involve problems unrelated to the information system or may involve ways that the information system might do more to support the work system, regardless of the original intentions. Some shortcomings are bugs. Important shortcomings must be corrected if users are to continue using an information system enthusiastically.

Handling of enhancement requests and bug fix requests is both a technical challenge and a delicate political issue for IS departments. The technical challenge is ensuring that changes don't affect other parts of the system in unanticipated ways. The traditional life cycle helps here because documentation and internal design methods enforce modularization and make it easier to understand the scope and impact of changes. The political issue for most IS departments is their inability to support even half of the enhancement requests they receive. For new or inadequately planned information systems, some departments have more enhancement requests than they can even analyze. In this environment, it requires both technical and political skill to keep users satisfied. Users are often frustrated by how long it takes to make changes. What might seem to be a simple change to a person who "programs" spreadsheets is often vastly more complex in a large information system. Changes often require retesting of other parts of the system and spawn changes in several levels of documentation.

The steps in each of the four phases of the traditional system life cycle have now been introduced. Table 12.3 outlines the steps in each phase and makes two major points in addition to the details it presents. First it shows that users are highly involved in three of the four phases. In other words, building information systems is not just technical work done by the technical staff. It also shows that each step has specific deliverables that document progress to date and help keep the project under control.

The traditional system life cycle is a tightly controlled approach designed to reduce the likelihood of mistakes or omissions. Despite its compelling logic, it has

TABLE 12.3

Steps and Deliverables in the Traditional System Life Cycle

PHASE/STEP	DEGREE OF USER PARTICIPATION	KEY DELIVERABLE, PLAN, OR DOCUMENT	KEY PARTICIPANTS
Initiation			
• Feasibility study	High	Functional specification	User representatives, management, and technical staff
• Project planning	Medium	Project plan	User representatives, management, and technical staff
Development			
• Detailed requirements analysis	High	External specification	User representatives, management, and technical staff
• Internal system design	None	Internal specification	Programmers and technical staff
• Hardware acquisition and installation	None	Hardware plan	Technical staff
• Programming	None	Hardware operational / Individual programs debugged	Programmers
• Documentation	Medium	User and programmer documentation	Technical staff and users
• System testing	Medium	Test plan / Completed system test	Programmers and users
Implementation			
• Implementation planning	High	Implementation plan	Training staff, users, and management
• Training	High	Training materials	Trainers and users
• Conversion	High	System in use	Users and project team
• Acceptance testing	High	System accepted	Users and project team
• Post-implementation audit	High	Audit report	Users and management
Operation and Maintenance			
• Ongoing operation and support	Low	Operations manual	Technical staff
	Low	Usage statistics	Technical staff and users
	High	Enhancement requests and bug fix requests	Technical staff and users
• Maintenance	Medium	Maintenance plan	Technical staff and users
• Absorption or termination	------------	------------	------------

both advantages and disadvantages. Adherence to fixed deliverables and signoffs improves control but guarantees a lengthy process. Having specific deliverables due at specific times makes it easier to monitor the work and take corrective actions early if the work starts to slip. But the schedule of deliverables sometimes takes on a life of its own and seems as important as the real project goals. Going through the motions of producing deliverables on schedule, participants may be tempted to turn in work that is incomplete and to approve documents they do not truly understand.

The traditional system life cycle is the standard against which other approaches are compared. Project managers who want to bypass some of its steps still need a way to deal with the issues they raise. The chapter looks next at three alternative approaches based on different assumptions and priorities: prototypes, application packages, and end-user development.

R E A L I T Y C H E C K   ✓

The Traditional System Life Cycle

The traditional system life cycle is organized around a sequence of steps and deliverables.

1. Assume you were buying or renting a house or apartment that you plan to live in for five years. You want to make a plan for this process. What will the steps be, and what will be the deliverable for each step?

2. Explain the ways your process reflects some of the ideas in the traditional system life cycle. (Because this is a different problem, your process should differ from the traditional life cycle in many ways.)

PROTOTYPES

The traditional system life cycle enforces tight controls to ensure that the resulting information system performs according to requirements and is maintainable. The prototype approach emphasizes a different issue. Prototypes are used when the precise requirements are difficult to visualize and define because an existing business process must be changed substantially or because a proposed business process in a new situation has never been used, as happens in new e-commerce applications.

A **prototype** information system is a working model built to learn about how an improved work system could operate if it included an improved information system. The prototype's goal is to test possible information system features as a way of determining what the requirements should be. Instead of asking users to imagine how a proposed work system and the supporting information system might operate, the prototype approach allows them to work actively with a model of the information system. This helps them identify the features they need. It also helps identify impractical features that originally seemed to be beneficial.

A prototype system's purpose is similar to that of a prototype automobile. For example, assume that an automobile designer wants to test a new type of steering. A prototype would be designed specifically to test the steering. The steering system and suspension would be produced carefully, but the prototype might not have a paint job, back seat, or radio. These features would be put in later when the design is completed.

A prototype information system might contain a rough model of the data entry screens but might lack error checking because this would not be necessary to demonstrate the concept of the system. Because only a small sample database would suffice for a demonstration, no effort would go into making the prototype efficient. If the system contained a model, it might calculate approximate results just to show the types of outputs the final system would produce. Later versions would check the inputs, make the model more elaborate, and make its outputs look more complete.

Prototype information systems are sometimes classified as throwaway prototypes or evolutionary prototypes.[12] A **throwaway prototype** is designed to be discarded after it is utilized to test ideas, and is especially useful for comparing alternative designs for parts of a system. These prototypes can be programmed for a personal computer even though the final system will use a vastly different approach. An **evolutionary prototype** is designed to be adapted for permanent use after the ideas are clarified, and should be built using the programming tools that will be used for the final information system.

The phases of building and using a prototype are covered next. Table 12.4 summarizes important characteristics of each phase.

Phases

The phases of a prototype approach differ from those of a traditional system life cycle because the approaches have different assumptions. The traditional system life cycle assumes users understand the requirements, and that the main issue is to guarantee that requirements are followed in a disciplined way. Prototyping assumes users either

TABLE 12.4

System Life Cycle Based on a Prototype	
Phase	**Characteristics**
Initiation	Users and developers agree to develop a prototype because they need experience with a working model before designing a final system.
Development	Working iteratively with users, a prototype is developed and improved. Later, decide whether to complete the prototype or switch to a traditional life cycle.
Implementation	Accomplish parts of implementation along with development as users work with the prototype system. Dispel skepticism about whether the system will meet users' needs.
Operation and maintenance	May be similar to a traditional life cycle. May require less maintenance because the system fits users' needs more accurately. May require more maintenance because the system is not constructed as well.

cannot say exactly what the proposed information system should do, or would have difficulty evaluating a written specification. Using a highly iterative approach, it proceeds by building a succession of "quick and dirty" versions of the system. The users look at each iteration and suggest improvements, continuing this way until they know what they want. At this point, they and the technical staff decide how to complete the project. Figure 12.5 shows the iterative process used in the prototype approach.

Initiation   The initiation phase begins with a request to build an information system in response to a business problem or opportunity. Because the problem isn't well understood, or because the users are unable to say exactly what they want, users and

FIGURE 12.5

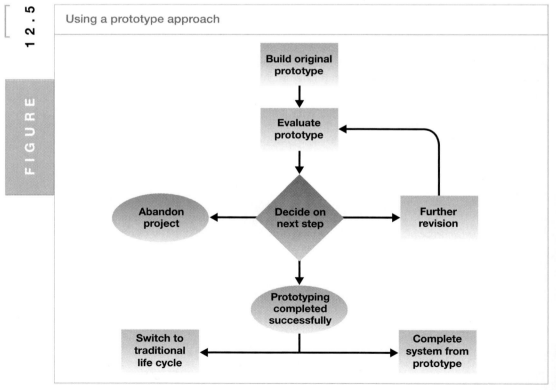

Using a prototype approach

Building an information system using a prototype is an iterative process. It involves evaluation and revision of a model system until the users and system builders understand the problem well enough to decide how to complete the project.

developers start by building a prototype instead of writing a functional specification. For this approach to succeed, the users must be willing and able to enter an iterative design process. Issues about completeness and consistency of the requirements are addressed as the users study successive versions.

Development   The development process emphasizes speed and rapid feedback. It begins by developing an initial prototype that demonstrates some of the desired processing but is far from complete. Next come a series of iterations, each modifying the prototype based on user comments about the most recent version. The technical approach for this process differs from what would be used in a traditional life cycle. Instead of using a programming language that would support high-volume transaction processing, a prototype might be built using a 4GL or DBMS for personal computers.

Once the requirements are clear, the users and technical staff must decide how to proceed. They might conclude that the project should be abandoned. Although no one wants to start a project only to abandon it, the prototype reduces the time and resources absorbed by a project that won't succeed. If the project is to continue, one approach is to complete the prototype using the code that has been generated thus far. Another is to shift to a traditional system life cycle by writing a functional specification and external specification based on what has been learned and then doing the internal design based on the desired level of information system performance. The shift to a traditional system life cycle is especially appropriate for an information system that will have a long life or will be critical to the business. If the system is primarily for management reporting, or if business problems are changing rapidly, extending the prototype might be a better choice.

Implementation   When using a prototype, part of the implementation is done in parallel with development. Users try out the prototype during successive iterations and become familiar with what it does and how it can help them. Systems developed this way may require less user training in the implementation phase. Active user participation in the development phase may offset skepticism about whether the results will be beneficial. For users who didn't participate in the prototyping, the training should be similar to the training they would have received in the traditional system life cycle. The conversion step should be similar to that of the traditional approach.

Operation and Maintenance   The operation and maintenance phase of an information system developed using a prototype should be similar to that of a system developed with the traditional life cycle. However, the characteristics of the development process contribute to both advantages and disadvantages that occur during the operation and maintenance phase.

Advantages and Disadvantages

The advantages of prototyping come from creating a more accurate idea of what the users really need. Starting from a better understanding has impacts on each remaining phase. During development, users have a tangible information system to work with instead of abstract specifications that may be difficult to visualize. This helps them provide useful feedback and may terminate an infeasible project before too much wasted effort. During implementation, the system may be more on target than it would have been otherwise. Early user involvement may also reduce skepticism and create a climate of acceptance about the new system. The impact during the operation and maintenance phase may be a reduced number of changes because of a better initial fit with user needs.

Building prototypes is much easier today than it was in the past because programming technology is much better. In particular, DBMSs, 4GLs, and CASE systems all contain screen generators (see Figure 12.6), report generators, and data dictionaries that make it easier to set up a model application quickly. Furthermore, because these same tools may be used for building the production version of the system, the transition from a prototype to a running system is much easier than it once was.

FIGURE   12.6

Creating a data input form

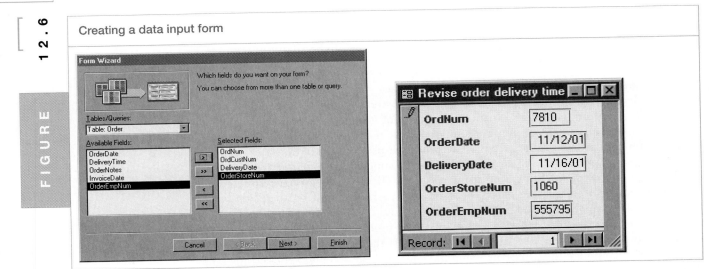

This Microsoft Access wizard permits a programmer to set up a data input form with minimal effort by automatically laying out a data input form after the programmer identifies the items that will appear on the form. It is an example of the programming advances that have made prototyping much easier.

Using prototypes has disadvantages, however. The process of developing a prototype may require greater involvement and commitment by key users who are already busy with their regular work. Continual changes while analyzing succeeding versions of the prototype may be difficult for these users. The succession of rapid changes may also require an unusual level of skill and commitment by the IS professionals. This process can be frustrating because the users are often saying that the prototype is not right. It can also be stressful because rapid iterations imply frequent deadlines in producing the next version. On the other hand, system developers often find building prototypes exciting because they produce tangible results quickly and get considerable feedback about their accomplishments.

The shortcuts that make rapid prototyping iterations possible sometimes undermine the final system's technical foundations. This is a problem for prototypes put into use without being revamped technically. Internal design, programming, and documentation are not as sound as they would have been under the traditional life cycle. As a result, information system performance and reliability may suffer, and the system may require more maintenance than if the traditional life cycle had been used. The users of a prototype may also fail to appreciate its fragility and may not understand why the IS staff insists on rebuilding a system that appears to work properly. Prototypes are built to demonstrate ideas. Even if the prototype eventually defines the final information system's general appearance, much more work must be done to assure reliability and adequate performance in real use. A prototype that looks good still is not successful in real use if it operates ten times too slowly, shuts down due to internal flaws, or has inadequate backup and recovery capabilities.

Prototypes are not the only alternative for bypassing parts of the traditional life cycle. Another is to purchase an application package previously developed by another firm.

APPLICATION PACKAGES

Although every company is unique in some ways, many information systems are similar across groups of companies. For example, the payroll systems in two small construction firms could be quite similar. Since there are thousands of such firms, this similarity leads to a business opportunity to develop and sell a payroll information system that many firms can use. Such systems typically start with custom work done for one or several firms. When the system works well for the original users, the software vendor markets it to other firms with similar requirements. The software vendor grad-

FIGURE 12.7

Example of a commercial application package

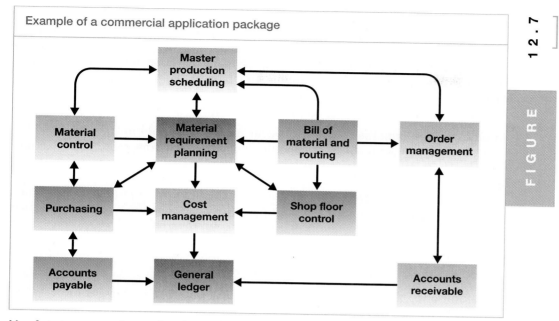

Manufacturing resource planning (MRP) systems such as this one are often application packages rather than internally built systems. The complexity of designing and integrating all the modules gives software vendors competitive advantage versus in-house IS groups in building and maintaining these systems.

ually adds more features to support a wider range of customers. Such systems often contain a number of modules and therefore are called application packages. The potential customers for most application packages have similar size and are in a particular market segment. For example, an appointment-scheduling system sold to clinics with several doctors might not fit large clinics, which need different business processes for scheduling appointments. Figure 12.7 shows relationships between the modules of a type of information system that commonly is purchased as an application package.

Purchasing an application package reduces the time delay until a system can be operational. It also reduces the amount of system development work that is needed. However, as will be apparent by looking at the phases of acquiring and using an application package, the life cycle for these systems still requires a great deal of effort and commitment. Table 12.5 shows some of the special characteristics of the phases of using an application package.

TABLE 12.5

System Life Cycle for Acquiring an Application Package

Phase	Characteristics
Initiation	May start with user's or manager's recognition of a business problem or with a sales call from a vendor.
Development	The vendor develops the software, although the purchaser still performs some typical development activities, such as determining detailed requirements. Development may include customization of the software and user documentation.
Implementation	Implementation starts by deciding exactly how the package will be used. It often relies on the vendor's staff because they have the greatest knowledge of the system.
Operation and maintenance	Operation occurs as it would with a traditional life cycle. Maintenance is different because the vendor maintains the software based on requests from customers and demands of the market.

Phases

It might seem that buying an application system from a vendor would bypass most of the work of building and maintaining the information system. In fact, the company's staff must still work on all four phases of the system to ensure that the right application package is selected, and is set up and supported properly. For large applications such as factory management systems, several years of effort may pass before the new information system is fully operational and delivering benefits.

Initiation   The initiation phase may occur much as it would in the traditional life cycle, with a business problem or opportunity motivating a proposal to develop a new system. It may also start with a software vendor's sales call trying to convince the firm's management that the firm could use the vendor's product.

Regardless of how the project begins, it is often useful to produce a functional specification just as is done in the traditional life cycle. The functional specification represents the firm's perception of the problem and the required information system capabilities. It helps in deciding which vendors to consider and in selecting a software package. Failure to produce a functional specification can give vendors too much leeway in shaping the firm's view of its own problems.

Development   Although purchasing an application package changes the development phase, many development activities are still required. It is still necessary to decide exactly what features are needed, to test the software, and to tailor parts of the documentation for use within the firm. The process of clarifying user requirements and evaluating packages from different vendors involves the same issues as the first part of the development phase in the traditional life cycle. Instead of writing a formal external specification, the project team invites vendors to present their products and to provide live demonstrations. These demonstrations may be set up like prototype installations, with a small number of users using the application package on real data to understand how it works.

The firm may perform benchmark testing. **Benchmarking** an application package involves running a test application with the same volumes of input, output, data access, and data manipulation that the final application will have. Benchmarking sometimes reveals that an application package performs the right processing but operates too slowly. To compare products systematically, the project team may issue a **request for proposal (RFP)**, which converts the ideas in the functional specification into a checklist of required capabilities and features. The vendors respond by explaining how their products meet the requirements.

Choosing among competing application packages is often difficult because each has advantages and disadvantages and few satisfy all user requirements. It may be unclear which features are or are not important. Business factors also matter, such as the vendor's financial strength and long-term viability. The selection process is based partially on information from vendors who emphasize their strengths and deemphasize weaknesses. Good vendors avoid selling poorly matched software, however, because unhappy customers usually hurt a vendor's reputation. Poorly matched software also has implementation problems that often waste vendor time and resources.

In competitive situations with large, expensive application packages, vendors often try to be the first one in the door and try to "help" the buyer analyze the business problem. They do this to influence the problem statement so that the vendor's product appears to be a better fit than a competitor's product. For example, if vendor A's product runs on the UNIX operating system and vendor B's runs on Windows NT, vendor A may try to influence the company to view a UNIX platform as a requirement. Simultaneously, vendor B might try to include features that are difficult to obtain through UNIX.

When all is said and done, it is always possible to argue about the requirements. In fact, they are the result of a process of learning about alternative ideas and deciding which ones seem most important. Different people doing the same task might come up with different requirements.

Regardless of how the requirements are developed, it is necessary to select a vendor and product. Consider a retailer deciding what payroll software to purchase. To make the selection, it has identified a series of important characteristics under various headings, including application features, technical features, vendor comparison, and economic comparison. The retailer wants to decide by evaluating each alternative in terms of each characteristic and then combining these scores. The more important characteristics have higher weighting in the final score. Box 12.2 illustrates this type of analysis. It weights each characteristic between 0 and 3 based on importance, evaluates each characteristic between 0 and 10 for each alternative, and calculates an overall score. Package B is preferred, but not by much.

In reality, the type of analysis in Box 12.2 is only an input to the decision and is often used as a sanity check to make sure that a significantly less preferable alternative is not chosen. One of many problems with over-reliance on a numerical comparison is that both the weightings and the ratings can be manipulated to some extent to give either of two close alternatives a slightly better score. Frequently, the real decision hinges on just several characteristics, such as whether the software runs on the right

---

SELECTING AN APPLICATION PACKAGE   BOX 12.2

The following table illustrates a common method for evaluating and comparing application packages. The results of this analysis are one of many types of information used in the selection. The table compares competing application packages A, B, and C based on four groups of characteristics. Each alternative has a score for each characteristic. For example, A has a score of 9 for completeness. Each characteristic also has a weight. For example, completeness has a weight of 2.5. The weighted score for each characteristic is the weight times the score. For example, the weighted score for completeness for A is 9 * 2.5 = 22.5. The total score for each alternative is the sum of its weighted scores. In this example, B is the preferred alternative with a total weighted score of 172.9.

CHARACTERISTIC	WEIGHT	A	B	C	A	B	C
			SCORE			WEIGHTED SCORE	
Application features							
completeness	2.5	9	7	8	22.5	17.5	20.0
quality of reports	1.0	9	5	9	9.0	5.0	9.0
ease of use	2.3	5	9	6	11.5	20.7	13.8
documentation	2.8	3	9	7	8.4	25.2	19.6
Technical features							
use of DBMS	2.8	8	7	3	22.4	19.6	8.4
transportability	0.8	2	5	6	1.6	4.0	4.8
expandability	1.2	4	5	5	4.8	6.0	6.0
Vendor comparison							
financial strength	2.0	9	7	5	18.0	14.0	10.0
management strength	1.3	6	9	8	7.8	11.7	10.4
commitment to product	2.6	4	7	9	10.4	18.2	23.4
Economic comparison							
purchase price	2.0	7	5	7	14.0	10.0	14.0
maintenance contract	1.5	7	7	8	10.5	10.5	12.0
consulting charges	0.6	5	6	8	3.0	3.6	4.8
conversion cost	2.3	5	3	5	11.5	6.9	11.5
Total weighted score					**155.4**	**172.9**	**167.7**

platform, whether the vendor is financially sound, and whether the vendor seems willing to change the software to suit the customer.

Implementation The implementation phase begins by deciding exactly how the application package will be set up and used. This decision is necessary because most application packages contain a broad range of options to satisfy different customers' needs. A typical approach is to set up a trial installation of the information system and compare the choices for the important options.

System documentation provided by the vendor must often be extended with a training manual tailored for a specific setting. For example, the vendor's manual may show how an order entry system works for a paper distributor. A hardware distributor's users will learn about it most easily if the examples in the training manual are about hardware products.

The conversion from the existing system to the new system requires the same types of planning and training needed in a traditional life cycle. One key difference is related to information system knowledge because the main experts on the purchased software are employees of the vendor rather than the firm that uses it. An expert on the software should be available during the implementation. The expert could be a vendor employee or a company employee who knows enough to troubleshoot problems that occur during implementation.

Operation and Maintenance Operation and maintenance for application packages is similar to this phase in the other approaches. Someone must be responsible for ensuring the information system operates efficiently on the computer and is used effectively in the organization. There must be a process for collecting enhancement requests and acting on them, and there must be a process for installing new software releases, starting with an analysis of their possible impact on users.

Application packages are unique because the vendor has the greatest expertise about the package and owns the responsibility for enhancing it. Most vendors enhance their products based on customer feedback and their own long-term plans. They typically send out new releases every 6 to 12 months. A **release** is an upgraded version of the software that the customer must install. Ideally, the vendor and customer should cooperate closely. The vendor should be available for questions and should base future enhancements on product usage. The vendor should respond quickly when bugs are found, especially if the bugs prevent users from doing their work. Figure 12.8 shows how the vendor's responsibilities fit into the phases of the system life cycle.

Product enhancements are a delicate issue in vendor-customer relationships. As happens with in-house development, vendors of application packages used in multiple sites soon have long lists of enhancement requests. Some of these require major prod-

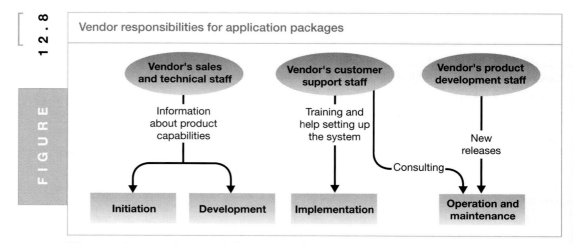

FIGURE 12.8

Vendor responsibilities for application packages

When an application package is used, the vendor's staff plays major roles at each phase of the system life cycle.

uct changes. Vendors usually work with their customers to identify the genuinely important enhancements. They also explain that many desired enhancements cannot be done. Managing relationships with vendors requires business and negotiation skills. These relationships require the ability to exert pressure to get the vendor to do what you want, but without having direct management authority over vendor personnel.

To protect themselves and their customers, vendors usually provide application packages under license agreements allowing the customer to use the software but not change it. To minimize dissatisfaction about receiving information in the wrong format, vendors usually provide database formats and links to 4GLs. These features help customers program their own reports, even if they are not permitted to change the transactions or database structure. Limiting customer changes prevents the customer from contaminating the database.

Advantages and Disadvantages

There are many reasons to purchase application packages. Benefits accrue sooner and the risks of cost and schedule overruns drop because the purchased software is available immediately, rather than months or years from now. Purchasing software helps a firm focus its resources on producing and selling whatever product or service it provides. Because the application package is the vendor's product, it will usually be documented and maintained better than in-house software. Vendors may also produce better features because they study the same problem in many companies. Finally, the firm's IS department may not have the knowledge, experience, or staffing necessary to produce the software.

With these advantages, purchasing an application package usually might seem a good choice. Unfortunately, the features in these products may not fit well. Firms using application packages often have to compromise on the business processes they want. As mentioned in reference to the Owens Corning and Kodak examples in Chapter 11, this has been an especially difficult issue for firms attempting to implement enterprise resource planning (ERP) systems. A rarely used alternative is to purchase application software and then modify it to suit local requirements. A key shortcoming of this alternative is that application vendors usually won't maintain software modified by customers. Even without customized changes, users of major application packages typically pay 10% to 15% of the package's purchase price per year for maintenance, support, and new releases.

Control of the long-term direction of the software is also an issue because the vendor makes that decision. Because many customers provide inputs about desired enhancements, individual customers may have little control over software that controls their business processes. In addition, there is the risk that the vendor will go out of business, leaving no reliable way to maintain the software.

Application packages require the company's IS staff to analyze, install, and maintain software developed elsewhere instead of developing new information systems themselves. IS professionals recognize that these evaluation and maintenance roles require knowledge and professionalism and are critical to the organization. However, these roles sometimes receive less professional credit and fewer accolades in the organization. Some IS staff members and users resent having to conform to product designs developed elsewhere. NIH ("not invented here") is often cited as a reason purchased software encounters problems.

Finally, although application packages can support specific data processing needs, they rarely provide sustainable competitive advantage because any competitor can usually buy the same package. Some firms have a strategy of using application packages for functions that don't provide competitive advantage but are necessary for running the business, such as accounting, payroll, and human resources. Acquiring application packages in these areas frees up resources for other applications that help differentiate the firm in its market.

The alternatives described thus far all assume that professional programmers will develop an information system for users. The next process assumes that the users are able to develop their own information systems.

END-USER DEVELOPMENT

In the 1980s, the term **end-user computing (EUC)** became popular as a description of computing that was truly the tool of the end user. EUC was originally viewed as the direct, hands-on use of computer systems by end users whose jobs go beyond entering data or processing transactions. The personal computer revolution of the 1980s made end-user computing possible through the use of personal productivity tools such as word processors, spreadsheets, online appointment calendars, electronic mail, and presentation software. Linkage of PCs into networks later permitted end-user computing to evolve and include many forms of everyday access to corporate data.

End-user development is a form of EUC in which users rather than programmers develop small data processing systems or models. Typical tools for end-user development include spreadsheets, DBMSs, 4GLs, and data analysis software. Figure 12.9 shows one of the capabilities that makes end-user development easier to perform.

End-user development became possible with the advent of spreadsheets and small DBMSs that could be used and controlled by people not trained as programmers. It is a partial solution to a severe overload problem in most IS departments, many of which have two-year backlogs of scheduled work. In this situation, users may feel it is pointless to request additional changes to existing systems, and the IS staff feels frustrated at not being able to provide good service. If the users could just change report formats or build small data processing systems, they would get more of what they want and the IS department's backlog would shrink. The technical staff would be more able to focus on major problems and opportunities, rather than continually changing old information systems. Table 12.6 outlines important aspects of this approach.

End-user development applies only where requirements for response time, reliability, and maintainability are not stringent; where the project is limited to a department and not on a critical path for other projects; and where proven technology is used. Unassisted end-user computing may be inappropriate even if high performance levels aren't needed. For example, the error rate in even simple spreadsheets is high because users often lack knowledge of testing methods needed to debug spreadsheets.

Phases

The phases of end-user development are based on the fact that the end user does the work and is responsible for the results.

Initiation   The user identifies a problem or opportunity that can be addressed with end-user technology. For example, a sales manager might need an information system

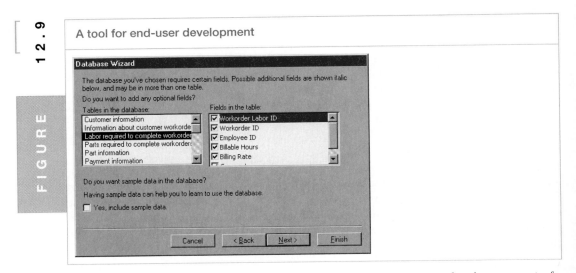

FIGURE 12.9

A tool for end-user development

In this example, tables from a sample service call management database are being used as the starting point for creating a service call management database tailored to a particular situation.

TABLE 12.6

System Life Cycle for End-User Development	
Phase	**Characteristics**
Initiation	Because the user will develop the information system, a formal functional specification is unnecessary.
Development	The user develops the system using tools that do not require a professional level of programming knowledge. Information systems that are critical to the company or have many users require more extensive testing, documentation, and usage procedures.
Implementation	Implementation is simplified because the developer is the user.
Operation and maintenance	End users are responsible. Long-term maintenance and technical quality become larger issues because the end users have other work to do and are not professional programmers.

for keeping track of sales prospects. Support staff may help in defining the problem more clearly and in identifying how the available tools can help. A functional specification is bypassed because the problem scope is small and because an explanation for someone else's approval is unnecessary.

Development   End users take responsibility for their own systems, deciding what they need and developing it using tools appropriate for them. Success often depends on the availability of IS staff who support the end-user developers with training and consulting. In most firms, end users must use computers and software supported by a central IS department. Figure 12.10 shows the various roles that the IS department plays in end-user development.

FIGURE 12.10

Roles in end-user development

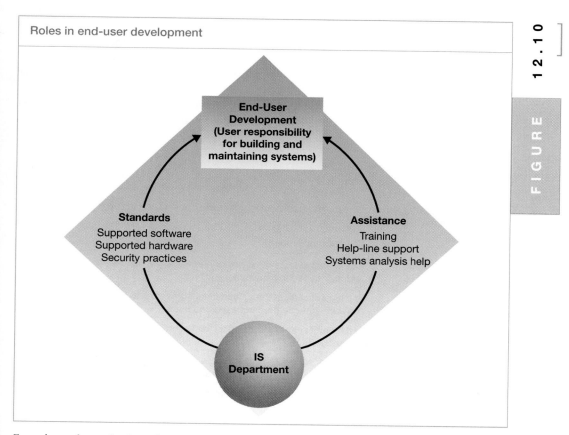

Even when end users develop and maintain systems, the IS staff plays many crucial roles in end-user development.

Implementation End-user development simplifies the implementation phase because the end user doesn't need training about the application. Training of other information system users is easier because an end user is an expert on both the system and how it fits into the department's business processes. Likewise, system acceptance may be less of an issue because end-user developers are so attuned to what is needed.

Operation and Maintenance End users are totally responsible for the operation and maintenance of systems developed through end-user development. They decide when and how these systems will be used and create whatever documentation is needed. They perform backups and are responsible for system security. End users also determine what enhancements and corrections are needed and make those changes. When those systems are critical to the company, controls must be enforced to establish system security and to maintain the systems.

Supporting the Users

Successful end-user computing must deal with a number of issues involving hardware, software, training, data availability, data security, and systems analysis (see Table 12.7).

Since end users are not hardware experts and have other work to do, the IS department typically supplies and manages computers and workstations. The IS staff produces guidelines about what equipment will be supported. This consistency makes the computers cheaper to acquire and service. Instead of acquiring computers and network components one at a time, firms can get volume discounts. Rather than trying to keep different types of computers operating, the firm's hardware staff can concentrate on one or several types. Similar issues arise for software. Although individuals might have their own favorite spreadsheet or word processor, using many different products is inefficient. Firms often arrange **site licenses**, blanket contracts covering the use of a particular software product at a particular site by a particular number of users. (The number of simultaneous users can be controlled through LANs that supply the software when needed.) Using only compatible software also makes it easier for users to work together. At minimum it eliminates obstacles to teamwork. Training is an area where restricting the hardware and software available to end users has important advantages. End-user training is often required for successful end-user computing. It is much easier to offer training and assistance for a small number of hardware and software choices.

Data availability is crucial when end-user applications need data residing on other computers. For example, consider a human resources manager who needs data to ana-

TABLE 12.7	Common Approaches to Issues in End-User Computing
	End-user computing raises many issues that should be handled consistently to avoid wasted effort by users and the IS staff.

Issue	Common approach
Hardware selection and maintenance	The IS staff selects the types of hardware that can be purchased and maintains the hardware.
Software selection	The IS staff selects the spreadsheet software and other end-user software that can be purchased and used.
Training	The IS staff provides training for end users on selected hardware and software.
Data availability	End users control their own data and share data using LANs. Corporate data are downloaded from central computers.
Data security	Limit access to only the data users need.
Systems analysis	Help end users with systems analysis and design where necessary. Provide help lines and other types of support.

lyze a proposed benefit program. Some of the data may reside elsewhere on a network and therefore may need to be downloaded. Greater access to data raises questions about data security. End-user computing entails security risks because end users have individual control over what they do with data. Downloading data to a workstation with a floppy disk drive makes it easier to steal data. Consequently, the data available to end users must be limited to what they legitimately need. This limitation is far from fool-proof, however, because many users need sensitive data, such as customer lists, pricing arrangements, and product design data.

End users often lack the system-related experience of IS professionals and need help in analyzing and designing systems and troubleshooting problems. Firms provide this help in various ways. Many deploy internal consultants to help end users by providing advice but not developing systems themselves. Many have set up help lines that can answer questions related to computers and systems. Many have established small groups that support end-user development by selecting and maintaining hardware and software, training end users, and providing consulting.

Advantages and Disadvantages

Compared to the complexity of the traditional life cycle, end-user development almost sounds too good to be true. It reduces the need for programmers and minimizes the problem of explaining requirements to people unfamiliar with the business. It eliminates the delays and political negotiations in resolving requirements and in implementing the system once it is developed.

Unfortunately, end-user development applies only to a limited set of situations. It works best where problems can be isolated from each other so that users can take full responsibility for both data and programs. Among other factors, the limitations of end-user development are related to the development tools used, the technical quality of the system, and the need for long-term maintenance. Because end users have other work to do and little time for learning to program, their tools are not the same as those designed for professional programmers. Many end users can use spreadsheets, small DBMSs, 4GLs, and statistical packages. Almost none can use programming languages or complex DBMSs requiring a professional level of involvement and understanding. Tools for trained programmers are needed to produce maintainable information systems involving shared databases and stringent response time or security requirements.

Technical quality is another issue for information systems built by end users. These systems are often less well designed and constructed than systems built by IS professionals. They are also more prone to bugs because end users are inexperienced in debugging. These issues may not be a problem in systems built for temporary, personal use by an individual, but matter greatly for systems with many users over a sustained period. Long-term maintenance is an especially important issue for complex applications involving many users. End-user developers may also find that long-term maintenance interferes with their primary job responsibilities. Like it or not, the support staff may be drawn into system maintenance roles when these situations occur.

R E A L I T Y C H E C K [✓]

End-User Development

This section explained end-user development and some of its advantages and disadvantages.

1. Think about your personal experience in developing spreadsheet models or doing other work related to computers. How comfortable would you feel if you had to develop a small system by yourself for keeping track of customers or calculating customer bills?

2. What kind of help do you think you would need?

DECIDING WHICH COMBINATION OF METHODS TO USE

The four system approaches described so far are idealized models, each involving different processes and emphasizing different issues. Understanding these issues helps in deciding what methods to use for a project. After comparing the advantages and disadvantages of the four alternatives, this section will conclude with ways to combine features of different processes into an approach appropriate for a particular situation.

Comparing Advantages and Disadvantages

Table 12.8 compares the advantages and disadvantages of the four alternatives. Many of the principal disadvantages of each approach are the mirror image of its principal advantages.

The traditional system life cycle establishes control to avoid developing information systems that miss the mark or are difficult to maintain. But these same controls are sometimes burdensome and may take on a life of their own. When this happens, the project team starts going through the motions of producing deliverables but puts less effort into responding to the users' changing needs.

Prototypes focus on helping users determine requirements based on real understanding. Rapid iterations of prototypes support this but often produce software that is more difficult to maintain than software designed carefully before programming begins. When the prototype takes shape, the users often wonder why they cannot put it into operation immediately. In addition, the process of simultaneously developing ideas and coding requires programmers and users who are willing and able to work iteratively.

Application packages keep company resources focused on the company's business, rather than on building information systems to support the company's business. But

TABLE 12.8

Advantages and Disadvantages of Four System Life Cycles

Life cycle	Advantages	Disadvantages
Traditional system life cycle	• Forces staff to be systematic by going through every step in an idealized process • Enforces quality by maintaining standards and reinforcing the expectation that the system will be produced to spec • Lower probability of missing important issues in the requirements analysis	• May produce excessive documentation; users feel buried in paperwork • Users are often unwilling or unable to study the specs that they approve • Takes too long to go from the original ideas to a working system • Users have trouble describing requirements for a proposed system
Prototype	• Helps clarify user requirements before the design is cast in concrete • Helps verify the feasibility of the design • Promotes genuine user participation in design • May produce part of the final information system	• May encourage inadequate problem analysis • User may not give up the prototype • May require "superprogrammers" • May generate confusion about whether or not the information system is complete and maintainable
Application package	• Software exists and can be tried out • Software has been used for similar problems elsewhere • Shortcuts delays for analysis, design, and programming • Has good documentation that will be maintained	• Controlled by another company that has its own priorities and business considerations • Package's limitations may prevent desired business processes • May be difficult to get needed enhancements if other companies using the package do not need those enhancements • Lack of intimate knowledge about how the software works and why it works that way
End-user development	• Bypasses the IS department and avoids delays • User controls the application and can change it as needed	• Creates fragile systems because an amateur does the programming • May eventually require consulting and maintenance assistance from the IS department

the company does not have complete control over how the package works. Business processes may have to change to conform to the logic built into the package. Furthermore, desired enhancements may never appear because the vendor's other customers may not find these enhancements important.

End-user development may be more responsive to end-user needs because it bypasses the IS department and avoids delays. However, it is only appropriate for systems that are limited in organizational scope, easy to debug, require little maintenance, and can be built using tools appropriate for end users.

Combining System Development Approaches

Although the four life cycle models might seem mutually exclusive, it is possible to combine their features into the approach for a given situation. Here are some ways to combine their features:

- Use a prototype as part of a traditional system life cycle. It may be difficult to produce a good functional specification or external specification without providing some hands-on experience. Therefore, include a prototyping phase in the original project plan, but insist that an internal specification be written as the basis for the internal design of the final information system.
- Use a small application package as a prototype. Shortcut the analysis process by purchasing an inexpensive application package and determining why it would or would not fit the situation. Identify required features it contains or lacks, as well as its unnecessary features. If it is well documented, use its documentation as a reference for clarifying business terminology and even helping the programmers understand an unfamiliar business situation.
- Adopt aspects of a traditional life cycle to purchasing an application package. Start with a functional specification. This makes it easier to evaluate alternative application packages. Purchasers of a packaged system can use appropriate parts of the traditional life cycle to be sure the problem is understood, the information system well tested, and the implementation well organized.
- Add an end-user development component to the traditional life cycle. Use the traditional life cycle to create the core of the information system based on a solid internal design and carefully controlled data updates. Develop user reports or inquiries using a 4GL that can be taught to users. Let the users develop their own reports using the original report programs as starting points and as demonstrations of good programming style. This maintains control of data while providing some of the advantages of end-user development. For complicated reporting requirements, use a programmer.

Other variations on the four life cycle models have been used but won't be covered in detail here. In the **phased approach**, the information system is built through a sequence of iterations of development, implementation, and operation. The idea is to address a small and manageable part of the problem, observe how this information system works, and then identify another small project that would lead to improvements but not have the risk of a lengthy project.

Joint application development (**JAD**) is another important variation. Its distinguishing feature is a carefully prepared two- to four-day meeting bringing together user representatives and IS staff members. At this meeting they analyze the business problem and come to a shared understanding of what must be done. JAD tries to eliminate misunderstandings that often persist despite lengthy user interviews during the analysis needed for functional specifications and external specifications. Bringing people together this way increases user participation and gives the user community a greater feeling of ownership for the information system. Some believe JAD also saves a lot of time that would be spent in a lengthy analysis.

However, some research on JAD has also found that JAD may not live up to its promise. In a genuine problem-solving dialogue, both business professionals and the system builders freely express their opinions, understandings, and concerns about the situation. One exploratory study found that JAD workshop activities were focused on system developers' models and terminology, and that the business area personnel were expected to participate on those terms with little or no training.[13]

There are clearly many ways to build systems. The four life cycle models are just that, models that express a particular approach. System builders applying any of these approaches should be aware of their advantages and disadvantages, and should develop a project plan that truly fits the situation.

CHAPTER CONCLUSION

What are the four phases of information system projects?

Any information system, regardless of how it is acquired, goes through four phases: initiation, development, implementation, and operation and maintenance. Initiation is the process of defining the need to change an existing work system, identifying the people who should be involved in deciding what to do, and describing in general terms how the work system should operate differently and how any information system that supports it should operate differently. Development is the process of building or acquiring and configuring hardware, software, and other resources needed to perform both the required IT-related functions and the required functions not related to IT. Implementation is the process of making a new or improved work system operational in the organization. Operation and maintenance is the ongoing operation of the work system and the information system, plus efforts directed at enhancing either system and correcting bugs.

What types of issues are addressed by the different system development processes?

The traditional system life cycle tries to solve a control problem by keeping the project on track. A prototype information system is a working model of the system built to learn about its true requirements. Firms acquire application packages to solve a resource and timing problem by using commercially available software that performs most of the functions desired. Firms use end-user development to solve a responsiveness problem involving the inability of information systems groups to keep up with changing information needs of individuals.

How does the traditional system life cycle solve the control problem of keeping a project on track?

The traditional system life cycle establishes a series of phases and steps with specific deliverables that must be completed before each step is completed. Key deliverables for the initiation phase include the functional specification and the project plan. For the development phase, they include the external and internal specifications, hardware plan, programs, testing plan, completion of system testing, and user and technical documentation. For implementation, they include the implementation plan, training materials, formal system acceptance, and post-implementation audit report. For operation and maintenance, they include the operations manual, maintenance plan, and completion of specific enhancements.

What are the advantages and disadvantages of prototypes?

The advantages of prototyping come from using a tangible working model instead of abstract specifications to clarify what the users need. During implementation, the system may be more on target than it would have been otherwise, and subsequent changes during operation may be reduced. However, developing a prototype may require exceptional developers and excessive involvement by key users. Users may not appreciate the incompleteness and technical fragility of a prototype.

What are the advantages and disadvantages of application packages?

Application packages reduce system development work, thereby reducing delays and helping a firm focus its resources on products or services it creates. They are often documented and maintained better than software built in-house and may provide better solutions. However, they often fit a firm's business processes only partially and the firm lacks long-term control of the package's direction.

What are the advantages and disadvantages of end-user development?

End-user development reduces the need for programmers, avoids the communication overhead of explaining the requirements to a technical staff, and eliminates the delays and political negotiations. However, it applies only to a limited set of situations and works best where problems can be isolated from each other so that users can take full responsibility for both data and programs. The resulting information systems are often less well-designed and more prone to bugs than systems built by IT professionals.

How is it possible to combine system development approaches into a system's life cycle?

A prototype can be used as part of a traditional system life cycle. A small application package can be used as a prototype to shortcut the analysis process. A structured approach can be used when purchasing an application package. An end-user development component can be added to the traditional life cycle.

runaway
initiation
development
implementation
operation and maintenance
traditional system life cycle
capability maturity model (CMM)
prototype
application package
end-user development
feasibility study
functional specification
project plan
detailed requirement analysis
external specification

internal system design
internal specification
hardware acquisition and
    installation
programming
unit testing
documentation
system testing
testing plan
implementation planning
training
conversion
phased approach
running in parallel
pilot implementation

acceptance testing
post-implementation audit
ongoing operation and support
operations manual
maintenance
throwaway prototype
evolutionary prototype
benchmarking
request for proposal (RFP)
release
end-user computing (EUC)
site license
phased approach
joint application development
    (JAD)

1. Identify the four phases any system goes through, and some of the common issues and problems that occur in each phase.

2. Why is it sometimes appropriate for a system project never to go past the initiation phase?

3. What are the links between the four phases and some of the reasons for rework of a previous phase?

4. Describe the four alternative approaches for building systems and the main issues addressed by each.

5. What different types of feasibility are considered in a feasibility study?

6. Identify the main deliverables from the development phase, and explain why other phases are necessary after development.

7. When in the traditional life cycle is user involvement greatest? Least?

8. What are the different approaches for converting from a previous system to a new system?

9. Explain reasons for using pilot implementations, acceptance testing, and post-implementation audits.

10. How is using a prototype different from using a traditional system life cycle?

11. What are the two types of prototypes?

12. Why is it still necessary for a firm to do a lot of systems analysis work when it purchases an application system?

13. What types of characteristics are considered when selecting among several application packages?

14. When working with an application package vendor with an established product, what might a firm expect to receive from the vendor during each of the four phases?

15. What are the advantages and disadvantages of using application packages?

16. Under what circumstances is end-user development appropriate?

17. Why do firms arrange site licenses with software vendors?

18. How is it possible to combine features of different life cycle models into the approach for building any particular system?

1. A code of ethics developed by three Swedish trade unions that organize computing personnel stated that computer professionals only take part in projects with the time and resources to do a good job, only develop systems in close collaboration with the user, and refrain from tasks aiming at control in ways that can be of harm to individuals.[14] Explain why you do or do not believe any computer professional would conform to these rules at all times.

2. Assume that your entire class had two months to write a single combined term paper. Within a broad guideline that the paper must be about some topic related to information systems, the class must decide on the topic and produce the paper. The class has asked you to decide how to do the project, what the steps will be, and who will do what work. What process would you propose? What problems or difficulties are likely to occur in this project as you have outlined it? Compare your approach to the traditional system life cycle, explaining major similarities and differences.

3. Based on the description of Microsoft's "synch and stabilize" model at the beginning of Chapter 9, explain where you think Microsoft is operating on the capability maturity model in Box 12.1.

4. The information systems manager at Balboa Hardware decided to take a stand. "We have had too many system failures. As of today, don't even think about a new information system unless you use a traditional system life cycle." Use the ideas in the chapter to explain the implications of this statement.

5. Should the development process for the different types of systems identified in Chapter 5 be different? If so, explain what the differences should be. If not, explain why there should be no differences. The answer in either instance should use ideas related to the alternative processes in this chapter.

6. Explain any relationships between the critical success factors method described in Chapter 11 and the various system development processes described in this chapter. If the relationships are unimportant, explain why.

Founded in Elkhart, Indiana, in 1904 as the Northern Indiana Brass Company, NIBCO Inc. is a leading provider of flow-control products such as fittings, pipe, valves, and actuators to residential and commercial construction, industrial, and irrigation markets. It is a privately held company with around 3,000 employees and revenues around $500 million.

In 1995 its management became concerned that its internal systems would not support the company's growth path because they relied on a hodge-podge of incompatible computer applications that could not communicate with each other. A strategic IT planning study with a consulting firm recommended that NIBCO replace its legacy systems with an ERP system on a client/server platform over a three- to five-year time frame. Further analysis by an internal committee led to a July 1996 recommendation that the company should go with SAP's R/3 system and should purchase modules for finance and controlling, material management and production planning, sales and distribution, and human resources. Contrary to consultant advice and prevailing wisdom, the committee recommended a "big bang" implementation in which all the modules (except human resources) would go live at the same time so that NIBCO could pursue its business goals without further delays. IBM was chosen as an implementation partner even though NIBCO believed it had not done a successful big-bang implementation up to that point. Three coleaders of the project were selected, with each focusing on one area but no one individual in charge. Business coordination and change management went to long-time NIBCO managers; technology went to an experienced CIO who had joined the company in 1995.[15]

Project kickoff occurred on September 30, 1996. The system was to go live at ten plants and four distribution centers on November 29, 1997, with a 30-day grace period. A great deal of the work would involve figuring out how to standardize what previously had been ten different ways of doing things in ten plants with ten different databases. The project team included three business process teams of seven or eight people, a change management team, and a technical team. The project team worked in a 50,000-square-foot open office. To avoid distractions, phones were in a hallway leading out of that area. Conversion from the existing legacy systems was an enormous task. Data from 85 files and a number of databases had to be cleaned up and loaded in order to test the data system with real data. No replacements were hired for important individuals who had moved from their primary responsibilities. This meant that others in their areas needed to take over the work they were previously doing. To compensate for the stress of doing so much extra work, the company created a bonus plan in which every salaried employee would receive a bonus depending on six criteria related to meeting the schedule and budget for the project. The November 29, 1997 date proved impossible because of delays in the consolidation of a number of distribution centers. In addition, it had been necessary to load the master data for manufacturing six times and more testing was needed.[16]

The new system did go live, on schedule, on December 30, 1997. The project leaders had worked hard on setting expectations around the difficulty of the project and the likelihood of disruptions. Transferring important managers to full-time project responsibility without replacing them did lead to lower productivity. Monthly shipments fell well below plan. According to one of the three project leaders, "It absolutely affected our financial performance. The business jogged; it didn't run." Ten weeks after the roll-out NIBCO was still in start-up mode in its financial, manufacturing, and sales management systems, and some users still wanted to go back to the way things were.[17]

Looking back on the project in late 1999, the CEO said, "We knew we wanted to go to an ERP system. . . . People hadn't heard the horror stories about SAP yet, but we've had no troubles. SAP has been well-suited to our needs. We rolled it out on Jan. 1, 1998, but getting there nearly killed us. We had at least 150 people assigned full-time to the project, and we brought it in on time and on budget. Our cost was $18 million, including training time, consultant time and our time. Our service to customers diminished during that time, but the pain was worth it."[18]

In July 2000, two and a half years after the big bang, NIBCO issued a statement in which its CEO said, "NIBCO has undergone a complete transformation in just a few years. We have integrated an SAP computer software infrastructure enterprise-wide, developed interactive Web sites with online ordering and other transactional capabilities for our customers, implemented

demand-pull manufacturing, focused on perfect order completion, and made other strategic moves to position NIBCO for leadership in the 21st century." The company called its new way of doing business eNIBCO. The CEO said this was a platform to provide better and stronger service. The platform includes

- NIBCO.com, an informational Web site providing complete product information, current price sheets, product brochures, catalogs, and specification guides
- NIBCOpartner.com, a secure Web site providing real-time access to customer-sensitive information and fast online order processing anytime, day or night
- EDI, which allows customers to enter orders via the exchange of standardized electronic business forms
- Vendor-managed inventory, which reduces customer overhead by transferring to NIBCO responsibility for customer inventory management, order entry, and forecasting.[19]

QUESTIONS

1. How is this case related to the issues raised in the previous chapter on IS planning?

2. How is this case related to the four phases of a system illustrated in Figure 12.1 and the four system life cycle approaches summarized in Table 12.2?

3. The text discussed some of the common issues in the implementation phase. Explain whether these issues were present in this case, whether other issues were present, and how they were handled.

4. In what ways do the developments described in the July 2000 statement seem to rely on the SAP implementation? In what ways do they not rely on it?

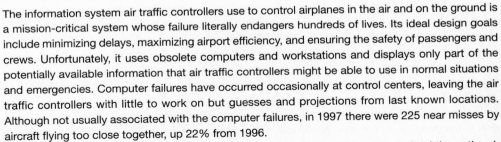

C A S E   **FAA: Trying to Overhaul the Air Traffic Control System**

The information system air traffic controllers use to control airplanes in the air and on the ground is a mission-critical system whose failure literally endangers hundreds of lives. Its ideal design goals include minimizing delays, maximizing airport efficiency, and ensuring the safety of passengers and crews. Unfortunately, it uses obsolete computers and workstations and displays only part of the potentially available information that air traffic controllers might be able to use in normal situations and emergencies. Computer failures have occurred occasionally at control centers, leaving the air traffic controllers with little to work on but guesses and projections from last known locations. Although not usually associated with the computer failures, in 1997 there were 225 near misses by aircraft flying too close together, up 22% from 1996.

In 1981 the Federal Aviation Administration (FAA) proposed a project to overhaul the entire air traffic control system by building the Advanced Automation System (AAS) with an initial installation in Seattle in 1992. In 1984 IBM Federal Systems and Hughes were chosen as finalists for the contract. After three years and $500 million of FAA expenditures on prototypes, the FAA selected IBM's $3.6 billion fixed-cost contract in 1988. The Government Accounting Office (GAO) warned that this was unrealistically low. The FAA pushed for an unprecedented 99.99999% reliability, no more than three seconds of downtime per year. Contrary to the wishes of the air traffic controllers, who wanted to retain paper strips they used to chart the progress of planes, the FAA wanted to accomplish the same type of function with a few keystrokes in a totally paperless environment. This was not achieved with the available technology. A report in 1992 found significant technical flaws in the work to date, including the inability to reach the required peak load of 210 coordinated consoles in a single facility. Six months later, IBM announced a 14-month delay. The FAA and IBM both proposed a number of changes and finally agreed to freeze technical requirements by April 1993. Later that year, Loral purchased IBM Federal Systems.

In 1994 a new FAA administrator revamped the AAS team and later threw out major portions of the AAS design, deciding to emphasize Display System Replacement (DSR) in a new contract with Loral. A mock-up of the new display caused major controversy at the 1995 air traffic controllers' convention because it did not adequately handle the paper strips used to chart the progress of the planes. In 1994 the FAA administrator also launched a project to use global positioning satellites to make sure that aircraft would not fly on collision courses. An initial system design by one contractor was deemed unreliable in 1995 and a $475 million contract went to Hughes Electronics in 1996 to continue the work. The FAA administrator left the government in 1996. During 1996 and 1997 the scope of the technical requirements expanded to include as many as six new satellites and additional navigation aids on each airplane, including 180,000 small, general aviation planes. By 1998 the future of this project was in doubt.[20, 21]

Meanwhile, work continued on the new terminals for air traffic controllers. On March 5, 1998, the next FAA administrator testified that the FAA was closer to solving what air traffic controllers described as a hazardous flaw in the new hardware and software the agency planned to install nationwide starting in late 1998 or 1999. The controllers had complained that the design of the Standard Terminal Automation Replacement System (STARS) might hinder air traffic control because the system's windowing software frequently blocks icons that represent aircraft on the screen. In February 1998, a human factors team had solved 87 of 98 remaining issues. The administrator said, "I am optimistic that all the human factors issues will be resolved."[22] In May 2000, the FAA announced it would spend $270 million to address long-standing complaints from air traffic controllers about the design of STARS. The decision to modify STARS came after two years of discussions by the FAA, STARS contractor Raytheon Co., the air traffic controllers, and air traffic systems specialists about "human factors" in the design of air traffic displays and workstations.[23]

QUESTIONS

1. How are these problems related to the ideas about planning and building information systems in Chapters 11 and 12?

2. Some observers cite the actual safety record of air traffic in arguing that the FAA's problems have not been a direct cause of airliner crashes and therefore are overstated. Explain why you agree or disagree.

3. What do you believe the FAA should do now?

E-Business Security and Control

chapter13

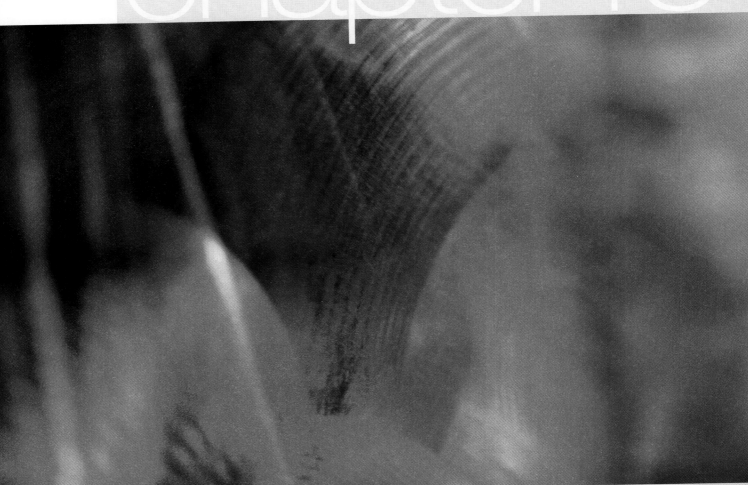

STUDY QUESTIONS

- What are the main types of risks of accidents related to information systems?
- What are the different types of computer crime?
- What issues magnify the vulnerability of information systems to accidents and crime?
- What measures can be taken to minimize accidents and computer crime?
- What are the different ways to control access to data, computers, and networks?
- What is public key encryption and what is its advantage over private key encryption?
- What is the role of a certification authority in e-commerce?

Threat of Accidents and Malfunctions
Operator Error
Hardware Malfunctions
Software Bugs
Data Errors
Accidental Disclosure of Information
Damage to Physical Facilities
Inadequate System Performance
Liability for System Failure

Threat of Computer Crime
Theft
Sabotage and Vandalism

Factors That Increase the Risks
The Nature of Complex Systems
Human Limitations
Pressures in the Business Environment

Methods for Minimizing Risks
Controlling Software Development and
Modifications

Providing Security Training
Maintaining Physical Security
Controlling Access to Data, Computers, and
Networks
Controlling Traditional Transaction Processing
Maintaining Security in Web-Based
Transactions
Motivating Efficient and Effective Operation
Auditing the Information System
Preparing for Disasters

Chapter Conclusion
Summary
Key Terms
Review Questions
Discussion Questions
Cases

E-Business Security and Control

OPENING CASE

VISA ADVISES EXTRA PRECAUTIONS FOR ONLINE MERCHANTS

According to a July 2000 survey by the Gartner Group, online merchants suffer 12 times the rate of credit card fraud that typical retail merchants suffer. About 1.1% of online credit card transactions involve stolen credit cards, and the online merchants have to absorb these losses themselves because credit card companies will not absorb losses unless the charge occurred in a face-to-face transaction that generated a signed receipt. First Data Corp., the largest U.S. credit card processor, said that 1.25% of all Internet transactions are disputed by customers, compared with 0.33% of catalog transactions by phone and mail and 0.14% of storefront retail transactions. An earlier survey by ActivMedia found a much lower level of credit card fraud in Web commerce and concluded that the Web sites most susceptible to fraud dealt in high-price merchandise that can easily be resold, such as electronics equipment and jewelry.[1, 2]

In an attempt to reduce the level of online credit card fraud, in August 2000 Visa U.S.A. announced "10 com-

mandments" for online merchants, and said merchants would have to follow their rules or suffer fines or other restrictions.[3] The requirements included maintaining a network firewall, keeping security patches current, encrypting stored data, using updated antivirus software, restricting data access on the basis of need to know, assigning a unique ID to each employee with data access, using original passwords, tracking data access by ID, and regularly testing security systems and processes.[4]

These commandments went beyond the previous Visa statements about how merchants should handle "card-not-present" transactions. Basic card acceptance procedures included asking for the card expiration date, asking for an additional validation number on the back of a Visa card, and using an address verification service to check the cardholder's billing address as a way to detect possible fraud. Another step is training employees to recognize suspicious behavior such as strange hesitation by the customer, unusual rush orders, customers unconcerned about product features, and suspicious shipping addresses.[5] Internet merchants were also advised to at least watch out for first-time shoppers, larger than normal orders, orders of big-ticket items, orders coming through free e-mail services that have no billing relationship or audit trail, and orders to international addresses that cannot be verified using an address verification service. With access to an internal history of transactions it could also be possible to watch for unusual characteristics such as multiple transactions shipped to a single address but made on multiple cards, multiple transactions over a very short period, and multiple cards used from a single IP address.[6]

WEB CHECK [✓]

Look at the Web sites for MasterCard and American Express to see whether they give advice to online merchants and whether it is different from the advice Visa offers.

DEBATE TOPIC

Guidelines such as the ones Visa suggests for its merchants cast suspicion on perfectly legitimate customers and may make their shopping experience unpleasant.

e ven though this book's first twelve chapters mentioned many problems that have occurred with computerized systems, those chapters emphasized the great progress that has been made not only in technology, but also in attaining personal and organizational benefits through information systems. To round out the picture, this chapter focuses on problems that may occur with these systems, and on approaches for minimizing these problems.

The Visa case is about Web-based purchase transactions, but it introduces many of the issues the chapter discusses. How can a company that relies on e-business assure the security of e-business systems? How can it avoid fraud? How can it do these things without establishing security procedures that undermine its business by absorbing too much attention and by causing too much inconvenience?

This chapter starts by discussing system threats that are related to accidental causes such as operator error and incorrect data. Next it looks at threats related to computer crime. It then explains a value chain for reducing those threats. The very large number of examples throughout the chapter illustrate the threats are widespread and are not restricted to situations involving inept management. No system is foolproof, but careful use of security and control methods reduces the risks substantially and increases the likelihood of enjoying the benefits.

THREAT OF ACCIDENTS AND MALFUNCTIONS

Many people assume that information systems will work as they are designed to work, that they will operate reliably, and that the information generated will be correct. When these assumptions are proven wrong, the consequences can be disastrous. This section looks at risks of accidents originating from eight causes: operator error, hardware malfunctions, software bugs, data errors, accidental disclosure of data, damage to physical facilities, inadequate system performance, and liability for system performance.

To help visualize the range of risks from accidents, Figure 13.1 assigns each type of risk to one element of the framework. Do not assume that each type of accident is totally caused by the element it is associated with, however. For example, saying that a particular accident involved operator error might seem to imply participants are at fault. But the technology might have been difficult to use and the business process might have been designed based on unrealistic assumptions about human capabilities. Interactions between causes of accidents is a key point as we look at each type of accident in turn.

W O R K   S Y S T E M   S N A P S H O T
Authorizing an online purchase transaction

CUSTOMERS

- Customers purchasing items online

PRODUCTS & SERVICES

- Completion of the online purchase transactions

BUSINESS PROCESS

- Customer decides what to buy and puts it in an online shopping cart.
- Online application calculates total price.
- Customer fills in credit card number, expiration date, shipping address, and other information relevant to the purchase.
- Merchant decides whether to authorize the purchase.
  - Check whether credit card is stolen
  - Check customer purchase history if available
  - Check the credit card's billing address, if appropriate
  - Identify any suspicious aspects of the order and take appropriate action

PARTICIPANTS	INFORMATION	TECHNOLOGY
• Customers purchasing items online • Order-processing staff at merchant	• Items in this purchase transaction • Shipping address • Customer purchase history • Credit card information • Additional validation information	• Customer's PC and browser • Merchant's server and e-commerce software • Internet infrastructure

Operator Error

A prime cause of accidents is **operator error**, a combination of inattention, nonconformance to procedures, or other error by participants in a system. A disastrous example occurred in 1995 when an American Airlines jet crashed into a mountain while approaching Cali, Colombia. Because winds were calm, an air traffic controller had offered the pilot an unusual route while descending into Cali to help make up time lost due to a delay taking off from Miami. The pilot or copilot tried to "reprogram the onboard computer using a radio beacon at an intermediate point, Rozo, but erroneously entered only the letter 'R,' not the full name, as is required for that beacon. The letter 'R' identified 'Romeo,' another beacon on the same frequency but 132 miles northeast of Cali." The pilot was supposed to verify the data, but did not, and the plane turned onto an incorrect course. About a minute later the crew recognized something was wrong and tried to turn back toward Cali. They continued their descent even though they did not find a navigational beacon that they should have passed. Although not blaming the air traffic controller, an inquiry's report noted "he knew something was wrong because the pilots' requests 'made little sense,' but he was unable to tell the pilots his suspicions 'because of limitations in his command of English.'"[7]

A careful study of accidents in complex systems such as nuclear plants, dams, tankers, and airplanes found that 60% to 80% of major accidents were attributed to operator error, but that many factors other than operator carelessness contributed to the problems. These factors included flawed system design, poor training, and poor

FIGURE 13.1

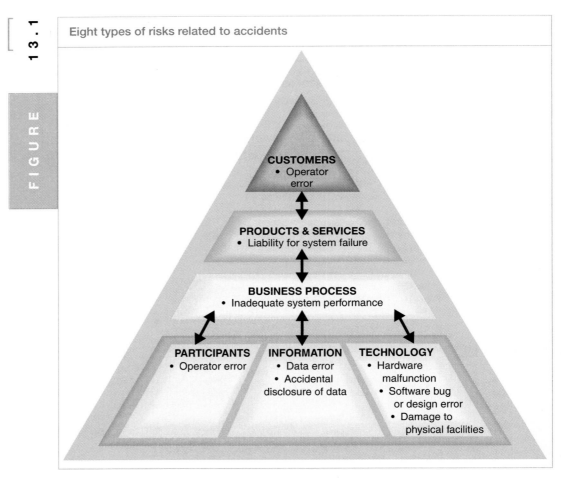

Eight types of risks related to accidents

Eight types of risks related to accidents can be associated with individual elements of the framework although the cause of the problem is often a combination of factors.

quality control.[8] One of that study's main examples was the partial meltdown at the Three Mile Island nuclear plant in Pennsylvania. A commission blamed the problem on operator error, but the operators were confronted with enormously complex technical systems, incomplete or contradictory information, and the necessity to make decisions quickly. The nature of the system increased the likelihood of operator error. The same thing happened in the flight to Cali. In fact, a federal jury found that American Airlines was only 75% responsible for the crash and assigned 17% of the blame to the navigational software company and 8% to the computer manufacturer because printed charts for the area contained information conflicting with the computer's database.[9]

Several factors magnify the risk of operator error. It is often difficult to anticipate how systems will really work in practice and how users will adapt to them. User adaptations and shortcuts may cause errors the designers never imagined. In addition, people tend to become complacent when a system seems to operate correctly. They begin to assume it will continue to operate correctly and put less energy and care into checking for errors. Who would anticipate that a pilot would enter the wrong code, or that the code R would stand for Romeo, 132 miles away, rather than Rozo, which was nearby? And who would have anticipated that an astronaut on the Mir space station would nearly cause a disaster by accidentally disconnecting a cable, thereby shutting down the computer that kept the Mir's solar panels facing the sun?[10] Obviously, "the system" should have prevented these things from happening. The main point is that all systems are vulnerable to human error.

R E A L I T Y C H E C K [✓]

Operator Error

This section mentioned that 60% to 80% of major accidents examined in one study were attributed to operator error, but that many factors other than carelessness contribute to operator error.

1. Identify times you or your acquaintances have been guilty of operator error in everyday life, for example by accidentally erasing an audio tape or by backing up when intending to go forward.

2. What factors caused the operator error in these cases? Was it ever caused by poor equipment design that somehow increased the likelihood of operator error?

Hardware Malfunctions

Although significant hardware malfunctions are becoming more and more infrequent as computer technology improves, these problems do occur occasionally. A highly embarrassing hardware flaw was publicized in late 1994 when Intel acknowledged that the division function of its Pentium microprocessor occasionally calculated incorrect answers on divisions involving more than five significant digits. Consider the following calculation:

$$4,195,835 - (4,195,835 / 3,145,727) * 3,145,727$$

Basic algebra says the answer should be zero since $a - (a \div b) * b = 0$, but the flawed Pentiums gave the answer 256. Intel had known about this problem for months before it became public but had downplayed it because most users don't do division calculations with five significant digits. Intel eventually took a $475 million write-off to account for replacing defective chips. The previous 386 and 486 chips also had math errors that were corrected.[11]

A far more frequent source of hardware malfunctions is incompatibilities between different components that are assembled in a single device or system. A *New York Times* reporter received an angry call from a colleague who had purchased an IBM Thinkpad 560 laptop based on his favorable comments about this product. The laptop crashed continually, often losing data. The IBM service facility replaced the motherboard under warranty, but the problem persisted. Eventually IBM found that the problem was an optional, non-IBM memory module the dealer had added. This module worked fine with other IBM notebooks but was incompatible with certain power-saving peculiarities of the Toshiba chips used in this particular model.[12]

Even very minor components sometimes cause significant problems. In October 2000, Dell recalled 27,000 Sanyo batteries for notebook PCs because those batteries could short circuit and cause a fire. Dell isn't the only PC maker to announce a recall in 2000. In May 2000, IBM and one of its suppliers announced a recall of 220,000 AC adapters used with its notebook computers.[13]

Another frequent and noticeable site for hardware failure is the electrical power and telecommunication networks that provide the infrastructure needed by computerized systems. For example, the entire NASDAQ stock exchange went down for 34 minutes in 1994 because a squirrel shorted out a power line despite the local electric utility's previous attempts "to improve the squirrel-proofing of power lines in the heavily wooded area" near the computer center.[14]

Vulnerability to hardware malfunctions is often magnified by user disbelief that hardware can malfunction. As evidenced by several airplane and nuclear plant accidents, it may be unclear whether the malfunction is in the hardware or in the warning system. Furthermore, as software functions are integrated into hardware, what is seen as hardware can have bugs just like software.

Software Bugs

A **software bug** is a flaw in a program that causes it to produce incorrect or inappropriate results. The Y2K problem introduced in Chapter 1 was an enormously expensive group of bugs related to the same problem—the fact that computers had been programmed to perform many date-related calculations incorrectly around the year 2000 because of the tradition of coding the year with two digits rather than four to save space in the computer's memory or in storage media. IS staffs of large companies with aging legacy systems looked forward to the year 2000 with trepidation because the transition from 1999 to 2000 might have revealed previously undetected bugs that had lain dormant for decades in undocumented programs. The U.S. Internal Revenue Service alone spent approximately one billion dollars on the Y2K problem. If it had not been fixed on time, tax returns would have gone unprocessed, refunds would not have been sent, and taxpayers might have been told they owe 99 years interest on disputed deductions. The project of reducing the likelihood of these problems required the IRS staff to analyze 88,000 programs containing 60,000,000 lines of computer code that was up to 30 years old.[15]

Isolated software bugs have caused significant financial losses even in large, well-run organizations. Examples mentioned earlier include the telecommunications software bug that crippled AT&T long distance networks for a day in 1990 and 1998 (see Chapter 6) and the guidance system bug that destroyed an Ariane 5 rocket in 1996 (see Chapter 9). Complex models are also susceptible to bugs. The Bank of Tokyo-Mitsubishi reported that its New York-based financial derivatives trading unit had lost $83 million in 1997 because its computer model undervalued its position.[16]

Software bugs are a fundamental problem with computerized systems because there are no infallible methods for proving that a program operates correctly. The best-tested software may still have bugs after testing is complete. Even if it were possible to prove that a program operates correctly relative to its design specs, there is no guarantee that it will operate correctly under unanticipated circumstances. This was certainly illustrated by the example in Chapter 3 concerning the missile detection system that warned of an impending nuclear attack after spotting the moon rising over the Soviet Union.

Data Errors

Data errors are another source of risk. Information systems in everyday life frequently contain errors such as incorrect phone numbers or addresses. It is possible to check for some errors automatically, such as determining whether a number is within a specified range or whether a ZIP code is valid. Unfortunately, validity checks such as these cannot detect many errors. For example, a system that checks whether an employee's age is between 18 and 70 usually cannot determine that 12/10/54 was entered accidentally instead of 10/12/45. This shows why many errors due to carelessness and inattention cannot be detected automatically.

Seemingly small data errors sometimes have major impacts. In 1996, the 20231 ZIP code used exclusively by the U.S. Patent and Trademark Office was somehow canceled by the Washington, D.C., post office. Nobody noticed for several weeks until Mobil Corporation called to ask why time-sensitive applications it had sent to the patent office had been returned unopened, but containing a stamp saying that the ZIP code had been discontinued. An estimated 50,000 letters to the patent office were returned this way before the problem was rectified.[17] An address-related problem also occurred at Network Solutions, Inc., the company that controls Internet addresses. Because a computer operator ignored alarms warning of problems with the computer that updates these addresses, corrupted address data was sent to ten other computers that transmit messages to machine addresses across the network. Thousands or even millions of attempts to send e-mail or access Web pages may have failed.[18]

Data errors have even impacted the stock market. A clerical error on March 25, 1993 caused a 12-point drop in the New York Stock Exchange's Dow Jones index in the last few minutes of trading. An institutional investor had sent Salomon Brothers a computerized order to sell $11,000,000 of stock spread over 400 companies. A Salomon

Brothers clerk entered this order incorrectly, typing 11,000,000 in the "shares" box rather than the "dollars" box on a data entry screen. The system automatically allocated the 11,000,000 shares among the companies and generated individual sell orders. The sell orders for under 99,999 shares of individual stocks on the New York Exchange were handled automatically by SuperDot, the Exchange's small-order system. Larger orders and orders for stocks on the NASDAQ exchange went to traders who looked at the size of the orders, concluded they were mistakes, and canceled them. The estimated cost of the error for Salomon Brothers was at least $1 million to repurchase shares sold and make up for lower prices received.[19]

Significant data errors are sometimes caused by malfunctions of automatic sensors. In a disastrous example in 1996, 70 people died in an Aeroperu plane crash because maintenance workers who were polishing the plane forgot to remove tape and paper covers applied over pressure sensors that are about one inch in diameter. Just before the crash, the pilot radioed that his instruments had gone haywire. One automatic system indicated the plane was flying too slowly and would fall out of the sky while another sounded an alarm because the plane was flying to fast. When the plane hit the water, the captain's instruments were showing an altitude of 9,500 feet. People examining the wreck found masking tape over the sensors. To avoid a repetition, Boeing planned to manufacture brightly colored covers for the pressure sensors.[20]

Some data errors are related to the incentives that motivate people to enter incorrect data. One manufacturer developed a system that consolidated all records by customer number. Late in the project it discovered that salespeople created a new customer number for each sale, even to existing customers, because they received larger commissions for opening new accounts. The company scrapped the project after discovering the database contained more than 7,000 customer numbers for McDonnell Douglas, a single large customer.[21]

Accidental Disclosure of Information

The widespread usage of the Web and e-mail have led to an increasing number of situations in which private data is accidentally disclosed to people who shouldn't have it. For example, the Internet retailer Buy.com accidentally disclosed a small amount of customer information when it installed a UPS online returns service that prints labels shoppers can attach to packages they want to return. The UPS application automatically generates a Web page containing the label, but when a customer changed a single number in that page's URL, another customer's data appeared. The glitch occurred because Buy.com initially provided the customer information to the UPS application in sequential order.[22]

In that case the problem involved the details of an interface between two systems and could be fixed easily. A number of other similar examples have occurred. H&R Block had to shut down its online tax service after an upgrade accidentally allowed several customers to import data belonging to other customers.[23] In another situation, the HMO Kaiser Permanente accidentally e-mailed personal medical information for 858 patients to 19 e-mail addresses when it tried to fix an e-mail response system that had become backlogged. Kaiser concluded the problem was a combination of human and technical mistakes.[24]

Damage to Physical Facilities

Physical facilities and equipment may be vulnerable to a wide range of environmental threats and external events. In the last few years, computer facilities have been damaged by fires, floods, hurricanes, and earthquakes. Computer and telecommunications equipment may be disabled by power failures and network breakdowns occurring far from the site. For example, 5,000 ATMs across the nation shut down for a week because a snowstorm collapsed the roof of an Electronic Data Systems data center in New Jersey.

Damage to physical facilities doesn't require a natural catastrophe. In 1991, a telephone maintenance crew accidentally cut a fiber optic cable that provided 40% of New

York City's long distance service. Because an AT&T operations center had not been notified that the work was being done, computers had not been programmed to give priority to data transmissions for air traffic control. Consequently, New York's three main airports lost their long-range radar for 102 minutes. Several days later, a U.S. Sprint cable broke, disrupting calls to and from Chicago.[25] In another example, airborne dust from a 1997 ceiling renovation made it hard to breathe at a New York air traffic control center, forcing it to rotate crews and operate on a limited basis for almost 10 hours. This set off cascading delays that affected air travel across the United States and caused the cancellation of 150 flights.[26] In all three cases, individuals and businesses were affected by events miles from their facilities. Firms relying on information systems need to protect their own facilities and need to prepare for impacts of problems elsewhere.

Damage to physical facilities can occur in space just as they occur on earth. As mentioned in a case following Chapter 1, computer malfunctions on a Galaxy 4 satellite operated by PanAmSat caused a communications satellite to face away from the earth. Until another satellite could be moved into a similar orbit, this mishap disrupted most of the pager service in the United States and disabled business operations, such as credit card payments at the gas pumps of 5,400 Chevron gas stations.[27, 28]

Inadequate System Performance

Inadequate system performance occurs when a system cannot handle the task that is required of it. The London Ambulance Service example at the end of this chapter is certainly a case in point. In that example, lives were lost because an ambulance-dispatching system could not get the ambulances to people who needed them. Another highly visible example occurred during the stock market crash of October 19, 1987. The New York Stock Market's "real-time" information system of stock prices ran two hours late as more than 500 million shares of stock were traded, three times the average daily volume at that time. Investments during the 1990s brought the NYSE's capacity to over 1.4 billion shares per day, but some delays were still experienced at the brokerage firms on the busiest days.

Inadequate uptime performance has become a bane of e-commerce firms. Schwab, eTrade, eBay, and many other leading firms have suffered a number of embarrassing outages during which their Web sites were not available for business. For example, when a 22-hour outage followed two other outages, eBay's stock dropped significantly and it had to refund $3 million to $5 million to customers who had listed goods on the site before it crashed. Some angry customers jumped to competitors, and Auctions, Amazon Auctions, and Auction Universe all reported a 50% increase in traffic in the days after the eBay crash.[29]

Liability for System Failure

Liability is legal responsibility for one's actions or products. Every type of accident mentioned thus far can result in a liability claim against a firm or individual. This is an especially serious potential problem in medical systems. One of the most widely repeated stories about the dangers of poorly debugged programs concerns several deaths and other severe injuries caused in the mid-1980s by the Therac-25, a computer-controlled linear accelerator used for radiation therapy. Due to a software bug, resetting the machine from one operational mode to another caused massive overdoses of radiation under some conditions.[30] Potential liability is one of the reasons most medical expert systems have remained research tools rather than common tools for doctors. Whoever created or sold such a system might be held liable if it produced an incorrect diagnosis.

Liability is also an issue in business software. In 1994, Kane Carpet Co. of Secaucus, N.J., sued in court to prove that after 22 consecutive profitable years and growth up to $90 million in sales, it had gone out of business due to flaws in an inventory system it purchased from McDonnell Douglas. Although the system seemed to work well at a flooring company in Houston, within a week of its installation in 1989

Kane experienced severe problems filling orders and quoting correct prices and credit terms.[31]

Liability for products sold through online auction sites is a major issue in e-commerce. For example, a California lawsuit asserted that eBay had the responsibility to ensure authenticity of sports memorabilia sold through its online auctions. The specific items in this case were baseballs and other items with forged signatures. EBay argued that it is only a venue for sales and that it couldn't possibly offer an auction market for consumers if it would have to verify every item auctioned. The outcome of the suit hinged on the judge's interpretation of two laws. A 1992 California law on sports memorabilia forbids dealers and auctioneers to represent items as collectibles if they contain forged signatures. The United States Telecommunications Act of 1996 says that ISPs are not liable for material sent over their networks.[32]

Liability related to information systems is complex because so many different things can go wrong. Given the potential for product liability lawsuits, software vendors are usually careful to avoid claiming their software is bug-free. Their license agreements usually state that any problems resulting from the use of the software are the user's fault.

The eight types of risk mentioned thus far are all related to things that go wrong accidentally. Before discussing security measures that reduce these risks, the next section will look at computer crime, which is anything but accidental.

REALITY CHECK ✓

Risks Related to Accidents

This section gave examples of eight different types of risks related to accidents.

1. Look at the categories and identify an example of each type of problem or something similar that you have personally encountered, regardless of whether a computer was involved.

2. Explain why you do or do not believe there is anything unique about the way these problems arise in relation to computerized systems.

THREAT OF COMPUTER CRIME

Computer crime is the use of computerized systems to perform illegal acts. It can be divided into two main areas: theft, and sabotage and vandalism. Computer pranks are included as illegal activities because they often have at least the potential for significant harm. Also, they may be difficult to differentiate from sabotage and other forms of destructive behavior.

Computer crime is growing more worrisome as computerized systems become more pervasive. The potential for significant damage to commercial interests and national defense through computer viruses and other forms of computerized sabotage has been demonstrated clearly. Weaknesses exploited often involve technical gaps between what a computer system is capable of enforcing and what it is expected to enforce. Other weaknesses involve gaps between computer policies, social policies, and human behavior.

Despite its seriousness, computer crime is not treated in the same way in our society as other types of crime. Perhaps this is because the perpetrators seem less physically threatening to victims than other criminals. Perhaps it is because companies victimized by computer crime are hesitant to suffer adverse publicity. Regardless of the cause, to date many convicted computer criminals have received mild treatment. In some cases, they have even taken jobs as security consultants after receiving minor punishments.

There is no single profile for computer criminals. They range from application programmers and clerical personnel to managers and accountants. In general, perpetrators of computer crime can be divided into employees, outsiders, and hackers. *Employees* use their knowledge of how a business operates to identify opportunities for theft or sabotage and to obtain easy access to the resources they need for their criminal activity. *Outsiders* often have a somewhat more difficult task because they must learn how to penetrate a system without having easy access to information about how it works. **Hackers** are less concerned about personal gains or damage they might cause. Instead, they may commit computer crime for the "fun" or intellectual challenge of breaking into a computer. Although outsiders and hackers tend to receive more attention in the press, employees are the perpetrators of most computer crimes.

As illustrated in Figure 13.2, the vulnerable points in computerized systems include people and procedures in addition to hardware, software, and data. A detailed look at many cases that are called computer crime reveals that the computer played a relatively small role compared to the role of bypassed procedures and forged transaction documents. Most of the following examples might have been stopped through better organizational procedures and safeguards.

Theft

Computer-related theft can be divided into six categories: theft of software and computer equipment, unauthorized use of access codes and financial passwords, theft by entering fraudulent transaction data, theft by stealing or modifying data, Internet hoaxes for illegal gains, and theft by modifying software.

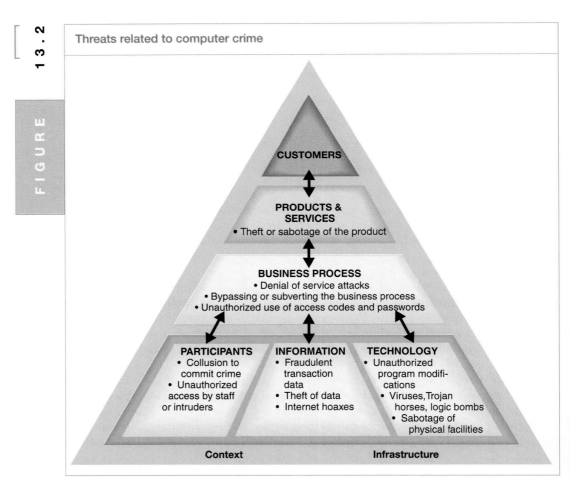

FIGURE 13.2

Threats related to computer crime

Various types of threats related to computer crime can be associated with individual elements of the framework although computer crimes often involve a combination of factors.

Theft of Software and Equipment   Theft of software and computer equipment has become a major problem for hardware and software manufacturers and for companies that use computer equipment. Part of the temptation is that software, chips, and computer equipment are both small and valuable. On November 10, 1997, armed robbers stole an estimated 200,000 certificates of authenticity and 100,000 CD-ROMs from a Microsoft manufacturing facility in Scotland. The certificates could have been worth as much as $16 million if affixed to counterfeit Microsoft operating system products.[33]

Theft of computers also causes problems because of the value of data on the computers. The theft of a desktop computer stolen from Visa International may have cost the company $6 million and caused headaches for thousands of credit card holders because the computer contained information on 314,000 credit card accounts. Several banks that issued the cards blocked the affected accounts and issued new cards, with Visa agreeing to cover the cost of around $20 per account.[34] In another example, a laptop containing proprietary company information was stolen from the CEO of Qualcomm, a leading telecommunications company. Responding to this incident, an insurance company specializing in computers and technology equipment said that 319,000 laptops were stolen in 1999.[35]

Unauthorized Use of Access Codes and Financial Passwords   Telephone credit card numbers, PBX access codes, ATM passwords, and regular credit card numbers have all become major targets of criminals. In 2000 the newsletter *Telcomine* estimated that unauthorized cell-phone use costs telecommunications companies $10 billion to $15 billion a year.[36] Many companies have been victimized by criminals stealing PBX access codes used to route telephone calls through the company's PBX to get reduced corporate rates and simplify accounting. Until the theft is detected and the access code switched off, it is used to make foreign long distance calls from pay phones and to arrange drug deals and other illegal activities.

Criminals steal telephone credit card numbers and PBX access codes in many ways. "Shoulder surfers" use binoculars, video cameras, or just good eyesight and number memory to spy on people entering telephone credit card numbers while making long distance calls in airports. Company insiders may also steal these codes. For example, an MCI Communications employee was arrested in 1994 for stealing 60,000 calling card numbers and selling them to an international crime ring. MCI officials estimated the entire loss was more than $50 million.[37]

Many schemes have been used to steal PIN (personal identification) numbers for ATMs. Criminals have scanned cordless and cellular telephone signals looking for people using bank-by-phone services. They have stolen data using wiretaps, thereby capturing data moving from one location to another. In 1998 a Russian citizen admitted to using passwords stolen from Citicorp customers to carry out illegal transfers from his apartment in St. Petersburg. He used the passwords to withdraw $400,000 of $12 million that was illegally transferred. Citibank stated it did not know how an accomplice stole the passwords.[38]

Theft by Entering Fraudulent Transaction Data   Entering fraudulent transaction data is the simplest and most common method of theft in computer-related crime. Box 13.1 lists major categories of transaction-related fraud. Such frauds are perpetrated by forging documents, bypassing procedures, or impersonating someone. The criminals who do this often know little about computers. In these cases, what is commonly called computer crime often relies less on knowledge of computers and much more on knowledge of how business systems operate. Many businesses have easy targets for this type of crime because their internal systems are managed carelessly.

As was clear from the chapter opening case about Visa's advice to online merchants, transaction fraud is an especially prevalent threat to online retailers. The problem became apparent as soon as online commerce began to take hold. For example, in 1995 the early e-retailer Cyber Source had a week in which fraudulent sales exceeded legitimate sales.[39] One of the biggest victims of credit card fraud so far has been the travel Web site Expedia. The company took a $4.1 million write-off in May 2000 to

EXAMPLES OF FRAUD COMMITTED USING TRANSACTION PROCESSING SYSTEMS

Listed are some of the many ways to commit fraud using transaction processing systems.[40] These types of fraud are usually perpetrated by insiders who generate fraudulent transaction data.

Forgery: The criminal produces fraudulent checks, ID cards, or even money. Desktop publishing technology such as scanners, drawing programs, and laser printers have made forgery easier than ever before. Figure 13.3 shows an example of this type of forgery. As long ago as 1992, the American Bankers Association estimated that counterfeiters aided by laser printers and color copiers forged $2 billion worth of checks annually.[41]

Impersonation fraud: The criminal impersonates someone else, accesses that person's account electronically, and steals money or information. One criminal recognized that bank computers handle deposits based on the magnetic account number at the bottom of deposit slips and not by the depositor's signature. This thief substituted specially coded deposit slips in the place of general deposit slips available in the bank lobby for customers who forget their own personalized slips. For the next three days, all deposits made with these fraudulent deposit slips were credited to the thief's account. The thief withdrew the money and vanished before the depositors' checks started to bounce.

Disbursements fraud: The criminal gets a company to pay for products or services it never received. This often is done by learning the procedures and paperwork through which purchases are made and receipt of material is verified. Pinkerton Security and Investigation Services suffered this type of fraud when an accounting employee transferred money out of a company bank account into accounts set up for bogus companies at another bank. This employee needed a superior's approval before making a transfer but was once asked to cancel a former superior's approval code. Instead of canceling it, she started using it herself. Normally the reconciliation of different accounts would have caught the discrepancies, but she was also supposed to do these reconciliations. Eventually caught in an audit, she pleaded guilty to stealing over $1 million and was sentenced to prison.[42]

Inventory fraud: The criminal modifies inventory records or causes inventory to be shipped to a location where it can be stolen. In one case, employees of a railroad changed the boxcar inventory file to indicate that over 200 boxcars were scrapped or destroyed. These boxcars were then shipped to another railroad company's yard and repainted.

Payroll fraud: The criminal pads an organization's payroll with nonexistent employees or leaves former employees on the payroll after termination. In one example, an employee of a welfare department's data center stole $2.75 million by creating a fictitious workforce. He used fake social security numbers and created input data that generated weekly checks through a payment system. He and several collaborators intercepted the checks and cashed them.

Pension fraud: The criminal embezzles funds from pension payments. Typically, the criminal keeps a deceased person on the file but sends that person's pension check to his own account. To test the existence of this problem, the State Retirement Board in Boston asked 14,500 pension recipients to submit proof they were still alive. They received responses from only 13,994.

Cashier fraud: Cashiers steal part of the cash payments received from customers. For example, a ticket clerk at the Arizona Veterans' Memorial Coliseum was caught issuing full-price basketball tickets, selling them, and then recording the transactions as half-price tickets by entering incorrect codes into the computer.

account for the large number of disputed charges on its site. Expedia's marketing director said that the site had been targeted by professional criminals who bought expensive airline tickets using stolen credit card numbers and then sold them to travelers.[43] It is no wonder that credit card companies hold merchants responsible for any fraudulent purchases made when the signature cannot be verified. It is also no wonder that Visa strongly encourages online merchants to adopt strong fraud detection practices.

Theft by Stealing or Modifying Data   Stealing or modifying data is yet another form of computer crime. One way to steal data is by removing physical media such as paper documents, tapes, or diskettes. There are many stories of salespeople taking a customer list when leaving a job. The pervasive use of personal computers and diskettes makes this easy to do. Product and process specifications are another valuable type of data that can be stolen this way. Unlike other forms of theft, it is often possible to steal computerized data without changing or moving it.

New communication technologies such as cellular telephones, electronic mail, and voice mail have created new possibilities for theft. In a 1993 federal court case in

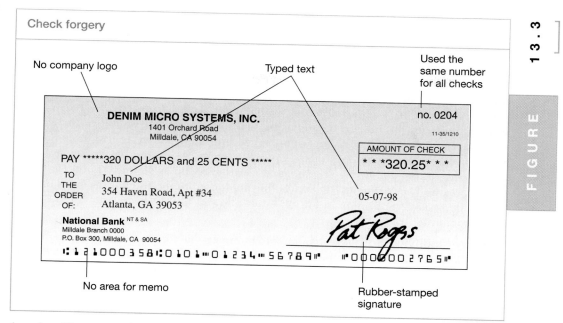

FIGURE 13.3

Check forgery

No company logo   Typed text   Used the same number for all checks

DENIM MICRO SYSTEMS, INC.
1401 Orchard Road
Milldale, CA 90054

no. 0204

11-35/1210

PAY *****320 DOLLARS and 25 CENTS *****

AMOUNT OF CHECK
* * *320.25* * *

TO THE ORDER OF: John Doe
354 Haven Road, Apt #34
Atlanta, GA 39053

05-07-98

National Bank NT & SA
Milldale Branch 0000
P.O. Box 300, Milldale, CA 90054

Pat Roggs

⑆ 1 2 ⑈ 0 0 0 3 5 8 ⑈: 0 1 0 1 ⑆ 0 1 2 3 4 ⑆ 5 6 7 8 9 ⑈   ⑈ 0 0 0 0 0 0 2 7 6 5 ⑈

No area for memo   Rubber-stamped signature

A number of flaws suggest that a check may be forged.

Boston, Standard Duplicating Machines (SDM) accused its rival Duplo Manufacturing of "a prolonged and surreptitious campaign of business espionage" by stealing voice-mail messages to steal business. The evidence involved recorded product inquiries on SDM's voice-mail system that were answered the next day by Duplo's salespeople. The lawsuit zeroed in on an employee hired by Duplo shortly after he was fired by SDM and was based on after-hours calls into SDM's toll-free 800 number from Duplo and from his home. Apparently SDM had not terminated telephone passwords for the terminated employee.[44]

The Web has also created many opportunities for computer criminals to steal credit card numbers. Kevin Mitnick, a hacker who had broken into many computers, was eventually caught after an Internet service provider (ISP) discovered he had stored 20,000 credit card numbers on its computer.[45] More recently, on September 9, 2000 the president of Western Union Financial Services sent a recorded message to thousands of customers saying that hackers had stolen 20,000 credit card and debit card numbers from the Western Union Web site. An employee had left a temporary breach while doing routine maintenance. Western Union shut down its servers immediately and urged its customers to cancel the exposed cards and request new ones.[46] This is not exactly what its customers had in mind when they provided their credit card numbers for use in money transfers.

Internet Hoaxes for Illegal Gain   Because the content of Internet sites is not controlled for accuracy, a large number of hoaxes and spoofs have occurred. Most have been inconsequential, but several in which individuals posted misleading messages to finance bulletin boards and chat rooms rocked the stock price of PairGain, Emulex, and other stocks. For example, in August 2000 a false rumor about management turmoil at the fiber-optics company Emulex appeared on the Internet as the market opened and was reported via news sources including Bloomberg News, Dow Jones Newswires, and CNBC-TV. Emulex stock plunged from $113 to as low as $43, and trading was halted. The stock price went back to over $100 later in the day after the false rumor was corrected, but not before a large number of investors had lost money by dumping the stock in response to the news. Several weeks later the FBI arrested a 23-year-old former employee of Internet Wire, Inc., a news-release service that unwittingly dispatched the bogus release. The suspect had allegedly made more than $240,000 by selling short just before the stock plunged.[47]

The U.S. Securities and Exchange Commission even fined a 16-year-old high school student for committing stock fraud. On 11 occasions he had purchased blocks of thinly traded small-company stocks and within hours had sent "numerous false and/or misleading unsolicited e-mail messages touting the stock he just purchased." Starting at age 14 he frequently contributed to financial message boards on Yahoo! and Silicon Investor, apparently providing no clue that he was a teenager. After buying substantial fractions of a day's volume in a small-cap stock, he posted hundreds of misleading messages on bulletin boards using fictitious names and sold the stocks when they went up. When the SEC first approached him, he claimed he had done nothing wrong because "Everyone does this." A prosecutor had a different view, saying it "was essentially a pump-and-dump scheme, and it was every bit as serious as other Internet fraud cases we have brought." The SEC fine amounted to the total of his gains on certain trades—$272,836, plus interest[48]—but allowed him to keep over $500,000 in gains from other trades.[49]

Theft by Modifying Software   Some programmers have committed computer crime by modifying software so it performs differently when it encounters a particular account number or other triggering condition. One of the early techniques used for this type of crime was to accumulate fractions of pennies on financial transactions and add them to a personal account. Presumably no one would notice and no one would be harmed. Because this technique involves shaving thin slices from transactions, it was sometimes called a *salami swindle.*

Individual criminals sometimes operate alone when they steal in this way, but software modification sometimes involves collusion with business executives. In what was called the largest criminal tax case in Connecticut history, top executives of Stew Leonard's, a sprawling dairy store that had received awards for entrepreneurship and customer service, pleaded guilty to conspiracy. They had stolen $17.5 million in cash receipts between 1981 and 1991 and used a computer program to modify the company's records to fool the auditors. The investigation began not through auditors' efforts, but when U.S. Customs agents stopped Leonard as he boarded a flight to a vacation home in the Caribbean with $80,000 in undeclared cash.[50]

Sabotage and Vandalism

Perpetrators of sabotage and vandalism try to invade or damage system hardware, software, or data. They may range from hackers to disgruntled employees to spies. Although some hackers may not intend to cause harm, sometimes they do so by making mistakes. This happened in a famous case in which a Cornell graduate student was convicted of a felony after trying to demonstrate a weakness in the Internet in 1988 by creating a worm that created copies of itself and transmitted them across the network. Although the worm was supposed to spread slowly, it spread rapidly due to a programming error and accidentally disrupted 6,000 computers and wasted nearly $100 million of time and effort. More recent examples, such as the Love Bug virus, have been even more expensive because the Internet is now used so widely. By some estimates the Love Bug virus caused over $10 billion in damage.[51]

Disgruntled employees who understand a computer system's operation and its weak points are especially dangerous perpetrators of computer crimes. Disgruntled employees have erased, modified, and even kidnapped data and programs. Although little is said about sabotage by spies, the fact that 14-year-olds have penetrated military networks surely implies there are possibilities for computer system sabotage by spies.

A number of programming techniques have been used for sabotage and vandalism:

A **trap door** is a set of instructions that permits a user to bypass the computer system's standard security measures. Trap doors are frequently put into programs by programmers to make it easier for them to modify the software. The Internet worm that disrupted 6,000 computers operated through a trap door left by programmers.

A **Trojan horse** is a program that appears to be valid and useful but contains hidden instructions that can cause damage. For example, a Trojan horse could identify

[L O O K   A H E A D]

The Love Bug Virus is discussed in a case at the end of the chapter.

a particular account number and bypass it or could accumulate differences due to rounding and place them in a particular account.

A **logic bomb** is a type of Trojan horse whose destructive actions are set to occur when a particular condition occurs, such as reaching a particular clock time or the initiation of a particular program. Logic bombs are sometimes used for computerized vandalism and revenge. In a 1998 federal court case, for example, prosecutors believed that an employee who had been fired by Omega Engineering of Bridgeport, New Jersey, created a logic bomb that went off 20 days later, deleting all of the company's design and production software and disabling its backup and recovery facilities. Total damage was estimated at $10 million. The suspect had been the company's chief computer network designer and the company's network administrator. Consequently, he knew the details of the network and also had the supervisory privileges to make network additions, changes, and deletions.[52]

A **virus** is a special type of Trojan horse that can replicate itself and spread, much like a biological virus. A virus attached to a program is loaded into the computer's memory when the program is loaded. The virus is programmed to insert a copy of itself into programs or files that do not contain it. When those programs are executed, the copy of the virus starts up and attempts to replicate the virus again. Another type of virus is a macro virus, which infects documents and can be transmitted via e-mail. Viruses are introduced into company computer systems in many different ways. Macro viruses are a common and serious threat because they can be transmitted accidentally if attached unknowingly to legitimate documents and e-mail. This is one of the reasons it is important to use a virus scanner on incoming documents before opening them. Other sources of virus infections include unauthorized disks, downloads from bulletin boards, sales demo disks, and repair or service people. Even Microsoft itself distributed a demonstration CD-ROM to journalists but had to follow immediately with a warning to throw it away because it was infected with a virus.[53]

A 1997 survey by the National Computer Security Association found that virtually all medium and large organizations in North America (99.33%) had experienced at least one computer virus infection, and that the average infection rate was 406 of 1,000 machines.[54] The cost of removing viruses and taking preventive measures has been estimated at several billion dollars a year. The chance of sabotage through viruses is also very real. Six years after the Chernobyl nuclear disaster contaminated an area the size of Delaware, a disgruntled employee inserted a virus into the computer system used to monitor a nuclear plant in Lithuania. Fortunately control room engineers saw indications that fuel rods were overheating. Whether or not this virus could have led to a meltdown, the mere fact that it could be introduced into the computer system shows the potential danger from lax security.[55] Earlier speculation that viruses might be used for warfare was proven valid in the Persian Gulf War. U.S. Intelligence agents in Amman, Jordan, replaced a computer chip in a French-made computer printer with a chip designed by the U.S. National Security Agency to disrupt a mainframe computer when the printer was used. The printer was attached to a mainframe used by Iraq's air defense system and caused data to vanish from computer screens.[56]

A **denial of service attack** is a method of sabotaging a Web site by flooding its ports and memory buffers with so many incoming messages that the Web site cannot provide service for its legitimate users. The basic concept is just like jamming a phone line with a huge number of incoming calls. In February 2000, coordinated denial of service attacks shut down a number of high-traffic Web sites, including Yahoo!, eBay, Amazon.com, Time Warner, ZDNet, and CNN. The sheer volume of these attacks suggested a coordinated effort using many computers running malicious software that had been planted secretly, thereby turning these computers into virtual zombies. "When the hacker is ready to attack, he will issue a master command that instructs all these zombie computers to try to simultaneously access a Web site. . . . Most Web firms and large companies have relatively secure systems, but some servers at universities and other institutions are vulnerable, for example. Even home PCs with high-speed Internet access can be used by the hackers, making their owners unwitting participants."[57]

Theft, sabotage, and vandalism are intentional threats to information systems whereas accidents (covered earlier) are unintentional threats. Many of the intentional and unintentional threats result from characteristics of systems, people, and the business environment. These causes of vulnerability are discussed next to lay the groundwork for the subsequent overview of measures to maintain system security.

FACTORS THAT INCREASE THE RISKS

Many examples of system-related accidents and crime have been presented to demonstrate the reality and breadth of the threat that must be countered by effective management and security measures. Although each example involved a unique situation, interrelated conditions such as carelessness, complacency, and inadequate organizational procedures increased the vulnerability to both accidents and crime. Table 13.1 shows particular conditions that increase vulnerability to each type of accident or crime.

Behind the conditions in Table 13.1 is a combination of issues related to three themes: the nature of complex systems, human limitations, and pressures in the business environment. Because most system security measures are related to these themes, they will be discussed before system security measures are presented.

The Nature of Complex Systems

Many complex systems rely on many different human, physical, and technical factors that all have to operate correctly to avoid catastrophic system failures. Consider how a simple power outage at a New York City AT&T switching station at 10 A.M. on September 19, 1991 was magnified by a combination of power equipment failure, alarm system failure, and management failure. When workers activated backup power at the station, a power surge and an overly sensitive safety device prevented diesel backup generators from providing power to the telephone equipment, which automatically started drawing power from emergency batteries. Workers disobeyed standard procedures by not checking that the diesel generators were working. Operating on battery power was an emergency situation, but over 100 people in the building that day did not notice the emergency alarms for various reasons: some alarm lights did not work; others were placed where they could not be seen; alarm bells had been inactivated due to false alarms; technicians were off-site at a training course. At 4:50 P.M. the batteries gave out, shutting down the hub's 2.1-million-call-per-hour capacity. Because communication between the region's airports went through this hub, regional airport operations came to a standstill, grounding 85,000 air passengers.[58, 59]

In addition to relying on everything to work correctly, computerized systems are often designed to hide things users don't want to be involved in, such as the details of data processing. Although usually effective, this approach makes it less likely that users will notice problems. In addition, users often try to bypass computerized systems by inventing new procedures that are convenient but that may contradict the system's original design concepts. The more flexible a system is, the more likely that it will be used in ways never imagined by its designers.

Information system decentralization and multivendor connectivity also affect security. As networked workstations become more common, the ability to access, copy, and change computerized data expands. Electronically stored data in offices is highly vulnerable because many offices are low-security or no-security environments where people can easily access and copy local data and data extracted from corporate databases. Laptop computers, PDAs, and storage media are easy to move. Data channels such as electronic message systems and bulletin boards may be poorly controlled. These areas of vulnerability all result from the worthwhile goal of making information and messages available and readily usable.

TABLE 13.1

Conditions That Increase Vulnerability

	Type of threat	Conditions that increase vulnerability
Threats from unintentional occurrences	Operator error	• Difficulty in anticipating how systems will really work in practice and how users and others will adapt to them • Complacency in assuming the system will operate as it is supposed to • Lack of energy and care in assuring systems work properly
	Hardware malfunction	• Disbelief that hardware can malfunction • Difficulty deciding whether the hardware or the warning system is malfunctioning
	Software bugs	• Inadequate design and testing • Unanticipated factors that affect system operation • Inability to prove software is correct
	Data errors	• Flaws in procedures • Inability of software to detect many types of errors • Carelessness and inattention
	Accidental disclosure of information	• Flaws in procedures • Carelessness and inattention
	Damage to physical facilities	• Inadequate backup • Inadequate physical security related to natural phenomena • Inadequate protection against failure of important external systems
	Inadequate system performance	• Inadequate design • Unanticipated peak loads or demand variations
	Liability	• Inadequate limitation on liability • Inadequate system quality
Threats from intentional actions	Theft	• Inadequate design of computer system or human processing • Existence of many easy targets for theft • Distributed systems
	Vandalism and sabotage	• Inadequate prevention of unauthorized access • Inadequate software change control • Inadequate organizational procedures

Human Limitations

To make things worse, many computer users are oblivious to system security and ignore it. Other human limitations increasing system vulnerability include complacency, carelessness, greed, and limited ability to understand complex systems.

Complacency and carelessness lead users and managers to assume systems work correctly. Pepsi-Cola's managers in the Philippines were certainly surprised when a "computer error" in their Numbers Fever promotion generated 800,000 winning numbers inside of bottle caps instead of 18. With a promised prize of one million pesos ($40,000) for each winner, Pepsi-Cola found itself in a public relations and legal nightmare. It certainly did not have $32 billion to pay the claimants and tried to appease them by spending $10 million to give 500 pesos ($20) to each claimant with a winning number.[60]

Complacency and carelessness also lead to lax enforcement of security systems. Controls designed to prevent disasters in computerized systems are often ignored by the people who are supposed to enforce them. A 1991 U.S. General Accounting Office (GAO) audit of U.S. stock markets turned up 68 security and control flaws. Three of the exchanges had no computer backup facilities; two had no alternative power supplies for trading floors; two had telecommunications equipment that could be used to modify data; combustible materials were found in a computer room.[61]

Greed and other human frailties increase vulnerability because they provide a motive for computer crime. People having personal problems related to drinking, drugs, gambling, or other difficulties may see computer crime as a way to solve their problems. People who want revenge on their employer or supervisor may also resort to computer crime.

Human limitations of system developers also have an impact. Even with the best CASE techniques, it is sometimes difficult to visualize exactly how a complicated information system will work. Many individuals understand parts of systems, but few understand all of a complex system. Inability to anticipate how the system will operate under all circumstances leads to accidents and increases the chances of computer crime.

Pressures in the Business Environment

The business environment increases vulnerability by adding pressures to complete systems rapidly with limited staffs. Information system vulnerability may not be considered adequately when development decisions are driven by needs to maximize return on investment. In the rush to meet deadlines with insufficient resources, features and testing that reduce vulnerability may be left out. Hallmarks of careful software development work may be curtailed, such as thorough documentation, careful design reviews, and complete testing. These things happen not only in information systems, but also in many other large projects. For example, after years of delays, the billion-dollar Hubble space telescope was launched into orbit with a warped mirror that had not been given a standard final test on earth.

Many Internet-based projects are especially susceptible to these threats because Web sites and intranets are often built quickly and modified frequently. For example, in 1999 an internal search at Boeing uncovered 2,300 intranet sites on more than 1,000 servers.[62] Managing so many intranets with proper security requires a combination of involvement by the IT group and cooperation by employees who create and maintain many of the sites.

METHODS FOR MINIMIZING RISKS

Many threats related to accidents and computer crime were covered to demonstrate why positive action to minimize these threats is essential. Figure 13.4 represents these actions as a series of business processes in a value chain for establishing and maintaining system security. The remainder of the chapter will use the following order to explain the basic sequence in developing the system, establishing security, controlling operations, and anticipating problems:

- Build the system correctly in the first place.
- Train users about security issues.
- Once the system is in operation, maintain physical security.
- Given that it is physically secure, prevent unauthorized access to computers, networks, and data.
- Having controlled access, make sure transactions are performed correctly.
- Even with transaction controls in place, motivate efficient and effective operation and find ways to improve.
- Even if the system seems secure, audit it to identify problems.
- Even with continuing vigilance, prepare for disasters.

None of the methods mentioned in the remainder of the chapter are foolproof because many problems cannot be foreseen. However, consistent and thorough attention to the security and control value chain reduces the likelihood of accidents, computer crime, and ineffective usage. As you read about these methods remember that security issues always involve trade-offs. Effort expended on security is often effort that would have been expended on providing value for customers or reducing internal costs. If security absorbs too much attention, it is difficult to get work done. If it receives too little attention, accidents and fraud become more likely.

Controlling Software Development and Modifications

Software quality control is the process of making sure that software is developed efficiently, debugged completely, and maintained carefully. Software quality control usu-

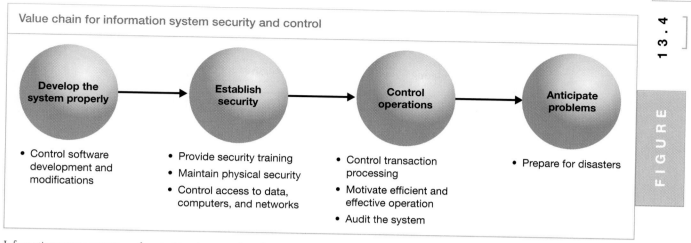

Value chain for information system security and control

Develop the system properly
- Control software development and modifications

Establish security
- Provide security training
- Maintain physical security
- Control access to data, computers, and networks

Control operations
- Control transaction processing
- Motivate efficient and effective operation
- Audit the system

Anticipate problems
- Prepare for disasters

FIGURE 13.4

Information system security and control involve a number of separate business processes that combine to reduce the risk of accidents, crime, and ineffective use.

ally implies strict adherence to a structured system life cycle, regardless of whether the software was built in-house or by a vendor.

Maintaining software quality also calls for careful testing of any vendor-supplied software before it is distributed in the organization. Although this may seem unnecessary because the software and computers should work properly, we have already seen many systems that did not work as intended. Problems and vulnerabilities of many systems are linked directly to bugs and design flaws that can be found through testing.

Another aspect of maintaining software quality is to prevent contact with computer viruses. Although there is no foolproof way to do this, effective measures include controlling access to the system, using only authorized, vendor-supplied software, and using vaccine programs to identify and eliminate known viruses. It is particularly dangerous to use programs from any sources that may not have been controlled carefully, such as public bulletin boards, public domain (free) software, pirated software, and diskettes or CD-ROMs that may be infected.

Software change control systems provide a procedural approach for maintaining software quality and preventing unwarranted changes. Software change control applies the idea of segregation of duties to the development and maintenance of computer systems. Figure 13.5 illustrates the sequence that occurs whenever a program is changed:

1. The programmer documents the change to be made and then checks out the programs to be changed. When these programs are checked out, no one else can check them out or change them.
2. The programmer changes the programs and tests them.
3. The programmer transfers the modified programs to another person authorized to check them. That person reads the documentation of the desired change, studies the before and after versions of the programs, tests them, and signs off that they are correct.
4. The system administrator replaces the old versions of the programs with the new revisions. A journal is kept detailing when each change was made, what it entailed, who revised the program, and who checked it.

Many variations on this sequence have been used. For example, many IS organizations use structured walk-throughs in which the programmer explains the code to other programmers to be sure it is consistent and easy to understand. As with other forms of quality review, this sequence is cumbersome and isn't foolproof. When enforced, however, it makes it more difficult for people to make careless changes or tamper with programs.

FIGURE 13.5

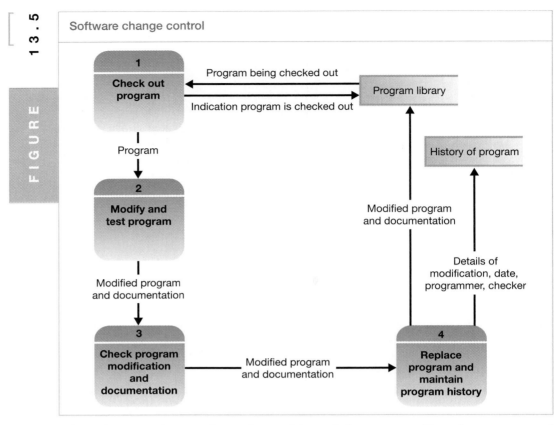

Software change control

Software change control creates a division of responsibility in which one person modifies and tests a program, and others check the changes and move the changes back into the program library.

Providing Security Training

Complacency, carelessness, and lack of awareness all increase the likelihood of accidents and computer crime. Companies should train employees to be aware of security concerns and to understand how these concerns are related to rules and procedures. Every employee who uses a computer or is at all involved with transaction processing should be familiar with the issues this chapter raises. They should also know some of the signs of suspicious activity and the company's procedures for reporting that activity.

Although the many examples presented here and the huge costs of telephone fraud and viruses show why this type of training and awareness is important, many companies do not follow through adequately. Large losses are not surprising when employees are unaware of the risks or know that company management doesn't care. A 1999 nuclear accident that killed several people and injured around 30 others at the Sumitomo Metal Mining Company in Japan illustrates the potential impact of inadequate training and knowledge about security risks. An uncontrolled nuclear chain reaction occurred when workers ignored a 5.2-pound limit and poured 35 pounds of uranium into a purification tank whose shape concentrated a critical mass of uranium in a way that is known to create nuclear chain reactions. In this case the reaction continued for 17 hours after an initial explosion. How to avoid nuclear reactions is one of the most fundamental things that uranium workers need to know, yet basic safety procedures related to the amount of uranium and the proper shape of vessels were not followed.[63] According to U.S. Energy Department officials who toured the plant three weeks later, the accident occurred "largely because managers counted on workers to follow rules but never explained why the rules were important." Japanese officials had previously performed a safety evaluation of the plant, and concluded that an accidental reaction was impossible. Based on that, the plant had no emergency plan.[64]

Maintaining Physical Security

Maintaining physical security is essential for protecting computing and communication facilities. Physical security measures should take into account threats including accidents, uncontrollable external events, and attacks by intruders. Physical security starts with simple measures, such as forbidding eating, drinking, and smoking near computer equipment. Just dropping a cup of coffee can damage equipment and erase data.

Physical access controls guard against physical access to computer facilities and data. The general guideline is to keep unauthorized people out of computer rooms, communication centers, and data storage locations. Contrary to that guideline, one author recalls a security consulting assignment in which his elevator accidentally stopped at the floor of a large casino's computer center at 11:00 P.M. He and an associate walked up to a locked door marked "Computer Center—No Admittance." They rang the bell, were admitted by a computer operator without saying a word, and wandered through the computer center for ten minutes before leaving. If they had been disgruntled heavy losers rather than security consultants, they might have done substantial damage.[65]

Firms go to great lengths to protect critical data processing facilities, and rightfully so. Concerns about physical security for its reservation system led American Airlines to build an underground facility in Tulsa, Oklahoma. With its extreme reliance on that system, foot-thick concrete walls and a 42-inch ceiling seemed justified.

Controlling Access to Data, Computers, and Networks

After providing for physical security, the next set of measures involves controlling access to data, computers, and networks. Security measures should restrict access to confidential information and enforce mandatory ground rules. Table 13.2 summarizes four aspects of access control: enforcing guidelines for manual data handling, defining access privileges, enforcing access privileges, and using encryption to make data meaningless to anyone who bypasses access controls.

TABLE 13.2

Controlling Access to Data, Computers, and Networks

Control technique	Example
Enforce manual data handling guidelines	• Lock desks • Shred discarded documents and manuals
Define access privileges	• Give different individuals different levels of privilege for using the computer • Give different individuals different levels of access to specific data files
Enforce access privileges	
What you know	• Password • Special personal data
What you have	• ID card • Key to physical facility
Where you are	• Call-back system
Who you are	• Fingerprint or handprint • Retina pattern or iris pattern • Voice pattern
Control incoming data from networks and other media	• Use firewalls • Scan for viruses
Make data meaningless to anyone lacking authorization	• Data encryption

Guidelines for Manual Data Handling   The way people handle data manually can constitute a security risk. Consider the common practice of going home and leaving work on top of your desk. Confidential or proprietary information lying on a desk is an easy target. Consequently, organizations may require people who work with sensitive information to lock it in their desks at night or whenever they leave.

Surprisingly, the handling of garbage also can be a security risk. Many organizations are careful to shred discarded documents and manuals instead of throwing them in the trash. Failure to do this led to one of the classic stories about computer crime and security. In 1971, a 19-year-old operated an illegal business based on information he obtained from a trash bin. The trash bin belonged to a supply office of Pacific Telephone and Telegraph (PT&T). In it, he found discarded equipment, which he refurbished. He also found manuals and the detailed operating and ordering procedures used by installation and repair crews. After posing as a freelance writer to get a plant tour, he impersonated a PT&T employee dialing orders into the PT&T computer. He drove to a PT&T facility in an old PT&T truck he had bought at an auction, picked up the equipment he had ordered, and sold it to other companies at discounted prices. Caught after stealing over $1,000,000 in inventory, he served 40 days in jail, paid an $8,500 fine, and later went to work as a security consultant.[66] If PT&T had shredded their operating procedure manuals instead of throwing them in the trash, this incident probably would not have happened. Although it is excessive to shred every document and printout that is no longer used, dumping ordering manuals, customer lists, and company plans into a trash bin invites unauthorized access to proprietary information.

Many IT users are unaware of a related fact, that deleting a document from a hard disk does not really mean that it is deleted, but rather that the directory information pointing to the document has been changed to indicate that the space currently used by the document is available for reuse. A product called Shredder software has been developed to over-write the information in deleted files, thereby ensuring that the deletion is complete.[67]

Access Privileges   Locking desks and shredding obsolete documents are security measures related to manual data handling. Security measures for computerized systems start with defining access privileges. **Access privileges** are precise statements of which computers and data an individual can access, and under what circumstances. The simplest way to define access privileges is with a list of all authorized users. Access lists are effective only if organizations enforce them strictly. Security-conscious organizations are especially concerned that all computer-related records and privileges are up to date for all employees. Such organizations ensure that all access to computers is canceled when an employee leaves.

The fact that someone can log onto a computer system doesn't mean that person should have access to all data in the system. Many systems use file access lists that grant individual users or groups of users different levels of access to specific files. Typical levels of access include: none, read only, read and copy, or read and update. For example, almost all users would have no direct access to the list of passwords. Some users would have read and copy access to a customer list. All users would have read and update access to their own personal information.

Regardless of whether the focus is physical facilities or computer networks, access controls require enforcement. We will look at ways to enforce access control based on four concepts: what you know, what you have, where you are, and who you are.

Access Control Based on What You Know   A **password** provides a simple form of protection. After logging on with an account number or user ID, the user enters a confidential password. Access is permitted only after the computer checks that this password goes with this account. Business people today may have separate passwords for electronic mail, voice mail, and several different computer networks, not to mention PIN numbers for ATMs and credit cards.

Unfortunately, password schemes have a variety of weaknesses. People who use many different computer systems often have to remember many different passwords.

Because it is hard to remember infrequently used passwords, people are tempted to use short passwords or passwords that can be guessed easily, such as the person's account number, a child's name, pet's name, or middle name. If a password is simple enough, it is easy to figure out by trial and error. This is especially true if a computer generates each trial password and tries it out automatically. Employers may forget to cancel passwords after employees leave a company. Where security is sloppy, terminated employees may be able to dial into an employer's computer months after being dismissed. Because the password list is just a file inside a computer, it may be possible to find and copy this list by working around the standard file security routines in the computer system. With all these shortcomings, passwords are certainly not foolproof. Nonetheless, they are useful as one part of an overall security system.

One of the most important shortcomings of passwords is that people literally give them away by writing passwords on the side of a workstation or by letting other people look over their shoulders. Many computer system break-ins occur because an operator has divulged a password to someone who appears to be authorized to receive it. The impostor often telephones, pretends to be a repair person, gains the unsuspecting operator's confidence, and then asks the operator to say or type the password as part of a supposed repair process. Computer hackers cynically call this **social engineering**. This type of approach has been used to steal passwords to Internet accounts. For example, some scams have used America Online's instant message feature to send messages such as "I am with the America Online customer service department and we are experiencing difficulties with our records. I need you to verify your log-on password to me so that I can validate you as a user, and fix our records promptly." Another common message is "You are eligible to have your account promoted to an Overhead Account . . . and it's totally free! All you have to do is change your password to 'Overhead' and e-mail us back."[68] All users of the Internet and other networked systems should understand this threat.

Access Control Based on What You Have   ID cards provide some security by making it more difficult for people to enter a physical facility or computer system. Simple ID card systems have many problems similar to those of passwords, however. The cards may be lost. The organization may fail to insist they be returned when an employee leaves. The card may be stolen or forged, as happens often with driver's licenses and passports. The technology for ID cards is becoming more powerful, and ID cards themselves can store data other than a name, number, and picture. ID cards that can be read by scanners can be used in combination with definitive personal identification to provide more advanced security methods.

Access Control Based on Where You Are   One way to prevent unauthorized access to computer systems is to make sure that a given user can access the system only from that user's terminal. This is accomplished using a **call-back system**, with which the user enters an account number and password and then is disconnected automatically. If the numbers match, the system then calls the user back at a phone number listed in an internal system directory. This prevents access by people who have stolen a password unless they are using the password from the password owner's location. Extending this idea, a device has been patented that instructs the user to repeat several words over the phone. Access would be granted only if the voice matches a stored voiceprint.

Access Control Based on Who You Are   For more definitive identification than is possible with passwords and ID cards, specialized equipment can sense a person's unique physical characteristics, such as fingerprints, voiceprints, blood-vessel patterns on the retina, or patterns in the iris of the eye. These are all forms of **biometric identification** because they use the individual's personal, biological characteristics. These systems are becoming competitive with magnetic card systems for restricting entrance to buildings. Hand and fingerprint identification are used to control access to high-security areas ranging from nuclear research labs to jewelry vaults and are now even available for unlocking car doors (see Figure 13.6). American Airlines has used a

FIGURE 13.6

Using your hand as a passport

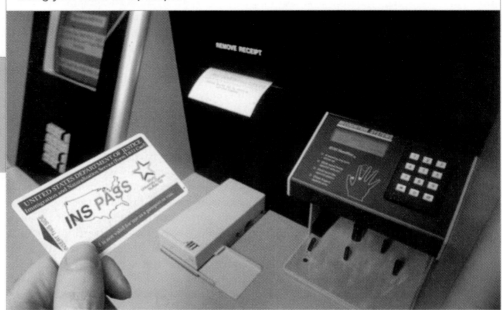

To reduce waiting time for frequent international travelers, the U.S. Immigration and Naturalization Service permits travelers at some airports to identify themselves using a hand scanner and an identification card.

retina scanner as part of the security system for its underground computer facility. The Cook County Jail in Chicago has used retina scanners to make sure prisoners don't attempt to exchange identities by memorizing each other's names, addresses, and personal information.[69]

All of the access control methods, even biometric identification, can be undermined by carelessness after the access control check is completed. For example, merely walking away from a computer terminal logged into a network can provide an opportunity for unauthorized access to data. A simple way to reduce this risk is to log off whenever you leave a terminal. To minimize unauthorized access, some computer systems apply an **automatic log off** to any terminal left unused for a fixed amount of time, such as five minutes.

Controlling Incoming Data Flowing through Networks and Other Media   In a highly networked world, access controls that focus on identifying people need to coexist with controls that focus on data flowing through networks. For example, a virus on a diskette might infect not only one personal computer, but also all the computers attached to the same network. A document attached to an incoming e-mail message might also bring a virus. Similarly, programs downloaded from the Internet might contain hidden code that finds, modifies, or transmits data on a hard disk without authorization.

A number of **virus protection** products are available commercially. These products automatically scan diskettes, e-mail attachments, and other possible sources of virus infection. They look for a wide range of known viruses and can also detect many abnormal situations that may indicate the presence of a virus whether or not the particular virus has been identified in the past. In many cases they can remove a virus and repair code affected by it. Virus protection software must be updated frequently because new viruses are being created all the time.

One of the basic tools for controlling incoming data is a **firewall**, a program that is like a lock on the front door. A firewall inspects each incoming data packet, decides whether it is acceptable based on the IP address it is coming from, sends acceptable messages to their destinations, and keeps track of all incoming messages that were stopped. Network administrators can program firewalls to accept messages that meet a variety of conditions, such as coming from a specific group of IP addresses or being generated by specific applications. This means that a firewall might stop a completely legitimate message (such as an e-mail attachment) that simply does not fit the desired profile. Firewalls and other filtering software are used wherever messages from the Internet or other public networks enter a private computer network. Figure 13.7 illustrates that firewalls, virus scanners, and other filters can be used at many different points within a private corporate network to make sure that only authorized access is permitted and to detect viruses before they spread. The issue here is not just detection of problems, but detection without causing excessive inefficiency. Firewall products compete on their ability to process a rapid stream of messages, to enforce a variety of controllable policies for accepting messages, and to protect against known vulnerabilities related to features of networking software.

Making the Data Meaningless to Unauthorized Users   Another way to protect data is to make it meaningless to unauthorized users. As Chapter 8 introduced, encryption is the encoding of data so that it can be decoded only by authorized parties. Encryption applies across a wide range of applications including data stored on computers (which might be accessed illegally), e-mail messages and cellular phone conversations (that might be intercepted), and electronic transactions (that might be monitored or performed fraudulently).

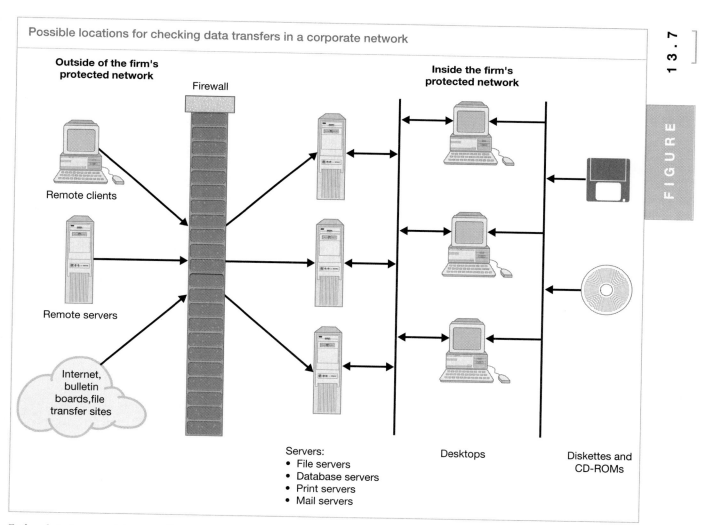

Possible locations for checking data transfers in a corporate network

FIGURE 13.7

Outside of the firm's protected network

Firewall

Inside the firm's protected network

Remote clients

Remote servers

Internet, bulletin boards, file transfer sites

Servers:
- File servers
- Database servers
- Print servers
- Mail servers

Desktops

Diskettes and CD-ROMs

Each node in the network is potentially a site for checking data transfers to avoid unauthorized access and virus propagation.

The difficult issue with encryption is to find a scheme that is difficult to break but is also practical to use. One possibility is to use an extremely long number as an encryption key, use a multiplication process to perform the encoding, and then a corresponding division process to perform the decoding. The problem with this approach is that both the sender and the receiver must have the same key, leaving questions about how the receiver will obtain the key in the first place and how the key will remain private. Consider, for example, sending the same encrypted message to 500 people. It would be very difficult to keep the key secret because each individual would need a copy.

The **public key encryption** method that is currently favored involves two keys for each user, a public key that is widely available (much like a phone number) and a private key that must be kept secret. The computer sending a message meant for only one individual uses that individual's public key to encrypt it. The computer receiving the message uses that individual's private key to decrypt it. Figure 13.8 illustrates the basic sequence in using public key encryption once an individual has a private key and public key. The calculations for determining a private key–public key pair are based on advanced mathematical methods invented in 1977. The approach is based on the fact that finding the factors of an extremely long odd number takes a long time, even with today's ultra-fast computers. In 1998 RSA Laboratories gave recommendations for the length of the modulus, the number that is the starting point for calculating a private key–public key pair. The modulus should be 768 bits for keys for personal use, 1,024 bits for typical corporate use, and 2,048 bits for extremely valuable keys such as the key pair of a certification authority. The recommendation said that a 768-bit key probably will be secure until the year 2004, when greater computing power may mean a longer key will be required to prevent theft.[70]

Because the computations for encrypting a long message are quite lengthy, a typical way to use public key encryption is to combine it with a secret key encryption system such as the Data Encryption Standard (DES) that was once a leading-edge technique. The method is to encrypt the message using a randomly selected DES key, encrypt the DES key using the recipient's public key, and send this combined message as a "digital envelope." The recipient's private key is used to decrypt the DES key and the DES key is then used to decrypt the message. This combines the much higher speed of the DES method with the greater key-management convenience of the public key method.[71] A similar method is used to create a **digital signature** that verifies the origin and content of a message and can be used for verifying that a message has not been changed. A mathematical procedure called "hashing" is used to create a digital signature. Both the digital signature and the message are encrypted and sent. If the message is modified later, the hashing function will not create the same digital signature.

Thus far, ways to control access to data have been described. Since insiders are responsible for most computer crime, it is clear that even people with authorized access may cause problems. The next level of control tries to make sure transactions are processed correctly.

R E A L I T Y   C H E C K   ✓

Controlling Access to Computers, Networks, and Data

This section described many ways to control access to computers, networks, and data.

1. Assume you have been hired in the patent department of an extremely security-conscious company. On your second day at work you see someone across the room who appears to be copying a password written on a slip of paper taped to the side of a workstation. Do you think you have a responsibility to do anything in this situation?

2. Several weeks later the company brings in a retina scanner to check the identity of anyone entering the patent department's office. How would you feel about undergoing a retina scan every time you enter the office?

Using public key encryption and digital signatures

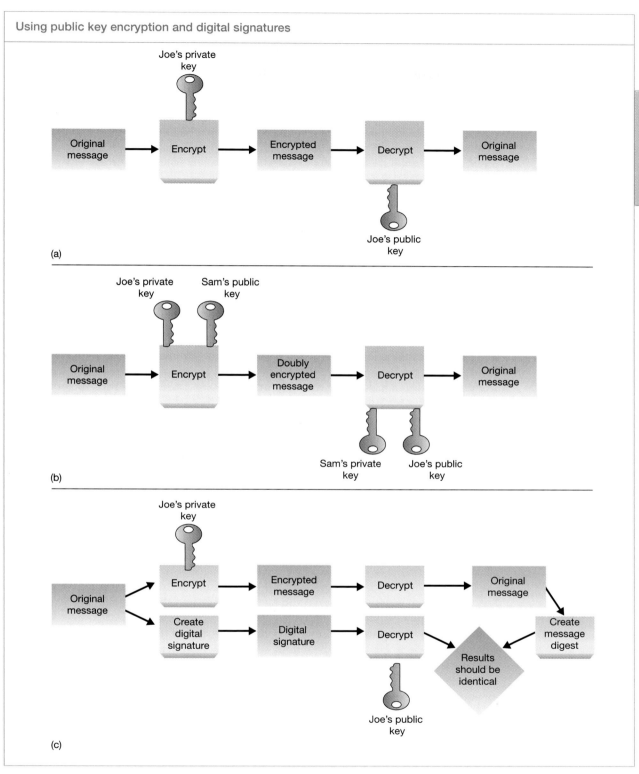

FIGURE 13.8

(a)

(b)

(c)

Public key encryption allows encryption and decryption without the necessity of distributing secret keys. The first case uses only the sender's key. The second case uses the recipient's key. (a) Joe wants to send a message to Sam and wants to assure Sam that the message came from him. Joe uses his private key to create an encrypted version of his message. Joe's public key is available to anyone. Sam uses it to decrypt the message. (b) Joe wants to send a message to Sam and wants to make sure only Sam can open the message. Joe uses his private key to create an encrypted version of his message, but further encrypts the message using Sam's public key so that only Sam will be able to decrypt the message. When Sam receives the message he performs the reverse process by using his own private key and Joe's public key. (c) Joe wants to send a message to Sam and Sam wants to make sure that no one has intercepted and modified it before it arrives. Joe uses his private key to encrypt the message and to create a digital signature for the message. Sam uses Joe's public key to decrypt the message and to extract a message digest from the digital signature. To verify the integrity of the message, Sam reconstructs a message digest from the decrypted message. The two message digests should be identical.

Controlling Traditional Transaction Processing

A company receives an order by fax. Why should or shouldn't it execute the order? Network Solutions, Inc. (NSI), the main registrar of Internet domain names, had to rethink its procedures around this simple question following an embarrassing incident. Someone sent it a fax requesting that it transfer "Internet.com" and 1,300 other domain names to Open SRS, a Canadian registrar of domain names. To the chagrin of the CEO of Internet.com, NSI promptly made the transfer. "There was no double-checking on the part of Network Solutions," he said. "What kind of business would fax in a letter saying, 'Just turn over these 1,300 domains'?" After the transfer was reversed, an NSI spokesman said that steps were being taken to avoid a recurrence.[72]

This incident concerned Web domain names, but was not really about the Web. Rather, it was about the methods a company could or should use to control its transaction processing. The typical control points for transaction processing include data preparation and authorization, data validation, error correction, and backup and recovery. After covering these we will look at control issues specifically related to Web-based transactions.

Data Preparation and Authorization   Data preparation and authorization creates the transaction data that will be entered into a transaction processing system. The story of Equity Funding Corporation shows the importance of controlling data preparation. Over the course of ten years, officers and computer programmers of Equity Funding colluded to make the company appear to be on a rapid growth path by issuing 60,000 fake insurance policies, accounting for about 65% of the company's total. The fake policies were sold to reinsurance companies. When the premiums were to be paid, Equity Funding generated more fake policies, sold them to reinsurers, and used the proceeds of the sale to pay premiums for policies sold earlier. In creating the fake policies, the programmers used statistical data from the company's legitimate policies to ensure that the fakes had the same profiles in coverage, premiums, policy cancellations, and benefits paid. When federal investigators asked to audit the files, the company delayed until it could forge health reports, contracts, and supporting documents. This fraud eventually cost investors $1 billion.[73] Collusion on the scale of the Equity Funding case is extraordinary because it requires the cooperation of so many people. Crime through fraudulent transaction data is much easier to perpetrate if it can be done by one person.

Segregation of duties is a control method that makes it more difficult to perpetrate one-person crimes and crimes of collusion. **Segregation of duties** is the division of responsibilities among two or more people to reduce the likelihood of theft or accidental misprocessing. For example, one person in an accounts payable department creates the expense voucher, another person authorizes it, and a third initiates the funds transfer. This does not assure honesty and accuracy, but it makes dishonesty and carelessness less likely.

Segregation of duties is used extensively in both computerized and noncomputerized systems. It is just as applicable in system development groups as it is in finance departments. Some computer frauds were possible only because an individual working in isolation from others could modify a program to put money into a particular account or perform other improper processing. IS organizations use software change control techniques (mentioned earlier) to improve software quality and avoid this problem. Although segregation of duties has advantages for security, it has disadvantages for efficiency because it requires multiple authorizations and the involvement of many people in processes that could be handled by one person. The extent of segregation of duties is a management choice based on this trade-off.

Data Validation   Data validation refers to checking transaction data for any errors or omissions that can be detected by looking at the data. Common computerized validation procedures include checking for missing data (such as a missing social security number), invalid data (such as an impossible ZIP code), and inconsistent data. As an example, Figure 13.9 shows a transaction screen from a hypothetical registration system at a college. Some validation checks are obvious, such as matching the student's

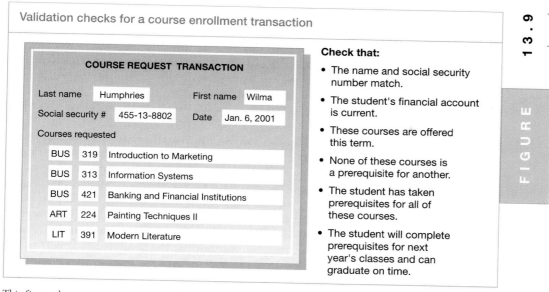

FIGURE 13.9

Validation checks for a course enrollment transaction

This figure shows a transaction screen from a hypothetical registration system and a list of automatic validation checks that might be used.

name and social security number or checking that the student's financial account is current. Others require more complex processing, such as determining whether the student has taken the prerequisite courses or whether the sequence of courses will permit graduation on time.

Although it is essential to validate transaction data to keep the database accurate and avoid wasting time correcting past errors, it is impossible to validate all the data in a system. For example, transpositions such as 56 instead of 65 are often difficult to catch because there may be no reason to suspect that 65 is more likely than 56. The army clerk who made such an error on a 13-digit part number ended up ordering a 7-ton anchor instead of a $6 incandescent lamp.[74] Better system design probably would have prevented this error. Instead of requiring the clerk to type a 13-digit number, an information system built today could easily permit the clerk to choose the item from a list of existing part numbers plus item descriptions.

Error Correction   **Error correction** is an essential component of any transaction processing system (TPS) because it is impossible to assure that all data in the system are correct, regardless of how carefully the data were validated when first entered. Error correction in many TPSs is surprisingly complicated due to the possibility of fraud. If erroneous data could be corrected by editing the data values (as would be done using a word processor), correct data could also be changed using the same techniques. Embezzlement would be rampant and the validity of most databases in doubt.

To control TPSs involving data related to financial accounting, error correction is usually handled as a separate transaction that is recorded and accounted for. The transaction history from the TPS therefore includes each normal transaction that occurred, such as payment of a bill or receipt of an order, as well as each error correction transaction, such as changing a customer's account balance because a bill contained the wrong price or because the merchandise was unsatisfactory.

Backup and Recovery   The last step in controlling transaction processing is to make sure that resumption of regular processing following a software or hardware crash will occur with the least possible inconvenience. The typical method for recovering from disruptions was illustrated in Figure 4.16, which shows the logic of performing periodic backups and using those backups to restore the transaction database to the point at which the disruption occurred. Because the topic of backup and recovery was explained in Chapter 4 it will not be repeated here.

Maintaining Security in Web-Based Transactions

As was implied by the opening case about Visa and online merchants, Web-based transactions face special challenges because the buyer and seller are typically strangers, might be anywhere, and do not have face-to-face contact. In this environment it is almost impossible to assure a transaction is legitimate, but a number of techniques using public key encryption have been developed to reduce risks.

These techniques use public key encryption in conjunction with a **public key infrastructure (PKI)** based on services provided by certification authorities that like to call themselves "trusted third parties." A **certification authority (CA)** is a company that issues computer-based records related to the identity of computers and the occurrence of computer-based transactions. The functions a CA may perform include maintaining lists of public keys and associated private keys and issuing digital certificates that identify individual computers, verify the identity of computers involved in specific transactions, and store transaction information to make sure the transaction cannot be repudiated by either party. A **digital certificate** is a computer-based record that identifies the certification authority, identifies the attribute of the sender that is being verified, contains the sender's public key, and is digitally signed by the certification authority. Possible types of digital certificates include identifying certificates, authorizing certificates, transactional certificates, and time stamps.

Transaction Privacy, Authentication, Integrity, and Nonrepudiation   Table 13.3 summarizes the way encryption and digital certificates can be used to address the issues of privacy, authentication, integrity, privacy, and nonrepudiation.

Transaction privacy results from ensuring that unauthorized individuals cannot obtain the transaction data, or if they obtain the data they cannot understand it. The public key encryption methods illustrated in Figure 13.8 address this issue in a general case. Transactions through Web browsers are encrypted using the **Secure Sockets Layer (SSL)** method initially developed by Netscape. This method encrypts Internet transmissions using a temporary encryption key generated automatically by the browser based on session information such as the time of day. SSL protects the transmission but does not authenticate the sender.

Transaction **authentication** is the process of verifying that the transaction participants are who they claim to be. Assume you were a Web merchant wanting to go beyond the type of guidelines provided by Visa in the chapter-opening case. Other than encryption, the methods mentioned in the section about controlling access to data and computers (see Table 13.2) do not apply directly to many Web-based e-commerce

TABLE 13.3

Maintaining Security in Web-Based Transactions	
Requirement for Web-based transactions	**Method related to this requirement**
Privacy: Ensuring that unauthorized individuals cannot obtain the transaction data.	Encryption: The transaction data is encrypted using a version of public key encryption that achieves the right trade-off between reliability and efficiency.
Authentication: Verifying that the transaction participants are who they claim to be.	Digital certificate: Digital certificates identifying the buyer and seller computers are used during transactions.
Integrity: Ensuring that the transaction data is not changed after the fact.	Digital signature: The buyer's private key is mathematically combined with the transaction data to create a transaction digest. Any change in the data would generate a different digest.
Nonrepudiation: Ensuring that neither party can claim the transaction did not occur.	Certification authority: A trusted third party stores the transaction data and the related digital signature.

transactions. For example, since anyone can obtain a password for a consumer-oriented e-commerce site, passwords provide little additional protection.

One possibility for better authentication in at least some cases is to focus on the specific computer that is being used and to use a certificate authority to verify that both buyer and seller are using computers that have been identified in advance. This can be done by using digital certificates previously assigned to each computer by the certificate authority and stored on those computers.

Transaction **integrity** involves ensuring that transaction information is not changed after the transaction is completed. The digital signature technique illustrated in Figure 13.8(c) is a method for ensuring transaction integrity. The transaction information is mathematically transformed by a hashing algorithm. The resulting message digest is encrypted with the buyer's private key to create the digital signature, and this is stored. If anyone tries to change the transaction, repeating the digital signature calculation will generate a different digital signature, an indication that the transaction data has been changed in some way.

Nonrepudiation means ensuring that neither party can deny that the transaction occurred. In a face-to-face credit card transaction, the signed receipt is used for non-repudiation (even though the signature might have been forged). In Web-based e-commerce, nonrepudiation relies on the digital records of the transaction. This is one of the areas where a certification authority can play a role, since it can store the transaction information and can issue a certificate to both parties stating that the transaction has occurred.

Difficulties with Security Methods for Web-Transactions   Security techniques based on digital signatures, digital certificates, and certificate authorities have been adopted to some extent, but have also encountered resistance. As with many security methods these techniques make transactions less efficient and more complicated. For example, transactions that use digital certificates must go through a certification authority, and this is not how most current transaction processes operate. Stronger security methods might reduce online credit card fraud, but the current level is apparently tolerable since the credit card companies and online merchants continue doing business.

Consider the **Secure Electronic Transaction (SET)** method proposed by Visa, MasterCard, American Express, and other leading credit card companies. SET would go far beyond SSL by establishing standards for encrypting and authenticating credit card transaction data. The merchants would have to follow prescribed processing standards including appropriate links to third parties during the transactions. The banks issuing the credit cards would have to establish mechanisms for issuing digital certificates to both cardholders and merchants. The necessary infrastructure and procedures would cost an estimated three dollars per cardholder, and many merchants don't believe the benefits of SET are worth the cost and inconvenience.[75]

An additional problem is that the entire public key infrastructure consists of business processes performed by people and technology. There is no guarantee that these processes will operate exactly the way they were intended to operate and will be immune to the many types of accidents and computer crime that were discussed earlier. Here are a few of the threats:

- What if someone else uses my key? For example, what if someone uses my computer while I have stepped away? Or what if someone breaks into my nonsecured computer and steals the digital certificate?
- How secure is the certificate authority's computer?
- Since others might have the same name that I have, how does the certificate authority know I am me when it assigns digital certificates in the first place?
- How secure are certificate practices?[76]

Motivating Efficient and Effective Operation

Topics already discussed, such as developing the information system properly, maintaining security, and controlling transaction processing, are all aspects of system management. Another side of system management is creating incentives for efficient and effective operation, especially by monitoring information system usage and by using chargeback to motivate efficiency.

Monitoring Information System Usage   Because it is difficult to manage things without measuring them, well-designed information systems contain measures of performance both for the business process being supported and for the information system itself. Consider a telemarketing firm's customer service information system. It might include measures of business process results, such as sales per hour and customer waiting time before speaking to an agent. It might also contain measures of information system efficiency, such as downtime, average response time for database inquiries, and weekly operating cost. Patterns of suspicious activity might also be recognized with the help of credit card companies.

Due to the prevalence of telephone fraud, all three types of monitoring are important for PBXs. User waiting time and cost savings on outside calls routed through the PBX are measures of the business process. PBX costs and downtime describe the information system's performance. Peculiar patterns of using one access code for frequent calls or unusual foreign calls could be a warning that an access code has been stolen.

Regardless whether the monitoring concerns business process performance, information system performance, or unusual activity, it has little value unless users and managers are willing and able to use the information. This is one of the reasons graphs of key measurements are often posted in the corridors going into factories. Posting the indicators makes sure everyone knows they are important and that everyone recognizes how well the factory is doing.

Charging Users to Encourage Efficiency   The lack of publicized measures for many computerized systems leads users to ignore their costs, use them inefficiently, and sometimes tolerate misuse. This is one of the reasons for charging users to encourage efficiency. **Chargeback systems** try to motivate efficient usage by assigning to user departments the costs of information systems. Impacts of chargeback systems on behavior are apparent in the way offices operate. If the telephone is treated as corporate overhead and therefore appears to be free to users, people will use the phone more than if they or their departments are charged directly. Likewise, disk storage on departmental computers is filled much more quickly if the users incur no storage charges. Even if resources aren't free, the way they are charged out affects how they are used. Consider a laser printer charged at 10¢ per page and a copier charged at 5¢ per page. If you had to make 45 copies, you would probably print one copy on the laser printer and make the other copies on the copier. But if the laser printer cost 5¢ or less, you would make all the copies there. Ideally, chargeback schemes should motivate people to use resources efficiently by reflecting the organization's true costs.

The key issue in charging for using information system resources is to affect people's decisions. If, for example, total computer costs are charged to departments based only on headcount, the charges probably won't affect decisions because the charges are the same regardless of how people use the computers. Instead of using this type of broad-brush allocation, chargeback schemes should use recognizable units of output that correspond closely to business activities. Directly controllable chargeable items include pages printed, transactions performed, and amount of data stored.

Some charging schemes also reflect resource scarcity to motivate usage only when those resources are needed. For example, most computer facilities are especially busy at particular times such as late morning and mid-afternoon and are underutilized other times. Rate differentials are sometimes used to shift some of the work to times of low utilization, thereby making it unnecessary to buy more capacity to cope with the peaks. With rate differentials, users are charged more when resources are scarcer. Resources such as CPU cycles or telephone minutes during busy periods could cost two or more times as much as they cost during slack periods. Although some users have no choice, rate differentials succeed in shifting some of the demand to times when resources would be underutilized.

Chargeback

Charging people for use of computer resources is one of the ways to motivate efficient usage.

1. Identify situations in your everyday life in which the way you are charged for something determines how efficiently you use it.

2. How do you think your university should encourage efficient usage of its internal telephone system and computers?

Auditing the Information System

Auditing standards and controls are designed to ensure that financial operations are neither misrepresented nor threatened due to defective procedures or accounting systems. With the advent of computer systems, the scope of auditing expanded to encompass both general controls over computer installations and application controls for assuring that the recording, processing, and reporting of data are performed properly.

Methods for verifying the phases of processing can be categorized as either "auditing around the computer" or "auditing through the computer." In **auditing around the computer**, the auditor typically selects source documents, traces associated entries through intermediate computer printouts, and examines the resultant entries in summary accounts. This approach basically treats the computer itself as a black box. Although it is useful in finding some errors, and is often cost-effective, it may not provide enough detail to catch crimes such as stealing a fraction of a penny on certain transactions. In **auditing through the computer**, the auditor attempts to understand and test the computer's processing in more detail. A common technique is to create test data and process the data through the system to observe whether the expected results occur. An important shortcoming of this approach is that only preconceived conditions are tested. Furthermore, it is impractical for the test data to represent every possible situation. If a program illegally transfers money every Thursday and the test data are processed on Tuesday, the problem will be missed.

An auditor's responsibility goes much further than just looking at how transactions are processed. Auditors must examine issues such as unauthorized access, controls on computerized data files, controls on data transmission, and procedures for recovering when the information system goes down unexpectedly.

Since privacy is a major concern of many Internet users, a large number of major Web sites have opened their operations to outside auditors so that they can say that their practices in storing and using customer information have been verified. The leader of the privacy practice at the Big Five accounting firm PricewaterhouseCoopers said that a vast majority of companies fail the early stages of the audit, either because of how their employees handle customer data or because their systems do not adequately protect that data. This seems to validate the fears expressed in a survey of Web-using households in which 92% said they do not trust online companies to keep their information private, no matter what they promise.[77]

Preparing for Disasters

You don't need to look at computer systems to understand the importance of genuine preparedness for possible disasters. Consider the oil tanker accident that polluted Prince William Sound in Alaska with 10 million gallons of oil. A large oil terminal was permitted in this area because a major accident seemed unlikely. Just in case, there was a 1,800-page contingency plan for handling a major spill. But when the accident occurred, almost nothing was done to contain and clean up the spilled oil during two days of calm seas, and almost nothing could be done after fierce winds spread the oil on the third day. Exxon, Alyeska Pipeline Service Co., and state officials blamed each other, citing reasons such as not having equipment ready or delaying authorization to use chemical dispersants. This example illustrates the necessity of genuine preparedness for disasters, not just having a plan on paper.

A **disaster plan** is a plan of action to recover from occurrences that shut down or harm major information systems. The need for such a plan is apparent from the potential impact of accidents, sabotage, and natural events such as floods and earthquakes. The nature and extent of an information systems disaster plan for a business depend on the role of information systems in the day-to-day operation of the business. Reliable online transaction processing systems are essential for banks, distributors, and airlines. For businesses such as these, any unplanned computer downtime can cut into customer service and revenues. These businesses may go to great expense maintaining redundant real-time databases in different locations, with several databases updated simultaneously whenever a transaction occurs. Even businesses that use information systems primarily for accounting and management reporting still need definitive plans for recovering from unexpected downtime.

A 1997 study done by Comdisco, a company selling disaster recovery services including disaster planning and emergency processing sites, found that only 45% of the 200 major companies in its survey had a disaster plan in place. Looking back five years at the World Trade Center bombing in New York City in 1993, the operations director at Fiduciary Trust Company International said that the company would have gone out of business if a remote data processing site had not been available for an emergency situation. At that time, the company moved 450 employees to Comdisco's site in New Jersey for three weeks. In the subsequent years, Fiduciary Trust set up leased line connections to a Comdisco site so that all its transactions and databases could be replicated immediately.[78] More recently, when a 1999 flood in Chicago cut power to Charles Schwab's option trading offices it switched its processing to a nearby Comdisco site without incident.[79]

CHAPTER CONCLUSION

SUMMARY

What are the main types of risks of accidents related to information systems?

The main types of risks of accidents include operator error, hardware malfunction, software bugs, data errors, accidental disclosure of information, damage to physical facilities, inadequate system performance, and liability for system failure.

What are the different types of computer crime?

Computer crime is the use of computerized systems to perform illegal acts. Computer crime can be divided into theft, sabotage, and vandalism. Thefts can be perpetrated through theft of software and equipment, unauthorized use of access codes, fraudulent transaction data, modification of software, and theft or modification of data. Entering fraudulent transaction data is the simplest and most common method of computer-related theft. Even without much computer knowledge, fraudulent data can be entered by forging documents, bypassing procedures, or impersonating someone.

What issues magnify the vulnerability of information systems to accidents and crime?

This vulnerability is magnified by the nature of complex systems, human limitations, and the business environment. Complex systems have many vulnerable points that may be difficult to identify in advance. Decentralization within systems decreases control. Human limitations such as complacency and carelessness increase opportunities for accidents and crime. Greed provides a motive for crime. Difficulty in visualizing how complex systems work makes it harder to anticipate accidents or guard against crime. The business environment's pressures for limiting staff and attaining immediate financial results reduce the time and effort devoted to making systems secure.

What measures can be taken to minimize accidents and computer crime?

The value chain for security starts by building the system right the first time, typically by adhering to a structured system life cycle and using software change control. The next step is training users about security issues to reduce carelessness. Once the system is in operation, maintain physical security and prevent unauthorized access to computers, networks, and data. Having controlled access, make sure transactions are performed correctly and monitor information system usage to ensure effectiveness and find ways to improve. Even if the system seems secure, audit it to identify problems and prepare for disasters.

What are the different ways to control access to data, computers, and networks?

There are five aspects of access control: enforcing guidelines for manual data handling, defining access privileges, enforcing access privileges, controlling incoming data from networks and other media, and using encryption to make the data meaningless to anyone who bypasses access controls. Guidelines for manual data handling range from rules about leaving work on top of desks to procedures for shredding sensitive documents. Access privileges are precise statements of which computers and data an individual can access and under what circumstances. It is possible to enforce access control based on four concepts: what you know (such as passwords); what you have (such as ID cards); where you are (such as permitting access only from a particular terminal); and who you are (such

as biometric identification). Control of incoming data is accomplished through firewalls and virus scanning.

What is public key encryption and what is its advantage over private key encryption?

Public key encryption involves two keys for each user, a public key that is widely available much like a phone number and a private key that must be kept secret. If a message is encrypted using one key it can be decrypted using the other. This makes it unnecessary to develop cumbersome and error-prone methods for distributing and using secret keys. Public key encryption can also be applied to create a document's digital signature, which can be used to verify the origin and content of a message and to verify that a message has not been changed.

What is the role of a certification authority in e-commerce?

A certification authority is a company that issues computer-based records related to the identity of computers and the occurrence of computer-based transactions. It issues digital certificates that identify individual computers, verify the identity of computers involved in specific transactions, and store transaction information to make sure the transaction cannot be repudiated by either party.

KEY TERMS

operator error
software bug
liability
computer crime
hacker
trap door
Trojan horse
logic bomb
virus
denial of service attack
software change control
physical access controls
access privileges

password
social engineering
call-back system
biometric identification
automatic log off
virus protection
firewall
public key encryption
digital signature
segregation of duties
data validation
error correction
public key infrastructure (PKI)

certification authority (CA)
digital certificate
Secure Sockets Layer (SSL)
authentication
integrity
nonrepudiation
Secure Electronic Transaction
   (SET)
chargeback system
auditing around the computer
auditing through the computer
disaster plan

REVIEW QUESTIONS

1. What are common reasons for project failure at each of the four phases of an information system project?

2. Identify the eight types of risks related to accidents rather than computer crime.

3. What factors make operator error more likely?

4. Why do software bugs occur?

6. How do software vendors limit their legal liability for software they sell?

7. What are the different types of computer crime, and which is most common?

8. Describe different ways to steal through fraudulent transaction data.

9. What programming techniques have been used to commit sabotage and vandalism?

10. How is system vulnerability related to the nature of complex systems, human limitations, and pressures in the business environment?

11. Identify the steps in the value chain for system security and control.

12. How does software change control operate?

13. What techniques are used for controlling access to data, computers, and networks?

14. Explain some of the shortcomings of passwords.

15. What do computer hackers mean when they use the term social engineering?

16. How does public key encryption work?

17. Describe the main methods for controlling transaction processing.

18. How do chargeback systems encourage efficiency?

19. What is the difference between SSL and SET?

20. Why is it important to have a disaster plan for information systems?

DISCUSSION QUESTIONS

1. The Business Software Alliance, a software-industry trade group, announced plans to offer a bounty of up to £2,500 ($3,900) to anyone in Great Britain who informed on companies using unlicensed software. Because around half the software used in Great Britain was thought to be unlicensed, many large firms would probably be named. Information about unlicensed use would be obtained through a toll-free number dubbed the Software Crimeline. The chairman of the Computer Users of Europe complained that this was "like the old East Bloc process of informing" and that he "could not see anyone who has any desire to continue his career feeling he could turn in his boss."[80] Explain how this example is related to this chapter's ideas about computer crime and system security.

2. A 20-year-old MIT junior was indicted for managing a computerized bulletin board allegedly used for illegal distribution of copyrighted software. He was not accused of posting software to it or of profiting from the alleged illegal activities. His defense revolved around the assertion that a computerized bulletin board is just a conduit for information and is not responsible for the information posted on it.[81] What are the ethical responsibilities of a person who runs a computerized bulletin board?

3. Your friend has been given a wonderful game program and wants to show you how it operates. He has used it on his computer without problems. Under what circumstances should you allow him to run it on your computer?

4. The night before the Space Shuttle Challenger blew up, killing the astronauts aboard, several engineers at Morton-Thiokol tried to have the launch delayed. They thought that the cold weather at Cape Canaveral might affect critical joints on the body of the booster and thereby endanger the spacecraft, but they were overruled. Identify any ideas in this chapter that might help explain why the Challenger was allowed to take off.

5. You are seated on an airplane about to take off and hear the following announcement after the instructions about fastening seat belts and the location of emergency exits: "This is your pilot. I want to congratulate you as the first group of passengers to benefit from our new autopilot system, which will control the entire flight from takeoff to landing. But don't worry, I'm still here just in case." How would you react to this announcement?

The Love Bug: How a Student Hack Caused $10 Billion in Damage

On May 4, 1999, people around the world began receiving e-mail messages with the title line ILOVEYOU and a message saying "Kindly check the attached LOVELETTER from me." The attachment was called LOVE-LETTER-FOR-YOU.TXT.vbs, meaning that it was a program written in Visual Basic. Anyone who opened the attached letter was in for a rude surprise, because the attachment contained a computer virus (technically, a VBScript worm) that destroyed artwork files ending with the letters jpg or jpeg, and modified MP3 files to make them inaccessible. It used Internet Explorer to visit a Web site in the Philippines, where another piece of malicious software, called WIN-BUGS-FIX.EXE was downloaded. That program searched the victim's hard drive for specific password files and sent them to an Internet account in the Philippines. The worm then used Microsoft Outlook to mail itself to everyone in the user's address book.[82] By various estimates the virus affected as many as 45,000,000 computers at a total cost of the wasted time and effort probably exceeding $10 billion.

The way the worm was addressed played a major role in its rapid spread. Even some computer users who were aware of virus threats were caught off guard because the message seemed to come from someone they knew and had the title ILOVEYOU. Later, when organizations started blocking messages with ILOVEYOU in their title, they may have inadvertently blocked messages that could have been helpful in analyzing the situation. Soon a number of mutations of the virus appeared, such as one called "Mother's Day Order Confirmation." With unintended bad timing, Williams Sonoma, Inc. sent legitimate e-mail to many of its customers marked "Great Gifts for Mom."

Events at Ford Motor Company exemplify what happened as companies around the world learned about the problem. The manager of a Ford computer center in England determined that a worm was spreading across Ford's global e-mail network. He suggested that the entire network should be shut down. In Europe alone, Ford had 1,000 infected computers and 30,000 salaried employees receiving 140,000 contaminated e-mail messages in the three hours before the network was shut down. Its factories kept running, but many employees could not access their electronic calendars. Members of Ford's network administration staff in Michigan stayed up most of the night writing corrective software that would be downloaded the next day to each desktop as it was reconnected to the network.[83] Other companies that did not use Microsoft Outlook had no problem with the Love Bug because it could not attach itself to the software they used.

The worm actually left a number of traces that made it easy to determine its source. The computer code contained the words "Manila, Philippines," and performed downloads from Web sites operated by Sky Internet in the Philippines. Computer logs at Sky Internet showed the password-stealing program was loaded on April 29 and that the programmer used Internet accounts from another Manila ISP. Incriminating chat-room logs traced to e-mail accounts also revealed several individuals chatting about hacking and the creation of virus programs. The clues were so numerous that some experts worried they might be false tips left to thwart investigators.[84]

The prime suspect was Onel de Guzman, 24, a computer-college student who had written his college thesis on a password-stealing program similar to the one used in the virus. He acknowledged during a May 1999 news conference that he might have released the virus by accident, but said he meant no harm. Although a Philippine law against computer hacking was passed after the Love Bug incident occurred, no such law existed in the Philippines at the time the Love Bug was launched, and all charges were dropped.[85] In an October 1999 interview (with his lawyer present), de Guzman admitted that he created viruses but didn't know if the Love Bug was one of his. He said he saw nothing wrong with stealing software from other computers, just as he has no moral qualms about the damage caused by viruses. He said software makers, notably Microsoft, were to blame for the Love Bug debacle because they licensed products vulnerable to sabotage.[86]

Continued

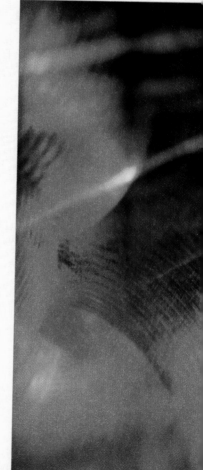

QUESTIONS

1. Review the value chain for system security and control. What are some typical measures aimed at protecting against this type of problem?

2. It has long been known that the use of e-mail attachments is riskier than just using plain text e-mail. Why should companies like Ford allow employees to receive e-mail with attachments? How should they weigh the benefits against the risks?

3. The suspect says that software makers are to blame. What could software makers do to minimize the threat of viruses?

C A S E　　**London Ambulance Service: A New System Causes a Disaster**

The London Ambulance Service (LAS) covers a population of 6.8 million people, carries over 5,000 patients every day, and receives up to 2,500 calls a day. Its goal is to respond to calls in an average of 14 minutes. A previous system for dispatching ambulances in response to medical emergencies had divided London into three separate zones and had communicated with ambulances through a combination of two-way radios, telephones, and computer displays in vehicles. Operators in the dispatching center received calls about emergencies and worked with local ambulance stations to identify the nearest available ambulance and then dispatch it to the site. A new system was developed to treat all of London as a single zone. It effectively did away with radio and telephone calls to stations and permitted the computer to dispatch ambulance crews automatically based on the location of the patient and of available ambulances. Unfortunately the new system had not been completely tested or debugged when it was put into operation on October 26, 1992. As the night progressed, calls were missed, several ambulances were dispatched to the same emergency, and operators in the dispatching center were swamped with computerized exception messages. Some emergency callers could not get through for up to 30 minutes. Between 10 and 20 people probably died because ambulances arrived up to three hours late. A spokesman for LAS called the situation "a complete nightmare."

A formal inquiry into this disaster concluded that neither the computerized parts of the system nor the human participants had been ready for full implementation. The software was neither complete nor fully tested. The computer system's performance under a full load had not been tested. The dispatching staff and ambulance crews had no confidence in the new information system and had not been fully trained. Physical changes in the dispatching room meant that the staff were working in unfamiliar positions without paper backup and were less able to collaborate on problems they had previously solved jointly. The automated dispatching approach required virtually perfect information, but the information it received was imperfect due to incomplete status reporting from the ambulance crews, poor coverage (black spots) in the radio system, a radio communications bottleneck, and technical inconsistencies between the mobile data terminals and the central computer. Imperfect data in the dispatching system caused inappropriate and duplicated allocations of ambulances to emergencies. A swarm of computerized exception messages plus an increased number of callbacks when ambulances did not arrive slowed the work even more. As the ambulance crews became more frustrated, they became less likely to press their status buttons in the right sequence, making the information even less accurate. Problems with the system had been predicted by the owner of a company whose bid to build the system had been unsuccessful. In several memos to LAS management he had warned that the planned system would be "an expensive disaster" and that its rule-based, analytical approach could not be as effective as an experienced operator in the small minority of difficult cases.

The next day the dispatching staff reverted to a semi-manual approach in which the computer stored data but the decisions were made while contacting an ambulance station near the incident. This approach worked well until November 4, when the computer system slowed down and then locked up and could not be rebooted. The dispatchers reverted entirely to manual dispatching. The computer problem turned out to be a software bug that prevented the computer from releasing a small amount of memory each time a vehicle mobilization was generated. This bug had little impact initially, but it gradually tied up more memory until the computer could no longer operate.[87, 88]

Continued

QUESTIONS

1. Explain how the value chain for security and control was or was not followed in this case.

2. Explain the extent to which you believe that better technology (such as cellular phones and global positioning satellites) adopted widely in the years since the LAS disaster would have minimized or eliminated the problems that occurred.

3. Assume the LAS could redo its testing phase before launching the new system. What should be tested and how?

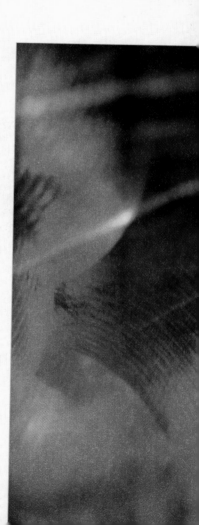

notes

Preface

1. Rebello, Kathy, "The Land of E-Everything," *Business Week, e-biz,* Nov. 1, 1999, p. EB8.
2. Alsop, Stewart, "E or Be Eaten," *Fortune,* Nov. 8, 1999, p. 86.
3. Price WaterhouseCoopers ad in *Business Week, e.biz,* Nov. 1, 1999, p. EB 5.
4. Narisetti, Raju. "IBM to Launch Global Web-Business Blitz," *Wall Street Journal,* Oct. 6, 1997, p. B11.
5. Wilder, Clinton, Bruce Caldwell, and Gregory Dalton. "More than Electronic Commerce," *Informationweek,* Dec. 15, 1997, pp. 30–40.

Chapter 1

1. Fisher, Lawrence M. "Slower Growth at Dell Leaves Sour Taste," *New York Times,* December 19, 1999.
2. *The Economist.* "Survey of E-Management: Enter the Eco-System," November 11, 2000, pp. 30–31.
3. Magretta, Joan. "The Power of Virtual Integration: An Interview with Dell Computer's Michael Dell," *Harvard Business Review,* March-April 1998, pp. 72–84.
4. *The Economist.* "Survey of E-Management: Inside the Machine," November 11, 2000, pp. 5–6.
5. Schwab, Charles R. "Foreword," Thomas M. Seibel and Pat House, *CyberRules: Strategies for Excelling at E-Business.* New York: Currency/Doubleday, 1999, p. viii.
6. Huff, Sid L., Michael Wade, Michael Parent, Scott Schneberger, and Peter Newson. *Cases in Electronic Commerce.* Boston: Irwin/McGraw-Hill, 2000, p. 4.
7. Bartels, Andrew. "The Difference between E-Business and E-Commerce," *Computerworld,* October 30, 2000, p. 41.
8. Laudon, Kenneth C., and Jane P. Laudon. *Essentials of Management Information Systems: Organization and Technology in the Networked Enterprise,* 4th ed. Upper Saddle River, NJ: Prentice Hall, 2001, p. 25.
9. Kalakota, Ravi, and Marcia Robinson. *E-Business: Roadmap for Success.* Reading, MA: Addison-Wesley, 1999, p. xvi.
10. El Sawy, Omar. *Redesigning Enterprise Processes for E-Business.* Boston: Irwin/McGraw-Hill, 2001, p. 7.
11. Stolee, Christopher. "E-Business—Just What Is It?" viewed at http://ebusiness.about.com/industry/, on October 22, 2000. Also: Alentis. "Where's the ASP Value in E-Business?" viewed at www.alentis.com/aspinfo.asp?aspinfoID=911&streamID=1, on October 22, 2000. Also: World Chambers Network. "Generating More Revenue through E-Business," viewed at http://209.208.234.83/benefits/, on October 22, 2000.
12. Shurety, Samantha. *E-Business with Net.Commerce.* Upper Saddle River, NJ: Prentice Hall PTR, 1999, p. 4.
13. IBM. "IBM E-Business," viewed at www-3.ibm.com/e-business/overview/28212.html, on October 22, 2000.
14. Hartman, Amir, John Sifonis, and John Kador. *Net Ready: Strategies for Success in the E-conomy.* New York: McGraw-Hill, 2000, pp. xvii–xviii.
15. Amor, Daniel. *The E-Business Revolution.* Upper Saddle River, NJ: Prentice Hall PTR, 2000, p. 7.
16. Harrington, H. J. *Business Process Improvement.* New York: McGraw-Hill, 1991.
17. Davenport, Thomas H. *Process Improvement: Reengineering Work through Information Technology.* Boston, MA: Harvard Business School Press, 1993.
18. Slater, Robert. The New GE: *How Jack Welch Revived an American Institution.* Homewood, IL: Irwin, 1993, p. 216.
19. Porter, Michael E., and Victor E. Millar. "How Information Gives You Competitive Advantage," *Harvard Business Review,* July-August, 1985, pp. 149–160.
20. Tran, Khanh T. L. "The Web @ Work/ Clorox Co." *Wall Street Journal,* October 9, 2000, p. B21.
21. Smith, Lee. "New Ideas from the Army," *Fortune,* September 19, 1994, pp. 203–212.
22. Gelsinger, Patrick, Paolo Gargini, Gerhard Parker, and Albert Yu. "2001: A Microprocessor Odyssey," pp. 95–113 in Derek Leebaert, *Technology 2001: The Future of Computing and Communications.* Cambridge, MA: The MIT Press, 1991, p. 100.
23. Murillo, Luis Eduardo. *The International DRAM Industry from 1970 to 1993.* Ph.D. Thesis, University of California, Berkeley, 1994, p. 539.
24. Reilly, Patrick M. "The Dark Side: Warning: Portable Devices Can Be Hazardous to Your Health," *Wall Street Journal,* November 16, 1992, p. R12.
25. Palfreman, Jon, and Doron Swade. *The Dream Machine: Exploring the Computer Age.* London: BBC Books, 1991.
26. "When Machines Screw Up," *Forbes,* June 7, 1993, pp. 110–111.
27. Edmondson, Gail. "Silicon Valley on the Rhine," *Business Week,* November 3, 1997, pp. 162–166.
28. Korper, Steffano, and Juanita Ellis. *The E-Commerce Book: Building the E-Empire.* San Diego, CA: Academic Press, 2000, p. 4.
29. Zuckerman, Laurence. "Many Reported Unready to Face Year 2000 Bug," *New York Times,* September 25, 1997, p. C3.
30. The Standish Group. *Chaos,* 1995 report available at www.standishgroup.com/chaos.html in June 1997.
31. Booth, Rose. "IT Project Failures Costly, TechRepublic/Gartner Study Finds," *TechRepublic,* www.techrepublic.com/, accessed on November 17, 2000.
32. Pear, Robert. "Modernization for Medicare Grinds to Halt," *New York Times,* September 16, 1997, p. A1+.
33. Ellul, Jacques. "The Technological Order." *Technology and Culture.* Fall 1962, p. 394. Quoted in Dizard, Wilson P., Jr., *The Coming Information Age.* New York: Longman, 1982.

34. deSola Pool, Ithiel. Ed., "Bell's Electrical Toy: What's the Use," in *The Social Impact of the Telephone*. Cambridge, MA: MIT Press, 1977, pp. 19–22.

35. Ofiesh, Gabriel. "The Seamless Carpet of Knowledge and Learning," pp. 299–319 in Lambert, Steve, and Suzanne Ropiequet, *CD ROM: The New Papyrus*. Redmond, WA: Microsoft Press, 1986.

36. Brand, Stewart. *The Media Lab*. New York: Viking Penguin, 1987, p. 256.

37. Smith, Douglas K., and Robert C. Alexander. *Fumbling the Future: How Xerox Invented, Then Ignored the First Personal Computer*. New York: William Morrow and Company, Inc., 1988, pp. 35–36.

38. Hammer, Michael, and James Champy. *Reengineering the Corporation: A Manifesto for Business Revolution*. New York: Harpers Business, 1993, p. 85.

39. Johnstone, Bob. "Case Study: Inventing the Laser Printer," *Wired*, October 1994, p. 99.

40. Simon, H. A., and Allen Newell. "Heuristic Problem Solving: The Next Advance in Operations Research," *Operations Research*, January-February 1958, pp. 7–8. Cited in Crevier, Daniel. *AI: The Tumultuous History of the Search for Artificial Intelligence*. New York: Basic Books, 1993, p. 108.

41. Armstrong, J. Scott. *Long Range Forecasting*. New York: John Wiley & Sons, 1985.

42. Keegan, Paul. "The Office That Ozzie Built," *The New York Times Magazine*, October 22, 1995, pp. 49–51.

43. Gartner Group. "Replace PCs with Network Computers? 'Over My Dead Body,' You Say?" *New York Times*, August 27, 1997, p. C5.

44. Caldwell, Bruce. "Trading Size 12 for a Custom Fit," *Information Week*, October 28, 1996.

45. Peppers, Don. "Banking on the Internet," *Inside 1 to 1*, April 15, 1999, www.1to1.com/articles/i1-041599/, accessed on November 17, 2000.

46. Slywotzky, Adrian. "How Digital Is Your Company?" *Fast Company*, February 1999, p. 94.

47. Kilarski, Doug. "Producing What Each Consumer Buys," *Consumer Goods Technology*, September/October 1998, www.consumergoods.com/archive/, accessed on November 17, 2000.

48. Zygmont, Jeff. "Mass Customization + the Web = Intimacy with Millions," *Consumer Goods Technology*, March 2000, www.consumergoods.com/archive/, accessed on November 17, 2000.

49. Waxer, Cindy. "501 Blues: The Seat-of-the-Pants Levi Strauss E-Commerce Effort Has Finally Gone to the Rag Basket," *Business 2.0*, January 1, 2000.

50. Boudette, Neal E. "SAP's U.S. Unit to Enhance Relations with Customers After Several Glitches," *Wall Street Journal*, November 4, 1999.

51. Nelson, Emily, and Evan Ramstad. "Hershey's Biggest Dud Is Its New Computer System," *Wall Street Journal*, October 29, 1999.

52. Branch, Shelly. "Hershey Foods Says It Expects to Miss Lowered 4th Quarter Earnings Target," *Wall Street Journal*, December 29, 1999.

53. Hershey's. "To Our Stockholders," *1999 Annual Report*. www.hersheys.com/annualreport/, viewed on November 17, 2000.

Chapter 2

1. "Barnes & Noble Sues Amazon.com," *Book News*, American Booksellers Association, www.bookweb.org/news/, May 19, 1997.

2. Hansell, Saul. "For Amazon, a Holiday Risk: Can It Sell Acres of Everything?" *New York Times*, November 28, 1999.

3. Carvajal, Doreen. "3 Online Book Retailers Cut Price on Best Sellers," *New York Times*, May 18, 1999.

4. Yourdon, Edward. *Decline and Fall of the American Programmer*. Englewood Cliffs, NJ: Prentice-Hall, 1992, p. 41.

5. Alter, Steven. "A General, Yet Useful Theory of Information Systems," *Communications of the AIS*, Volume 1, Article 13, March 1999.

6. Alter, Steven. "Same Words, Different Meanings: Are Basic IS/IT Concepts Our Self-Imposed Tower of Babel?" *Communications of the AIS*, Volume 3, Article 10, April 2000, http://cais.isworld.org./articles/.

7. Alter, "Theory of Information Systems," 1:13.

8. Quinn, James Brian. *Intelligent Enterprise: A Knowledge and Service Based Paradigm for Industry*. New York: Free Press, 1992, p. 329.

9. Hope, Tony, and Jeremy Hope. *Transforming the Bottom Line: Managing Performance with the Real Numbers*, Boston, MA: Harvard Business School Press, 1996.

10. Markus, M. Lynne, and Mark Keil. "If We Built It, They Will Come: Designing Information Systems That People Want to Use," *Sloan Management Review*, Summer 1994, pp. 11–25.

11. Van Natta, Jr., Don. "Gore Lawyers Focus on Ballot in Palm Beach County," *New York Times*, November 16, 2000, p. A25.

12. Broadbent, Marianne, and Peter Weill. "Management by Maxim: How Business and IT Managers Can Create IT Infrastructures," *Sloan Management Review*, Spring 1997, pp. 77–92.

13. Brown, John Seeley. "Reinventing the Corporation." *Harvard Business Review*, January-February 1991, p. 108.

14. Pfeffer, Jeffrey. *Competitive Advantage through People: Unleashing the Power of the Work Force*. Boston, MA: Harvard Business School Press, 1994, p. 177.

15. Darnton, Geoffrey, and Sergio Giacoletto. *Information in the Enterprise*. Digital Press, 1992, p. i.

16. Aramark Uniform Services. "Rent, Purchase, Lease. What's Right for You?" www.aramark-uniform.com/, viewed on November 18, 2000.

17. Aramark Uniform Services. "New Customer Invoice," www.aramark-uniform.com/news/, accessed on November 18, 2000.

18. Klebnikov, Paul. "Paper Jam," *Forbes Magazine*, March 3, 2000.

19. Biddle, Frederic M., John Lippman, and Stephanie N. Mehta. "One Satellite Fails, and the World Goes Awry," *Wall Street Journal*, May 21, 1998, p. B1.

20. Zuckerman, Laurence. "Satellite Failure Is Rare, and Therefore Unsettling," *New York Times*, May 21, 1998, p. C3.

21. Orbit Communication Corp. "C-Band News," www.orbitsat.com/News/, viewed on November 17, 2000.

Chapter 3

1. Taptich, Brian E. "Thanks to Fleet Teamwork, Charles Schwab & Company Is Still Pioneering Online Finance," *Red Herring*, September 1999, www.redherring.com/mag/.

2. Charles Schwab. "Welcome to Charles Schwab," www.aboutschwab.com/, accessed on November 1, 2000.

3. Heins, John. "After Cost Cuts, What?" *Forbes*, May 1, 1989, p. 46.

4. Barboza, David, "On-Line Trade Fees Falling Off the Screen," *New York Times*, March 1, 1998, p. B4.

5. Charles Schwab. "Schwab Signature Services Overview," www.schwab.com/SchwabNOW/, accessed on November 1, 2000.

6. Barnett, Megan. "Charles Schwab Goes Upscale," *The Standard,* Jan. 13, 2000.

7. Multex.com. "Charles Schwab Corp: Stock Snapshot," October 29, 2000, www.multexinvestor.com/data/.

8. Harrington, H. J. *Business Process Improvement.* New York: McGraw-Hill, 1991.

9. Davenport, Thomas H. *Process Improvement: Reengineering Work through Information Technology.* Boston, MA: Harvard Business School Press, 1993.

10. Harris, Catherine L. "Office Automation: Making It Pay Off," *Business Week,* October 12, 1987, pp. 134–146.

11. Hammer, Michael. "Reengineering Work: Don't Automate, Obliterate," *Harvard Business Review,* July-August 1990, pp. 104–112.

12. Davenport, Thomas H., and Short, James E. "The New Industrial Engineering: Information Technology and Business Process Redesign," *Sloan Management Review,* Summer 1990, pp. 11–27.

13. Hammer, Michael, and James Champy. *Reengineering the Corporation: A Manifesto for Business Revolution.* New York: Harper Business, 1993.

14. Uchitelle, Louis. "It's Just the Beginning," *New York Times,* Special section on e-commerce, June 7, 2000.

15. Nelson, Emily, and Ann Zimmerman. "How Kimberly-Clark Keeps Client Costco in Diapers," *Wall Street Journal,* September 7, 2000.

16. Malone, T. W., and Crowston, K. "The Interdisciplinary Study of Coordination," *ACM Computing Surveys,* 1994.

17. Seybold, Patricia B. "Delivering a Branded Customer Experience," excerpt from *Creating a Positive Customer Experience,* research report by Patricia Seybold, May 15, 2000, www.psgroup.com/doc/products/.

18. Perrow, Charles. *Normal Accidents: Living with High-Risk Technologies.* New York: Basic Books, 1984.

19. Eisenhardt, Kathleen M., and Shona L. Brown. "Time Pacing: Competing in Markets That Won't Stand Still," *Harvard Business Review,* March-April 1998, pp. 59–69.

20. Maznevski, Martha L., and Katherine M. Chuboda, "Bridging Space over Time: Virtual Team Dynamics and Effectiveness," *Organization Science,* Vol. 11, No. 5, September-October 2000.

21. Yang, Catherine, and Howard Gleck. "How to File: Even Accountants Don't Know for Sure," *Business Week,* March 7, 1988, p. 88.

22. Hitt, Greg. "Favored Companies Get 11th-Hour Tax Breaks," *Wall Street Journal,* July 30, 1997, p. A2.

23. Herman, Tom. "A Special Summary and Forecast of Federal and State Tax Developments," *Wall Street Journal,* July 30, 1997, p. A1.

24. Tully, Shawn. "A Boom Ahead in Company Profits," *Fortune,* April 6, 1992, pp. 76–84.

25. Hammer, Michael, and James Champy. *Reengineering the Corporation: A Manifesto for Business Revolution.* New York: Harper Business, 1993, p. 55.

26. Carley, William M. "Jet Near-Crash Shows 747s May Be at Risk of Autopilot Failure," *Wall Street Journal,* April 26, 1993, p. A1.

27. Forester, Tony, and Perry Morrison. *Computer Ethics: Cautionary Tales and Ethical Dilemmas in Computing.* Cambridge, MA: MIT Press, 1994, p. 108.

28. Neumann, Peter G. *Computer-Related Risks.* Reading, MA: Addison-Wesley Publishing Company, 1995, pp. 68–69.

29. Ross, Philip E. "The Day the Software Crashed," *Forbes,* April 25, 1994, pp. 142–156.

30. Wald, Matthew L. "Appalled by Risk, Except in the Car," *New York Times,* June 15, 1997, p. E4.

31. Brody, Herbert. "Reforming the Pentagon: An Inside Job," *Technology Review,* April 1994, pp. 31–36.

32. Womack, James P., and Daniel T. Jones. *Lean Thinking: Banish Waste and Create Wealth in Your Corporation.* New York: Simon & Schuster, 1996, pp. 15 and 314.

33. Roach, Stephen S. "Services Under Siege—The Restructuring Imperative," *Harvard Business Review,* September-October 1991, pp. 82–90.

34. Brynjolfsson, Erik. "The Productivity Paradox of Information Technology," *Communications of the ACM,* December 1993, pp. 67–77.

35. Bulkeley, Wiliam M. "The Data Trap: How PC Users Waste Time," *Wall Street Journal,* January 4, 1993, p. B2.

36. Heygate, Richard. "Technophobes, Don't Run Away Yet," *Wall Street Journal,* August 15, 1994, p. A8.

37. Blackburn, Joseph D. "New Product Development: The New Time Wars," in Joseph D. Blackburn, ed., *Time-Based Competition: The Next Battleground in American Manufacturing.* Homewood, Ill.: Business One Irwin, 1991, pp.121–165.

38. Weiss, Todd, R. "Walmart.com Site Back Online after 28-Day Overhaul," *Computerworld Online,* October 31, 2000.

39. Sager, Ira. "CyberCrime," *Businessweek Online,* February 21, 2000.

40. Weiner, Tim. "No One Loses C.I.A. Job in Case of Double Agent," *New York Times,* September 29, 1994, p. A1.

41. Pounds, William. "The Process of Problem Finding," *Industrial Management Review,* Vol. 11, No. 1, 1969, pp. 1–20.

42. Simon, Herbert. *The New Science of Management Decision.* New York: Harper & Row, 1960.

43. Tversky, Amos, and Daniel Kahneman. "The Framing of Decisions and the Psychology of Choice," *Science,* Vol. 211, January 30, 1981, pp. 453–458.

44. Slovic, Paul, Baruch Fischhoff, and Sarah Lichtenstein. "Risky Assumptions," *Psychology Today,* June 1990, pp. 44–48.

45. Rubin, John. "The Dangers of Overconfidence," *Technology Review,* July 1989, pp. 11–12.

46. Janis, Irving L. *Groupthink: Psychological Studies of Policy Decisions and Fiascoes.* Boston: Houghton Mifflin, 1983.

47. Smart, Tim. "A Day of Reckoning for Bean Counters," *Business Week,* March 14, 1994, pp. 75–76.

48. Keen, P. G. W. "Information Technology and the Management Difference: A Fusion Map," *IBM Systems Journal,* Vol. 32, No. 1, 1993, pp. 17–39.

49. Bulkeley, William M. "Replaced by Technology: Job Interviews," *Wall Street Journal,* August 22, 1994, p. B1.

50. Pitney Bowes. "DocuMatch Integrated Mail System," www.pb.com/products_serv/, viewed on November 18, 2000.

51. Haskin, David. "Will E-Postage Stamp Out the Postal Meter?" *Business Week Online,* August 11, 1999.

52. E-Stamp Corporation. "Welcome to E-Stamp," www.estamp.com/, viewed on November 18, 2000.

53. Haskin, op. cit.

54. E-Stamp Corporation. "E-Stamp Corporation Announces Second Quarter 2000 Results," July 20, 2000, www.estamp.com/, viewed on November 18, 2000.

55. Hammer, Ben. "E-Stamp to Cancel Web Sales," *The Industry Standard,* November 27, 2000, www.thestandard.com/.

56. Thurm, Scott. "Eating Their Own Dog Food: Cisco Goes Online to Buy, Sell, and Hire," *Wall Street Journal*, April 19, 2000.

57. Brown, Eryn. "9 Ways to Win on the Web," *Fortune*, May 24, 1999.

Chapter 4

1. www.eBay.com, viewed on September 28, 2000.

2. Guernsey, Lisa. "The Powers Behind the Auctions," *New York Times*, August 20, 2000.

3. www.eBay.com, viewed on September 28, 2000.

4. Guernsey, Lisa. "A New Caveat for eBay Users: Seller Beware," *New York Times*, August 2, 2000.

5. Dobrzynski, Judith H. "In Online Auctions, Rings of Bidders," *New York Times*, June 2, 2000.

6. Leonard, Dorothy, and Jeffrey F. Rayport. "Spark Innovation through Empathic Design," *Harvard Business Review*, November-December 1997, pp. 102–113.

7. Hirsch, James S. "Renting Cars Abroad Can Drive You Nuts," *Wall Street Journal*, December 10, 1993, p. B1.

8. Chen, P. P. "The Entity-Relationship Model—Toward a Unified View of Data," *ACM Transactions on Database Systems*, Vol. 1, No. 1, March 1976.

9. Microsoft Product Support Services. "ACC: Database Normalization Basics," http://support.microsoft.com/support/, accessed on November 16, 2000.

10. Lexis-Nexis. "Introducing nexis.com," advertisement, *New York Times*, September 27, 2000, p. A15.

11. Greising, David. "Washington's Hot Potato," *Business Week*, December 16, 1996, pp. 30–33.

12. Galbraith, Craig S., and Gregory B. Merrill, "The Politics of Forecasting: Managing the Truth," *California Management Review*, Vol. 38, No. 2, Winter 1996, pp. 29–43.

13. LeFauve, Richard G., and Arnoldo Hax. "Saturn—The Making of the Modern Corporation," pp. 257–281 in Stephen P. Bradley, Jerry A. Hausman, and Richard L. Nolan, eds., *Globalization, Technology, and Competition*. Boston: Harvard Business School Press, 1993.

14. Transcript of Election 2000 Vice Presidential Debate, October 5, 2000. Viewed at www.cspan.org/campaign2000/ on October 11, 2000.

15. Geyelin, Milo. "Reynolds Sought Specifically to Lure Young Smokers Years Ago, Data Suggest," *Wall Street Journal*, January 15, 1998, p. A4.

16. Kuntz, Phil, and Eva M. Rodriguez. "New Videotape Shows Clinton Thanking Donors for Contributions at Fund-Raiser," *Wall Street Journal*, October 16, 1997, p. A4.

17. Hudson, Richard L. "Frankness of European Doctors Differs from One Country to Next, Survey Shows," *Wall Street Journal*, February 18, 1993, p. B7D.

18. Fialka, John J. "Supersecret Complex Outside Capital Is a $310 Million Surprise to Congress," *Wall Street Journal*, August 9, 1994, p. B2.

19. U.S. House of Representatives, *H.R. 3605, Patients' Bill of Rights Act of 1998, Section 112*, March 31, 1998.

20. Weinstein, Michael. "In Health Care, Be Careful What You Wish For," *New York Times*, May 31, 1998, Sec. 4, p. 1.

21. Myers, Steven Lee. "China Rejects U.S. Actions on Bombing of Embassy," *New York Times*, April 11, 2000.

22. Myers, Steven Lee. "Chinese Embassy Bombing: A Wide Net of Blame," *New York Times*, April 17, 2000.

23. Schmidt, Eric. "In a Fatal Error, C.I.A. Picked a Bombing Target Only Once: The Chinese Embassy," *New York Times*, July 23, 1999.

24. Myers, Steven Lee. "C.I.A. Fires Officer Blamed in Bombing of China Embassy," *New York Times*, April 9, 2000.

25. Ibid.

Chapter 5

1. Petroski, Henry. *Invention by Design: How Engineers Get from Thought to Thing*. Cambridge, MA: Harvard University Press, 1996.

2. Belden, Tom. "CATIA: The Computer Heart and Soul of Aircraft Design," *The Seattle Times*, February 11, 1997.

3. IBM. "CATIA Solutions: Digital Product Definition and Simulation," www-3. ibm.com/solutions/, accessed on November 1, 2000.

4. Sliwa, Carol. "Net Used to Extend EDI's Reach," *Computerworld*, February 12, 1998, p. 1.

5. Davenport, Thomas H., and James E. Short. "The New Industrial Engineering: Information Technology and Business Process Redesign," *Sloan Management Review*, Summer 1990, pp. 11–27.

6. Bylinsky, Gene. "The Race to the Automatic Factory," *Fortune*, February 21, 1983, pp. 53–64.

7. Fisher, Marshall. "What Is the Right Supply Chain for Your Product?" *Harvard Business Review*, March-April 1997, pp. 105–116.

8. Blattberg, Robert C., and John Deighton. "Interactive Marketing: Exploiting the Age of Addressability," *Sloan Management Review*, Fall 1991, pp. 5–14.

9. Frank, Stephen E. "Eager Banks Say Walk Right In," *Wall Street Journal*, October 22, 1997, p. B12.

10. Alwang, Greg. "Unified Messaging," *PC Magazine*, July 20, 1999.

11. Weber, Thomas E. "Instant Messages Aren't Just for Chat," *Wall Street Journal*, March 13, 2000.

12. Guernsey, Lisa. "The Web Discovers Its Voice," *New York Times*, October 21, 1999.

13. Johansen, Robert. *Groupware: Computer Support for Teams*. New York: Free Press, 1988.

14. Gilpin, Kenneth N. "E.D.S. Wins Record $7 Billion Contract for Navy Computer Network," *New York Times*, October 7, 2000, p. B1.

15. Anthes, Gary H. "Learning How to Share," *Computerworld*, February 23, 1998, pp. 76–79.

16. Jurvis, Jeff. "Serving Up Knowledge," *Information Week*, November 17, 1997, pp. 141–157.

17. Davenport, Thomas H., and Lawrence Prusak. *Working Knowledge: How Organizations Manage What They Know*. Boston: Harvard Business School Press, 1998, p. 21.

18. Pfeffer, Jeffrey. "Ask the Expert: Managing People for a Competitive Advantage," *CIO Online*, posted December 28, 1998.

19. Dennis, Alan R., Joey F. George, Len M Jessup, Jay F. Nunamaker, Jr., and Douglas R. Vogel. "Information Technology to Support Meetings," *MIS Quarterly*, December 1988, pp. 591–624.

20. Nunamaker, Jay, Doug Vogel, Alan Heminger, Ben Martz, Ron Brohowski, and Chris McGoff. "Experiences at IBM with Group Support Systems: A Field Study," *Decision Support Systems*, Vol. 5, No. 2, June 1989, pp. 183–196.

21. Trombly, Maria. "Bigger Than Y2K, *Computerworld Online*, September 25, 2000.

22. Mason, Richard. "Information Systems Technology and Corporate Strategy: A Historical Overview." In F. Warren McFarlan, ed., *The Information Systems Research Challenge. Proceedings.* Boston: Harvard Business School Press, 1984, pp. 261–278.

23. Mintzberg, Henry. *The Nature of Managerial Work.* New York: Harper & Row, 1973.

24. Peters, T. J., and R. H. Waterman, Jr. *In Search of Excellence.* New York: Harper & Row, 1982.

25. Verity, John W. "Coaxing the Meaning Out of Data," *Business Week,* February 3, 1997, pp. 134–137.

26. Stedman, Chris. "Data Mining Despite the Dangers," *Computerworld,* December 29, 1997/January 5, 1998, pp. 61–62.

27. Gwynne, Peter. "Making the Right Decision," *Beyond Computing,* September 2000, pp. 42–45.

28. Hulbert, Mark. "In the Data Mine, There Is Seldom a Pot of Gold," *New York Times,* October 1, 2000.

29. Davis, Randall. "Amplifying Expertise with Expert Systems." In Patrick H. Winston and Karen A. Prendergast, eds., *The AI Business: Commercial Uses of Artificial Intelligence.* Cambridge, MA: MIT Press, 1984, pp. 17–39.

30. Stipp, David. "Computer Researchers Find 'Neural Networks' Help Mimic the Brain," *Wall Street Journal,* September 9, 1988, p. 1.

31. Loofbourrow, T. H. "Expert Systems and Neural Networks: The Hatfields and the McCoys?" *Expert Systems,* Fall 1990.

32. McNeill, Daniel, and Paul Freiberger. *Fuzzy Logic: The Revolutionary Computer Technology That is Changing the World.* New York: Touchstone, 1993.

33. Munakata, Toshinori, and Jani Yashvant. "Fuzzy Systems: An Overview," *Communications of the ACM,* March 1994, pp. 69–76.

34. Allen, Bradley P. "Case-Based Reasoning: Business Applications," *Communications of the ACM,* March 1994, pp. 40–42.

35. Minsky, Marvin. *The Society of Mind.* New York: Simon & Schuster, 1986.

36. Davenport, Thomas P. "Putting the Enterprise into the Enterprise System," *Harvard Business Review,* July-August 1998, pp. 121–131.

37. Williamson, Miryam. "From SAP to Nuts," *Computerworld,* November 10, 1997.

38. Bylinsky, Gene. "Computers That Learn by Doing," *Fortune,* September 6, 1993, pp. 96–102.

39. Steward, Thomas D. "Owens Corning: Back from the Dead," *Fortune,* May 26, 1997, pp. 118–126.

40. Koch, Christopher. "Flipping the Switch: The Big Bang Theory," *CIO,* June 15, 1996.

41. O'Reilly, Brian. "The Power Merchant," *eCompany,* April 2000, www.ecompany.com/articles/.

42. King, Julia, and Gary H. Anthes. "Enron Hits the Gas," *Computerworld,* November 20, 2000, p. 1+.

43. Mullen, Theo. "Enron Breaks into E-Biz Big Leagues," *Internetweek Online,* May 11, 2000, www.internetwk.com/lead/.

Chapter 6

1. Ives, Blake, and Michael P. Vitale. "After the Sale: Leveraging Maintenance with Information Technology," *MIS Quarterly,* March 1988, pp. 7–21.

2. Venkatraman, N. "IT-Enabled Business Transformation: From Automation to Business Scope Redefinition," *Sloan Management Review,* Winter 1994, pp. 73–87.

3. Otis Elevator Company. *Otis.com,* viewed on November 7, 2000.

4. Wald, Matthew L. "Reference Disks Speak Volumes," *New York Times,* February 26, 1998, p. D12.

5. Davis, Stan, and Christopher Meyer. *Blur: The Speed of Change in the Connected Economy.* Reading, MA: Addison-Wesley, 1998, p. 19.

6. Levitin, Anany V., and Thomas C. Redman. "Data as a Resource: Properties, Implications, and Prescriptions," *Sloan Management Review,* Fall 1998, pp. 89–101.

7. Adobe Corporation. "How DRM Works," www.adobe.com/epaper/, viewed on November 21, 2000.

8. Shapiro, Carl, and Hal R. Varian. "Versioning: The Smart Way to Sell Information," *Harvard Business Review,* November-December 1998, pp. 106–114.

9. Gutek, Barbara A. *The Dynamics of Service: Reflections on the Changing Nature of Customer/Provider Interactions.* San Francisco: Jossey-Bass Publishers, 1995, pp. 7–8.

10. Lazarus, David. "Charting the Course: Global Business Sets Its Goals," *Fortune,* August 4, 1997, p. A-41.

11. Chapman, Katy. "Body Scanning Empowers Mass Production," *American Sportswear & Knitting Times,* June/July 2000.

12. Slatalla, Michelle. "Wonder How You'd Look in Yellow Eye Shadow?" *New York Times,* August 17, 2000.

13. Canedy, Dana. "Wish You Weren't Here," *New York Times,* November 20, 1997, p. C1 +.

14. Davis, *op cit,* pp. 16–21.

15. Alter, Steven. "Shopping.com: When Ecommerce Isn't a Bargain," *Communications of the Association for Information Systems,* Vol. 2, Article 22, November 1999.

16. Mossberg, Walter S. "Amazon.com Still Remains a Web Shopping Model," *Wall Street Journal,* September 21, 2000.

17. Burton, Jonathan. "Creating Ways to Cut the Delivery Time from Mouse to House," *New York Times,* June 7, 2000.

18. Arnaut, Gordon. "No Frills, Just Service with a Screen," *New York Times,* January 26, 1998, p. C5.

19. Driscoll, Lisa. "Think of It as Insurance for Insurers," *Business Week,* January 8, 1990, p. 44E.

20. Champy, James. *Reengineering Management: The Mandate for New Leadership.* New York: HarperBusiness, 1995, p. 133.

21. Mehta, Stephanie N. "AT&T Is Seeking Cause of Big Outage in Data Network Used by Corporations," *Wall Street Journal,* April 15, 1998, p. B8.

22. Sims, Calvin. "Disruption of Phone Service Laid to Computer Program," *New York Times,* January 17, 1990, p. A1.

23. Pearl, Daniel. "A Power Outage Snarls Air Traffic in Chicago Region." *Wall Street Journal,* September 15, 1994, p. A4.

24. Morris, Charles R., and Charles H. Ferguson. "How Architecture Wins Technology Wars," *Harvard Business Review,* March-April 1993, pp. 86–97.

25. Porter, Michael. *Competitive Advantage: Creating and Sustaining Superior Performance.* London: Free Press, 1985.

26. Freudenheim, Milt. "Oxford Health Drops 62% as Quarterly Loss Is Seen," *New York Times,* October 28, 1997, p. C9.

27. Klebnikov, Paul. "Paper Jam," *Forbes,* March 20, 2000.

28. Clemons, Eric K., and Michael Row. "A Strategic Information System: McKesson Drug Company's Economost," *Planning Review,* September-October 1988, pp. 14–19.

29. Johnston, H. Russell, and Michael R. Vitale. "Creating Competitive Advantage with Interorganizational Information Systems," *MIS Quarterly,* June 1988, pp. 153–165.

30. Diebold, John. *The Innovators.* New York: E. P. Dutton, 1990.

31. Wiseman, Charles. "Attack & Counterattack: The New Game in Information Technology." *Planning Review,* Vol. 16, No. 15, September-October 1988, p. 6.

32. Christie, James. "Reality Strands Airlines in Orbitz," *Redherring.com,* September 13, 2000.

33. Stuart, Anne. "Clicks & Bricks," *CIO,* March 15, 2000.

34. Farmer, Melanie Austria. "Barnes & Noble to Offer In-Store Access to Web Site," *CNET News.com,* October 26, 2000.

35. Rosencrance, Linda. "FTC Warns Online Retailers to Keep Holiday Shipping Promises," *Computerworld Online,* November 17, 2000.

36. Woolley, Scott. "E-muscle," *Forbes,* March 9, 1998, p. 204.

37. Eisenberg, Anne. "In Online Auctions of the Future, It'll Be Bot vs. Bot vs. Bot," *Wall Street Journal,* August 17, 2000.

38. Weiss, Todd R. "Amazon Apologizes for Price-Testing Program That Angered Customers," *Computerworld Online,* September 28, 2000.

39. Afuah, Allan, and Christopher L. Tucci. *Internet Business Models and Strategies.* Boston: Irwin/McGraw-Hill, 2001, pp. 54–55.

40. Brain, Marshall. "How E-Commerce Works," http://www.howstuffworks.com/ecommerce.htm, viewed on November 23, 2000.

41. Perman, Stacy. "E-Tailing Survival Guide: OK, Forget the Whole Damn Thing," *eCompany,* December 2000.

42. Brain, Marshall. "How Internet Cookies Work," www.howstuffworks.com/cookie.htm, accessed on November 5, 2000.

43. WhatIs?.com. "Definition of Cookie," www.whatis.com, accessed on November 5, 2000.

44. Eichelberger, Lori. "The Cookie Controversy," www.cookiecentral.com, accessed on November 5, 2000.

45. Luftman, Jerry N. "Applying the Strategic Alignment Model," pp. 43–69. Also Davidson, William H., and Joseph F. Movizzo. "Managing the Business Transformation Process," pp. 322–358. In Jerry N. Luftman, ed., *Competing in the Information Age: Strategic Alignment in Practice.* New York: Oxford University Press, 1996.

46. Hafner, Katie. "Are Customers Ever Right? Service's Decline and Fall," *New York Times,* July 20, 2000.

47. Ibid.

48. Brady, Diane. "Why Service Stinks," *Business Week,* October 23, 2000, pp. 118–128.

49. Drucker, Jesse. "Passengers Find They May Be Saving Money, but Losing Time," *Wall Street Journal,* August 25, 2000.

50. Zeitlin, Minda. "E-Customer Service Gets Real," *Computerworld Online,* October 30, 2000.

51. Ho, Rodney. "Online Auction Start-Up Auctiva Stirs EBay's Wrath with Its Web Strategy," *Wall Street Journal,* October 24, 2000.

52. Gillen, Mary. "French Attempt Yahoo Nazi Blockade," *PC Magazine,* November 2000.

53. Stolberg, Sheryl Gay, and Jeff Gerth. "High-Tech Stealth Being Used to Sway Doctor Prescriptions," *New York Times,* November 16, 2000, p. A1.

54. Ernst & Young LLP. "Ernie," www.ernie.ey.com, viewed September 20, 1998.

55. *Business Innovation Journal.* "Selling Knowledge on the 'Net'," Issue 1, 1998, www.businessinnovation.ey.com/journal/, viewed on September 20, 1998.

56. Gartner Group. "Online Advisory Services: A New Model," June 12, 2000, www.gartner.com/public/, viewed on November 20, 2000.

57. Tapscott, Don, and David Ticoll. "Retail Evolution," *The Standard,* July 17, 2000.

58. Multex.com. "Webvan Group, Inc.," *Market Guide,* http://yahoo.marketguide.com/mgi/, viewed on November 23, 2000.

59. Helft, Miguel. "Webvan Fails to Deliver," *The Standard,* October 18, 2000.

60. Sandoval, Greg. "Webvan Running Out of Thanksgiving Goodies," *CNET News.com,* November 20, 2000.

Chapter 7

1. Petersen, Andrea. "DoubleClick Reverses Course After Outcry on Privacy Issue," *Wall Street Journal,* March 3, 2000.

2. Tedeschi, Bob. "DoubleClick Reverses on Using Personal Data," *New York Times,* March 2, 2000.

3. Rewick, Jennifer. "DoubleClick's Buy of Abacus Unit Shows Signs of Strategic Letdown," *Wall Street Journal,* October 19, 2000.

4. Ellul, Jacques. *The Technological Bluff.* Grand Rapids, MI: William B. Eerdmans Publishing Company, 1990, p. 39.

5. Perrow, Charles. *Normal Accidents: Living with High-Risk Technologies.* New York: Basic Books, 1984.

6. Norman, Donald A. *Things That Make Us Smart: Defending Human Attributes in the Age of the Machine.* Reading, MA: Addison-Wesley Publishing Company, 1993, pp. 233–236.

7. Turkle, Sherry. *The Second Self: Computers and the Human Spirit.* New York: Simon & Schuster, 1984, p. 271.

8. Sheff, David. *Game Over: How Nintendo Zapped an American Industry, Captured Your Dollars, and Enslaved Your Children.* New York: Random House, 1993, p. 10.

9. Rosenbaum, David E. "Panel Documents How Violent Fare Is Aimed at Youth," *New York Times,* September 12, 2000.

10. Karasek, Robert, and Tores Theorell. *Healthy Work.* New York: Basic Books, 1990.

11. "Healthy Lives: A New View of Stress," *University of California, Berkeley Wellness Letter,* June 1990, pp. 4–5.

12. Winslow, Ron. "Lack of Control Over Job Is Seen as Heart Risk," *Wall Street Journal,* July 25, 1997, p. B1.

13. Varian, Hal R. "The Information Economy: How Much Will Two Bits Be Worth in the Digital Marketplace?" *Scientific American,* September 1995, pp. 200–201.

14. Schlefer, Jonathan. "Office Automation and Bureaucracy." *Technology Review,* July 1983, pp. 32–40.

15. McKay, Colin J. "Work with Visual Display Terminals: Psychosocial Aspects and Health," *Journal of Occupational Medicine,* Vol. 31, No. 12, December 1989, pp. 957–966.

16. Brody, Jane E. "Health Watch: Women Under Stress," *New York Times,* June 11, 1997, p. B10.

17. Office of Technology Assessment. *The Electronic Supervisor: New Technology, New Tensions.* Washington, DC: U.S. Congress, Office of Technology Assessment, 1987.

18. Hutheesing, Nikhil. "What Are You Doing on That Porn Site?" *Forbes,* November 3, 1997, pp. 368–369.

19. Matthews, Anna Wilde. "New Gadgets Trace Truckers' Every Move," *Wall Street Journal,* July 14, 1997, p. B1.

20. Rosencrance, Linda. "Truckers Critical of NTSB Plan for Onboard Electronic Data Recorders," *Computerworld Online,* October 30, 2000.

21. Alter, Steven L. "Equitable Life: A Computer-Assisted Underwriting System," *Decision Support Systems.* Reading, MA: Addison-Wesley, 1980.

22. Stockton, William. "New Airliners Make Experts Ask: How Advanced Is Too Advanced?" *New York Times,* December 12, 1988.

23. Dreyfus, Joel. "The Three R's on the Shop Floor," *Fortune,* Vol. 121, No. 2, Spring 1990, pp. 86–89.

24. Zuboff, Shoshanna. *In the Age of the Smart Machine: The Future of Work and Power,* New York: Basic Books, 1988, p. 135.

25. Zuboff, Shoshana. "New Worlds of Computer-Mediated Work," *Harvard Business Review,* September-October 1982, pp. 142–152.

26. Zuboff, *In the Age of the Smart Machine: The Future of Work and Power.*

27. Zuboff, Shoshana. "Problems of Symbolic Toil," *Dissent,* Winter 1982, pp. 51–61.

28. Markoff, John. "Portrait of a Newer, Lonelier Crowd Is Captured in an Internet Survey," *New York Times,* February 16, 2000.

29. Bloomberg News, "Manufacturers See Lack of Basic Skills," *New York Times,* November 16, 1997, p. 10.

30. Garson, Barbara. *The Electronic Sweatshop.* New York: Penguin Books, 1989.

31. Ives, Blake, and Margrethe H. Olson. "User Involvement and MIS Success: A Review of Research," *Management Science,* Vol. 30, No. 5, May 1984, pp. 586–603.

32. Sviokla, John J. "Knowledge Workers and Radically New Technology," *Sloan Management Review,* Summer 1996, pp. 25–40.

33. Keen, Peter G. W. "Information Systems and Organizational Change," *Communications of the ACM,* Vol. 24, No. 1, January 1981, pp. 24–33.

34. Markus, M. Lynne. "Power, Politics, and MIS Implementation," *Communications of the ACM,* Vol. 26, No. 6, June 1983, pp. 430–444.

35. Mason, Richard. "Four Ethical Issues of the Information Age," *MIS Quarterly,* Vol. 10, No. 1, January 1986.

36. Chase, Marilyn. "If the Screenplay Doesn't Shake You, the Sound Might," *Wall Street Journal,* July 21, 1997, p. B1.

37. Carnevale, Mary Lu. "Telemarketers Fight Banning of Autodialers," *Wall Street Journal,* January 20, 1993, p. B1.

38. *New York Times.* "Court Blocks Caller ID," March 23, 1992, p. C8.

39. Duff, Christina. "Pick Up on This: Just Don't Answer, Let Freedom Ring," *Wall Street Journal,* January 14, 1998, p. A1.

40. Warren, Samuel D., and Louis D. Brandeis. "The Right to Privacy," *Harvard Law Review,* Vol. 4, December 15, 1890.

41. Ito, Youichi, and Takaaki Hattori. "Mass Media Ethics in Japan," pp. 168–180 in Thomas W. Cooper, *Communications Ethics and Global Change.* White Plains, NY: Longman, 1989.

42. Asenjo, Porfirio Barroso. "Spanish Media Ethics," pp. 69–84 in Thomas W. Cooper, *Communications Ethics and Global Change.* White Plains, NY: Longman, 1989.

43. Toppo, Greg. "FTC Announces Toysmart Settlement," *Excite News,* July 21, 2000.

44. Guidera, Jerry, and Frank Byrt. "Judge Rejects Toysmart's Agreement with FTC Because of Lack of a Buyer," *Wall Street Journal,* August 18, 2000.

45. Amazon.com. "Amazon.com Privacy Notice," www.amazon.com, accessed on November 7, 2000.

46. Broder, John M. "F.T.C. Opens Hearings on Computers' Threat to Americans' Right to Privacy," *New York Times,* June 11, 1997, p. A20.

47. Bernstein, Nina. "OnLine, High-Tech Sleuths Find Private Facts," *New York Times,* September 15, 1997, p. A1.

48. Calandra, Thom. "'Privacy for Sale': Tales of Data Rape," *San Francisco Chronicle,* September 12, 1992, p. E1.

49. Betts, Mitch. "Driver Privacy on the Way?" *Computerworld,* February 28, 1994, p. 29.

50. Sandberg, Jared. "Ply and Pry: How Business Pumps Kids on the Web," *Wall Street Journal,* June 9, 1997, p. B1.

51. *Wall Street Journal.* "New Rule to Protect Child Privacy on the Internet to Take Effect." April 21, 2000.

52. Hilts, Philip J. "Cigarette Makers Dispute Reports on Addictiveness," *New York Times,* April 15, 1994, p. A1.

53. McGinley, Laurie. "New Labeling Doesn't Tell All About Nutrition," *Wall Street Journal,* May 6, 1994, p. B1.

54. Hilts, Philip J. "Big Flaw Cited in Federal Test on Cigarettes," *New York Times,* May 2, 1994, p. A1.

55. Knecht, G. Bruce. "Reports of Mrs. Rissmiller's Death Have Been Greatly Exaggerated," *Wall Street Journal,* April 20, 1994, p. B1.

56. O'Brien. Timothy L. "Aided by Internet, Identify Theft Soars," *Wall Street Journal,* April 3, 2000.

57. Thurow, Lester C. "Needed: A New System of Intellectual Property Rights," *Harvard Business Review,* September-October 1997, pp. 95–103.

58. Kaplan, Carl S. "DVD Case Will Test Reach of Digital Copyright Law," *New York Times,* Cyber Law Journal, July 14, 2000.

59. Harmon, Amy. "Copyright Office Backs Digital Law," *New York Times,* October 30, 2000.

60. Flynn, Laurie J. "Trademarks Winning Domain Fights," *New York Times,* September 4, 2000.

61. Quick, Rebecca. "Framing Muddies Issue of Content Ownership," *Wall Street Journal,* January 30, 1997, p. B6.

62. "Times of London in Web Dispute," *Computerworld,* December 15, 1997, p. 8.

63. Landry, Julie. "Will the Web Wilt Wal-Mart?" *Red Herring,* September 25, 1999.

64. Wolverton, Troy. "Amazon.com, Wal-Mart Settle Lawsuit," *CNN News.com,* April 5, 1999.

65. Betts, Mitch. "Ruling Opens Door to Software Patents," *Computerworld,* September 5, 1994, p. 73.

66. Angwin, Julia. "Business-Method Patents Create Growing Controversy," *Wall Street Journal,* October 3, 2000.

67. Iowa Department for the Blind. "How Does a Screen Reader Work?" www.blind.state.ia.us/access/, viewed on November 7, 2000.

68. Collett, Stacy. "Group Sues AOL Over Access for the Blind," *Online News,* November 5, 1999.

69. Coxeter, Ruth. "A Computerized Overseer for the Truck Drivin' Man," *Business Week,* September 19, 1994, p. 90.

70. Betts, Mitch. "Computerized Records: An Open Book?" *Computerworld,* August 9, 1993, p. 1.

71. Bjerklie, David. "E-mail: The Boss Is Watching," *Technology Review,* April 1993, p. 14.

72. Cespedes, Frank V., and H. Jeff Smith. "Database Marketing: New Rules for Policy and Practice," *Sloan Management Review,* Summer 1993, pp. 7–22.

73. Branscomb, Anne Wells. *Who Owns Information: From Privacy to Public Access.* New York: Basic Books, 1994.

74. Pear, Robert. "U.S. Inaugurating a Vast Database of All New Hires," *New York Times,* September 22, 1997, p. A1+.

75. Betts, Michael. "Personal Data More Public Than You Think," *Computerworld*, March 9, 1992, p. 1.

76. Associated Press. "Bill Would Tell I.R.S. Workers Not to Snoop," *New York Times*, April 8, 1997, p. A9.

77. Polaroid Corporation. "Polaroid and Visionics Team Up to Provide Facial Recognition Solutions for Departments of Motor Vehicles," Press release, Boston, April 15, 1998.

78. Visionics Corporation, Visionics Corporation web site, www.faceit.com, viewed on November 20, 2000.

Chapter 8

1. Gomes, Lee. "Napster's Legal Strategy Relies on 1984 Sony Betamax Ruling," *Wall Street Journal*, September 13, 2000.

2. Associated Press. "U.S. Copyright Office Rejects the Defense Offered by Napster, Says the Law Is Violated," *Wall Street Journal*, September 11, 2000.

3. Greenman, Catherine. "Taking Sides in the Napster War," *New York Times*, August 31, 2000.

4. Ewing, Jack. "Bertlesmann: A New Net Powerhouse?" *Business Week*, November 13, 2000.

5. *New York Times on the Web*. "Court Gives Napster Deadline to Block Copyrighted Songs," March 6, 2001. www.nytimes.com/.

6. Bulkeley, William M., and Mark Maremont. "IBM to Rebrand Its Corporate Computers," *Wall Street Journal*, October 3, 2000, p. B8.

7. Sager, Ira. "A Bare-Bones Box for Business," *Business Week*, May 26, 1997, p. 136.

8. Lohr, Steve. "The Network Computer as the PC's Evil Twin," *New York Times*, November 4, 1996.

9. Hillis, Danny. "The Bandwidth Bomb," *Harvard Business Review*, September-October 2000, pp. 179–186.

10. Port, Otis. "The Silicon Age? It's Just Dawning," *Business Week*, December 9, 1996, pp. 148–152.

11. Hill, G. Christian. "Bringing It Home," *Wall Street Journal*, June 16, 1997, p. R4.

12. Gilheany, Steve, "Moore's Law and Knowledge Management," www.archivebuilders.com/whitepapers/, viewed on September 18, 2000.

13. Grove, Andrew, "A Revolution in Progress," Keynote speech at Comdex, November 18, 1996, www.intel.com/pressroom/.

14. Intel Corporation. "Intel Completes 0.13 Micron Process Technology Development," Press release, November 7, 2000, viewed at www.intel.com/pressroom/ on November 20, 2000.

15. Biersdorfer, J. D. "Apple Breaks the Mold," *New York Times*, September 14, 2000.

16. Pitta, Julia. "Victim of Success," *Forbes*, December 10, 1990, pp. 278–280.

17. Williams, Molly. "National Semiconductor to Ship Long-Awaited 'System-on-a-Chip'," *Wall Street Journal*, September 18, 2000.

18. Straub, Detmar. "The Effect of Culture on IT Diffusion: E-Mail and FAX in Japan and the U.S.," *Information System Research*, Vol. 5, No. 1, March 1994, pp. 23–47.

19. *PC Magazine*. "Voice Recognition," November 5, 1999, www.zdnet.com/products/.

20. Carey, John. "Thinking Flat in Washington," *Business Week*, May 9, 1994, p. 36.

21. Woollacott, Emma. "IBM Deserts Transmeta's Crusoe," vnunet.com, November 6, 2000, www.vnunet.com/Analysis/, viewed on November 20, 2000.

22. Transmeta Corporation, "The Crusoe Processor Family," www.transmeta.com/crusoe/, viewed on November 20, 2000.

23. Transmeta Corporation. "Crusoe Technology," www.transmeta.com/crusoe/, viewed on November 20, 2000.

24. Hughes, Rob. "Transmeta's Crusoe Microprocessor," Geek.com: ChipGeek, January 20, 2000, www.ugeek.com/procspec/, viewed on November 20, 2000.

25. Ticehurst, Jo. "IBM Ditches Transmeta Notebook Plans," vnunet.com, November 1, 2000, www.vnunet.com/News/, viewed on November 20, 2000.

26. Ticehurst, Jo. "Transmeta's Crusoe Not Ready for Mainstream," vnunet.com, November 7, 2000, www.vnunet.com/News/, viewed on November 20, 2000.

27. Reid, Calvin. "Publishers Embrace Gemstar's E-Book," Publisher's Weekly.com, October 16, 2000, www.publishersweekly.com/, viewed on November 20, 2000.

28. Seyboldreports.com. "Gemstar Announces E-Book Titles," October 12, 2000, www.seyboldreport.com/News/, viewed on November 20, 2000.

29. ABC News.com. "Web Spinner: Stephen King's New Tale Hits the Internet," July 24, 2000, www.abcnews.go.com/sections/, viewed on November 20, 2000.

30. Webopedia. "Tech Glossary: Electronic Paper," http://webopedia.lycos.com/Mobile_Computing/, viewed on November 20, 2000.

31. D'Amico, Mary Lisbeth and Marc Ferranti, "Xerox Crafts Electronic Paper," IDG News Service, June 30, 1999, www.pcworld.com/news/, viewed on November 20, 2000.

32. E Ink Corporation. "What Is Electronic Ink?" www.eink.com/technology/, viewed on November 20, 2000.

Chapter 9

1. Cusumano, Michael A., and Richard W. Selby. "How Microsoft Builds Software," *Communications of the ACM*, June 1997, Vol. 40, No. 6, pp. 53–61.

2. Panko, Raymond R. "What We Know About Spreadsheet Errors," *Journal of End User Computing*, Vol. 10, No. 2. Spring 1998, pp. 15–21.

3. Clark, Don. "'Bug Hunting' Emerges as Hot Campus Sport," *Wall Street Journal*, March 14, 1997, p. B1.

4. Gleick, James. "Little Bug, Big Bang," *New York Times Sunday Magazine*, December 1, 1996, pp. 38–40.

5. Williams, Laurie A., and Robert R. Kessler. "All I Really Need to Know About Pair Programming I Learned in Kindergarten," *Communications of the ACM*, Vol. 43, No. 5, May 2000, pp. 109–114.

6. Webopedia. "Java," http://webopedia.internet.com/, viewed on November 23, 2000.

7. Rada, Roy. "Corporate Shortcut to Standardization," *Communications of the ACM*, January 1998, Vol. 41, No. 1, pp. 11–14.

8. IBM. "Is There More to Java Than Coffee Jokes?" *Forbes*, January 26, 1998, pp. 74–75.

9. Hof, Robert D. "Java Can Be a Contender – If Sun Lets It," *Business Week*, April 6, 1998, p. 42.

10. Freeman, David. "How to Make Spreadsheets Error-Proof," *Journal of Accountancy*, 181(5), May 1996, pp. 75–77.

11. Savitz, E. J. "Magellan Loses Its Compass," *Barron's* (84:50), December 12, 1994.

12. Zachary, G. Pascal. "Agony and Ecstasy of 200 Code Writers Beget Windows NT," *Wall Street Journal*, May 26, 1993, p. A1.

13. Shirky, Clay. "Darwin, Linux, and Radiation," *Business 2.0*, October 24, 2000, p. 102.

14. Lohr, Steve, with John Markoff. "Why Microsoft Is Taking a Hard Line with the Government," *New York Times*, January 12, 1998, p. C1.

15. Ross, Philip E. "The Day the Software Crashed," *Forbes*, April 25, 1994, pp. 142–156.

16. Weinberg, Gerry. *The Psychology of Computer Programming* (Silver Anniversary Edition). Dorset House Publishing, 1998.

17. Williams and Kessler, *op. cit.*

18. Siddiqi, Jawed. "An Exposition of XP But No Position on XP," *eXtreme Programming Pros and Cons: What Questions Remain?* IEEE Computer Society Dynabook, http://computer.org/seweb/, viewed on November 27, 2000.

19. Cockburn, Alistair. "Characterizing People as Non-Linear, First Order Components in Software Development," October 1999, http://members.aol.com/humansandt/papers/, viewed on November 27, 2000.

20. Highsmith, Jim. "Extreme Programming," *e-business application delivery*, February 2000, http://cutter.com/ead/, viewed on November 27, 2000.

21. Beck, Kent, Ward Cunningham, Ron Jeffries, and Martin Fowler. "A Gentle Introduction to Extreme Programming," viewed on Google's cache of http://delza.alliances.org/muse/extreme/, viewed on November 27, 2000.

22. Siddiqi, Jawed. "An Exposition of XP But No Position on XP," *eXtreme Programming Pros and Cons: What Questions Remain?* IEEE Computer Society Dynabook, http://computer.org/seweb/dynabook/, viewed on November 27, 2000.

23. "Cthree Project Terminated" viewed at http://c2.com/cgi/wiki?CthreeProject Terminated, on November 27, 2000, within Cunningham & Cunningham, Inc., "Extreme Programming Roadmap," www.c2.com/cgi/wiki?ExtremeProgramming Roadmap.

24. IBM developerWorks staff. "Java Poll Results: Question: What Are Your Thoughts on Extreme Programming?" October 2000, www-4.ibm.com/software/developer/, viewed on November 27, 2000.

25. Cycorp. "Cycorp: Company Overview," http://www.cyc.com/overview.html, viewed on November 25, 2000.

26. Cycorp, Inc. "The CYC Technology," www.cyc.com/tech.html, viewed on June 2, 1998.

27. Lenat, Douglas B. "CYC: A Large-Scale Investment in Knowledge Infrastructure," *Communications of the ACM*, November 1995, pp. 33–38.

28. Moody, Sid. "The Brain Behind Cyc," *Austin Chronicle*, December 28, 1999, www.weeklywire.com/, viewed on November 25, 2000.

Chapter 10

1. Shapiro, Eileen C. *Fad Surfing in the Boardroom: Reclaiming the Courage to Manage in the Age of Instant Answers*. Reading, MA: Addison-Wesley, 1995, pp. 101–102.

2. Janah, Monua, and Clinton Wilder. "Networking—Special Delivery—Think FedEx Is Only About Shipping Packages? Think Again," *Information Week*, October 27, 1997.

3. FedEx. "FedEx eBusiness Tools," viewed at www.fedex.com/us/ebusiness, on October 16, 2000.

4. Violino, Bob. "Challenges Galore," *Information Week*, January 6, 1997, p. 70.

5. Lewis, Peter H. "Picking the Right Data Superhighway," *New York Times*, November 11, 1999.

6. Blumenstein, Rebecca. "Who's on First? A Road Map of the Bewildering World of Telecommunications," *Wall Street Journal*, September 18, 2000, p. R4.

7. Stallings, William, and Richard van Slyke. *Business Data Communications*, 3rd ed. New York: Macmillan College Publishing Company, 1998, p. 85.

8. Lucent Technologies. "Bell Labs Scientists Demo First Long Distance Triple Terabit Transmission," March 16, 2000, viewed at www.bell-labs.com/news/.

9. Ziegler, Bart. "Building the Highway: New Obstacles, New Solutions," *Wall Street Journal*, p. B1.

10. Banks, Howard. "The Law of the Photon," *Forbes*, October 6, 1997, pp. 66–73.

11. Owens, Cynthia. "The Developing Leap," *Wall Street Journal*, February 11, 1994, p. R15.

12. Pitta, Julia. "Format Wars," *Fortune*, July 7, 1997, p. 263.

13. Steinberg, Steve G. "Schumpeter's Lesson: What Really Happened in Digital Technology in the Last Five Years," *Wired*, January 1998, pp. 80–84.

14. Davis, Beth, with Gregory Dalton. "VPNs Set to Take Off," *Information Week*, January 5, 1998, pp. 85–86.

15. Sliwa, Carol. "Net Used to Extend EDI's Reach," *Computerworld*, February 23, 1998, p. 1.

16. Panko, Raymond R. *Business Data Communications and Networking*. Upper Saddle River, NJ: Prentice Hall, pp. 149–159.

17. Ibid, p. 370.

18. "Wireless Repairmen," Mobile Computing Briefs, *Computerworld*, February 23, 1998, p. 65.

19. Girard, Kim. "Wireless Revolution Fizzles," *Computerworld*, February 23, 1998, p. 6.

20. Pringle, David. "WAP Standard Runs into Trouble with Incompatible Technologies," *Wall Street Journal*, May 9, 2000.

21. Pringle, David. "The Anytime, Anywhere Net," *Wall Street Journal*, July 5, 2000.

22. Guth, Robert A., "Regaining the Glory," *Wall Street Journal*, September 25, 2000.

23. Franklin, Curt. "How the Bluetooth Short Range Radio System Works," www.howstuffworks.com, October 2, 2000.

24. Blumenstein, Rebecca. "AT&T Group to Buy Net2Phone Stake in a Turning Point for Web Telephony," *Wall Street Journal*, April 3, 2000.

25. Schiesel, Seth. "A U.S. Judge Strikes Down Parts of the '96 Telecommunications Act," *New York Times*, January 1, 1998, p. 1.

26. Auckerman, William. "Japan Moves Closer to Low-Cost Home Access," *Internet News.com*, August 17, 1999.

27. Carroll, Jill. "U.S. Regulators Open Inquiry into Nature of Cable-Net Service," *Wall Street Journal*, September 29, 2000.

28. Carroll, Jill. "FCC Proposes Opening AOL's Messaging to Rivals as Part of Time Warner Deal," *Wall Street Journal*, September 13, 2000.

29. Arnst, Catherine. "The Global Free-for-All," *Business Week*, September 26, 1994, pp. 118–126.

30. Webopedia. "DoCoMo," http://webopedia.internet.com/, viewed on November 27, 2000.

31. *Wall Street Journal Interactive Edition*. "Issue Briefing: The Wireless Web," July 5, 2000.

32. Zohar, Mark. "NTT DoCoMo Sets the Mobile Internet Standard," *Forrester Brief*, February 15, 2000.

33. Stiles, Shane. "Getting Connected with DoCoMo's I-Mode," *Gate39*, April 9, 2000, www.gate39.com/business/, viewed on November 27, 2000.

34. Scuka, Daniel. "NTT DoCoMo Officially Ties Up with AOL," *Japan, Inc.* September 27, 2000, www.japaninc.net/online/sc/ntt/, viewed on November 27, 2000.

35. O' Regan, Rob. "Ellen Hancock: Moving Exodus Beyond the Data Center," *eWeek,* June 2, 2000, www.zdnet.com/eweek/, viewed on November 27, 2000.

36. Koblentz, Evan. "Web Hosting Partner Keeps Stone Site Rolling," *PC Week,* October 29, 2000, www.zdnet.com/eweek, viewed on November 27, 2000.

37. Cone, Edward. "Exodus Thrives on ASPs," *Inter@ctive Week,* September 26, 2000, www.zdnet.com/intweek, viewed on November 27, 2000.

38. O' Regan, Rob. "Ellen Hancock: Moving Exodus Beyond the Data Center," *eWeek,* June 2, 2000, www.zdnet.com/eweek/, viewed on November 27, 2000.

39. Koblentz, Evan. "Web Host Rivals Offer Different MSP Recipes," *PC Week,* October 27, 2000, www.zdnet.com/eweek, viewed on November 27, 2000.

Chapter 11

1. Sliwa, Carol. "Kmart Names New CIO," *Computerworld Online,* September 15, 2000.

2. Songini, Marc L. "IT Changes Hit Supply Chains," *Computerworld Online,* October 16, 2000.

3. Muller, Joann. "A Kmart Special: Better Service," *Businessweek Online,* September 4, 2000.

4. Lund, Brian. "Kmart Inches Forward," *Motley Fool QuickNews,* www.fool.com, March 6, 2000.

5. Muller. "A Kmart Special."

6. Smith, Tom. "Kmart's Plan to Light Up the Web," *InternetWeek,* July 21, 2000.

7. Shook, David. "Comparing the Big Three of Clicks-and-Bricks," *Businessweek Online,* October 5, 2000.

8. Hopper, Max D. "Rattling SABRE—New Ways to Compete on Information," *Harvard Business Review,* May-June 1990, pp. 118–125.

9. Parker, Marilyn M. *Strategic Transformation and Information Technology: Paradigms for Performing While Transforming.* Upper Saddle River, NJ: Prentice Hall, 1996, pp. 72–74.

10. Henderson, John C., N. Venkatraman, and Scott Oldach. "Aligning Business and IT Strategies," pp. 21–42 in Jerry N. Luftman, ed., *Competing in the Information Age: Strategic Alignment in Practice.* New York: Oxford University Press, 1996.

11. Parker, *Strategic Transformation and Information Technology,* p. 222.

12. Goff, Leslie, and Michael Puttre. "Business Strategies Misaligned with MIS Resources," *MIS Week,* November 6, 1989, p. 38.

13. Rockart, John F. "Chief Executives Define Their Own Data Needs," *Harvard Business Review,* March/April 1979, pp. 81–92.

14. Boynton, Andrew C., and Robert W. Zmud. "An Assessment of Critical Success Factors," *Sloan Management Review,* Summer 1984, pp. 17–27.

15. Hammer, Michael, and James Champy. *Reengineering the Corporation: A Manifesto for Business Revolution.* New York: Harper Business, 1993.

16. Ibid.

17. Stewart, Thomas A. "Reengineering: The Hot New Management Tool," *Fortune,* August 23, 1993, pp. 41–48.

18. Strassmann, Paul A. "Re-engineering: An emetic in a perfume bottle?" *Computerworld,* August 16, 1993, p. 33.

19. Cafasso, Rosemary. "Rethinking Re-engineering," *Computerworld,* March 15, 1993, pp. 102–105.

20. Martin, Michael H. "Smart Managing: Best Practices, Careers, and Ideas," *Fortune,* February 2, 1998, pp. 149–151.

21. Stein, Tom. "ERP Links to Supply Chain," *Information Week,* January 5, 1998, pp. 103–104.

22. Losee, Stephanie. "Burned by Technology," *Fortune,* September 9, 1996, pp. 105–112.

23. Battles, Brett E., and David Mark. "Companies That Just Don't Get IT," *Wall Street Journal,* December 9, 1996, p. A14.

24. Broadbent, Marianne, and Peter Weill. "Management by Maxim: How Business and IT Managers Can Create IT Infrastructures," *Sloan Management Review,* Spring 1997, pp. 77–92.

25. Ibid.

26. Ross, Jeanne. "Johnson & Johnson: Building an Infrastructure to Support Global Operations," MIT Center for Information Systems Research, CISR Working Paper #283, 1995.

27. Anthes, Gary H. "Avoiding ASP Angst," *Computerworld Online,* October 16, 2000.

28. Kerstetter, Jim. "Software Shakeout," *BusinessWeek Online,* March 5, 2001.

29. Lacity, Mary Cecelia, and Rudy Hirschheim. *Information Systems Outsourcing: Myths, Metaphors, and Realities.* Chichester, UK: John Wiley & Sons, 1993.

30. Lacity, Mary C., Leslie P. Willcocks, and David F. Feeny. "IT Outsourcing: Maximize Flexibility and Control," *Harvard Business Review,* May-June 1995, pp. 84–93.

31. Lovelace, Herbert. "1998: Year of Conversions," *Information Week,* January 5, 1998, p. 121.

32. Dalton, Gregory. "Ready to Go Global?" *Information Week,* February 9, 1998, pp. 49–60.

33. Markoff, John. "Internet in Japan Is Riding a Wireless Wave," *New York Times,* August 14, 2000.

34. Moffett, Matt. "Callbacks Cut Telephone Bills of Users Abroad," *Wall Street Journal,* June 21, 1994, p. B1.

35. Andrews, Edmund L. "Europe's Cheap Phone Calls (Via U.S.) to Get Dearer," *Wall Street Journal,* January 11, 1997, p. 25.

36. Cespedes, Frank V., and H. Jeff Smith. "Database Marketing: New Rules for Policy and Practice," *Sloan Management Review,* Summer 1993, pp. 7–22.

37. Weber, Thomas E. "Views on Protecting Privacy Diverge in U.S. and Europe," *Wall Street Journal Interactive,* June 19, 2000.

38. Alter, Steven. "Implementation Risk Analysis," pp. 103–119 in R. Doktor, R. L. Schultz, and D. P. Sleven, eds., *TIMS Studies in Management Sciences,* Vol. 13. Amsterdam: North Holland Publishing Company, 1979.

39. Hartman, Amir, and John Sifonis with John Kador. *Net Ready: Strategies for Success in the E-conomy.* New York: McGraw-Hill, 2000, p. 246.

40. Copeland, Thomas E., and Philip T. Kennan. "How Much Is Flexibility Worth?" *The McKinsey Quarterly,* 1998, No. 2, pp. 38–49.

41. Feigenbaum, Edward, Pamela McCorduck, and Penny H. Nii. *The Rise of the Expert Company.* New York: Times Books, 1988.

42. The Standish Group. "Chaos," Sample research paper, originally published in 1995, viewed on October 19, 2000 at www.standishgroup.com/visitor/.

43. Anthes, Gary H. "No More Creeps!" *Computerworld,* May 2, 1994, pp. 107–110.

44. Boehm, Barry W. "Improving Software Productivity," *Computer,* September 1987, pp. 43–57.

45. Brooks, Frederick P., Jr. "The Mythical Man-Month." *Datamation,* December 1974, pp. 44–52.

46. Yourdon, Edward. *Decline & Fall of the American Programmer.* Englewood Cliffs, NJ: Yourdon Press, 1992, p. 162.

47. Boynton, A. C., B. Victor, and B. J. Pine II. "New Competitive Strategies: Challenges to Organizations and Information Technology," *IBM Systems Journal,* Vol. 32, No. 1, 1993, pp. 40–64.

48. Keen, Peter G. W. *Shaping the Future: Business Design Through Information Technology.* Boston, MA: Harvard Business School Press, 1991, p. 141.

49. The Economist Group. "Five Year Summary," http://www.economistgroup.com/, viewed on November 27, 2000.

50. The Economist Group. "The Economist Intelligence Unit," www.economistgroup.com/, viewed on November 27, 2000.

51. EIU ViewsWire. "About the EIU ViewsWire," www.viewswire.com/, viewed on November 27, 2000.

52. Lovelock, Peter, and Ali F. Farhoomand. "EIU's ViewsWire: New Wine in a New Bottle," pp. 768–784 in Soon, Ang, Helmut Krcmar, Wanda Orlikowski, Peter Weill, and Janice I. DeGross, eds, *Proceedings of ICIS, the Twenty-First Annual International Conference on Information Systems.* Brisbane, Australia, December 10–13, 2000.

53. Rozenberg, Dino. "Cemex: A System for Worldwide Manufacturing," *Manufactura,* May 1998 edition, www.cemex.com/articles/manueng.htm, viewed on June 2, 1998.

54. Dolan, Kerry A. "Cyber-cement," *Forbes,* June 15, 1998, pp. 60–61.

55. Dombey, Daniel. "Well Built Success," *Industry Week,* May 5, 1997, www.cemex.com/articles/indeng.htm, viewed on June 3, 1998.

56. Cemex. "Why Cemex Is Different: Technology," www.cemex.com/03021.html, viewed on November 28, 2000.

57. Cemex. "Cemex Launches E-Business Strategy," News Release, September 13, 2000, www.cemex.com/nr_090900.html, viewed on November 28, 2000.

Chapter 12

1. Yahoo Store. "Pricing," viewed at http://store.yahoo.com/pric.html, on October 20, 2000.

2. Yahoo Store. "The Fastest, Easiest Way to Open an Online Store," viewed at http://store.yahoo.com/, on October 20, 2000.

3. Cringely, Robert X. "When Disaster Strikes IS," *Forbes ASAP,* August 29, 1994, pp. 58–64.

4. The Standish Group. "Chaos," Sample research paper, originally published in 1995, viewed on October 19, 2000 at www.standishgroup.com/visitor/.

5. Pollack, Andrew. "Two Teams, Two Measures Equaled One Lost Spacecraft," *New York Times,* October 1, 1999.

6. Markus, M. Lynne, and Mark Keil. "If We Build It, They Will Come: Designing Information Systems That People Want to Use," *Sloan Management Review,* Summer 1994, pp. 11–25.

7. Hersleb, James et al. "Software Quality and the Capability Maturity Model," *Communications of the ACM,* June 1997, pp. 30–40.

8. Anthes, Gary H. "Capable and Mature," *Computerworld,* December 15, 1997, p. 76.

9. Frantz, Douglas. "B of A's Plans for Computer Don't Add Up," pp. 161–169 in Rob Kling, ed., *Computerization and Controversy: Value Conflicts and Social Choice,* 2nd edition, San Diego: Academic Press, 1996.

10. Collett, Stacy. "SAP: Whirlpool's Rush to Go Live Led to Shipping Snafus," *Online News,* November 4, 1999.

11. Greenstein, Irwin. "Imaging System Snafu Snarls Calif. Banks." *MIS Week,* June 19, 1989, pp. 1+.

12. Fournier, Roger. *Practical Guide to Structured System Development and Maintenance.* Englewood Cliffs, NJ: Yourdon Press, 1991.

13. Davidson, Elizabeth J. "An Exploratory Study of Joint Application Design (JAD) in Information Systems Delivery," pp. 271–283 in Degross, Janice I., Robert P. Bostrom, and Daniel Robey, eds., *Proceedings of the Fourteen International Conference on Information Systems.* Orlando, FL, 1993.

14. Dahlbom, Bo, and Lars Mathiassen. "A Scandinavian View on the ACM's Code of Ethics," *Computers and Society,* Vol. 24, No. 2, June 1994, pp. 14–15.

15. Brown, Carol V., and Iris Vessey. "NIBCO's Big Bang," p. 790 in Soon, Ang, Helmut Krcmar, Wanda Orlikowski, Peter Weill, and Janice I. DeGross, eds, *Proceedings of ICIS, the Twenty-First Annual International Conference on Information Systems,* Brisbane, Australia, December 10–13, 2000.

16. Ibid.

17. Stedman, Craig. "Short-Term Sacrifices: Big-Bang R/3 Roll-Out Forced Compromises," *Computerworld Online,* http://www.computerworld.com/cwi/story/0,1199,NAV47_STO30212,00.html.

18. Glasser, Perry, "NIBCO's Rex Martin," *CIO Enterprise Magazine,"* October 15, 1999.

19. NIBCO, Inc. "Transformed NIBCO Positioned for E-Business Leadership," July 19, 2000, http://www.nibco.com/news/E-businessLeadership.shtml, viewed on November 28, 2000.

20. Cole, Jeff. "How Major Overhaul of Air-Traffic Control Lost Its Momentum," *Wall Street Journal,* March 2, 1998, p. A1.

21. Bourlas, Stephen. "Anatomy of a Runaway: What Grounded AAS," *IEEE Software,* January and March 1996, reprinted in Robert L. Glass, *Software Runaways.* Upper Saddle River, NJ: Prentice Hall, 1998, pp. 56–64.

22. O'Hara, Colleen. "FAA Works with Controllers to Solve Unsafe STARS Design," *Federal Computer Week,* March 6, 1998, www.fcw.com/pubs/fcw/1998/0302/web-stars-3-2-1998.html, viewed on June 3, 1998.

23. Trimble, Paula Shaki. "FAA Agrees to $270M Fix," *Federal Computer Week,* May 8, 2000, www.fcw.com/fcw/articles/, viewed on November 28, 2000.

Chapter 13

1. Rosencrance, Linda. "Survey: Retail Fraud More Prevalent for Online Vendors," *Computerworld Online,* July 24, 2000.

2. Angwin, Julia. "Credit Card Fraud Has Become a Nightmare for E-Merchants," *Wall Street Journal,* September 19, 2000.

3. Trombley, Maria. "Visa Issues 10 'Commandments' for Online Merchants," *Computerworld Online,* August 11, 2000.

4. Visa. "Do Business Online—Security," www.visabrc.com/, accessed on October 17, 2000.

5. Visa. "Card-Not-Present Transactions: Basic Card Acceptances and Fraud Control Procedures," www.visabrc.com/, accessed on October 17, 2000.

6. Visa. "Card-Not-Present Transactions: Best Practices for Internet Merchants," www.visabrc.com/, accessed on October 17, 2000.

7. Wald, Matthew L. "Colombians Attribute Cali Crash to Pilot Error," *New York Times*, September 26, 1996, p. 12.

8. Perrow, Charles. *Normal Accidents: Living with High-Risk Technologies*. New York: Basic Books, 1984.

9. McCartney, Scott. "Makers of Flight Computer, Software Partly Liable for Colombia Crash," *Wall Street Journal*, June 14, 2000.

10. Gordon, Michael R. "Astronaut Error Adds New Anxiety on Space Station," *New York Times*, July 18, 1997, p. A1.

11. Markoff, John. "Flaw Undermines Accuracy of Pentium Chips," *New York Times*, November 24, 1994, p. C1.

12. Manes, Stephen. "As Snug as a Bug in the System," *New York Times*, October 15, 1996, p. B6.

13. Rosencrance, Linda. "Dell Recalls 27,000 Notebook PC Batteries," *Computerworld Online*, October 13, 2000.

14. Getler, Warren. "Errant Squirrel Causes Another Nasdaq Outage," *Wall Street Journal*, August 2, 1994, p. C1.

15. Gleckman, Howard. "Hey, I Owe 99 Years in Back Taxes," *Business Week*, February 23, 1998, pp. 119–120.

16. McGee, Suzanne. "Bank of Tokyo Blames Loss on Bad Model," *Wall Street Journal*, March 28, 1997, p. A3.

17. "Postal Service Misplaces Patent Office's ZIP Code," *Wall Street Journal*, August 9, 1996, p. A4.

18. Markoff, John. "Network Problem Disrupts Internet," *New York Times*, July 18, 1997, p. A1.

19. Norris, Floyd. "Salomon's Error Went Right to Floor," *New York Times*, March 27, 1993.

20. Wald, Matthew L. "Peru Crash Is Attributed to Maintenance Error," *New York Times*, November 16, 1996, p. 9.

21. Bulkeley, William M. "Databases Are Plagued by Reign of Error," *Wall Street Journal*, May 26, 1992, p. B6.

22. Rosencrance, Linda. "Glitch Temporarily Exposes Some Buy.com Customer Data," *Computerworld Online*, October 13, 2000.

23. Ohlson, Kathleen. "Glitch Exposes Customer Tax Records," *Computerworld Online*, February 16, 2000.

24. Martinez, Barbara. "Kaiser E-Mail Glitch Highlights Pitfalls of Placing Personal-Health Data Online," *Wall Street Journal*, August 11, 2000.

25. Bradsher, Keith. "How AT&T Accident Snowballed," *New York Times*, January 14, 1991, p. C1.

26. Wald, Matthew L. "Dust at Center for Air Control Disrupts Travel," *New York Times*, October 16, 1997, p. A1.

27. Biddle, Frederic M., John Lippman, and Stephanie N. Mehta. "One Satellite Fails, and the World Goes Awry," *Wall Street Journal*, May 21, 1998, p. B1.

28. Zuckerman, Laurence. "Satellite Failure Is Rare, and Therefore Unsettling," *New York Times*, May 21, 1998, p. C3.

29. Cohen, Jackie. "Flirting with Disaster," *The Standard*, September 6, 1999.

30. Jacky, Jonathan. "Safety-Critical Computing: Hazards, Practices, Standards, and Regulation," pp. 767–792 in Rob Kling, ed., *Computerization and Controversy*. San Diego, CA: Academic Press, 1991.

31. Ross, Philip E. "The Day the Software Crashed," *Forbes*, April 25, 1994, pp. 142–156.

32. Guernsey, Lisa. "EBay Faces Suit on Sale of Fake Goods," *New York Times*, October 16, 2000, p. C6.

33. Dow Jones Newswires. "Microsoft Gear Is Stolen from Scottish Plant," *Wall Street Journal*, November 19, 1997, p. B4.

34. "Computer's Theft May Cost Visa More Than $6 Million," *Wall Street Journal*, November 19, 1996, p. B4.

35. Fox, Pimm. "Analysis: Qualcomm's CEO Should Have Known Better," *Computerworld Online*, September 25, 2000.

36. Schaff, William. "Identix Has a Finger on the Future," *Information Week Between the Lines*, October 10, 2000, betweenthelines@daily.informationweek.com, viewed on October 12, 2000.

37. Booker, Ellis, and Anthes, Gary H. "Toll Fraud Rings in High Cost," *Computerworld*, October 10, 1994, p. 1.

38. Starkman, Dean. "Russian Hacker Enters Fraud Plea in Citicorp Case," *Wall Street Journal*, January 26, 1998, p. B9A.

39. Hansell, Saul. "Internet Merchants Try to Fight Fraud in Software Purchases," *New York Times*, November 17, 1997, p. C1.

40. Allen, Brandt. "Embezzler's Guide to the Computer," *Harvard Business Review*, July-August 1975, pp. 79–89.

41. Fenyvesi, Charles. "Washington Whispers: Forging Ahead," *U.S. News & World Report*, August 3, 1992. p. 20.

42. Carley, William M. "Rigging Computers for Fraud or Malice Is Often an Inside Job," *Wall Street Journal*, August 27, 1992, p. A1.

43. Angwin, Julia. "Credit-Card Fraud Has Become a Nightmare for E-Merchants," *Wall Street Journal*, September 19, 2000, p. B1.

44. Bulkeley, William M. "Voice Mail May Let Competitors Dial 'E' for Espionage," *Wall Street Journal*, September 28, 1993, p. B1.

45. Markoff, John. "How a Computer Sleuth Traced a Digital Trail," *New York Times*, February 16, 1995.

46. Salkever, Alex. "Online Banking: The Nightmare," *Business Week Online*, October 9, 2000.

47. Ewing, Terzah, Matthew Rose, Rhonda Rundle, and Gary Fields. "FBI Arrests Man on Charges Related to Press-Release Hoax," *Wall Street Journal*, September 1, 2000.

48. Schroeder, Michael, Ruth Simon, and Aaron Elstein. "Teenage Trader Runs Afoul of SEC in Stock-Fraud Case," *Wall Street Journal Interactive Edition*, September 21, 2000.

49. Schroeder, Michael, and Ruth Simon. "Teenage Stock Manipulator Got Away with Most Trades," *Wall Street Journal*, October 20, 2000.

50. Levy, Clifford. "Founder of Renowned Store Pleads Guilty in Fraud Case," *New York Times*, July 23, 1993, p. A11.

51. Lander, Mark. "A Filipino Linked to 'Love Bug' Talks About his License to Hack," *New York Times*, October 21, 2000.

52. DiDio, Laura. "Ex-Employee Nabbed in $10M Hack Attack," *Computerworld*, February 23, 1998, p. 6.

53. Wildstrom, Stephen H. "Out, Out, Damned Virus," *Business Week*, July 22, 1996, p. 19.

54. National Computer Security Association. "NCSA Computer Virus Prevalence Survey," 1997.

55. Reichlin, Igor. "Many Chernobyls Just Waiting to Happen," *Business Week*, March 16, 1992.

56. *U.S. News & World Report*. "The Gulf War Flu." January 20, 1992, p. 50.

57. Loftus, Peter. "In the Wake of Attacks, Web Sites Turn to Law Enforcement," *Dow Jones Newswires*, February 9, 2000.

58. Horwitt, Elizabeth. "N.Y. Sites Unfazed by Outage," *Computerworld*, September 23, 1991, p. 1+.

59. Anthes, Gary H. "FCC Blasts AT&T for New York Blowout," *Computerworld,* November 18, 1991, p. 58.

60. "Edwards, Tamala M. "Numbers Nightmare: A Pepsi Promotion Misfires in the Philippines," *Time,* August 9, 1993, p. 53.

61. Anthes, Gary H. "GAO Finds Security Lax at U.S. Stock Exchanges," *Computerworld,* September 2, 1991, p. 99.

62. Sliwa, Carol. "Maverick Intranets a Challenge for IT," *Computerworld Online,* March 15, 1999.

63. French, Howard W. "Japanese Fuel Plant Spews Radiation After Accident," *New York Times,* October 1, 1999.

64. Wald, Matthew L. "Experts Say Lapses Led to Japan's A-Plant Failure," *New York Times,* October 23, 1999.

65. Ball, Leslie D. "Computer Crime," *Technology Review,* April 1982, pp. 21–30.

66. Time-Life Books. *Computer Security.* Alexandria, VA: Time-Life Books, 1986.

67. Davies, Erin. "Great Tool for the Paranoid," *Fortune,* February 16, 1998, p. 129.

68. Sandberg, Jared. "Hackers Prey on AOL Users with Array of Dirty Tricks," *Wall Street Journal,* January 5, 1998, p. B1.

69. Booker, Ellis. "Retinal Scanners Eye-Identify Inmates," *Computerworld,* March 23, 1992, p. 28.

70. RSA Laboratories. "FAQ 3.0 on Cryptography," www.rsa.com/rsalabs/newfaq/, 1998.

71. RSA Laboratories. "FAQ 3.0," www.rsa.com/rsalabs/newfaq/.

72. Bicknell, Craig. "NSI's Webjacking Epidemic," *Wired News,* June 8, 2000.

73. Time-Life Books. *Computer Security.* Alexandria, VA: Time-Life Books, 1986.

74. "A 7-Ton Clerical Fluke: Anchor Arrives Instead of Lamp," *Washington Post,* April 13, 1985.

75. Greenstein, Marilyn, and Todd M. Feinman. *Electronic Commerce: Security Risk Management and Control.* Boston: Irwin/McGraw-Hill, 2000, p. 304.

76. Ellison, Carl, and Schneier, Bruce. "Ten Risks of PKI: What You're Not Being Told About Public Key Infrastructure," viewed on October 18, 2000, at http://xent.ics.uci.edu/FoRK-archive/nov99/.

77. Tedeschi, Bob. "Sellers Hire Auditors to Verify Policies and Increase Trust," *New York Times,* September 18, 2000.

78. Hoffman, Thomas. "Denial Stalls Disaster Recovery Plans," *Computerworld,* February 23, 1998, p. 10.

79. Cohen, Jackie. "Flirting with Disaster," *The Standard,* September 6, 1999.

80. Hudson, Richard L. "Know Anybody Using Pirated Software? That's Information Worth Some Money," *Wall Street Journal,* October 11, 1994, p. B5.

81. Braudel, William. "Licensing Stymies Users," *Computerworld,* April 18, 1994, p. 12.

82. Bridis, Ted. "Virus Gives 'Love' a Bad Name, Leads to Vast E-Mail Shutdown," *Wall Street Journal,* May 5, 2000.

83. Bradsher, Keith. "With Its E-Mail Infected, Ford Scrambled and Caught Up," *New York Times,* May 8, 2000.

84. Bridis, Ted. "Philippine Officials Raid Apartment of Suspected Creator of Computer Virus," *Wall Street Journal,* May 8, 2000.

85. Frank, Robert. "Phillipine Prosecutors Drop Charges in Love Bug Case," *Wall Street Journal,* August 22, 2000.

86. Landler, Mark. "A Filipino Linked to 'Love Bug' Talks About His License to Hack," *New York Times,* October 21, 2000.

87. "London Ambulance Dispatch Computer," Forum on Risks to the Public in Computers and Related Systems, *ACM Committee on Computers and Public Policy, Peter G. Neumann, moderator,* Vol. 14, Issue 2, November 9, 1992.

88. "Report of the Inquiry into the London Ambulance Service, February 1993," Forum on Risks to the Public in Computers and Related Systems, *ACM Committee on Computers and Public Policy,* Peter G. Neumann, moderator, Vol. 14, Issue 48, April 7, 1993.

credits

Text

Box 2.1 Reprinted from "Punching Two or More in Palm Beach County," *New York Times*, November 16, 2000. Used with permission of the *New York Times*.

Figure 7.6 Reprinted from "Knowledge Workers and Radically New Technology," by John Sviokla, *Sloan Management Review*, Summer 1996, by permission of the publisher. Copyright 1996 by Sloan Management Review Association. All Rights Reserved.

Photos

About the Author
Courtesy of Steven Alter.

Chapter 1
1.8a The Computer Museum. 1.8b Intel Corporation Pressroom Photo Archives. 1.9 Fisher/Thatcher/Hulton Archive. 1.11 Chuck Nacke/Woodfin Camp & Associates. 1.12a Courtesy of International Business Machines Corporation. Unauthorized use not permitted. 1.12b Samsung Electronics/AP/Wide World Photos. 1.13 Corbis-Bettmann.

Chapter 2
2.1a Romilly Lockyer/The Image Bank. 2.1b Courtesy of Steven Alter. 2.9 Michael Grecco/Stock Boston.

Chapter 3
3.8 John Blaustein/Woodfin Camp & Associates. 3.12 © Alan Becker/The Image Bank. 3.14 Liaison/Tim Chapman/Newsmakers/OnlineUSA.

Chapter 4
4.1b Howard Sochurek/Corbis/Stock Market. 4.1c Dario Lopez-Mills/Brazilian Institute for Space/AP/Wide World Photos. 4.6 Courtesy of Steven Alter. 4.7 Courtesy of Steven Alter. 4.8 Courtesy of English Wizard. 4.11 Courtesy of MapInfo. 4.12 Courtesy of Prentice-Hall. 4.17 Courtesy of NASA. 4.20 © Chris Salvo/FPG International.

Chapter 5
5.1a © Will and Deni McIntyre/Photo Researchers, Inc. 5.1b © Cindy Charles/Photo Edit. 5.1c © Jeff Mermelstein. 5.3a © Louis Psihoyos/Matrix International, Inc. 5.3b © Louis Psihoyos/Matrix International, Inc. 5.4a © Ulf E. Wallin/The Image Bank. 5.4b © Bruce Ayers/Tony Stone Images. 5.5 Courtesy Professor Tuominen, Lappeenranta University of Technology, Lappeenranta, Finland. 5.6 Courtesy of Oracle. 5.8 Courtesy of Steven Alter. 5.10a Courtesy of the San Francisco Police Department. 5.10b Courtesy of Steven Alter.

Chapter 6
6.1 AP/Wide World Photos. 6.2a Myrleen Ferguson/PhotoEdit. 6.2b Courtesy Britannica, Inc. 6.7 © Lands' End. 6.8 © Elena Dorfman. 6.10 Courtesy of Hertz. 6.11 © Michelle Bridwell MR/Photo Edit. 6.13 Britannica.com, Inc.

Chapter 7
7.2 Courtesy of Apple Computer, Inc. 7.3 Electronic Publishing Services, Inc. 7.4 Courtesy of Boeing. 7.5 © David Graham/Black Star. 7.7a © Lebrun-Photo News/Gamma Liaison. 7.7b Courtesy of Kurzweil Educational Systems, Inc. 7.7c © Reuters/Fred Prouser/Archive Photos.

Chapter 8
8.2a Courtesy of International Business Machines Corporation. Unauthorized use not permitted. 8.2b Courtesy of Canon Computer Systems. 8.3 2001 Brad Trent. 8.11a Courtesy of International Business Machines Corporation. Unauthorized use not permitted. 8.11b Tony Freeman/Photo Edit. 8.11c David K. Crow/Photo Edit. 8.12 Courtesy of International Business Machines Corporation. Unauthorized use not permitted. 8.13 Courtesy Epson America. 8.14a © Steve Firebaugh. 8.14b Courtesy of International Business Machines Corporation. Unauthorized use not permitted. 8.14c © Frank Wing/The Image Bank. 8.14d Imation Enterprises. 8.15a SuperStock, Inc. 8.15b © Steve Firebaugh. 8.15c Ed Kashi.

Chapter 9
9.9 Courtesy of Steven Alter. 9.10a The Bettmann Archive. 9.10b Motion Picture and TV Archive.

Chapter 10
10.5 © T. Tracy/FPG International. 10.11 © Hank Morgan/Photo Researchers, Inc. 10.17 Fredrik D. Bodin/Stock Boston.

Chapter 11
11.2 © John Storey. 11.10 Courtesy of Steven Alter.

Chapter 12
12.6 Courtesy of Steven Alter. 12.9 Courtesy of Steven Alter.

Chapter 13
13.6 © Larry Ford.

company index

A

Abacus Direct, 267
Adobe, 232
Airborne Express, 4
Akamai Technologies, 16
Alyeska Pipeline Service Co., 543
Amazon.com, 15, 16, 41, 44, 116, 254, 260, 289, 294, 525
American Airlines, 251, 432, 433, 513–514, 531, 533–534
American Baby, 186
American Express, 541
American Hospital Supply, 432
American Online (AOL), 16, 195, 260, 296, 533
Ameritech, 420
Anderson Consulting, 256
Applied Expert Systems, 283
Aramark Uniform Services, 82
Ariba, 16
AskJeeves, 16
At Home Corp., 16
AT&T, 247, 254, 373, 400, 420, 516, 518, 526
AT&T Universal Card Services, 246
Auctiva, 262

B

Baby Bells, 420
Bank of America, 433
Bank of Tokyo-Mitsubishi, 516
Bank One, 195
Bann, 443
Barnes & Noble, 16, 41, 253, 294
Battelie Memorial Institute, 34
Baxter International, 241, 432–433
Bell Atlantic, 420
Bell Canada, 339
BellSouth, 420
Bizrate.com, 256
BMW, 267
Boeing, 179–180, 182, 231
Boise Cascade, 417
Borders Books, 264
Boston Consulting Group, 241
British Airways, 427
Burlington Industries, 184
Buy.com, 16, 116

C

CDnow, 253
Cemex, 468
Charles Schwab, 16, 85–86, 94, 116, 189, 253, 257, 260, 518, 544
Chase Manhattan Bank, 207
Chemical Bank, 433
Chrysler, 381

Cisco Systems, 130–131, 242, 457
Citicorp, 521
Clorox, 14
CNET.com, 16
CNN, 83, 116, 525
Comdisco, 544
CommerceOne, 16
Compaq, 444
CompuSys, 477
Continental, 251
Costco, 100
Covisint, 251
Cummins Engine, 417
Cyber Source, 521
Cycorp, Inc., 382–383

D

DaimlerChrysler, 251
Dassault, 179
Dell Computer, 3–4, 5–7, 9, 10, 15, 18, 216, 259, 260, 326, 443, 515
Delta Airlines, 251
Digex, 427, 450
Digital Equipment, 34, 327, 373
Dilliard's Department Stores, 184
Disney, 16
Dockers, 38
Dollar Rent-A-Car, 143
DoubleClick, 258, 267–268
DRI/McGraw-Hill, 164
Drugstore.com, 294
Du Pont, 105

E

Earthlink, 16
eBay, 16, 116, 133–134, 239, 260, 262, 427, 518
Economist Group, 467–468
Eddie Bauer, 16
E*Direct, 226, 237
E*display, 226
Edmunds.com, 253
Egghead.com, 16
Electronic Data Systems (EDS), 196
Elizabeth Arden, 237
eMakeover.com, 237
Emulex, 523
Encyclopedia Britannica, 228, 229
Equifax, 289
Equity Funding Corporation, 538
Ernst & Young, 263–264
E*Service, 226
E-Stamp, 129–130
E-Trade, 16, 116, 518
EuroDollar, 143
Exodus Communications, 16, 427

Expedia, 16, 294, 521
Experian, 289
Exxon, 543
EZface.com, 237

F

Farm Journal, 186
Farmland Industries, 443
FedEx, 112, 241, 385–386, 387, 389, 418
Fiduciary Trust Company International, 544
First Data Corp., 512
First Union, 259
First USA, 292
Ford Motor, 88, 90–91, 251, 253, 547
Foxmeyer Drug, 443
Freemarkets, Inc., 16

G

The Gap, 16
Gartner Group, 318
GE Americom, 83
Gemstar International, 344
General Electric, 10, 14, 34
General Motors, 105, 106, 133, 185, 203, 251, 444
Google, 16
GTE, 31

H

Hacker Quarterly, 293
Haggar, 184
Hallmark, 238
Handspring Visors, 418
Hershey Foods, 39
Hewlett-Packard, 315
Home Depot, 103
Honda, 449
Honeywell, 100
H&R Block, 517
Hughes Electronics, 508, 509

I

IBM, 34, 39, 198, 258, 326, 329, 335–336, 348, 366, 373, 374, 507, 515
IBM Credit, 99, 115
IBM Federal Systems, 508
Intel, 23, 326, 327
Internal Revenue Service (IRS), 241
Internet.com, 538
Internet Wire, Inc., 523

J

J. D. Edwards, 216, 443
Jiffy Lube, 100
J&J's, 449–450
Johnson & Johnson, 427

K

Kaiser Permanente, 517
Kane Carpet Co., 518
Kimberly-Clark, 100
KMart, 429–430
Kodak, 443, 497
KPMG Peat Marwick, 472

L

Lands End, 237
Legacy systems, 444
Levi Strauss, 38
Libero, 453
Lockhead, 477
London Ambulance Service, 548–549
Lotus Development Corporation, 34
Lotus Notes, 444
Lufthansa Airbus, 109
Lutheran Brotherhood, 283
Lycos, 16

M

Macys.com, 253
MakeoverStudio.com, 237
Mars, Inc., 291
MasterCard, 541
Matsushita Electric, 235
Mazda, 88
McDonald's, 282, 331
McDonnell Douglas, 517, 518
MCI, 4, 207, 245, 420, 521
McKesson systems, 250
Mercedes Benz, 34
Merrill Lynch, 16, 250, 294, 427
Metropolitan Life, 276
Microsoft, 16, 34, 195, 319, 347–348, 374, 421, 444, 521
Mobil Corporation, 516
Morgan Stanley Dean Witter, 16
Motorola, 113
Mrs. Fields Cookies, 294

N

Napstar.com, 305–306, 322
National Federation of the Blind, 296
National Mutual, 283
National Semiconductor, 386
Netscape, 306
Network Solutions, Inc., 516, 538
News Index, 293
New York Cash Exchange (NYCE), 251
New York Times, 16
NFO Interactive, 239
Nibco, 507–508
Nintendo, 272

Nissan, 136
Northern Lights, 16
Northwest, 251
NTT DoCoMo, 426, 452
NUMMI, 106, 185
Nynex, 420

O

Office Depot, 16
Omaha Steaks, 386
One-Click, 294
Open SRS, 538
Oracle, 216, 443
Orbitz, 251
Oshkosh, 450
Otis Elevator, 225, 243
Owens Corning, 216, 222, 443, 497
Oxford Health Plans, 249

P

Pacific Bell, 288
Pacific Southwest Airlines, 117
Pacific Telephone and Telegraph (PT&T), 532
Pacific Telesis, 420
PairGain, 523
Palm Pilot, 21, 418
PanAmSat, 83
Pandesic LLC, 450
PBS broadcasting, 83
PC Magazine, 333–334
Peoplesoft, 216, 443
Pepsi-Cola, 527
Pez, 133
Phillip Morris, 291
Platform, 444
Pottery Barn, 237
Priceline.com, 239, 294
PricewaterhouseCoopers, 543
Procter & Gamble, 241
Prodential, 283

Q

Qualcomm, 25, 521

R

R. J. Reynolds, 168
Raytheon Co., 509
Remington Rand, 34
Renault/Nissan, 251
RSA Laboratories, 536

S

SAP, 30, 216, 443
SDBT Corp., 115
Sears, 259, 418

Sesame Street, 430
Shiseido, 237
SIM, 442
Sky Internet, 547
Soloman Brothers, 516–517
Southwestern Bell, 420
Sprint, 420
Standard Duplicating Machines (SDM), 523
Stew Leonard's, 524
Sumitomo Metal Mining Company, 530
Sun Alliance Insurance Group, 283
Sun Microsystems, 319, 374
SuperDot, 517

T

Target, 429
Time Warner, 525
TotalNews, Inc., 293
Toyota, 106, 185
Toysrus.com, 253
Transmeta Corporation, 343
Trans Union, 289
Travelocity.com, 16
Turner Classic Movies, 83

U

United Airlines, 251, 259
United Parcel Service (UPS), 4, 112, 241, 517
USAA, 258

V

VerticalNet, 16
ViewsWire, 467
Visa, 512–513, 521, 541

W

Wall Street Journal, 16
Wal-Mart, 83, 116, 241, 247, 294, 429–430
Webvan, 264–265
WinVista, 276

X

Xerox Corporation, 34, 64, 82, 250

Y

Yahoo!, 16, 116, 262, 427, 471–472, 473, 524
Yellow Freight System, 195

Z

ZDNet, 525

author index

A

Afuah, Allan, 255n
Alexander, Robert C., 34n
Allen, Bradley P., 213n
Allen, Brandt, 522n
Allen, Randy L., 429
Alter, Steven, 47n, 52n, 58n, 278n, 456n
Alwang, Greg, 195n
Ames, Aldrich, 117–118
Amor, Daniel, 6n
Andrews, Edmund L., 452n
Angwin, Julia, 295n, 511n, 522n
Anthes, Gary H., 197n, 223n, 450n, 461n, 480n, 521n, 526n, 527n
Armstrong, J. Scott, 34n
Arnaut, Gordon, 242n
Arnst, Catherine, 425n
Asenjo, Porfirio Barroso, 289n
Athes, Gary H., 443
Auckerman, William, 421n

B

Ball, Leslie D., 531n
Banks, Howard, 407n
Barnett, Megan, 86n
Bartels, Andrew, 6n
Battles, Brett E., 448n
Beck, Kent, 381n
Belden, Tom, 180n
Bell, Alexander Graham, 34, 288
Berners-Lee, Tim, 152
Bernstein, Nina, 290n
Betts, Mitch, 290n, 294n, 301n, 302n
Bicknell, Craig, 538n
Biddle, Frederic M., 83, 518n
Biersdorfer, J. D., 328n
Bjerklie, David, 301n
Blackburn, Joseph D., 115n
Blattberg, Robert C., 187n
Blumenstein, Rebecca, 404n, 419n
Boehm, Barry W., 461n
Booker, Ellis, 521n, 534n
Booth, Rose, 31n
Borders, Louis, 264
Bork, Robert, 290
Borwn, Shona L., 99
Bostrom, Robert P., 504n
Boudette, Neal E., 39n
Bourlas, Stephen, 509n
Boynton, Andrew C., 441n, 467n
Bradley, stephen P., 165n
Bradsher, Keith, 518n, 547n
Brady, Diane, 259n
Brain, Marshall, 256n, 258n
Branch, Shelly, 39n

Brand, Stewart, 34n
Brandeis, Louis D., 288n
Branscomb, Anne Wells, 301n
Braudel, William, 546n
Bridis, Ted, 547n
Broadbent, Marianne, 74, 449n
Broder, John M., 289n
Brody, Herbert, 113n
Brody, Jane E., 275n
Brohowski, Ron, 198n
Brooks, Frederick P., Jr., 462n
Brown, Carol V., 507n
Brown, Eryn, 131n
Brown, John Seeley, 81n
Brynjolfsson, Erik, 115n
*Buchanan, 70
Bulkeley, William M., 115n, 128n, 315n, 517n, 523n
Burton, Jonathan, 241n
Bush, George W., 70
Bylinsky, Gene, 185n, 221n
Byrt, Frank, 289n

C

Cafasso, Rosemary, 442n
Calandra, Thorn, 290n
Caldwell, Bruce, 38n
Canedy, Dana, 238n
Carey, John, 342n
Carley, William M., 106n, 522n
Carlson, Chester, 34
Carnevale, Mary Lu, 288n
Carroll, Jill, 419, 420, 421n
Carvajal, Doreen, 42n
Cespedes, Frank V., 301n, 452n
Champy, James, 34n, 99n, 105n, 246n, 433, 442n
Chapman, Katy, 237n
Chase, Marilyn, 288n
Chen, P. P., 144n
Cheney, Dick, 166
Christie, James, 251n
Christopher, Koch, 222n
Chuboda, Katherine M., 104n
Clark, Don, 355n
Clemons, Eric K., 250n
Clinton, Bill, 31, 168
Cockburn, Alistair, 381n
Cohen, Jackie, 518n, 544n
Cole, Jeff, 509n
Collett, Stacy, 297n, 484n
Cone, Edward, 427n
Conway, Chuck, 429
Copeland, Thomas E., 457n
Corley, Eric, 293

Coxeter, Ruth, 301n
Cringely, Robert X., 472n
Crowston, K., 102n
Cunningham, Ward, 381n
Cusumano, Michael A., 348n

D

Dahlbom, Bo, 506n
Dalton, Gregory, 416n, 452n
D'Amico, Mary Lisbeth, 344n
Darnton, Geoffrey, 81
Davenport, Thomas H., 10n, 86n, 88n, 184n, 197n
Davenport, Thomas P., 215n
Davidson, Elizabeth J., 504n
Davies, Erin, 532n
Davis, Beth, 416n
Davis, Randall, 209n, 238n
Davis, Stan, 229
DeGross, Janice I., 468n, 504n
Deighton, John, 187n
Dell, Michael, 3, 5
Dennis, Alan R., 198n
deSola Pool, Ithiel, 34n
DiDio, Laura, 525n
Diebold, John, 251n
Dizard, Wilson P., Jr., 32n
Dobrzynski, Judith H., 133n
Doktor, R., 456n
Dolan, Kerry A., 469n
Dombey, Daniel, 469n
Dreyfus, Joel, 279n
Driscoll, Lisa, 246n
Drucker, Jesse, 259n
Duff, Christina, 288n

E

Edmonson, Gail, 30n
Edwards, Tamala M., 527n
Eichelberger, Lori, 258n
Eisenberg, Anne, 254n
Eisenhardt, Kathleen M., 104n
Ellis, Juanita, 32n
Ellison, Carl, 541n
Ellul, Jacques, 32, 268n
El Sawy, Omar, 6n
Elstein, Aaron, 524n
Ewing, Jack, 306n
Ewing, Terzah, 523n

F

Fanning, Shawn, 305
Farhoomand, Ali F., 468n
Farmer, Melanie Austria, 253n
Feeny, David F., 450n

Feigenbaum, Edward, 457n
Feinman, Todd M., 541n
Fenyvesi, Charles, 522n
Ferguson, Charles H., 247n
Ferranti, Marc, 344n
Fialka, John J., 174n
Fields, Gary, 523n
Fischhoff, Baruch, 124n
Fisher, Lawrence M., 3n
Fisher, Marshall, 185n
Flynn, Laurie J., 293n
Forester, Tony, 107n
Fournier, Roger, 489n
Fowler, Martin, 381n
Fox, Pimm, 521n
Frank, Robert, 547n
Frank, Stephen E., 194n
Franklin, Curt, 418n
Frantz, Douglas, 484n
Freeman, David, 368n
Freiberger, Paul, 212n
French, Howard W., 530n

G

Galbraith, Craig S., 164n
Gargini, Paolo, 24n
Garson, Barbara, 282n
Gates, Bill, 319
Gelsinger, Patrick, 24n
George, Joey F., 198n
Gerth, Jeff, 263n
Getler, Warren, 515n
Geyelin, Milo, 168n
Giacoletto, Sergio, 81
Gillen, Mary, 262n
Gilpin, Kenneth N., 196n
Girard, Kim, 418n
Glasser, Perry, 507n
Gleck, Howard, 105n
Gleckman, Howard, 516n
Gleick, James, 356n
Goff, Leslie, 440n
Gomes, Lee, 305n
Gordon, Michael R., 514n
Gore, Al, 70
Greenman, Catherine, 305n
Greenstein, Irwin, 486n
Greenstein, Marilyn, 541n
Greising, David, 164n
Grove, Andrew, 328
Guernsey, Lisa, 133n, 195n, 519n
Guidera, Jerry, 289n
Gutek, Barbara A., 232n
Guth, Robert A., 418n
Guzman, Onel de, 547
Gwynne, Peter, 208n

H

Hafner, Katie, 259n
Hall, Arsenio, 290
Hammer, Ben, 128, 130n
Hammer, Michael, 34n, 88n, 99n, 105n, 433, 441–442
Hancock, Ellen, 427
Hansell, Saul, 42n, 521n

Harmon, Amy, 293n
Harrington, H. J., 10n, 86n
Harris, Catherline L., 88n
Hartman, Amir, 6n, 457n
Haskin, David, 129n
Hattori, Takaaki, 289n
Hausman, Jerry A., 165n
Hax, Arnoldo, 165n
Helft, Miguel, 265n
Heminger, Alan, 198n
Henderson, John C., 440n
Herman, Tom, 105n
Hersleb, James, 480n
Heygate, Richard, 115n
Highsmith, Jim, 381n
Hill, G. Christian, 328n
Hillis, Danny, 323n
Hilts, Philip J., 291n
Hirsch, James S., 143n
Hirschheim, Rudy, 450n
Hitt, Greg, 105n
Ho, Rodney, 262n
Hof, Robert D., 366n
Hoffman, Thomas, 544n
Hopper, Max D., 432n
Horwitt, Elizabeth, 526n
Hudson, Richard L., 174n, 546
Huff, Sid L., 6n
Hughes, Rob, 343n
Hulbert, Mark, 208n
Hutheesing, Nikhil, 276n

I

Ito, Youichi, 289n
Ives, Blake, 225n, 283n

J

Jackson, Thomas Penfield, 374
Jacky, Jonathan, 518n
Janah, Monua, 386n
Janis, Irving L., 124n
Jeffries, Ron, 381n
Jessup, Len M., 198n
Johansen, Robert, 195n
Johnston, H. Russell, 250n
Johnstone, Bob, 34n
Jones, Daniel T., 114n
Jurvis, Jeff, 197n

K

Kador, John, 6n, 457n
Kahneman, Daniel, 123n
Kalakota, Ravi, 6n
Kaplan, Carl S., 293n
Karasek, Robert, 273n
Kasparov, Garry, 348
Keegan, Paul, 34n
Keen, Peter G. W., 128n, 284n, 467n
Keil, Mark, 68, 478n
Kennan, Philip T., 457n
Kennedy, John F., 124
Kerstetter, Jim, 450n
Kessler, Robert R., 356n, 381n
Kilarski, Doug, 38n
King, Julia, 223n
Klebnikov, Paul, 82, 250n

Knecht, G. Bruce, 292n
Koblentz, Evan, 427n
Korper, Steffano, 30n
Krcmar, Helmut, 468n
Kuntz, Phil, 168n

L

Lacity, Mary C., 448, 451n
*Lander, Mark, 524n
*Landler, Mark, 547n
Landry, Julie, 294n
Laudon, Jane P., 6n
Laudon, Kenneth C., 6n
Lazarus, David, 235n
LeFauve, Richard G., 165n
Lenat, Douglas B., 383n
Leonard, Dorothy, 136n
Levitin, Anany V., 231n
Levy, Clifford, 524n
Lewis, Peter H., 403n
Lichtenstein, Sarah, 124n
Lieberman, Joseph, 166
Lippman, John, 83, 518n
Loftus, Peter, 526n
Lohr, Steve, 319n, 374n
Loofbourrow, T. H., 212n
Losee, Stephanie, 444n
Lovelace, Herbert, 452n
Lovelock, Peter, 468n
Luftman, Jerry N., 258n, 440n
Lund, Brian, 430n

M

Magretta, Joan, 4n
Malone, T. W., 102n
Manes, Stephen, 515n
Mark, David, 448
Markoff, John, 280n, 374n, 452n, 515n, 516n, 523n
Markus, M. Lynne, 68, 285n, 478n
Martin, Michael H., 443n
Martinez, Barbara, 517n
Martz, Ben, 198n
Mason, Richard, 201n, 287n
Mathiassen, Lars, 506n
Matsushita, Konosuke, 235
Matthews, Anna Wilde, 277n
Maznevski, Martha L., 104n
McCartney, Scott, 514n
McCorduck, Pamela, 452
McGee, Suzanne, 516n
McGinley, Laurie, 291n
McGoff, Chris, 198n
McKay, Colin J., 275n
McNealy, Scott, 319
McNeill, Daniel, 212n
*McReynolds, 70
Mehta, Stephanie N., 247n, 518n
Merrill, Gregory B., 164n
Meyer, Christopher, 229
Millar, Victor E., 12
Milosevic, S, 178
Minsky, Marvin, 214n
Mintzberg, Henry, 203, 204n
Mitnick, Kevin, 523
Moffett, Matt, 452n

Moody, Sid, 383n
Moore, Gordon, 23
Morris, Charles R., 247n
Morrison, Perry, 107n
Mossberg, Walter S., 239n
Mullen, Theo, 223n
Muller, Joann, 429n, 430n
Munakata, Toshinori, 213n
Murillo, Luis Eduardo, 24n
Myers, Steven Lee, 176n, 177n

N

Nehta, Stephanie N., 83
Nelson, Emily, 39n, 100n
Neumann, John von, 312
Neumann, Peter G., 109n, 548n
Newell, Allen, 34
Newson, Peter, 6n
Nii, Penny H., 452
Nixon, Richard, 168
Nolan, Richard L., 165n
Norman, Donald A., 270n
Norris, Floyd, 517n
Nunamaker, Jay, 198n

O

O'Brien, Timothy L., 292n
O'Connor, Kevin, 268n
Ofiesh, Gabriel, 34n
O'Hara, Colleen, 509n
Ohlson, Kathleen, 517n
Ohno, Taaichi, 114
Oldach, Scott, 440n
Olson, Ken, 34
Olson, Margrethe H., 283n
Omidyar, Pierre, 133
O'Regan, Rob, 427n
O'Reilly, Brian, 223n
Orlikowski, Wanda, 468n
Owens, Cynthia, 411n

P

Palfreman, Jon, 29n
Panko, Raymond R., 354n, 414n, 417n
Parent, Michael, 6n
Parker, Herhard, 24n
Parker, Marilyn M., 430, 433n, 440n
Pear, Robert, 32n, 302n
Pearl, Daniel, 247n
Peppers, Don, 38n
Perman, Stacy, 256n
Perrow, Charles, 104n, 270n
Peters, T. J., 204n
Petersen, Andrea, 268n
Petroski, Henry, 180n
Pfeffer, Jeffrey, 81, 197
Pine, B. J., II, 467n
Pitta, Julia, 329n, 412n
Pollack, Andrew, 477n
Port, Otis, 327n
Porter, Michael, 12n, 249n
Pottruck, David, 253
Pounds, William, 121n
Pringle, David, 418n
Prusak, Lawrence, 197n
Puttre, Michael, 440n

Q

Quayle, Dan, 290
Quick, Rebecca, 293n
Quinn, James Brian, 64

R

Ramstad, Evan, 39n
Randa, Roy, 366n
Rather, Dan, 290
Rayport, Jeffrey F., 136n
Redman, Thomas C., 231n
Reichlin, Igor, 525n
Reid, Calvin, 344n
Reilly, Patrick M., 25n
Rewick, Jennifer, 268n
Reynolds, R. J., 168
Rissmiller, Edna, 292
Roach, Stephen S., 115n
Robey, Daniel, 504n
Robinson, Marcia, 6n
Rochart, John F., 441n
Rodriguez, Eva M., 168n
Rose, Matthew, 523n
Rosenbaum, David E., 272n
Rosencrance, Linda, 253n, 277n, 511n, 515n, 517n
Ross, Jeanne, 450n
Ross, Philip E., 109n, 380n, 519n
Rothfeder, Jeffrey, 290
Row, Michael, 250n
Rozenberg, Dino, 468n
Rubin, John, 124n
Rundle, Rhonda, 523n

S

Sager, Ira, 116n, 318n
Salkever, Alex, 523n
Samatha, Shurety, 6n
Sandberg, Jared, 291n, 533n
Sandoval, Greg, 265n
Savitz, E. J., 368n
Schaff, William, 521n
Schiesel, Seth, 420n
Schlefer, Jonathan, 274n
Schmidt, Eric, 176n
Schneberger, Scott, 6n
Schneier, Bruce, 541n
Schroeder, Michael, 524n
Schultz, R. L., 456n
Schwab, Charles, 5`, 86n
Schwartzkopf, Norman, 25
Scuka, Daniel, 426n
Selby, Richard W., 348n
Seybold, Patricia B., 103n
Shapiro, Carl, 232n
Shapiro, Eileen C., 386n
Sheff, David, 272n
Shirky, Clay, 370n
Shook, David, 430n
Short, James E., 88n, 184n
Siddiqi, Jawed, 381n
Sifonis, John, 6n, 457n
Simon, Herbert, 34, 122n
Simon, Ruth, 524n
Sims, Calvin, 247n
Slatalla, Michelle, 237n

Slater, Robert, 10n
Sleven, D. P., 456n
Sliwa, Carol, 184n, 417n, 429n, 528n
Slovic, Paul, 124n
Slyke, Richard van, 407n
Slywotzky, Adrian, 38n
Smart, Tim, 128n
Smith, Douglas K., 34n
Smith, H. Jeff, 301n, 452n
Smith, Lee, 22n
Smith, Tom, 430n
Son, Masayoshi, 421
Songini, Marc L., 429n
Soon, Ang, 468n
Stallings, William, 407n
Starkman, Dean, 521n
Starkweather, Garry, 34
Stedman, Chris, 208n
Stedman, Craig, 507n
Stein, Tom, 443n
Steinberg, Steve G., 414n
Steven, Alter, 239n
Steward, Thomas D., 222n
Stewart, Martha, 430
Stewart, Thomas A., 440n
Stiles, Shane, 426n
Stipp, David, 212n
Stockton, William, 278n
Stolberg, Sheryl Gay, 263n
Stolee, Christopher, 6n
Strassmann, Paul, 442
Straub, Detmar, 331n
Stuart, Anne, 253n
Sviokla, John J., 284n
Swade, Doron, 29n

T

Tapich, Brian E., 85n
Tapscott, Don, 264n
Tedeschi, Bob, 268n, 543n
Theorell, Tores, 273n
Thurm, Scott, 130n
Thurow, Lester C., 293n
Ticehurst, Jo, 343n
Ticoll, David, 264n
Toppo, Greg, 289n
Tran, Khanh T. L., 14n
Trimble, Paula Shaki, 509n
*Trombley, Maria, 511n
*Trombly, Maria, 200n
Tucci, Christopher L., 255n
Tully, Shawn, 105n
Turing, Alan, 375
Turkle, Sherry, 271n
Tversky, Amos, 123n

U

Uchitelle, Louis, 100n
Umetnosti, Bulevar, 178

V

Van Natta, Don, Jr., 70
Varian, Hal R., 232n, 274n
Venkatraman, N., 226n, 440n
Verity, John W., 207n
Vessey, Iris, 507n

Victor, C. B., 467n
Violino, Bob, 396n
Vitale, Michael P., 225n
Vitale, Michael R., 250n
Vogel, Doug, 198n

W

Wade, Michael, 6n
Wald, Matthew L., 110n, 228n, 517n, 518n, 530n
Warren, Samuel D., 288n
Waterman, R. H., Jr., 204n
Watson, Thomas, Sr., 34
Waxer, Cindy, 38n
Weber, Thomas E., 195n, 453n
Weill, Peter, 74, 449n, 468n
Weinberg, Gerry, 381n
Weiner, Tim, 118n
Weinstein, Michael, 174n

Weiss, Todd R., 116n, 254n
Wilder, Clinton, 386n
Wildstrom, Stephen H., 525n
Willcocks, Leslie P., 450n
Williams, Laurie A., 356n, 381n
Williams, Molly, 329n
Williamson, Miryam, 216n
Winslow, Ron, 273n
Wiseman, Charles, 251n
Wolverton, Troy, 294n
Womack, James P., 113n
Woollacott, Emma, 343n
Woolley, Scott, 254n

Y

Yang, Catherine, 105n
Yashvant, Jani, 213n
Yourdon, Edward, 45n, 462n
Yu, Albert, 24n

Z

Zachary, G. Pascal, 371n
Zadeh, Lofti, 212
Zambrano, Lorenzo, 468
Zeitlin, Minda, 259n
Ziegler, Bart, 408n
Zimmerman, Ann, 100n
Zmud, Robert W., 430
Zohar, Mark, 425n
Zuboff, Shoshanna, 279n
Zuckerman, Laurence, 30n, 83, 518n
Zygmont, Jeff, 38n

glossary/index

A

Abacus Direct, 268

Abstractness of work. Extent to which work is abstract, which some people enjoy and others find uncomfortable, 279

Acceptance testing. At the end of an information system's implementation phase, final testing by users to decide whether they accept the new system, 486

Access, 295
  control of, 532–534
  direct, 158–159
  indexed, 159
  to information, 297
  sequential, 157–158

Access codes, unauthorized use of, 521

Access privileges. Precise statements of which computers and data an individual can access and under what circumstances, 532

Access restriction. The procedures and techniques used for controlling who can access what information under what circumstances, 168

Accidents, threat of, in information systems, 512–519

Accuracy of data, 163

Accuracy of information. The extent to which information represents what it is supposed to represent, 291–292

Acquisition costs, 435

Activity rates. The number of interim work steps that are performed per unit time, 112
  variability in, 112

Ada, 363, 364

Addressability. The ability to direct specific marketing messages to specific individuals or groups in a marketing effort, 186–187

Ad hoc access, 141

Admissibility of information. Extent to which the use of specific information is required or prohibited in a particular situation, 167

Ads, banner, 255

Affiliate program. Arrangement between a Web site and a firm engaged in e-commerce. The Web site displays links to the other firm's e-commerce site and receives a commission for sales initiated through these links, 256

Age of data. The amount of time that has passed since the data were produced, 166

AIX, 373

Alpha Chip, 327

American Consumer Satisfaction Index, 258

Americans with Disabilities Act, 296

Analog data, transmitting digital data versus, 401–404

Analog encoding, 404

Analog signals. Signals that vary continuously in a wave pattern mimicking the shape of the original data, 402–403

Anonymous communication. Communication in which the sender's identity is purposely hidden, 120

Anthropomorphize. Ascribe human attributes to an animal or object, 271

Applet. Small program, typically written in Java, that operates on data transmitted to a Web browser as part of a Web page, 153, 365

Application packages. Commercially available software that addresses a specific type of business process, such as sales tracking, general ledger, or inventory control, 479–480, 492–493, 502–503
  advantages and disadvantages of, 497
  phases of, 494–497

Application programmers, 439

Application service provider (ASP). An outsourcing vendor that operates a firm's application software on remote servers on a wide area network, thereby making it unnecessary for the firm to install and maintain the software on its own servers, 388, 450

Application software. Software that defines the tasks the computer should perform and expresses that processing from a user or business perspective, 350–351

Architecture (of a work system). How the current or proposed system operates mechanically; summarized in terms of its components, the way the components are linked, and the way the components operate together, 63

Artificial Intelligence (AI). The field of research related to the demonstration of intelligence by machines, 375

ASCII (American Standard Code for Information Interchange). One of several standard codes for representing letters, digits, and special characters on computer systems, 323–324

ASIC (Application specific integrated circuit). A chip tailored to a particular application such as controlling a machine or video game, 329

ASP. *See* Application service providers (ASP)

Assemblers, 361

Assembly languages. Second generation programming languages permitting naming of variables rather than specifying data locations in the computer, 361–362
  comparison of machine language and, 362

Asymmetric digital subscriber line (ADSL), 403

Asynchronous transfer mode (ATM). A form of high bandwidth switching that attempts to combine the features of circuit switching with the robustness and efficiency of packet switching, 417–418

Attenuation, 408

Attributes. The specific data items related to specific entities in a database, 141

Auctions, 254–255

Audio. Data in the form of sounds, 136
  output of, 339–340

Audio conferencing. A single telephone call involving three or more people participating from at least two locations, 193

Audiographic conferencing. An extension of audio conferencing permitting dispersed participants to view pictures or graphical material at the same time, 193

Audio Home Recording Act (1992), 305–306

Auditing around the computer. Auditing process in which the auditor views the computer system as a black box and audits inputs and outputs to the system, 543

Auditing through the computer. Auditing process in which the auditor attempts to understand and test the computer system's processing by tracing transactions through it, 543

Authentication. Process of verifying that the transaction participants are who they claim to be, 540–541

Automatic log off. Security measure of logging off any terminal that has not been used for a specified amount of time, 534

Automatic translation programs, 377

Autonomy. The degree if discretion individuals of groups have in planning, regulating, and controlling their own work, 275

Availability of information. The extent to which information exists and can be accessed effectively by people who need it., 166–167

B

B2B (business-to-business). A form of e-commerce that uses the Internet as a primary channel for selling, distributing, and servicing products that are sold to other businesses, 15, 254

B2C (business-to-consumer). A form of e-commerce that uses the Internet as a primary channel for selling products to consumers, 15, 254

B2G (business-to-government), 15

Backup Storing additional copies of data in case something goes wrong with the original data, 160, 539

Backward chaining. In an expert system, a goal-oriented process of starting with a tentative conclusion and then looking for facts in the database that support that conclusion, 208

Bandwidth. The capacity of the telecommunications channel stated in megabits or gigabits per second, 406–407

Banner ads. Web-based advertisement that invites Web users to click on the advertisement to go to a different site offering products and services not offered on the current site, 255

Bar code readers, 332

Bar codes, 21–22

Baseband. Use of the entire capacity of a network to transmit one digitally coded signal at a time, 415–416

BASIC (Beginner's All-purpose Symbolic Instruction Code), 363, 364

Basic rate interface (BRI), 417

Batch processing. Transaction processing in which information for individual transactions is gathered and stored but isn't processed immediately, 200

Baud. Rate of signal changes per second in digital data transmission; equal to bits per second if the signal has only two states, 0 and 1, 310, 403

Benchmarking (an application package). Running a test application with the same volumes of input, output, data access, and data manipulation that the final application will have, 494

Benign neglect, 284

Beta testing. Real-world testing of a preliminary release of software to identify bugs and other problems not identified in earlier testing within the programming group, 356

Bias (in data). Systematic inaccuracy due to methods used for collecting, processing, or presenting data, 164–165

Binary representation
of numbers, 323
of text, 323–324

Biometric identification. Identification of an individual based on unique biological characteristics, 533–534

Bit. A binary digit, namely, a 0 or 1, 310

Bits per second (bps). A measure of speed of data transmission, 310

Bluetooth. A short range wireless technology that operates over distances of less than 10 meters, 418

Bottleneck. An essential work step where a temporary or long-term capacity storage delays work on most of the items being produced or processed, 115

Boundary (of a system). Border between what is inside the system and what is outside, 9

Bounded rationality. Description of the common practice of making decisions in a limited amount of time, based on limited information, and with limited ability to process that information, 123

Bridge. A combination of hardware and software that links two networks by converting the addressing data from one into addressing data in the appropriate protocol for the other, 416

Broadband. Division of the capacity of a network to permit it to carry several signals at the same time, 416

Browser. Software that supports the user's interface to the Web and displays Web pages to the user, 152, 153

Bug. A flaw in a program that causes it to produce incorrect or inappropriate results, 354–356
software, 516

Bug fixes (as a type of project). Projects directed at correcting bugs in existing systems, 438

Bulletin boards, 526

Business
functional areas of, 10–11
local area networks in, 392–393
operation of through systems, 7–18
strategic alignment of, and IT, 440–453
in work system framework, 46

Business-driven IT infrastructure, 448–450

Business environment, pressures in, 528

Business process. A related group of steps or activities that use people, information, and other resources to create value for internal or external customers, 10–11, 68, 86
activity rate in, 112
attention to errors and exceptions, 108–110
characteristics of, 94–110
communication in, 118–121
complexity of, 105
consistency in, 112–114
decision-making in, 121–125
degree of reliance on machines, 106–107
degree of structure, 96–99
describing, organization and hierarchy, 88–91
downtime in, 116
evaluating performance, 110–118
flexibility of, 113
idealized, 93
level of integration, 100–104
output rate in, 112
process modeling in documenting, 87–94
productivity in, 114–115
programming as a, 352–359
prominence of planning and control, 107–108
range of involvement, 99–100
rhythm of, 104
security of, 117–118

Business process reengineering (BPR). The fundamental rethinking and radical redesign of business processes using information technology to achieve dramatic improvements in critical measures of performance, 87, 442

Business professional. A person in a business or government organization who manages other people or works as a professional in fields such as engineering, sales, manufacturing, consulting, and accounting, 4

Bus topology. Network topology in which each node is attached to a central channel called a bus, 415

Byte 8 bits, sufficient to represent 256 different characters, 310

C

Cable modems. A device that permits Internet access through cable television connections, 403

CAD. *See* Computer-aided design (CAD)

Call-back system. Access control system in which the user enters an account number and password and is then disconnected and called back automatically, 533

Caller ID. An optional feature in current telephone systems that displays the caller's telephone number on a special unit attached to a telephone, 288

Capability maturity model (CMM). A model for describing and measuring the extent to which an IT organization uses predictable, manageable processes for building information systems., 479

Capacity. The theoretical limit of the output a system can produce in a given time period, 112

Carrier signal. In telecommunications, an oscillatory signal that carries the encoded data and is recognized by both the sending and receiving equipment, 402

CASE. *See* Computer-aided software engineering

Case-based reasoning. A decision support method based on the idea of finding past cases most similar to the current situation in which a decision must be made, 213–214, 375

Case manager approach. Organizing a business process around a single individual who performs different information-related tasks that might have been assigned to many different individuals in the past, 99

Cashier fraud, 522

CATIA, 179

CDMA. *See* Code division multiple access (CDMA)

CD-R. Compatible disk—recordable. Like a CD-ROM except that a CD-R drive can record information on it once (but cannot rewrite over data recorded in any particular location on the disk, 337

CD-ROM. Compact Disk Read Only Memory, a 650 megabyte optical disk used for storing and retrieving data; the original versions were read only, but subsequent versions permit modification of data, 337

CD-RW. Compact disk-rewriteable; like a CD-ROM except that a CD-RW drive can record information on it and can rewrite over data recorded in a particular location on the disk, 337

Cell phones, 411

Centralization versus decentralization, 445–448

Centralized computing. Computing in which all the processing for multiple users is done by a large central computer, 316, 317

Central processing unit (CPU). Component of a computer that executes machine language instructions, 312

Certification authority (CA). A company whose business consists of issuing digital certificates that provide an independent confirmation of an attribute claimed by a person offering a digital signature, 540

Champion. In relation to an information system, an individual who makes sure the system is recognized as important by others in the organization, 437

Channel. Physical path along which data transmission occurs, 398

Chargeback systems. Accounting system that motivates efficient system usage by assigning to user organizations costs for information systems and related resources, 542

Chat room. An informal computer conference that someone can join, participate in, and then leave, 195

Checking accounts, 188

Chief information officer (CIO). Title of the head of the information systems department in some firms, 437

Children's Online Privacy Protection Act (1998), 291

Chip. A small piece of silicon onto which an electronic circuit or component has been etched, 327

Choice. Third phase of decision making; the selection of the preferred alternative, 122

CIM. *See* Computer-integrated manufacturing (CIM)

Circuit switching. Process of setting up a temporary circuit between the source and destination for telephone calls, 405–406

CISC (complex instruction set computer). Microprocessor design in which the microprocessor may perform hundreds of basic instructions instead of using a reduced instruction set, 329

C language, 363, 364

C++ language, 351, 363, 364

CLASH, 179–180, 182

Clicks and bricks. A business strategy of using e-commerce while maintaining store- or office-based channels, 252–253

Client/server architecture. Computer system architecture consisting of client devices that send requests for service and server devices that perform the request processing, 319–322

Clock speed, measuring, 310–311

Coaxial cable. Type of cable used for local area networks and other data transmission covering less than 10 miles, 409

COBOL (Common Business Oriented Language), 351, 363, 364, 365, 366, 367

Code-division multiple access (CDMA). One of several technical standards for transmitting cellular phone calls, 414

Code generators, 370

Code of Fair Information Practices, 290–291

Collaboration. A form of process integration involving such strong coordination and interdependence between processes that their unique identity begins to disappear, 102, 103

Collision. Calculation of the same location for two different records while storing or retrieving data in a computer system, 158

Commodity-information component, 230

Commodity-service component, 230

Common culture. A minimal form of process integration involving shared understandings and beliefs, 102

Common sense. A shared understanding of how things work in everyday life, 376

Common standards. A minimal form of process integration involving the use of consistent terminology and procedures to make business processes easier to maintain and interface, 102

Communications
anonymous, 120
basic concepts in, 118–120
convergence of computing and, 388–390
data, 387
impersonal, 120
nonverbal, 119
personal, 119–120
time, place, and direction of, 120

Communication systems. Information systems that help people communicate, 180, 191–199

Compatibility. The extent to which the characteristics and features of a particular technology fit with those of other technologies relevant to the situation, 309

Competitive advantage. Competitive situation in which one firm's value chain produces products and services that are superior to those of other firms in terms of cost, features, or other characteristics, 249
information systems and, 249–251

Competitive necessity. In relation to systems, the need to use or provide a particular type of system in order to remain competitive, 251

Compiler. A program that translates higher-level language programs into machine language, 363

Completeness (of information).. The extent to which the available information seems adequate for the task, 165–166

Complexity. How complicated a system is, based on a combination of how many types of elements the system contains and the number and nature of their interactions, 105
managing, 105

Computer. A programmable device that can execute previously stored instructions, 312
clock speed, 310–311
compatibility, 309

controlling access to, 531
in data manipulation, 322–330
data storage and processing, 310
ease of use, 309
functional capabilities and limitations, 309
host, 401
maintainability, 309
making, intelligent, 374–377
operating speed, 310
rate of data transfer, 310
reliance of telecommunications on, 388
role of telecommunications in, 388–389
speed of executing instructions, 311
technology performance, 311
transmission frequency, 310–311
types of, 312–315

Computer-aided design (CAD). Use of computers and specialized software to support a design process, 179–180, 182, 185, 231

Computer-aided manufacturing (CAM), 238

Computer-aided software engineering (CASE). Use of computerized systems to improve the process of analyzing, designing, developing, and maintaining information systems, 73, 91, 351, 358, 368–370
systems in, 491
techniques in, 528
tools in, 483

Computer conferencing. The exchange of text messages typed into computers from various locations to discuss a particular issue, 195–196

Computer crime. The use of computerized systems to perform illegal acts, 519
threat of, 519–526

Computer-integrated manufacturing (CIM). Use of computers and communication technology to integrate design, manufacturing, planning, and other business functions, 185

Computerized systems, 14

Computer-mediated work. Work done through computers, rather than through direct physical contact with the object of the task, 279, 280

Computer operators, 439

Computer output microfilm. Form of computer output that bypasses paper and shrinks pages of output to tiny images stored on firm, 335–336

Computer program. A set of instructions in a programming language that specifies the processing to be performed by the computer, 352

Computer-readable form, 333

Computer-related theft, 520

Computer system. A system consisting of computers and computer-controlled devices that process data by executing programs, 312
basic model of, 312
overview, 312–315

Computing
centralized, 317
convergence of communications and, 388–390

distributed, 318
network, 318–319
new combinations of data and, 389–390
in organizations, 315–322
personal, 317–318
Confidentiality, 194
Conformance to standards and regulations. Degree of adherence to standards and regulations imposed by external bodies such as major customers, industry groups, or the government, 247–248
Connectivity. In an organization, the ability to access and use geographically dispersed data and resources. In computerized systems, the technical ability to transmit data between devices, 25–26, 397
Consistency (of business processes). Applying the same techniques in a prescribed manner to obtain prescribed results, 112–114
Constraints, 56
Context (of a work system). The organizational, competitive, technical, and regulatory realm within which a work system operates, including external stakeholders, the organization's policies, practices, and culture, and competitive and regulatory issues, 46, 74–76
Context diagram. Data flow diagram verifying the scope of a system by showing the sources and destinations of data it uses and generates, 88–89
Controlling. The process of using information about past work performance to assure that goals are attained and plans carried out, 107–108
Convergence of computing and communications. Historical trend through which communication capabilities became essential to many computer systems and computing capabilities became essential to communication systems, 26
Conversion. Process of converting from a previous system, 486
Cookie. A small text file that a Web browser stores in a folder on a Web user's PC to facilitate repeat usage of a Web site by recording user preferences, the time of the most recent session, and other information about past use of the Web site, 258, 267
Coordination. As a form of integration, managing dependencies between processes through negotiation and exchange of messages, thereby permitting separate but independent processes to respond to each other's needs and limitations, 102
Copyright law, 294
Cordless phones, 411
Cost. The totality of what an internal or external customer must give up in order to obtain, use, and maintain the product of a business process, customer satisfaction and, 245–246

Cost/benefit analysis. The process of evaluating proposed projects by comparing estimated benefits and costs, 453–456
Cost-effectiveness, 308–309
of computing equipment, 329
Cost leadership strategy. A strategy based on competing on lower costs, 249
CP/M, 370
Credit cards, 188
Critical success factors (CSF). Approach for identifying critical business factors that should have very high priority in information system development, 440–441
Crosstalk noise, 408
Culture, organizational, 76
Customer(s), 65–67
attracting, to e-commerce, 255–256
criteria, for evaluating products and services, 244–249
diverse concerns of different, 248–249
evaluation of product by, 67–68
external, 65
internal, 65
internal and external, 65
multiple, with different concerns, 66
transforming, into participants, 66–67
view of products and service, 226–235
in work system framework, 46
Customer experience. A customer's entire involvement with a product (or service); defining the requirements, acquiring the product, using the product, maintaining it, and retiring it, 13, 235–243
Customer relationship management (CRM). Commercial software that addresses planning, controlling, and scheduling of pre-sales and post-sales activities, 187, 252–253
Customer service, rationing resources, 259
Customization, 233–234
exercising, choices, 238
Cybersquatting. Registering a Web domain name in order to sell it later to a company or person that wants to use it, 293
Cycle time (of business processes). The length of time between the start of the process and its completion, 115–116

D

Data. Facts, images, or sounds that may or may not be pertinent or useful for a particular task, 69–72. *See also* Information
access to, 156–160, 531
accuracy of, 163
availability of, in end-user development, 500–501
backup and recovery of, 160–161
basic ideas for describing, 136–141
capturing, 330–334, 398–399
compression of, 325–326
computers in manipulation of, 322–330
controlling and organizing to enhance value of, 156–161
controlling incoming, 534–535
in databases, 137–138
defining and organizing, 141–144

directing, from source to destination, 404–406
displaying, 338–340
encryption of, 326
errors in, 516–517
evaluating, as a resource, 162–168
files in, 138–139
generating, 398–401
guidelines for manual handling of, 532
hard, 71–72
identifying, in a database, 142–144
input of, 330–334
location of, in corporation, 445–446
logical versus physical views of, 139–140
making, meaningless to unauthorized users, 535–536
measuring amounts of, 310
new combinations of computing and, 389–390
organizing, as a file, 138
output of, 338–340
precision of, 163
preparation and authorization of, 538
preprogrammed access to, 141
process of accessing, 140–141
receiving, 400–401
soft, 71–72
storing and retrieving, 334–337
theft by entering fraudulent transaction, 521–522
theft by stealing or modifying, 522–523
timeliness of, 166
transmitting, through wire and wireless media, 406–412
types of, 135–136
Data analysis software, 498
Database. A structured collection of data items stored, controlled, and accessed through a computer based on predefined relationships between predefined types of data items related to a specific business, situation, or problem
defined, 137–138
distributed, 160
hypermedia, 152–155
identifying the data in, 142–144
image, 152
multidimensional, 146–147
query programs for, 377
relational, 145–148
text, 149, 151
Database administration. The process of managing a database, 161, 439
Database management systems (DBMSs). An integrated set of programs used to define, update, and control databases, 73, 138, 156–161, 450, 491, 498, 501
backup and recovery, 160–161
controlling distributed databases, 160
defining the database and access to data, 156–157
methods for accessing data in a computer system, 157–160
processing transactions, 160
supporting database administration, 161
Data channels, 526

Data communications. The transmission of computerized data between devices in different locations, 387

Data dictionary. A central repository for defining data in a database management system, 157

Data Encryption Standard (DES), 536

Data flow diagram (DFD). Diagram using four standardized symbols to represent flows of data between processes or subprocesses in a business, 87, 88–91, 90, 481

Data independence. Characteristic of programs whereby data organization and format are defined outside of programs and inserted automatically, 358

Data loss. Loss of data during transmission due to the physical properties of the data channel or distortion from other signals, 408

Data mart. A small data warehouse or a subset of a larger data warehouse devoted to a particular business function or department, 149

Data mining. The use of data analysis tools to try to find the patterns in large transaction databases, 207–208

Data model. A sufficiently detailed description of the structure of the data to help the user or programmer think about the data, 139–140

Data modeling. The process of identifying the types of entities in a situation, relationships between those entities, and the relevant attributes of these entities, 141–144

Data validation. The checking of transaction data for any errors or omissions that can be detected by looking at the data, 538–539

Data warehouse. Hardware and software that extracts data from a transaction database and stores it separately for analysis and archival purposes rather than transaction processing, 149

Debit cards, 188

Debugging. The process of finding and correcting bugs, flaws that cause programs to produce incorrect or inappropriate results, 354

Decentralization versus centralization, 445–448

Decision-making
   automatic, 124–125
   common flaws in, 123–124
   rationality in, 122
   satisficing in, 123
   steps in, 121–122

Decision support system (DSS). An interactive information system that provides information, models, and data manipulation tools to help make decisions in semistructured and unstructured situations, 180, 191–192, 205–215

Decoding. Process of converting data from a form used for a transmission back into a form for use by people, 399–400

Dedicated line. A telephone line used exclusively by a particular firm fro

transmitting voice or computerized data between two locations, 404

De facto standards. Standards established by the fact that a product dominates a particular market, 412

Degree of structure. The degree of predetermined correspondence between the inputs and outputs of business process, 96–99

De jure standards. Standards defined by industry groups or by the government, 412

Deliverables (in a project). Tangible work products, such as documents, plans, or computer programs, 459

Delivery, taking, 241

Denial of service attack. Method of sabotaging a Web site by flooding a server's ports and memory buffers with so many incoming messages that the Web site cannot provide service for its legitimate users, 525–526

Design. Second phase of decision making; a systematic study of the problem, creation or alternatives, and evaluation of outcomes, 122
   human-centered, 269
   machine-centered, 269–270

De-skilling. Use of technology or process changes that reduce the value of skills previously needed to do specific types of work, 277

Detailed requirements analysis. Process of creating a user-oriented description of exactly what a proposed information system will do, 482

Development. Second phase of an information system project. The transformation of system requirements into hardware and software that accomplish the required functions, 19–20, 472
   in application package, 494–496
   in end-user development, 499
   in information system, 476–477
   in prototype, 491
   in traditional system life cycle, 481–484

Different-time (asynchronous) communication, 120

Digital certificate. A computer-based record used to verify the sender of an electronic message, 540

Digital data, transmitting analog data versus, 401–404

Digital encoding, 404

Digital purse. Computerized record that plays the role of a smart card in an online transaction, 240

Digital rights management (DRM). Methods for controlling distribution and usage of information products, 232

Digital signal(s). In telecommunications, signals represented by a series of 0's and 1's, 402

Digital signal processor (DSP). Specialized, single-purpose microprocessor devoted to processing voice or video signals, 329

Digital signature. A digital record that validates a transaction by serving the purpose of a signature, 536

Digital subscriber line (DSL). Digital technology for achieving high speed data communications using copper telephone lines, 392, 403–404

Digital versatile disk (DVD). An optical disk that holds 4.7 gigabytes of data, 337

Digitization. The process of generating a series of numbers that approximately represents a particular image or sound, 26

Direct access. Data access method for finding an individual item in a file by calculating its location in a computer system, 158–159

Direct access storage devices (DASDs), 336

Direct marketing. The process of selling through mail or other forms of communication addressed to specific individuals, 186

Disaster plan. For information system, a plan of action to recover from occurrences that shut down or harm major information systems, 543–544

Disbursements fraud, 522

Discount rate, 456

Display System Replacement (DSR), 508

Distributed computing. Computing in which individuals do their own work on personal computers and use a telecommunications network to link to other devices., 316, 318

Distributed databases. Database that is spread across more than one location, 160

Documentation. Formal, written explanation of how a system operates, 483–484

Downsizing. Reduction in both total staffing and layers of management, 442

Downtime. The amount or percentage of time during which a process or machine is out of operation, 116

Dumb terminals. Terminal that serves only as an input/output mechanism linking users with the central computer, 317

Dynamic pricing, 254

E

Ease of use. Ease of learning how to use a technology, ease of setting it up, ease of becoming proficient, and ease of using it directly, 309

e-business. The practice of performing and coordinating critical business processes such as designing products, obtaining supplies, manufacturing, selling, fulfilling orders, and providing services through the extensive use of computer and communication technologies and computerized data, 5–6
   tools for, 386
   trend toward, 14–18, 106
   vital role of telecommunications in, 387–388

e-commerce. Electric commerce, use of the Web and other electronic means for selling, distributing, and servicing products, 14, 251–260

achieving profitability and sustainable differentiation, 259–260
attracting customers, 255–256
establishing and integrating systems, 252–253
providing an effective self-service environment, 256–257
providing excellent customer service, 258–259
setting prices for, 253–255
tools for, 386
eCommerce Builder, 386
Economic feasibility, 481
EDI, 105
Effectiveness. The extent to which a system accomplishes the right goals, 64
Efficiency. The ratio between outputs and inputs for a particular task, regardless of whether the task itself is the right task to perform, 64
charging users to encourage, 542
Electronically enhanced products, 241
Electronic cameras, 333
Electronic cash. Means of transferring funds for small purchases through the use of computers, 188
Electronic communication systems, 192
Electronic data interchange (EDI). The electronic transmission of business data such as purchase orders and invoices from one firm's computerized information system to that of another firm, 184, 248, 416–417, 443
Electronic encyclopedias, 228
Electronic funds transfer (EFT). Using electronic messages representing funds transfers to settle accounts between banks and other businesses, 188
Electronic junk mail, 194
Electronic message systems, 526
Electronic publishing, 232
E-mail, 194
E-marketplace, 388
Embedded computer. A computer that is an internal component of another machine, 312
Encoding (data). Process of converting data from an original form into a form for transmission, 398
analog, 404
digital, 404
Encryption. Process of coding data to make it meaningless to anyone who steals it, 168, 535–536
End-user computing (EUC). Direct, hands-on use of computer systems by end users whose jobs go beyond entering data into a computer or processing transactions, 498
End-user development. The development of information systems by work system participants (end users) rather than information system professionals, 480, 498, 503
advantages and disadvantages, 501
phases in, 498–500
supporting the users, 500–501

End-user software. General-purpose tools designed for end users without assistance by programers, 351
Enhancement. Concerning information systems, improvements in an existing system's function without changing its fundamental concepts or operation, 438
Enterprise resource planning (ERP) system information system that uses an integrated database to provide a common, integrated infrastructure for typical business processes within functional areas and consistent information across areas, 215–219, 497
Enterprise systems, 180, 191–192, 215–216, 443. *See also* Enterprise resource planning (ERP) system
Entity. A specific thing about which an information system collects information, 141
Entity-relationship diagram (ERP). Diagram identifying the entity types in a situation and diagramming the relationships between those entity types, 141–144, 144, 481
Entity type. A kind of thing an information system collects information about, 141
Environment (of a system). Everything pertinent to the system that is outside of its boundaries, 9
E-retailers, 388
Ergonomics. Study of the interplay of human characteristics and characteristics of machines people use, 274
Error(s). *See also* Bugs
attention to, in business process, 108–110
data, 516–517
logic, 354–355
operator, 513–514
random, 165
syntax, 354
Error correction. Process of correcting incorrect data that has been entered into a computerized system, 539
eShipping tools, 386
Ethical dilemmas. Difficult choices related to ethical issues that may or may not be covered by laws, 286
Ethical theories. Principles that can be used as a basis for deciding what to do in ethical dilemmas, 287
Ethics. A branch of philosophy dealing with the principles of right and wrong behavior related to other people, 286
Evolutionary prototype. A prototype designed to be adapted for permanent use after the ideas are clarified, 489
Executing. The process of doing work (as opposed to planning the work or controlling it), 107–108
Executive information system (EIS). A highly interactive system providing managers and executives flexible access to information for monitoring operating results and general business conditions, 191–192, 202–205
Expert systems. Information system that uses rules and other representations of

knowledge to support the work of professionals in bounded, but complex situations in which recognized experts do better than nonexperts, 208–210, 375
Explanation module. Part of an expert system that explains how a particular fact was inferred or why a particular question is being asked, 208
Explicit knowledge. Precisely and formally articulated knowledge that is often codified in databases of corporate procedures and best practices, 197
Extensible markup language (XML). An extension of HTML containing tags that define data in a manner similar to data definitions in databases, 152
External customers. People who receive and use work system outputs that go outside the firm, 65
External specifications. A document explaining the results produced by the detailed requirements analysis, 482
Extranet. Private network that operates similarly to an Intranet but is directed at customers or suppliers rather than at employees, 196

F
Fax, 194–195
Feasibility study. A user-oriented overview of a proposed information system's purpose and feasibility, 481
Federal Aviation Administration (FAA), 508–509
Federal Communication Commission (FCC), 421
Federal Trade Commission, 253
Fiber optic cable. Type of cable that transmits data using a core of ultra-pure glass, 398–399, 409
Field. In a file, a group of characters that have a predefined meaning, 138
File. A set of related records, 138–139
File server. A specialized computer dedicated to retrieving data from a database, 319
Finance systems, 188–189
Financial passwords, 521
Firewall. A program that inspects incoming messages from a network, decides whether they are legitimate, sends legitimate messages to their destinations, and keeps track of messages that were stopped, 534–535
Flash memory. A semiconductor device that stores and modifies data while the computer is operating, but that also retains data when the computer is turned off, 337
Flexibility (of a business process). The ease with which a business process can be adjusted to meet immediate customer needs and adapted over the long term as business conditions change, 113
FLOPS (Floating point operations per second). Operations per second involving decimal numbers rather than just integers, 309, 311

Flowchart. Diagram expressing the sequence and logic of procedures using standardized symbols to represent different types of input/output, processing, and data storage, 87, 91–94

Focus strategy. A strategy whereby a company sells its product or service into a restricted market niche with limited competition, 249

Forgery, 522

Format (of information). The way information is organized and expressed for personation to a user, 167

FORTRAN (FORmula TRANslator), 363, 364

Forward chaining. In an expert system, starting with data and trying to draw all possible conclusions from the data, 208

Fourth generation language (4GLs). Loosely defined group of programming languages that make programming less procedural than third generation languages, 366–367, 483, 491, 497, 498, 501

Frame relay. A form of packet switching that is a popular technology for public switched data networks, 417

Framework. A brief set of ideas for organizing a thought process about a particular type of thing or situation, 43
  need for, 43–44
  work system, 45–47

Fraud, 253
  cashier, 522
  committed using transaction processing systems, 522
  disbursements, 522
  impersonation, 522
  inventory, 522
  payroll, 522
  pension, 522
  telephone, 542

Free version of a product. Version of a product given the customer for free in the hope that in the future the customer will pay for the product itself, its updates, or related services, 232

Front-end processor. A computer that handles network communication for another computer such as a mainframe that processes the data, 401

Functional areas of business. Large subsystems of a firm related to specific business disciplines, such as production, marketing, and finance, 10–11
  information system categories related to, 181–218

Functional capabilities. The types of processing a particular type of technology can perform and the degree of capability it has, 308

Functional silos. Term for functional areas of business; used in discussing common tendency to focus internally within a function (silo) rather than emphasizing coordinated results for the entire firm, 10

Functional specification. Overview of the business problem addressed by a proposed system, the way business processes will change, and the project's benefits, costs and risk, 481

Fuzzy logic. A form of reasoning that makes it possible to combine conditions stated in an imprecise form similar to completion times and resource requirements, 212–213, 375

G

Gantt charts. Chart representing a schedule visually by displaying tasks along with their planned and actual start and completion times and resource requirements, 459–461

Gateway. A combination of hardware and software permitting communication between computers on incompatible networks, 416

Generations of programming languages. Historical succession of different types of computer languages, 361

Geographic information systems. Information system permitting users to access data based on spatial or geographic coordinates, 149

Gigabyte, 310

Global system for mobile communication (GSM). One of several technical standards for transmitting cellular phone calls, 414

Graphical user interface (GUI). User interface using icons to represent objects, a pointing device to select operations, and graphical imagery to represent relationships, 317–318

Group support systems (GSS). A form of groupware devoted to facilitating meetings through a variety of capabilities related to brainstorming, topic commenting, issue analysis, voting, and evaluation of alternatives, 197–199

Groupware systems. Commercial software that help groups and teams work together by sharing information and controlling work flows, 192, 195–196

H

Hackers. People who enjoy playing with computers, a small minority of whom commit computer crime for the challenge of breaking into a computer system, 520, 547–548

Hard data. Clearly defined data generated by formal systems (as opposed to soft data), 71–72

Hard disk. Device that stores and retrieves data using magnetized regions on a rotating disk, 336
  increased storage capacity, 22

Hardware. Physical devices and connections in a computer system, 72, 312
  location of, in corporation, 445–446
  malfunctions of, 515
  theft of, 521

Hardware acquisition and installation. During the development phase of an information system, the process of acquiring and installing whatever required hardware is not previously in place, 483

High definition television (HDTV). A new standard for broadcasting and receiving television signals, 404

Higher level languages. Computer languages developed to permit people to program at a higher level than machine language or assembly language, 362–363, 365–366

Home network, 392

Host computer. Computer that performs central processing for a telecommunications network, 401

HP/UX, 373

HTML (hypertext markup language). Standard for coding Web pages, 152, 414

HTTP (Hypertext Transfer Protocol). A key application-level standard for coding and displaying pages on the World Wide Web, 414

Human-centered design. Design of a technology or process with the primary goal of making the participants' work as effective and satisfying as possible, 269

Human infrastructure, 73–74

Human limitations, and system-related accidents, 527–528

Human side of technology use, 436

Hypermedia database. A database that uses hypertext links to organize documents that may include any combination of text, images, data files, audio, video, and executable computer programs, 152
  Web and, 152–155

Hypertext. Approach to data management and access by storing data in a network of nodes connected by links and accessed through an interactive browsing system, documents in, 151

I

Idealized business process. The way a business process is supposed to be performed assuming that work system participants follow the rules that are supposed to govern the process, 93

Ideas, organizing, 352–354

Identity theft. Use of someone else's personal identification information to impersonate that individual in order to commit crimes, 292

If-then rules. Expert system rules stated in the form: If certain conditions are true, then certain conclusions should be drawn, 208

Image. Data in the form of a picture, 136

Image database. A database that stores images and their descriptions rather than just predefined data items or text, 152

Image processing systems, 190

I-mode, 452

Impersonal communication. Communication in which the identity and personality of the sender and recipient affect the communication minimally, 120

Impersonation fraud, 522

Implementation. In decision making, the process of putting the decision into effect. In the information system project, the process of making a new work system operational in the organization, 20, 122, 472
   in application package, 496
   in end-user development, 500
   in information system, 477–478
   in traditional system life cycle, 484–487
Implementation planning. The process of creating plans for training, conversion, and acceptance testing, 484
Inappropriate staffing, 284
Incentives, 75–76
Index. A list organized to locate information related to specific topics, 154
Indexed access. Method for finding data using an index, 159
Indexed sequential access method (ISAM). Data access method that uses indexes to perform both sequential and direct access processing efficiently, 159–160
Individuals, impact of information systems on, 272–281
Inference engine. Part of an expert system that uses the knowledge base plus facts in the database to draw inferences and decide what to do next, 208
Information. Data whose form and content are appropriate for a particular use, 69–72. *See also* Data
   accidental disclosure of, 517
   accuracy of, 291–292
   age of, 166
   completeness of, 165–166
   converting any type of, to bits, 323
   infrastructure for, 74
   providing, for management, 200–205
   value of, 162
   in work system framework, 46
Information accessibility. How easy it is to obtain and manipulate the information, regardless of information quality, 162, 166–167, 297
Information Age, 282
Information content of products. The degree to which the value of products resides in information rather than in just physical objects, 185
Information overload. Overabundance of data, some of which may be unsolicited or irrelevant, 194, 273–274
Information presentation. The level of summarization and format for presentation to the user, regardless of information quality and accessibility, 162, 167
Information privacy. The ability of an individual to determine when, how, and to what extent personal information is communicated to others, 287–291
Information product. Product deriving most of its value from the information it contains, 227, 228
   characteristics of, 231–232
Information quality. How good the information is, based on its accuracy,

precision, completeness, timeliness, and source, 162–166
Information security. The extent to which information is controlled and protected from inappropriate, unauthorized, or illegal access and use, 162, 167–168
Information sharing. A limited form of integration involving mutual access to data by business processes that operate independently, 101, 102
Information superhighway. The idea that everyone should have virtually unlimited network-based access to information in electronic form, 407
Information system (IS) A particular type of work system that uses information technology to capture, transmit, store, retrieve, manipulate, or display information, thereby supporting one or more other work systems, 6, 181–218
   allocating resources between new and old, 437–438
   alternative approaches for building, 479–480
   application packages, 492–497
   applying principle-based systems analysis to, 58
   architecture of, 444–445
   auditing, 543
   challenges in projects, 461–462
   communication systems, 191–199
   competitive advantage and, 249–251
   deciding which system to use, 502–504
   decision support system, 191–192, 205–215
   dependence on people for success of, 281–285
   difficulty building and modifying, 30–31
   difficulty integrating, 31–32
   difficulty maintaining performance, 433–434
   end-user development, 498–501
   enterprise systems, 191–192, 215–216
   executive information system, 191–192, 202–205
   factors that increase the risks, 526–528
   finance systems, 188–189
   impacts of, 272–281
   in imposing structure, 97–99
   information sources for analyzing, 462–463
   international issues in planning for, 451–453
   investing in, 453–457
   issues and problems in each phase, 475
   limitations and uses of catorgies in, 216–218
   management information system, 191–192, 200–205
   manufacturing systems, 185
   methods for minimizing risks, 528–542(?)
   models as components of, 168–170
   monitoring, usage, 542
   office automation systems, 190, 191–192
   phases of, 472–473, 474–479
   process performance variables and related roles of, 111
   product design systems, 182
   prototypes in, 489–492
   relationships between work systems and, 50–52

sales and marketing systems, 186–187
   supply chain systems, 182–184
   threat of accidents and malfunctions, 512–519
   traditional system life cycle, 480–488
   transaction processing system, 191–192, 199–200
   as work systems, 47
Information system architecture. Basic blueprint showing how a firm's data processing systems, telecommunications networks, and data are integrated, 444–445
Information system department
   division of labor between users and, 458–459
   planning role of, 436–437
Information system plan, 431–432
Information system planning. The part of business planning concerned with deploying the firm's information systems resources, including people, hardware, and software
   principles for, 435–436
   process of, 431–440
   user roles in, 437
Information system professionals, project roles of, 438–439
Information system staff, position of the, 445–448
Information system steering committee. Committee whose goal is to make sure an IS effort reflects business priorities; often includes knowledgeable representatives from user groups, 437
Information technology (IT). The hardware and software used by information systems, 72
   access to, 295–297
   as driving force for innovation, 21–29
   obstacles when applying, in the real world, 29–34
   performance variables for, 307–309
   role of, 13–14
   strategic alignment of business and, 440–453
Information technology infrastructure. Shared technical and human resources used to build, operate, and maintain information systems included in the firm's IS infrastructure, 438
Information technology professionals, difficulty collaborating with, 434–435
Infrastructure (of a work system). The human and technical resources the work system depends on and shares with other systems, 72–74
   business-driven, 448–450
   distinguishing between technology and, 73
   human, 73–74
   information, 74
   information technology, 438
   public key, 540
   in work system framework, 46
Initiation. First phase of an information system project: the process of defining the need, identifying who should be involved,

and describing in general terms how the work system and information system should operate differently input device differently, 19, 472
in application package, 494
in end-user development, 498
in information system, 475–476
in prototype, 490–491
in traditional system life cycle, 481
Innovation, information technology as driving force for, 21–29
Input device. Devices used for entering instructions and data into computers, 312
Inputs (to a system). The physical objects and information that cross the boundary to enter it from its environment, 9
data, 330–334
Instant messaging. Communication capabilities making it possible to instantly contacting anyone who is currently online who is a member of a computer user's buddy list", 195
Instruction set, improved, 329
Intangible benefits. Benefits that affect performance but are difficult to measure, 454
Integrated circuit. Entire electronic circuit embedded on a single small piece of silicon, 23, 327
Integrated service digital network (ISDN). A set of standards to handle voice and computer data in telephone networks, providing additional telephone capabilities without scrapping existing copper telephone lines, 417
Integration. Mutual responsiveness and collaboration between distinct activities or processes, 100
impact of, on performance, 327–329
levels of, 100–103
problems in, 31–32
tradeoffs in, 103–104
Integrity. In e-business, characteristic of transaction data whereby that data has not bee modified covertly after the transaction was completed, 541
Intellectual property, ownership rights for, 294
Intellectual skills, 295
Intelligence. First phase of decision-making; the collection and analysis of data related to the problem identified in the problem - finding stage, 122
Intelligent agents. An autonomous, goal-directed computerized process launched into a computer system or network to perform work while other processes are continuing, 214–215, 375
Interactive product. A product that provides immediate responses to interactive commands, 234
Internal customers. In relation to a work system, work system customers who work inside the same organization as the work system participants, 65
Internal process performance, evaluation of, 473

Internal rate of return (IRR). Interest rate one would have to receive on a project's cost stream to produce the same ultimate return as the project, 457
Internal specification. A technical blueprint for the information system; produced by the internal system design step of the development phase of an information system, 483
Internal system design. Within the development phase of an information system, the process of deciding how the data processing will be configured on the computer, 483
International issues in information systems planning, 451–453
International Standards Organization, 413
Internet, from a user's viewpoint, 396
Internet and telecommunications software firms, 388
Internet content providers, 388
Internet Explorer, 152, 153, 366, 374
Internet hoaxes for illegal gain, 523–524
Internet service providers (ISPs). Company providing links and computer processing needed by consumers in order to use the Internet, 388, 416
Internet Tax Freedom Act (1998), 74
Internet telephony. The use of the. Internet to carry on voice conversations while bypassing traditional telephone company billing systems, 418–419
Interoperability. The ability of heterogeneous hardware and software components to work together conveniently and inexpensively, 26, 309
Interorganizational information systems. Information system that links a firm with customers, suppliers, alliance partners, or other external organizations, 443
Interpreter. A computer program that translates and executes each successive line of a program, 363
Interviews, 462, 463–464
Intranet. Private communication network that uses the type of interface popularized by the Web but is accessibility only by authorized employees, contractors, and customers, 196
Inventory fraud, 522
ISO (International Organization for Standardization), 366

J
Java, 363, 364
Joint application development (JAD). A system development strategy in which users and information systems staff members spend 2 to 4 days together in a carefully prepared meeting to come to a shared understanding of the business problem early in the project, 503–504
JPEG, 326
Junk mail, electronic, 194
Just-in-time (JIT), 104

K
Key. A field that uniquely identifies which person, thing, or event is described by a record in a file, 138
Keyboard. Term that describes a general area of information in which a document or Web site may be classified, 331
Keywords, 155
Kilobyte, 310
Knowledge. A combination of instincts, ideas, rules, and procedures that guide actions and decisions, 70
Knowledge base. Part of an expert system consisting of facts and if-then rules supplied by an expert, 208
Knowledge-based systems. System that represents knowledge in an explicit form so that it can be used in a problem solving process, 208
Knowledge management systems. Communication system designed to facilitate the sharing of knowledge rather than just information, 196–197

L
Languages
assembly, 361–362
fourth generation, 366–367, 483, 491, 497, 498, 501
generations of, 361
higher level, 362–363, 364, 365–366
machine, 361
special-purpose, 367
third generation, 362
Laptop computer. A portable PC that fits into a briefcase, 313
Last mile. A general term for the communication link between a high-speed public communication network and the consumer's home or the corporate user's office, 394
Lava, 365–366
Legacy system. Old, and often technically obsolete, information system that still exists because it performs essential data processing such as accounting and customer billing, 444
Level of summarization. A comparison between the number of individual items on which data are based and the number of items in the data presented, 167
LEXIS-NEXIS database, 151
Liability. Legal responsibility for one's actions of products, for system failure, 518–519
Life cycle costs, 435
Ligand Pharmaceuticals, 292
Linux, 371
Local area network (LAN). Network connecting personal computers and other equipment within a local area to help people share equipment, data, and software, 415–416
in business, 392–393
Locking. The ability to lock a specific page or record temporarily, thereby preventing access by any other process until it is unlocked, 160

Logical reference. Within a computer program, a reference to specific data that identifies the data the programmer wants but doesn't say exactly how to find the data, 160

Logical view of data. View of data expressing the way the user or programmer thinks about the data, 139–140

Logic bomb. A type of Trojan horse whose destructive actions occur based on a particular condition, such as the initiation of a particular program, 525

Logic errors. Bug that causes a program to perform incorrect processing even though the program is syntactically correct, 354–355

Lossless compression. A method of data compression for typical business data and text that does not affect data quality, 326

Lossy compression. A method of data compression that causes some degradation in data quality but still suffices for some audio, video, and image applications, 326

Love bug, 547–548

Lower-CASE (computer aided software engineering). A set of CASE tools used by programmers to facilitate the programming process, 369

Low value variations. Different versions of processes, technologies, and information that exist within an organization based on historical accident rather than conscious design, 105

M

Machine-centered design. Design of a technology or process with the primary goal of simplifying what machines must do, 269–270

Machine independence. Ultimate of software portability, whereby a program written in a particular language can be executed on any brand of computer with roughly similar capacity level, 358

Machine language. The internal programming language for a particular chip, 326–327, 361

comparison of assembly language and, 362

Machines, degree of reliance on, 106–107

MAC OS, 371

Macro viruses, 525

Magnetic disks, 336

Magnetic ink character recognition (MICR). Data input technology based on the automatic recognition of magnetic ink, 331

Magnetic tape. Sequential data storage medium that uses the magnetization and demagnetization of tiny regions on a plastic tape, 336

Mainframe computer. Computer used to control large databases, perform high volume transaction processing, and generate reports from large databases, 314

Maintainability. Ease with which users or technical specialists can keep the technology running and upgrade it to suit the changing needs of the situation, 309

Maintenance. The process of modifying the information system over time after it has been implemented, 20, 487

supporting, 243

Malfunction, threat of, in information systems, 512–519

Management by maxim. A framework for aligning IT with business needs by identifying business maxims and defining related IT maxims, 448

Management information system (MIS). Information system that provides information for managing an organization, 180, 191–192, 200–205

Manufacturing systems, 185

Marketplaces, 254–255

Market segmentation, 254

Mass customization. The use of mass production techniques to produce customized products or services, 185

Material requirement planning (MRP) systems, Commercial software packages that tries to integrate purchasing and production activities by starting with an output schedule and working backward to calculate a schedule of how many units of what types of products must be purchased and produced, and when this must happen in order to meet the output schedule., 183

Mathematical model. A series of equations or graphs that describe precise relationships between variables, 170

M-commerce, 21

Meaningfulness, of work, 279

Megabyte, 310

Memory chips, 23

capacity of, 24

Mental models. The unwritten assumptions and beliefs that people use when they think about a topic, 169–170

Messages, 397

Metadata. Data defining the date in a database, 157

Meta tags, 256

Microfiche, 335–336

Micron. One millionth of a meter, 327

Microprocessor. An integrated circuit that combines control logic and memory on a single chip, 327

Middleware. Software controlling communication between clients and servers in a client server network and performing whatever translation is necessary to make a client's request understandable to a server device, 321–322

Midrange computers. Previously called minicomputers; centralized computers typically shared by a department for processing transactions, accessing corporate databases and generating reports, 313–314

Miniaturization. Replacement of existing products with smaller products having equal or greater functionality, 22–23

advances in, 26, 28

impact of, on performance, 327–329

Minicomputers, 314

MIPS. Abbreviation for "million instructions per second," 309, 311

Misinterpretation, danger of, 194

Mission-critical information system. Information system whose failure would prevent or delay critical business activities such as selling to customers, processing orders, and manufacturing, 249–250

Mobile commerce (m-commerce). A form of e-commerce in which the merchant communicates with customers using wireless technologies such as cell phones and personal digital assistants, 21

Modeling language. Special purpose language for developing models, used extensively in decision support systems, 367

Models, 44

as components of information systems, 168–170

need for, 43–44

optimization, 207

simulation, 207

Modem (modulator/demodulator). A device for encoding and decoding computer-generated digital data so it can be transmitted over an analog telephone line, 402–403

cable, 403

Modularity. Design of technology in the form of separate components, such of which can be developed, tested, and understood independently and then plugged into other related components to create a system or device, 309

greater, 358

Module. Self-contained subsystem that produces predictable outputs from known inputs, 353

Moore's Law. Gordon Moore's prediction in the early 1970s that the storage capacity of computer memory chips would double approximately every 18 months, 23

Mouse, 331

MP3, 326

MS-DOS, 370, 371

Multidimensional database. Database consisting of a single file each of whose fields can be considered a separate dimension for analysis, 147

Multimedia. The use of multiple types of data, such as text, pictures, and sounds, within the same application, 28

Multiplexer. Device that collects signals from multiple terminals and interweaves these signals so that they can be transmitted more economically on a single high-speed channel, 405–406

Multitasking. Concurrent execution of several different programs by a computer, 372

current limits on, 372

Multiuser computer systems, operating systems for, 373

Mythical man-month. Term coined to explain that people are interchangeable only in projects that require little communication or learning, 462

N

Natural language. Language as it is spoken by people, 377
processing of, 375
Negative impacts, balancing positive impacts and, 297

Net present value (NPV). The estimated amount of money the project is worth to the firm, taking into account the cost and benefit streams and the time value of money, 456
Netscape Navigator, 152, 153, 366
NetWare, 373

Network. A series of devices plus communications channels linked to transmit data between the devices, 397
controlling access to, 531
types of, 392–396

Network computer (NC). Stripped down personal computer that does not contain a hard disk and is designed to be controlled through a network, 318

Network computing. Computing in which some of the computing is done on each user's computer, but the processing is controlled centrally, 316, 318–319

Network management. The process of monitoring the network's operations and reallocating its workload to use its capacity efficiently, 400

Network operating system. Operating system that controls the operation of a network, 373
Network technology, 414–419

Neural network. An information system that recognizes objects or patterns based on examples that have been used to train it, 210–212, 375

Newsgroup. Simple form of computer conferencing though the Internet, 196

Node. Any sending, receiving, or processing device in a telecommunications network, 397
Noise, 165
crosstalk, 408
Nonimpact printers, 338–339

Nonprocedural. Description of a program that specifies what should be accomplished, but not the procedures for doing it, 357
Nonprocedurality, 357–358

Nonrepudiation. Inability of either party to a transaction to deny that the transaction occurred, 541

Nonverbal communication. Communication through facial expressions, eye contact, gestures, body language, and other nonverbal means, 119

Normalization. Technique for eliminating redundancies from the tables in a

relationship database and paring them down to their simplest form, 145–146

Notebook computer. A portable PC that fits into a briefcase and is about the size of a notebook, 313
Note-taking systems, 190
Numbers, binary representation of, 323
Numerical representation of sounds and pictures, 324–325

O

Object code. Machine language program that has been translated automatically from a higher level language for execution by a computer, 363

Object-oriented programming (OOP). Programming method that treats data and programs as if they are tightly intertwined and operates based on concepts of object, classes, inheritance, methods, message passing, and polymorphism, 359
major concepts of, 360
trend toward, 358–359
Obsolete products, retiring, 243

Office automation system (OAS). Information system that facilities everyday data processing task in offices and business organizations, 180, 190, 191–192

Ongoing operation and support. The process of ensuring that the technical system components operate correctly and that the information system is used effectively, 487

Online analytical processing (OLAP). The use of online data analysis tools to explore large databases of transaction data, 207
Online auctions, for personal property, 133–134
On-site observation, 463
Open-ended questions, 464

Open standards. Published technical standards that can be used by anyone, 414
Open systems, 26

Open Systems Interface (OSI) reference model. A framework for defining telecommunications standards, 412–413

Operating system. Complex program that controls the operation of computers and networks by controlling execution of other programs, communication with peripheral devices, and use of disk space and other computer system resources, 370
examples of, 371
importance of, 373–374
for Multiuser computer systems, 373
for personal computers, 370, 372
Operation, 20
motivating efficient and effective, 541–542

Operations and maintenance phase. Final phase of an information system project; the ongoing operation of the work system and the information system, plus efforts directly as enhancing either system and correcting bugs, 472
in application package, 496–497
in end-user development, 500

in information system, 478
in prototype, 491
in traditional system life cycle, 487–488

Operations manual. A document that specifies when day-to-day computer operations should be done, 487
Operator, 270

Operator error. A mistake by someone operating technology, 513–514

Optical character recognition (OCR). Data input technology for converting a printed document into electronic text by scanning the document and identifying specific letters and numbers, 331–333
Optical disks, 336–337

Optimization model. Mathematical model that starts with an optimization criterion and uses mathematical search techniques to determine optimal decisions based on the criteria and any constraints that apply, 207

Organizational culture. The shared understandings about relationships and work practices that determine how things are done in a workplace, 76
Organizational feasibility, 481

Organizational inertia. The tendency to continue doing things in the same way and therefore to resist change, 32–33
OS/2, 371
OS/2 WARP, 371
Otisline, 225, 226, 235, 237

Output device. Device that displays data to people, 112, 312
variability in, 112

Output rate. The amount of output (completions) that a process produces per unit of time, 112

Outputs (of a system). The physical objects and information that go from a system into its environment, 9
data, 338–340
Outright piracy, 293

Outsourcing. Process of purchasing products or services from another firm, 450–451

P

Packet switching. Technique for high volume data transfer based on dividing messages into small packets, transmitting them across a network, and later recombining them, 405–406

Palmtop computer. Small, handheld device for storing personal information such as address and phone lists, to-do lists, and current documents. May include cell phone and Internet capabilities, 313
Paper, 335–336
Paper outputs, 338–339

Parallel processing. Computing method in which a larger computation or query is divided into smaller computations or queries performed simultaneously, 330
Participants, 68
difference between, and users, 68–69
impacts on, 69

incentives of system, 75–76
number of, 99
transforming customers into, 66–67
in work system framework, 46
Pascal, 363, 364
Password. Secret series of characters keyed into a computer system to verify a user's identity, 532–533
Patients' Bill of Rights Act (1998), 175–176
Payback period. The time until the project's net benefit becomes positive, 457
Payroll fraud, 522
PBX, 542
Peer-to-peer architecture. Network architecture in which each workstation can communicate directly with every other workstation on the network without going though a specialized server, 322
Pension fraud, 522
People
   dependence on, for information system success, 281–285
   technology and, 268–272
Performance. How well a work system, its components, or its products operate, 63
   evaluation of, for business processes, 110–118
Peripherals. Input, output, and storage devices, usually considered to be options separate from the computer itself, 312
Personal communication. Communication in which the personal relationship between the sender and receiver affects both form and content, 119–120
Personal computer (PC). A single-user computer that sits on a desktop or can be carried around by the user, 313
   operating systems for, 370, 372
Personal computerizing. Form of computing in which the computer is available as a tool for individual work at any time, 316
Personal computing, 317–318
Personal database systems, 190
Personal digital assistant (PDA). Small, handheld device for storing personal information such as address and phone lists, to-do lists, and current documents. May include cell phone and Internet capabilities, 25, 313, 418
Personal property, online auctions for, 133–134
Phased approach. System implementation approach based on using the new information system and work system for a limited subset of the processing while continuing to use old methods for the rest of the processing, 486
Phased approach (combining system development approaches).. The information system is built through a sequence of iterations of development, implementation, and operation, 503
Physical access controls. Security measures that guard against physical access to computer facilities and data, 531
Physical facilities, damage to, 517–518

Physical privacy. The ability of an individual to avoid unwanted intrusions into personal time, space, and property, 287–288
Physical product. A product that has no significant information or service components, 227
Physical security, maintaining, 531
Physical view of data. View of data focusing on how a machine can find and retrieve specific data, expressed as locations in storage devices plus internal techniques for finding data, 140
Pictures
   capturing, 333–334
   numerical representation of, 324–325
Pilot implementation. Trial implementation with a small group of users, 486
Pilot project. A limited, experimental application of a new method or technology to get experience with it, 438
Piracy, information, 293
Pixel. Picture element, a numerically coded element of an image that has been represented as a two-dimensional array of numbers, 324
Planning. The process of deciding what work to do and what outputs to produce when, 107–108
   challenges in, 432–435
Platform. The basic type of computer, operating system, and network that an information system uses, 444–445
PL/I, 363, 364
Pointing devices, 331
Point-of-sale (POS) system. Systems that use bar codes to record orders and generate customer bills, 186
Portability. The ability of computers and communications devices to be carried conveniently and used in different places, 23
Positive impacts, balancing negative impacts and, 297
Post-implementation audit. Retrospective look at system development, implementation, and operations to *see* what can be learned from a project's history, 486–487
Power. The ability to get other people to do things, 275
Power relationships, 194
Precision. The fineness of detail in the portrayal of data, 163
Predefined data items. Numerical or alphabetical data items whose meaning and format are specified explicitly, 136
Preprogrammed access, to data, 141
Presentation packages, 190
Presentation technologies. Devices and techniques used to help communicate ideas more effectively, 120
Price(s)
   for e-commerce, 253–255
   finding good, 239

Price performance. The relationship between the price of technology and the performance it provides, 308–309
Primary processes. Processes that directly create the value the firm's customer perceives, 12
Primary rate interface (PRI), 417
Principle-based systems analysis (PBSA). A systems analysis approach business professionals can use for analyzing systems at whatever level of depth is appropriate in a particular situation. It applies the work system framework and related work system principles, 53–62
   applying, to work systems, information systems, and projects, 58
   ideas and vocabulary that support steps in, 77–79
   limitations and pitfalls in, 58, 61–62
   organizing analysis around work system principles, 54–57
   systems analysis in, 53–54
Priorities. Statements about the relative importance of different goals, 56
making recommendations that support, 57
Privacy, 194, 287–291
   information, 288–291
   physical, 287–288
Private branch exchange (PBX). A special-purpose computer that controls telephone switching at a company site, 394, 405
Problem expansion, 284
Problem-finding. The process of identifying and formulating problems that should be solved, 121
Problem-solving. The process of using information, knowledge, and intuition to solve a problem that has been defined previously, 122
Procedural. Description of a program that specifies the procedures for how something should be done, 357
Process characteristics, 94–110
   attention to errors and exceptions, 108–110
   complexity, 105
   degree of reliance on machines, 106–107
   degree of structure, 96–99
   impacts of excess or deficiency, 95–96
   level of integration, 100–104
   link between, and process performance, 68
   prominence of planning and control, 107–108
   range of involvement, 99–100
   rhythm, 104
Process modeling. Naming business processes, subdividing them into their basic elements, and defining their internal linkages so that they can be studied and improved, 87–94
Process performance, link between process characteristics and, 68
Product design systems, 182
Product differentiation strategy. A strategy of competing by providing more value than competitors or eliminating the competitor's differentiation, 249

Productivity. The relationship between the amount of output produced by a business process and the amount of money, time, and effort it consumes, 114–115

Products, 67
acquiring, 238–239
customer's criteria for evaluating, 244–249
customers evaluation of, 67–68
customer's view of, 226–235
evaluation of performance, 473
learning about options and benefits, 237
maintaining and retiring, 243
maintenance systems for, 243
providing information on, 242–243
in work system framework, 46

Program. A set of instructions in a programming language that specifies the data processing to be performed by a computer, 312
testing, 354–356

Programmable product, 234

Programmer-analysts, 439

Programming. Coding, testing, and documentation of computer programs during the development phase of an information system project, 483
changing nature of, 356–358
major developments, 367–370
making more efficient, 156
tighter links between analysis and, 358
as a translation process, 352
viewing as a business process, 352–359

Program trading. A technique whereby large firms automate some buy and sell decisions related to stocks, bonds, or commodities by using real time access to the latest price information, 189

Project. A work system designed to produce a particular product and then go out of existence
applying principle-based systems analysis to, 58
management of, 439, 458–464
success or failure of, 20–21
as work systems, 47

Project goal. A result that should occur if the project is carried out successfully, 459

Project plan. Summary of a project that divides it into sub-projects with start and completion times and identifies staffing, resource requirements, and dependencies between project steps, 481

Project schedule. A terse project description identifying the timing of major steps and who will do the work, 459

Property, 292–295

Proprietary standards. Technical standards that are owned by a corporation and licensed to others, 414

Protocol. Precisely defined rules, codes, and procedures for linking devices or transmitting data between devices, 413

Prototype. A working model of an information system built to learn about the system's true requirements and how an improved work system could operate if it included an improved information system, 479, 489, 502, 503
advantages and disadvantages of, 491–492
evolutionary, 489
phases in, 449–491
throwaway, 489

Pseudocode, 92

Public key encryption. Access control method involving two keys for each user, a public key that is widely available and a mathematically related private key that must be kept secret, 536, 537

Public key infrastructure (PKI). Infrastructure related to making public key encryption feasible; includes certification authorities, 540

Public switched data network (PSDN). A public data network managed by telecommunications carrier, 417

Pull system. An information system in which the user must request the information explicitly each time it is to be used, 140–141

Purchase transactions, performing, 239–241

Purpose (of a system). The system for a system's existence and the reference point for measuring its success, 9

Push system. An information system in which information is provided to the user automatically, 140–141

Q

Quality (In reference to a product) the customer's perception that the product has desired features and that these features are in line with the product's costs, 246
customer satisfaction and, 246

Query language. Special-purpose computer language used to provide immediate, online answers to user questions, 366

Questionnaires, 463

Qwerty keyboard, 331

R

Radio frequencies, 421

Random access memory (RAM). A type of silicon chip that stores instructions and data currently being used by a computer, 312

Random error. Inaccuracy due to inherent variability in whatever is being measured or the way it is being measured. Also called noise, 165

Range of involvement. The organizational span of people involved in a business process, 99–100

Rate of data transfer, measuring, 310

Rationality. Traditional model for explaining how people should make decisions by gathering and evaluating all of the pertinent information, 122

Read only memory (ROM). Chips whose contents cannot be changed by a user's programs because it stores programs controlling internal computer operations such as the way the computer boots up when it is turned on, 312

Real options. Investment decision-making technique that uses decision trees to account for the possibility that projects or subprojects can be deferred, modified, expanded, or abandoned based on initial accomplishments and problems, 457

Real-time processing. Transaction processing in which each transaction is processed immediately, 189, 200

Record. Set of fields treated as a unit because each is related to the same thing, person, or event, 138
keeping, 280

Recovery (from data loss). The ability to restore a database to the state it was in when a problem stopped further database processing, 160, 539

Reduced Instruction Set Computer (RISC). A method for attaining high-speed computation by using a simple processor that operates very fast microprocessor, 329

Redundant arrays of independent disks (RAID). Data storage method in which the same data is stored on several different disks to protect against the possibility of losing data in a disk crash, 336

Reengineering, 441–442

Regulations. Rules based on laws administered by federal, state, local governments, and international bodies, 247
conformance to, 247–248

Relation. In a relational database, a keyed table consisting of records, 145

Relational database. Database that provides users with a logical view of data consisting of a series of two-dimensional tables that can be manipulated and combined, 145–148

Relationship, 141

Release. An upgraded version of the software that replaces a previous version, 496

Reliability. Likelihood that a system or product will not experience operational failure, customer satisfaction and, 246

Remote monitoring. Use of information technology to observe a building, business operation, person, or computer from a distance, 243

Repair processes, supporting, 243

Repetitive strain injury (RSI). Injury caused by repetitive movement, 274

Replication. Database management process that maintains complete or partial copies of a master database at remote locations, 160

Report generators. Program that makes it comparatively easy for users or programmers to generate reports by describing specific report components and features, 366, 369–370

Request for proposal (RFP). Document sent to application vendors asking for their responses to checklists of required capabilities and features, 494

Requirements creep. Continual increases in project scope that make project completion a moving target, 461

Research projects, 438

Resistance to change. Any action or inaction that obstructs a change process, 284–285

Resource, evaluating data as, 162–168

Responsiveness. Timely action based on what the customer wants, customer satisfaction and, 246

Reusability. Design of software modules so that they can be modified to be used in many different situations, 358

Rewriteable CD-RW disks, 337

Rhythm, 104

Ring topology. Network topology in which the nodes are linked directly without a central server, 415

Router. A combination of hardware and software that links two parts of the same LAN or two compatible LANs by directing messages to the correct node, 416

Runaway. A project that is grossly over budget, extremely late, and typically produces little of value, 472

Running in parallel. The simultaneous use of the old system and the new system during conversion, 486

S

Sabotage, 524–526

Safety systems, inadequacies of, 109–110

Sales and marketing systems, 186–187

Sales force automation (SFA). Commercial software that supports sales-related data handling and data retrieval tasks such as personal scheduling, opportunity tracking, contact management, note and information sharing, and tracking the progress of sales cycles, 187

Same-time (synchronous) communication, 120

Satisficing. Common practice of choosing a satisfactory alternative rather than searching for an optimal alternative, 123

Scalability. The ability to significantly increase or decrease capacity without major disruption or excessive costs, 112, 309

Schema. The data definition for a database, 157

Screen outputs, 338

Screen reader. A software program that allows a blind person to use text on a screen and to identify graphics such as desktop icons by means of a speech synthesizer, 295

Search engine. A program that finds documents or Web pages that seem to be related to groups of words or phrases supplied by the user, 154–155

Secure Electronic Transaction (SET). Proposed standard for the process of encrypting and authenticating credit card transaction data, 541

Secure Sockets Layer (SSL). Method of encrypting Internet transmissions using a temporary encryption key generated automatically by the browser based on session information such as the time of day, 540

Security (of business processes). The likelihood that a business process is not vulnerable to unauthorized uses, sabotage, or criminal activity, 117–118, 253

maintaining, in web-based transactions, 540, 541

Security training, providing, 530

Segregation of duties. The division of responsibilities among two or more people to reduce the likelihood of theft or accidental misprocessing, 538

Self-service work systems. Work system in which customers are participants who perform important steps in the business process, 66–67

Semistructured task. Task for which the information requirements and procedures are generally known, although some aspects of the task still rely on the judgment of the person doing the task, 96

Sensitivity analysis. Using an organized sequence of what-if questions to study the model's outputs under different circumstances, 170

Sequential access. Data access method in which individual records in a file are processed in sequence, 157–158

Server. Specialized computer linked to other computers on a network in order to perform specific types of tasks requested through those computers, 314–315

Service product. Product consisting of actions that provide value to a customer who receives neither information nor physical things, 227

Services, 67

  characteristics of, 232–233

  customer's criteria for evaluating, 244–249

  customers evaluation of product, 67–68

  customer's view of, 226–235

  providing better, 242

  in work system framework, 46

Shopbot. Program that searches the Web or a particular e-commerce database for the best price on a particular product or highest current bid for particular items at auctions, 214–215, 254

Shredder software, 532

Simulation model. Mathematical model that simulates the outcome of tentative decisions and assumptions entered by the user, 207

Site license. Blanket contract covering the use of a particular software product at a particular site by a particular number of users, 500

Slicing and dicing selecting specific subsets of data during the process of analyzing a database from different viewpoints to understand important phenomena reflected in the data, 147

Smart card. Plastic card containing magnetically or optically coded data that can be changed, 188, 240, 337

Smart product. A product preprogrammed to obtain information from its environment and act appropriately, 234

Social context. The situation and relationships within which communication takes place, 119, 194

Social engineering. A computer hacker's attempt to acquire a password or other restricted information by pretending to have authorization and convincing an operator to type or otherwise reveal the information, 533

Social inertia. The tendency of organizations to continue doing things in the same way and, therefore, to resist change, 282

Social presence. The extent to which the recipient of communication perceives it as personal interaction with another person, 119

Social relationships, 280

Soft data. Intuitive or subjective information obtained by informal means such as talking to people or interpreting stories and options, 71–72

Software. Programs that control the processing performed by a computer system, 72, 312

  current limits of, 348–350

  quality control for, 528–529

  theft of, 521, 524

  types of, 350–351

Software bug. A flaw in a program that causes it to produce incorrect or inappropriate results, 516

Software change control. Approach for maintaining software quality and preventing unwarranted changes in systems by enforcing segregation of duties when software is changed, 529

Software techniques, 28–29

Solaris, 373

Sounds

  capturing, 333–334

  numerical representation of, 324–325

Source (of data). The person or organization that produced the data, 166

Source code. Computer program produced in higher-level language by a programmer and later translated automatically into object code for execution on a computer, 363

Spamming. The sending of unsolicited electronic junk mail, 287

Special-purpose languages, 367

Speed of executing instructions, measuring, 311

Sponsor. In relation to an information system, a senior manager who recognizes the importance of the system and makes sure resources are allocated for building and maintaining it, 437

Spreadsheet programs, 190

Spreadsheets, 367–368, 498

Stakeholders. People with a personal stake in the system and its outputs even if they are neither its participants nor its customers, 76

Standards. Widely publicized rules governing the size, shape, and operating characteristics of products or processes, 247–248

  auditing, 543

  common, 102

conformance to, 247–248
de facto, 412
de jure, 412
open, 414
telecommunications, 412–414

Star topology. Network topology in which all messages go through a central node that serves as a switch, receiving messages and forwarding them to a destination node, 415

Statistical packages, 501

Storage device. Devise that stores programs and data for future processing, 312

Strategic information systems. Information system designed to play a major role in an organization's competitive strategy, 250

Structured English. Constrained form of English used to specify the precise logic that will be coded as a computer program, 91–94

Structured programming. A disciplined style of programming based on successive decomposition, 354, 483

Structured Query Language (SQL). The industry standard programming language for expressing data access and manipulation in relational databases, 140, 321–322, 354, 366

Structured task. A task that is so well understood that it is possible to say exactly how to perform it and how to evaluate whether it has been performed well, 96

Subprocess. Part of a process that is a process in its own right, 10

Subschema. A system component that is a system in its own right, 157

Subsystem, 8–9

Success factors. Situational characteristics that are usually associated with system or project success or whose absence is associated with system or project failure, 58

Successive decomposition. Problem solving strategy of breaking problems into successively smaller subproblems, 352

Supercomputer. Computer designed for exceptionally high volume, high-speed calculations, particularly for complex analysis problems, 314

Supplier-customer encounter. Interaction between a customer an a provider in which a personal relationship is unimportant, 232

Supplier-customer relationship Situation in which a customer has repetitive contact with a particular provider and in which the customer and provider get to know each other personally, 232

Supply chain. The transactions, coordination, and movement of goods between a firm's supplier and the firm, 13

Supply chain management (SCM). The overall system of coordinating closely with suppliers so that both the firm and its suppliers reap the benefits of smaller inventories, smoother production, and less waste, 184

Supply chain systems, 182–184

Support processes. Processes that add value indirectly by making it easier for others to perform the primary processes, 12

Sustainable competitive advantage. Competitive advantage other firms cannot count effectively, 251

Switch. A special-purpose computer that performs switching within a network by directly incoming messages along an appropriate path, 404–405

Switching. The process of directing a signal from its source to its destination, 398

Syntax error. Programming error involving incorrect use of programming language, 354

System(s). Sets of interacting components that operate together to accomplish a purpose, 8
    boundaries of, 9
    development of, 503, 528–529
    environment of, 9
    ethics and, 286–297
    inadequate performance of, 518
    inputs of, 9
    liability for failure of, 518–519
    need for balanced view of, 52
    operation of business through, 7–8
    outputs of, 9
    phases in building and maintaining, 19–21
    purpose of, 9
System managers, 439

Systems analysis. A very general process of defining a problem, gathering pertinent information, developing alternative solutions, and choosing among those solutions, 53–54, 439
    organizing, around work system principles, 54–57
    tighter links between programming and, 35839

System software. Software that controls the internal operation of the computer system, thereby performing the background work that makes it possible for application software to run on computer hardware, 350, 351

Systems programmers, 439

System testing. Testing of an entire computer system after individual programs have been tested, 356, 484

T

Tacit knowledge. Knowledge that is acquired and shared through experience and social interaction and is understood and applied unconsciously, 197

Tangible benefits. Benefits that can be measured directly to evaluate system performance, 454

Tasks
    semistructured, 96
    structured, 96
    unstructured, 96

Task scope. The size of the task relative to the overall purpose of the organization, 279

Task variety. The range of different types of things people do at work, 279

TCP/IP (Transmission Control Protocol/Internet Protocol). A set of standards for sharing data between different computers running incompatible operating systems, 414

Technical feasibility, 481

Technical writers, 439

Technological change, 268

Technology, 72
    distinguishing between, and infrastructure, 73
    as metaphor and influence, 271–272
    people and, 268–272
    performance of, from a business viewpoint, 311
    units of measure for operation, 309–311
    in work system framework, 46

Telecommunications. The transmission of data between devices in different locations, 387
    reliance of, on computers, 388
    role of, in computing, 388–389
    vital role of, in e-business, 387–388

Telecommunications Act (1996), 420

Telecommunications equipment manufacturers, 388

Telecommunications networks, functions and components of, 397–412

Telecommunications policy, 419–422

Telecommunications standards, 412–414

Telecommunications systems, terminology in, 390–392

Telecommuting. Using telecommunications technology as a substitute for travel to bring the work to the workers rather than the workers to the work, 272

Teleconferencing. The use of electronic transmission to permit same-time, different-place meetings, 192, 193–194

Telemarketing. The process of selling products and services by telephone, 187

Telephone and cable companies, 388

Telephone fraud, 542

Telephone network, 394, 396

Terabyte, 310

Testing. The process of determining whether a program or system operates in the desired manner, 354

Testing plan. A precise statement of exactly how the information system will be tested, 484

Text. A series of letters, numbers, and other characters whose combined meaning does not depend on a prespecified format or definition of individual items, 136
    binary representation of, 323–324

Text chat, 259

Text database. A set of text documents stored on a computer so that individual documents and information within the documents can be retrieved, 149, 151

Text processing systems, 190

Theft
    identity, 292
    for software and equipment, 521

Thin client. A client computer in a client-server environment that puts more of the processing in the server, 318

Third generation languages (3GLs), 362

32-bit addressing. The ability of the machine to address over 16 million (232) internal locations directly, 327

Throwaway prototype. A prototype designed to be discarded after it is utilized to test ideas, 489

Time, measuring, 310

Time-division multiple access (TDMA). One of several technical standards for transmitting cellular phone calls, 414

Timelines, 166

Timeliness (of data). The extent to which the age of the data is appropriate for the task and user, 166

Token passing. Method for sending messages between nodes of a LAN, 415

Total cost of ownership (TCO). The total cost of acquiring and owning something, including money, time, effort, and attention that could be used for other purposes, 245, 454–455

Total quality management (TQM), 99, 112, 463

Touch screen, 331

Toysmart.com, 289

Traditional system life cycle. Building a system by dividing the project into a series of steps, each of which has a standard set of deliverables, 479, 480–488, 502, 503

Training. The process of ensuring that system participants know what they need to know about both the work system and the information system, 485–486
  providing security, 530

Transaction data, theft by entering fraudulent, 521–522

Transaction integrity, 541

Transaction privacy, 540

Transaction processing, controlling, 538–541

Transaction processing systems (TPS). A system that collects and stores data about transactions and sometimes control decisions made as part of a transaction, 180, 191–192, 199–200
  fraud committed using, 522

Transistor, 312

Translation process, programming as a, 352

Transmission frequency, measuring, 310–311

Trap door. A set of instructions that permits a programmer to bypass the computer system's standard security measures, 524

Trojan horse. A program that appears to be valid and useful but contains hidden instructions than can cause damage, 524–525

Twisted pair. A pair of copper telephone wires that are twisted to help minimize distortion of the signal by other telephone lines in the same sheath of cable, 408–409

U

Unanticipated innovations, 285

Unified messaging. Communication capabilities related to combining e-mail, voice mail, and sometimes fax into a single mail box that can be assessed from any location, 195

Uniform resource locator (URL). An address that defines the route to obtain a web page from a specific server, 152, 153

United States Telecommunications Act (1996), 519

Unit testing. The debugging of an individual program by testing it under a wide range of conditions, 356, 483

UNIX, 371, 373, 494

Unstructured task. A task that is so poorly understood that the information to be used, the method of using the information, and the criteria for deciding whether the task is being done well cannot be specified, 96

Upper-CASE (computer aided software engineering). Tools used by business and IT professionals to describe business processes and the data needed by those processes, 369

User(s)
  charging, to encourage efficiency, 542
  difference between participants and, 68–69
  division of labor between IS department and, 458–459

User department, planning role of, 436–437

User friendly. Characteristic of technology whereby most users can use it easily and successfully with minimal start-up time and training, 270–271

User hostile. Characteristic of technology whereby technology is difficult to use and makes users feel inept, 271

User involvement. Degree to which users are involved in the design and implementation of an information system, 282

User-support projects. Projects such as helping users with applications developed by the IS department, with applications purchased from outside vendors, and with performing individual work on personal computers, 437–438

User support staffs, 439

V

Value added. The amount of value a business process creates for its internal or external customer, 10

Value added network (VAN). Public data network that adds value by transmitting data and by providing access to commercial databases and software, 416–417

Value chain. The set of processes a firm uses to create value for its customers, 10, 12

Valued skills, 277–279

Value of information. Monetary measure of the relevance of data, expressed in terms of the monetary differences in the expected outcome with and without the information, 162

Vandalism, 524–526

Very small aperture terminals (VSATs), 411

Video, 136
  capturing, 333–334

Video conferencing. An interactive meeting involving two or more groups of people who can view each other using television screens, 193–194, 390

Video display terminals, 274–275, 280, 338

Video Privacy Protection Act (1988), 290

Virtual organization. Organization in which major aspects of core processes such as design, production, and delivery are outsourced to other organizations that specialize in these areas, 444

Virtual private network (VPN). A private network configured within a public network, 416

Virtual reality. A simulation of reality that engages the participant's senses and intellect by permitting the participant to interact with the simulated environment, 170–171

Virus. A special type of Trojan horse that can replicate itself and spread, much like a biological virus, 525
  macro, 525

Virus protection. Process of protecting against computer viruses using software that automatically scans incoming data and messages that might be sources of virus infection, 534

VisiCalc, 327–328

Visual BASIC, 363, 364

Voice chat. Using chat room capabilities but talking into a microphone and listening using the computer's loudspeakers, 195

Voice mail, 194–195, 390

Voice messages, 136

Voice recognition. Use of software to convert from spoken words to text by matching the sound patterns of spoken words with previously stored sound patterns, 333–334

VSAT. Very small aperture terminal for satellite communication, 411

W

Waste. Loss of resources resulting from activity that uses resources without adding value, 114

Web-based transactions, maintaining security in, 540

Web browsers, 351

Web page. A hypertext document directly accessible via the World Wide Web, 152

Web servers, 319

Web-transactions, difficulties with security methods for, 541

What-if question. Question posed and answered (typically using a mathematical model) to understand the effect of different assumptions or different decision, 170

Wide area network (WAN). Telecommunications network that spans a wide geographical area such as a state or country, 396, 416

Windows 95, 371

Windows 98, 371

Windows 2000, 371

Windows ME (Millennium Edition), 371

Windows NT, 370, 371
Wire and wireless transmission, 389, 406–412
Wireless application protocol (WAP). A standard technology framework for the wireless Internet, 418
Wireless markup language (WMI), 418
Wireless networking, 418
Work, meaningfulness of, 279
Workaround, 93–94
Workstation. A powerful single-user computer used for computing intensive work such as complex data analysis, graphic design, and engineering, 313
Work system. A system in which human participants perform a business process using information, technology, and other resources to produce products for internal or external customers, 6, 45
applying principle-based systems analysis to, 58
architecture for, 63
balance between the elements of, 47
business process in, 68
clarifications related to the elements of, 65–76
contest in, 74–76
customers in, 65–67
defining, 55–56
in depth, 76–79
information in, 69–72
infrastructure in, 72–74

measuring, performance, 63–64
need for balanced view of, 52
participants in, 68–69
phases in building and maintaining, 19–21
principle-based systems analysis method, 53–62
products in, 67–68
relationships between information systems and, 50–52
self-service, 66–67
services in, 67–68
technology in, 72
use of databases by, 138
viewing information systems and projects as, 47
Work system framework. A framework for summarizing, describing, and analyzing a work system by focusing on eight elements— the customers, products and services, business process, participants, information, and technology, 7–8, 45–47
definition of elements of, 46
Work system principals. A set of seven principles that apply to any work system, 48–49
organizing system analysis around, 54–57
using, to explore the situation and search for possible improvements, 56–57
Work system snapshot. A summary of a work system (or information system or project) designed to clarify the system's scope in

terms of the following six elements: customers, product and services, business process, participants, information, and technology, 55–56, 62
World Intellectual Property Organization, 293
World Wide Web (WWW), invention of, 33

X

X.25. A public switched data network technology hat was used in the first commercial packet switched networks, 417
XML. *See* Extensible markup language (XML)

Y

Year 2000 (Y2K) problem. Widespread problem that caused some information system failures around January 1, 2000 (and potentially could have caused many others) due to the programming practice of using two digits to identify the year portion of a date, 30–31, 516
Yield management. The process of trying to maximize revenue by selling the same product (such as a seat on a flight) to different customers at different prices, 254

Z

Zip drives, 312

NOTES

NOTES

NOTES

NOTES

NOTES

NOTES

NOTES